LIVES THROUGH LITERATURE

LIVES THROUGH LITERATURE

A Thematic Anthology

Third Edition

Helane Levine Keating

Pace University

Walter Levy

Pace University

Upper Saddle River, New Jersey 07458

Library of Congress Cataloging-in-Publication Data

Lives through literature : a thematic anthology [edited by] Helane Levine Keating, Water Levy.—3rd ed.
    p.   cm.
   Includes bibliographical refererences and index.
   ISBN 0-13-017006-2
   1. Literature   2. Life—Literary collections.   I. Levine-Keating, Helane.   II. Levy, Walter.
PN6014.L64   2000
808.8—dc21

                                        00-028338

VP, Editorial Director: Laura Pearson
Editor-in-Chief: Leah Jewell
Senior Acquisition Editor: Carrie Brandon
Editorial Assistant: Sandy Hrasdzira
Managing Editor: Mary Rottino
Project Liaison: Fran Russello
Project Manager: Publications Development Company of Texas
Prepress and Manufacturing Buyer: Lynn Pearlman
Cover Art Director: Jayne Conte
Cover Designer: Bruce Kenselaar
Marketing Manager: Brandy Dawson

Cover illustration: An abstract painting by Todd Gipstein.

This book was set in 10/12 Fairfield Light by Publications Development Company of Texas and was printed and bound by Courier Companies, Inc.
The cover was printed by Phoenix Color Corp.

Credits and copyright acknowledgments appear on pages 1303–1310 that constitute an extension of the copyright page.

© 2001, 1995, 1991 by Helane Levine Keating and Walter Levy
A Division of Pearson Education
Upper Saddle River, New Jersey 07458

Printed in the United States of America

10 9 8 7 6 5 4 3 2 1

ISBN 0-13-017006-2

Prentice-Hall International (UK) Limited, *London*
Prentice-Hall of Australia Pty. Limited, *Sydney*
Prentice-Hall Canada Inc., *Toronto*
Prentice-Hall Hispanoamericana, S.A., *Mexico*
Prentice-Hall of India Private Limited, *New Delhi*
Prentice-Hall of Japan, Inc., *Tokyo*
Pearson Education Asia Pte. Ltd., *Singapore*
Editora Prentice-Hall do Brasil, Ltda., *Rio de Janeiro*

Contents

Short Stories   43

Poems   91

Drama 117

PART 1: PARENTS AND CHILDREN:
CROSS-GENRE DISCUSSION AND WRITING TOPICS   190

PART 2

SISTERS AND BROTHERS 193

Myths, Parables, and Folktales 194

Essays 213

Short Stories 230

Poems   271

Drama   286

PART 2: SISTERS AND BROTHERS:
CROSS-GENRE DISCUSSION AND WRITING TOPICS   340

PART 3

PEOPLE IN LOVE   343

Myths, Parables, and Folktales   345

Essays 371

Short Stories 388

Poems 432

Drama   464

PART 3: PEOPLE IN LOVE:
CROSS-GENRE DISCUSSION AND WRITING TOPICS   512

PART 4

WIVES AND HUSBANDS 515

Myths and Folktales 517

Essays   537

Short Stories   543

Poems   587

Drama   612

PART 5
FRIENDS AND ENEMIES   679

Myths and Folktales   681

Essays   691

Short Stories 710

Poems 795

Drama 814

PART 6
STUDENTS AND TEACHERS   865

Myths, Parables, and Folktales   867

Essays   881

Short Stories   903

Poems 932

Drama 948

PART 6: STUDENTS AND TEACHERS:
CROSS-GENRE DISCUSSION AND WRITING TOPICS   1036

PART 7

PEOPLE ALONE 1039

Myths, Parables, and Folktales 1041

Essays 1044

Short Stories 1055

Poems 1131

Drama   1153

PART 7: PEOPLE ALONE:
CROSS-GENRE DISCUSSION AND WRITING TOPICS   1192

PART 8
READING AND ANALYZING FICTION   1193

PART 9
READING AND ANALYZING POETRY   1207

PART 10
READING AND ANALYZING DRAMA   1221

PART 11
READING, ANALYZING, AND WRITING ESSAYS   1231

Glossary   1251

Alternate Contents

ARRANGED CHRONOLOGICALLY AND BY GENRE

Myths, Parables, and Folktales

Essays

Short Stories

Poems

Preface to the
Third Edition

> *Our debt to tradition through reading and conversation is so massive, our protest or private addition so rare and insignificant—and this commonly on the ground of reading or hearing—that, in a large sense, one would say there is no pure originality. All minds quote. Old and new make the warp and woof of every moment.*
>
> —Ralph Waldo Emerson's "Quotation and Originality"

Lives Through Literature is designed to teach literature and encourage writing. It is a thematic anthology interweaving literary texts that demonstrate interrelationships of life experience as expressed in both sacred and secular myths, parables, folktales, fiction, nonfiction, poetry, and drama. The anthology is aimed primarily at students in the freshman and sophomore English sequences. Selections are drawn from many civilizations and cultures so that we provide a solid core of world literature from the ninth century B.C.E. to the present. We hope that this anthology becomes a catalyst for critical thinking and writing, as well as a source of multicultural literacy.

SEVEN UNIVERSAL THEMES

> *But there remains the indefeasible persistency of the individual to be himself. One leaf, one blade of grass, one meridian, does not resemble another. Every mind is different; and the more it is unfolded, the more pronounced is that difference.*
>
> —Ralph Waldo Emerson, "Quotation and Originality"

We have chosen seven universal themes that we believe are immediately appealing and relevant to our students' experience as well as to the instructor's experience: Parents and Children, Sisters and Brothers, People in Love, Wives and Husbands, Friends and Enemies, Students and Teachers, and People Alone. Since it is likely that these are the very relationships students are struggling with as they enter and proceed through college, we believe that literature of both immediate and lasting relevance will encourage their active participation in the study of literature and critical thinking and writing. The variety of selections included within each theme reveal a multiplicity of points of view as reflected in the differences in age, culture, class, gender, ethnicity, race, religion, sexual orientation, and philosophy.

The themes are arranged in a progressive order that loosely follows the path of growth and development that is an integral part of the process of maturation and individuation. Within each theme, material is grouped by genre, and within each genre material is organized to create a dialogue between selections that precede or follow. Part 1, "Parents and Children," focuses on aspects of relationships between parents and children from the perspective of each, such as coming of age, separation, and death. Part 2, "Sisters and Brothers," portrays the nature of sibling loyalty, jealousy, rivalry, and competitiveness. Part 3, "People in Love," and Part 4, "Wives and Husbands," differentiate the experience of love from that of marriage. Focuses include the role time and timing plays in relationships, the experience of falling in love, the nature of love when both partners are single or married, the difficulties caused by unrequited love or love outside a marriage, and so on. Our intent is not to imply that love and marriage are mutually exclusive, but to suggest that they are complex subjects with many facets for analysis and interpretation. Part 5, "Friends and Enemies," explores different types of friendship and the sources of enmity that arise between friends or explode between foes. Part 6, "Students and Teachers," raises fundamental questions regarding how and from whom we learn, the nature of the lesson, and the profound connection between students and teachers. Finally, we have added to the third edition Part 7, "People Alone" which addresses the singularity of the individual in society and family, one's relationship with oneself rather than with others, the distinction between solitude and loneliness, and the ways in which individuals face death.

INTERRELATED TEXTS

> *Some collaboration has to take place in the mind between the woman and the man before the act of creation can be accomplished. Some marriage of opposites has to be consummated. The whole mind must lie wide open if we are to get the sense that the writer is communicating his experience with perfect fullness.*
>
> —Virginia Woolf, *A Room of One's Own*

We have been most concerned to select texts that elucidate the main themes of *Lives Through Literature* and to place them where they will generate dynamic literary discussion and stimulating writing topics. Our criteria are that all works represent literary excellence, a wide range of cultures, and multiple possibilities for juxtaposition, comparison, and contrast. We recognize the arguments over what constitutes the modern canon, and in light of this, we have chosen classic and respected authors such as Homer, Rumi, Shakespeare, Ibsen, Chekhov, Tolstoy, Kafka, Woolf, and Joyce as well as contemporary authors such as Carver, Plath, Hughes, Coover, Munro, Sexton, and Morrison and less widely recognized writers such as Lalla, Yezierska, Hayden, Petry, North, Alvarez, and O'Hagan. Selections range from the traditional to the experimental, from classic to post-modern, from realistic to surreal. Our selections are culturally diverse and sensitive to issues of gender, race, ethnicity, class religion, age, and sexual orientation.

SUBJECT CLUSTERS

> *Mythology is no man's work; but what we daily observe in regard to the bon-mots that circulate in society—that every talker helps a story in repeating it, until at last, from the slenderest filament of fact a good fable is constructed—the same growth befalls mythology: the legend is tossed from believer to poet, from poet to believer, everybody adding a grace or dropping a fault, or rounding the form until it gets an ideal truth.*
> —Ralph Waldo Emerson, "Quotation and Originality"

By design, we have included a cluster of selections that share similar subject matter but expose quite different points of view. The exploration of multiple views and interpretations is one of the strengths of this anthology. Whereas some clusters appear within one genre of a thematic grouping, others are woven through several genres or even several thematic groupings. For instance, the myth of Daedalus and Icarus appears in several very different forms, first in "Parents and Children" and later in "People in Love" and in "Students and Teachers." Cross-genre clusters on Demeter and Persephone, the Prodigal Son, and Snow White also appear in "Parents and Children." "Sisters and Brothers" has cross-genre clusters portraying the Cain and Abel relationship and the relationship of Hansel and Gretel. "People in Love" includes a cross-genre cluster on The Lady of Shalott, while "Wives and Husbands" has clusters on the relationship between Penelope and Odysseus, the story of Lot's Wife, and the existence of "marriage factories." This section also juxtaposes the Orpheus and Eurydice myth with its American Indian counterpart, "Coyote and the Shadow People," which forms a cluster with H. D.'s poem "Eurydice" and Jorie Graham's poem "Orpheus and Eurydice." "Friends and Enemies" has a cluster of texts portraying the archetype of the double, or shadow. "Students and Teachers" clusters four Zen parables with a poem by a student of Zen. Several poems focusing on the animal as unexpected friend or teacher appear in both "Friends and Enemies" and "Students and Teachers." In "People Alone," the original ancient Greek myth of Sisyphus is juxtaposed with Albert Camus's famous essay, "The Myth of Sisyphus." The literary motif of blindness and inner sight appears and reappears throughout the anthology, in fiction by Raymond Carver, in Sophocles' great drama *Oedipus The King,* and in excerpts from the autobiographical writing of Helen Keller. Other clusters and subthemes center on the role of a secret in relationships, the pleasures of solitude, the experience of rebirth and regeneration, the trials of being an immigrant, rites of passage, and the history and evolution of romantic love. Additional information on these thematic groupings is available in the inside cover of *Lives Through Literature* and in the *Instructor's Manual.*

INTRODUCTIONS TO THEMATIC SECTIONS

Each thematic introduction opens with a short introduction, elucidating the theme and its variations. These brief introductions can be used as a point of departure for a general discussion that will generate a more intense examination of the selections. Within each thematic section the material is arranged so that there is a progression of experience leading toward some significant moment in life. We have situated each selection within its genre to encourage it to be seen in the context of the selections that precede and follow it.

VERSATILITY

Like its other two editions, the third edition of *Lives Through Literature* is extremely versatile allowing selections and themes to be used in any order. It offers a wide variety of literary styles and an interesting array of subthemes and cross-genre connections. Although each thematic part may be discussed as an entity, order of reading and discussion is dependent on the decision of the instructor and the design of the course in which *Lives Through Literature* is being used. Because each part of the anthology is divided into discrete genres, an instructor may focus on a particular genre for an in-depth look at theme, style, and technique. The nine plays, for example, provide a basic course in the history of drama including Sophocles, Shakespeare, Ibsen, Wilde, Shaw, Glaspell, Ionesco, Hellman, Miller, and Williams. The poetry offers a range of styles and techniques from Homer and *The Bhagavad Gita* to Li Po, Shakespeare, Wordsworth, Keats, Browning, Dickinson, Whitman, Rilke, T. S. Eliot, Auden, Plath, and Hughes. Folktales, legends, myths, and parables provide a unique and popular way to examine universal myth and social and interpersonal relationships as well as provide a multicultural perspective. The essays include both the personal memoir and the more objective and scholarly essay that examines a specific subject, thus offering two very distinct modes of nonfiction prose as well as many examples of the use of rhetorical modes. The wide scope of short stories displays various narrative techniques, levels of diction, settings, and approaches to plot.

ALTERNATE CHRONOLOGICAL CONTENTS

For convenience in using the anthology, we have included an Alternate Chronological Contents grouped by genre. This provides another avenue for exploring the anthology's range of themes and genres.

QUESTIONS AND TOPICS FOR WRITING

We have provided questions and topics for writing aimed at eliciting thought, discussion, and general knowledge. We ask basic questions regarding character, plot, setting, and narration, as well as style, diction, technique, and use of symbols and figurative language. Topics for writing are graduated and range from discussions of plot and character to more challenging discussions of figurative language, symbolism, and the uses of irony. Questions and topics for writing are designed to avoid leading readers to predetermined interpretations or conclusions.

READING AND WRITING ABOUT LITERATURE

Lives Through Literature's parallel purpose is to introduce readers to literary analysis, terminology, technique, and literary essay composition. Parts 8 through 11 provide a brief handbook for readers and writers that will make the texts in the anthology more accessible. Part 8: "Reading and Analyzing Fiction," Part 9: "Reading and Analyzing Poetry," Part 10: "Reading and Analyzing Drama," and Part 11: "Reading, Analyzing, and Writing Essays" are written for both beginning and more advanced students. Each part provides descriptions and examples of literary devices and a sample analysis of a selection from each genre. Our aim is to provide specific practical examples for students to use with classroom discussion and writing assignments. "Reading, Analyzing, and Writing Essays," in particular, discusses strategies for writing literary analyses. It includes sample thesis statements for the most common sorts of essays used in the classroom. These parts provide practical support for readers with concrete advice about conceptualizing, planning, and organizing essays.

NOTES

Notes are provided for difficult or obscure terms, allusions, and geographical locations. We hope that these notes will help improve the flow of reading and allow readers maximum comprehension and enjoyment of themes and selections.

ILLUSTRATIONS

Lives Through Literature includes seven illustrations that match specific selections or illuminate a particular theme. These illustrations help make themes and selections more concrete. They also provide another resource for discussion of themes, subthemes, and genres.

SHORT AUTHOR BIOGRAPHIES

A short biography of each author provides readers with a means of locating each author in terms of importance and accomplishments. These biographies appear in alphabetical order at the end of *Lives Through Literature*. Each biography notes the author's place of birth, education, publications, major awards, and individual qualities.

GLOSSARY

A glossary of literary terms is provided to serve as a brief handbook of the vocabulary of literature.

INSTRUCTOR'S MANUAL

The Instructor's Manual includes a brief analysis of each text, its theme, subject, plot, point of view, character, setting, imagery, symbolism, and distinctive use of figurative language. We suggest thematic clusters and other ways for linking texts in a particular part or by genre, style, syntax, and diction.

PROFESSIONAL ACKNOWLEDGMENTS

When we first began this project, we believed that we had created an exciting thematic anthology and looked forward to teaching it. We were grateful to have the opportunity to rethink the anthology when we prepared the second edition, and now we are so pleased that it has been accepted by so many professors and their students. We think that this third edition of *Lives Through Literature* is the best yet, and we are indebted to everyone who has provided encouragement, thoughtful suggestions, and information. A good text is a collaboration between publisher and author, and we thank Prentice Hall and the Pearson Group for its commitment to our endeavor. We are deeply appreciative of Carrie Brandon, our editor, whose encouragement, good ideas, and faith in *Lives Through Literature* has brought us this far. We also thank her former editorial assistant Gianna Caradonna and her present assistant Sandy Hrasdzira. At Publications Development Company of Texas, we thank Nancy Land and Celeste Johns for their attention to our manuscript. We are also grateful to Fred Courtright, our permissions editor, for his expertise and good cheer. We are indebted to the following colleagues, whose editorial comments helped to shape this text: Marsha R. Nourse, Dean College; Walter L. Reed, Emory University; Jeffrey A. Skillings, Dean College; and Steve R. Smith, Pacific University.

We thank our colleagues and friends for suggestions, support, and good answers to our innumerable questions: Neil Baldwin, Bruce Bassett, Rita Bradshaw-Beyers, Linda Chase, William A. Clary, Laura Hapke, Tom Henthorne, Mark Hussey, Jean McConochie, Charles North, Tom O'Sullivan, Sherman Raskin, Eugene Richie, and Priscilla Valk. We are grateful to the staff of the Henry Birnbaum Library of Pace University for their unfailing courteous assistance. We also thank Thaddeus (Kermit) Valk for his help in cutting and pasting.

PERSONAL ACKNOWLEDGMENTS

We wish to thank our families and loved ones for their special support. Helane Levine Keating is especially grateful to Daniel Galliduani for his enthusiastic encouragement and unfailing moral support, his insightful suggestions, and his deep understanding. I have kept my son, Noah Keating, in mind when choosing selections, since he is now in college, and I thank him for his stimulating comments and good humor. I also thank my parents, Marion and Martin Levine, for their loving thoughts as I worked on this third edition of *Lives Through Literature*. And to Fran Faulkner and Barbara Condon, the kind and patient postmasters of the New Kingston Post Office, a special thanks for all their help.   H.L.K.

Walter Levy thanks Gene Moncrief for her tireless cheerfulness and perceptive criticisms. It was my original hope that Alexander and Matthew Levy, Katherine and Jerrold Freitag and Kristina Wronski and Matthew Starle would use *Lives Through Literature* in their college English courses, but life never works out that way. Ironically, though they have graduated, they still look forward to reading *Lives Through Literature,* if only to see what I'll write in this space.   W.L.

Kahlo, Frida (1907–1954). *My Grandparents, My Parents, and I (Family Tree)* (1936). Oil and tempera on metal panel, 12⅛ × 13⅝″ (30.7 × 34.5 cm). The Museum of Modern Art, New York. Gift of Allan Roos, M.D., and B. Mathieu Roos. Photograph © 2000. The Museum of Modern Art, New York.

PART 1

PARENTS AND CHILDREN

The parent-child relationship is filled with constant change and deep emotion that can accompany us throughout our lives. The mystery of who our parents really are exists for most of us, whether we think we know our parents very well or have never met them. And for parents, children are a constant source of amazement and surprise. Writers are often drawn to the parent-child relationship as a rich source of conflict and resolution. Included in this section are myths, essays, stories, poems, a play, a parable, and a folktale that bring the reader to a new awareness of the primal human relationship.

Pregnancy and birthing, the first stages of parenthood, can be filled with joy, anxiety, ambivalence, and, sometimes, sadness. Sylvia Plath's "Metaphors" and Audre Lorde's "Now That I Am Forever with Child" show this range of emotion. The process of coming of age can cause conflict, with parents struggling to accept this growing independence of their children and children struggling to become independent. The ancient Greek "Myth of Demeter and Persephone," which depicts the maiden Persephone's abduction from her mother Demeter, signals Persephone's coming of age and the necessary separation of mother and daughter. While the Greek myth focuses on Demeter's experience of this separation, as does Eavan Boland's poem "The Pomegranate," Persephone's perspective can be seen in Louise Glück's poem "Pomegranate." In the folktale "Snow-White," a stepmother cannot bear the growing beauty of her young stepdaughter. A mother's guilt and love suffuse Tillie Olsen's story "I Stand Here Ironing," and a mother's protectiveness emerges in Alice Walker's story "Everyday Use." Doris Lessing's story "Through the Tunnel" shows a boy separating from his mother when he dares himself to swim through a tunnel and succeeds. In this manner, he completes his rite of passage on his way to manhood. "The Myth of Daedalus and Icarus" shows a father who must watch his son dare but fatally fail, while the connection between father and son before Icarus's fall is the subject of Alastair Reid's poem "Daedalus." In Luke's "The Parable of the Prodigal Son," as well as Robert Bly's "The Prodigal Son" and Elizabeth Bishop's "The Prodigal," the love and forgiveness of a father for his son is explored.

A child's view of a parent is often filled with conflict, ambivalence, love, and hate: witness Hisaye Yamamoto's story "Seventeen Syllables," Chinua Achebe's story "Marriage

1

Is a Private Affair," and poems such as Theodore Roethke's "My Father's Waltz," Sharon Olds's "I Go Back to May 1937," Sandra Cisneros's "His Story," Sylvia Plath's "Daddy," and Muriel Rukeyser's "Ms. Lot."

Can these parent-child relationships be resolved before or after a parent's death? Robert Hayden's poem "Those Winter Sundays," Stanley Kunitz's poem "The Portrait," and W. S. Merwin's poem "Yesterday" each reflect an adult's guilt regarding a dead parent; each also reflects the haunting desire for resolution with one's parents even after death.

The quest to know one's parents takes many forms. The memoirs of Julia Alvarez and Maxine Hong Kingston portray the search for the true identities of their immigrant parents. Understanding the relationships with our parents and children brings a greater understanding of ourselves and of those whom we love or do not love.

Myths, Parables, and Folktales

The Myth of Demeter and Persephone

From the Homeric Hymns
translated by Andrew Lang

Of fair-tressed Demeter,[1] Demeter holy Goddess, I begin to sing: of her and her slim-ankled daughter whom Hades[2] snatched away, the gift of wide-beholding Zeus; but Demeter knew it not, she that bears the Seasons, the giver of goodly crops. For her daughter was playing with the deep-bosomed maidens of Oceanus,[3] and was gathering flowers—roses, and crocuses, and fair violets in the soft meadow, and lilies, and hyacinths, and the narcissus which the earth brought forth as a snare to the fair-faced maiden, by the counsel of Zeus[4] and to pleasure the Lord with many guests. Wondrously bloomed the flower, a marvel for all to see, whether deathless gods or deathly men. From its root grew forth a hundred blossoms, and with its fragrant odor the wide heaven above and the whole earth laughed, and the salt wave of the sea. Then the maiden marvelled, and stretched forth both her hands to seize the fair plaything, but the wide-wayed earth gaped in the Nysian plain, and up rushed the Prince, the host of many guests, the many-named son of Cronos,[5] with his immortal horses. Against her will he seized her, and drove her off weeping in his golden chariot, but she shrilled aloud, calling on Father Cronides, the highest of gods and the best.

---

[1] Demeter: mother goddess of Earth, the chief goddess of agriculture, also known as the corn goddess; also referred to as Lady Deo.
[2] Hades: god of the dead who presides over the Underworld; also known as Aidoneus.
[3] Oceanus: the god of all rivers and a personification of the seas.
[4] Zeus: the greatest of the gods; the god of light who presided over all other gods on Mount Olympus; also called Cronides or Croneon. The etherial region inhabited by the gods whether or not they are on Mt. Olympus is also called Olympus.
[5] Cronos: the chief of the Titans who ruled before the age of Zeus. Zeus, Cronos' eldest son, overthrew him.

But no immortal god or deathly man heard the voice of her, . . . save the daughter of Persaeus, Hecate[6] of the shining headgear, as she was thinking delicate thoughts, who heard the cry from her cave and Prince Helios,[7] the glorious son of Hyperion,[8] the maiden calling on Father Cronides. But he far off sat apart from the gods in his temple haunted by prayers, receiving goodly victims from mortal men. By the design of Zeus did the brother of Zeus lead the maiden away, the lord of many, the host of many guests, with his deathless horses; right sore against her will, even he of many names the son of Cronos. Now, so long as the Goddess beheld the earth, and the starry heaven, and the tide of the teeming sea, and the rays of the sun, and still hoped to behold her mother dear, and the tribes of the eternal gods; even so long, despite her sorrow, hope warmed her high heart; then rang the mountain peaks, and the depths of the sea to her immortal voice, and her lady mother heard her. Then sharp pain caught at her heart, and with her hands she tore the wimple about her ambrosial hair, and cast a dark veil about her shoulders, and then sped she like a bird over land and sea in her great yearning; but to her there was none that would tell the truth, none, either of Gods, or deathly men, nor even a bird came near her, a soothsaying messenger. Thereafter for nine days did Lady Deo roam the earth, with torches burning in her hands, nor ever in her sorrow tasted she of ambrosia and sweet nectar, nor laved her body in the baths. But when at last the tenth morn came to her with the light, Hecate met her, a torch in her hands, and spoke a word of tidings, and said:

"Lady Demeter, thou that bring the Seasons, thou giver of glad gifts, which of the heavenly gods or deathly men has ravished away Persephone,[9] and brought thee sorrow: for I heard a voice but I saw not who the ravisher might be?"

So spoke Hecate, and the daughter of fair-tressed Rhea[10] answered her not, but swiftly rushed on with her, bearing torches burning in her hands. So came they to Helios that watches both for gods and men, and stood before his car, and the lady Goddess questioned him:

"Helios, have pity on me that am a goddess, if ever by word or deed I gladdened thy heart. My daughter, whom I bore, a sweet plant and fair to see; it was her shrill voice I heard through the air unharvested, even as of one violently entreated, but I saw her not with my eyes. But do thou that look down with thy rays from the holy air upon all the land and sea, do thou tell me truly concerning my dear child, if thou did behold her; who it is that has gone off and ravished her away from me against her will, who is it of gods or mortal men?"

So spoke she, and Hyperionides answered her:

"Daughter of fair-tressed Rhea, Queen Demeter, thou shall know it; for greatly do I pity and revere thee in thy sorrow for thy slim-ankled child. There is none other guilty of the Immortals but Zeus himself that gathers the clouds, who gave thy daughter to Hades, his own brother, to be called his lovely wife; and Hades has ravished her away in

---

[6] Hecote: beneficent goddess associated with the Underworld after her connection with Persephone.
[7] Helios: a Titan who is the god of the sun; often pictured as a young man who travels across the sky in a chariot of fire drawn by horses.
[8] Hyperion: a Titan, the father of Helios; often referred to as the god of the sun.
[9] Persephone: Demeter's daughter by Zeus.
[10] Rhea: married to Cronos and the mother of Zeus, Hades, Poseidon, Demeter, Hera, and Hestia.

his chariot, loudly shrilling, beneath the dusky gloom. But, Goddess, cease from thy long lamenting. It behooves not thee thus vainly to cherish anger unassuaged. No unseemly lord for thy daughter among the Immortals is Aidoneus, the lord of many, thine own brother and of one seed with thee, and for his honor he won, since when was made the threefold division, to be lord among those with whom he dwells."

So spoke he, and called upon his horses, and at his call they swiftly bore the fleet chariot on like long winged birds. But grief more dread and bitter fell upon her, and angry thereafter was she with Cronion that has dark clouds for his dwelling. She held apart from the gathering of the Gods and from tall Olympus, and disfiguring her form for many days she went among the cities and rich fields of men. Now no man knew her that looked on her, nor no deep-bosomed woman, till she came to the dwelling of Celeus, who then was Prince of fragrant Eleusis. There sat she at the wayside in sorrow of heart, by the Maiden Well whence the townsfolk came to draw water. In the shade she sat; above her grew a thick olive-tree; and in fashion she was like an ancient crone who knows no more of child-bearing and the gifts of Aphrodite, the lover of garlands. Such she was as are the nurses of the children of law-pronouncing kings. Such are the house-keepers in their echoing halls.

Now the daughters of Celeus beheld her as they came to fetch the fair-flowing water, to carry in bronze vessels to their father's home. Four were they, like unto goddesses, all in the bloom of youth, Callidice, and Cleisidice, and winsome Demo, and Callithoe the eldest of them all, nor did they know her, for the Gods are hard to be known by mortals, but they stood near her and spoke winged words:

"Who art thou and whence, old woman, of ancient folk, and why were thou wandering apart from the town, nor do draw near to the houses where are women of thine own age, in the shadowy halls, even such as thou, and younger women, too, who may kindly entreat thee in word and deed?"

So spoke they, and the lady Goddess answered:

"Dear children, whoever ye be, of womankind I bid you hail, and I will tell you my story. Seemly it is to answer your questions truly. Deo is my name that my lady mother gave me; but now, look you, from Crete am I come hither over the wide ridges of the sea, by no will of my own, nay, by violence have sea-rovers brought me hither under duress, who thereafter touched with their ship at Thoricos where the women and they themselves embarked on land. Then were they busy about supper beside the hawsers of the ship, but my heart heeded not delight of supper; no, stealthily setting forth through the dark land I fled from these overweening masters, that they might not sell me whom they had never bought and gain my price. Thus hither have I come in my wandering, nor know I at all what land is this, nor who they be that dwell therein. But to you may all they that hold mansions in Olympus give husbands and lords, and such children to bear as parents desire; but me do ye maidens pity in your kindness, till I come to the house of woman or of man, that there I may work zealously for them in such tasks as fit a woman of my years. I could carry in my arms a new-born babe, and nurse it well, and keep the house, and strew my master's bed within the well-builded chambers, and teach the maids their tasks."

So spoke the Goddess, and straightway answered her the maid unwed, Callidice, the fairest of the daughters of Celeus:

"Mother, what things soever the Gods do give must men, though sorrowing, endure, for the Gods are far stronger than we; but this will I tell thee clearly and truly, namely, what men they are who here have most honor, and who lead the people, and by their counsels and just laws do safeguard the bulwarks of the city. Such are wise Triptolemus, Diocles, Polyxenus, and noble Eumolpus, and Dolichus, and our lordly father. All their wives keep their houses, and not one of them would at first sight condemn thee and thrust thee from their halls, but gladly they will receive thee: for thine aspect is divine. So, if thou will, abide here, that we may go to the house of my father, and tell out all this tale to my mother, the deep-bosomed Metaneira, if perchance she will bid thee come to our house and not seek the homes of others. A dear son born in her later years is nurtured in the well-built hall, a child of many prayers and a welcome. If thou would nurse him till he comes to the measure of youth, then whatsoever woman saw thee should envy thee; such gifts of fosterage would my mother give thee."

So spoke she and the Goddess nodded assent. So rejoicing they filled their shining pitchers with water and bore them away. Swiftly they came to the high hall of their father, and quickly they told their mother what they had heard and seen, and speedily she bade them run and call the strange woman, offering goodly hire. Then as deer or calves in the season of Spring leap along the meadow, when they have had their fill of pasture, so lightly they tucked up the folds of their lovely gowns, and ran along the hollow chariot-way, while their hair danced on their shoulders, in color like the crocus flower. They found the glorious Goddess at the wayside, even where they had left her, and led her to their father's house. But she paced behind in heaviness of heart, her head veiled, and the dark robe floating about her slender feet divine. Speedily they came to the house of Celeus, the fosterling of Zeus, and they went through the corridor where their lady mother was sitting by the doorpost of the well-wrought hall, with her child in her lap, a young blossom, and the girls ran up to her, but the Goddess stood on the threshold, her head touching the roof-beam, and she filled the doorway with the light divine. Then wonder, and awe, and pale fear seized the mother, and she gave place from her high seat, and bade the Goddess be seated. But Demeter the bearer of the Seasons, the Giver of goodly gifts, would not sit down upon the shining high seat. Nay, in silence she waited. Casting down her lovely eyes, till the wise Iambe set for her a well-made stool, and cast over it a glistening fleece. Then sat she down and held the veil before her face: long in sorrow and silence sat she so, and spoke to no man nor made any sign, but smileless she sat, nor tasted meat nor drink, wasting with long desire for her deep-bosomed daughter.

So abode she till wise Iambe with jests and many mockeries beguiled the lady, the holy one, to smile and laugh and hold a happier heart, and pleased her moods even thereafter. Then Metaneira filled a cup of sweet wine and offered it to her, but she refused it, saying, that it was not permitted for her to drink red wine; but she bade them mix meal and water with the tender herb of mint, and give it to her to drink. Then Metaneira made a potion and gave it to the Goddess as she bade, and Lady Deo took it and made libation, and to them fair-girdled Metaneira said:

"Hail, lady, for methinks thou art not of mean parentage, but goodly born, for grace and honor shine in thine eyes as in the eyes of law-dealing kings. But the gifts of the Gods, even in sorrow, we men of necessity endure, for the yoke is laid upon our necks; yet now that thou art come hither, such things as I have shall be thine. Rear me this child that the gods have given in my later years and beyond my hope; and he is to me a child of many prayers. If thou rear him, and he come to the measure of youth, verily each woman that sees thee will envy thee, such shall be my gifts of fosterage."

Then answered her again Demeter of the fair garland:

"And may thou too, lady, fare well, and the Gods give thee all things good. Gladly will I receive thy child that thou bid me nurse. Never, methinks, by the folly of his nurse shall charm or sorcery harm him; for I know an antidote stronger than the wild wood herb, and a goodly salve I know for the venomed spells."

So spoke she, and with her immortal hands she placed the child on her fragrant breast, and the mother was glad at heart. So in the halls she nursed the goodly son of wise Celeus, even Demophoon, whom deep-breasted Metaneira bare, and he grew like a god, upon no mortal food, nor on no mother's milk. For Demeter anointed him with ambrosia as though he had been a son of a God, breathing sweetness over him, and keeping him in her bosom. So worked she by day, but at night she hid him in the force of fire like a brand, his dear parents knowing it not. Nay, to them it was great marvel how flourished he and grew like the Gods to look upon. And, verily, she would have made him exempt from age and death forever, had not fair-girdled Metaneira, in her witlessness, spied on her in the night from her fragrant chamber. Then wailed she, and smote both her thighs, in terror for her child, and in anguish of heart, and lamenting she spoke winged words: "My child Demophoon, the stranger is concealing thee in the heart of the fire; bitter sorrow for me and lamentation."

So spoke she, wailing, and the lady Goddess heard her. Then in wrath did the fair-garlanded Demeter snatch out of the fire with her immortal hands and cast upon the ground that woman's dear son, whom beyond all hope she had borne in the halls. Dread was the wrath of Demeter, and she spoke to fair-girdled Metaneira. "Oh ill-advised and uncounselled race of men, that know not beforehand the fate of coming good or coming evil. For, lo, thou has wrought upon thyself a bane incurable, by thine own witlessness; for by the oath of the Gods, the relentless water of Styx,[11] I would have made thy dear child deathless and exempt from age forever, and would have given him glory imperishable. But now in nowise may he escape the Fates and death, yet glory imperishable will ever be his, since he has lain on my knees and slept within my arms; but as the years go round, and in his day, the sons of the Eleusinians will ever wage war and dreadful strife one upon the other. Now I am honored Demeter, the greatest good and gain of the Immortals to deathly men. But, come now, let all the people build me a great temple and an altar thereby, below the town, and the steep wall, above Callichorus on the jutting rock. But the rites I myself will prescribe, that in time to come ye may pay them duly and appease my power."

Therewith the Goddess changed her shape and height and cast off old age, and beauty breathed about her, and the sweet scent was breathed from her fragrant robes, and afar shone the light from the deathless body of the Goddess, the yellow hair flowing

---

[11] Styx: a spring that, when it flowed underground, became a chief river in the Underworld. The water of the spring had magical properties and when Achilles was dipped in it he became nearly invulnerable.

about her shoulders, so that the goodly house was filled with the splendor as of lightning fire, and forth from the halls went she.

But anon the knees of the woman were loosened, and for long time she was speechless, nay, nor did she even mind of the child, her best beloved, to lift him from the floor. But the sisters of the child heard his pitiful cry, and leapt from their fair-strewn beds; one of them, lifting the child in her hands, laid it in her bosom; and another lit fire, and the third ran with smooth feet to take her mother forth from the fragrant chamber. Then gathered they about the child, and bathed and clad him lovingly, yet his mood was not softened, for meaner nurses now and handmaids held him.

They the long night through were adoring the renowned Goddess, trembling with fear, but at the dawning they told truly to mighty Celeus all that the Goddess had commanded; even Demeter of the goodly garland. Thereon he called into the marketplace the many people, and bade them make a rich temple, and an altar to fair-tressed Demeter, upon the jutting rock. Then they heard and obeyed his voice, and as he bade they builded. And the child increased in strength by the Goddess's will.

Now when they had done their work, and rested from their labors, each man started for his home, but yellow-haired Demeter, sitting there apart from all the blessed Gods, abided, wasting away with desire for her deep-bosomed daughter. Then the most dread and terrible of years did the Goddess bring for mortals upon the fruitful earth, nor did the earth send up the seed, for Demeter of the goodly garland concealed it. Many crooked ploughs did the oxen drag through the furrows in vain, and much white barley fell fruitless upon the land. Now would the whole race of mortal men have perished utterly from the stress of famine, and the Gods that hold mansions in Olympus would have lost the share and renown of gift and sacrifice, if Zeus had not conceived a counsel within his heart.

First he roused Iris of the golden wings to speed forth and call the fair-tressed Demeter, the lovesome in beauty. So spoke Zeus, and Iris obeyed Zeus, the son of Cronos, who has dark clouds for his tabernacle, and swiftly she sped down the space between heaven and earth. Then came she to the citadel of fragrant Eleusis, and in the temple she found Demeter clothed in dark raiment, and speaking winged words addressed her: "Demeter, Father Zeus, whose counsels are imperishable, bids thee back unto the tribes of the eternal Gods. Come thou, then, lest the word of Zeus be of no avail." So spoke she in her prayer, but the Goddess yielded not. Thereafter the Father sent forth all the blessed Gods, all of the Immortals, and coming one by one they bade Demeter return, and gave her many splendid gifts, and all honors that she might choose among the immortal Gods. But none availed to persuade by turning her mind and her angry heart, so stubbornly she refused their sayings. For she deemed no more forever to enter fragrant Olympus, and no more to allow the earth to bear her fruit, until her eyes should behold her fair-faced daughter.

But when far-seeing Zeus, the lord of the thunder-peal, had heard the thing, he sent to Erebus[12] the slayer of Argus, the God of the golden wand, to win over Hades

---

[12] Erebus: a place of extreme darkness through which souls passed on the way to Hades; personified as a shade or dweller in the Underworld.

with soft words, and persuade him to bring up holy Persephone into the light, and among the Gods, forth from the murky gloom, so that her mother might behold her, and that her anger might relent. And Hermes[13] disobeyed not, but straightway and speedily went forth beneath the hollow places of the earth, leaving the home of Olympus. That King he found within his dwelling, sitting on a couch with his chaste bedfellow, who sorely grieved for desire of her mother, that still was cherishing a fell design against the ill deeds of the Gods. Then the strong slayer of Argos drew near and spoke: "Hades of the dark locks, thou Prince of men outworn, Father Zeus bade me bring the dread Persephone forth from Erebus among the Gods, that her mother may behold her, and relent from her anger and terrible wrath against the Immortals, for now she contrives a mighty deed, to destroy the feeble tribes of earth-born men by withholding the seed under the earth. Thereby the honors of the Gods are lessened and fierce is her wrath, nor mingles she with the Gods, but sits apart within the fragrant temple in the steep citadel of Eleusis."[14]

So spoke he, and smiling were the brows of Aidoneus, Prince of the dead, nor did he disobey the commands of King Zeus, as speedily he bade the wise Persephone: "Go, Persephone, to thy dark-mantled mother, go with a gentle spirit in thy breast, nor be thou beyond all other folk disconsolate. Verily I shall be no unseemly lord of thine among the Immortals, I that am the brother of Father Zeus, and while thou art here shall thou be mistress over all that lives and moves, but among the Immortals shall thou have the greatest renown. Upon them that wrong thee shall vengeance be unceasing, upon them that solicit not thy power with sacrifice, and pious deeds, and every acceptable gift."

So spoke he, and wise Persephone was glad; and joyously and swiftly she arose, but the God himself, stealthily looking around her, gave her sweet pomegranate seed to eat, and this he did that she might not abide forever beside revered Demeter of the dark mantle. Then openly did Aidoneus, the Prince of all, get ready the steeds beneath the golden chariot, and she climbed up into the golden chariot, and beside her the strong Slayer of Argus took reins and whip in hand, and drove forth from the halls, and gladly sped the two horses. Speedily they devoured the long way: nor sea, nor rivers, nor grassy glades, nor cliffs, could stay the rush of the deathless horses; nay, far above them they cleft the deep air in their course. Before the fragrant temple he drove them, and checked them where dwelt Demeter of the goodly garland, who, when she beheld them, rushed forth like a Maenad[15] down a dark mountain woodland.

Persephone on the other side rejoiced to see her mother dear, and leaped to meet her; but the mother said, "Child, in Hades hast thou eaten any food? for if thou hast not then with me and thy father the son of Cronos, who has dark clouds for his tabernacle, shall thou ever dwell honored among all the Immortals. But if thou hast tasted food,

---

[13] Hermes: protector of heroes, a god of travel and commerce. He invented the lyre and pipes. Hermes usually is depicted as wearing distinctive winged shoes and a broad-brimmed hat, and carrying a winged staff. He is known as the messenger of the gods.

[14] Eleusis: an Ancient Greek city in Attica, near Athens, where Demeter and Persephone were honored. The rites, a means for seeking immortality, were a mystery of which only initiates were knowledgeable.

[15] Maenad, or Bacchante: a female follower of Dionysus, the god of fertility and wine. Worship of Dionysus usually involved drunken and orgiastic behavior.

thou must return again, and beneath the hollows of the earth must dwell in Hades a third portion of the year; yet two parts of the year thou shall abide with me and the other Immortals. When the earth blossoms with all manner of fragrant flowers, then from beneath the murky gloom shall thou come again, a mighty marvel to Gods and to mortal men. Now tell me by what wile the strong host of many guests deceived thee? . . ."

Then fair Persephone answered her august mother: "Behold, I shall tell thee all the truth without fail. I leaped up for joy when good Hermes, the swift messenger, came from my father Cronides and the other heavenly Gods, with the message that I was to return out of Erebus, so that thou mightest behold me, and cease thine anger and dread wrath against the Immortals. Thereon Hades himself compelled me to taste of a sweet pomegranate seed against my will. And now I will tell thee how, through the crafty device of Cronides my father, he ravished me, and bore me away beneath the hollows of the earth. All that thou askest I will tell thee. We were all playing in the lovely meadows. We were playing there, and plucking beautiful blossoms with our hands; crocuses mingled, and iris, and hyacinth, and roses, and lilies, a marvel to behold, and narcissus, that the wide earth bore, a wile for my undoing. Gladly was I gathering them when the earth gaped beneath, and therefrom leaped the mighty Prince, the host of many guests, and he bore me against my will despite my grief beneath the earth, in his golden chariot; and shrilly did I cry. This all is true that I tell thee."

So the livelong day in oneness of heart did they cheer each other with love, and their minds ceased from sorrow, and great gladness did either win from other. Then came to them Hecate of the fair wimple, and often did she kiss the holy daughter of Demeter, and from that day was her queenly comrade and handmaiden; but to them for a messenger did far-seeing Zeus of the loud thunder-peal send fair-tressed Rhea to bring dark-mantled Demeter among the Gods, with pledge of what honor she might choose among the Immortals. He vowed that her daughter, for the third part of the revolving year, should dwell beneath the murky gloom, but for the other two parts she should abide with her mother and the other gods.

Thus he spoke, and the Goddess disobeyed not the commands of Zeus. Swiftly she sped down from the peaks of Olympus, and came to fertile Rarion; fertile of old, but now no longer fruitful; for fallow and leafless it lay, and hidden was the white barley grain by the device of fair-ankled Demeter. Nonetheless with the growing of the Spring the land was to teem with tall ears of corn, and the rich furrows were to be heavy with corn, and the corn to be bound in sheaves. There first did she land from the unharvested ether, and gladly the Goddesses looked on each other, and rejoiced in heart, and thus first did Rhea of the fair wimple speak to Demeter:

"Hither, child; for he called thee, far-seeing Zeus, the lord of the deep thunder, to come among the Gods, and has promised thee such honors as thou wish, and has decreed that thy child, for the third of the rolling year, shall dwell beneath the murky gloom, but the other two parts with her mother and the rest of the Immortals. So does he promise that it shall be and thereto nods his head; but come, my child, obey, and be not too unrelenting against the Son of Cronos, the lord of the dark cloud. And do thou increase the grain that brings life to men."

So spoke she, and Demeter of the fair garland obeyed. Speedily she sent up the grain from the rich field, and the wide earth was heavy with leaves and flowers: and she hastened, and showed the thing to the kings, the dealers of law; to Triptolemus and Diocles the charioteer, and mighty Eumolpus, and Celeus the leader of the people; she showed them the manner of her rites, and taught them her goodly mysteries, holy mysteries which none may violate, or search into, or noise abroad, for the great curse from the Gods restrains the voice. Happy is he among deathly men who hath beheld these things! and he that is uninitiate, and has no lot in them, has never equal lot in death beneath the murky gloom.

Now when the Goddess had given instruction in all her rites, they went to Olympus, to the gathering of the other Gods. There the Goddesses dwell beside Zeus the lord of the thunder, holy and revered are they. Right happy is he among mortal men whom they dearly love; speedily do they send as a guest to his lofty hall Plutus,[16] who giveth wealth to mortal men. But come thou that holdest the land of fragrant Eleusis, and sea-girt Paros, and rocky Antron, come, Lady Deo! Queen and giver of goodly gifts, and bringer of the Seasons; come thou and thy daughter, beautiful Persephone, and of your grace grant me goodly substance in requital of my song; but I will mind me of thee, and of other minstrelsy.

(C. 550 B.C.E.)

QUESTIONS

1. Why does Demeter refuse to return to Olympus and how does she finally force Zeus to intervene?

2. Explain how Demeter's behavior in Eleusis is linked to the abduction of her daughter.

3. How does the relationship between Demeter and Persephone illustrate the relationship between a mother and daughter?

4. Why do you think that the Greeks used this myth illustrative of family relationships to explain the rotation of the year from season to season, from summer to winter and summer again?

---

[16] Plutus: refers to Hades.

The Myth of Dædalus and Icarus

Edited by Thomas Bulfinch (1796–1867)

The labyrinth from which Theseus escaped by means of the clew of Ariadne was built by Dædalus, a most skilful artificer. It was an edifice with numberless winding passages and turnings opening into one another, and seeming to have neither beginning nor end, like the river Mæander, which returns on itself, and flows now onward, now backward, in its course to the sea. Dædalus built the labyrinth for King Minos, but afterwards lost the favor of the king, and was shut up in a tower. He contrived to make his escape from his prison, but could not leave the island by sea, as the king kept strict watch on all the vessels, and permitted none to sail without being carefully searched. "Minos may control the land and sea," said Dædalus, "but not the regions of the air. I will try that way." So he set to work to fabricate wings for himself and his young son Icarus. He wrought feathers together, beginning with the smallest and adding larger, so as to form an increasing surface. The larger ones he secured with thread and the smaller with wax, and gave the whole a gentle curvature like the wings of a bird. Icarus, the boy, stood and looked on, sometimes running to gather up the feathers which the wind had blown away, and then handling the wax and working it over with his fingers, by his play impeding his father in his labors. When at last the work was done, the artist, waving his wings, found himself buoyed upward, and hung suspended, poising himself on the beaten air. He next equipped his son in the same manner, and taught him how to fly, as a bird tempts her young ones from the lofty nest into the air. When all was prepared for flight he said, "Icarus, my son, I charge you to keep at a moderate height, for if you fly too low the damp will clog your wings, and if too high the heat will melt them. Keep near me and you will be safe." While he gave him these instructions and fitted the wings to his shoulders, the face of the father was wet with tears, and his hands trembled. He kissed the boy, not knowing that it was for the last time. Then rising on his wings, he flew off, encouraging him to follow, and looked back from his own flight to see how his son managed his wings. As they flew the ploughman stopped his work to gaze, and the shepherd leaned on his staff and watched them, astonished at the sight, and thinking they were gods who could thus cleave the air.

They passed Samos and Delos[1] on the left and Lebynthos on the right, when the boy, exulting in his career, began to leave the guidance of his companion and soar upward as if to reach heaven. The nearness of the blazing sun softened the wax which held the feathers together, and they came off. He fluttered with his arms, but no feathers remained to hold the air. While his mouth uttered cries to his father it was submerged in the blue waters of the sea, which thenceforth was called by his name. His father cried, "Icarus, Icarus, where are you?" At last he saw the feathers floating on the water, and

---

[1] Delos: islands in the Aegean Sea, off the southeastern coast of Greece.

bitterly lamenting his own arts, he buried the body and called the land Icaria in memory of his child. Dædalus arrived safe in Sicily, where he built a temple to Apollo, and hung up his wings, an offering to the god.

Dædalus was so proud of his achievements that he could not bear the idea of a rival. His sister had placed her son Perdix under his charge to be taught the mechanical arts. He was an apt scholar and gave striking evidences of ingenuity. Walking on the seashore he picked up the spine of a fish. Imitating it, he took a piece of iron and notched it on the edge, and thus invented the *saw*. He put two pieces of iron together, connecting them at one end with a rivet, and sharpening the other ends, and made a *pair of compasses*. Dædalus was so envious of his nephew's performances that he took an opportunity, when they were together one day on the top of a high tower, to push him off. But Minerva,[2] who favors ingenuity, saw him falling, and arrested his fate by changing him into a bird called after his name, the Partridge. This bird does not build his nest in the trees, nor take lofty flights, but nestles in the hedges, and mindful of his fall, avoids high places.

(Pre-6th Century B.C.E.)

Questions

1. By observing Dædalus's character traits, what can you tell about him and his relationship with his son Icarus?

2. What foreshadows the ending of the story?

3. What parallels can be drawn between Dædalus and Icarus and parents and children today?

---

[2] Minerva: the Roman name for Athene, a virgin warrior-goddess, who wears a helmet, carries a spear and a goat-skin shield. Athena was supposed to have been born by springing forth from the head of Zeus, her father. She presides over the arts, literature, philosophy, and music. She is patron of Athens, Greece, which is named in her honor.

LUKE 15:11–32*

The Parable of the Prodigal Son*

And he said, A certain man had two sons: And the younger of them said to *his* father, Father, give me the portion of goods that falleth *to me*. And he divided unto them *his* living. And not many days after the younger son gathered all together, and took his journey into a far country, and there wasted his substance with riotous living. And when he had spent all, there arose a mighty famine in that land; and he began to be in want. And he went and joined himself to a citizen of that country; and he sent him into his fields to feed swine. And he would fain have filled his belly with the husks that the swine did eat: and no man gave unto him. And when he came to himself, he said, How many hired servants of my father's have bread enough and to spare, and I perish with hunger! I will arise and go to my father, and will say unto him, Father, I have sinned against heaven, and before thee, And am no more worthy to be called thy son: make me as one of thy hired servants. And he arose, and came to his father. But when he was yet a great way off, his father saw him, and had compassion, and ran, and fell on his neck, and kissed him. And the son said unto him, Father, I have sinned against heaven, and in thy sight, and am no more worthy to be called thy son. But the father said to his servants, Bring forth the best robe, and put *it* on him; and put a ring on his hand, and shoes on *his* feet: And bring hither the fatted calf, and kill *it*: and let us eat, and be merry: For this my son was dead, and is alive again; he was lost, and is found. And they began to be merry. Now his elder son was in the field: and as he came and drew nigh to the house, he heard music and dancing. And he called one of the servants, and asked what these things meant. And he said unto him, Thy brother is come; and thy father hath killed the fatted calf, because he hath received him safe and sound. And he was angry, and would not go in: therefore came his father out, and entreated him. And he answering said to *his* father, Lo, these many years do I serve thee, neither transgressed I at any time thy commandment; and yet thou never gavest me a kid, that I might make merry with my friends: But as soon as this thy son was come, which hath devoured thy living with harlots, thou hast killed for him the fatted calf. And he said unto him, Son, thou art ever with me, and all that I have is thine. It was meet that we should make merry, and be glad: for this thy brother was dead, and is alive again; and was lost, and is found.

(C. 90)

---

* King James Version of the Bible.

QUESTIONS

1. Why does the Prodigal Son leave his father and his home? What happens to him when he is away that he doesn't anticipate, and what prompts him to return home?

2. What does the father's reaction to his prodigal son reveal about his understanding of what it means to be a parent?

3. What lesson is the father's answer to the elder son meant to teach?

Jacob Grimm (1785–1863) and Wilhelm Grimm (1786–1859)

Snow-White

Translated by Lucy Crane

It was the middle of winter, and the snowflakes were falling like feathers from the sky, and a queen sat at her window working, and her embroidery frame was of ebony. And as she worked, gazing at times out on the snow, she pricked her finger, and there fell from it three drops of blood on the snow. And when she saw how bright and red it looked, she said to herself, "Oh that I had a child as white as snow, as red as blood, and as black as the wood of the embroidery frame!"

Not very long after she had a daughter, with a skin as white as snow, lips as red as blood, and hair as black as ebony, and she was named Snow-White. And when she was born the queen died.

After a year had gone by the king took another wife, a beautiful woman, but proud and overbearing, and she could not bear to be surpassed in beauty by any one. She had a magic looking-glass, and she used to stand before it, and look in it, and say,

> "Looking-glass upon the wall,
> Who is fairest of us all?"

And the looking-glass would answer,

> "You are fairest of them all."

And she was contented, for she knew that the looking-glass spoke the truth.

Now, Snow-White was growing prettier and prettier, and when she was seven years old she was as beautiful as day, far more so than the queen herself. So one day when the queen went to her mirror and said,

> "Looking-glass upon the wall,
> Who is fairest of us all?"

It answered,

> "Queen, you are full fair, 'tis true,
> But Snow-White fairer is than you."

This gave the queen a great shock, and she became yellow and green with envy, and from that hour her heart turned against Snow-White, and she hated her. And envy and pride like ill weeds grew in her heart higher every day, until she had no peace day or night. At last she sent for a huntsman, and said,

"Take the child out into the woods, so that I may set eyes on her no more. You must put her to death, and bring me her heart for a token."

The huntsman consented, and led her away; but when he drew his cutlass to pierce Snow-White's innocent heart, she began to weep and to say,

"Oh, dear huntsman, do not take my life; I will go away into the wild wood, and never come home again."

And as she was so lovely the huntsman had pity on her, and said,

"Away with you then, poor child"; for he thought the wild animals would be sure to devour her, and it was as if a stone had been rolled away from his heart when he spared to put her to death. Just at that moment a young wild boar came running by, so he caught and killed it, and taking out its heart, he brought it to the queen for a token. And it was salted and cooked, and the wicked woman ate it up, thinking that there was an end of Snow-White.

Now, when the poor child found herself quite alone in the wild woods, she felt full of terror, even of the very leaves on the trees, and she did not know what to do for fright. Then she began to run over the sharp stones and through the thorn bushes, and the wild beasts after her, but they did her no harm. She ran as long as her feet would carry her; and when the evening drew near she came to a little house, and she went inside to rest. Everything there was very small, but as pretty and clean as possible. There stood the little table ready laid, and covered with a white cloth, and seven little plates, and seven knives and forks, and drinking-cups. By the wall stood seven little beds, side by side, covered with clean white quilts. Snow-White, being very hungry and thirsty, ate from each plate a little porridge and bread, and drank out of each little cup a drop of wine, so as not to finish up one portion alone. After that she felt so tired that she lay down on one of the beds, but it did not seem to suit her; one was too long, another too short, but at last the seventh was quite right; and so she lay down upon it, committed herself to heaven, and fell asleep.

When it was quite dark, the masters of the house came home. They were seven dwarfs, whose occupation was to dig underground among the mountains. When they had lighted their seven candles, and it was quite light in the little house, they saw that some one must have been in, as everything was not in the same order in which they left it. The first said,

"Who has been sitting in my little chair?"

The second said,

"Who has been eating from my little plate?"

The third said,

"Who has been taking my little loaf?"

The fourth said,

"Who has been tasting my porridge?"

The fifth said,

"Who has been using my little fork?"

The sixth said,

"Who has been cutting with my little knife?"

The seventh said,
"Who has been drinking from my little cup?"
Then the first one, looking round, saw a hollow in his bed, and cried,
"Who has been lying on my bed?"
And the others came running, and cried,
"Some one has been on our beds too!"
But when the seventh looked at his bed, he saw little Snow-White lying there asleep. Then he told the others, who came running up, crying out in their astonishment, and holding up their seven candles to throw a light upon Snow-White.

"O goodness! O gracious!" cried they, "what beautiful child is this?" and were so full of joy to see her that they did not wake her, but let her sleep on. And the seventh dwarf slept with his comrades, an hour at a time with each, until the night had passed.

When it was morning, and Snow-White awoke and saw the seven dwarfs, she was very frightened; but they seemed quite friendly, and asked how she came to be in their house. And she related to them how her step-mother had wished her to be put to death, and how the huntsman had spared her life, and how she had run the whole day long, until at last she had found their little house. Then the dwarfs said,

"If you will keep our house for us, and cook, and wash, and make the beds, and sew and knit, and keep everything tidy and clean, you may stay with us, and you shall lack nothing."

"With all my heart," said Snow-White; and so she stayed, and kept the house in good order. In the morning the dwarfs went to the mountain to dig for gold; in the evening they came home, and their supper had to be ready for them. All the day long the maiden was left alone, and the good little dwarfs warned her, saying,

"Beware of your step-mother, she will soon know you are here. Let no one into the house."

Now the queen, having eaten Snow-White's heart, as she supposed, felt quite sure that now she was the first and fairest, and so she came to her mirror, and said,

> "Looking-glass upon the wall,
> Who is fairest of us all?"

And the glass answered,

> "Queen, thou art of beauty rare,
> But Snow-White living in the glen
> With the seven little men
> Is a thousand times more fair."

Then she was very angry, for the glass always spoke the truth, and she knew that the huntsman must have deceived her, and that Snow-White must still be living. And she thought and thought how she could manage to make an end of her, for as long as she was not the fairest in the land, envy left her no rest. At last she thought of a plan; she painted her face and dressed herself like an old peddler woman, so that no one would have known her. In this disguise she went across the seven mountains, until she came to the house of the seven little dwarfs, and she knocked at the door and cried,

"Fine wares to sell! fine wares to sell!"

Snow-White peeped out of the window and cried,

"Good-day, good woman, what have you to sell?"

"Good wares, fine wares," answered she, "laces of all colours"; and she held up a piece that was woven of variegated silk.

"I need not be afraid of letting in this good woman," thought Snow-White, and she unbarred the door and bought the pretty lace.

"What a figure you are, child!" said the old woman, "come and let me lace you properly for once."

Snow-White, suspecting nothing, stood up before her, and let her lace her with the new lace; but the old woman laced so quick and tight that it took Snow-White's breath away, and she fell down as dead.

"Now you have done with being the fairest," said the old woman as she hastened away.

Not long after that, towards evening, the seven dwarfs came home, and were terrified to see their dear Snow-White lying on the ground, without life or motion; they raised her up, and when they saw how tightly she was laced they cut the lace in two; then she began to draw breath, and little by little she returned to life. When the dwarfs heard what had happened they said,

"The old peddler woman was no other than the wicked queen; you must beware of letting any one in when we are not here!"

And when the wicked woman got home she went to her glass and said,

> "Looking-glass upon the wall,
> Who is fairest of us all?"

And it answered as before,

> "Queen, thou art of beauty rare,
> But Snow-White living in the glen
> With the seven little men
> Is a thousand times more fair."

When she heard that she was so struck with surprise that all the blood left her heart, for she knew that Snow-White must still be living.

"But now," said she, "I will think of something that will be her ruin." And by witchcraft she made a poisoned comb. Then she dressed herself up to look like another different sort of old woman. So she went across the seven mountains and came to the house of the seven dwarfs, and knocked at the door and cried.

"Good wares to sell! good wares to sell!"

Snow-White looked out and said,

"Go away, I must not let anybody in."

"But you are not forbidden to look," said the old woman, taking out the poisoned comb and holding it up. It pleased the poor child so much that she was tempted to open the door; and when the bargain was made the old woman said,

"Now, for once your hair shall be properly combed."

Poor Snow-White, thinking no harm, let the old woman do as she would, but no sooner was the comb put in her hair than the poison began to work, and the poor girl fell down senseless.

"Now, you paragon of beauty," said the wicked woman, "this is the end of you," and went off. By good luck it was now near evening, and the seven little dwarfs came home. When they saw Snow-White lying on the ground as dead, they thought directly that it was the step-mother's doing, and looked about, found the poisoned comb, and no sooner had they drawn it out of her hair than Snow-White came to herself, and related all that had passed. Then they warned her once more to be on her guard, and never again to let any one in at the door.

And the queen went home and stood before the looking-glass and said,

> "Looking-glass upon the wall,
> Who is fairest of us all?"

And the looking-glass answered as before,

> "Queen, thou art of beauty rare,
> But Snow-White living in the glen
> With the seven little men
> Is a thousand times more fair."

When she heard the looking-glass speak thus she trembled and shook with anger.

"Snow-White shall die," cried she, "though it should cost me my own life!" And then she went to a secret lonely chamber, where no one was likely to come, and there she made a poisonous apple. It was beautiful to look upon, being white with red cheeks, so that any one who should see it must long for it, but whoever ate even a little bit of it must die. When the apple was ready she painted her face and clothed herself like a peasant woman, and went across the seven mountains to where the seven dwarfs lived. And when she knocked at the door Snow-White put her head out of the window and said,

"I dare not let anybody in; the seven dwarfs told me not."

"All right," answered the woman; "I can easily get rid of my apples elsewhere. There, I will give you one."

"No," answered Snow-White, "I dare not take anything."

"Are you afraid of poison?" said the woman, "look here, I will cut the apple in two pieces; you shall have the red side, I will have the white one."

For the apple was so cunningly made, that all the poison was in the rosy half of it. Snow-White longed for the beautiful apple, and as she saw the peasant woman eating a piece of it she could no longer refrain, but stretched out her hand and took the poisoned half. But no sooner had she taken a morsel of it into her mouth than she fell to the earth as dead. And the queen, casting on her a terrible glance, laughed aloud and cried,

"As white as snow, as red as blood, as black as ebony! this time the dwarfs will not be able to bring you to life again."

And when she went home and asked the looking-glass,

"Looking-glass upon the wall,
Who is fairest of us all?"

at last it answered,

"You are the fairest now of all."

Then her envious heart had rest, so far as an envious heart can have rest.

The dwarfs, when they came home in the evening, found Snow-White lying on the ground, and there came no breath out of her mouth, and she was dead. They lifted her up, sought if anything poisonous was to be found, cut her laces, combed her hair, washed her with water and wine, but all was of no avail, the poor child was dead, and remained dead. Then they laid her on a bier, and sat all seven of them round it, and wept and lamented three whole days. And then they would have buried her, but that she looked still as if she were living, with her beautiful blooming cheeks. So they said,

"We cannot hide her away in the black ground." And they had made a coffin of clear glass, so as to be looked into from all sides, and they laid her in it, and wrote in golden letters upon it her name, and that she was a king's daughter. Then they set the coffin out upon the mountain, and one of them always remained by it to watch. And the birds came too, and mourned for Snow-White, first an owl, then a raven, and lastly, a dove.

Now, for a long while Snow-White lay in the coffin and never changed, but looked as if she were asleep, for she was still as white as snow, as red as blood, and her hair as black as ebony. It happened, however, that one day a king's son rode through the wood and up to the dwarf's house, which was near it. He saw on the mountain the coffin, and beautiful Snow-White within it, and he read what was written in golden letters upon it. Then he said to the dwarfs,

"Let me have the coffin, and I will give you whatever you like to ask for it."

But the dwarfs told him that they could not part with it for all the gold in the world. But he said,

"I beseech you to give it me, for I cannot live without looking upon Snow-White; if you consent I will bring you to great honor, and care for you as if you were my brethren."

When he so spoke the good little dwarfs had pity upon him and gave him the coffin, and the king's son called his servants and bid them carry it away on their shoulders. Now it happened that as they were going along they stumbled over a bush, and with the shaking the bit of poisoned apple flew out of her throat. It was not long before she opened her eyes, threw up the cover of the coffin, and sat up, alive and well.

"Oh dear! where am I?" cried she. The king's son answered, full of joy, "You are near me," and, relating all that had happened, he said,

"I would rather have you than anything in the world; come with me to my father's castle and you shall be my bride."

And Snow-White was kind, and went with him, and their wedding was held with pomp and great splendor.

But Snow-White's wicked step-mother was also bidden to the feast, and when she had dressed herself in beautiful clothes she went to her looking-glass and said,

> "Looking-glass upon the wall,
> Who is fairest of us all?"

The looking-glass answered,

> "O Queen, although you are of beauty rare,
> The young bride is a thousand times more fair."

Then she railed and cursed, and was beside herself with disappointment and anger. First she thought she would not go to the wedding; but then she felt she should have no peace until she went and saw the bride. And when she saw her she knew her for Snow-White, and could not stir from the place for anger and terror. For they had ready red-hot iron shoes, in which she had to dance until she fell down dead.

(1812)

QUESTIONS

1. What does this folktale suggest about the value of a woman's beauty in many cultures?

2. Why is the stepmother portrayed as wicked? Besides Snow-White's beauty, what other reasons can you think of for the stepmother's jealousy of Snow-White?

3. Where is Snow-White's father, the king, during his wife's attacks on his daughter? Why doesn't he intervene to protect Snow-White?

4. What do the happy ending for Snow-White and the prince and the brutal ending for the stepmother suggest about the values and lessons implicit in this folktale?

Writing Topics for Myths, Parables, and Folktales

1. Persephone's forced separation from her mother is often regarded as a symbol of the separation occurring when a daughter leaves home and her mother's protection. Contrast this Greek myth with the biblical story of "The Parable of the Prodigal Son." What conclusions can you draw about attitudes toward the universal problem of maturation and the desire for independence?

2. Analyze whether or not "The Parable of the Prodigal Son" and the myth of "Dædalus and Icarus" reflect a male experience. To what extent does each reinforce the notion of obedience to authority?

3. Discuss each myth and folktale as "a story with a lesson." What lesson does each one teach? What universal truths are embedded in each?

Essays

Sandra M. Gilbert (b. 1936) and Susan Gubar (b. 1944)

Snow White and Her Wicked Stepmother

*   *   *

As the legend of Lilith[1] shows, and as psychoanalysts from Freud and Jung onward have observed, myths and fairy tales often both state and enforce culture's sentences with greater accuracy than more sophisticated literary texts. If Lilith's story summarizes the genesis of the female monster in a single useful parable, the Grimm tale of "Little Snow White" dramatizes the essential but equivocal relationship between the angel-woman and the monster-woman. * * * "Little Snow White," which Walt Disney entitled "Snow White and the Seven Dwarves," should really be called Snow White and Her Wicked Stepmother, for the central action of the tale—indeed, its only real action—arises from the relationship between these two women: the one fair, young, pale, the other just as fair, but older, fiercer; the one a daughter, the other a mother; the one sweet, ignorant, passive, the other both artful and active; the one a sort of angel, the other an undeniable witch.

Significantly, the conflict between these two women is fought out largely in the transparent enclosures into which * * * both have been locked: a magic looking glass, an enchanted and enchanting glass coffin. Here, wielding as weapons the tools patriarchy suggests that women use to kill themselves into art, the two women literally try to kill each other with art. Shadow fights shadow, image destroys image in the crystal prison. * * *

The story begins in midwinter, with a Queen sitting and sewing, framed by a window. As in so many fairy tales, she pricks her finger, bleeds, and is thereby assumed into the cycle of sexuality William Blake called the realm of "generation," giving birth "soon

---

[1] Lilith: according to legend, first wife of Adam.

23

after" to a daughter "as white as snow, as red as blood, and as black as the wood of the window frame."[2] All the motifs introduced in this prefatory first paragraph—sewing, snow, blood, enclosure—are associated with key themes in female lives (hence in female writing), and they are thus themes we shall be studying throughout this book. But for our purposes here the tale's opening *is* merely prefatory. The real story begins when the Queen, having become a mother, metamorphoses also into a witch—that is, into a wicked "step" mother: ". . . when the child was born, the Queen died," and "After a year had passed the King took to himself another wife."

When we first encounter this "new" wife, she is framed in a magic looking glass, just as her predecessor—that is, her earlier self—had been framed in a window. To be caught and trapped in a mirror rather than a window, however, is to be driven inward, obsessively studying self-images as if seeking a viable self. The first Queen seems still to have had prospects; not yet fallen into sexuality, she looked outward, if only upon the snow. The second Queen is doomed to the inward search that psychoanalysts like Bruno Bettelheim censoriously define as "narcissism,"[3] but which * * * is necessitated by a state from which all outward prospects have been removed.

That outward prospects *have* been removed—or lost or dissolved away—is suggested not only by the Queen's mirror obsession but by the absence of the King from the story as it is related in the Grimm version. The Queen's husband and Snow White's father (for whose attentions, according to Bettelheim, the two women are battling in a feminized Oedipal struggle) never actually appears in this story at all, a fact that emphasizes the almost stifling intensity with which the tale concentrates on the conflict in the mirror between mother and daughter, woman and woman, self and self. At the same time, though, there is clearly at least one way in which the King *is* present. His, surely, is the voice of the looking glass, the patriarchal voice of judgment that rules the Queen's— and every woman's—self-evaluation. He it is who decides, first, that his consort is "the fairest of all," and then, as she becomes maddened, rebellious, witchlike, that she must be replaced by his angelically innocent and dutiful daughter, a girl who is therefore defined as "more beautiful still" than the Queen. To the extent, then, that the King, and only the King, constituted the first Queen's prospects, he need no longer appear in the story because, having assimilated the meaning of her own sexuality (and having, thus, become the second Queen) the woman has internalized the King's rules: his voice resides now in her own mirror, her own mind.

But if Snow White is "really" the daughter of the second as well as of the first Queen (i.e., if the two Queens are identical), why does the Queen hate her so much? The traditional explanation—that the mother is as threatened by her daughter's "budding sexuality" as the daughter is by the mother's "possession" of the father—is helpful but does not seem entirely adequate, considering the depth and ferocity of the Queen's rage. It is true, of course, that in the patriarchal Kingdom of the text these women inhabit the Queen's life can be literally imperiled by her daughter's beauty, and true (as we shall see

---

[2] "Little Snow White." All references are to the text as given in *The Complete Grimm's Fairy Tales* (New York: Random House) 1972.

[3] Bruno Bettelheim, *The Uses of Enchantment: The Meaning and Importance of Fairy Tales* (New York: Knopf) 1976, pp. 202–03.

throughout this study) that, given the female vulnerability such perils imply, female bonding is extraordinarily difficult in patriarchy: women almost inevitably turn against women because the voice of the looking glass sets them against each other. But, beyond all this, it seems as if there is a sense in which the intense desperation with which the Queen enacts her rituals of self-absorption causes (or is caused by) her hatred of Snow White. Innocent, passive, and self-lessly free of the mirror madness that consumes the Queen, Snow White represents the ideal of renunciation that the Queen has already renounced at the beginning of the story. Thus Snow White is destined to replace the Queen *because* the Queen hates her, rather than vice versa. The Queen's hatred of Snow White, in other words, exists before the looking glass has provided an obvious reason for hatred.

For the Queen, as we come to see more clearly in the course of the story, is a plotter, a plot-maker, a schemer, a witch, an artist, an impersonator, a woman of almost infinite creative energy, witty, wily, and self-absorbed as all artists traditionally are. On the other hand, in her absolute chastity, her frozen innocence, her sweet nullity, Snow White represents precisely the ideal of "contemplative purity" we have already discussed, an ideal that could quite literally kill the Queen. An angel in the house of myth, Snow White is not only a child but (as female angels always are) childlike, docile, submissive, the heroine of a life that *has no story.* But the Queen, adult and demonic, plainly wants a life of "significant action," by definition an "unfeminine" life of stories and storytelling. And therefore, to the extent that Snow White, as her daughter, is a part of herself, she wants to kill the Snow White *in herself,* the angel who would keep deeds and dramas out of her own house.

The first death plot the Queen invents is a naively straightforward murder story: she commands one of her huntsmen to kill Snow White. But, as Bruno Bettelheim has shown, the huntsman is really a surrogate for the King, a parental—or, more specifically, patriarchal—figure "who dominates, controls, and subdues wild ferocious beasts" and who thus "represents the subjugation of the animal, asocial, violent tendencies in man."[4] In a sense, then, the Queen has foolishly asked her patriarchal master to act for her in doing the subversive deed she wants to do in part to retain power over him and in part to steal his power from him. Obviously, he will not do this. As patriarchy's angelic daughter, Snow White is, after all, *his* child, and he must save her, not kill her. Hence he kills a wild boar in her stead, and brings its lung and liver to the Queen as proof that he has murdered the child. Thinking that she is devouring her ice-pure enemy, therefore, the Queen consumes, instead, the wild boar's organs; that is, symbolically speaking, she devours her own beastly rage, and becomes (of course) even more enraged.

When she learns that her first plot has failed, then, the Queen's storytelling becomes angrier as well as more inventive, more sophisticated, more subversive. Significantly, each of the three "tales" she tells—that is, each of the three plots she invents—depends on a poisonous or parodic use of a distinctively female device as a murder weapon, and in each case she reinforces the sardonic commentary on "femininity" that such weaponry makes by impersonating a "wise" woman, a "good" mother, or, as Ellen Moers would put it, an "educating heroine."[5] As a "kind" old pedlar woman, she offers to

---

[4] Bettelheim, p. 205.
[5] See Ellen Moers, *Literary Women* (New York: Doubleday) 1976, pp. 211–42.

lace Snow White "properly" for once—then suffocates her with a very Victorian set of tight laces. As another wise old expert in female beauty, she promises to comb Snow White's hair "properly," then assaults her with a poisonous comb. Finally, as a wholesome farmer's wife, she gives Snow White a "very poisonous apple," which she has made in "a quite secret, lonely room, where no one every came." The girl finally falls, killed, so it seems, by the female arts of cosmetology and cookery. Paradoxically, however, even though the Queen has been using such feminine wiles as the sirens' comb and Eve's apple subversively, to destroy angelic Snow White so that she (the Queen) can assert and aggrandize herself, these arts have had on her daughter an opposite effect from those she intended. Strengthening the chaste maiden in her passivity, they have made her into precisely the eternally beautiful, inanimate *objet d'art* patriarchal aesthetics want a girl to be. From the point of view of the mad, self-assertive Queen, conventional female arts *kill*. But from the point of view of the docile and selfless princess, such arts, even while they kill, confer the only measure of power available to a woman in a patriarchal culture.

Certainly when the kindly huntsman-father saved her life by abandoning her in the forest at the edge of his kingdom, Snow White discovered her own powerlessness. Though she had been allowed to live because she was a "good" girl, she had to find her own devious way of resisting the onslaughts of the maddened Queen, both inside and outside her self. In this connection, the seven dwarves probably represent her own dwarfed powers, her stunted selfhood, for, as Bettelheim points out, they can do little to help save the girl from the Queen. At the same time, however, her life with them is an important part of her education in submissive femininity, for in serving them she learns essential lessons of service, of selflessness, of domesticity. Finally, that at this point Snow White is a housekeeping angel in a *tiny* house conveys the story's attitude toward "woman's world and woman's work": the realm of domesticity is a miniaturized kingdom in which the best of women is not only like a dwarf but like a dwarf's servant.

Does the irony and bitterness consequent upon such a perception lead to Snow White's few small acts of disobedience? Or would Snow White ultimately have rebelled anyway, precisely because she *is* the Queen's true daughter? The story does not, of course, answer such questions, but it does seem to imply them, since its turning point comes from Snow White's significant willingness to be tempted by the Queen's "gifts," despite the dwarves' admonitions. Indeed, the only hint of self-interest that Snow White displays throughout the whole story comes in her "narcissistic" desire for the stay-laces, the comb, and the apple that the disguised murderess offers. As Bettelheim remarks, this "suggests how close the stepmother's temptations are to Snow White's inner desires."[6] Indeed, it suggests that, as we have already noted, the Queen and Snow White are in some sense one: while the Queen struggles to free herself from the passive Snow White in herself, Snow White must struggle to repress the assertive Queen in herself. That both women eat from the same deadly apple in the third temptation episode merely clarifies and dramatizes this point. The Queen's lonely art has enabled her to contrive a two-faced fruit—one white and one red "cheek"—that represents her ambiguous relationship to this angelic girl who is both her daughter and her enemy, her self and

---

[6] Bettelheim, p. 211.

her opposite. Her intention is that the girl will die of the apple's poisoned red half—red with her sexual energy, her assertive desire for deeds of blood and triumph—while she herself will be unharmed by the passivity of the white half.

But though at first this seems to have happened, the apple's effect is, finally, of course, quite different. After the Queen's artfulness has killed Snow White into art, the girl becomes if anything even more dangerous to her "step" mother's autonomy than she was before, because even more opposed to it in both mind and body. For, dead and self-less in her glass coffin, she is an object, to be displayed and desired, patriarchy's marble "opus," the decorative and decorous Galatea[7] with whom every ruler would like to grace his parlor. Thus, when the Prince first sees Snow White in her coffin, he begs the dwarves to give "it" to him as a gift, "for I cannot live without seeing Snow White. I will honor and prize her as my dearest possession." An "it," a possession, Snow White has become an idealized image of herself, and as such she has definitively proven herself to be patriarchy's ideal woman, the perfect candidate for Queen. At this point, therefore, she regurgitates the poison apple (whose madness had stuck in her throat) and rises from her coffin. The fairest in the land, she will marry the most powerful in the land; bidden to their wedding, the egotistically assertive, plotting Queen will become a former Queen, dancing herself to death in red-hot iron shoes.

What does the future hold for Snow White, however? When her Prince becomes a King and she becomes a Queen, what will her life be like? Trained to domesticity by her dwarf instructors, will she sit in the window, gazing out on the wild forest of her past, and sigh, and sew, and prick her finger, and conceive a child white as snow, red as blood, black as ebony wood? Surely, fairest of them all, Snow White has exchanged one glass coffin for another, delivered from the prison where the Queen put her only to be imprisoned in the looking glass from which the King's voice speaks daily. There is, after all, no female model for her in this tale except the "good" (dead) mother and her living avatar the "bad" mother. And if Snow White escaped her first glass coffin by her goodness, her passivity and docility, her only escape from her second glass coffin, the imprisoning mirror, must evidently be through "badness," through plots and stories, duplicitous schemes, wild dreams, fierce fictions, mad impersonations. The cycle of her fate seems inexorable. Renouncing "contemplative purity," she must now embark on that life of "significant action" which, for a woman, is defined as a witch's life because it is so monstrous, so unnatural. * * * She will become a murderess bent on the self-slaughter implicit in her murderous attempts against the life of her own child. Finally, in fiery shoes that parody the costumes of femininity as surely as the comb and stays she herself contrived, she will do a silent terrible death-dance out of the story, the looking glass, the transparent coffin of her own image. Her only deed, this death will imply, can be a deed of death, her only action the pernicious action of self-destruction.

In this connection, it seems especially significant that the Queen's dance of death is a silent one. In "The Juniper Tree" [190–97] a version of "Little Snow White" in which a *boy's* mother tries to kill him (for different reasons, of course) the dead boy is transformed not into a silent art object but into a furious golden bird who sings a song of

---

[1] Galatea: the name of the statue sculpted by Pygmalion that was eventually transformed into a living woman. (See Ovid's "The Myth of Pygmalion," p. 352 in Part 3: People in Love.)

vengeance against his murderess and finally crushes her to death with a millstone. The male child's progress toward adulthood is a growth toward both self-assertion and self-articulation. "The Juniper Tree" implies, a development of the *powers* of speech. But the girl child must learn the arts of silence either as herself a silent image invented and defined by the magic looking glass of the male-authored text, or as a silent dancer of her own woes, a dancer who enacts rather than articulates. * * *

*   *   *

(1979)

QUESTIONS

1. Why do Gilbert and Gubar suggest that Snow White's stepmother is so eager to destroy her? What does Snow White symbolize to her stepmother?

2. What do the following symbolize: the window through which Snow White's mother looks, the mirror into which her stepmother looks, and the glass coffin in which the "dead" Snow White is placed? What do the window, mirror, and glass coffin have in common?

3. Explain why Gilbert and Gubar see Snow White's mother and stepmother as the same person and even go so far as to suggest that the wicked Queen and Snow White are halves of the same whole? (You might want to consult von Franz's essay, "The Realization of the Shadow," p. 691, in Part 5: "Friends and Enemies," for a better understanding of the shadow.)

4. Do you agree or disagree with Gilbert and Gubar's opinion that Snow White is an example of "patriarchal repression"?

MAXINE HONG KINGSTON (B. 1940)

The Woman Warrior

Memoirs of a Childhood Among Ghosts*

Once in a long while, four times so far for me, my mother brings out the metal tube that holds her medical diploma. On the tube are gold circles crossed with seven red lines each—"joy" ideographs in abstract. There are also little flowers that look like gears for a gold machine. According to the scraps of labels with Chinese and American addresses, stamps, and postmarks, the family airmailed the can from Hong Kong in 1950. It got crushed in the middle, and whoever tried to peel the labels off stopped because the red and gold paint came off too, leaving silver scratches that rust. Somebody tried to pry the end off before discovering that the tube pulls apart. When I open it, the smell of China flies out, a thousand-year-old bat flying heavy-headed out of the Chinese caverns where bats are as white as dust, a smell that comes from long ago, far back in the brain. Crates from Canton, Hong Kong, Singapore, and Taiwan have that smell too, only stronger because they are more recently come from the Chinese.

Inside the can are three scrolls, one inside another. The largest says that in the twenty-third year of the National Republic, the To Keung School of Midwifery, where she has had two years of instruction and Hospital Practice, awards its Diploma to my mother, who has shown through oral and written examination her Proficiency in Midwifery, Pediatrics, Gynecology, "Medecine," "Surgary," Therapeutics, Ophthalmology, Bacteriology, Dermatology, Nursing and Bandage. This document has eight stamps on it: one, the school's English and Chinese names embossed together in a circle; one, as the Chinese enumerate, a stork and a big baby in lavender ink; one, the school's Chinese seal; one, an orangish paper stamp pasted in the border design; one, the red seal of Dr. Wu Pak-liang, M.D., Lyon, Berlin, president and "Ex-assistant étranger à la clinique chirugicale et d'accouchement de l'université de Lyon"; one, the red seal of Dean Woo Yin-kam, M.D.; one, my mother's seal, her chop mark larger than the president's and the dean's; and one, the number 1279 on the back. Dean Woo's signature is followed by "(Hackett)." I read in a history book that Hackett Medical College for Women at Canton[1] was founded in the nineteenth century by European women doctors.

The school seal has been pressed over a photograph of my mother at the age of thirty-seven. The diploma gives her age as twenty-seven. She looks younger than I do, her eyebrows are thicker, her lips fuller. Her naturally curly hair is parted on the left, one wavy wisp tendrilling off to the right. She wears a scholar's white gown, and she is not thinking about her appearance. She stares straight ahead as if she could see me and past me to her grandchildren and grandchildren's grandchildren. She has spacy eyes, as all people recently from Asia have. Her eyes do not focus on the camera. My mother is

---

* This selection is an excerpt from *The Woman Warrior: Memoirs of a Childhood Among Ghosts* (New York: Alfred A. Knopf, Inc.) 1975.

[1] Canton: now Guangzhou, a major city in southern China on the Pearl River.

not smiling; Chinese do not smile for photographs. Their faces command relatives in foreign lands—"Send money"—and posterity forever—"Put food in front of this picture." My mother does not understand Chinese-American snapshots. "What are you laughing at?" she asks.

The second scroll is a long narrow photograph of the graduating class with the school officials seated in front. I picked out my mother immediately. Her face is exactly her own, though forty years younger. She is so familiar, I can only tell whether or not she is pretty or happy or smart by comparing her to the other women. For this formal group picture she straightened her hair with oil to make a chinlength bob like the others'. On the other women, strangers, I can recognize a curled lip, a sidelong glance, pinched shoulders. My mother is not soft; the girl with the small nose and dimpled underlip is soft. My mother is not humorous, not like the girl at the end who lifts her mocking chin to pose like Girl Graduate. My mother does not have smiling eyes; the old woman teacher (Dean Woo?) in front crinkles happily, and the one faculty member in the western suit smiles westernly. Most of the graduates are girls whose faces have not yet formed; my mother's face will not change anymore, except to age. She is intelligent, alert, pretty. I can't tell if she's happy.

The graduates seem to have been looking elsewhere when they pinned the rose, zinnia, or chrysanthemum on their precise black dresses. One thin girl wears hers in the middle of her chest. A few have a flower over a left or a right nipple. My mother put hers, a chrysanthemum, below her left breast. Chinese dresses at that time were dartless, cut as if women did not have breasts; these young doctors, unaccustomed to decorations, may have seen their chests as black expanses with no reference points for flowers. Perhaps they couldn't shorten that far gaze that lasts only a few years after a Chinese emigrates. In this picture too my mother's eyes are big with what they held—reaches of oceans beyond China, land beyond oceans. Most emigrants learn the barbarians' directness—how to gather themselves and stare rudely into talking faces as if trying to catch lies. In America my mother has eyes as strong as boulders, never once skittering off a face, but she has not learned to place decorations and phonograph needles, nor has she stopped seeing land on the other side of the oceans. Now her eyes include the relatives in China, as they once included my father smiling and smiling in his many western outfits, a different one for each photograph that he sent from America.

He and his friends took pictures of one another in bathing suits at Coney Island beach, the salt wind from the Atlantic blowing their hair. He's the one in the middle with his arms about the necks of his buddies. They pose in the cockpit of a biplane, on a motorcycle, and on a lawn beside the "Keep Off the Grass" sign. They are always laughing. My father, white shirt sleeves rolled up, smiles in front of a wall of clean laundry. In the spring he wears a new straw hat, cocked at a Fred Astaire angle. He steps out, dancing down the stairs, one foot forward, one back, a hand in his pocket. He wrote to her about the American custom of stomping on straw hats come fall. "If you want to save your hat for next year," he said, "you have to put it away early, or else when you're riding the subway or walking along Fifth Avenue, any stranger can snatch it off your head and put his foot through it. That's the way they celebrate the change of seasons here." In the winter he wears a gray felt hat with his gray overcoat. He is sitting on a rock in Central Park. In one snapshot he is not smiling; someone took it when he was studying, blurred in the glare of the desk lamp.

There are no snapshots of my mother. In two small portraits, however, there is a black thumbprint on her forehead, as if someone had inked in bangs, as if someone had marked her.

"Mother, did bangs come into fashion after you had the picture taken?" One time she said yes. Another time when I asked, "Why do you have fingerprints on your forehead?" she said, "Your First Uncle did that." I disliked the unsureness in her voice.

The last scroll has columns of Chinese words. The only English is "Department of Health, Canton," imprinted on my mother's face, the same photograph as on the diploma. I keep looking to see whether she was afraid. Year after year my father did not come home or send for her. Their two children had been dead for ten years. If he did not return soon, there would be no more children. ("They were three and two years old, a boy and a girl. They could talk already.") My father did send money regularly, though, and she had nobody to spend it on but herself. She bought good clothes and shoes. Then she decided to use the money for becoming a doctor. She did not leave for Canton immediately after the children died. In China there was time to complete feelings. As my father had done, my mother left the village by ship. There was a sea bird painted on the ship to protect it against shipwreck and winds. She was in luck. The following ship was boarded by river pirates, who kidnapped every passenger, even old ladies. "Sixty dollars for an old lady" was what the bandits used to say. "I sailed alone," she says, "to the capital of the entire province." She took a brown leather suitcase and a seabag stuffed with two quilts.

At the dormitory the school official assigned her to a room with five other women, who were unpacking when she came in. They greeted her and she greeted them. But no one wanted to start friendships until the unpacking was done, each item placed precisely to section off the room. My mother spotted the name she had written on her application pinned to a headboard, and the annoyance she felt at not arriving early enough for first choice disappeared. The locks on her suitcase opened with two satisfying clicks; she enjoyed again how neatly her belongings fitted together, clean against the green lining. She refolded the clothes before putting them in the one drawer that was hers. Then she took out her pens and inkbox, an atlas of the world, a tea set and tea cannister, sewing box, her ruler with the real gold markings, writing paper, envelopes with the thick red stripe to signify no bad news, her bowl and silver chopsticks. These things she arranged one by one on her shelf. She spread the two quilts on top of the bed and put her slippers side by side underneath. She owned more—furniture, wedding jewelry, cloth, photographs—but she had left such troublesome valuables behind in the family's care. She never did get all of it back.

The women who had arrived early did not offer to help unpack, not wanting to interfere with the pleasure and the privacy of it. Not many women got to live out the daydream of women—to have a room, even a section of a room, that only gets messed up when she messes it up herself. The book would stay open at the very page she had pressed flat with her hand, and no one would complain about the field not being plowed or the leak in the roof. She would clean her own bowl and a small, limited area; she would have one drawer to sort, one bed to make.

To shut the door at the end of the workday, which does not spill over into evening. To throw away books after reading them so they don't have to be dusted. To go through boxes on New Year's Eve and throw out half of what is inside. Sometimes for extravagance to pick a bunch of flowers for the one table. Other women besides me must have this daydream about a carefree life. I've seen Communist pictures showing a contented woman sitting on her bunk sewing. Above her head is her one box on a shelf. The words stenciled on the box mean "Fragile," but literally say, "Use a little heart." The woman looks very pleased. The Revolution put an end to prostitution by giving women what they wanted: a job and a room of their own.

Free from families, my mother would live for two years without servitude. She would not have to run errands for my father's tyrant mother with the bound feet or thread needles for the old ladies, but neither would there be slaves and nieces to wait on her. Now she would get hot water only if she bribed the concierge. When I went away to school my mother said, "Give the concierge oranges."

Two of my mother's roommates, who had organized their corners to their satisfaction, made tea and set a small table with their leftover travel food. "Have you eaten, Lady Scholar?" they invited my mother. "Lady Scholar, come drink tea," they said to each of the others. "Bring your own cup." This largess moved my mother—tea, an act of humility. She brought out meats and figs she had preserved on the farm. Everyone complimented her on their tastiness. The women told which villages they came from and the names they would go by. My mother did not let it be known that she had already had two children and that some of these girls were young enough to be her daughters.

Then everyone went to the auditorium for two hours of speeches by the faculty. They told the students that they would begin with a text as old as the Han empire, when the prescription for immortality had not yet been lost. Chang Chung-ching, father of medicine, had told how the two great winds, *yang* and *yin,* blew through the human body. The diligent students would do well to begin tonight memorizing his book on colds and fevers. After they had mastered the ancient cures that worked, they would be taught the most up-to-date western discoveries. By the time the students graduated—those of them who persevered—their range of knowledge would be wider than that of any other doctor in history. Women have now been practicing medicine for about fifty years, said one of the teachers, a woman, who complimented them for adding to their growing number and also for coming to a school that taught modern medicine. "You will bring science to the villages." At the end of the program, the faculty turned their backs to the students, and everyone bowed the three bows toward the picture of Doctor Sun Yat-sen,[2] who was a western surgeon before he became a revolutionary. Then they went to the dining hall to eat. My mother began memorizing her books immediately after supper.

There were two places where a student could study: the dining hall with its tables cleared for work, everyone chanting during the common memorization sessions; or the table in her own room. Most students went to the dining hall for the company there. My mother usually stayed in her room or, when a roommate wanted the privacy of it also, went to a secret hiding place she had hunted out during the first week of school. Once in a while she dropped by the dining hall, chanted for a short while with the most advanced group, not missing a syllable, yawned early, and said good-night. She quickly

---

[2] Doctor Sun Yat-sen (1866–1925): a medical doctor and a leader of the revolution against the Manchus in 1912, bringing about their collapse.

built a reputation for being brilliant, a natural scholar who could glance at a book and know it.

"The other students fought over who could sit next to me at exams," says my mother. "One glimpse at my paper when they got stuck, and they could keep going."

"Did you ever try to stop them from copying your paper?"

"Of course not. They only needed to pick up a word or two, and they could remember the rest. That's not copying. You get a lot more clues in actual diagnosis. Patients talk endlessly about their ailments. I'd feel their pulses knocking away under my very fingertips—so much clearer than the paperdolls in the textbooks. I'd chant the symptoms, and those few words would start a whole chapter of cures tumbling out. Most people don't have the kind of brains that can do that." She pointed at the photograph of the thirty-seven graduates. "One hundred and twelve students began the course at the same time I did."

She suspected she did not have the right kind of brains either, my father the one who can recite whole poems. To make up the lack, she did secret studying. She also gave herself twenty years' headstart over the young girls, although she admitted to only ten, which already forced her to push. Older people were expected to be smarter; they are closer to the gods. She did not want to overhear students or teachers say, "She must be exceedingly stupid, doing no better than anyone else when she is a generation older. She's so dumb, she has to study day and night."

"I studied far in advance," says my mother. "I studied when the breathing coming from the beds and coming through the wood walls was deep and even. The night before exams, when the other students stayed up, I went to bed early. They would say, 'Aren't you going to study?' and I'd say, 'No, I'm going to do some mending,' or, 'I want to write letters tonight.' I let them take turns sitting next to me at the tests." The sweat of hard work is not to be displayed. It is much more graceful to appear favored by the gods.

(1975)

Questions

1. What do Hong Kingston's tone and descriptive phrases reveal about her affection for her mother and father?

2. What does each photograph reveal about the parent from the daughter's point of view?

3. How does Hong Kingston's description of the unrolling of the three scrolls and the order in which they are opened give structure to the essay?

JULIA ALVAREZ (B. 1950)

El Doctor

"Lights! At this hour?" my father asks, looking up from his empty dinner plate at the glowing lamp my mother has just turned on above the table. "Are we in Plato's cave,[1] Mother?" He winks at me; as the two readers in the family we show off by making allusions my mother and sisters don't understand. He leans his chair back and picks up the hem of the curtain. A dim gray light falls into the room. "See, Mother. It's still light out there!"

"Ya, ya!" she snaps, and flips the switch off.

"Your mother is a wonder," he announces, then he adds, "El Doctor[2] is ready for bed." Dinner is over; every night my father brings the meal to a close with a third-person goodnight before he leaves the room.

Tonight he lingers, watching her. She says nothing, head bent, intent on her mashed plantains with oil and onions. "Yessir," he elaborates, "El Doctor—" The rest is garbled, for he's balled up his napkin and rubbed his lips violently as if he meant to erase them from his face. Perhaps he shouldn't have spoken up? She is jabbing at the few bites of beefsteak on her plate. Perhaps he should have just let the issue drop like water down his chest or whatever it is the Americans say. He scrapes his chair back.

Her scowl deepens. "Eduardo, please." And then, because he already knows better, she adds only, "The wax finish."

"Por supuesto,"[3] he says, his voice full of false concern as he examines her spotless kitchen floor for damages. Then, carefully, he lifts his chair up and tucks it back in its place. "This old man is ready for bed." He leans over and kisses the scowl off her face. "Mother, this country agrees with you. You look more beautiful every day. Doesn't she, girls?" And with a wink of encouragement to each of us, he leaves us in the dark.

I remember my mother mornings, slapping around in her comfortable slippers, polishing her windows into blinding panes of light. But I remember him mostly at night, moving down the dark halls, undressing as he climbed the dark stairs to bed.

I want to say there were as many buttons on his vest as stairs up to the bedroom: it seemed he unbuttoned a button on each step so that by the time he reached the landing, his vest was off. His armor, I thought, secretly pleased with all I believed I understood about him. But his vest couldn't have had more than six buttons, and the stairs were long and narrow. Of course, I couldn't see well in the dark he insisted on.

"I'm going to take this dollar," he showed me, holding a bill in one hand and a flickering lighter in the other, "and I'm going to set fire to it." He never actually did. He spoke in parables, he complained in metaphor because he had never learned to say things directly. I already knew what he meant, but I had my part to play.

---

[1] Plato's cave: an allusion to the "Allegory of the Cave" from *The Republic* by the Greek philosopher Plato (C. 427–347 B.C.E.).
[2] *El Doctor:* "The Doctor."
[3] *Por supuesto:* "Of course."

"Why would you want to do something like that?" I asked.

"Exactly! Why burn up my money with all these lights in the house!"

As we grew up, confirmed in our pyromania, he did not bother to teach us to economize, but went through the house, turning off lights in every room, not noticing many times that we were there, reading or writing a letter, and leaving us in the dark, hurt that he had overlooked us.

At the bedroom door he loosened his tie and, craning his neck, undid the top button of his shirt. Then he sat at the edge of the bed and turned on his bedside lamp. Not always; if a little reflected sun dappled the room with shadowy light, if it was late spring or early fall or summertime, he waited until the last moment to turn on the lamp, sometimes reading in the dark until we came in and turned it on for him, "Papa, you're going to ruin your eyes," we scolded.

Once I worked it out for him with the pamphlet the electric company sent me. Were he to leave his bedside light, say, burning for the rest of his evenings—and I allowed him a generous four decades ("I won't need it for that long," he protested; I insisted)—the cost (side by side we multiplied, added, carried over to the next column) would be far less than if he lost his eyesight, was forced to give up his practice, and had to spend the next four decades—

"Like your friend Milton,"[4] he said, pleased with the inspired possibilities of blindness. Now that I was turning out to be the family poet, all the greats were my personal friends. "'When I consider how my light is spent,'" he began. He loved to recite, racing me through poems to see who would be the first one to finish.

"'How my light is spent,'" I echoed and took the lead, "'Ere half my days, in this dark world and wide . . .'"

Just as I was rounding the linebreak to the last line, he interjected it, "'They also serve who only stand and wait.'"

I scowled. How dare he clap the last line on after I had gone through all the trouble of reciting the poem! "Not every blind man is a Milton," I said, and I gave him the smirk I wore all through adolescence.

"Nutrition," he said mysteriously.

"What about nutrition?"

"Good nutrition, we're starting to see the effects: children grow taller; they have better teeth, better bones, better minds than their elders." And he reached for his book on the bedside table.

Actually, the reading came later. First there is the scene that labels him immigrant and shows why I could never call him, sweetly, playfully, *Daddy*. He took from his back pocket a wad of bills so big his hand could not close over it. And he began to count. If at this point we disturbed him, he waved us away. If we called from downstairs, he did not answer. All over the bed he shared with my mother were piles of bills: I do not know the system; no one ever did. Perhaps all the fives were together, all the tens? Perhaps each pile was a specific amount? But this was the one private moment he insisted on. Not even catching him undressing, which I never did, seems as intimate a glimpse of him.

---

[4] John Milton (1608–1674): one of England's greatest poets and author of the epic *Paradise Lost*.

After the counting came the binding and marking: each pile was held together with rubber bands he saved from the rolled-up *New York Times,* and the top bill was scribbled on. He marked them as a reminder of how much was in each pile, I'm sure, but I can't help thinking it was also his way of owning what he had earned, much as ranchers brand their cattle. The Secretary of the Treasury had signed this twenty; there was Andrew Jackson's picture; he had to add his hand to it to make it his—to try to convince himself that it was his, for he never totally believed it was. Even after he was a successful doctor in New York with a house in the suburbs and lands at "home," his daughters in boarding schools and summer camps, a second car with enough gadgets to keep him busy in bad traffic, he was turning off lights, frequenting thrift shops for finds in ties, taking the 59th Street bridge even if it was out of his way to avoid paying a toll to cross the river.

He could not afford the good life, he could only pass it on. And he did. Beneath the surface pennypinching, his extravagance might have led him to bankruptcy several times had mother not been there to remind him that the weather was apt to change. "Save for a snowy day," she advised him.

"Julie! Isn't it rainy day?" he enlisted me. He was always happy to catch his wife at an error since she spoke English so much better than he did. "Save it for a rainy day?"

Eager to be an authority on anything, I considered Arbiter of Clichés a compliment to my literary talent. "Save it for a rainy day," I agreed.

"See, Mother."

She defended herself. "Snow is much worse than rain. For one thing, you need to own more clothes in the winter . . . ."

Out from his pocket came a ten when we needed small change for the subway. Away at college I opened the envelope, empty but for the money order for fifty, a hundred; typed out in the blank beside *for* was his memo: "Get yourself a little something in my name." It was the sixties and parental money was under heavy suspicion; my friends needed me as a third world person to be a good example of poverty and oppression by the capitalist, military-industrial complex. I put my little somethings quietly in the bank. By the time I graduated from college, I had a small corrupt fortune.

But my rich father lived in the dark, saving string, going the long way. I've analyzed it with my economist friends. Perhaps since his fortune came from the same work which in his country had never earned him enough, he could never believe that his being well-to-do wasn't an I.R.S. oversight. My psychologist friends claim that it is significant that he was the youngest of twenty-five children. Coming after so many, he would always fear that the good things would run out. And indeed he had a taste for leftovers, which made his compliments come a day or two after a special meal. Whenever we had chicken, he insisted on the wings and the neck bone because those had been the portions left by the time the platter got to him, the baby. He liked the pale, bitter center of the lettuce. ("The leaves were gone when I got the salad bowl.") And when we had soup, he was surprised to find a piece of meat bobbing at the surface. "Someone missed this one."

Unlike mother, he saved for a sunny day. Extravaganza! On his birthday, on Christmas, on his saint's day which was never celebrated for anyone else, his presents multiplied before us. Beside the one we had bought for him, there were always other glossy packages, ribboned boxes which dwarfed ours. The cards were forged: "To my dearest father from his loving daughter." "Which of you gave me this?" he asked with mock surprise and real delight. Cordelias[5] all, we shook our heads as he unwrapped a silk lounging jacket or a genuine leather passport case. I wish he had allowed someone to give him something.

Perhaps we did on those evenings after the money was counted and put away, and he was ready for company. With an instinct for his rituals, we knew when it was time to come into the bedroom. We heard the bathroom door click shut; he was undressing, putting on his pajamas. The hamper lid clapped on its felt lip. We heard steps. The bed creaked. We found him in the darkening room with a book. "Papi, you're ruining your eyes!" and we turned on the bedside lamp for him since he could not give himself the luxury of that light. "Oh my God, it's gotten dark already," he almost thanked us.

He wanted company, not conversation. He had us turn on the television so we could learn our English. This after years here, after his money had paid for the good private schools which unrolled our r's and softened our accents; after American boyfriends had whispered sweet colloquialisms in our ears. As the television's cowboys and beauty queens and ladies with disappointing stains in their wash droned on in their native English, he read the usual: a history book in Spanish. We sat at the edge of the king-size bed and wondered what he wanted from us. He wanted presences: Walter Cronkite,[6] his children, his wife, the great gods from the past, Napoleon, Caesar, Maximilian.[7] If one of us, bored with his idea of company, got up to leave, he lowered his book. "Did you know that in the campaign of 1808, Napoleon left his General behind to cut off the enemy from the rear, and the two divisions totally missed each other?" That was the only way he knew to ask us to stay, appealing to history and defeat, to wintry campaigns, bloody frost-bitten feet, a field strewn with war dead.

I taste the mints that he gave us, one each. He kept a stash of them in a drawer next to his bed like a schoolboy and ate exactly one each night and gave away four. That was the other way he kept us there if we got up to go after Napoleon's troops had been annihilated. "Don't you want a mint?" He didn't mean right then and there. It was a promise we had to wait for, perhaps until the chapter ended or the Roman empire fell or he was sure we had given up on the evening and decided to stay, talking in code with each other about school, our friends, our wild (for that room) adventures.

We were not fooled into rash confessions there, for at the merest hint of misadventure, the book came down like a coffin lid on Caesar or Claudius.[8] Oh, we confessed, we were just exaggerating! Of course we didn't raid the dorm kitchen at midnight, our friends did. "Tell me who your friends are," he said in Spanish, "and I'll tell you who *you* are." No, we hadn't gotten help on our math. "The man who reaches the summit following another's trail will not find his way back to his own valley." If he

---

[5] Cordelia: the loving daughter of King Lear, the protagonist of William Shakespeare's tragedy *King Lear*. Lear's other daughters feigned love and betrayed him.

[6] Walter Cronkite (b. 1916): broadcast journalist, foreign correspondent and anchorman for CBS News.

[7] Napoleon Bonaparte (1769–1821): emperor of the Holy Roman Empire; Julius Caesar (100–44 B.C.E.), emperor of the Roman Empire; and Maximilian (1832–1867), emperor of Mexico.

[8] Julius Caesar (100–44 B.C.E.) and Claudius (10 B.C.E.–54 C.E.): Roman emperors.

caught us, hurrying, scurrying, here, there, he stopped us mid-flight to tell us what Napoleon had said to his valet, "Dress me slowly, I'm in a hurry."

But why look beyond one's own blood for good examples? "You come from good stock," he bragged when I came home from boarding school, my pride wounded. I'd been called ugly names by some great-great-granddaughters of the American Revolution. "You tell them your great-grandfather was the son of a count." He had paid a lot of money on a trip to Barcelona to find that out from a man who claimed he was licensed to do family trees. The elaborate chart, magnificently framed in curlicued wood, hung in the waiting room of his office in Spanish Brooklyn along with his medical degrees. His patients, I suppose, were meant to be reassured that their ailments would be treated, not only by the valedictorian of the faculty of medicine of La Universidad de Santo Domingo, but also by the descendant of a count. "We were in this hemisphere before they were. In fact, the first group of Puritans—"

"You don't understand, you don't understand," I wailed, hot tears welling in my eyes. And I closed the door of my room, forbidding anyone to enter.

"What's she doing in there, Mother?" I heard him ask her.

"I don't know. Writing poetry or something."

"Are you sure? You think she's all right?"

I had been reading Sylvia Plath[9] and my talk was spiked with suicide.

"These girls are going to drive us crazy!" My mother said, "That's what I'm sure of. One of them has to have straight hair. Straight hair, at this stage of the game! Another wants to spend the weekend at a boy's school. All the other girls get to! This one wants to die young and miserable!" Then she yelled at father. "I'm going to end up in Bellevue.[10] And then you're all going to be very sorry!" I heard the rushed steps down the stairs, the bang of the screen door, finally the patter of the hose as she watered the obedient grass in the growing dark.

He knocked first. "Hello?" he asked tentatively, the door ajar. "Hello, hello, Edgar Allan Poe,"[11] he teased, entering. He sat at the foot of my bed and told me the story of his life.

"The point is," he concluded. *"'La vida es sueño y los sueños, sueños son.'"*[12] He stood by the window and watched my mother watering her fussy bushes as if she could flush roses out of them. "My father," he turned to me, "used to say that to my mother: Life is a dream, Mauran, and dreams are dreams."

He came across the shadowy room as if he did not want anyone to overhear. It was getting late. In the darkening garden she would be winding the hose into drooping coils. "Always, always," he said. "I always wanted to be a poet. *'La vida es sueño.'* 'They also serve who only stand and wait.' 'To be or not to be.' Can you imagine! To say such things! My God! Everyone gets a little something." He cupped his hands towards me. I nodded, too stunned at his flood of words to ask him what he meant. "And some make a building," he made a building with a wave of his hand. "Some," he rubbed his thumb and

---

[9] Sylvia Plath (1932–1963): an American poet who committed suicide. (See p. 91, p. 103, and p. 273.)

[10] Bellevue: a New York City hospital famous for its psychiatric ward.

[11] Edgar Allan Poe (1809–1849): an American writer. (See p. 885.)

[12] Spanish for "Life is a dream, and dreams are dreams."

index finger together, "make money. Some make friends, connections, you know. But some, some make something that can change the thinking of mankind! Oh my God!" He smacked his forehead with his palm in disbelief. "Think of the Bible. Think of your friend Edgar Allan Poe. But then," he mused, "then you grow older, you discover. . . ." He looked down at me. I don't know what he saw in my eyes, perhaps how young I still was, perhaps his eyes duplicated in my face. He stopped himself.

"You discover?" I said.

But he was already half way across the room. "Papi?" I tried to call him back.

"Your mother," he explained, letting himself out of the room and the revelation. "I think she is calling for me."

A few days later as I sat in his bedroom after supper, waiting for him to fall asleep, I tried to get him to finish his sentence. He couldn't remember what he was about to say, he said, but speaking of discoveries, "We're descended from the conquistadores, you know? Your grandfather traveled the whole north coast on horseback. Now there was a great man!" The supporting evidence was slim. "He looked like an Irishman. Ah, he was big and pink-tinted—what is that word, Julie? *Rowdy?*"

"You mean *ruddy?*" I said, knowing Don José de Jesus was probably ruddy with drink and rowdy with women. He had sired twenty-five children, widowed once, and kept four or five mistresses who raised the figure to thirty-five children. Of course, father never told us that; mother did when she explained how one of our uncles could be born within two months of father's birthday. She cautioned us never ever to mention to father what she had told us.

The youngest did, pretending ignorance, practicing addition. If Teolinda, the first wife, had ten children, and Mauran, the second one, had fifteen, and four of the kids had already died, then how come there were still thirty uncles and aunts left? "They were not hijos de padre y madre,"[13] he explained. "You know where that term came from? *Hijos de padre y madre?* When the Spaniards—"

"Where did the extra uncles and aunts come from?" She was not one to be diverted by a red herring twitching in the sun when a skeleton was rattling in the closet.

So, so he said. The time had come. The uncles and aunts were half brothers and sisters. The mothers *were* wives, yes, in the eyes of God, where it really mattered.

When we raised our eyebrows and pressed the smile out of our lips, he would have none of it. Customs changed. Our grandfather was a patriotic man. There had been a terrible epidemic, the island was underpopulated, the birthrate was low, the best men did what they had to do. "So," he looked pointedly at each of us. "There's a good *ejemplo*[14] for you. Always put in that extra little bit in whatever you do," he said, lifting up the history of Constantinople or Machu Picchu or Rome.

His mother? He sighed. Don't talk to him about his mother! A saint! Sweet, very religious, patience personified, always smiling. They didn't make them like that anymore, with a few exceptions, he winked at me.

But since Mauran knew about the half children, and being very religious, she must have believed her husband and she would spend eternity separated. I imagined her

---

[13] Spanish for "Children of both the father and mother."
[14] *ejemplo:* "example."

as a dour and dowdy woman alternately saying her rosary when her husband transgressed or having his children when he didn't.

"Does mother remind you of her?" I asked, thinking that leading questions might help him remember what he had been about to say in my room a few nights ago.

"Your mother is a wonder," he said. A good woman, so devoted, so thorough, a little nervous, so giving, a little forceful, a good companion, a little too used to her own way, so generous. "Every garland needs a few thorns," he added.

"I heard that," she said, coming into the room, "What was that about too used to my own way?"

"Did I say that, girls?" father turned to us. "No, Mami, you misheard."

"Then what did you say?"

"What did I say, girls?"

We shrugged, leaving him wide open.

"I said, Mother," he said, unwrapping a rare second mint and putting it in his mouth to buy time. "I said: so used to giving to others. Mother, you're too generous!"

"Ay, put gravy on the chicken." She waved him off, terribly pleased as father winked at our knowing looks.

A few nights later, still on the track of his secret self, I asked him, "Papi, how do you see yourself?" Only I, who had achieved a mild reputation as a deep thinker, could get away with such questions.

"You ask deep questions," he mused, interrupting Napoleon's advance across the Russian steppes. "I like that."

He offered me my mint and unwrapped his. "I am the rock," he said, nodding.

"Ay, Papi, that's too impersonal. How do you perceive yourself? What kind of man are you?" I was young and thought such definitions could be given and trusted. I was young and ready to tear loose, but making it harder for myself by trying to understand those I was about to wound.

"I am a rock," he repeated, liking his analogy. "Mother, you girls, my sisters, everyone needs my support. I am the strong one!"

That admission put a mermaid on the rock, luring me back with a delicate song about loss and youth's folly and the loneliness of the father. "But, Papi," I whispered as I moved from the armchair to the foot of his bed, "you don't always have to be strong."

That was my mistake. The conversation was over. He hated touching scenes; they confused him. Perhaps as the last child of an older, disappointed woman, he was used to diffuse attention, not intimacy. To take hold of a hand, to graze a cheek and whisper an endearment were beyond him. Tenderness had to be mothered by necessity: he was a good doctor. Under the cover of Hippocrates' oath,[15] with the stethoscope around his neck and the bright examination light flushing out the personal and making any interchange terribly professional, he was amazingly delicate: tapping a bone as if it were the fontenelle of a baby, easing a patient back on a pillow like a lover his sleeping beloved, stroking hair away from a feverish forehead. But now he turned away.

---

[15] Hippocrates (c. 460–370 b.c.e.): a Greek physician, is called the father of medicine. The oath is a code of ethical conduct for physicians formulated in Ancient Greece and still administered to medical students upon graduation in many universities.

He fell asleep secretly in that room full of presences, my mother beside him. No one knew exactly when it happened. We looked to him during a commercial or when a slip had implicated us in some forbidden adventure, and the book had collapsed like a card house on his chest and his glasses rode the bridge of his nose like a schoolmarm's. Though if we got up to leave and one of us reached for his glasses he woke with a start, "I'm not asleep!" he lied. "Don't go yet, it's early."

He fell asleep in the middle of the Hundred Days while Napoleon marched towards Waterloo or, defeated, was shipped off to St. Helena. We stifled our giggles at his comic-book snores, the sheets pulled over his head, his nose poking out like a periscope. Very quietly, widening our eyes at each other as if that might stop any noise, we rose. One turned off the set and threw a kiss at mother, who put her finger to her lips from her far side of the bed. Another and another kiss traveled across the hushed room. A scolding wave from mother hurried my sisters out.

I liked to be the one who stayed, bending over the bedside table strewn with candy wrappers, slipping a hand under the tassled shade. I turned the switch over, once. The room burst into brighter light, the tassels swung madly, mother signaled to me, crossly, Out! Out at once! I shrugged apologies. Her scowl deepened. Father groaned. I bent closer. I turned again. The room went back into economical dark.

(1982)

QUESTIONS

1. What do the anecdotes Alvarez relates reveal about her father? What age is she in these reflections? How do you know if the memoir is related from that age or from when she's older?

2. How would you characterize the author's relationship with her father? With her mother? Why is the father a figure of the evening in the author's memories, whereas the mother is a morning or daytime figure?

3. How is the father defined by his immigrant experience? By his class? By his gender? By his profession?

4. Why does the father never explain why he didn't become a poet? If he were to have answered, what do you expect his answer would have been?

Writing Topics for Essays

1. Discuss the theme of mortality as it appears in both Alvarez's "El Doctor" and Hong Kingston's "The Woman Warrior."

2. Discuss the attitudes toward women that are revealed in Hong Kingston's "The Woman Warrior" and Alvarez's "El Doctor." Do the daughters in each essay see themselves as freer to define themselves than their mothers were? How do you see these essays in relationship to Gilbert and Gubar's "Snow White and Her Wicked Stepmother"?

3. According to Gilbert and Gubar's "Snow White and Her Wicked Stepmother," the woman artist must rebel against her docile training if she is going to create art. Write an essay showing how art requires the woman artist to "go against the grain" if she is going to be original. (You might also want to include Woolf's essay, "Shakespeare's Sister," p. 227, in your analysis.)

4. Do you think that you will follow in the path of your parents? If this does not seem probable to you, consider what makes you think that you can break the bonds of family and culture that identify you as a person in a family and in society?

Short Stories

DORIS LESSING (B. 1919)

Through the Tunnel

Going to the shore on the first morning of the vacation, the young English boy stopped at a turning of the path and looked down at a wild and rocky bay, and then over to the crowded beach he knew so well from other years. His mother walked on in front of him, carrying a bright striped bag in one hand. Her other arm, swinging loose, was very white in the sun. The boy watched that white naked arm, and turned his eyes, which had a frown behind them, towards the bay and back again to his mother. When she felt he was not with her, she swung around. "Oh, there you are, Jerry!" she said. She looked impatient, then smiled. "Why, darling, would you rather not come with me? Would you rather—" She frowned, conscientiously worrying over what amusements he might secretly be longing for, which she had been too busy or too careless to imagine. He was very familiar with that anxious, apologetic smile. Contrition sent him running after her. And yet, as he ran, he looked back over his shoulder at the wild bay; and all morning, as he played on the safe beach, he was thinking of it.

Next morning, when it was time for the routine of swimming and sunbathing, his mother said, "Are you tired of the usual beach, Jerry? Would you like to go somewhere else?"

"Oh, no!" he said quickly, smiling at her out of that unfailing impulse of contrition—a sort of chivalry. Yet, walking down the path with her, he blurted out, "I'd like to go and have a look at those rocks down there."

She gave the idea her attention. It was a wild-looking place, and there was no one there; but she said, "Of course, Jerry. When you've had enough, come to the big beach. Or just go straight back to the villa, if you like." She walked away, that bare arm, now slightly reddened from yesterday's sun, swinging. And he almost ran after her again, feeling it unbearable that she should go by herself, but he did not.

She was thinking, Of course he's old enough to be safe without me. Have I been keeping him too close? He mustn't feel he ought to be with me. I must be careful.

He was an only child, eleven years old. She was a widow. She was determined to be neither possessive nor lacking in devotion. She went worrying off to her beach.

As for Jerry, once he saw that his mother had gained her beach, he began the steep descent to the bay. From where he was, high up among red-brown rocks, it was a scoop of moving blueish green fringed with white. As he went lower, he saw that it spread among small promontories and inlets of rough, sharp rock, and the crisping, lapping surface showed stains of purple and darker blue. Finally, as he ran sliding and scraping down the last few yards, he saw an edge of white surf and the shallow, luminous movement of water over white sand, and, beyond that, a solid, heavy blue.

He ran straight into the water and began swimming. He was a good swimmer. He went out fast over the gleaming sand, over a middle region where rocks lay like discoloured monsters under the surface, and then he was in the real sea—a warm sea where irregular cold currents from the deep water shocked his limbs.

When he was so far out that he could look back not only on the little bay but past the promontory that was between it and the big beach, he floated on the buoyant surface and looked for his mother. There she was, a speck of yellow under an umbrella that looked like a slice of orange peel. He swam back to shore, relieved at being sure she was there, but all at once very lonely.

On the edge of a small cape that marked the side of the bay away from the promontory was a loose scatter of rocks. Above them, some boys were stripping off their clothes. They came running, naked, down to the rocks. The English boy swam towards them, but kept his distance at a stone's throw. They were of that coast; all of them were burned smooth dark brown and speaking a language he did not understand. To be with them, of them, was a craving that filled his whole body. He swam a little closer; they turned and watched him with narrowed, alert dark eyes. Then one smiled and waved. It was enough. In a minute, he had swum in and was on the rocks beside them, smiling with a desperate, nervous supplication. They shouted cheerful greetings at him; and then, as he preserved his nervous, uncomprehending smile, they understood that he was a foreigner strayed from his own beach, and they proceeded to forget him. But he was happy. He was with them.

They began diving again and again from a high point into a well of blue sea between rough, pointed rocks. After they had dived and come up, they swam around, hauled themselves up, and waited their turn to dive again. They were big boys—men, to Jerry. He dived, and they watched him; and when he swam around to take his place, they made way for him. He felt he was accepted and he dived again, carefully, proud of himself.

Soon the biggest of the boys poised himself, shot down into the water, and did not come up. The others stood about, watching. Jerry, after waiting for the sleek brown head to appear, let out a yell of warning; they looked at him idly and turned their eyes back towards the water. After a long time, the boy came up on the other side of a big dark rock, letting the air out of his lungs in a sputtering gasp and a shout of triumph. Immediately the rest of them dived in. One moment, the morning seemed full of chattering boys; the next, the air and the surface of the water were empty. But through the heavy blue, dark shapes could be seen moving and groping.

Jerry dived, shot past the school of underwater swimmers, saw a black wall of rock looming at him, touched it, and bobbed up at once to the surface, where the wall was a low barrier he could see across. There was no one visible; under him, in the water, the dim shapes of the swimmers had disappeared. Then one, and then another of the boys came up on the far side of the barrier of rock, and he understood that they had swum through some gap or hole in it. He plunged down again. He could see nothing through the stinging salt water but the blank rock. When he came up the boys were all on the diving rock, preparing to attempt the feat again. And now, in a panic of failure, he yelled up, in English, "Look at me! Look!" and he began splashing and kicking in the water like a foolish dog.

They looked down gravely, frowning. He knew the frown. At moments of failure, when he clowned to claim his mother's attention, it was with just this grave, embarrassed inspection that she rewarded him. Through his hot shame, feeling the pleading grin on his face like a scar that he could never remove, he looked up at the group of big brown boys on the rock and shouted *"Bonjour! Merci! Au revoir! Monsieur, monsieur!"*[1] while he hooked his fingers round his ears and waggled them.

Water surged into his mouth; he choked, sank, came up. The rock, lately weighted with boys, seemed to rear up out of the water as their weight was removed. They were flying down past him now, into the water; the air was full of falling bodies. Then the rock was empty in the hot sunlight. He counted one, two, three . . .

At fifty, he was terrified. They must all be drowning beneath him, in the watery caves of the rock! At a hundred, he stared around him at the empty hillside, wondering if he should yell for help. He counted faster, faster, to hurry them up, to bring them to the surface quickly, to drown them quickly—anything rather than the terror of counting on and on into the blue emptiness of the morning. And then, at a hundred and sixty, the water beyond the rock was full of boys blowing like brown whales. They swam back to the shore without a look at him.

He climbed back to the diving rock and sat down, feeling the hot roughness of it under his thighs. The boys were gathering up their bits of clothing and running off along the shore to another promontory. They were leaving to get away from him. He cried openly, fists in his eyes. There was no one to see him, and he cried himself out.

It seemed to him that a long time had passed, and he swam out to where he could see his mother. Yes, she was still there, a yellow spot under an orange umbrella. He swam back to the big rock, climbed up, and dived into the blue pool among the fanged and angry boulders. Down he went, until he touched the wall of rock again. But the salt was so painful in his eyes that he could not see.

He came to the surface, swam to shore and went back to the villa to wait for his mother. Soon she walked slowly up the path, swinging her striped bag, the flushed, naked arm dangling beside her. "I want some swimming goggles," he panted, defiant and beseeching.

She gave him a patient, inquisitive look as she said casually, "Well, of course, darling."

But now, now, now! He must have them this minute, and no other time. He nagged and pestered until she went with him to a shop. As soon as she had bought the

---

[1] French for "Hello! Thank you! Goodbye! Mister, mister!"

goggles, he grabbed them from her hand as if she were going to claim them for herself, and was off, running down the steep path to the bay.

Jerry swam out to the big barrier rock, adjusted the goggles, and dived. The impact of the water broke the rubber-enclosed vacuum, and the goggles came loose. He understood that he must swim down to the base of the rock from the surface of the water. He fixed the goggles tight and firm, filled his lungs, and floated, face down, on the water. Now he could see. It was as if he had eyes of a different kind—fish eyes that showed everything clear and delicate and wavering in the bright water.

Under him, six or seven feet down, was a floor of perfectly clean, shining white sand, rippled firm and hard by the tides. Two greyish shapes steered there, like long, rounded pieces of wood or slate. They were fish. He saw them nose towards each other, poise motionless, make a dart forward, swerve off, and come around again. It was like a water dance. A few inches above them the water sparkled as if sequins were dropping through it. Fish again—myriads of minute fish, the length of his fingernail—were drifting through the water, and in a moment he could feel the innumerable tiny touches of them against his limbs. It was like swimming in flaked silver. The great rock the big boys had swum through rose sheer out of the white sand—black, tufted lightly with greenish weed. He could see no gap in it. He swam down to its base.

Again and again he rose, took a big chestful of air, and went down. Again and again he groped over the surface of the rock, feeling it, almost hugging it in the desperate need to find the entrance. And then, once, while he was clinging to the black wall, his knees came up and he shot his feet out forward and they met no obstacle. He had found the hole.

He gained the surface, clambered about the stones that littered the barrier rock until he found a big one, and, with this in his arms, let himself down over the side of the rock. He dropped, with the weight, straight to the sandy floor. Clinging tight to the anchor of stone, he lay on his side and looked in under the dark shelf at the place where his feet had gone. He could see the hole. It was an irregular, dark gap; but he could not see deep into it. He let go of his anchor, clung with his hands to the edges of the hole, and tried to push himself in.

He got his head in, found his shoulders jammed, moved them in sidewise, and was inside as far as his waist. He could see nothing ahead. Something soft and clammy touched his mouth; he saw a dark frond moving against the greyish rock, and panic filled him. He thought of octopuses, of clinging weed. He pushed himself out backward and caught a glimpse, as he retreated, of a harmless tentacle of seaweed drifting in the mouth of the tunnel. But it was enough. He reached the sunlight, swam to shore, and lay on the diving rock. He looked down into the blue well of water. He knew he must find his way through that cave, or hole, or tunnel, and out the other side.

First, he thought, he must learn to control his breathing. He let himself down into the water with another big stone in his arms, so that he could lie effortlessly on the bottom of the sea. He counted. One, two, three. He counted steadily. He could hear the movement of blood in his chest. Fifty-one, fifty-two. . . . His chest was hurting. He let go of the rock and went up into the air. He saw that the sun was low. He rushed to the villa and found his mother at her supper. She said only "Did you enjoy yourself?" and he said "Yes."

All night the boy dreamed of the water-filled cave in the rock, and as soon as breakfast was over he went to the bay.

That night, his nose bled badly. For hours he had been underwater, learning to hold his breath, and now he felt weak and dizzy. His mother said, "I shouldn't overdo things, darling, if I were you."

That day and the next, Jerry exercised his lungs as if everything, the whole of his life, all that he would become, depended upon it. Again his nose bled at night, and his mother insisted on his coming with her the next day. It was a torment to him to waste a day of his careful self-training, but he stayed with her on that other beach, which now seemed a place for small children, a place where his mother might lie safe in the sun. It was not his beach.

He did not ask for permission, on the following day, to go to his beach. He went, before his mother could consider the complicated rights and wrongs of the matter. A day's rest, he discovered, had improved his count by ten. The big boys had made the passage while he counted a hundred and sixty. He had been counting fast, in his fright. Probably now, if he tried, he could get through that long tunnel, but he was not going to try yet. A curious, most unchildlike persistence, a controlled impatience, made him wait. In the meantime, he lay underwater on the white sand, littered now by stones he had brought down from the upper air, and studied the entrance to the tunnel. He knew every jut and corner of it, as far as it was possible to see. It was as if he already felt its sharpness about his shoulders.

He sat by the clock in the villa, when his mother was not near, and checked his time. He was incredulous and then proud to find he could hold his breath without strain for two minutes. The words "two minutes," authorised by the clock, brought close the adventure that was so necessary to him.

In another four days, his mother said casually one morning, they must go home. On the day before they left, he would do it. He would do it if it killed him, he said defiantly to himself. But two days before they were to leave—a day of triumph when he increased his count by fifteen—his nose bled so badly that he turned dizzy and had to lie limply over the big rock like a bit of seaweed, watching the thick red blood flow on to the rock and trickle slowly down to the sea. He was frightened. Supposing he turned dizzy in the tunnel? Supposing he died there, trapped? Supposing—his head went around, in the hot sun, and he almost gave up. He thought he would return to the house and lie down, and next summer, perhaps, when he had another year's growth in *him— then* he would go through the hole.

But even after he had made the decision, or thought he had, he found himself sitting up on the rock and looking down into the water; and he knew that now, this moment, when his nose had only just stopped bleeding, when his head was still sore and throbbing—this was the moment when he would try. If he did not do it now, he never would. He was trembling with fear that he would not go; and he was trembling with horror at the long, long tunnel under the rock, under the sea. Even in the open sunlight, the barrier rock seemed very wide and very heavy; tons of rock pressed down on where he would go. If he died there, he would lie until one day—perhaps not before next year— those big boys would swim into it and find it blocked.

He put on his goggles, fitted them tight, tested the vacuum. His hands were shaking. Then he chose the biggest stone he could carry and slipped over the edge of the rock until half of him was in the cool enclosing water and half in the hot sun. He looked up once at the empty sky, filled his lungs once, twice, and then sank fast to the bottom with the stone. He let it go and began to count. He took the edges of the hole in his hands and drew himself into it, wriggling his shoulders in sidewise as he remembered he must, kicking himself along with his feet.

Soon he was clear inside. He was in a small rock-bound hole filled with yellowish-grey water. The water was pushing him up against the roof. The roof was sharp and pained his back. He pulled himself along with his hands—fast, fast—and used his legs as levers. His head knocked against something; a sharp pain dizzied him. Fifty, fifty-one, fifty-two. . . . He was without light, and the water seemed to press upon him with the weight of rock. Seventy-one, seventy-two. . . . There was no strain on his lungs. He felt like an inflated balloon, his lungs were so light and easy, but his head was pulsing.

He was being continually pressed against the sharp roof, which felt slimy as well as sharp. Again he thought of octopuses, and wondered if the tunnel might be filled with weed that could tangle him. He gave himself a panicky, convulsive kick forward, ducked his head, and swam. His feet and hands moved freely, as if in open water. The hole must have widened out. He thought he must be swimming fast, and he was frightened of banging his head if the tunnel narrowed.

A hundred, a hundred and one. . . . The water paled. Victory filled him. His lungs were beginning to hurt. A few more strokes and he would be out. He was counting wildly; he said a hundred and fifteen, and then, a long time later, a hundred and fifteen again. The water was a clear jewel-green all around him. Then he saw, above his head, a crack running up through the rock. Sunlight was falling through it, showing the clean, dark rock of the tunnel, a single mussel shell, and darkness ahead.

He was at the end of what he could do. He looked up at the crack as if it were filled with air and not water, as if he could put his mouth to it to draw in air. A hundred and fifteen, he heard himself say inside his head—but he had said that long ago. He must go on into the blackness ahead, or he would drown. His head was swelling, his lungs cracking. A hundred and fifteen, a hundred and fifteen pounded through his head, and he feebly clutched at rocks in the dark, pulling himself forward leaving the brief space of sunlit water behind. He felt he was dying. He was no longer quite conscious. He struggled on in the darkness between lapses into unconsciousness. An immense, swelling pain filled his head, and then the darkness cracked with an explosion of green light. His hands, groping forward, met nothing; and his feet, kicking back, propelled him out into the open sea.

He drifted to the surface, his face turned up to the air. He was gasping like a fish. He felt he would sink now and drown; he could not swim the few feet back to the rock. Then he was clutching it and pulling himself up onto it. He lay face down, gasping. He could see nothing but a red-veined, clotted dark. His eyes must have burst, he thought; they were full of blood. He tore off his goggles and a gout of blood went into the sea. His nose was bleeding, and the blood had filled the goggles.

He scooped up handfuls of water from the cool, salty sea, to splash on his face, and did not know whether it was blood or salt water he tasted. After a time, his heart quieted, his eyes cleared, and he sat up. He could see the local boys diving and playing half a mile away. He did not want them. He wanted nothing but to get back home and lie down.

In a short while, Jerry swam to shore and climbed slowly up the path to the villa. He flung himself on his bed and slept, waking at the sound of feet on the path outside. His mother was coming back. He rushed to the bathroom, thinking she must not see his face with bloodstains, or tearstains, on it. He came out of the bathroom and met her as she walked into the villa, smiling, her eyes lighting up.

"Have a nice morning?" she asked, laying her hand on his warm brown shoulder a moment.

"Oh, yes, thank you," he said.

"You look a bit pale." And then, sharp and anxious, "How did you bang your head?"

"Oh, just banged it," he told her.

She looked at him closely. He was strained; his eyes were glazed-looking. She was worried. And then she said to herself, Oh, don't fuss! Nothing can happen. He can swim like a fish.

They sat down to lunch together.

"Mummy," he said, "I can stay underwater for two minutes—three minutes, at least." It came bursting out of him.

"Can you, darling?" she said. "Well, I shouldn't overdo it. I don't think you ought to swim any more today."

She was ready for a battle of wills, but he gave in at once. It was no longer of the least importance to go to the bay.

(1955)

QUESTIONS

1. Why does the mother let Jerry go swimming alone? Does the reader know what she is feeling? More important, does Jerry know?

2. Describe Jerry's feelings as he tries to get through the tunnel. Why doesn't Jerry need to tell his mother, or anyone else, what he has achieved?

3. What role does setting play in influencing the conflict, climax, and resolution of the story's plot?

4. If you experienced a "rite of passage" or "initiation," did your parents encourage it, know about it, or was it something you did on your own?

HISAYE YAMAMOTO (B. 1920)

Seventeen Syllables

The first Rosie knew that her mother had taken to writing poems was one evening when she finished one and read it aloud for her daughter's approval. It was about cats, and Rosie pretended to understand it thoroughly and appreciate it no end, partly because she hesitated to disillusion her mother about the quantity and quality of Japanese she had learned in all the years now that she had been going to Japanese school every Saturday (and Wednesday, too, in the Summer). Even so, her mother must have been skeptical about the depth of Rosie's understanding, because she explained afterwards about the kind of poem she was trying to write.

See, Rosie, she said, it was a *haiku*, a poem in which she must pack all her meaning into seventeen syllables only, which were divided into three lines of five, seven, and five syllables. In the one she had just read, she had tried to capture the charm of a kitten, as well as comment on the superstition that owning a cat of three colors meant good luck.

"Yes, yes, I understand. How utterly lovely," Rosie said, and her mother, either satisfied or seeing through the deception and resigned, went back to composing.

The truth was that Rosie was lazy; English lay ready on the tongue but Japanese had to be searched for and examined, and even then put forth tentatively (probably to meet with laughter). It was so much easier to say yes, yes, even when one meant no, no. Besides, this was what was in her mind to say: I was looking through one of your magazines from Japan last night, Mother, and towards the back I found some *haiku* in English that delighted me. There was one that made me giggle off and on until I fell asleep—

> It is morning, and lo!
> I lie awake, comme il faut,
> sighing for some dough.

Now, how to reach her mother, how to communicate the melancholy song? Rosie knew formal Japanese by fits and starts, her mother had even less English, no French. It was much more possible to say yes, yes.

It developed that her mother was writing the *haiku* for a daily newspaper, the *Mainichi Shinbun,* that was published in San Francisco. Los Angeles, to be sure, was closer to the farming community in which the Hayashi family lived and several Japanese vernaculars were printed there, but Rosie's parents said they preferred the tone of the northern paper. Once a week, the *Mainichi* would have a section devoted to *haiku,* and her mother became an extravagant contributor, taking for herself the blossoming pen name, Ume Hanazono.

So Rosie and her father lived for awhile with two women, her mother and Ume Hanazono. Her mother (Tome Hayashi by name) kept house, cooked, washed, and, along with her husband and the Carrascos, the Mexican family hired for the harvest, did her ample share of picking tomatoes out in the sweltering fields and boxing them in tidy strata in the cool packing shed. Ume Hanazono, who came to life after the dinner dishes were done, was an earnest, muttering stranger who often neglected speaking when spoken to and stayed busy at the parlor table as late as midnight scribbling with pencil on scratch paper or carefully copying characters on good paper with her fat, pale green Parker.

The new interest had some repercussions on the household routine. Before, Rosie had been accustomed to her parents and herself taking their hot baths early and going to bed almost immediately afterwards, unless her parents challenged each other to a game of flower cards or unless company dropped in. Now, if her father wanted to play cards, he had to resort to solitaire (at which he always cheated fearlessly), and if a group of friends came over, it was bound to contain someone who was also writing *haiku,* and the small assemblage would be split in two, her father entertaining the nonliterary members and her mother comparing ecstatic notes with the visiting poet.

If they went out, it was more of the same thing. But Ume Hanazono's life span, even for a poet's, was very brief—perhaps three months at most.

One night they went over to see the Hayano family in the neighboring town to the west, an adventure both painful and attractive to Rosie. It was attractive because there were four Hayano girls, all lovely and each one named after a season of the year (Haru, Natsu, Aki, Fuyu), painful because something had been wrong with Mrs. Hayano ever since the birth of her first child. Rosie would sometimes watch Mrs. Hayano, reputed to have been the belle of her native village, making her way about a room, stooped, slowly shuffling, violently trembling (*always* trembling), and she would be reminded that this woman, in this same condition, had carried and given issue to three babies. She would look wonderingly at Mr. Hayano, handsome, tall, and strong, and she would look at her four pretty friends. But it was not a matter she could come to any decision about.

On this visit, however, Mrs. Hayano sat all evening in the rocker, as motionless and unobtrusive as it was possible for her to be, and Rosie found the greater part of the evening practically anaesthetic. Too, Rosie spent most of it in the girls' room, because Haru, the garrulous one, said almost as soon as the bows and other greetings were over, "Oh, you must see my new coat!"

It was a pale plaid of grey, sand, and blue, with an enormous collar, and Rosie, seeing nothing special in it, said, "Gee, how nice."

"Nice?" said Haru, indignantly. "Is that all you can say about it? It's gorgeous! And so cheap, too. Only seventeen-ninety-eight, because it was a sale. The saleslady said it was twenty-five dollars regular."

"Gee," said Rosie. Natsu, who never said much and when she said anything said it shyly, fingered the coat covetously and Haru pulled it away.

"Mine," she said, putting it on. She minced in the aisle between two large beds and smiled happily. "Let's see how your mother likes it."

She broke into the front room and the adult conversation, and went to stand in front of Rosie's mother, while the rest watched from the door. Rosie's mother was properly envious. "May I inherit it when you're through with it?"

Haru, pleased, giggled and said yes, she could, but Natsu reminded gravely from the door, "You promised me, Haru."

Everyone laughed but Natsu, who shamefacedly retreated into the bedroom. Haru came in laughing, taking off the coat. "We were only kidding, Natsu," she said. "Here, you try it on now."

After Natsu buttoned herself into the coat, inspected herself solemnly in the bureau mirror, and reluctantly shed it, Rosie, Aki, and Fuyu got their turns, and Fuyu, who was eight, drowned in it while her sisters and Rosie doubled up in amusement. They all went into the front room later, because Haru's mother quaveringly called to her to fix the tea and rice cakes and open a can of sliced peaches for everybody. Rosie noticed that her mother and Mr. Hayano were talking together at the little table—they were discussing a *haiku* that Mr. Hayano was planning to send to the *Mainichi*, while her father was sitting at one end of the sofa looking through a copy of *Life*, the new picture magazine. Occasionally, her father would comment on a photograph, holding it toward Mrs. Hayano and speaking to her as he always did—loudly, as though he thought someone such as she must surely be at least a trifle deaf also.

The five girls had their refreshments at the kitchen table, and it was while Rosie was showing the sisters her trick of swallowing peach slices without chewing (she chased each slippery crescent down with a swig of tea) that her father brought his empty teacup and untouched saucer to the sink and said, "Come on, Rosie, we're going home now."

"Already?" asked Rosie.

"Work tomorrow," he said.

He sounded irritated, and Rosie, puzzled, gulped one last yellow slice and stood up to go, while the sisters began protesting, as was their wont.

"We have to get up at five-thirty," he told them, going into the front room quickly, so that they did not have their usual chance to hang onto his hands and plead for an extension of time.

Rosie, following, saw that her mother and Mr. Hayano were sipping tea and still talking together, while Mrs. Hayano concentrated, quivering, on raising the handleless Japanese cup to her lips with both her hands and lowering it back to her lap. Her father, saying nothing, went out the door, onto the bright porch, and down the steps. Her mother looked up and asked, "Where is he going?"

"Where is he going?" Rosie asked. "He said we were going home now."

"Going home?" Her mother looked with embarrassment at Mr. Hayano and his absorbed wife and then forced a smile. "He must be tired," she said.

Haru was not giving up yet. "May Rosie stay overnight?" she asked, and Natsu, Aki, and Fuyu came to reinforce their sister's pleas by helping her make a circle around Rosie's mother. Rosie, for once, having no desire to stay, was relieved when her mother, apologizing to the perturbed Mr. and Mrs. Hayano for her father's abruptness at the same time, managed to shake her head no at the quartet, kindly but adamant, so that they broke their circle to let her go.

Rosie's father looked ahead into the windshield as the two joined him. "I'm sorry," her mother said. "You must be tired." Her father, stepping on the starter, said nothing. "You know how I get when it's *haiku*," she continued, "I forget what time it is." He only grunted.

As they rode homeward, silently, Rosie sitting between, felt a rush of hate for both, for her mother for begging, for her father for denying her mother. I wish this old Ford would crash, right now, she thought, then immediately, no, no, I wish my father would laugh, but it was too late: already the vision had passed through her mind of the green pick-up crumpled in the dark against one of the mighty eucalyptus trees they were just riding past, of the three contorted, bleeding bodies, one of them hers.

Rosie ran between two patches of tomatoes, her heart working more rambunctiously than she had ever known it to. How lucky it was that Aunt Taka and Uncle Gimpachi had come tonight, though, how very lucky. Otherwise, she might not have really kept her half-promise to meet Jesus Carrasco. Jesus, who was going to be a senior in September at the same school she went to, and his parents were the ones helping with the tomatoes this year. She and Jesus, who hardly remembered seeing each other at Cleveland High, where there were so many other people and two whole grades between them, had become great friends this Summer—he always had a joke for her when he periodically drove the loaded pick-up up from the fields to the shed where she was usually sorting while her mother and father did the packing, and they laughed a great deal together over infinitesimal repartee during the afternoon break for chilled watermelon or ice cream in the shade of the shed.

What she enjoyed most was racing him to see which could finish picking a double row first. He, who could work faster, would tease her by slowing down until she thought she would surely pass him this time, then speeding up furiously to leave her several sprawling vines behind. Once he had made her screech hideously by crossing over, while her back was turned, to place atop the tomatoes in her green-stained bucket a truly monstrous, pale green worm (it had looked more like an infant snake). And it was when they had finished a contest this morning, after she had pantingly pointed a green finger at the immature tomatoes evident in the lugs at the end of his row and he returned the accusation (with justice), that he had startlingly brought up the matter of their possible meeting outside the range of both their parents' dubious eyes.

"What for?" she had asked.

"I've got a secret I want to tell you," he said.

"Tell me now," she demanded.

"It won't be ready till tonight," he said.

She laughed. "Tell me tomorrow then."

"It'll be gone tomorrow," he threatened.

"Well, for seven hakes, what is it?" she had asked, more than twice, and when he had suggested that the packing shed would be an appropriate place to find out, she had cautiously answered maybe. She had not been certain she was going to keep the appointment until the arrival of her mother's sister and her husband. Their coming seemed a sort of signal of permission, of grace, and she had definitely made up her mind to lie and leave as she was bowing them welcome.

So, as soon as everyone appeared settled back for the evening, she announced loudly that she was going to the privy outside. "I'm going to the *benjo!*" and slipped out the door. And now that she was actually on her way, her heart pumped in such an undisciplined way that she could hear it with her ears. It's because I'm running, she told herself, slowing to a walk. The shed was up ahead, one more patch away, in the middle of the fields. Its bulk, looming in the dimness, took on a sinisterness that was funny when Rosie reminded herself that it was only a wooden frame with a canvas roof and three canvas walls that made a slapping noise on breezy days.

Jesus was sitting on the narrow plank that was the sorting platform and she went around to the other side and jumped backwards to seat herself on the rim of a packing stand. "Well, tell me," she said, without greeting, thinking her voice sounded reassuringly familiar.

"I saw you coming out the door," Jesus said. "I heard you running part of the way, too."

"Uh-huh," Rosie said, "Now tell me the secret."

"I was afraid you wouldn't come," he said.

Rosie delved around on the chicken-wire bottom of the stall for number two tomatoes, ripe, which she was sitting beside, and came up with a left-over that felt edible. She bit into it and began sucking out the pulp and seeds. "I'm here," she pointed out.

"Rosie, are you sorry you came?"

"Sorry? What for?" she said. "You said you were going to tell me something."

"I will, I will," Jesus said, but his voice contained disappointment, and Rosie, fleetingly, felt the older of the two, realizing a brand-new power which vanished without category under her recognition.

"I have to go back in a minute," she said. "My aunt and uncle are here from Wintersburg. I told them I was going to the privy."

Jesus laughed. "You funny thing," he said. "You slay me!"

"Just because you have a bathroom *inside*," Rosie said. "Come on, tell me."

Chuckling, Jesus came around to lean on the stand facing her. They still could not see each other very clearly, but Rosie noticed that Jesus became very sober again as he took the hollow tomato from her hand and dropped it back into the stall. When he took hold of her empty hand, she could find no words to protest; her vocabulary had become distressingly constricted and she thought desperately that all that remained intact now was yes and no and oh, and even these few sounds would not easily out. Thus, kissed by Jesus, Rosie fell, for the first time, entirely victim to a helplessness delectable beyond speech. But the terrible, beautiful sensation lasted no more than a second, and the reality of Jesus' lips and tongue and teeth and hand made her pull away with such strength that she nearly tumbled.

Rosie stopped running as she approached the lights from the windows of home. How long since she had left? She could not guess, but gasping yet, she went to the privy in back and locked herself in. Her own breathing deafened her in the dark, close space, and she sat and waited until she could hear at last the nightly calling of the frogs and crickets. Even then, all she could think to say was, oh, my, and the pressure of Jesus' face against her face would not leave.

No one had missed her in the parlor, however, and Rosie walked in and through quickly, announcing that she was next going to take a bath. "Your father's in the bathhouse," her mother said, and Rosie, in her room, recalled that she had not seen him when she entered. There had been only Aunt Taka and Uncle Gimpachi with her mother at the table, drinking tea. She got her robe and straw sandals and crossed the parlor again to go outside. Her mother was telling them about the *haiku* competition in the *Mainichi* and the poem she had entered.

Rosie met her father coming out of the bathhouse. "Are you through, Father?" she asked. "I was going to ask you to scrub my back."

"Scrub your own back," he said shortly, going toward the main house.

"What have I done now?" she yelled after him. She suddenly felt like doing a lot of yelling. But he did not answer, and she went into the bathhouse. Turning on the dangling light, she removed her denims and T-shirt and threw them in the big carton for dirty clothes standing next to the washing machine. Her other things she took with her into the bath compartment to wash after her bath. After she had scooped a basin of hot water from the square wooden tub, she sat on the grey cement of the floor and soaped herself at exaggerated leisure, singing "Red Sails in the Sunset" at the top of her voice and using da-da-da where she suspected her words. Then, standing, still singing, for she was possessed by the notion that any attempt now to analyze would result in spoilage and she believed that the larger her volume the less should be able to hear herself think, she obtained more hot water and poured it on until she was free of lather. Only then did she allow herself to step into the steaming vat, one leg first, then the remainder of her body inch by inch until the water no longer stung and she could move around at will.

She took a long time soaking, afterwards remembering to go around outside to stoke the embers of the tin-lined fireplace beneath the tub and to throw on a few more sticks so that the water might keep its heat for her mother, and when she finally returned to the parlor, she found her mother still talking *haiku* with her aunt and uncle, the three of them on another round of tea. Her father was nowhere in sight.

At Japanese school the next (Wednesday, it was), Rosie was grave and giddy by turns. Preoccupied at her desk in the row for students on Book Eight, she made up for it at recess by performing wild mimicry for the benefit of her friend Chizuko. She held her nose and whined a witticism or two in what she considered the manner of Fred Allen; she assumed intoxication and a British accent to go over the climax of the Rudy Vallee recording of the pub conversation about William Ewart Gladstone; she was the child Shirley Temple[1] piping "On the Good Ship Lollipop"; she was the gentleman soprano of the Four Inkspots trilling "If I Didn't Care." And she felt reasonably satisfied when Chizuko wept and gasped, "Oh, Rosie, you ought to be in the movies!"

Her father came after her at noon, bringing her sandwiches of minced ham and two nectarines to eat while she rode, so that she could pitch right into the sorting when they got home. The lugs were piling up, he said, and the ripe tomatoes in them would probably have to be taken to the cannery tomorrow if they were not ready for the produce haulers tonight. "This heat's not doing them any good. And we've got no time for a break today."

---

[1] Allen: American comedian who conducted popular radio programs during the 1930s–1950s; Vallee: popular American singer and actor during the 1930s and 1940s; Gladstone: an English statesman and prime minister (1809–1898); and Temple: popular American child actress, born in 1928.

It *was* hot, probably the hottest day of the year, and Rosie's blouse stuck damply to her back even under the protection of the canvas. But she worked as efficiently as a flawless machine and kept the stalls heaped, with one part of her mind listening in to the parental murmuring about the heat and the tomatoes and with another part planning the exact words she would say to Jesus when he drove up with the first load of the afternoon. But when at last she saw that the pick-up was coming, her hands went berserk and the tomatoes started falling in the wrong stalls, and her father said, "Hey, hey! Rosie, watch what you're doing!"

"Well, I have to go to the *benjo*," she said, hiding panic.

"Go in the weeds over there," he said, only half-joking.

"Oh, Father" she protested.

"Oh, go on home," her mother said. "We'll make out for awhile."

In the privy, Rosie peered through a knothole toward the fields, watching as much as she could of Jesus. Happily she thought she saw him look in the direction of the house from time to time before he finished unloading and went back toward the patch where his mother and father worked. As she was heading for the shed, a very presentable black car purred up the dirt driveway to the house and its driver motioned to her. Was this the Hayashi home, he wanted to know. She nodded. Was she a Hayashi? Yes, she said, thinking that he was a good-looking man. He got out of the car with a huge, flat package and she saw that he warmly wore a business suit. "I have something here for your mother then," he said, in a more elegant Japanese than she was used to.

She told him where her mother was and he came along with her, patting his face with an immaculate white handkerchief and saying something about the coolness of San Francisco. To her surprised mother and father, he bowed and introduced himself as, among other things, the *haiku* editor of the *Mainichi Shinbun,* saying that since he had been coming as far as Los Angeles anyway, he had decided to bring the first prize she had won in the recent contest.

"First prize?" her mother echoed, believing and not believing, pleased and overwhelmed. Handed the package with a bow, she bobbed her head up and down numerous times to express her utter gratitude.

"It is nothing much," he added, "but I hope it will serve as a token of our great appreciation for your contributions and our great admiration of your considerable talent."

"I am not worthy," she said, falling easily into his style. "It is I who should make some sign of my humble thanks for being permitted to contribute."

"No, no, to the contrary," he said, bowing again.

But Rosie's mother insisted, and then saying that she knew she was being unorthodox, she asked if she might open the package because her curiosity was so great. Certainly she might. In fact, he would like her reaction to it, for personally, it was one of his favorite *Hiroshiges.*[2]

Rosie thought it was a pleasant picture, which looked to have been sketched with delicate quickness. There were pink clouds, containing some graceful calligraphy, and a

---

[2]Hiroshige (1767–1858): a Japanese painter noted for his series *Fifty-three Stages of the Tokaido Highway* (1833).

sea that was a pale blue except at the edges, containing four sampans with indications of people in them. Pines edged the water and on the far-off beach there was a cluster of thatched huts towered over by pine-dotted mountains of grey and blue. The frame was scalloped and gilt.

After Rosie's mother pronounced it without peer and somewhat prodded her father into nodding agreement, she said Mr. Kuroda must at least have a cup of tea, after coming all this way, and although Mr. Kuroda did not want to impose, he soon agreed that a cup of tea would be refreshing and went along with her to the house, carrying the picture for her.

"Ha, your mother's crazy!" Rosie's father said, and Rosie laughed uneasily as she resumed judgment on the tomatoes. She had emptied six lugs when he broke into an imaginary conversation with Jesus to tell her to go and remind her mother of the tomatoes, and she went slowly.

Mr. Kuroda was in his shirtsleeves expounding some *haiku* theory as he munched a rice cake, and her mother was rapt. Abashed in the great man's presence, Rosie stood next to her mother's chair until her mother looked up inquiringly, and then she started to whisper the message, but her mother pushed her gently away and reproached, "You are not being very polite to our guest."

"Father says the tomatoes . . ." Rosie said aloud, smiling foolishly.

"Tell him I shall only be a minute," her mother said, speaking the language of Mr. Kuroda.

When Rosie carried the reply to her father, he did not seem to hear and she said again, "Mother says she'll be back in a minute."

"All right, all right," he nodded, and they worked again in silence. But suddenly, her father uttered an incredible noise, exactly like the cork of a bottle popping, and the next Rosie knew, he was stalking angrily toward the house, almost running, in fact, and she chased after him crying "Father! Father! What are you going to do?"

He stopped long enough to order her back to the shed. "Never mind!" he shouted. "Get on with the sorting!"

And from the place in the fields where she stood, frightened and vacillating, Rosie saw her father enter the house. Soon Mr. Kuroda came out alone, putting on his coat. Mr. Kuroda got into his car and backed out down the driveway, onto the highway. Next her father emerged, also alone, something in his arms (it was the picture, she realized), and going over to the bathhouse woodpile, he threw the picture on the ground and picked up the axe. Smashing the picture, glass and all (she heard the explosion faintly), he reached over the kerosene that was used to encourage the bath fire and poured it over the wreckage. I am dreaming, Rosie said to herself, I am dreaming, but her father, having made sure that his act of cremation was irrevocable, was even then returning to the fields.

Rosie ran past him and toward the house. What had become of her mother? She burst into the parlor and found her mother at the back window, watching the dying fire. They watched together until there remained only a feeble smoke under the blazing sun. Her mother was very calm.

"Do you know why I married your father?" she said, without turning.

"No," said Rosie. It was the most frightening question she had ever been called upon to answer. Don't tell me now, she wanted to say, tell me tomorrow, tell me next week, don't tell me today. But she knew she would be told now, that the telling would combine with the other violence of the hot afternoon to level her life, her world (so various, so beautiful, so new?) to the very ground.

It was like a story out of the magazines, illustrated in sepia, which she had consumed so greedily for a period until the information had somehow reached her that those wretchedly unhappy autobiographies, offered to her as the testimonials of living men and women, were largely inventions: Her mother, at nineteen, had come to America and married her father as an alternative to suicide.

At eighteen, she had been in love with the first son of one of the well-to-do families in her village. The two had met whenever and wherever they could, secretly, because it would not have done for his family to see him favor her—her father had no money; he was a drunkard and a gambler besides. She had learned she was with child; an excellent match had already been arranged for her lover. Despised by her family, she had given premature birth to a stillborn son, who would be seventeen now. Her family did not turn her out, but she could no longer project herself in any direction without refreshing in them the memory of her indiscretion. She wrote to Aunt Taka, her favorite sister, in America, threatening to kill herself if Aunt Taka would not send for her. Aunt Taka hastily arranged a marriage with a young man, but lately arrived from Japan, of whom she knew, a young man of simple mind, it was said, but of kindly heart. The young man was never told why his unseen betrothed was so eager to hasten the day of meeting.

The story was told perfectly, with neither groping for words nor untoward passion. It was as though her mother had memorized it by heart, reciting it to herself so many times over that its nagging vileness had long since gone.

"I had a brother then?" Rosie asked, for this was what seemed to matter now; she would think about the other later, she assured herself, pushing back the illumination which threatened all that darkness that had hitherto been merely mysterious or even glamorous. "A half-brother?"

"Yes."

"I would have liked a brother," she said.

Suddenly, her mother knelt on the floor and took her by the wrists. "Rosie," she said urgently, "promise me you will never marry!" Shocked more by the request than the revelation, Rosie stared at her mother's face. Jesus, Jesus, she called silently, not certain whether she was invoking the help of the son of the Carrascos or of God, until there returned sweetly the memory of Jesus' hand, how it had touched her and where. Still her mother waited for an answer, holding her wrists so tightly that her hands were going numb. She tried to pull free. "Promise," her mother whispered fiercely, "promise." "Yes, yes, I promise," Rosie said. But for an instant she turned away, and her mother, hearing the familiar glib agreement, released her. Oh, you, you, you, her eyes and twisted mouth said, you fool. Rosie, covering her face, began at last to cry, and the embrace and consoling hand came much later than she expected.

(1949)

QUESTIONS

1. How does Rosie's mother's devotion to writing *haiku* affect the rest of the family? Why does Rosie's father disapprove of her mother's new interest?

2. Why is it significant that the story of Rosie's mother takes place at the same time that Rosie feels the stirring of first love?

3. What connection might there be between Rosie's mother's success as a poet and the story of why she married Rosie's father?

4. Why does Rosie's mother beg her not to get married at the end of the story?

CHINUA ACHEBE (B. 1930)

Marriage Is a Private Affair

"Have you written to your dad yet?" asked Nene one afternoon as she sat with Nnaemeka in her room at 16 Kasanga Street, Lagos.[1]

"No. I've been thinking about it. I think it's better to tell him when I get home on leave!"

"But why? Your leave is such a long way off yet—six whole weeks. He should be let into our happiness now."

Nnaemeka was silent for a while, and then began very slowly as if he groped for his words: "I wish I were sure it would be happiness to him."

"Of course it must," replied Nene, a little surprised. "Why shouldn't it?"

"You have lived in Lagos all your life, and you know very little about people in remote parts of the country."

"That's what you always say. But I don't believe anybody will be so unlike other people that they will be unhappy when their sons are engaged to marry."

"Yes. They are most unhappy if the engagement is not arranged by them. In our case it's worse—you are not even an Ibo."[2]

This was said so seriously and so bluntly that Nene could not find speech immediately. In the cosmopolitan atmosphere of the city it had always seemed to her something of a joke that a person's tribe could determine whom he married.

At last she said, "You don't really mean that he will object to your marrying me simply on that account? I had always thought you Ibos were kindly disposed to other people."

"So we are. But when it comes to marriage, well, its not quite so simple. And this," he added, "is not peculiar to the Ibos. If your father were alive and lived in the heart of Ibibio-land he would be exactly like my father."

"I don't know. But anyway, as your father is so fond of you, I'm sure he will forgive you soon enough. Come on then, be a good boy and send him a nice lovely letter . . ."

"It would not be wise to break the news to him by writing. A letter will bring it upon him with a shock. I'm quite sure about that."

"All right, honey, suit yourself. You know your father."

As Nnaemeka walked home that evening he turned over in his mind the different ways of overcoming his father's opposition, especially now that he had gone and found a girl for him. He had thought of showing his letter to Nene but decided on second thoughts not to, at least for the moment. He read it again when he got home and couldn't help smiling to himself. He remembered Ugoye quite well, an Amazon of a girl[3] who used to beat up all the boys, himself included, on the way to the stream, a complete dunce at school.

---

[1] Lagos: the capital and largest city of Nigeria.
[2] Ibo: an ethnic group in southeast Nigeria.
[3] An allusion to the mythical tribe of warrior women called Amazons.

I have found a girl who will suit you admirably—Ugoye Nweke, the eldest daughter of our neighbour, Jacob Nweke. She has a proper Christian upbringing. When she stopped schooling some years ago her father (a man of sound judgment) sent her to live in the house of a pastor where she has received all the training a wife could need. Her Sunday School teacher has told me that she reads her Bible very fluently. I hope we shall begin negotiations when you come home in December.

On the second evening of his return from Lagos Nnaemeka sat with his father under a cassia tree. This was the old man's retreat where he went to read his Bible when the parching December sun had set and a fresh, reviving wind blew on the leaves.

"Father," began Nnaemeka suddenly, "I have come to ask forgiveness."

"Forgiveness? For what, my son?" he asked in amazement.

"It's about this marriage question!"

"Which marriage question."

"I can't—we must—I mean it is impossible for me to marry Nweke's daughter."

"Impossible? why?" asked his father.

"I don't love her."

"Nobody said you did. Why should you?" he asked.

"Marriage today is different . . ."

"Look here, my son," interrupted his father, "nothing is different. What one looks for in a wife are a good character and a Christian background."

Nnaemeka saw there was no hope along the present line of argument.

"Moreover," he said, "I am engaged to marry another girl who has all of Ugoye's good qualities, and who . . ."

His father did not believe his ears. "What did you say?" he asked slowly and disconcertingly.

"She is a good Christian," his son went on, "and a teacher in a Girls' School in Lagos."

"Teacher, did you say? If you consider that a qualification for a good wife I should like to point out to you, Emeka, that no Christian women should teach. St. Paul in his letter to the Corinthians says that women should keep silence." He rose slowly from his seat and paced forwards and backwards. This was his pet subject, and he condemned vehemently those church leaders who encouraged women to teach in their schools. After he had spent his emotion on a long homily he at last came back to his son's engagement, in a seemingly milder tone.

"Whose daughter is she, anyway?"

"She is Nene Atang."

"What!" All the mildness was gone again. "Did you say Neneataga, what does that mean?"

"Nene Atang from Calabar.[4] She is only girl I can marry." This was a very rash reply and Nnaemeka expected the storm to burst. But it did not. His father merely walked away into his room. This was most unexpected and perplexed Nnaemeka. His father's

---

[4] Calabar: a town on the Calabar River in southeastern Nigeria.

silence was infinitely more menacing than a flood of threatening speech. That night the old man did not eat.

When he sent for Nnaemeka a day later he applied all possible ways of dissuasion. But the young man's heart was hardened, and his father eventually gave him up as lost.

"I owe it to you, my son, as a duty to show you what is right and what is wrong. Whoever put this idea into your head might as well have cut your throat. It is Satan's work." He waved his son away.

"You will change your mind, Father, when you know Nene."

"I shall never see her," was the reply. From that night the father scarcely spoke to his son. He did not, however, cease hoping that he would realize how serious was the danger he was heading for. Day and night he put him in his prayers.

Nnaemeka, for his own part, was very deeply affected by his father's grief. But he kept hoping that it would pass away. If it had occurred to him that never in the history of his people had a man married a woman who spoke a different tongue, he might have been less optimistic. "It has never been heard," was the verdict of an old man speaking a few weeks later. In that short sentence he spoke for all of his people. This man had come with others to commiserate with Okeke when news went round about his son's behaviour. By that time the son had gone back to Lagos.

"It has never been heard," said the old man again with a sad shake of his head.

"What did Our Lord say?" asked another gentleman. "Sons shall rise against their Fathers; it is there is the Holy Book."

"It is the beginning of the end," said another.

The discussion thus tending to become theological, Madubogwu, a highly practical man, brought it down once more to the ordinary level.

"Have you thought of consulting a native doctor about your son?" he asked Nnaemeka's father.

"He isn't sick," was the reply.

"What is he then? The boy's mind is diseased and only a good herbalist can bring him back to his right senses. The medicine he requires is *Amalile,* the same that women apply with success to recapture their husbands' straying attention."

"Madubogwu is right," said another gentleman. "This thing calls for medicine."

"I shall not call in a native doctor." Nnaemeka's father was known to be obstinately ahead of his more superstitious neighbours in these matters. "I will not be another Mrs. Ochuba. If my son wants to kill himself let him do it with his own hands. It is not for me to help him."

"But it was her fault," said Madubogwu. "She ought to have gone to an honest herbalist. She was a clever woman, nevertheless."

"She was a wicked murderess," said Jonathan who rarely argued with his neighbours because, he often said, they were incapable of reasoning. "The medicine was prepared for her husband, it was his name they called in its preparation and I am sure it would have been perfectly beneficial to him. It was wicked to put it into the herbalist's food, and say you were only trying it out."

Six months later, Nnaemeka was showing his young wife a short letter from his father:

It amazes me that you could be so unfeeling as to send me your wedding picture. I would have sent it back. But on further thought I decided just to cut off your wife and sent it back to you because I have nothing to do with her. How I wish that I had nothing to do with you either.

When Nene read through this letter and looked at the mutilated picture her eyes filled with tears, and she began to sob.

"Don't cry, my darling," said her husband. "He is essentially good-natured and will one day look more kindly on our marriage." But years passed and that one day did not come.

For eight years, Okeke would have nothing to do with his son, Nnaemeka. Only three times (when Nnaemeka asked to come home and spend his leave) did he write to him.

"I can't have you in my house," he replied on one occasion. "It can be of no interest to me where or how you spend your leave—or your life, for that matter."

The prejudice against Nnaemeka's marriage was not confined to his little village. In Lagos, especially among his people who worked there, it showed itself in a different way. Their women, when they met at their village meeting were not hostile to Nene. Rather, they paid her such excessive deference as to make her feel she was not one of them. But as time went on, Nene gradually broke through some of this prejudice and even began to make friends among them. Slowly and grudgingly they began to admit that she kept her home much better than most of them.

The story eventually got to the little village in the heart of the Ibo country that Nnaemeka and his young wife were a most happy couple. But his father was one of the few people who knew nothing about this. He always displayed so much temper whenever his son's name was mentioned that everyone avoided it in his presence. By a tremendous effort of will he had succeeded in pushing his son to the back of his mind. The strain had nearly killed him but he had persevered, and won.

Then one day he received a letter from Nene, and in spite of himself he began to glance through it perfunctorily until all of a sudden the expression on his face changed and he began to read more carefully.

. . . Our two sons, from the day they learnt that they have a grandfather, have insisted on being taken to him. I find it impossible to tell them that you will not see them. I implore you to allow Nnaemeka to bring them home for a short time during his leave next month. I shall remain here in Lagos . . .

The old man at once felt the resolution he had built up over so many years falling in. He was telling himself that he must not give in. He tried to steel his heart against all emotional appeals. It was a reenactment of that other struggle. He leaned against a window and looked out. The sky was overcast with heavy black clouds and a high wind began to blow filling the air with dust and dry leaves. It was one of those rare occasions when even Nature takes a hand in a human fight. Very soon it began to rain, the first rain in the year. It came down in large sharp drops and was accompanied by the lightning and thunder which mark a change of season. Okeke was trying hard not to think of his two grandsons. But he knew he was now fighting a losing battle. He tried to hum a favourite hymn but the pattering of large rain drops on the roof broke up the tune. His mind immediately returned to the children. How could he shut his door against them? By a curious mental process he imagined them standing, sad and forsaken, under the harsh angry weather—shut out from his house.

That night he hardly slept, from remorse—and a vague fear that he might die without making it up to them.

(1972, 1973)

QUESTIONS

1. Explain why Okeke is so opposed to Nnaemeka's engagement to Nene.

2. What finally cracks Okeke's determination to have no contact with his son?

3. How does the weather reflect the story's outcome?

4. What value system sustains Okeke's decision to cut off his son from all contact with him? What does this story suggest about the clash between old and new values in many cultures?

TILLIE OLSEN (B. 1913)

I Stand Here Ironing

I stand here ironing, and what you asked me moves tormented back and forth with the iron.

"I wish you would manage the time to come in and talk with me about your daughter. I'm sure you can help me understand her. She's a youngster who needs help and whom I'm deeply interested in helping."

"Who needs help." . . . Even if I came, what good would it do? You think because I am her mother I have a key, or that in some way you could use me as a key? She has lived for nineteen years. There is all that life that has happened outside of me, beyond me.

And when is there time to remember, to sift, to weigh, to estimate, to total? I will start and there will be an interruption and I will have to gather it all together again. Or I will become engulfed with all I did or did not do, with what should have been and what cannot be helped.

She was a beautiful baby. The first and only one of our five that was beautiful at birth. You do not guess how new and uneasy her tenancy in her now-loveliness. You did not know her all those years she was thought homely, or see her poring over her baby pictures, making me tell her over and over how beautiful she had been—and would be, I would tell her—and was now, to the seeing eye. But the seeing eyes were few or nonexistent. Including mine.

I nursed her. They feel that's important nowadays. I nursed all the children, but with her, with all the fierce rigidity of first motherhood, I did like the books then said. Though her cries battered me to trembling and my breasts ached with swollenness, I waited till the clock decreed.

Why do I put that first? I do not even know if it matters, or if it explains anything.

She was a beautiful baby. She blew shining bubbles of sound. She loved motion, loved light, loved color and music and textures. She would lie on the floor in her blue overalls patting the surface so hard in ecstasy her hands and feet would blur. She was a miracle to me, but when she was eight months old I had to leave her daytimes with the woman downstairs to whom she was no miracle at all, for I worked or looked for work and for Emily's father, who "could no longer endure" (he wrote in his good-bye note) "sharing want with us."

I was nineteen. It was the pre-relief, pre-WPA[1] world of the depression. I would start running as soon as I got off the streetcar, running up the stairs, the place smelling sour, and awake or asleep to startle awake, when she saw me she would break into a clogged weeping that could not be comforted, a weeping I can hear yet.

---

[1] WPA, the Works Projects Administration (1935–1943): a U.S. government agency that sponsored building projects to provide work for the unemployed during the Great Depression.

After a while I found a job hashing at night so I could be with her days, and it was better. But it came to where I had to bring her to his family and leave her.

It took a long time to raise the money for her fare back. Then she got chicken pox and I had to wait longer. When she finally came, I hardly knew her, walking quick and nervous like her father, looking like her father, thin, and dressed in a shoddy red that yellowed her skin and glared at the pockmarks. All the baby loveliness gone.

She was two. Old enough for nursery school they said, and I did not know then what I know now—the fatigue of the long day, and the lacerations of group life in the kinds of nurseries that are only parking places for children.

Except that it would have made no difference if I had known. It was the only place there was. It was the only way we could be together, the only way I could hold a job.

And even without knowing, I knew. I knew the teacher that was evil because all these years it has curdled into my memory, the little boy hunched in the corner, her rasp, "why aren't you outside, because Alvin hits you? that's no reason, go out, scaredy." I knew Emily hated it even if she did not clutch and implore "don't go Mommy" like the other children, mornings.

She always had a reason why we should stay home. Momma, you look sick. Momma, I feel sick. Momma, the teachers aren't there today, they're sick. Momma, we can't go, there was a fire there last night. Momma, it's a holiday today, no school, they told me.

But never a direct protest, never rebellion. I think of our others in their three-, four-year-oldness—the explosions, the tempers, the denunciations, the demands—and I feel suddenly ill. I put the iron down. What in me demanded that goodness in her? And what was the cost, the cost to her of such goodness?

The old man living in the back once said in his gentle way: "You should smile at Emily more when you look at her." What *was* in my face when I looked at her? I loved her. There were all the acts of love.

It was only with the others I remembered what he said, and it was the face of joy, and not of care or tightness or worry I turned to them—too late for Emily. She does not smile easily, let alone almost always as her brothers and sisters do. Her face is closed and sombre, but when she wants, how fluid. You must have seen it in her pantomimes, you spoke of her rare gift for comedy on the stage that rouses a laughter out of the audience so dear they applaud and applaud and do not want to let her go.

Where does it come from, that comedy? There was none of it in her when she came back to me that second time, after I had had to send her away again. She had a new daddy now to learn to love, and I think perhaps it was a better time.

Except when we left her alone nights, telling ourselves she was old enough.

"Can't you go some other time, Mommy, like tomorrow?" she would ask. "Will it be just a little while you'll be gone? Do you promise?"

The time we came back, the front door open, the clock on the floor in the hall. She rigid awake. "It wasn't just a little while. I didn't cry. Three times I called you, just three times, and then I ran downstairs to open the door so you could come faster. The clock talked loud. I threw it away, it scared me what it talked."

She said the clock talked loud again that night I went to the hospital to have Susan. She was delirious with the fever that comes before red measles, but she was fully conscious all the week I was gone and the week after we were home when she could not come near the new baby or me.

She did not get well. She stayed skeleton thin, not wanting to eat, and night after night she had nightmares. She would call for me, I would rouse from exhaustion to sleepily call back: "You're all right, darling, go to sleep, it's just a dream," and if she still called, in a sterner voice, "now go to sleep, Emily, there's nothing to hurt you." Twice, only twice, when I had to get up for Susan anyhow, I went in to sit with her.

Now when it is too late (as if she would let me hold and comfort her like I do the others) I get up and go to her at once at her moan or restless stirring. "Are you awake, Emily? Can I get you something?" And the answer is always the same: "No, I'm all right, go back to sleep, Mother."

They persuaded me at the clinic to send her away to a convalescent home in the country where "she can have the kind of food and care you can't manage for her, and you'll be free to concentrate on the new baby." They still send children to that place. I see pictures on the society page of sleek young women planning affairs to raise money for it, or dancing at the affairs, or decorating Easter eggs or filling Christmas stockings for the children.

They never have a picture of the children so I do not know if the girls still wear those gigantic red bows and the ravaged looks on the every other Sunday when parents can come to visit "unless otherwise notified"—as we were notified the first six weeks.

Oh it is a handsome place, green lawns and tall trees and fluted flower beds. High up on the balconies of each cottage the children stand, the girls in their red bows and white dresses, the boys in white suits and giant red ties. The parents stand below shrieking up to be heard and the children shriek down to be heard, and between them the invisible wall "Not To Be Contaminated by Parental Germs or Physical Affection."

There was a tiny girl who always stood hand in hand with Emily. Her parents never came. One visit she was gone. "They moved her to Rose Cottage" Emily shouted in explanation. "They don't like you to love anybody here."

She wrote once a week, the labored writing of a seven-year-old. "I am fine. How is the baby. If I write my leter nicly I will have a star. Love." There never was a star. We wrote every other day, letters she could never hold or keep but only hear read—once. "We simply do not have room for children to keep any personal possessions," they patiently explained when we pieced one Sunday's shrieking together to plead how much it would mean to Emily, who loved so to keep things, to be allowed to keep her letters and cards.

Each visit she looked frailer. "She isn't eating," they told us.

(They had runny eggs for breakfast or mush with lumps, Emily said later, I'd hold it in my mouth and not swallow. Nothing ever tasted good, just when they had chicken.)

It took us eight months to get her released home, and only the fact that she gained back so little of her seven lost pounds convinced the social worker.

I used to try to hold and love her after she came back, but her body would stay stiff, and after a while she'd push away. She ate little. Food sickened her, and I think much of life too. Oh she had physical lightness and brightness, twinkling by on skates, bouncing like a ball up and down up and down over the jump rope, skimming over the hill; but these were momentary.

She fretted about her appearance, thin and dark and foreign-looking at a time when every little girl was supposed to look or thought she should look a chubby blonde replica of Shirley Temple. The doorbell sometimes rang for her, but no one seemed to come and play in the house or be a best friend. Maybe because we moved so much.

There was a boy she loved painfully through two school semesters. Months later she told me how she had taken pennies from my purse to buy him candy. "Licorice was his favorite and I brought him some every day, but he still liked Jennifer better'n me. Why, Mommy?" The kind of question for which there is no answer.

School was a worry to her. She was not glib or quick in a world where glibness and quickness were easily confused with ability to learn. To her overworked and exasperated teachers she was an overconscientious "slow learner" who kept trying to catch up and was absent entirely too often.

I let her be absent, though sometimes the illness was imaginary. How different from my now-strictness about attendance with the others. I wasn't working. We had a new baby, I was home anyhow. Sometimes, after Susan grew old enough, I would keep her home from school, too, to have them all together.

Mostly Emily had asthma, and her breathing, harsh and labored, would fill the house with a curiously tranquil sound. I would bring the two old dresser mirrors and her boxes of collections to her bed. She would select beads and single earrings, bottle tops and shells, dried flowers and pebbles, old postcards and scraps, all sorts of oddments; then she and Susan would play Kingdom, setting up landscapes and furniture, peopling them with action.

Those were the only times of peaceful companionship between her and Susan. I have edged away from it, that poisonous feeling between them, that terrible balancing of hurts and needs I had to do between the two, and did so badly, those earlier years.

Oh there are conflicts between the others too, each one human, needing, demanding, hurting, taking—but only between Emily and Susan, no, Emily toward Susan that corroding resentment. It seems so obvious on the surface, yet it is not obvious. Susan, the second child, Susan, golden- and curly-haired and chubby, quick and articulate and assured, everything in appearance and manner Emily was not; Susan, not able to resist Emily's precious things, losing or sometimes clumsily breaking them; Susan telling jokes and riddles to company for applause while Emily sat silent (to say to me later: that was *my* riddle, Mother, I told it to Susan); Susan, who for all the five years' difference in age was just a year behind Emily in developing physically.

I am glad for that slow physical development that widened the difference between her and her contemporaries, though she suffered over it. She was too vulnerable for that terrible world of youthful competition, of preening and parading, of constant measuring of yourself against every other, of envy, "If I had that copper hair," "If I had that skin. . . ." She tormented herself enough about not looking like the others, there was enough of the unsureness, the having to be conscious of words before you speak, the constant caring—what are they thinking of me? without having it all magnified by the merciless physical drives.

Ronnie is calling. He is wet and I change him. It is rare there is such a cry now. That time of motherhood is almost behind me when the ear is not one's own but must always be racked and listening for the child cry, the child call. We sit for a while and I hold him, looking out over the city spread in charcoal with its soft aisles of light. "*Shoogily*," he breathes and curls closer. I carry him back to bed, asleep. *Shoogily*. A funny word, a family word, inherited from Emily, invented by her to say: comfort.

In this and other ways she leaves her seal, I say aloud. And startle at my saying it. What do I mean? What did I start to gather together, to try and make coherent? I was at the terrible, growing years. War years. I do not remember them well. I was working, there were four smaller ones now, there was not time for her. She had to help be a mother, and housekeeper, and shopper. She had to set her seal. Mornings of crisis and near hysteria trying to get lunches packed, hair combed, coats and shoes found, everyone to school or Child Care on time, the baby ready for transportation. And always the paper scribbled on by a smaller one, the book looked at by Susan then mislaid, the homework not done. Running out to that huge school where she was one, she was lost, she was a drop; suffering over the unpreparedness, stammering and unsure in her classes.

There was so little time left at night after the kids were bedded down. She would struggle over books, always eating (it was in those years she developed her enormous appetite that is legendary in our family) and I would be ironing, or preparing food for the next day, or writing V-mail[2] to Bill, or tending the baby. Sometimes, to make me laugh, or out of her despair, she would imitate happenings or types at school.

I think I said once: "Why don't you do something like this in the school amateur show?" One morning she phoned me at work, hardly understandable through the weeping: "Mother, I did it. I won, I won; they gave me first prize; they clapped and clapped and wouldn't let me go."

Now suddenly she was Somebody, and as imprisoned in her difference as she had been in anonymity.

She began to be asked to perform at other high schools, even in colleges, then at city and statewide affairs. The first one we went to, I only recognized her that first moment when thin, shy, she almost drowned herself into the curtains. Then: Was this Emily? The control, the command, the convulsing and deadly clowning, the spell, then the roaring, stamping audience, unwilling to let this rare and precious laughter out of their lives.

Afterwards: You ought to do something about her with a gift like that—but without money or knowing how, what does one do? We have left it all to her, and the gift has as often eddied inside, clogged and clotted, as been used and growing.

She is coming. She runs up the stairs two at a time with her light graceful step, and I know she is happy tonight. Whatever it was that occasioned your call did not happen today.

"Aren't you ever going to finish the ironing, Mother? Whistler[3] painted his mother in a rocker. I'd have to paint mine standing over an ironing board." This is one of her communicative nights and she tells me everything and nothing as she fixes herself a plate of food out of the icebox.

---

[2] V-mail, victory mail: mail sent to American soldiers during World War II (1941–1945).
[3] James Abbott McNeill Whistler (1834–1903): an American artist, perhaps best known for his painting *Arrangement in Gray and Black*, popularly known as *Whistler's Mother*.

She is so lovely. Why did you want me to come in at all? Why were you concerned? She will find her way.

She starts up the stairs to bed. "Don't get me up with the rest in the morning." "But I thought you were having midterms." "Oh, those," she comes back in, kisses me, and says quite lightly, "in a couple of years when we'll all be atom-dead they won't matter a bit."

She has said it before. She *believes* it. But because I have been dredging the past, and all that compounds a human being is so heavy and meaningful in me, I cannot endure it tonight.

I will never total it all. I will never come in to say: She was a child seldom smiled at. Her father left me before she was a year old. I had to work her first six years when there was work, or I sent her home and to his relatives. There were years she had care she hated. She was dark and thin and foreign-looking in a world where the prestige went to blondeness and curly hair and dimples, she was slow where glibness was prized. She was a child of anxious, not proud, love. We were poor and could not afford for her the soil of easy growth. I was a young mother, I was a distracted mother. There were the other children pushing up, demanding. Her younger sister seemed all that she was not. There were years she did not want me to touch her. She kept too much in herself, her life was such she had to keep too much in herself. My wisdom came too late. She has much to her and probably little will come of it. She is a child of her age, of depression, of war, of fear.

Let her be. So all that is in her will not bloom—but in how many does it? There is still enough left to live by. Only help her to know—help make it so there is cause for her to know—that she is more than this dress on the ironing board, helpless before the iron.

(1954)

QUESTIONS

1. Why do you think Olsen decided to have the mother stand ironing, as opposed to doing any other chore, while she thinks about the life of her oldest child?

2. How does the mother's hard life affect the daughter's personality and sense of self?

3. What type of narration does Olsen use in the story, and how does the point of view of the narrator make you feel about the mother and daughter?

4. To what extent does the voice of the mother illustrate her deepest feelings about whether or not she really believes that Emily turned out "well," despite everything she recalls to the contrary?

ALICE WALKER (B. 1944)

Everyday Use

For Your Grandmama

I will wait for her in the yard that Maggie and I made so clean and wavy yesterday afternoon. A yard like this is more comfortable than most people know. It is not just a yard. It is like an extended living room. When the hard clay is swept clean as a floor and the fine sand around the edges lined with tiny, irregular grooves anyone can come and sit and look up into the elm tree and wait for the breezes that never come inside the house.[1]

Maggie will be nervous until after her sister goes: she will stand hopelessly in corners homely and ashamed of the burn scars down her arms and legs, eyeing her sister with a mixture of envy and awe. She thinks her sister has held life always in the palm of one hand, that "no" is a word the world never learned to say to her.

You've no doubt seen those TV shows where the child who has "made it" is confronted, as a surprise, by her own mother and father, tottering in weakly from backstage. (A pleasant surprise, of course: What would they do if parent and child came on the show only to curse out and insult each other?) On TV mother and child embrace and smile into each other's faces. Sometimes the mother and father weep, the child wraps them in her arms and leans across the table to tell how she would not have made it without their help. I have seen these programs.

Sometimes I dream a dream in which Dee and I are suddenly brought together on a TV program of this sort. Out of a dark and soft-seated limousine I am ushered into a bright room filled with many people. There I meet a smiling, gray, sporty man like Johnny Carson who shakes my hand and tells me what a fine girl I have. Then we are on the stage and Dee is embracing me with tears in her eyes. She pins on my dress a large orchid, even though she has told me once that she thinks orchids are tacky flowers.

In real life I am a large, big-boned woman with rough, man-working hands. In the winter I wear flannel nightgowns to bed and overalls during the day. I can kill and clean a hog as mercilessly as a man. My fat keeps me hot in zero weather. I can work all day, breaking ice to get water for washing. I can eat pork liver cooked over the open fire minutes after it comes steaming from the hog. One winter I knocked a bull calf straight in the brain between the eyes with a sledge hammer and had the meat hung up to chill before nightfall. But of course all this does not show on television. I am the way my daughter would want me to be: a hundred pounds lighter, my skin like an uncooked barley pancake. My hair glistens in the hot bright lights. Johnny Carson has much to do to keep up with my quick and witty tongue.

---

[1] A swept yard is a tradition in some African-American communities in Georgia.

But that is a mistake. I know even before I wake up. Who ever knew a Johnson with a quick tongue? Who can even imagine me looking a strange white man in the eye? It seems to me I have talked to them always with one foot raised in flight, with my head turned in whichever way is farthest from them. Dee, though. She would always look anyone in the eye. Hesitation was no part of her nature.

"How do I look, Mama?" Maggie says, showing just enough of her thin body enveloped in pink skirt and red blouse for me to know she's there, almost hidden by the door.

"Come out into the yard," I say.

Have you ever seen a lame animal, perhaps a dog run over by some careless person rich enough to own a car, sidle up to someone who is ignorant enough to be kind to him? That is the way my Maggie walks. She has been like this, chin on chest, eyes on ground, feet in shuffle, ever since the fire that burned the other house to the ground.

Dee is lighter than Maggie, with nicer hair and a fuller figure. She's a woman now, though sometimes I forget. How long ago was it that the other house burned? Ten, twelve years? Sometimes I can still hear the flames and feel Maggie's arm sticking to me, her hair smoking and her dress falling off her in little black papery flakes. Her eyes seemed stretched open, blazed open by the flames reflected in them. And Dee. I see her standing off under the sweet gum tree she used to dig gum out of; a look of concentration on her face as she watched the last dingy gray board of the house fall in toward the red-hot brick chimney. Why don't you do a dance around the ashes? I'd wanted to ask her. She had hated the house that much.

I used to think she hated Maggie, too. But that was before we raised the money, the church and me, to send her to Augusta to school. She used to read to us without pity; forcing words, lies, other folks' habits, whole lives upon us two, sitting trapped and ignorant underneath her voice. She washed us in a river of make-believe, burned us with a lot of knowledge we didn't necessarily need to know. Pressed us to her with the serious way she read, to shove us away at just the moment, like dimwits, we seemed about to understand.

Dee wanted nice things. A yellow organdy dress to wear to her graduation from high school; black pumps to match a green suit she'd made from an old suit somebody gave me. She was determined to stare down any disaster in her efforts. Her eyelids would not flicker for minutes at a time. Often I fought off the temptation to shake her. At sixteen she had a style of her own: and knew what style was.

I never had an education myself. After second grade the school was closed down. Don't ask me why: in 1927 colored asked fewer questions than they do now. Sometimes Maggie reads to me. She stumbles along good-naturedly but can't see well. She knows she is not bright. Like good looks and money, quickness passed her by. She will marry John Thomas (who has mossy teeth in an earnest face) and then I'll be free to sit here and I guess just sing church songs to myself. Although I never was a good singer. Never could carry a tune. I was always better at a man's job. I used to love to milk till I was hoofed in the side in '49. Cows are soothing and slow and don't bother you, unless you try to milk them the wrong way.

I have deliberately turned my back on the house. It is three rooms, just like the one that burned, except the roof is tin; they don't make shingle roofs any more. There are no real windows, just some holes cut in the sides, like the portholes in a ship, but not round and not square, with rawhide holding the shutters up on the outside. The house is in a pasture, too, like the other one. No doubt when Dee sees it she will want to tear it down. She wrote me once that no matter where we "choose" to live, she will manage to come see us. But she will never bring her friends. Maggie and I thought about this and Maggie asked me, "Mama, when did Dee ever *have* any friends?"

She had a few. Furtive boys in pink shirts hanging about on washday after school. Nervous girls who never laughed. Impressed with her they worshiped the well-turned phrase, the cute shape, the scalding humor that erupted like bubbles in lye. She read to them.

When she was courting Jimmy T. she didn't have much time to pay to us, but turned all her faultfinding power on him. He *flew* to marry a cheap gal from a family of ignorant flashy people. She hardly had time to recompose herself.

When she comes I will meet—but there they are!

Maggie attempts to make a dash for the house, in her shuffling way, but I stay her with my hand. "Come back here," I say. And she stops and tries to dig a well in the sand with her toe.

It is hard to see them clearly through the strong sun. But even the first glimpse of leg out of the car tells me it is Dee. Her feet were always neat-looking, as if God himself had shaped them with a certain style. From the other side of the car comes a short, stocky man. Hair is all over his head a foot long and hanging from his chin like a kinky mule tail. I hear Maggie suck in her breath. "Uhnnnh," is what it sounds like. Like when you see the wriggling end of a snake just in front of your foot on the road. "Uhnnnh."

Dee next. A dress down to the ground, in this hot weather. A dress so loud it hurts my eyes. There are yellows and oranges enough to throw back the light of the sun. I feel my whole face warming from the heat waves it throws out. Earrings, too, gold and hanging down to her shoulders. Bracelets dangling and making noises when she moves her arm up to shake the folds of the dress out of her armpits. The dress is loose and flows, and as she walks closer, I like it. I hear Maggie go "Uhnnnh" again. It is her sister's hair. It stands straight up like the wool on a sheep. It is black as night and around the edges are two long pigtails that rope about like small lizards disappearing behind her ears.

"Wa-su-zo-Tean-o!"[2] she says, coming on in that gliding way the dress makes her move. The short stocky fellow with the hair to his navel is all grinning and he follows up with "Asalamalakim,[3] my mother and sister!" He moves to hug Maggie but she falls back, right up against the back of my chair. I feel her trembling there and when I look up I see the perspiration falling off her chin.

"Don't get up," says Dee. Since I am stout it takes something of a push. You can see me trying to move a second or two before I make it. She turns, showing white heels through her sandals, and goes back to the car. Out she peeks next with a Polaroid. She stoops down quickly and lines up picture after picture of me sitting there in front of the

---

[2] *Wa-su-zo-Tean-o:* Swahili greeting.
[3] *Asalamalakim:* "Hello, peace."

house with Maggie cowering behind me. She never takes a shot without making sure the house is included. When a cow comes nibbling around the edge of the yard she snaps it and me and Maggie *and* the house. Then she puts the Polaroid in the back seat of the car, and comes up and kisses me on the forehead.

Meanwhile Asalamalakim is going through the motions with Maggie's hand. Maggie's hand is as limp as a fish, and probably as cold, despite the sweat, and she keeps trying to pull it back. It looks like Asalamalakim wants to shake hands but wants to do it fancy. Or maybe he don't know how people shake hands. Anyhow, he soon gives up on Maggie.

"Well," I say. "Dee."

"No, Mama," she says. "Not 'Dee.' Wangero Leewanika Kemanjo!"

"What happened to 'Dee'?" I wanted to know.

"She's dead." Wangero said. "I couldn't bear it any longer being named after the people who oppress me."

"You know as well as me you was named after your aunt Dicie," I said. Dicie is my sister. She named Dee. We called her "Big Dee" after Dee was born.

"But who was *she* named after?" asked Wangero.

"I guess after Grandma Dee," I said.

"And who was she named after?" asked Wangero.

"Her mother," I said, and saw Wangero was getting tired. "That's about as far back as I can trace it," I said. Though, in fact, I probably could have carried it back beyond the Civil War through the branches.

"Well," said Asalamalakim, "there you are."

"Uhnnnh," I heard Maggie say.

"There I was not," I said, "before 'Dicie' cropped up in our family, so why should I try to trace it that far back?"

He just stood there grinning, looking down on me like somebody inspecting a Model A car. Every once in a while he and Wangero sent eye signals over my head.

"How do you pronounce this name?" I asked.

"You don't have to call me by it if you don't want to," said Wangero.

"Why shouldn't I?" I asked. "If that's what you want us to call you, we'll call you."

"I know it might sound awkward at first," said Wangero.

"I'll get used to it," I said. "Ream it out again."

Well, soon we got the name out of the way. Asalamalakim had a name twice as long and three times as hard. After I tripped over it two or three times he told me to just call him Hakim-a-barber. I wanted to ask him was he a barber, but I didn't really think he was, so I didn't ask.

"You must belong to those beef-cattle peoples down the road," I said. They said "Asalamalakim" when they met you, too, but they didn't shake hands. Always too busy: feeding the cattle, fixing the fences, putting up salt-lick shelters, throwing down hay. When the white folks poisoned some of the herd the men stayed up all night with rifles in their hands. I walked a mile and a half just to see the sight.

Hakim-a-barber said, "I accept some of their doctrines, but farming and raising cattle is not my style." (They didn't tell me, and I didn't ask, whether Wangero [Dee] had really gone and married him.)

We sat down to eat and right away he said he didn't eat collards and pork was unclean. Wangero, though, went on through the chitlins and corn bread, the greens and everything else. She talked a blue streak over the sweet potatoes. Everything delighted her. Even the fact that we still used the benches her daddy made for the table when we couldn't afford to buy chairs.

"Oh, Mama!" she cried. Then turned to Hakim-a-barber. "I never knew how lovely these benches are. You can feel the rump prints," she said, running her hands underneath her and along the bench. Then she gave a sigh and her hand closed over Grandma Dee's butter dish. "That's it!" she said. "I knew there was something I wanted to ask you if I could have." She jumped up from the table and went over in the corner where the churn stood, the milk in its clabber by now. She looked at the churn and looked at it.

"This churn top is what I need," she said. "Didn't Uncle Buddy whittle it out of a tree you all used to have?"

"Yes," I said.

"Uh huh," she said happily. "And I want the dasher, too."

"Uncle Buddy whittle that, too?" asked the barber.

Dee (Wangero) looked up at me.

"Aunt Dee's first husband whittled the dash," said Maggie so low you almost couldn't hear her. "His name was Henry, but they called him Stash."

"Maggie's brain is like an elephant's," Wangero said, laughing. "I can use the churn top as a centerpiece for the alcove table," she said, sliding a plate over the churn, "and I'll think of something artistic to do with the dasher."

When she finished wrapping the dasher the handle stuck out. I took it for a moment in my hands. You didn't even have to look close to see where hands pushing the dasher up and down to make butter had left a kind of sink in the wood. In fact, there were a lot of small sinks; you could see where thumbs and fingers had sunk into the wood. It was beautiful light yellow wood, from a tree that grew in the yard where Big Dee and Stash had lived.

After dinner Dee (Wangero) went to the trunk at the foot of my bed and started rifling through it. Maggie hung back in the kitchen over the dishpan. Out came Wangero with two quilts. They had been pieced by Grandma Dee and then Big Dee and me had hung them on the quilt frames on the front porch and quilted them. One was in the Lone Star pattern. The other was Walk Around the Mountain. In both of them were scraps of dresses Grandma Dee had worn fifty and more years ago. Bits and pieces of Grandpa Jarrell's Paisley shirts. And one teeny faded blue piece, about the size of a penny matchbox, that was from Great Grandpa Ezra's uniform that he wore in the Civil War.

"Mama," Wangero said sweet as a bird. "Can I have these old quilts?"

I heard something fall in the kitchen, and a minute later the kitchen door slammed.

"Why don't you take one or two of the others?" I asked "These old things was just done by me and Big Dee from some tops your grandma pieced before she died."

"No," said Wangero. "I don't want those. They are stitched around the borders by machine."

"That's make them last better," I said.

"That's not the point," said Wangero. "These are all pieces of dresses Grandma used to wear. She did all this stitching by hand. Imagine!" She held the quilts securely in her arms, stroking them.

"Some of the pieces, like those lavender ones, come from old clothes her mother handed down to her," I said, moving up to touch the quilts. Dee (Wangero) moved back just enough so that I couldn't reach the quilts. They already belonged to her.

"Imagine!" she breathed again, clutching them closely to her bosom.

"The truth is," I said, "I promised to give them quilts to Maggie, for when she marries John Thomas."

She gasped like a bee had stung her.

"Maggie can't appreciate these quilts!" she said. "She'd probably be backward enough to put them to everyday use."

"I reckon she would," I said. "God knows I been saving 'em for long enough with nobody using 'em. I hope she will!" I didn't want to bring up how I had offered Dee (Wangero) a quilt when she went away to college. Then she had told me they were old-fashioned, out of style.

"But they're *priceless!*" she was saying now, furiously, for she has a temper. "Maggie would put them on the bed and in five years they'd be in rags. Less than that!"

"She can always make some more," I said. "Maggie knows how to quilt."

Dee (Wangero) looked at me with hatred. "You just will not understand. The point is these quilts, *these* quilts!"

"Well," I said, stumped. "What would *you* do with them?"

"Hang them," she said. As if that was the only thing you *could* do with quilts.

Maggie by now was standing in the door. I could almost hear the sound her feet made as they scraped over each other.

"She can have them, Mama," she said, like somebody used to never winning anything, or having anything reserved for her. "I can 'member Grandma Dee without the quilts."

I looked at her hard. She had filled her bottom lip with checkerberry snuff and it gave her face a kind of dopey, hangdog look. It was Grandma Dee and Big Dee who taught her how to quilt herself. She stood there with her scarred hands hidden in the folds of her skirt. She looked at her sister with something like fear but she wasn't mad at her. This was Maggie's portion. This was the way she knew God to work.

When I looked at her like that something hit me in the top of my head and ran down to the soles of my feet. Just like when I'm in church and the spirit of God touches me and I get happy and shout. I did something I never had done before: hugged Maggie to me, then dragged her on into the room, snatched the quilts out of Miss Wangero's hands and dumped them into Maggie's lap. Maggie just sat there on my bed with her mouth open.

"Take one or two of the others," I said to Dee.

But she turned without a word and went out to Hakim-a-barber.

"You just don't understand," she said, as Maggie and I came out to the car.

"What don't I understand?" I wanted to know.

"Your heritage," she said. And then she turned to Maggie, kissed her, and said, "You ought to try to make something of yourself, too, Maggie. It's really a new day for us. But from the way you and Mama still live you'd never know it."

She put on some sunglasses that hid everything above the tip of her nose and her chin.

Maggie smiled; maybe at the sunglasses. But a real smile, not scared. After we watched the car dust settle I asked Maggie to bring me a dip of snuff. And then the two of us sat there just enjoying, until it was time to go in the house and go to bed.

(1973)

QUESTIONS

1. Does the mother favor Dee over Maggie, or does she love them both? How does this love relate to the significance of the subtitle of the story, "For Your Grandmama"?

2. Explain the significance of the fire, the burned house, and the dirt yard. How can they be seen symbolically as well as literally?

3. Why does Dee want the quilt so badly and why doesn't her mother want her to have it? Compare the quilt's connotations for Dee with those of her mother.

4. What does the quilt symbolize in the story?

JAMES JOYCE (1882–1941)

Counterparts

The bell rang furiously and, when Miss Parker went to the tube, a furious voice called out in a piercing North of Ireland accent:

—Send Farrington here!

Miss Parker returned to her machine, saying to a man who was writing at a desk:

—Mr Alleyne wants you upstairs.

The man muttered *Blast him!* under his breath and pushed back his chair to stand up. When he stood up he was tall and of great bulk. He had a hanging face, dark wine-coloured, with fair eyebrows and moustache: his eyes bulged forward slightly and the whites of them were dirty. He lifted up the counter and, passing by the clients, went out of the office with a heavy step.

He went heavily upstairs until he came to the second landing, where a door bore a brass plate with the inscription *Mr Alleyne*. Here he halted, puffing with labour and vexation, and knocked. The shrill voice cried:

—Come in!

The man entered Mr Alleyne's room. Simultaneously Mr Alleyne, a little man wearing gold-rimmed glasses on a clean-shaven face, shot his head up over a pile of documents. The head itself was so pink and hairless that it seemed like a large egg reposing on the papers. Mr Alleyne did not lose a moment:

—Farrington? What is the meaning of this? Why have I always to complain of you? May I ask you why you haven't made a copy of that contract between Bodley and Kirwan? I told you it must be ready by four o'clock.

—But Mr Shelley said, sir—

—*Mr Shelley said, sir*. . . . Kindly attend to what I say and not to what *Mr Shelley says, sir*. You have always some excuse or another for shirking work. Let me tell you that if the contract is not copied before this evening I'll lay the matter before Mr Crosbie. . . . Do you hear me now?

—Yes, sir.

—Do you hear me now? . . . Ay and another little matter! I might as well be talking to the wall as talking to you. Understand once and for all that you get a half an hour for your lunch and not an hour and a half. How many courses do you want, I'd like to know. . . . Do you mind me, now?

—Yes, sir.

Mr Alleyne bent his head again upon his pile of papers. The man stared fixedly at the polished skull which directed the affairs of Crosbie & Alleyne, gauging its fragility. A spasm of rage gripped his throat for a few moments and then passed, leaving after it a sharp sensation of thirst. The man recognized the sensation and felt that he must have a good night's drinking. The middle of the month was passed and, if he could get the copy done in time, Mr Alleyne might give him an order on the cashier. He stood still, gazing fixedly at the head upon the pile of papers. Suddenly Mr Alleyne began to upset all the papers, searching for something. Then, as if he had been unaware of the man's presence till that moment, he shot up his head again, saying:

—Eh? Are you going to stand there all day? Upon my word, Farrington, you take things easy!

—I was waiting to see . . .

—Very good, you needn't wait to see. Go downstairs and do your work.

The man walked heavily towards the door and, as he went out of the room, he heard Mr Alleyne cry after him that if the contract was not copied by evening Mr Crosbie would hear of the matter.

He returned to his desk in the lower office and counted the sheets which remained to be copied. He took up his pen and dipped it in the ink but he continued to stare stupidly at the last words he had written: *In no case shall the said Bernard Bodley be* . . . The evening was falling and in a few minutes they would be lighting the gas; then he could write. He felt that he must slake the thirst in his throat. He stood up from his desk and, lifting the counter as before, passed out of the office. As he was passing out the chief clerk looked at him inquiringly.

—It's all right, Mr Shelley, said the man, pointing with his finger to indicate the objective of his journey.

The chief clerk glanced at the hat-rack but, seeing the row complete, offered no remark. As soon as he was on the landing the man pulled a shepherd's plaid cap out of his pocket, put it on his head and ran quickly down the rickety stairs. From the street door he walked on furtively on the inner side of the path towards the corner and all at once dived into a doorway. He was now safe in the dark snug of O'Neill's shop, and, filling up the little window that looked into the bar with his inflamed face, the colour of dark wine or dark meat, he called out:

—Here, Pat, give us a g.p.,[1] like a good fellow.

The curate brought him a glass of plain porter.[2] The man drank it at a gulp and asked for a caraway seed. He put his penny on the counter and, leaving the curate[3] to grope for it in the gloom, retreated out of the snug as furtively as he had entered it.

Darkness, accompanied by a thick fog, was gaining upon the dusk of February and the lamps in Eustace Street had been lit. The man went up by the houses until he reached the door of the office, wondering whether he could finish his copy in time. On the stairs a moist pungent odour of perfumes saluted his nose: evidently Miss Delacour had come while he was out in O'Neill's. He crammed his cap back again into his pocket and re-entered the office, assuming an air of absent-mindedness.

—Mr Alleyne has been calling for you, said the chief clerk severely. Where were you?

The man glanced at the two clients who were standing at the counter as if to intimate that their presence prevented him from answering. As the clients were both male the chief clerk allowed himself a laugh.

---

[1] g.p.: glass of porter.
[2] porter: a kind of beer, of a dark brown color and bitterish taste, drunk by the lower class of laborers.
[3] curate: in Ireland, a "spirit-grocer's" assistant, one who helps in selling alcoholic beverages.

—I know that game, he said. Five times in one day is a little bit. . . . Well, you better look sharp and get a copy of our correspondence in the Delacour case for Mr Alleyne.

This address in the presence of the public, his run upstairs and the porter he had gulped down so hastily confused the man and, as he sat down at his desk to get what was required, he realized how hopeless was the task of finishing his copy of the contract before half past five. The dark damp night was coming and he longed to spend it in the bars, drinking with his friends amid the glare of gas and the clatter of glasses. He got out the Delacour correspondence and passed out of the office. He hoped Mr Alleyne would not discover that the last two letters were missing.

The moist pungent perfume lay all the way up to Mr Alleyne's room. Miss Delacour was a middle-aged woman of Jewish appearance. Mr Alleyne was said to be sweet on her or on her money. She came to the office often and stayed a long time when she came. She was sitting beside his desk now in an aroma of perfumes, smoothing the handle of her umbrella and nodding the great black feather in her hat. Mr Alleyne had swivelled his chair round to face her and thrown his right foot jauntily upon his left knee. The man put the correspondence on the desk and bowed respectfully but neither Mr Alleyne nor Miss Delacour took any notice of his bow. Mr Alleyne tapped a finger on the correspondence and then flicked it toward him as if to say: *That's all right: you can go.*

The man returned to the lower office and sat down again at his desk. He stared intently at the incomplete phrase: *In no case shall the said Bernard Bodley be* . . . and thought how strange it was that the last three words began with the same letter. The chief clerk began to hurry Miss Parker, saying she would never have the letters typed in time for post. The man listened to the clicking of the machine for a few minutes and then set to work to finish his copy. But his head was not clear and his mind wandered away to the glare and rattle of the public-house. It was a night for hot punches. He struggled on with his copy, but when the clock struck five he had still fourteen pages to write. Blast it! He couldn't finish it in time. He longed to execrate aloud, to bring his fist down on something violently. He was so enraged that he wrote *Bernard Bernard* instead of *Bernard Bodley* and had to begin again on a clean sheet.

He felt strong enough to clear out the whole office singlehanded. His body ached to do something, to rush out and revel in violence. All the indignities of his life enraged him. . . . Could he ask the cashier privately for an advance? No, the cashier was no good, no damn good: he wouldn't give an advance. . . . He knew where he would meet the boys: Leonard and O'Halloran and Nosey Flynn. The barometer of his emotional nature was set for a spell of riot.

His imagination had so abstracted him that his name was called twice before he answered. Mr Alleyne and Miss Delacour were standing outside the counter and all the clerks had turned round in anticipation of something. The man got up from his desk. Mr Alleyne began a tirade of abuse, saying that two letters were missing. The man answered that he knew nothing about them, that he had made a faithful copy. The tirade continued: it was so bitter and violent that the man could hardly restrain his fist from descending upon the head of the manikin before him.

—I know nothing about any other two letters, he said stupidly.

—*You—know—nothing.* Of course you know nothing, said Mr Alleyne. Tell me, he added, glancing first for approval to the lady beside him, do you take me for a fool? Do you think me an utter fool?

The man glanced from the lady's face to the little egg-shaped head and back again; and, almost before he was aware of it, his tongue had found a felicitous moment:

—I don't think, sir, he said, that that's a fair question to put to me.

There was a pause in the very breathing of the clerks. Everyone was astounded (the author of the witticism no less than his neighbours) and Miss Delacour, who was a stout amiable person, began to smile broadly. Mr Alleyne flushed to the hue of a wild rose and his mouth twitched with a dwarf's passion. He shook his fist in the man's face till it seemed to vibrate like the knob of some electric machine:

—You impertinent ruffian! You impertinent ruffian! I'll make short work of you! Wait till you see! You'll apologize to me for your impertinence or you'll quit the office instanter! You'll quit this, I'm telling you, or you'll apologize to me!

*   *   *

He stood in a doorway opposite the office watching to see if the cashier would come out alone. All the clerks passed out and finally the cashier came out with the chief clerk. It was no use trying to say a word to him when he was with the chief clerk. The man felt that his position was bad enough. He had been obliged to offer an abject apology to Mr Alleyne for his impertinence but he knew what a hornet's nest the office would be for him. He could remember the way in which Mr Alleyne had hounded little Peake out of the office in order to make room for his own nephew. He felt savage and thirsty and revengeful, annoyed with himself and with everyone else. Mr Alleyne would never give him an hour's rest; his life would be a hell to him. He had made a proper fool of himself this time. Could he not keep his tongue in his cheek? But they had never pulled together from the first, he and Mr Alleyne, ever since the day Mr Alleyne had overheard him mimicking his North of Ireland accent to amuse Higgins and Miss Parker: that had been the beginning of it. He might have tried Higgins for the money, but sure Higgins never had anything for himself. A man with two establishments to keep up, of course he couldn't. . . .

He felt his great body again aching for the comfort of the public-house. The fog had begun to chill him and he wondered could he touch Pat in O'Neill's. He could not touch him for more than a bob—and a bob was no use. Yet he must get money somewhere or other; he had spent his last penny for the g.p. and soon it would be too late for getting money anywhere. Suddenly, as he was fingering his watch-chain, he thought of Terry Kelly's pawn-office in Fleet Street. That was the dart! Why didn't he think of it sooner?

He went through the narrow alley of Temple Bar quickly, muttering to himself that they could all go to hell because he was going to have a good night of it. The clerk in Terry Kelly's said *A crown!* but the consignor held out for six shillings; and in the end the six shillings was allowed him literally. He came out of the pawn-office joyfully, making a little cylinder of the coins between his thumb and fingers. In Westmoreland Street the footpaths were crowded with young men and women returning from business and ragged urchins ran here and there yelling out the names of the evening editions. The man passed through the crowd, looking on the spectacle generally with proud satisfaction and staring masterfully at the office-girls. His head was full of the noises of tram-gongs and swishing trolleys and his nose already sniffed the curling fumes of punch. As he walked on he preconsidered the terms in which he would narrate the incident to the boys:

—So, I just looked at him—coolly, you know, and looked at her. Then I looked back at him again—taking my time, you know. *I don't think that that's a fair question to put to me,* says I.

Nosey Flynn was sitting up in his usual corner of Davy Bryne's and, when he heard the story, he stood Farrington a half-one, saying it was as smart a thing as ever he heard. Farrington stood a drink in his turn. After a while O'Halloran and Paddy Leonard came in and the story was repeated to them. O'Halloran stood tailors of malt, hot, all round and told the story of the retort he had made to the chief clerk when he was in Callan's of Fownes's Street; but, as the retort was after the manner of the liberal shepherds in the eclogues,[4] he had to admit that it was not so clever as Farrington's retort. At this Farrington told the boys to polish off that and have another.

Just as they were naming their poisons who should come in but Higgins! Of course he had to join in with the others. The men asked him to give his version of it, and he did so with great vivacity for the sight of five small hot whiskies was very exhilarating. Everyone roared laughing when he showed the way in which Mr Alleyne shook his fist in Farrington's face. Then he imitated Farrington, saying, *And here was my nabs,*[5] *as cool as you please,* while Farrington looked at the company out of his heavy dirty eyes, smiling and at times drawing forth stray drops of liquor from his moustache with the aid of his lower lip.

When that round was over there was a pause. O'Halloran had money but neither of the other two seemed to have any; so the whole party left the shop somewhat regretfully. At the corner of Duke Street Higgins and Nosey Flynn bevelled off to the left while the other three turned back towards the city. Rain was drizzling down on the cold streets and, when they reached the Ballast Office, Farrington suggested the Scotch House. The bar was full of men and loud with the noise of tongues and glasses. The three men pushed past the whining matchsellers at the door and formed a little party at the corner of the counter. They began to exchange stories. Leonard introduced them to a young fellow named Weathers who was performing at the Tivoli as an acrobat and knockabout *artiste.* Farrington stood a drink all round. Weathers said he would take a small Irish and Apollinaris.[6] Farrington, who had definite notions of what was what, asked the boys would they have an Apollinaris too; but the boys told Tim to make theirs hot. The talk became theatrical. O'Halloran stood a round and then Farrington stood another round, Weathers protesting that the hospitality was too Irish. He promised to get them in behind the scenes and introduce them to some nice girls. O'Halloran said that he and Leonard would go but that Farrington wouldn't go because he was a married man; and Farrington's heavy dirty eyes leered at the company in token that he understood he was being chafed. Weathers made them all have just one little tincture at his expense and promised to meet them later on at Mulligan's in Poolbeg Street.

When the Scotch House closed they went round to Mulligan's. They went into the parlour at the back and O'Halloran ordered small hot specials all around. They were all beginning to feel mellow. Farrington was just standing another round when Weathers

---

[4] eclogues: short poems, especially pastoral dialogues.
[5] my nabs: slang for "my gentleman," meaning "myself."
[6] Apollinaris: an effervescent mineral water.

came back. Much to Farrington's relief he drank a glass of bitter this time. Funds were running low but they had enough to keep them going. Presently two young women with big hats and a young man in a check suit came in and sat at a table close by. Weathers saluted them and told the company that they were out of the Tivoli. Farrington's eyes wandered at every moment in the direction of one of the young women. There was something striking in her appearance. An immense scarf of peacock-blue muslin was wound round her hat and knotted in a great bow under her chin; and she wore bright yellow gloves, reaching to the elbow. Farrington gazed admiringly at the plump arm which she moved very often and with much grace; and when, after a little time, she answered his gaze he admired still more her large dark brown eyes. The oblique staring expression in them fascinated him. She glanced at him once or twice and, when the party was leaving the room, she brushed against his chair and said *O, pardon!* in a London accent. He watched her leave the room in the hope that she would look back at him, but he was disappointed. He cursed his want of money and cursed all the rounds he had stood, particularly all the whiskies and Apollinaris which he had stood to Weathers. If there was one thing that he hated it was a sponge. He was so angry that he lost count of the conversation of his friends.

When Paddy Leonard called him he found that they were talking about feats of strength. Weathers was showing his biceps muscle to the company and boasting so much that the other two had called on Farrington to uphold the national honour. Farrington pulled up his sleeve accordingly and showed his biceps muscle to the company. The two arms were examined and compared and finally it was agreed to have a trial of strength. The table was cleared and the two men rested their elbows on it, clasping hands. When Paddy Leonard said *Go!* each was to try to bring down the other's hand on to the table. Farrington looked very serious and determined.

The trial began. After about thirty seconds Weathers brought his opponent's hand slowly down on to the table. Farrington's dark wine-coloured face flushed darker still with anger and humiliation at having been defeated by such a stripling.

—You're not to put the weight of your body behind it. Play fair, he said.

—Who's not playing fair? said the other.

—Come on again. The two best out of three.

The trial began again. The veins stood out on Farrington's forehead, and the pallor of Weathers' complexion changed to peony. Their hands and arms trembled under the stress. After a long struggle Weathers again brought his opponent's hand slowly on to the table. There was a murmur of applause from the spectators. The curate, who was standing beside the table, nodded his red head toward the victor and said with loutish familiarity:

—Ah! that's the knack!

—What the hell do you know about it? said Farrington fiercely, turning on the man. What do you put in your gab for?

—Sh, sh! said O'Halloran, observing the violent expression of Farrington's face. Pony up, boys. We'll have just one little smahan[7] more and then we'll be off.

---

[7] smahan: a drop to drink, a taste or a nip.

A very sullen-faced man stood at the corner of O'Connell Bridge waiting for the little Sandymount tram to take him home. He was full of smouldering anger and revengefulness. He felt humiliated and discontented; he did not even feel drunk; and he had only twopence in his pocket. He cursed everything. He had done for himself in the office, pawned his watch, spent all his money; and he had not even got drunk. He began to feel thirsty again and he longed to be back again in the hot reeking public-house. He had lost his reputation as a strong man, having been defeated twice by a mere boy. His heart swelled with fury and, when he thought of the woman in the big hat who had brushed against him and said *Pardon!* his fury nearly choked him.

His tram let him down at Shelbourne Road and he steered his great body along in the shadow of the wall of the barracks. He loathed returning to his home. When he went in by the side-door he found the kitchen empty and the kitchen fire nearly out. He bawled upstairs:

—Ada! Ada!

His wife was a little sharp-faced woman who bullied her husband when he was sober and was bullied by him when he was drunk. They had five children. A little boy came running down the stairs.

—Who is that? said the man, peering through the darkness.

—Me, pa.

—Who are you? Charlie?

—No, pa. Tom.

—Where's your mother?

—She's out at the chapel.

—That's right. . . . Did she think of leaving any dinner for me?

—Yes, pa. I—

—Light the lamp. What do you mean by having the place in darkness? Are the other children in bed?

The man sat down heavily on one of the chairs while the little boy lit the lamp. He began to mimic his son's flat accent, saying half to himself: *At the chapel. At the chapel, if you please!* When the lamp was lit he banged his fist on the table and shouted:

—What's for my dinner?

—I'm going . . . to cook it, pa, said the little boy.

The man jumped up furiously and pointed to the fire.

—On that fire! You let the fire out! By God, I'll teach you to do that again!

He took a step to the door and seized the walking-stick which was standing behind it.

—I'll teach you to let the fire out! he said, rolling up his sleeve in order to give his arm free play.

The little boy cried *O, pa!* and ran whimpering round the table, but the man followed him and caught him by the coat. The little boy looked about him wildly but, seeing no way of escape, fell upon his knees.

—Now, you'll let the fire out the next time! said the man, striking at him viciously with the stick. Take that, you little whelp!

The boy uttered a squeal of pain as the stick cut his thigh. He clasped his hands together in the air and his voice shook with fright.

—O, pa! he cried. Don't beat me, pa! And I'll ... I'll say a *Hail Mary*[8] for you. . . . I'll say a *Hail Mary* for you, pa, if you don't beat me. . . . I'll say a *Hail Mary*. . . .

(1914)

QUESTIONS

1. Why is Farrington so pleased with himself for talking back to Mr Alleyne?

2. In what ways might it be said that Farrington is self-destructive? In what ways might his actions be seen as a product of his class?

3. What are the causes of Farrington's "smouldering anger" by the end of the evening?

4. How would you describe Farrington's view of his role as a father?

5. What do you think Joyce had in mind when he gave this story the title "Counterparts"?

---

[8] Hail Mary: opening words of a Catholic prayer said with rosary beads.

Nadine Gordimer (b. 1923)

The Moment Before the Gun Went Off

Marais Van der Vyver shot one of his farm labourers, dead. An accident, there are accidents with guns every day of the week—children playing a fatal game with a father's revolver in the cities where guns are domestic objects, nowadays, hunting mishaps like this one, in the country—but these won't be reported all over the world. Van der Vyver knows his will be. He knows that the story of the Afrikaner[1] farmer—regional Party leader and Commandant of the local security commando—shooting a black man who worked for him will fit exactly *their* version of South Africa, it's made for them. They'll be able to use it in their boycott and divestment campaigns, it'll be another piece of evidence in their truth about the country. The papers at home will quote the story as it has appeared in the overseas press, and in the back-and-forth he and the black man will become those crudely-drawn figures on anti-apartheid banners, units in statistics of white brutality against the blacks quoted at the United Nations—he, whom they will gleefully be able to call 'a leading member' of the ruling Party.

People in the farming community understand how he must feel. Bad enough to have killed a man, without helping the Party's, the government's, the country's enemies, as well. They see the truth of that. They know, reading the Sunday papers, that when Van der Vyver is quoted saying he is 'terribly shocked,' he will 'look after the wife and children,' none of those Americans and English, and none of those people at home who want to destroy the white man's power will believe him. And how they will sneer when he even says of the farm boy (according to one paper, if you can trust any of those reporters), 'He was my friend, I always took him hunting with me.' Those city and overseas people don't know it's true: farmers usually have one particular black boy they like to take along with them in the lands; you could call it a kind of friend, yes, friends are not only your own white people, like yourself, you take into your house, pray with in church and work with on the Party committee. But how can those others know that? They don't want to know it. They think all blacks are like the big-mouth agitators in town. And Van der Vyver's face, in the photographs, strangely opened by distress—everyone in the district remembers Marais Van der Vyver as a little boy who would go away and hide himself if he caught you smiling at him, and everyone knows him now as a man who hides any change of expression round his mouth behind a thick, soft moustache, and in his eyes by always looking at some object in hand, leaf of a crop fingered, pen or stone picked up, while concentrating on what he is saying, or while listening to you. It just goes to show what shock can do; when you look at the newspaper photographs you feel like apologizing, as if you had stared in on some room where you should not be.

There will be an inquiry; there had better be, to stop the assumption of yet another case of brutality against farm workers, although there's nothing in doubt—an

---

[1] Afrikaner: an Afrikaans-speaking South African of European ancestry, especially one descended from seventeenth century Dutch settlers.

accident, and all the facts fully admitted by Van der Vyver. He made a statement when he arrived at the police station with the dead man in his bakkie.[2] Captain Beetge knows him well, of course; he gave him brandy. He was shaking, this big, calm, clever son of Willem Van der Vyver, who inherited the old man's best farm. The black was stone dead, nothing to be done for him. Beetge will not tell anyone that after the brandy Van der Vyver wept. He sobbed, snot running onto his hands, like a dirty kid. The Captain was ashamed, for him, and walked out to give him a chance to recover himself.

Marais Van der Vyver left his house at three in the afternoon to cull a buck from the family of kudu[3] he protects in the bush areas of his farm. He is interested in wildlife and sees it as the farmers' sacred duty to raise game as well as cattle. As usual, he called at his shed workshop to pick up Lucas, a twenty-year-old farmhand who had shown mechanical aptitude and whom Van der Vyver himself had taught to maintain tractors and other farm machinery. He hooted, and Lucas followed the familiar routine, jumping onto the back of the truck. He liked to travel standing up there, spotting game before his employer did. He would lean forward, braced against the cab below him.

Van der Vyver had a rifle and .300 ammunition beside him in the cab. The rifle was one of his father's, because his own was at the gunsmith's in town. Since his father died (Beetge's sergeant wrote 'passed on') no one had used the rifle and so when he took it from a cupboard he was sure it was not loaded. His father had never allowed a loaded gun in the house; he himself had been taught since childhood never to ride with a loaded weapon in a vehicle. But this gun was loaded. On a dirt track, Lucas thumped his fist on the cab roof three times to signal: look left. Having seen the white-ripple-marked flank of a kudu, and its fine horns raking through disguising bush, Van der Vyver drove rather fast over a pot-hole. The jolt fired the rifle. Upright, it was pointing straight through the cab roof at the head of Lucas. The bullet pierced the roof and entered Lucas's brain by way of his throat.

That is the statement of what happened. Although a man of such standing in the district, Van der Vyver had to go through the ritual of swearing that it was the truth. It has gone on record, and will be there in the archive of the local police station as long as Van der Vyver lives, and beyond that, through the lives of his children, Magnus, Helena and Karel—unless things in the country get worse, the example of black mobs in the towns spreads to the rural areas and the place is burned down as many urban police stations have been. Because nothing the government can do will appease the agitators and the whites who encourage them. Nothing satisfies them, in the cities: blacks can sit and drink in white hotels, now, the Immorality Act[4] has gone, blacks can sleep with whites . . . It's not even a crime any more.

Van der Vyver has a high barbed security fence round his farmhouse and garden which his wife, Alida, thinks spoils completely the effect of her artificial stream with its tree-ferns beneath the jacarandas. There is an aerial soaring like a flag-pole in the back yard. All his vehicles, including the truck in which the black man died, have aerials that

---

[2] bakkie: jeep.
[3] kudu: large African antelope with a brown coat and vertical white stripes.
[4] Immorality Act: South African law under apartheid stating that it was illegal for whites to marry non-whites.

swing their whips when the driver hits a pot-hole: they are part of the security system the farmers in the district maintain, each farm in touch with every other by radio, twenty-four hours out of twenty-four. It has already happened that infiltrators from over the border have mined remote farm roads, killing white farmers and their families out on their own property for a Sunday picnic. The pot-hole could have set off a land-mine, and Van der Vyver might have died with his farm boy. When neighbours use the communications system to call up and say they are sorry about 'that business' with one of Van der Vyver's boys, there goes unsaid: it could have been worse.

It is obvious from the quality and fittings of the coffin that the farmer has provided money for the funeral. And an elaborate funeral means a great deal to blacks; look how they will deprive themselves of the little they have, in their lifetime, keeping up payments to a burial society so they won't go in boxwood to an unmarked grave. The young wife is pregnant (of course) and another little one, wearing red shoes several sizes too large, leans under her jutting belly. He is too young to understand what has happened, what he is witnessing that day, but neither whines nor plays about; he is solemn without knowing why. Blacks expose small children to everything, they don't protect them from the sight of fear and pain the way whites do theirs. It is the young wife who rolls her head and cries like a child, sobbing on the breast of this relative and that.

All present work for Van der Vyver or are the families of those who work; and in the weeding and harvest seasons, the women and children work for him, too, carried—wrapped in their blankets, on a truck, singing—at sunrise to the fields. The dead man's mother is a woman who can't be more than in her late thirties (they start bearing children at puberty) but she is heavily mature in a black dress between her own parents, who were already working for old Van der Vyver when Marais, like their daughter, was a child. The parents hold her as if she were a prisoner or a crazy woman to be restrained. But she says nothing, does nothing. She does not look up; she does not look at Van der Vyver, whose gun went off in the truck, she stares at the grave. Nothing will make her look up; there need be no fear that she will look up; at him. His wife, Alida, is beside him. To show the proper respect, as for any white funeral, she is wearing the navy-blue-and-cream hat she wears to church this summer. She is always supportive, although he doesn't seem to notice it; this coldness and reserve—his mother says he didn't mix well as a child—she accepts for herself but regrets that it has prevented him from being nominated, as he should be, to stand as the Party's parliamentary candidate for the district. He does not let her clothing, or that of anyone else gathered closely, make contact with him. He, too, stares at the grave. The dead man's mother and he stare at the grave in communication like that between the black man outside and the white man inside the cab the moment before the gun went off.

The moment before the gun went off was a moment of high excitement shared through the roof of the cab, as the bullet was to pass, between the young black man outside and the white farmer inside the vehicle. There were such moments, without explanation, between them, although often around the farm the farmer would pass the young man without returning a greeting, as if he did not recognize him. When the bullet went off what Van der Vyver saw was the kudu stumble in fright at the report and gallop away. Then he heard the thud behind him, and past the window saw the young man fall out of the vehicle. He was sure he had leapt up and toppled—in fright, like the buck. The farmer was almost laughing with relief, ready to tease, as he opened his door, it did not seem possible that a bullet passing through the roof could have done harm.

The young man did not laugh with him at his own fright. The farmer carried him in his arms, to the truck. He was sure, sure he could not be dead. But the young black man's blood was all over the farmer's clothes, soaking against his flesh as he drove.

How will they ever know, when they file newspaper clippings, evidence, proof, when they look at the photographs and see his face—guilty! guilty! they are right!—how will they know, when the police stations burn with all the evidence of what has happened now, and what the law made a crime in the past. How could they know that *they do not know.* Anything. The young black callously shot through the negligence of the white man was not the farmer's boy; he was his son.

(1991)

QUESTIONS

1. What are the significant character traits of Marais Van der Vyver? How does Van der Vyver usually hide himself from directly dealing with another person?

2. Can you find examples of foreshadowing of Lucas's death in this story?

3. The official version of the shooting is that it is an accident, but given the relationships between blacks and whites in South Africa during apartheid, explain how appearances can be misleading.

4. Did you find the surprise ending of the story effective and consistent with the rest of the story?

Writing Topics for Short Stories

1. Working with the idea of the device of using mothers as narrators, compare the point of view of the mothers in Olsen's "I Stand Here Ironing" and Walker's "Everyday Use." Why do you think Walker and Olsen, both feminists, have chosen the iron and the quilt as symbols for the role of the mother?

2. The roles of the mothers in Olsen's "I Stand Here Ironing," Lessing's "Through the Tunnel," and Walker's "Everyday Use" are central to each one. What does each story suggest about a mother's moral and maternal obligations?

3. Lessing's "Through the Tunnel" and Achebe's "Marriage Is a Private Affair" depict sons making decisions for themselves that separate them from a parent. Explain how each of these stories demonstrates that the successful completion of a major step in developing autonomy requires the acquiescence or approbation of a parent.

4. Compare the problems caused by an "arranged marriage" in Achebe's "Marriage Is a Private Affair" and Yamamoto's "Seventeen Syllables." What role does love play in each story? (See the Chinese folktale "Faithful Even in Death," p. 354, and Pound's poem "The River-Merchant's Wife: A Letter," p. 590, for further consideration of arranged marriages.)

5. Analyze the literal and figurative function of the setting in Gordimer's "The Moment Before the Gun Went Off," Lessing's "Through the Tunnel," Joyce's "Counterparts," or Yamamoto's "Seventeen Syllables." Explain how setting adds depth of meaning to the central conflict of each story.

6. Discuss the function and outcome of "lies of omission" as depicted in Gordimer's "The Moment Before the Gun Went Off," Lessing's "Through the Tunnel," or Yamamoto's "Seventeen Syllables."

7. A parent's unhappiness can generate the suffering of his or her child. Compare how and why this occurs in Joyce's "Counterparts" and Yamamoto's "Seventeen Syllables."

Poems

SYLVIA PLATH (1932–1963)

Metaphors

I'm a riddle in nine syllables,
An elephant, a ponderous house,
A melon strolling on two tendrils.
O red fruit, ivory, fine timbers!
This loaf's big with its yeasty rising.
Money's new-minted in this fat purse.
I'm a means, a stage, a cow in calf.
I've eaten a bag of green apples,
Boarded the train there's no getting off.

(1958)

QUESTIONS

1. What imagery in this poem reveals that the speaker is female?

2. What event is she describing, and how many ways does she create metaphors for describing it?

3. What is the tone of the poem? Explain how the figurative language of the poem determines the tone.

AUDRE LORDE (1934–1992)

Now That I Am Forever with Child

How the days went
while you were blooming within me
I remember   each upon each
the swelling changed planes of my body

how you first fluttered   then jumped
and I thought it was my heart.

How the days wound down
and the turning of winter
I recall   you
10   growing heavy against the wind.
I thought   now her hands
are formed   her hair
has started to curl
now her teeth are done
now she sneezes.

Then the seed opened.
I bore you one morning
just before spring
my head rang like a fiery piston
20   my legs were towers between which
a new world was passing.
Since then
I can only distinguish
one thread within running hours
you   flowing through selves
toward You.

(1963)

QUESTIONS

1. As the speaker looks back, to whom is she speaking? What similes and metaphors are used to convey the experience of pregnancy and childbirth?

2. What is the general mood of the poem? How does the mood shift in the final stanza affect your reading of the poem?

LANGSTON HUGHES (1902–1967)

Mother to Son

Well, son, I'll tell you:
Life for me ain't been no crystal stair.
It's had tacks in it,
And splinters,
And boards torn up,
And places with no carpet on the floor—
Bare.
But all the time
I'se been a-climbin' on,
10   And reachin' landin's,
And turnin' corners,
And sometimes goin' in the dark
Where there ain't been no light.
So boy, don't you turn back.
Don't you set down on the steps
'Cause you finds it's kinder hard.
Don't you fall now—
For I'se still goin', honey,
I'se still climbin',
20   And life for me ain't been no crystal stair.

(1926)

QUESTIONS

1. What is the mother's metaphor for life?

2. What does the mother mean when she says that "life for me ain't been no crystal stair"? Why hasn't it been?

ROBERT HAYDEN (1913–1980)

Those Winter Sundays

Sundays too my father got up early
and put his clothes on in the blueblack cold,
then with cracked hands that ached
from labor in the weekday weather made
banked fires blaze. No one ever thanked him.

I'd wake and hear the cold splintering, breaking.
When the rooms were warm, he'd call,
and slowly I would rise and dress,
fearing the chronic angers of that house,

10   Speaking indifferently to him,
who had driven out the cold
and polished my good shoes as well.
What did I know, what did I know
of love's austere and lonely offices?

(1962)

QUESTIONS

1. What need on the speaker's part is the driving force behind the poem?

2. What do you think is meant by the phrase "love's austere and lonely offices" in the last line?

LOUISE GLÜCK (B. 1943)

Pomegranate[1]

First he gave me
his heart. It was
red fruit containing
many seeds, the skin

---

[1] Pomegranate: a red, thick-skinned fruit the size of an apple. The pulp is filled with seeds and has an acid flavor.

leathery, unlikely.
I preferred
to starve, bearing
out my training.
Then he said Behold
10   how the world looks, minding
your mother. I
peered under his arm:
What had she done
with color & odor?
Whereupon he said Now *there*
is a woman who loves
with a vengeance, adding
Consider she is in her element:
the trees turning to her, whole
20   villages going under
although in hell
the bushes are still
burning with pomegranates.
At which
he cut one open & began
to suck. When he looked up at last
it was to say My dear
you are your own
woman, finally, but examine
30   this grief your mother
parades over our heads
remembering
that she is one to whom
these depths were not offered.

(1975)

Questions

1. What images does the man in the poem use to characterize the woman's mother?

2. How does his depiction of Demeter compare with the way Demeter is portrayed in the Ancient Greek "Myth of Demeter and Persephone"? (See p. 3.) How does Glück's poem also focus on a certain stage of growing-up? What images support this?

3. Why do you think that Glück never actually names Demeter, Persephone, or Hades? How does the title of the poem make the allusion to the myth understandable?

EAVAN BOLAND (B. 1944)

The Pomegranate[1]

The only legend I have ever loved is
The story of a daughter lost in Hell.
And found and rescued there.
Love and blackmail are the gist of it.
Ceres[2] and Persephone[3] the names.
And the best thing about the legend is
I can enter it anywhere. And have.
As a child in exile in
A city of fogs and strange consonants,
10   I read it first and at first I was
An exiled child in the crackling dusk of
The underworld, the stars blighted. Later
I walked out in a summer twilight
Searching for my daughter at bedtime.
When she came running I was ready
To make any bargain to keep her.
I carried her back past whitebeams.
And wasps and honey-scented buddleias.
But I was Ceres then and I knew
20   Winter was in store for every leaf
On every tree on that road.
Was inescapable for each one we passed.
And for me.
          It is winter
And the stars are hidden.
I climb the stairs and stand where I can see
My child asleep beside her teen magazines,
Her can of Coke, her plate of uncut fruit.
The pomegranate! How did I forget it?
30   She could have come home and been safe
And ended the story and all
Our heartbroken searching, but she reached
Out a hand and plucked a pomegranate.
She put out her hand and pulled down

---

[1] Pomegranate: a red, thick-skinned fruit the size of an apple. The pulp is filled with seeds and has an acid flavor.
[2] Ceres: the Roman name for Demeter.
[3] Persephone: the daughter of Demeter and Zeus, who was abducted by Hades. (See "The Myth of Demeter and Persephone," p. 3.)

The French sound for apple[4] and
The noise of stone and the proof
That even in the place of death,
At the heart of legend, in the midst
Of rocks full of unshed tears
40   Ready to be diamonds by the time
The story was told, a child can be
Hungry. I could warn her. There is still a chance.
The rain is cold. The road is flint-colored.
The suburb has cars and cable television.
The veiled stars are aboveground.
It is another world. But what else
Can a mother give her daughter but such
Beautiful rifts in time?
If I defer the grief I will diminish the gift.
50   The legend will be hers as well as mine.
She will enter it. As I have.
She will wake up. She will hold
The papery, flushed skin in her hand.
And to her lips. I will say nothing.

(1993)

QUESTIONS

1. What is the time frame of each stanza? What is still possible for the speaker in the first stanza that is no longer possible in the second?

2. What does the pomegranate represent?

ALASTAIR REID (B. 1926)

Daedalus[1]

My son has birds in his head.

I know them now. I catch
the pitch of their calls, their shrill
cacophonies, their chitterings, their coos.
They hover behind his eyes, and come to rest

---

[4] *Pomme:* French word for "apple."
[1] Daedalus: an allusion to the father of Icarus. (See "The Myth of Dædalus and Icarus," p. 12.)

on a branch, on a book, grow still,
claws curled, wings furled.
His is a bird world.

I learn the flutter of his moods,
10   his moments of swoop and soar.
From the ground I feel him try
the limits of the air—
sudden lift, sudden terror—
and move in time to cradle
his quivering, feathered fear.

At evening, in the tower,
I see him to sleep, and see
the hooding over of eyes,
the slow folding of wings.
20   I wake to his morning twitterings,
to the *croomb* of his becoming.

He chooses his selves—wren, hawk,
swallow, or owl—to explore
the trees and rooftops of his heady wishing.
Tomtit, birdwit.
Am I to call him down, to give him
a grounding, teach him gravity?
Gently, gently.
Time tells us what we weigh, and soon enough
30   his feet will reach the ground.
Age, like a cage, will enclose him.
So the wise men said.

My son has birds in his head.

(1967)

QUESTIONS

1. What makes this a "persona" poem? Compare the tone of voice of this Daedalus with the image you have of Daedalus in the Ancient Greek myth. (See p. 12).

2. Discuss the theme of mortality as it runs through the poem. How and for what purpose does Reid change the Greek myth in Daedalus's portrait of Icarus?

3. How do visual imagery and bird metaphors reinforce meaning in the poem?

ROBERT HAYDEN (1913–1980)

O Daedalus, Fly Away Home[1]

(For Maia and Julie)

Drifting night in the Georgia pines,
coonskin drum and jubilee banjo.[2]
     Pretty Malinda, dance with me.

Night is juba,[3] night is conjo.[4]
     Pretty Malinda, dance with me.

Night is an African juju man[5]
weaving a wish and a weariness together
     to make two wings.

    O fly away home fly away

10   Do you remember Africa?

     O cleave the air fly away home

My gran,[6] he flew back to Africa,
just spread his arms and
     flew away home.

Drifting night in the windy pines;
night is a laughing, night is a longing.
     Pretty Malinda, come to me.

Night is a mourning juju man
weaving a wish and a weariness together
20   to make two wings.

    O fly away home fly away

               (1966)

---

[1] An allusion to "The Myth of Dædelus and Icarus." (See p. 12.)
[2] jubilee banjo: joyous banjo.
[3] juba: a dance accompanied by hand-clapping.
[4] conjo: ritual objects used in shamanistic or magic ceremonies. Shamanism is the conjuring of gods, demons, or ancestral spirits.
[5] jujuman: a shaman, a medicine man or woman, or a magician.
[6] gran: grandparent or ancestor.

QUESTIONS

1. Why does Hayden relate "The Myth of Daedelus and Icarus" to African-American suffering under slavery?

2. What is the function of the refrain, "O fly away home"?

3. How is this poem simultaneously light-hearted and heavy-hearted, full of love and full of sadness?

ELIZABETH BISHOP (1911–1979)

The Prodigal[1]

The brown enormous odor he lived by
was too close, with its breathing and thick hair,
for him to judge. The floor was rotten; the sty
was plastered halfway up with glass-smooth dung.
Light-lashed, self-righteous, above moving snouts,
the pigs' eyes followed him, a cheerful stare—
even to the sow that always ate her young—
till, sickening, he leaned to scratch her head.
But sometimes mornings after drinking bouts
10 (he hid the pints behind a two-by-four),
the sunrise glazed the barnyard mud with red;
the burning puddles seemed to reassure.
And then he thought he almost might endure
his exile yet another year or more.

But evenings the first star came to warn.
The farmer whom he worked for came at dark
to shut the cows and horses in the barn
beneath their overhanging clouds of hay,
with pitchforks, faint forked lightnings, catching light,
20 safe and companionable as in the Ark.
The pigs stuck out their little feet and snored.
The lantern—like the sun, going away—
laid on the mud a pacing aureole.[2]
Carrying a bucket along a slimy board,
he felt the bats' uncertain staggering flight,

---

[1] The Prodigal: an allusion to "The Parable of the Prodigal Son." (See p. 14.)
[2] aureole: a halo or crown.

his shuddering insights, beyond his control,
touching him. But it took him a long time
finally to make his mind up to go home.

(1976)

QUESTIONS

1. How does the speaker's characterization of the Prodigal Son compare with the son's portrayal in the parable from the Bible? (See p. 14 for "The Parable of the Prodigal Son," Luke, 15:11–32.)

2. How does the poem's imagery suggest the kind of life the Prodigal Son leads?

ROBERT BLY (B. 1926)

The Prodigal Son[1]

The Prodigal Son is kneeling in the husks.
He remembers the man about to die
who cried, "Don't let me die, Doctor!"
The swine go on feeding in the sunlight.

When he folds his hands, his knees on corncobs,
he sees the smoke of ships
floating off the isles of Tyre and Sidon,[2]
and father beyond father beyond father.

An old man once, being dragged across the floor
10   by his shouting son, cried:
"Don't drag me any farther than that crack on the floor—
I only dragged my father that far!"

My father is seventy-five years old.
How difficult it is,
bending the head, looking into the water.
Under the water there's a door the pigs have gone through.

(1987)

---

[1] The Prodigal Son: an allusion to "The Parable of the Prodigal Son." (See p. 14.)
[2] Tyre and Sidon: port cities in ancient Phoenicia, now Lebanon.

QUESTIONS

1. How does Bly use "The Parable of the Prodigal Son" as a way of commenting more generally about the relationships between fathers and sons?

2. What does the speaker reveal about his own relationship with his father?

THEODORE ROETHKE (1908–1963)

My Papa's Waltz

The whiskey on your breath
Could make a small boy dizzy;
But I hung on like death:
Such waltzing was not easy.

We romped until the pans
Slid from the kitchen shelf;
My mother's countenance
Could not unfrown itself.

The hand that held my wrist
10   Was battered on one knuckle;
At every step you missed
My right ear scraped a buckle.

You beat time on my head
With a palm caked hard by dirt,
Then waltzed me off to bed
Still clinging to your shirt.

(1942)

QUESTIONS

1. How do rhyme and meter contribute to the poem's meaning and vitality?

2. What does the speaker reveal about his childhood and his feelings for his father? Which images best depict the boy's feelings?

3. How is the waltz used ironically here? Is this a portrait of a happy family?

SYLVIA PLATH (1932–1963)

Daddy

The poem is spoken by a girl with an Electra complex.[1] Her father died while she thought he was God. Her case is complicated by the fact that her father was also a Nazi and her mother very possibly part Jewish. In the daughter the two strains marry and paralyze each other—she has to act out the awful little allegory before she is free of it.

—Sylvia Plath

You do not do, you do not do
Any more, black shoe
In which I have lived like a foot
For thirty years, poor and white
Barely daring to breathe or Achoo.

Daddy, I have had to kill you.
You died before I had time——
Marble-heavy, a bag full of God,
Ghastly statue with one gray toe[2]
10   Big as a Frisco seal

And a head in the freakish Atlantic
Where it pours bean green over blue
In the waters off beautiful Nauset.[3]
I used to pray to recover you.
Ach, du.

In the German tongue, in the Polish town[4]
Scraped flat by the roller
Of wars, wars, wars.
But the name of the town is common.
20   My Polack friend

Says there are a dozen or two.
So I never could tell where you
Put your foot, your root,
I never could talk to you.
The tongue stuck in my jaw.

---

[1] Electra complex: a psychological term, refers to a girl's tendency to be attracted to her father and hostile to her mother, the equivalent of the Oedipus complex, a psychological term referring to a boy's love for his mother and hostility toward his father.
[2] Refers to the ravages of diabetes, which eventually caused Plath's father's death.
[3] Nauset: a beach on the eastern coast of Cape Cod.
[4] Polish town: Plath's father, Otto Plath, was born in Grasbow, Poland.

It stuck in a barb wire snare.
Ich, ich, ich, ich,[5]
I could hardly speak.
I thought every German was you.
30   And the language obscene

An engine, an engine
Chuffing[6] me off like a Jew.
A Jew to Dachau, Auschwitz, Belsen.[7]
I began to talk like a Jew.
I think I may well be a Jew.

The snows of the Tyrol,[8] the clear beer of Vienna[9]
Are not very pure or true.
With my gipsy ancestress and my weird luck
And my Taroc pack and my Taroc[10] pack
40   I may be a bit of a Jew.

I have always been scared of *you,*
With your Luftwaffe,[11] your gobbledygoo.
And your neat mustache
And your Aryan eye, bright blue.
Panzer-man,[12] panzer-man, O You—

Not God but a swastika[13]
So black no sky could squeak through.
Every woman adores a Fascist,
The boot in the face, the brute
50   Brute heart of a brute like you.

You stand at the blackboard,[14] daddy,
In the picture I have of you,
A cleft in your chin instead of your foot
But no less a devil for that, no not
Any less the black man who

---

[5] *Ich:* means "I" in German.
[6] *Chuffing:* onomatopoetic word, used to indicate the sound of a locomotive pulling the boxcars of Jews to the concentration camps.
[7] Dachau, Auschwitz, Belsen: extermination camps in Poland and Germany.
[8] Tyrol: an Alpine region along the border of Austria and Italy.
[9] Vienna: the capital and largest city in Austria situated on the Danube River.
[10] Taroc: tarot cards used to tell fortunes.
[11] *Luftwaffe:* the German Air Force.
[12] *Panzer:* elite German tank divisions.
[13] swastika: The original swastika cross is found in Eurasian and Native American cultures. A backwards version was used by Adolf Hitler (1889–1945) as a symbol of the Nazi party.
[14] Otto Plath was a professor of biology.

Bit my pretty red heart in two.
I was ten when they buried you.
At twenty I tried to die
And get back, back, back to you.[15]
60 I thought even the bones would do.

But they pulled me out of the sack,
And they stuck me together with glue.
And then I knew what to do.
I made a model of you,
A man in black with a Meinkampf[16] look

And a love of the rack and the screw.
And I said I do, I do.
So daddy, I'm finally through.
The black telephone's off at the root,
70 The voices just can't worm through.

If I've killed one man, I've killed two——
The vampire who said he was you
And drank my blood for a year,
Seven years, if you want to know.
Daddy, you can lie back now.

There's a stake in your fat black heart
And the villagers never liked you.
They are dancing and stamping on you.
They always *knew* it was you.
80 Daddy, daddy, you bastard, I'm through.

(1963)

QUESTIONS

1. What metaphors does the speaker use to convey her feelings about her father? How do these metaphors intensify the poem's impact?

2. Why do you think the speaker is so negative about her father and her husband?

3. From what is the speaker really trying to free herself?

4. How do rhyme and rhythm contribute to the overall effect of this poem?

---

[15] Plath attempted suicide.
[16] Meinkampf: an allusion to Adolf Hitler's autobiography *Mein Kampf* (*My Struggle*), published in 1925, which outlined his political ideology.

SANDRA CISNEROS (B. 1954)

His Story

I was born under a crooked star.
So says my father.
And this perhaps explains his sorrow.

An only daughter
whom no one came for
and no one chased away.

It is an ancient fate.
A family trait we trace back
to a great aunt no one mentions.

10   Her sin was beauty.
She lived mistress.
Died solitary.

There is as well
the cousin with the famous
how shall I put it?
profession.

She ran off with the colonel.
And soon after,
the army payroll.

20   And, of course,
grandmother's mother
who died a death of voodoo.
There are others.

For instance,
my father explains,
in the Mexican papers

a girl with both my names
was arrested for audacious crimes
that began by disobeying fathers.

30   Also, and here he pauses,
the Cubano who sells him shoes
says he too knew a Sandra Cisneros
who was three times cursed a widow.

You see.
An unlucky fate is mine
to be born woman in a family of men.

Six sons, my father groans,
all home.
And one female,
40   gone.

(1987)

QUESTIONS

1. Explain the irony of the poem's title. What is the play on words?

2. Why does the speaker's father disapprove of her? What are his expectations and how are they linked to her gender?

3. Discuss the ways in which the speaker's culture is embedded in the language, cadence, and imagery of the poem. What does she mean by "crooked star"?

MURIEL RUKEYSER (1913–1980)

Ms. Lot[1]

Well, if he treats me like a young girl still,
That father of mine, and here's my sister
And we're still traveling into the hills—
But everyone on the road knows he offered us
To the Strangers when all they wanted was men,
And the cloud of smoke still over the twin cities
And mother a salt lick the animals come to—
Who's going to want me now?
Mother did not even know
10   She was not to turn around and look.
God spoke to Lot, my father.
She was hard of hearing. He knew that.
I don't believe he told her, anyway.
What kind of father is that, or husband?
He offered us to those men. They didn't want women.
Mother always used to say:
Some normal man will come along and need you.

(1976)

---

[1] Ms. Lot: an allusion to "The Story of Lot." (See p. 517.)

QUESTIONS

1. How is Lot himself portrayed in the poem? In the Bible? Why are Lot's daughters and his wife unnamed in both the Bible and the poem?

2. In what ways does the story of Lot and his family reveal the position of women in the family and in the society of their day? (See p. 517.)

3. How has Rukeyser changed the biblical version? How does Rukeyser's retelling of the story make a political statement about the position of women in society both then and now?

4. What is the effect of the anachronistic use of the term *Ms.*?

SHARON OLDS (B. 1942)

I Go Back to May 1937

I see them standing at the formal gates of their colleges,
I see my father strolling out
under the ochre sandstone arch, the
red tiles glinting like bent
plates of blood behind his head, I
see my mother with a few light books at her hip
standing at the pillar made of tiny bricks with the
wrought-iron gate still open behind her, its
sword-tips black in the May air,
10 they are about to graduate, they are about to get married,
they are kids, they are dumb, all they know is they are
innocent, they would never hurt anybody.
I want to go up to them and say Stop,
don't do it—she's the wrong woman,
he's the wrong man, you are going to do things
you cannot imagine you would ever do,
you are going to do bad things to children,
you are going to suffer in ways you never heard of,
you are going to want to die. I want to go
20 up to them there in the late May sunlight and say it,
her hungry pretty blank face turning to me,
her pitiful beautiful untouched body,
his arrogant handsome blind face turning to me,
his pitiful beautiful untouched body,
but I don't do it. I want to live. I
take them up like the male and female

paper dolls and bang them together
at the hips like chips of flint as if to
strike sparks from them, I say
30 Do what you are going to do, and I will tell about it.

(1987)

QUESTIONS

1. What emotions do the photographs evoke for the speaker?

2. How does point of view influence the way the speaker views these photographs?

3. What is the speaker's dilemma at the end of the poem? How does the fact that she is a writer play into this dilemma? Discuss the role of hindsight in this poem.

RAINER MARIA RILKE (1875–1926)

Portrait of My Father as a Young Man

Translated by Stephen Mitchell

In the eyes: dream. The brow as if it could feel
something far off. Around the lips, a great
freshness—seductive, though there is no smile.
Under the rows of ornamental braid
on the slim Imperial officer's uniform:
the saber's basket-hilt. Both hands stay
folded upon it, going nowhere, calm
and now almost invisible, as if they
were the first to grasp the distance and dissolve.
10 And all the rest so curtained with itself,
so cloudy, that I cannot understand
this figure as it fades into the background—

Oh quickly disappearing photograph
in my more slowly disappearing hand.

(1907)

QUESTIONS

1. Explain why the poem's title is crucial to understanding the poem.

2. What does the speaker withhold until the final stanza?

3. Discuss the way that the photograph serves as a metaphor.

W. S. MERWIN (B. 1927)

Yesterday

My friend says I was not a good son
you understand
I say yes I understand

he says I did not go
to see my parents very often you know
and I say yes I know

even when I was living in the same city he says
maybe I would go there once
a month or maybe even less
10   I say oh yes

he says the last time I went to see my father
I say the last time I saw my father

he says the last time I saw my father
he was asking me about my life
how I was making out and he
went into the next room
to get something to give me

oh I say
feeling again the cold
20   of my father's hand the last time

he says and my father turned
in the doorway and saw me
look at my wristwatch and he
said you know I would like you to stay
and talk with me

oh yes I say

but if you are busy he said
I don't want you to feel that you

have to
30   just because I'm here

I say nothing

he says my father
said maybe

you have important work you are doing
or maybe you should be seeing
somebody I don't want to keep you

I look out the window
my friend is older than I am
he says and I told my father it was so
40   and I got up and left him then
you know

though there was nowhere I had to go
and nothing I had to do

(1983)

Questions

1. How many speakers are there in the poem? How does Merwin differentiate the voices in the dialogue?

2. Analyze the reason for the "gap" between father and son. How old do you imagine the father and son are when their dialogue takes place? Why does age add significance to the poem's meaning?

3. Does the son agree with his friend's opinion that he "was not a good son"? Is there really a friend, or is "the friend" a manifestation of the speaker's conscience?

Stanley Kunitz (b. 1905)

The Portrait

My mother never forgave my father
for killing himself,
especially at such an awkward time
and in a public park,
that spring
when I was waiting to be born.
She locked his name
in her deepest cabinet

and would not let him out,
10   though I could hear him thumping.
When I came down from the attic
with the pastel portrait in my hand
of a long-lipped stranger
with a brave moustache
and deep brown level eyes,
she ripped it into shreds
without a single word
and slapped me hard.
In my sixty-fourth year
20   I can feel my cheek
still burning.

(1971)

QUESTIONS

1. Whose image is in the "portrait" of the poem and of whom is the poem a portrait?

2. What emotion is expressed in the last three lines?

3. What does the mother's "deepest cabinet" stand for? Explain why you empathize with her behavior and secret reason for keeping the portrait all these years, her son's behavior, both, or neither.

HELANE LEVINE KEATING (B. 1948)

The Envious Heart

*Then her envious heart had rest
so far as an envious heart can have rest.*

—The Brothers Grimm,
"Snow White"

Apples are the fruit of autumn
the season I detest. That was when
he married me, never letting on.
He said she was simply a girl,
a thin thing with straight hair.
He said he rarely saw her
although she was his daughter.

You are my only queen, he said.
Look in this mirror—
10   *it is yours.*

I look, but all I see is
her sneering face, her wide lips
mimicking mine. Instead of a little girl
there's a woman not much younger than myself.
When they're together she's his queen,
that black-eyed slut, calling him Daddy
with her bone-dry lust, looking
over her shoulder at him
till he turns from me, transfixed.

20   She'll stop at nothing,
making him tell her stories
about her mother, the same ones
over and over. How can I
cover my ears?

Now everywhere I go
voices whisper
proclaiming her loveliest.
Who remembers my beauty?
Each night beneath his body
30   her shadow erases me.
In my mirror I am invisible.

(1983)

QUESTIONS

1. What does the stepmother say and do to suggest that she feels betrayed? Do you think that her feelings are based on vanity?

2. By analyzing the images used to depict the stepdaughter, is it possible that stepdaughters are "wicked" and stepmothers are not, despite what folktales tell us? How might the father be responsible for the conflict?

3. How has the poet transformed the persona of the poem from the expected to the unexpected? What is the shift in symbolism of the stepmother as a result?

Dylan Thomas (1914–1953)

Do Not Go Gentle into That Good Night

Do not go gentle into that good night,
Old age should burn and rave at close of day;
Rage, rage against the dying of the light.

Though wise men at their end know dark is right,
Because their words had forked no lightning they
Do not go gentle into that good night.

Good men, the last wave by, crying how bright
Their frail deeds might have danced in a green bay,
Rage, rage against the dying of the light.

10　Wild men who caught and sang the sun in flight,
And learn, too late, they grieved it on its way,
Do not go gentle into that good night.

Grave men, near death, who see with blinding sight
Blind eyes could blaze like meteors and be gay,
Rage, rage against the dying of the light.

And you, my father, there on the sad height,
Curse, bless, me now with your fierce tears, I pray.
Do not go gentle into that good night.
Rage, rage against the dying of the light.

(1951)

Questions

1. What is the speaker urging his ailing father to do? Why does the behavior of "wise men," "good men," "wild men," and "grave men" help further the poem's argument?

2. How does the use of repetition, alliteration, assonance, end rhyme, and internal rhyme link related words in the poem, reinforce meaning, and add music and intensity to the poem?

MURIEL RUKEYSER (1913–1980)

Myth

Long afterward, Oedipus,[1] old and blinded, walked the
roads.   He smelled a familiar smell.   It was
the Sphinx.[2]   Oedipus said, "I want to ask one question.
Why didn't I recognize my mother?"   "You gave the
wrong answer," said the Sphinx.   "But that was what
made everything possible," said Oedipus.   "No," she said.
"When I asked, What walks on four legs in the morning,
two at noon, and three in the evening, you answered,
Man.   You didn't say anything about woman."
10   "When you say Man," said Oedipus, "you include women
too. Everyone knows that."   She said, "That's what
you think."

(1973)

QUESTIONS

1. What is the point of Rukeyser's adaptation of the myth of Oedipus?

2. Why does the Sphinx have the last word here?

3. How can the poem's title be seen as a pun?

Writing Topics for Poems

1. How do Lorde's "Now That I Am Forever with Child" and Plath's "Metaphors" challenge conventional attitudes toward motherhood? Discuss how you feel about motherhood.

2. Compare the point of view of the speakers of Glück's "Pomegranate" and Boland's "The Pomegranate." How and for what purpose does each poet transform "The Myth of Demeter and Persephone" (p. 3)?

3. Discuss the ambivalence or anger toward a parent or parents experienced by adult children as depicted in Plath's "Daddy," Cisneros's "His Story," Rukeyser's "Ms. Lot," Olds's "I Go Back to May 1937," and Kunitz's "The Portrait."

---

[1] Oedipus: an allusion to King Oedipus of Thebes. (See Sophocles' play *Oedipus the King*, p. 1153.)

[2] Sphinx: a monster with the face of a woman, the chest and legs of a lion, and the wings of a bird of prey. The Sphinx killed travelers to Thebes who could not answer her riddle: "What walks on four legs in the morning, two legs at noon, and three legs in the evening?" When Oedipus solved this riddle, the Sphinx killed herself by jumping from a cliff.

4. "The Myth of Dædalus and Icarus" is central to Reid's "Daedalus," Hayden's "O Daedalus, Fly Away Home," Rukeyser's "Waiting for Icarus" (Part 3, "People in Love" (p. 448), and Auden's "Musée de Beaux Arts" (Part 6, "Students and Teachers," p. 939). Analyze how each poet derives new meanings from the original myth by retelling it for a contemporary audience.

5. Explain how the theme of guilt infused in Kunitz's "The Portrait," Merwin's "Yesterday," and Rilke's "Portrait of My Father as a Young Man" relates to each speaker's relationship with his father.

6. "The Parable of the Prodigal Son" (Luke 15:11-32, p. 14) is appealing because it illustrates spiritual awareness and forgiveness. What changes do Bly ("The Prodigal Son") and Bishop ("The Prodigal") make in their poetic revisions of the parable? Is it significant that Bly is male and Bishop female in their ways of retelling of this story?

7. Compare Hughes's "Mother to Son" with Hayden's "Those Winter Sundays." How does each speaker reveal his parent's value system? What emotions do you think each speaker reveals?

Drama

WILLIAM SHAKESPEARE (1564–1616)

The Tempest

THE PERSONS OF THE PLAY

ALONSO, *King of Naples*
SEBASTIAN, *his brother*
PROSPERO, *the right Duke of Milan*
ANTONIO, *his brother, the usurping Duke of Milan*
FERDINAND, *son to the King of Naples*
GONZALO, *an honest old councillor*
ADRIAN *and* FRANCISCO, *lords*
CALIBAN, *a savage and deformed slave*
TRINCULO, *a jester*
STEPHANO, *a drunken butler*

MASTER OF A SHIP
BOATSWAIN
MARINERS
MIRANDA, *daughter to Prospero*
ARIEL, *an airy spirit*
IRIS
CERES
JUNO } *personated by spirits*
NYMPHS
REAPERS

The scene: an uninhabited island

1.1 *A tempestuous noise of thunder and lightning heard.*
Enter a Ship-master and a Boatswain.

MASTER. Boatswain!
BOATSWAIN. Here, master. What cheer?

1.1 The scene takes place on a ship at sea.   **0.1** *noise . . . lightning* Here as throughout the text, the stage directions tend to be descriptive, and seem designed for a reader rather than for an acting company preparing a production. It has been suggested that they were revised and amplified by Ralph Crane when he copied the text for publication. The usage is characteristically loose: Jacobean theatres had lightning machines, and a *noise of thunder and lightning heard* need not imply that no visual effects accompanied the sound of thunder.

MASTER. Good—speak to th' mariners. Fall to't yarely, or we run ourselves aground. Bestir, bestir!   *Exit*

    Enter MARINERS

BOATSWAIN. Hey, my hearts! Cheerly, cheerly, my hearts! Yare, yare! Take in the topsail. Tend to th' master's whistle. (*To the storm*)—Blow till thou burst thy wind, if room enough.

    Enter ALONSO, SEBASTIAN, ANTONIO, FERDINAND, GONZALO, *and others*

ALONSO. Good boatswain, have care. Where's the master?
    (*To the* MARINERS) Play the men.
10   BOATSWAIN. I pray now, keep below.
ANTONIO. Where is the master, bos'n?
BOATSWAIN. Do you not hear him? You mar our labour. Keep your cabins—you do assist the storm.
GONZALO. Nay, good, be patient.
BOATSWAIN. When the sea is. Hence! What cares these roarers for the name of king? To cabin; silence! Trouble us not.
GONZALO. Good, yet remember whom thou hast aboard.
BOATSWAIN. None that I love more than myself. You are a councillor; if you can command these elements to silence, and work the peace of the present, we will not
20   hand a rope more—use your authority. If you cannot, give thanks you have lived so long, and make yourself ready in your cabin for the mischance of the hour, if it so hap. (*To the* MARINERS)—Cheerly, good hearts! (*To the courtiers*)—Out of our way, I say!   *Exit*
GONZALO. I have great comfort from this fellow. Methinks he hath no drowning mark upon him—his complexion is perfect gallows. Stand fast, good Fate, to his hanging, make the rope of his destiny our cable, for our own doth little advantage. If he be not born to be hanged, our case is miserable.   *Exeunt*

    Enter BOATSWAIN

---

3 Good Not good cheer, but either an expression of satisfaction at the boatswain's presence ('good, you're here') or a contraction of 'good fellow,' as below, ll. 14 and 17; **yarely** quickly, smartly. **5 Cheerly** F's 'cheerly,' perhaps trisyllabic and equivalent to the modern 'cheerily.' **6 Tend** pay attention. **6 Blow . . . wind** i.e. do your worst. **6–7 if room enough** so long as there is enough open sea, without reefs or rocks, for the ship to ride out the storm. **7.1 *Alonso*** a variant of Alphonso, which is the normal English form. For a discussion of possible historical models for Alonso, Ferdinand and Prospero. ***Sebastian, Antonio*** previously coupled as the names of a shipwreck victim and his adoring benefactor in *Twelfth Night*. **9 Play the men** Act like men: the remark is officious and condescending, but Alonso *is* the king. **15 roarers** roaring winds and waves, with an overtone of rioters. **18 None . . . myself** 'I am nearest to myself' was proverbial. **18 councillor** The Folio spelling, counsellor, implies not only a member of the Privy Council, but an adviser and persuader. **22 Cheerly** See l. 5 and note. **24–5 he . . . gallows** The proverb was 'he that is born to be hanged shall never be drowned.' **25 complexion** character, as indicated by the physiognomy. **26 doth little advantage** is of little use to us.

BOATSWAIN. Down with the topmast! Yare! Lower, lower! Bring her to try with main-course. (*A cry within*) A plague upon this howling! They are louder than the weather
30   or our office.

    Enter SEBASTIAN, ANTONIO, *and* GONZALO

Yet again? What do you here? Shall we give o'er and drown? Have you a mind to sink?
SEBASTIAN. A pox o' your throat, you bawling, blasphemous, incharitable dog!
BOATSWAIN. Work you, then.
ANTONIO. Hang, cur, hang, you whoreson insolent noisemaker! We are less afraid to be drowned than thou art.
GONZALO. I'll warrant him for drowning, though the ship were no stronger than a nut-shell and as leaky as an unstanched wench.
BOATSWAIN. Lay her a-hold, a-hold! Set her two courses off to sea again; lay her off!

    Enter MARINERS *wet*

MARINERS. All lost! To prayers, to prayers! All lost!   *Exeunt*
40   BOATSWAIN. What, must our mouths be cold?
GONZALO.
    The King and Prince at prayers, let's assist them,
    For our case is as theirs.
SEBASTIAN.   I'm out of patience.
ANTONIO.
    We are merely cheated of our lives by drunkards.
    This wide-chopped rascal—would thou mightst lie drowning
    The washing of ten tides!   *Exit* BOATSWAIN
GONZALO.   He'll be hanged yet,
    Though every drop of water swear against it,
    And gape at wid'st to glut him.

    A confused noise within

    'Mercy on us!'—'We split, we split!'—'Farewell,
    my wife and children!'—'Farewell, brother!'
50   —'We split! we split! we split!'
ANTONIO. Let's all sink wi' th' King.
SEBASTIAN. Let's take leave of him.   *Exit with* ANTONIO
GONZALO. Now would I give a thousand furlongs of sea for an acre of barren ground—long heath, brown furze, anything. The wills above be done, but I would fain die a dry death.   *Exit*

---

29 They the passengers.   **30 our office** we at our work.   **31 give o'er** give up.   **36 for against:** Gonzalo re-peats his joke of ll. 24–5.   **38 Lay her a-hold** Bring the ship close to the wind so as to hold it; to do this more sail must be set, hence the order immediately following. (*course* = sail)   **38 lay her off** get her out to sea.
40 must our mouths be cold To be cold in the mouth, i.e. dead, was proverbial.   **43 merely** completely.
44 wide-chopped big-mouthed.   **47 glut** swallow.   **54 long heath, brown furze** heather and gorse; the pas-sage has suffered much interpretation.

1.2   *The island.*
Enter PROSPERO *and* MIRANDA

MIRANDA.

If by your art, my dearest father, you have
Put the wild waters in this roar, allay them.
The sky, it seems, would pour down stinking pitch,
But that the sea, mounting to th' welkin's cheek,
Dashes the fire out. O, I have suffered
With those that I saw suffer: a brave vessel—
Who had, no doubt, some noble creature in her—
Dashed all to pieces! O, the cry did knock
Against my very heart—poor souls, they perished.

10 Had I been any god of power, I would
Have sunk the sea within the earth or ere
It should the good ship so have swallowed, and
The fraughting souls within her.

PROSPERO.   Be collected.
No more amazement. Tell your piteous heart
There's no harm done.

MIRANDA.   O, woe the day!

PROSPERO.   No harm.
I have done nothing but in care of thee,
Of thee, my dear one, thee, my daughter, who
Art ignorant of what thou art; naught knowing
Of whence I am, nor that I am more better

20 Than Prospero, master of a full poor cell,
And thy no greater father.

1.2.0.1 Prospero The name means 'fortunate' or 'prosperous' (literally 'according to one's hopes'). Jonson used it and Stephano in *Every Man in his Humour* (1601), in which, according to the cast list in the Jonson folio, Shakespeare performed.   **Miranda** literally 'wonderful,' 'to be wondered at.'   **1 art** used throughout to refer to Prospero's magic powers, and in the Folio text capitalized throughout.   **3 pitch** implying chiefly its smell and blackness here, but also with moral overtones ('pitch defiles') and possibly an ironic ambiguity as well: its practical use was for caulking ships.   **4 welkin** The word originally meant either cloud or sky. By Shakespeare's time the cloud meaning had dropped out, and the word was, in southern English, exclusively literary;   **cheek** common in personifications of both heaven and the sea.   **5 fire** the lightning, imagined as boiling the pitch of l. 3.   **6 brave** fine, noble.   **10 god of power** The power is both Prospero's magic generally, and, specifically, the raising of storms.   **11 or ere** The two words are cognate, both meaning 'before.' The doubling is for emphasis. See Abbott 131.   **13 fraughting** 'that forms freight or cargo' (*OED*); not normally used of people.   **14 amazement** both overwhelming fear and overwhelming wonder comprising, with the *piteous heart* immediately following, the full Aristotelian response to tragedy;   **piteous** here, feeling pity; Shakespeare also uses the word to mean 'pitiful.'   **19 more better** higher in rank.   **20 cell** technically a single-chamber dwelling, often with monastic implications; by the late-sixteenth century used poetically for 'a small and humble dwelling, a cottage.'

MIRANDA.   More to know
  Did never meddle with my thoughts.
PROSPERO.   'Tis time
  I should inform thee farther. Lend thy hand
  And pluck my magic garment from me.

  MIRANDA *helps him to disrobe*

                                      So.
  Lie there, my art.—Wipe thou thine eyes; have comfort.
  The direful spectacle of the wreck, which touched
  The very virtue of compassion in thee,
  I have with such provision in mine art
  So safely ordered that there is no soul,
30 No, not so much perdition as an hair
  Betid to any creature in the vessel
  Which thou heard'st cry, which thou saw'st sink. Sit down,
  For thou must now know farther.

  They sit

MIRANDA.   You have often
  Begun to tell me what I am, but stopped,
  And left me to a bootless inquisition,
  Concluding, 'Stay, not yet.'
PROSPERO.   The hour's now come;
  The very minute bids thee ope thine ear.
  Obey, and be attentive. Canst thou remember
  A time before we came unto this cell?
40 I do not think thou canst, for then thou wast not
  Out three years old.
MIRANDA.   Certainly, sir, I can.
PROSPERO.
  By what? By any other house or person?
  Of anything the image tell me that
  Hath kept with thy remembrance.
MIRANDA.   'Tis far off,
  And rather like a dream than an assurance

---

22 meddle with The original meaning is 'mix with' with a sexual connotation persisting until well into the seventeenth century. The modern pejorative usage, 'interfere with,' appears to be the most common one by Shakespeare's time. It is, therefore, worth noting both the passiveness Miranda claims for her thoughts here, and the clear contradiction of that claim in her recollection of her frequent 'bootless inquisition,' l. 35.   **24–5 magic garment . . . Lie there, my art.** Prospero refers to his cloak of office.   **26 spectacle** The predominant meaning is 'theatrical display or pageant,' 'safely ordered' by Prospero as presenter, l. 29.   **29 no soul** an anacoluthon. The omitted verb, 'perished,' is implied in 'perdition.'   **35 bootless** unsuccessful;   **inquisition** a formal or legal process of inquiry; like 'perdition,' l. 30, rhetorical usage.   **41 Out** beyond, hence 'fully.'   **42 By what** i.e. by what image (in your memory).   **43 Of . . . me** describe to me whatever: the memory is assumed to be visual.

That my remembrance warrants. Had I not
Four or five women once that tended me?
PROSPERO.
Thou hadst, and more, Miranda; but how is it
That this lives in thy mind? What seest thou else
50   In the dark backward and abyss of time?
If thou rememb'rest aught ere thou cam'st here,
How thou cam'st here thou mayst.
MIRANDA.   But that I do not.
PROSPERO.
Twelve year since, Miranda, twelve year since,
Thy father was the Duke of Milan, and
A prince of power—
MIRANDA.   Sir, are you not my father?
PROSPERO.
Thy mother was a piece of virtue, and
She said thou wast my daughter; and thy father
Was Duke of Milan, and his only heir
And princess no worse issued.
MIRANDA.   O, the heavens!
60   What foul play had we that we came from thence?
Or blessèd was't we did?
PROSPERO.   Both, both, my girl.
By foul play, as thou sayst, were we heaved thence,
But blessedly holp hither.
MIRANDA.   O, my heart bleeds
To think o'th' teen that I have turned you to,
Which is from my remembrance. Please you, farther.
PROSPERO.
My brother, and thy uncle, called Antonio—
I pray thee mark me, that a brother should
Be so perfidious—he whom next thyself
Of all the world I loved, and to him put
70   The manage of my state, as at that time
Through all the signories it was the first,
And Prospero the prime duke, being so reputed
In dignity, and for the liberal arts
Without a parallel; those being all my study,
The government I cast upon my brother,

---

46 **warrants** guarantees as true.   50 **backward** 'the past portion (of time).'   54 **Milan** accented on the first syllable.   59 **no worse issued** was no less nobly descended.   63 **holp** helped (shortened form of the old p.p. *holpen*).   64 **teen** trouble.   65 **from** away from, not present in.   70 **manage** administration.   71 **signories** both lordships and domains, specifically applied to the Italian city-states.   73 **liberal arts** technically those 'considered "worthy of a free man"; opposed to *servile* or *mechanical* . . . [arts] suitable to persons of superior social station.'

And to my state grew stranger, being transported
And rapt in secret studies. Thy false uncle—
Dost thou attend me?
MIRANDA.   Sir, most heedfully.
PROSPERO.
Being once perfected how to grant suits,
80   How to deny them, who t'advance, and who
To trash for overtopping, new created
The creatures that were mine, I say: or changed 'em,
Or else new formed 'em; having both the key
Of officer and office, set all hearts i'th' state
To what tune pleased his ear, that now he was
The ivy which had hid my princely trunk,
And sucked my verdure out on't—thou attend'st not!
MIRANDA.
O, good sir, I do!
PROSPERO.   I pray thee mark me:
I thus neglecting worldly ends, all dedicated
90   To closeness and the bettering of my mind
With that which, but by being so retired,
O'er-prized all popular rate, in my false brother
Awaked an evil nature, and my trust,
Like a good parent, did beget of him
A falsehood in its contrary as great
As my trust was, which had, indeed, no limit,
A confidence sans bound. He being thus lorded,
Not only with what my revenue yielded,
But what my power might else exact, like one
100   Who, having into truth by telling of it,
Made such a sinner of his memory
To credit his own lie, he did believe

---

76 state the dukedom—either the office or the country.   **76–7 transported | And rapt** Both words literally mean 'physically carried away': Prospero describes his studies as a prefiguration of his abduction and dispatch to the island.   **79 perfected** completely versed in, coming to a mastery of (the word is accented on the first and third syllables).   **81 trash** 'to check (a hound) by a cord or leash';   **overtopping** gaining too much power or authority.   **82 creatures** dependants (whose offices have been *created*).   **82–3 or changed 'em, | Or else new formed 'em** either changed (the allegiance and/or the duties of) existing officials, or else created new ones. *Changed* is equivalent to *new created* in l. 81, and in contrast to *new formed* in l. 83.   **83–4 both . . . office** control over both officials and administration.   **83 key** The keys of his office become, with 'set . . . to what tune,' the keys of musical notation.   **85 that** so that   **86–7 ivy . . . on't** a familiar topos, usually representing the perils of symbiotic relationships.   **87 verdure** sap, vitality, hence power.   **90 closeness** privacy.   **91 but** merely.   **92 O'er-prized all popular rate** exceeded the common people's understanding (*o'er-prized* = were priced beyond the reach of). The point is that what was incomprehensible and disruptive was the fact of retirement and secrecy, and the elitism these implied, not anything inherently mysterious about the studies themselves (they were, after all, 'the liberal arts').   **97 sans** without, a common loan-word at this time;   **lorded** turned into a lord.   **98 revenue** pronounced revènue.   **100–2 Who . . . lie** The syntax is, 'who, having made of his memory such a sinner against (*into*) truth as to credit his own lie by telling it.'

He was indeed the duke, out o'th' substitution
And executing th'outward face of royalty
With all prerogative. Hence his ambition growing—
Dost thou hear?

MIRANDA.   Your tale, sir, would cure deafness.

PROSPERO.

To have no screen between this part he played
And him he played it for, he needs will be
Absolute Milan. Me, poor man, my library
110   Was dukedom large enough. Of temporal royalties
He thinks me now incapable; confederates—
So dry he was for sway—with' King of Naples
To give him annual tribute, do him homage,
Subject his coronet to his crown, and bend
The dukedom yet unbowed—alas, poor Milan!—
To most ignoble stooping.

MIRANDA.   O, the heavens!

PROSPERO. Mark his condition, and th'event; then tell me
If this might be a brother.

MIRANDA.   I should sin
To think but nobly of my grandmother:
Good wombs have borne bad sons.

120   PROSPERO.   Now the condition.
This King of Naples, being an enemy
To me inveterate, hearkens my brother's suit,
Which was that he, in lieu o'th' premises
Of homage and I know not how much tribute,
Should presently extirpate me and mine
Out of the dukedom, and confer fair Milan,
With all the honours, on my brother; whereon,
A treacherous army levied, one midnight
Fated to th' purpose did Antonio open

---

103 out o'th' substitution as a consequence of having taken my place. **107–8 To have no screen . . . for** to have no barrier between his role and himself, to act for himself. The metaphor is confusing because it in fact characterizes Prospero's situation, not Antonio's: it is Prospero who set up Antonio as a screen between himself and his office. **108–11 will be . . . thinks . . . confederates** As Prospero relives the experience, his tenses change from past to present and future. **109 Absolute** 'free from all external restraint or interference; unrestricted, unlimited, independent'; **Me** for me, or as for me. **110 temporal royalties** the prerogatives of rule, as opposed to the spiritual prerogatives afforded by his intellectual pursuits. **111 confederates** conspires: clearly pejorative here, though generally not so in the period. **112 dry** thirsty, hence eager. **115 yet** hitherto. **117 his condition, and th'event** the terms of his agreement with Naples and its outcome. **118–20 I should sin . . . bad sons** Miranda takes Prospero's attack on Antonio to imply an accusation of adultery against Prospero's mother. **123 in lieu o'th' premises** in return for the conditions agreed upon. **125 presently** immediately; **extirpate** literally, 'uproot'; the word could mean either exterminate or drive off. **129 Fated** appointed by fate; Prospero subsequently claims that 'bountiful Fortune' is 'Now my dear lady,' ll. 178–9.

130   The gates of Milan, and i'th' dead of darkness
       The ministers for th' purpose hurried thence
       Me and thy crying self.

MIRANDA.   Alack, for pity!
       I not rememb'ring how I cried out then
       Will cry it o'er again—it is a hint
       That wrings mine eyes to't.

PROSPERO.   Hear a little further,
       And then I'll bring thee to the present business
       Which now's upon's; without the which this story
       Were most impertinent.

MIRANDA.   Wherefore did they not
       That hour destroy us?

PROSPERO.   Well demanded, wench:
140   My tale provokes that question. Dear, they durst not,
       So dear the love my people bore me, nor set
       A mark so bloody on the business; but
       With colours fairer painted their foul ends.
       In few, they hurried us aboard a barque,
       Bore us some leagues to sea, where they prepared
       A rotten carcase of a butt, not rigged,
       Nor tackle, sail, nor mast—the very rats
       Instinctively have quit it. There they hoist us
       To cry to th' sea that roared to us, to sigh
150   To th' winds, whose pity, sighing back again,
       Did us but loving wrong.

MIRANDA.   Alack, what trouble
       Was I then to you!

PROSPERO.   O, a cherubin
       Thou wast that did preserve me. Thou didst smile,
       Infusèd with a fortitude from heaven,
       When I have decked the sea with drops full salt,
       Under my burden groaned, which raised in me
       An undergoing stomach to bear up

---

131 ministers agents.   **134 hint** occasion (literally 'something one seizes on'). Compare 2.1.3.   **138 impertinent** 'not pertaining to the matter at hand' (*OED* 2).   **139 wench** originally a young woman or girl child; also, in Shakespeare's time, 'a familiar or endearing form of address; used chiefly in addressing a daughter, wife or sweetheart.'   **144 few** i.e. few words;   **a barque** In fact, Milan is not a port.   **146 carcase** 'The decaying skeleton of a vessel';   **butt** literally a barrel or tub; but (unlike tub) not recorded as a slang term for a boat. The word is apparently etymologically unrelated to Italian *botto,* a kind of sloop, or to French *boute,* a leathern vessel; but Shakespeare may be using it in the belief that it is.   **152 cherubin** originally a plural, but used as the normal singular in English until the seventeenth century.   **155 decked** adorned.   **156–7 Under my burden . . . An undergoing stomach** *Undergoing stomach* = courage to endure; *stomach* implies variously the inmost part, temper, especially 'spirit, courage, valour, bravery.'

Against what should ensue.

MIRANDA.   How came we ashore?

PROSPERO. By providence divine;

160   Some food we had, and some fresh water, that
A noble Neapolitan, Gonzalo,
Out of his charity, who being then appointed
Master of this design, did give us, with
Rich garments, linens, stuffs, and necessaries,
Which since have steaded much; so of his gentleness,
Knowing I loved my books, he furnished me
From mine own library with volumes that
I prize above my dukedom.

MIRANDA.   Would I might
But ever see that man!

PROSPERO (*rising*).   Now I arise.

170   Sit still, and hear the last of our sea-sorrow:
Here in this island we arrived, and here
Have I, thy schoolmaster, made thee more profit
Than other princes can that have more time
For vainer hours, and tutors not so careful.

MIRANDA.
Heavens thank you for't. And now I pray you, sir,
For still 'tis beating in my mind, your reason
For raising this sea-storm.

PROSPERO.   Know thus far forth:
By accident most strange, bountiful Fortune,
Now my dear lady, hath mine enemies

180   Brought to this shore; and by my prescience
I find my zenith doth depend upon
A most auspicious star, whose influence
If now I court not, but omit, my fortunes
Will ever after droop. Here cease more questions:
Thou art inclined to sleep. 'Tis a good dulness,
And give it way—I know thou canst not choose.

        MIRANDA *sleeps*

---

165 steaded been useful or advantageous;   **gentleness** both kindness and nobility.   **169 Now I arise** both literally, as Prospero prepares to exercise his control over the shipwreck victims, and figuratively, as he sees his fortunes turn (compare 'my zenith . . . ,' l. 181). There is no clear indication of when he resumes his magic cloak, but 'I am ready now' (l. 187) provides an appropriate point.   **170 Sit still** remain seated.   **172 profit** the verb, not the noun.   **174 careful** both caring and taking trouble.   **178–9 Fortune, | Now my dear lady** Fortuna was characteristically fickle.   **181 zenith** technically the highest point of the celestial sphere, and also, here, the top of Fortune's wheel; hence, the culmination of Prospero's good fortune.   **182 influence** astrological powers.   **183 omit** disregard, 'fail or forbear to use.'   **185 dulness** drowsiness.

(*Calling*) Come away, servant, come.
　　　[*Puts on his cloak*]　　　　　　I am ready now.
　Approach, my Ariel. Come.

　　　Enter ARIEL

ARIEL.
　　All hail, great master, grave sir, hail! I come
190　To answer thy best pleasure, be't to fly,
　　To swim, to dive into the fire, to ride
　　On the curled clouds; to thy strong bidding task
　　Ariel and all his quality.
PROSPERO.　　　　　　　　Hast thou, spirit,
　　Performed to point the tempest that I bade thee?
ARIEL.　To every article.
　　I boarded the King's ship; now on the beak,
　　Now in the waist, the deck, in every cabin,
　　I flamed amazement. Sometime I'd divide
　　And burn in many places; on the topmast,
200　The yards and bowsprit would I flame distinctly,
　　Then meet and join. Jove's lightning, the precursors
　　O'th' dreadful thunder-claps, more momentary
　　And sight-outrunning were not; the fire and cracks
　　Of sulphurous roaring the most mighty Neptune
　　Seem to besiege and make his bold waves tremble,
　　Yea, his dread trident shake.
PROSPERO.　　　　　　　　My brave spirit!
　　Who was so firm, so constant, that this coil
　　Would not infect his reason?
ARIEL.　　　　　　　　　　Not a soul
　　But felt a fever of the mad, and played
210　Some tricks of desperation. All but mariners
　　Plunged in the foaming brine and quit the vessel,
　　Then all afire with me: the King's son Ferdinand,
　　With hair up-staring—then like reeds, not hair—

---

187 I am The metre suggests that Crane may be expanding 'I'm' here.　**188.1 Ariel** literally 'lion of God,' used by Isaiah as an epithet for Jerusalem (29: 1). The name appears as a spirit in many magical texts. **190–2 be't . . . clouds** Ariel declares himself at home in the fluid and volatile elements; Prospero adds 'earth' at l. 255.　**193 quality** either fraternity, i.e. the other spirits, or abilities.　**194 Performed to point** presented in exact detail.　**195 article** The metaphor is of a legal document.　**196 beak** prow.　**197 in the waist** amidships;　**deck** 'In early craft there was a deck only at the stern, so that sixteenth-century writers sometimes use *deck* as equivalent to *poop*.'　**198 flamed amazement** appeared as flame, producing terror. Here and at l. 200, most editors refer to St. Elmo's fire and cite various travel narratives, in which, however, the phenomenon is generally treated as a comforting omen.　**204 sulphurous** Sulphur was popularly associated with thunder and lightning, from its use in explosives.　**207 coil** tumult, confusion.　**209 a fever of the mad** such a fever as the mad feel.　**213 up-staring** standing on end.

Was the first man that leapt, cried 'Hell is empty,
And all the devils are here.'

PROSPERO.   Why, that's my spirit.
But was not this nigh shore?

ARIEL.   Close by, my master.

PROSPERO.
But are they, Ariel, safe?

ARIEL.   Not a hair perished.
On their sustaining garments not a blemish,
But fresher than before; and as thou bad'st me,
220   In troops I have dispersed them 'bout the isle.
The King's son have I landed by himself,
Whom I left cooling of the air with sighs
In an odd angle of the isle, and sitting,
His arms in this sad knot.

PROSPERO.   Of the King's ship
The mariners say how thou hast disposed,
And all the rest o'th' fleet.

ARIEL.   Safely in harbour
Is the King's ship, in the deep nook where once
Thou called'st me up at midnight to fetch dew
From the still-vexed Bermudas, there she's hid;
230   The mariners all under hatches stowed,
Who, with a charm joined to their suffered labour,
I have left asleep; and for the rest o'th' fleet,
Which I dispersed, they all have met again,
And are upon the Mediterranean float,
Bound sadly home for Naples,
Supposing that they saw the King's ship wrecked,
And his great person perish.

PROSPERO.   Ariel, thy charge
Exactly is performed; but there's more work.
What is the time o'th' day?

ARIEL.   Past the mid-season.

PROSPERO.
240   At least two glasses. The time 'twixt six and now

---

215 devils often monosyllabic, and possibly so here.   **217 Not a hair perished** Ariel repeats Prospero's re-assurance to Miranda: see 1.2.30.   **218 sustaining garments** They were buoyed up by their clothing, either because of the magical quality of the wreck, or naturally and briefly like Ophelia (*Hamlet* 4.7.175–83), but in this case long enough to enable them to reach the nearby shore.   **223 angle** corner.   **224 this sad knot** Ariel folds his arms, implying sorrow.   **228 midnight . . . dew** the appropriate time and a common sub-stance for the performance of magic. Caliban credits Sycorax with the use of 'wicked dew' at l. 321. **229 still-vexed** always troubled by storms;   **Bermudas** the only reference to Bermuda in the play. **231 their suffered labour** the toil they have undergone.   **234 float** sea.   **240 two glasses** i.e. two hours past noon. The reference here and at 5.1.223 is to hour glasses, not to the half-hour glasses used by mariners.

Must by us both be spent most preciously.

ARIEL.

Is there more toil? Since thou dost give me pains,
Let me remember thee what thou hast promised,
Which is not yet performed me.

PROSPERO.   How now? Moody?
What is't thou canst demand?

ARIEL.   My liberty.

PROSPERO.

Before the time be out? No more.

ARIEL.   I prithee,
Remember I have done thee worthy service,
Told thee no lies, made no mistakings, served
Without or grudge or grumblings. Thou did promise
To bate me a full year.

250   PROSPERO.   Dost thou forget
From what a torment I did free thee?

ARIEL.   No.

PROSPERO.

Thou dost, and think'st it much to tread the ooze
Of the salt deep,
To run upon the sharp wind of the north,
To do me business in the veins o'th' earth
When it is baked with frost.

ARIEL.   I do not, sir.

PROSPERO.

Thou liest, malignant thing! Hast thou forgot
The foul witch Sycorax, who with age and envy
Was grown into a hoop? Hast thou forgot her?

ARIEL.

No, sir.

260   PROSPERO. Thou hast. Where was she born? Speak; tell me.

ARIEL.

Sir, in Algiers.

PROSPERO.   O, was she so—I must
Once in a month recount what thou hast been,
Which thou forget'st. This damned witch Sycorax,

---

242 pains tasks: the complaint anticipates Caliban's charges against Prospero.   **243 remember** remind.
244 Moody the first indication of Ariel's characteristic rebelliousness.   **250 bate me** deduct from my time.
255 veins either mineral deposits ('veins of ore') or the channels of underground streams.   **256 baked** The operative meaning of bake is 'to harden as frost does.'   **258 Sycorax** The name has never been satisfactorily explained. It is usually etymologized from the Greek *sus* (pig) and *korax* (raven); only the latter of these seems right. The figure is largely derived from Ovid's account of Medea in *Metamorphoses* 7, and the name sounds like an epithet for Medea, the Scythian raven. The account of Sycorax's career is presented as deriving from Prospero's memory, but in fact the memory is Ariel's. Prospero never saw Sycorax, who died before he came to the island.

For mischiefs manifold and sorceries terrible
To enter human hearing, from Algiers
Thou know'st was banished—for one thing she did
They would not take her life. Is not this true?
ARIEL. Ay, sir.
PROSPERO.
This blue-eyed hag was hither brought with child,
270   And here was left by th' sailors. Thou, my slave,
As thou report'st thyself, was then her servant,
And for thou wast a spirit too delicate
To act her earthy and abhorred commands,
Refusing her grand hests, she did confine thee,
By help of her more potent ministers
And in her most unmitigable rage,
Into a cloven pine, within which rift
Imprisoned thou didst painfully remain
A dozen years; within which space she died
280   And left thee there, where thou didst vent thy groans
As fast as mill-wheels strike. Then was this island—
Save for the son that she did litter here,
A freckled whelp, hag-born—not honoured with
A human shape.
ARIEL.   Yes, Caliban, her son.
PROSPERO.
Dull thing, I say so: he, that Caliban
Whom now I keep in service. Thou best know'st
What torment I did find thee in. Thy groans
Did make wolves howl, and penetrate the breasts
Of ever-angry bears—it was a torment
290   To lay upon the damned, which Sycorax
Could not again undo. It was mine art,
When I arrived and heard thee, that made gape
The pine and let thee out.

---

266 for one thing she did She was pregnant (see l. 269), and pregnancy required the commutation of a capital sentence. Editorial debate over the *one thing* was energetic until the early years of this century, most critics resisting the idea that Sycorax's pregnancy saved her life. The problematic element in the passage is not its meaning, but the obliqueness of Prospero's reference to it.   **269 blue-eyed** generally explained as 'with blue eyelids,' implying pregnancy.   **273 earthy** and therefore antithetical to Ariel's volatile nature.   **274 hests** behests.   **275 ministers** agents.   **279** Sycorax, then, died sometime before Prospero came to the island, and thus more than twelve years ago. Caliban is therefore at least twenty-four at the time of the play, and was at least thirteen when Prospero arrived with the three-year old Miranda.   **281 as mill-wheels strike** as the blades of water-wheels strike the water. Kittredge suggested that the reference was to the mill's clapper, a device which shakes the hopper so as to move the grain down to the millstones; but there is no evidence that a clapper was ever referred to as a mill-wheel.   **285 Dull thing, I say so** Prospero's vexation continues: 'Don't parrot what I say!'   **288–9 penetrate the breasts | Of** i.e. arouse sympathy in.   **291–3 Could . . . out** Prospero thus demonstrates that his magic is more powerful than Sycorax's.

ARIEL.   I thank thee, master.

PROSPERO.

   If thou more murmur'st, I will rend an oak

   And peg thee in his knotty entrails till

   Thou hast howled away twelve winters.

ARIEL.   Pardon, master.

   I will be correspondent to command

   And do my spriting gently.

PROSPERO.   Do so, and after two days

   I will discharge thee.

ARIEL.   That's my noble master.

300   What shall I do? Say what: what shall I do?

PROSPERO.

   Go, make thyself like a nymph o'th'sea.

   Be subject to no sight but thine and mine, invisible

   To every eyeball else. Go, take this shape,

   And hither come in't; go! Hence, with diligence!

Exit ARIEL

(*To* MIRANDA) Awake, dear heart, awake. Thou hast slept well.

   Awake.

MIRANDA. The strangeness of your story put

   Heaviness in me.

PROSPERO.   Shake it off. Come on;

   We'll visit Caliban, my slave, who never

   Yields us kind answer.

MIRANDA.   'Tis a villain, sir,

   I do not love to look on.

310 PROSPERO.   But as 'tis,

   We cannot miss him. He does make our fire,

   Fetch in our wood, and serves in offices

   That profit us. What ho, slave! Caliban!

   Thou earth, thou, speak!

CALIBAN (*within*).   There's wood enough within.

PROSPERO.

   Come forth, I say; there's other business for thee.

   Come, thou tortoise, when?

---

297 correspondent responsive. **298 gently** graciously. **301 like a nymph o'th' sea** The disguise is, of course, logically pointless if Ariel is invisible to everyone except Prospero. But he is visible to the audience, and the costume is the appropriate one to adopt in singing to Ferdinand on the shore. **307 Heaviness** drowsiness. **311 miss** do without. **314 earth** in contrast to Prospero's other servant, the spirit of air; *within* i.e. within the discovery place at the back of the stage. Caliban's 'hard rock' dwelling (l. 343) may have been a small movable property erected either inside or immediately in front of this alcove, but the discovery place itself may just as well have served as his den.

Enter ARIEL *like a water-nymph*

Fine apparition! My quaint Ariel,
Hark in thine ear. (*whispers*)

ARIEL.   My lord, it shall be done.   *Exit*

PROSPERO.

Thou poisonous slave, got by the devil himself
320 · Upon thy wicked dam, come forth!

Enter CALIBAN

CALIBAN.

As wicked dew as e'er my mother brushed
With raven's feather from unwholesome fen
Drop on you both! A south-west blow on ye
And blister you all o'er!

PROSPERO.

For this be sure tonight thou shalt have cramps,
Side-stitches that shall pen thy breath up. Urchins
Shall, for that vast of night that they may work,
All exercise on thee. Thou shalt be pinched
As thick as honeycomb, each pinch more stinging
Than bees that made 'em.

330 CALIBAN.   I must eat my dinner.

This island's mine by Sycorax my mother,
Which thou tak'st from me. When thou cam'st first,
Thou strok'st me and made much of me; wouldst give me
Water with berries in't, and teach me how
To name the bigger light and how the less,
That burn by day and night; and then I loved thee,
And showed thee all the qualities o'th' isle,
The fresh springs, brine pits, barren place and fertile—

---

317 quaint The word includes the senses of ingenious and skillful, curious in appearance, and elegant.
319–20 got by the devil himself | Upon thy wicked dam alluding to stories of sexual liaisons between
witches and the devil. The identity of Caliban's father is mentioned nowhere else in the play, though Prospero
calls him a 'demi-devil' and a bastard at 5.1.270–1. It is not clear whether Prospero's expostulation is mere in-
vective or a literal account of Caliban's conception; and indeed, its dramatic purpose is amply served by leaving us in doubt. See the Introduction, p. 25.   **321 wicked** both harmful and foul.   **321–2 dew . . . raven's
feather** Dew was a common ingredient of magical potions, required by Prospero as well as Sycorax: see l. 228.
The raven was especially associated with witchcraft, and its Greek and Latin name, *korax/corax*, is clearly related to the unexplained name Sycorax.   **323 south-west** Southerly winds were associated with warm, damp
weather, and considered unwholesome.   **326 Urchins** goblins, so called 'from the supposition that they occasionally assumed the form of a hedgehog.' Compare 2.2.5.   **327 vast** great stretch (normally of space, not
time).   **328–9 pinched | As thick as honeycomb** covered with pinches as thoroughly as the honeycomb
has cells; the image perhaps derives from the notion that bees mould their wax by pinching it into shape.
331 Caliban bases his claim to the island on inheritance. If he is, as Prospero asserts, illegitimate, the claim
would be invalid.   **335 bigger . . . less** echoing Genesis 1:16; in the Geneva Bible, 'God then made two
great lights: the greater light to rule the day, and the less light to rule the night.' No English Bible reads 'bigger.'

Cursed be I that did so! All the charms
340   Of Sycorax, toads, beetles, bats light on you!
For I am all the subjects that you have,
Which first was mine own king, and here you sty me
In this hard rock, whiles you do keep from me
The rest o'th' island.

PROSPERO.   Thou most lying slave,
Whom stripes may move, not kindness, I have used thee—
Filth as thou art—with humane care, and lodged thee
In mine own cell, till thou didst seek to violate
The honour of my child.

CALIBAN.   O ho, O ho! Would't had been done!
Thou didst prevent me—I had peopled else
This isle with Calibans.

350 MIRANDA.   Abhorrèd slave,
Which any print of goodness wilt not take,
Being capable of all ill! I pitied thee,
Took pains to make thee speak, taught thee each hour
One thing or other. When thou didst not, savage,
Know thine own meaning, but wouldst gabble like
A thing most brutish, I endowed thy purposes
With words that made them known. But thy vile race—
Though thou didst learn—had that in't which good natures
Could not abide to be with; therefore wast thou
360 Deservedly confined into this rock,
Who hadst deserved more than a prison.

CALIBAN.
You taught me language, and my profit on't
Is I know how to curse. The red plague rid you
For learning me your language!

PROSPERO.   Hag-seed, hence!
Fetch us in fuel, and be quick, thou'rt best,
To answer other business—shrug'st thou, malice?
If thou neglect'st, or dost unwillingly
What I command, I'll rack thee with old cramps,
Fill all thy bones with achës, make thee roar,
That beasts shall tremble at thy din.

370 CALIBAN.   No, pray thee.

---

339 charms spells.   **342 sty me** pen me up like a pig.   **346 humane** F's spelling, not distinguished in the period from *human*, and accented until the eighteenth century on the first syllable.   **351 print** imprint. The metaphor alludes at once to coinage, wax seals, and typography.   **352 capable of** susceptible (only) to.   **357 race** 'Natural or inherited disposition.'   **363 red** 'Applied to various diseases marked by evacuation of blood or cutaneous eruptions.'   **364 learning** teaching.   **366 answer other business** perform other tasks.   **368 old cramps** the cramps of old age.   **369 achës** Until the seventeenth century, the noun was pronounced *atch*, the verb *ake*.

(*Aside*) I must obey. His art is of such power,
It would control my dam's god Setebos
And make a vassal of him.
PROSPERO.   So, slave, hence!

Exit CALIBAN

Enter FERDINAND, *and* ARIEL *invisible, playing and singing*

ARIEL (*sings*).
          Come unto these yellow sands,
            And then take hands;
          Curtsied when you have, and kissed
            The wild waves whist,
          Foot it featly here and there,
            And sweet sprites bear
380   The burden. Hark, hark!
               (*Burden, dispersedly*) Bow-wow.
            The watch dogs bark.
               (*Burden, dispersedly*) Bow-wow.
            Hark, hark! I hear
          The strain of strutting Chanticleer
            Cry cock a diddle dow.
               (*Burden, dispersedly*) Cock a diddle dow.
FERDINAND.
    Where should this music be?—i'th' air or th' earth?
    It sounds no more; and sure it waits upon
390   Some god o'th' island. Sitting on a bank,
    Weeping again the King my father's wreck,
    This music crept by me upon the waters,
    Allaying both their fury and my passion
    With its sweet air. Thence I have followed it,
    Or it hath drawn me rather; but 'tis gone.
    No, it begins again.
ARIEL (*sings*).
          Full fathom five thy father lies,
            Of his bones are coral made;

---

372 Setebos The name is found in accounts of Magellan's voyages as that of a 'great devil' of the Patagonians.
373.1 invisible Ariel is dressed as a sea-nymph; his invisibility is presumably established simply by Prospero's
instructions at l. 302 and by Ferdinand's failure to see him. Henslowe's papers list as a property of the Lord
Admiral's Men a 'robe for to goo invisibell,' but such a garment would be unnecessary here, and awkward in
conjunction with the nymph's wings; ***playing*** probably a lute; later Ariel plays a tabor and pipe (3.2.122.1).
376–7 kissed . . . whist either 'kissed the wild waves into silence' or 'kissed (each other) until the wild waves
are silent.' **378 featly** both neatly and elegantly. **381 *burden*** refrain; ***dispersedly*** i.e. not in unison.
389 waits attends. **393 passion** literally, suffering. **397 fathom** originally the measure of a man's out-
stretched arms from fingertip to fingertip, reckoned as 6 feet. The drowned father is thus 30 feet deep.

Those are pearls that were his eyes;
400 Nothing of him that doth fade,
But doth suffer a sea-change
Into something rich and strange.
Sea-nymphs hourly ring his knell.
                    (*Burden*) Ding dong.
Hark, now I hear them, ding dong bell.

FERDINAND.
The ditty does remember my drowned father.
This is no mortal business, nor no sound
That the earth owes—I hear it now above me.

PROSPERO (*to* MIRANDA).
The fringéd curtains of thine eye advance,
And say what thou seest yond.

410 MIRANDA.   What is't?—a spirit?
Lord, how it looks about! Believe me, sir,
It carries a brave form. But 'tis a spirit.

PROSPERO.
No, wench, it eats and sleeps, and hath such senses
As we have—such. This gallant which thou seest
Was in the wreck, and but he's something stained
With grief—that's beauty's canker—thou mightst call him
A goodly person. He hath lost his fellows,
And strays about to find 'em.

MIRANDA.   I might call him
A thing divine, for nothing natural
I ever saw so noble.

420 PROSPERO (*aside*). It goes on, I see,
As my soul prompts it. (*To* ARIEL) Spirit, fine spirit, I'll free thee
Within two days for this.

FERDINAND.   Most sure, the goddess
On whom these airs attend. Vouchsafe my prayer
May know if you remain upon this island,
And that you will some good instruction give
How I may bear me here. My prime request,
Which I do last pronounce, is—O you wonder!—

---

406 ditty a song, especially its verbal element;   **remember** commemorate.   **407 mortal** both human, and pertaining to death: Ferdinand's perception grows as he muses on the song.   **408 owes** owns.   **414 gallant** 'A man of fashion and pleasure; a fine gentleman,' especially 'a ladies' man.'   **415 but** except for the fact that; **something** somewhat.   **416 grief—that's beauty's canker** A canker is variously a spreading sore; rust; a disease, especially of fruit trees; a destructive larva; and, from these, the general sense of 'anything that frets, corrodes, corrupts or consumes slowly and secretly'; *grief—that's beauty's canker* means either that grief is a disease especially disfiguring to the beautiful, or that grief is attracted especially to the beautiful as the larva is to the rose, precisely because of its beauty.   **419 natural** as opposed to the artificial creations of, e.g., Prospero's masque.   **420 It** my plan.   **423 airs** Ariel's songs.   **424 remain** dwell.   **426 bear me** conduct myself.   **427 wonder** The epithet puns on Miranda's name.

If you be maid or no?

MIRANDA.   No wonder, sir,
But certainly a maid.

FERDINAND.   My language! Heavens!
430   I am the best of them that speak this speech,
Were I but where 'tis spoken.

PROSPERO.   How? The best?
What wert thou if the King of Naples heard thee?

FERDINAND.
A single thing, as I am now, that wonders
To hear thee speak of Naples. He does hear me,
And that he does, I weep: myself am Naples,
Who with mine eyes, never since at ebb, beheld
The King my father wrecked.

MIRANDA.   Alack, for mercy!

FERDINAND.
Yes, faith, and all his lords, the Duke of Milan
And his brave son being twain.

PROSPERO (*aside*).   The Duke of Milan
440   And his more braver daughter could control thee
If now 'twere fit to do't. At the first sight
They have changed eyes. Delicate Ariel,
I'll set thee free for this.—A word, good sir:
I fear you have done yourself some wrong; a word.

MIRANDA.
Why speaks my father so ungently? This
Is the third man that e'er I saw, the first
That e'er I sighed for. Pity move my father
To be inclined my way!

FERDINAND.   O, if a virgin,
And your affection not gone forth, I'll make you
The Queen of Naples.

450 PROSPERO.   Soft, sir, one word more.
(*Aside*) They are both in either's powers; but this swift business
I must uneasy make lest too light winning
Make the prize light.—One word more: I charge thee
That thou attend me. Thou dost here usurp

---

428 maid a girl, as opposed to either a goddess or a married woman.   **434, 435 Naples** the King of Naples.
434 He does hear me i.e. because I am he.   **436 never since at ebb** continually weeping.   **439 his brave son** Antonio's son is mentioned nowhere else in the play.   **440 control** challenge, refute.   **442 changed** interchanged: 'they can't take their eyes off one another'; **Delicate** graceful, artful.   **444 you have done yourself some wrong** i.e. in claiming to be King of Naples. The tone is ironic, but Prospero is, of course, quite correct.   **452 uneasy** difficult.   **452–3 light . . . light** easy . . . cheap, with perhaps an overtone of 'promiscuous' in the second instance. Prospero's explanation of his behaviour has generally been found unconvincing.

The name thou ow'st not, and hast put thyself
Upon this island as a spy, to win it
From me, the lord on't.
FERDINAND.   No, as I am a man!
MIRANDA.
    There's nothing ill can dwell in such a temple.
    If the ill spirit have so fair a house,
    Good things will strive to dwell with't.
460   PROSPERO.   Follow me.—
    Speak not you for him: he's a traitor.—Come,
    I'll manacle thy neck and feet together.
    Sea-water shall thou drink; thy food shall be
    The fresh-brook mussels, withered roots, and husks
    Wherein the acorn cradled. Follow.
FERDINAND.   No;
    I will resist such entertainment till
    Mine enemy has more power.

        He draws, and is charmed from moving

MIRANDA.   O dear father,
    Make not too rash a trial of him, for
    He's gentle, and not fearful.
PROSPERO.   What, I say—
470   My foot my tutor? Put thy sword up, traitor,
    Who mak'st a show but dar'st not strike, thy conscience
    Is so possessed with guilt. Come from thy ward,
    For I can here disarm thee with this stick
    And make thy weapon drop.
MIRANDA.   Beseech you, father—
PROSPERO.
    Hence! Hang not on my garments.
MIRANDA.   Sir, have pity;
    I'll be his surety.
PROSPERO.   Silence! One word more
    Shall make me chide thee, if not hate thee. What,
    An advocate for an imposter? Hush!
    Thou think'st there is no more such shapes as he,

---

455 ow'st own'st.   **458 temple** 'Any place regarded as occupied by the divine presence; *spec.* the person or body of a Christian.'   **459–60 If the ill spirit . . . dwell with't** and, being stronger, expel it. Miranda's assertion is conventional Renaissance Platonic doctrine; equally conventional in the period, however, are observations about the deceptiveness of attractive exteriors. In the dramatic circumstances, Miranda's speech expresses more naïveté than Platonism. Compare 5.1.181–4.   **464 fresh-brook mussels** Fresh-water mussels are inedible.   **466 entertainment** treatment.   **469 gentle, and not fearful** noble, and therefore not a coward.   **470 My foot my tutor?** 'Shall the lowest of my appendages teach me how to act?'   **472 ward** defensive posture.

480 Having seen but him and Caliban. Foolish wench,
To th' most of men this is a Caliban,
And they to him are angels.

MIRANDA.   My affections
Are then most humble. I have no ambition
To see a goodlier man.

PROSPERO (*to* FERDINAND). Come on, obey.
Thy nerves are in their infancy again
And have no vigour in them.

FERDINAND.   So they are.
My spirits, as in a dream, are all bound up.
My father's loss, the weakness which I feel,
The wreck of all my friends, nor this man's threats,

490 To whom I am subdued, are but light to me,
Might I but through my prison once a day
Behold this maid. All corners else o' th' earth
Let liberty make use of—space enough
Have I in such a prison.

PROSPERO (*aside*).   It works (*To* FERDINAND) Come on.—
(*To* ARIEL) Thou hast done well, fine Ariel. Follow me;
Hark what thou else shalt do me.

MIRANDA (*to* FERDINAND).   Be of comfort.
My father's of a better nature, sir,
Than he appears by speech. This is unwonted
Which now came from him.

PROSPERO (*to* ARIEL).   Thou shalt be as free

500 As mountain winds; but then exactly do
All points of my command.

ARIEL.   To th' syllable.

PROSPERO (*to* FERDINAND).
Come, follow. (*To* MIRANDA)—Speak not for him.   *Exeunt.*

2.1 *Enter* ALONSO, SEBASTIAN, ANTONIO, GONZALO, ADRIAN, FRANCISCO.

GONZALO (*to* ALONSO).
Beseech you, sir, be merry. You have cause—
So have we all—of joy, for our escape
Is much beyond our loss. Our hint of woe
Is common: every day some sailor's wife,

---

481 To compared to.   **485 nerves** sinews.   **490 but** merely, otherwise than.   **492 All corners** any parts
'whatsoever, even the smallest, most distant and secluded.'   **496 do me** do for me.   **500 then** i.e. if that is
to be so.
3 beyond more important than;   **hint** occasion.

The masters of some merchant, and the merchant
Have just our theme of woe; but for the miracle—
I mean our preservation—few in millions
Can speak like us. Then wisely, good sir, weigh
Our sorrow with our comfort.

ALONSO.   Prithee, peace.

10   SEBASTIAN (*aside to* ANTONIO). He receives comfort like cold porridge.

ANTONIO. The visitor will not give him o'er so.

SEBASTIAN. Look, he's winding up the watch of his wit. By and by it will strike.

GONZALO. Sir,—

SEBASTIAN. One. Tell.

GONZALO.   —when every grief is entertained
     That's offered, comes to th' entertainer—

SEBASTIAN. A dollar.

GONZALO. Dolour comes to him indeed. You have spoken truer than you purposed.

SEBASTIAN. You have taken it wiselier than I meant you should.

20   GONZALO. Therefore, my lord,—

ANTONIO. Fie, what a spendthrift is he of his tongue!

ALONSO (*to* GONZALO). I prithee, spare.

GONZALO. Well, I have done. But yet—

SEBASTIAN. He will be talking.

ANTONIO. Which, of he or Adrian, for a good wager, first begins to crow?

SEBASTIAN. The old cock.

ANTONIO. The cockerel.

SEBASTIAN. Done. The wager?

ANTONIO. A laughter.

30   SEBASTIAN. A match!

ADRIAN. Though this island seem to be desert—

ANTONIO. Ha, ha, ha!

SEBASTIAN. So, you're paid!

ADRIAN. Uninhabitable, and almost inaccessible—

SEBASTIAN. Yet—

ADRIAN. Yet—

ANTONIO. He could not miss't.

---

5 The masters . . . the merchant either the officers or the owners of some merchantman, and either the vessel itself or the merchant to whom the cargo belongs. **9, 10 peace, porridge** punning on 'pease-porridge.' **10–12** Antonio's and Sebastian's opening exchange should probably be treated as a private conversation; but for the most part throughout this scene their insulting banter is designed to be overheard. **11 visitor** Gonzalo is compared with the church functionary charged with comforting the sick of the parish. **give him o'er** leave him alone. **14 One. Tell.** His watch has struck one. Keep count. **17 A dollar** i.e. in payment: Sebastian quibbles on *entertainer* = performer. **25–7 which, . . . cockerel** Compare the proverb 'the young cock crows as he the old hears.' **29 A laughter** The proverb is 'he laughs that wins'; a laughter is also 'the whole number of eggs laid by a fowl before she is ready to sit.' s. laughter 2. **31 desert** uninhabited. **32–3 Ha . . . paid** F gives the laugh to Sebastian, l. 38 to Antonio. But, since Antonio has won the bet and the prize is a laugh, it seems clear that the speech headings have been reversed. Sebastian's line means 'you've had your laugh.'

ADRIAN. It must needs be of subtle, tender, and delicate temperance.

ANTONIO. Temperance was a delicate wench.

40   SEBASTIAN. Ay, and a subtle, as he most learnedly delivered.

ADRIAN. The air breathes upon us here most sweetly.

SEBASTIAN. As if it had lungs, and rotten ones.

ANTONIO. Or as 'twere perfumed by a fen.

GONZALO. Here is everything advantageous to life.

ANTONIO. True, save means to live.

SEBASTIAN. Of that there's none or little.

GONZALO. How lush and lusty the grass looks! How green!

ANTONIO. The ground indeed is tawny.

SEBASTIAN. With an eye of green in't.

50   ANTONIO. He misses not much.

SEBASTIAN. No, he doth but mistake the truth totally.

GONZALO. But the rarity of it is, which is indeed almost beyond credit—

SEBASTIAN. As many vouched rarities are.

GONZALO. That our garments, being, as they were, drenched in the sea, hold notwithstanding their freshness and gloss, being rather new-dyed than stained with salt water.

ANTONIO. If but one of his pockets could speak, would it not say he lies?

SEBASTIAN. Ay, or very falsely pocket up his report.

GONZALO. Methinks our garments are now as fresh as when we put them on first in

60   Afric, at the marriage of the King's fair daughter Claribel to the King of Tunis.

SEBASTIAN. 'Twas a sweet marriage, and we prosper well in our return.

ADRIAN. Tunis was never graced before with such a paragon to their queen.

GONZALO. Not since widow Dido's time.

ANTONIO. Widow? A pox o' that. How came that widow in? Widow Dido!

SEBASTIAN. What if he had said 'widower Aeneas' too? Good lord, how you take it!

ADRIAN. 'Widow Dido' said you? You make me study of that. She was of Carthage, not of Tunis.

GONZALO. This Tunis, sir, was Carthage.

---

38 subtle gentle;   **temperance** 'mildness of weather or climate.'   **39 Temperance . . . wench** Antonio takes Temperance to be a girl's name; hence *delicate* = given to pleasure.   **40 subtle** Sebastian develops the theme of delicacy: *subtle* here implies craftiness and (sexual) expertise; and, with *learnedly*, plays on the sense of acute or speculative.   **47 lush** The relevant meaning current in Shakespeare's time is 'soft, tender.'   **48 The . . . tawny** not a contradiction: Antonio is mocking Gonzalo's compulsion to remark on everything.   **49 eye** 'slight shade, tinge.'   **50 He . . . much** i.e. Gonzalo's is the 'eye of green.'   **52, 53 rarity, rarities** exceptional quality, unique phenomena.   **54–6 our garments . . . water** Compare Ariel, 1.2.218–19: 'On their sustaining garments not a blemish, | But fresher than before.'   **57 If . . . lies** Since Ariel has testified to the condition of the garments, Antonio is presumably being merely perverse; but the line also contributes to a general sense that the quality of the island and of experience on it is perceived diversely and subjectively by the various characters.   **58 pocket up** conceal or suppress.   **64, 65 Widow Dido, widower Aeneas** Dido was the widow of Sychaeus; Aeneas' wife Creusa died in the sack of Troy. Recollections of and allusions to the *Aeneid* provide an important undercurrent throughout the play.   **68 This . . . was Carthage** Gonzalo is correct in the sense that, though Carthage and Tunis were always separate cities, after the destruction of Carthage Tunis took its place as the political and commercial centre of the region. This is presumably what Antonio and Sebastian are quibbling about.

ADRIAN. Carthage?

70 GONZALO. I assure you, Carthage.

ANTONIO. His word is more than the miraculous harp.

SEBASTIAN. He hath raised the wall, and houses too.

ANTONIO. What impossible matter will he make easy next?

SEBASTIAN. I think he will carry this island home in his pocket and give it his son for an apple.

ANTONIO. And sowing the kernels of it in the sea, bring forth more islands.

GONZALO. Ay.

ANTONIO. Why, in good time.

GONZALO (*to* ALONSO). Sir, we were talking that our garments seem now as fresh as

80 when we were at Tunis at the marriage of your daughter, who is now queen.

ANTONIO. And the rarest that e'er came there.

SEBASTIAN. Bate, I beseech you, widow Dido.

ANTONIO. O, widow Dido? Ay, widow Dido.

GONZALO. Is not, sir, my doublet as fresh as the first day I wore it? I mean, in a sort.

ANTONIO. That sort was well fished for.

GONZALO. When I wore it at your daughter's marriage.

ALONSO.

    You cram these words into mine ears against

    The stomach of my sense. Would I had never

    Married my daughter there, for coming thence

90   My son is lost, and, in my rate, she too,

    Who is so far from Italy removed

    I ne'er again shall see her. O thou mine heir

    Of Naples and of Milan, what strange fish

    Hath made his meal on thee?

FRANCISCO.   Sir, he may live.

    I saw him beat the surges under him

    And ride upon their backs; he trod the water,

    Whose enmity he flung aside, and breasted

    The surge most swoll'n that met him; his bold head

    'Bove the contentious waves he kept, and oared

100 Himself with his good arms in lusty stroke

    To th' shore, that o'er his wave-worn basis bowed,

    As stooping to relieve him. I not doubt

    He came alive to land.

ALONSO.   No, no, he's gone.

---

78 in good time ironic: 'at long last.' **82 Bate . . . Dido** either 'except widow Dido' or 'don't mention widow Dido again.' **84 in a sort** to some extent, in some way. **85 sort** lot: Antonio's metaphor is of drawing lots. **87–8 You . . . sense** Alonso complains that he is being force-fed; *stomach* = temper, disposition; *sense* means both intention and perception. **90 rate** estimation. **94–103 Sir . . . land** The contrast of tone is important. Alonso's crudeness is answered with the high, heroic rhetoric of the Roman plays. **101 his** its; **basis** the foot of the cliff above the shore.

SEBASTIAN.

    Sir, you may thank yourself for this great loss,

    That would not bless our Europe with your daughter,

    But rather lose her to an African,

    Where she, at least, is banished from your eye,

    Who hath cause to wet the grief on't.

ALONSO.   Prithee, peace.

SEBASTIAN.

    You were kneeled to and importuned otherwise

110   By all of us, and the fair soul herself

    Weighed between loathness and obedience at

    Which end o'th' beam should bow. We have lost your son,

    I fear, for ever. Milan and Naples have

    More widows in them of this business' making

    Than we bring men to comfort them.

    The fault's your own.

ALONSO.   So is the dear'st o'th' loss.

GONZALO.

    My lord Sebastian,

    The truth you speak doth lack some gentleness,

    And time to speak it in—you rub the sore

    When you should bring the plaster.

120 SEBASTIAN.   Very well.

ANTONIO.

    And most chirurgeonly!

GONZALO (*to* ALONSO).

    It is foul weather in us all, good sir,

    When you are cloudy.

SEBASTIAN.   Foul weather?

ANTONIO.   Very foul.

GONZALO (*to* ALONSO).

    Had I plantation of this isle, my lord,—

ANTONIO.

    He'd sow't with nettle-seed.

SEBASTIAN.   Or docks, or mallows.

GONZALO.

    —And were the king on't, what would I do?

---

108 wet the grief on't weep over the sorrow of it. **109 importuned** accented on the second syllable. **111–12 Weighed . . . bow** *Weigh* is used both in its literal sense and in the sense of 'ponder, consider.' The construction is a double one, combining 'hung balanced between loathing and obedience' and 'pondered at which end of the (scale's) beam (she) should bow.' **115 Then we bring men** Sebastian assumes both their return from the island and the loss of the rest of the fleet. **121 chirurgeonly** like a surgeon. **124 plantation** the right to colonize; Antonio and Sebastian take it in the sense of 'planting.' **125 docks** 'coarse weedy herbs'; **mallows** another weed, but also another antidote for Gonzalo's nettles: mallow roots were used to make a soothing ointment.

SEBASTIAN.
  'Scape being drunk, for want of wine.
GONZALO.
  I'th' commonwealth I would by contraries
  Execute all things, for no kind of traffic
130 Would I admit; no name of magistrate;
  Letters should not be known; riches, poverty,
  And use of service, none; contract, succession,
  Bourn, bound of land, tilth, vineyard, none;
  No use of metal, corn, or wine, or oil;
  No occupation, all men idle, all,
  And women too, but innocent and pure;
  No sovereignty—
SEBASTIAN.   Yet he would be king on't.
ANTONIO. The latter end of his commonwealth forgets the beginning.
GONZALO.
  All things in common nature should produce
140 Without sweat or endeavour. Treason, felony,
  Sword, pike, knife, gun, or need of any engine
  Would I not have, but nature should bring forth
  Of it own kind all foison, all abundance
  To feed my innocent people.
SEBASTIAN.
  No marrying 'mong his subjects?
ANTONIO.
  None, man, all idle—whores and knaves.
GONZALO.
  I would with such perfection govern, sir,
  T'excel the golden age.
SEBASTIAN. 'Save his majesty!
150 ANTONIO. Long live Gonzalo!
GONZALO. And—do you mark me, sir?
ALONSO.
  Prithee no more. Thou dost talk nothing to me.

128–48 This passage is closely related to a section of Montaigne's essay 'Of the Cannibals' in John Florio's translation (1603). **128 by contraries** in a manner opposite to what is usual. **129 traffic** commerce. **131 Letters** literature, erudition. **132 use of service** keeping servants; **succession** inheritance. **133 Bourn, bound of land** These are synonyms, like 'foison' and 'abundance'; **tilth** raising crops. **134 corn . . . oil** Noble (p. 80) points to an echo of the version of Psalm 4:8 in the Psalter of the *Book of Common Prayer*: '. . . since the time that their corn, and wine, and oil, increased.' **135–6 idle . . . but innocent and pure** countering the proverb 'Idleness begets lust.' **139 in common** for communal use. **139 Without sweat** The prelapsarian qualities implied in Montaigne become explicit in Gonzalo's commonwealth: compare Genesis 3:19. **141 engine** 'A machine or instrument used in warfare.' **143 it** its; **foison** plenty, abundance, specifically a 'plentiful crop or harvest.' **145 No marrying** presumably not: marriage is a 'contract' (l. 149), and irrelevant to 'innocent people' (l. 162). **149 'Save** for 'God save,' possibly shortened in deference to the statute forbidding oaths.

GONZALO. I do well believe your highness, and did it to minister occasion to these gentlemen, who are of such sensible and nimble lungs that they always use to laugh at nothing.

ANTONIO. 'Twas you we laughed at.

GONZALO. Who in this kind of merry fooling am nothing to you; so you may continue, and laugh at nothing still.

ANTONIO. What a blow was there given!

160 SEBASTIAN. An it had not fall'n flat-long.

GONZALO. You are gentlemen of brave mettle; you would lift the moon out of her sphere if she would continue in it five weeks without changing.

Enter ARIEL *invisible, playing solemn music*

SEBASTIAN. We would so, and then go a-bat-fowling.

ANTONIO. Nay, good my lord, be not angry.

GONZALO. No, I warrant you, I will not adventure my discretion so weakly. Will you laugh me asleep, for I am very heavy?

ANTONIO. Go sleep, and hear us.

All sleep except ALONSO, SEBASTIAN, *and* ANTONIO

ALONSO.
What, all so soon asleep? I wish mine eyes
Would, with themselves, shut up my thoughts. I find
They are inclined to do so.

170 SEBASTIAN. Please you, sir,
Do not omit the heavy offer of it.
It seldom visits sorrow; when it doth,
It is a comforter.

ANTONIO. We two, my lord,
Will guard your person while you take your rest,
And watch your safety.

ALONSO. Thank you. Wondrous heavy.

ALONSO *sleeps. Exit* ARIEL

---

153 minister occasion provide an opportunity (to laugh). **154 sensible** sensitive; **use** are accustomed. **160 An** if; **flat-long** on the flat of the sword, hence harmlessly. **161 mettle** the same word as *metal* (F's spelling is 'mettal'), continuing Sebastian's sword metaphor. **161–2 you would lift . . . changing** (a) You would try to steal the moon if it held still long enough; (b) the moon would have to stop changing before you would do anything extraordinary. The retort probably alludes to the proverb 'The moon keeps her course for all the dogs' barking': Gonzalo sneers at the two courtiers' arrogance and ineffectuality. **163 a-bat-fowling** (a) 'the catching of birds by night when at roost,' here using the moon as a lantern; 'swindling, victimizing the simple.' **165 adventure my discretion so weakly** put my good judgment at risk by such weak behaviour. **166 heavy** sleepy. **167 Go . . . as** 'Compose yourself for sleep, and we will do our part by laughing.' **171 omit** disregard; **heavy** here including the sense 'serious.'

SEBASTIAN.
  What a strange drowsiness possesses them!
ANTONIO.
  It is the quality o'th' climate.
SEBASTIAN.   Why
  Doth it not then our eyelids sink? I find not
  Myself disposed to sleep.
ANTONIO.   Nor I; my spirits are nimble.
180 They fell together all, as by consent;
  They dropped as by a thunder-stroke. What might,
  Worthy Sebastian, O what might—? No more.
  And yet methinks I see it in thy face,
  What thou shouldst be. Th' occasion speaks thee, and
  My strong imagination sees a crown
  Dropping upon thy head.
SEBASTIAN.   What? Art thou waking?
ANTONIO.
  Do you not hear me speak?
SEBASTIAN.   I do, and surely
  It is a sleepy language, and thou speak'st
  Out of thy sleep. What is it thou didst say?
190 This is a strange repose, to be asleep
  With eyes wide open—standing, speaking, moving,
  And yet so fast asleep.
ANTONIO.   Noble Sebastian,
  Thou let'st thy fortune sleep—die, rather; wink'st
  Whiles thou art waking.
SEBASTIAN.   Thou dost snore distinctly.
  There's meaning in thy snores.
ANTONIO.
  I am more serious than my custom. You
  Must be so too, if heed me; which to do
  Trebles thee o'er.
SEBASTIAN.   Well? I am standing water.
ANTONIO.
  I'll teach you how to flow.
SEBASTIAN.   Do so—to ebb
  Hereditary sloth instructs me.
200 ANTONIO.   O!

---

180 consent common agreement, consensus.   **184 Th'occasion speaks thee** the opportunity proclaims to
thee.   **186 waking** awake.   **193 wink'st** you close your eyes (to this opportunity).   **194 distinctly** articu-
lately, 'so as to be clearly perceived or understood.'   **198 Trebles thee o'er** makes thee three times greater.
198 standing water i.e. waiting to be moved.   **199–200 to ebb . . . me** (a) My natural laziness prompts me
to withdraw; (b) The idleness imposed on me by my birth (i.e. by being Alonso's younger brother) teaches me to
hold back.

If you but knew how you the purpose cherish
Whiles thus you mock it, how in stripping it
You more invest it—ebbing men, indeed,
Most often do so near the bottom run
By their own fear or sloth.

SEBASTIAN.   Prithee say on.
The setting of thine eye and cheek proclaim
A matter from thee, and a birth, indeed,
Which throes thee much to yield.

ANTONIO.   Thus, sir:
Although this lord of weak remembrance, this,
210   Who shall be of as little memory
When he is earthed, hath here almost persuaded—
For he's a spirit of persuasion, only
Professes to persuade—the King his son's alive,
'Tis as impossible that he's undrowned
As he that sleeps here swims.

SEBASTIAN.   I have no hope
That he's undrowned.

ANTONIO.   O, out of that no hope
What great hope have you! No hope that way is
Another way so high a hope that even
Ambition cannot pierce a wink beyond,
220   But doubt discovery there. Will you grant with me
That Ferdinand is drowned?

SEBASTIAN.   He's gone.

ANTONIO.   Then tell me,
Who's the next heir of Naples?

SEBASTIAN.   Claribel.

ANTONIO.
She that is Queen of Tunis; she that dwells
Ten leagues beyond man's life; she that from Naples
Can have no note unless the sun were post—

201–2 If . . . mock it 'If you only understood your true feelings, realized that your mockery reveals how great your desire is.'   **202–3 in stripping it | You more invest it** The more you put it off the more important it becomes to you. *Invest* suggests a ceremonial robing.   **206 setting** fixed expression, 'set.'   **207 A matter** something important.   **208 throes thee much to yield** gives you much pain to produce.   **209 of weak remembrance** whose memory is weak (alluding presumably to l. 155).   **211 earthed** buried.   **212 spirit of persuasion** quintessentially a persuader.   **212–3 only | Professes to persuade** giving counsel is his sole profession.   **219–20 Ambition . . . there** The sense is that ambition cannot conceive of anything higher than the hope of a crown, but the syntax is confused, and when Antonio says that 'ambition cannot *but* doubt discovery' he is in fact saying the opposite of what the meaning requires.   **219 pierce a wink** catch a glimpse.   **224 Ten leagues beyond man's life** i.e. farther than a man can travel in a lifetime. A league was a variable measure, usually about 3 miles, 'never in regular use in England, but often occurring in poetical or rhetorical statements of distance.' Compare Antonio's use of 'cubit,' l. 234. The actual distance from Tunis to Naples is about 300 miles.   **225 note** information;   **post** messenger.

The man i' th' moon's too slow—till newborn chins
Be rough and razorable; she that from whom
We all were sea-swallowed, though some cast again—
And by that destiny, to perform an act
230   Whereof what's past is prologue, what to come
In yours and my discharge.
SEBASTIAN.   What stuff is this? How say you?
'Tis true my brother's daughter's Queen of Tunis,
So is she heir of Naples, 'twixt which regions
There is some space.
ANTONIO.   A space whose every cubit
Seems to cry out, 'How shall that Claribel
Measure us back to Naples? Keep in Tunis,
And let Sebastian wake.' Say this were death
That now hath seized them, why, they were no worse
Than now they are. There be that can rule Naples
240   As well as he that sleeps, lords that can prate
As amply and unnecessarily
As this Gonzalo; I myself could make
A chough of as deep chat. O, that you bore
The mind that I do, what a sleep were this
For your advancement! Do you understand me?
SEBASTIAN.
Methinks I do.
ANTONIO.   And how does your content
Tender your own good fortune?
SEBASTIAN.   I remember
You did supplant your brother Prospero.
ANTONIO.   True;
And look how well my garments sit upon me,
250   Much feater than before. My brother's servants
Were then my fellows, now they are my men.
SEBASTIAN. But for your conscience?

---

226 moon's too slow The point is that the moon requires a month to complete its cycle, whereas the sun takes only a day.   **227 from** coming from.   **228 cast** cast up (on shore); the word is also apparently related to the theatrical metaphor of ll. 228. *Cast* in the sense of 'assign parts in a play' is not recorded by the *OED* before the eighteenth century.   **229 And by that destiny** F's parentheses make Johnson's emendation, 'And that by destiny,' attractive. But Antonio's argument is not merely that they were cast up by destiny, but that destiny has also singled them out to perform the murders he is proposing.   **231 discharge** performance.   **234 cubit** a measure originally derived from the length of the forearm, 'varying at different times and places, but usually about 18–22 inches.' Compare 'league,' l. 224.   **236 Measure us** traverse us (cubits);   **Keep** stay.   **237 wake** Compare ll. 214–15.   **242–3 I . . . chat** I could teach a jackdaw to speak as profoundly as he does. *Chough:* 'a bird of the crow family, formerly applied somewhat widely to all the smaller chattering species, but especially to the common jackdaw.'   **246 content** liking.   **247 Tender** regard with either favour or fear. The question is, are you inclined to look favourably on your good fortune or not?   **250 feater** i.e. they suit me better.

ANTONIO.
    Ay, sir, where lies that? If 'twere a kibe
    'Twould put me to my slipper, but I feel not
    This deity in my bosom. Twenty consciences
    That stand 'twixt me and Milan, candied be they,
    And melt ere they molest! Here lies your brother,
    No better than the earth he lies upon,
    If he were that which now he's like—that's dead—
260   Whom I with this obedient steel, three inches of it,
    Can lay to bed for ever; whiles you, doing thus,
    To the perpetual wink for aye might put
    This ancient morsel, this Sir Prudence, who
    Should not upbraid our course. For all the rest,
    They'll take suggestion as a cat laps milk;
    They'll tell the clock to any business that
    We say befits the hour.
SEBASTIAN.   Thy case, dear friend,
    Shall be my precedent: as thou got'st Milan,
    I'll come by Naples. Draw thy sword—one stroke
270   Shall free thee from the tribute which thou payest,
    And I the King shall love thee.
ANTONIO.   Draw together,
    And when I rear my hand do you the like
    To fall it on Gonzalo.
SEBASTIAN.   O, but one word.

    They talk apart.

    Enter ARIEL, *invisible, with music and song*

ARIEL.
    My master through his art foresees the danger
    That you, his friend, are in, and sends me forth—
    For else his project dies—to keep them living.

253–5 If . . . bosom If it were a chilblain (kibe) on my heel it would force me to wear a slipper, but conscience causes me no inner discomfort. **256 candied** The sense is probably 'congealed, frozen solid,' rather than 'turned to sugar, glazed.' **257 melt** possibly an apocope for 'melted'; **molest** interfere with me. **261 doing thus** Antonio mimes stabbing Gonzalo. **262 To . . . put** might put to sleep forever. **263 morsel** choice dish. **265 suggestion** 'prompting or incitement to evil'; **as . . . milk** i.e. naturally and eagerly. **266–7 tell . . . hour** say it is time to do whatever business we say is apropos. **273.2 invisible, with music** Ariel is no longer dressed as a water nymph; *invisible* implies nothing about his costume, but only that the other characters cannot see him. *With music* may mean that he carries an instrument on which to accompany himself in the song, as he did at 1.2.374, or it may mean that he is accompanied by a musical consort—compare the music that Ferdinand hears 'above me,' 1.2.408. **274–6 My master . . . living** Ariel acts briefly as a chorus. The lines are addressed not to the sleeping Gonzalo but to the audience (the song that wakes Gonzalo is perceived by him only as 'a humming,' l. 294). **276 project** The word combines the meanings of both scheme and purpose.

He sings in GONZALO's *ear*

> While you here do snoring lie,
> Open-eyed conspiracy
>   His time doth take.
> If of life you keep a care,
> Shake off slumber, and beware.
>   Awake, awake!

280

ANTONIO.
    Then let us both be sudden.
GONZALO (*waking*).   Now, good angels
    Preserve the King!

The others wake

ALONSO.
    Why, how now, ho! Awake? Why are you drawn?
    Wherefore this ghastly looking?
GONZALO.   What's the matter?
SEBASTIAN.
    Whiles we stood here securing your repose,
    Even now, we heard a hollow burst of bellowing,
    Like bulls, or rather lions—did't not wake you?
    It struck mine ear most terribly.

290

ALONSO.   I heard nothing.
ANTONIO.
    O, 'twas a din to fright a monster's ear,
    To make an earthquake. Sure, it was the roar
    Of a whole herd of lions.
ALONSO.   Heard you this, Gonzalo?
GONZALO.
    Upon mine honour, sir, I heard a humming,
    And that a strange one too, which did awake me.
    I shaked you, sir, and cried. As mine eyes opened
    I saw their weapons drawn. There was a noise,
    That's verily. 'Tis best we stand upon our guard,
    Or that we quit this place. Let's draw our weapons.
ALONSO.

300

    Lead off this ground, and let's make further search
    For my poor son.
GONZALO.   Heavens keep him from these beasts!
    For he is sure i' th' island.
ALONSO.   Lead away.

———————

286 ghastly full of fear.   **287 securing** guarding.

ARIEL.
Prospero my lord shall know what I have done.
So, King, go safely on to seek thy son.   *Exeunt*

2.2   *Enter* CALIBAN *with a burden of wood*

CALIBAN.
All the infections that the sun sucks up
From bogs, fens, flats, on Prosper fall, and make him
By inchmeal a disease!

    A noise of thunder heard

               His spirits hear me,
And yet I needs must curse. But they'll nor pinch,
Fright me with urchin-shows, pitch me i'th' mire,
Nor lead me like a firebrand in the dark
Out of my way, unless he bid 'em; but
For every trifle are they set upon me,
Sometime like apes that mow and chatter at me,
10   And after bite me; then like hedgehogs, which
Lie tumbling in my barefoot way, and mount
Their pricks at my footfall; sometime am I
All wound with adders, who with cloven tongues
Do hiss me into madness—
    Enter TRINCULO   Lo, now, lo,
Here comes a spirit of his, and to torment me
For bringing wood in slowly. I'll fall flat.
Perchance he will not mind me.

    He lies down and covers himself with his cloak

TRINCULO. Here's neither bush nor shrub to bear off any weather at all, and another
    storm brewing—I hear it sing i' th' wind. Yon same black cloud, yon huge one, looks
20   like a foul bombard that would shed his liquor. If it should thunder as it did before, I
    know not where to hide my head—yon same cloud cannot choose but fall by pailfuls.

---

304 *Exeunt* Ariel probably departs in a different direction from the rest.
2.2.2 flats swamps.   **3 By inchmeal** inch by inch.   **5 urchin-shows** goblin shows; apparitions in the shape
of hedgehogs (compare 1.2.326–8 and 2.2.10).   **6 firebrand** literally a piece of wood kindled at the fire; not
recorded as a term for a will-o'-the-wisp. Shakespeare's use is metaphorical.   **9 mow** make mouths or gri-
maces.   **10 like hedgehogs** the *urchin-shows* of l. 5.   **13 wound with** entwined by.   **14 Trinculo** The
name is related to Italian *trincare*, drink deeply, and *trincone*, a drunkard.   **17 mind** notice.   **18 bear off**
keep off.   **21 bombard** the earliest kind of cannon, and thence 'a leather jug or bottle for liquor . . . probably
from some resemblance to the early cannons.' The connotation of offensive weaponry is still clearly present in
Shakespeare's usage.

What have we here—a man or a fish?—dead or alive? A fish, he smells like a fish; a very ancient and fish-like smell; a kind of not-of-the-newest poor-John. A strange fish! Were I in England now, as once I was, and had but this fish painted, not a holiday-fool there but would give a piece of silver. There would this monster make a man—any strange beast there makes a man. When they will not give a doit to relieve a lame beggar, they will lay out ten to see a dead Indian. Legged like a man, and his fins like arms! Warm, o'my troth! I do now let loose my opinion, hold it no longer: this is no fish, but an islander, that hath lately suffered by a thunderbolt. (*Thunder*) Alas, the
30 storm is come again! My best way is to creep under his gaberdine—there is no other shelter hereabout. Misery acquaints a man with strange bedfellows. I will here shroud till the dregs of the storm be past.

> *He crawls under* CALIBAN's *cloak*

> *Enter* STEPHANO *singing, a bottle in his hand*

STEPHANO.
> I shall no more to sea, to sea,
> Here shall I die ashore—

This is a very scurvy tune to sing at a man's funeral.
Well, here's my comfort. (*Drinks*)

(*Sings*)

> The master, the swabber, the boatswain, and I,
> The gunner, and his mate,
> Loved Moll, Meg, and Marian, and Margery,
40 > But none of us cared for Kate;
> For she had a tongue with a tang,
> Would cry to a sailor, 'Go hang!'
> She loved not the savour of tar nor of pitch,
> Yet a tailor might scratch her where'er she did itch.
> Then to sea, boys, and let her go hang!

This is a scurvy tune too, but here's my comfort.

> *He drinks*

CALIBAN. Do not torment me! O!

---

23 poor-John dried, salted fish; poor food.   **24 had . . . painted** on a sign, to attract spectators.   **25 make a man** both 'make a man's fortune' and 'be considered a man.'   **26 doit** a coin of small value, originally equivalent to half a farthing.   **27 a dead Indian** The display of New-World natives, living and dead, had been a popular and lucrative enterprise since the early sixteenth century. Sir Martin Frobisher brought back and exhibited live Indians in 1576 and 1577. **29 suffered** perished. **30 gaberdine** cloak of coarse cloth. **31 Misery . . . bedfellows** not recorded as a proverb. **32 dregs** continuing the 'bombard' metaphor of l. 20. **37 swabber** seaman who cleans the decks. **41 tang** sting; originally 'the tongue of a serpent, formerly thought to be a stinging organ.' **44 tailor** Tailors were conventionally supposed to be unmanly; **scratch . . . itch** implying the gratification of sensual desire.

STEPHANO. What's the matter? Have we devils here? Do you put tricks upon's with savages and men of Ind? Ha? I have not scaped drowning to be afeard now of your four
50   legs; for it hath been said, 'As proper a man as ever went on four legs cannot make
him give ground'; and it shall be said so again, while Stephano breathes at' nostrils.
CALIBAN. The spirit torments me! O!
STEPHANO. This is some monster of the isle with four legs, who hath got, as I take it, an
ague. Where the devil should he learn our language? I will give him some relief, if it
be but for that. If I can recover him, and keep him tame, and get to Naples with him,
he's a present for any emperor that ever trod on neat's-leather.
CALIBAN. Do not torment me, prithee! I'll bring my wood home faster.
STEPHANO. He's in his fit now, and does not talk after the wisest. He shall taste of my
bottle. If he have never drunk wine afore, it will go near to remove his fit. If I can
60   recover him and keep him tame, I will not take too much for him; he shall pay for him
that hath him, and that soundly.
CALIBAN. Thou dost me yet but little hurt; thou wilt anon, I know it by thy trembling.
Now Prosper works upon thee.
STEPHANO. Come on your ways. Open your mouth—here is that which will give language to you, cat. Open your mouth—this will shake your shaking, I can tell you, and
that soundly. (CALIBAN *drinks*) You cannot tell who's your friend—open your chops
again.
TRINCULO. I should know that voice. It should be—but he is drowned, and these are
devils—O defend me!
70   STEPHANO. Four legs and two voices; a most delicate monster! His forward voice now is
to speak well of his friend, his backward voice is to utter foul speeches and to detract.
If all the wine in my bottle will recover him, I will help his ague. Come. (CALIBAN
drinks again) Amen! I will pour some in thy other mouth.
TRINCULO. Stephano!
STEPHANO. Doth thy other mouth call me? Mercy, mercy! This is a devil, and no monster. I will leave him; I have no long spoon.
TRINCULO. Stephano! If thou beest Stephano, touch me, and speak to me; for I am
Trinculo—be not afeard—thy good friend Trinculo.
STEPHANO. If thou beest Trinculo, come forth. I'll pull thee by the lesser legs—if any be
80   Trinculo's legs, these are they. (*Pulls him from under the cloak*) Thou art very Trinculo
indeed! How cam'st thou to be the siege of this mooncalf? Can he vent Trinculos?

---

48 What's the matter? What's going on?   **48 Do . . . upon's** 'To put a trick upon' someone was proverbial.
50–1 As . . . ground The proverbial formula is 'As good a man as ever went on two legs,' but Stephano adapts
it to the four-legged monster he sees.   **54 ague** Commonly used for the shivering stage of fever, hence any fit
of shaking or quaking, as Caliban is doing under his gaberdine.   **55 recover** cure.   **56 neat's-leather**
cowhide.   **58 after the wisest** in the wisest fashion.   **59 go near** to do much to.   **60 I will not take too**
much for him No price will be too high for him.   **62 thy trembling** Trinculo is now quaking with fear.
64–5 here . . . cat the proverbial 'liquor that would make a cat speak.'   **66 Your . . . friend** Presumably Caliban dislikes his first taste.   **70 delicate** exquisitely made.   **72 If . . . him** if it takes all the wine in my bottle
to cure him.   **75 call me** speak my name (implying supernatural knowledge).   **76 I . . . spoon** The proverb
is 'He must have a long spoon that will eat with the devil.'   **81 siege** excrement;   **mooncalf** monstrosity (regarded as having been produced by the influence of the moon at its birth); also a 'born fool';   **vent** defecate.

TRINCULO. I took him to be killed with a thunder-stroke. But art thou not drowned, Stephano? I hope now thou art not drowned. Is the storm overblown? I hid me under the dead mooncalf's gaberdine for fear of the storm. And art thou living, Stephano? O, Stephano, two Neapolitans scaped!

STEPHANO. Prithee do not turn me about; my stomach is not constant.

CALIBAN (*aside*). These be fine things, an if they be not sprites. That's a brave god, and bears celestial liquor. I will kneel to him.

STEPHANO. How didst thou scape? How cam'st thou hither? Swear by this bottle how
90   thou cam'st hither—I escaped upon a butt of sack which the sailors heaved o'er-board—by this bottle, which I made of the bark of a tree with mine own hands since I was cast ashore.

CALIBAN. I'll swear upon that bottle to be thy true subject, for the liquor is not earthly.

STEPHANO. Here; swear then how thou escaped'st.

TRINCULO. Swum ashore, man, like a duck. I can swim like a duck, I'll be sworn.

STEPHANO. Here, kiss the book. (*He gives* TRINCULO *the bottle*)
Though thou canst swim like a duck, thou art made like a goose.

TRINCULO. O Stephano, hast any more of this?

STEPHANO. The whole butt, man. My cellar is in a rock by the seaside, where my wine
100   is hid. How now, mooncalf, how does thine ague?

CALIBAN. Hast thou not dropped from heaven?

STEPHANO. Out o' th' moon, I do assure thee. I was the man i' th' moon when time was.

CALIBAN. I have seen thee in her, and I do adore thee. My mistress showed me thee, and thy dog and thy bush.

STEPHANO. Come, swear to that: kiss the book. I will furnish it anon with new contents. Swear.

CALIBAN *drinks*

TRINCULO. By this good light, this is a very shallow monster. I afeard of him? A very weak monster! The man i' th' moon? A most poor, credulous monster! Well drawn, monster, in good sooth!
110   CALIBAN. I'll show thee every fertile inch o' th' island—and I will kiss thy foot. I prithee be my god.

---

86 turn me about Presumably Stephano, in his relief, is attempting a kind of dance with Trinculo. **87 sprites, celestial liquor** It is tempting to see throughout this scene a continuing play on 'spirits' as liquor produced by distillation. The term in this precise sense seems not to have been in use until the later seventeenth century. **87 That's a brave god** Caliban's reaction to Stephano parallels Miranda's to Ferdinand ('a thing divine') and Ferdinand's to Miranda ('most sure, the goddess . . .'), 1.2.419 ff. **90 sack** The term was applied to any of a variety of white wines imported from Spain and the Canary Islands. **94 Here . . . escaped'st** Stephano ignores Caliban until l. 99. **96 kiss the book** alluding both to kissing the Bible to confirm an oath and to the proverbial 'Kiss the cup.' **97 goose** Referring to Trinculo's posture as he drinks, but also, the term was a byword for giddiness and unsteadiness on the feet. **102–4 man . . . bush** The man, according to the folktale, was banished to the moon, variously for stealing a bundle of kindling (his thorn bush), or for gathering kindling on the sabbath. Belief in the man in the moon was energetically attacked by reforming zealots in the fifteenth century, and later by Puritans. **102 when time was** once upon a time. **107 this good light** i.e. the sun. **108 Well drawn** a good draft, well drunk. **110 I'll . . . island** as he had done for Prospero: compare 1.2.337 ff.

TRINCULO. By this light, a most perfidious and drunken monster. When's god's asleep, he'll rob his bottle.

CALIBAN. I'll kiss thy foot. I'll swear myself thy subject.

STEPHANO. Come on, then, down and swear.

TRINCULO. I shall laugh myself to death at this puppy-headed monster. A most scurvy monster! I could find in my heart to beat him—

STEPHANO. Come, kiss.

TRINCULO. —But that the poor monster's in drink. An abominable monster!

CALIBAN.

120   I'll show thee the best springs; I'll pluck thee berries;
       I'll fish for thee, and get thee wood enough.
       A plague upon the tyrant that I serve!
       I'll bear him no more sticks, but follow thee,
       Thou wondrous man.

TRINCULO. A most ridiculous monster, to make a wonder of a poor drunkard!

CALIBAN.

       I prithee let me bring thee where crabs grow,
       And I with my long nails will dig thee pig-nuts,
       Show thee a jay's nest, and instruct thee how
       To snare the nimble marmoset. I'll bring thee
130   To clust'ring filberts, and sometimes I'll get thee
       Young scamels from the rock. Wilt thou go with me?

STEPHANO. I prithee now lead the way without any more talking. Trinculo, the King and all our company else being drowned, we will inherit here. (*To* CALIBAN) Here, bear my bottle. Fellow Trinculo, we'll fill him by and by again.

CALIBAN. [*sings drunkenly*] Farewell, master, farewell, farewell!

TRINCULO. A howling monster; a drunken monster!

CALIBAN. No more dams I'll make for fish,
            Nor fetch in firing
            At requiring,
140   Nor scrape trenchering, nor wash dish:
            'Ban, 'Ban, Ca-Caliban
       Has a new master—get a new man!
       Freedom, high-day! High-day, freedom! Freedom, high-day, freedom!

STEPHANO. O brave monster! Lead the way!   *Exeunt*

124–5 wondrous . . . wonder Caliban's reaction to Stephano again parallels Ferdinand's to Miranda: compare 'O you wonder,' 1.2.427.   **126 crabs** Shakespeare uses the word for both crabapples and crustaceans.   **127 pig-nuts** edible tubers (*burnium flexuosum*), also called earth-nuts and earth chestnuts.   **128 jay's nest** Jays were prized for their plumage, and the nests tend to be well hidden.   **129 marmoset** a small monkey, common as a pet.   **130 filberts** hazelnuts.   **131 scamels** This creature has provoked endless debate. The context requires a crustacean, bird, or a fish of the sort 'frequenting rocks . . . , such as the black goby or sea-gudgeon, the striped bass, the wrasse, etc.'   **138 firing** firewood.   **140 trenchering** trenchers collectively (a sense not recorded elsewhere).   **141 'Ban** abbreviating Caliban.   **142 get a new man** addressed to the old master, Prospero.   **143 high-day** holiday.

3.1 *Enter* Ferdinand *bearing a log.*

Ferdinand.

    There be some sports are painful, and their labour
    Delight in them set off; some kinds of baseness
    Are nobly undergone; and most poor matters
    Point to rich ends. This my mean task
    Would be as heavy to me, as odious, but
    The mistress which I serve quickens what's dead,
    And makes my labours pleasures. O, she is
    Ten times more gentle than her father's crabbed,
    And he's composed of harshness. I must remove
10   Some thousands of these logs and pile them up,
    Upon a sore injunction. My sweet mistress
    Weeps when she sees me work, and says such baseness
    Had never like executor. I forget.
    But these sweet thoughts do even refresh my labours,
    Most busil'est when I do it.

      Enter Miranda *and* Prospero *at a distance, unseen*

Miranda.   Alas, now pray you
    Work not so hard. I would the lightning had
    Burnt up those logs that you are enjoined to pile!
    Pray set it down, and rest you. When this burns,
    'Twill weep for having wearied you. My father
20   Is hard at study. Pray now, rest yourself;
    He's safe for these three hours.
Ferdinand.   O most dear mistress,
    The sun will set before I shall discharge
    What I must strive to do.
Miranda.   If you'll sit down
    I'll bear your logs the while. Pray give me that;
    I'll carry it to the pile.
Ferdinand.   No, precious creature,
    I had rather crack my sinews, break my back,
    Than you should such dishonour undergo
    While I sit lazy by.
Miranda.   It would become me
    As well as it does you, and I should do it
30   With much more ease, for my good will is to it,

---

3 most poor poorest.   **4 mean** lowly.   **5 but** except that.   **11 sore** harsh.   **12–13 such . . . executor** Such base labour was never performed by one so noble.   **13 I forget** i.e. to work at my task.   **14–15 these . . . do it** My thoughts of Miranda are most active when I am busiest at my work.   **19 'Twill weep** by exuding resin.   **21 He's safe** i.e. we are safe from him.

And yours it is against.

PROSPERO (*aside*).   Poor worm, thou art infected!
This visitation shows it.

MIRANDA.   You look wearily.

FERDINAND.
No, noble mistress, 'tis fresh morning with me
When you are by at night. I do beseech you—
Chiefly that I might set it in my prayers—
What is your name?

MIRANDA.   Miranda.—O my father,
I have broke your hest to say so.

FERDINAND.   Admired Miranda,
Indeed the top of admiration, worth
What's dearest to the world! Full many a lady
40   I have eyed with best regard, and many a time
Th' harmony of their tongues hath into bondage
Brought my too diligent ear. For several virtues
Have I liked several women, never any
With so full soul but some defect in her
Did quarrel with the noblest grace she owed,
And put it to the foil. But you, O you,
So perfect and so peerless, are created
Of every creature's best.

MIRANDA.   I do not know
One of my sex, no woman's face remember,
50   Save from my glass, mine own; nor have I seen
More that I may call men than you, good friend,
And my dear father. How features are abroad
I am skilless of; but by my modesty,
The jewel in my dower, I would not wish
Any companion in the world but you;
Nor can imagination form a shape
Besides yourself to like of. But I prattle
Something too wildly, and my father's precepts
I therein do forget.

FERDINAND.   I am, in my condition,

---

31 worm any small creature; used variously to express affection, as here, or contempt; also, a source of infection.   **32 visitation** punning both on the sense of 'plague' and on the pastoral or charitable visit to the sick.
37 hest command;   **Admired Miranda** punning on her name.   **39 dearest** most valuable.   **42 diligent** attentive.   **42, 43 several** various, different.   **45 owed** owned.   **46 put it to the foil** either foiled it, overthrew it, or, taken with *quarrel* (l. 45), challenged it, as at a fencing match.   **47–8 So . . . best** 'Alluding to the picture of Venus by Apelles': this was a synthesis of the most perfect features of the most beautiful women the painter could find.   **48 creature** created being.   **52–3 How . . . of** I do not know what people look like elsewhere.   **53 skilless** ignorant.   **modesty** virginity.   **54 dower** (here) dowry.   **59 condition** rank.

60   A prince, Miranda; I do think a king—
     I would not so!—and would no more endure
     This wooden slavery than to suffer
     The flesh-fly blow my mouth. Hear my soul speak:
     The very instant that I saw you did
     My heart fly to your service, there resides
     To make me slave to it, and for your sake
     Am I this patient log-man.
MIRANDA.   Do you love me?
FERDINAND.
     O heaven, O earth, bear witness to this sound,
     And crown what I profess with kind event
70   If I speak true; if hollowly, invert
     What best is boded me to mischief: I,
     Beyond all limit of what else i' th' world,
     Do love, prize, honour you.
MIRANDA.   I am a fool
     To weep at what I am glad of.
PROSPERO (*aside*).   Fair encounter
     Of two most rare affections! Heavens rain grace
     On that which breeds between 'em!
FERDINAND.   Wherefore weep you?
MIRANDA.
     At mine unworthiness, that dare not offer
     What I desire to give, and much less take
     What I shall die to want. But this is trifling,
80   And all the more it seeks to hide itself,
     The bigger bulk it shows. Hence, bashful cunning,
     And prompt me, plain and holy innocence!
     I am your wife if you will marry me;
     If not, I'll die your maid. To be your fellow
     You may deny me, but I'll be your servant
     Whether you will or no.
FERDINAND.   My mistress, dearest,
     And I thus humble ever.

     He kneels

---

61 would not wish it were not.   **63 flesh-fly** fly that deposits its eggs in dead flesh;   **blow** corrupt ('said of flies and other insects: to deposit eggs.'   **69 event** outcome.   **70 hollowly** insincerely, falsely.   **70–1 invert . . . mischief** turn whatever good fortune is foretold for me to evil.   **72 what** whatever.   **77–81 that dare not offer . . . cunning** The *offer* is unconsciously sexual; with *this is trifling* Miranda realizes her indiscretion, acknowledges the *bashful cunning* (81) of her language, and undertakes to confront its implications.   **79 want** lack.   **81 bashful cunning** dissimulating bashfulness.   **84 maid** (a) virgin; (b) servant.   **86 mistress** 'A woman who has command over a man's heart,' in this context without illicit overtones.

MIRANDA. My husband then?
FERDINAND.   Ay, with a heart as willing
   As bondage e'er of freedom. Here's my hand.
MIRANDA.
90   And mine, with my heart in't. And now farewell
   Till half an hour hence.
FERDINAND.   A thousand-thousand!

Exeunt FERDINAND *and* MIRANDA *separately*

PROSPERO.
   So glad of this as they I cannot be,
   Who are surprised withal, but my rejoicing
   At nothing can be more. I'll to my book,
   For yet ere suppertime must I perform
   Much business appertaining.   *Exit*

3.2   *Enter* CALIBAN, STEPHANO, *and* TRINCULO

STEPHANO (*to* TRINCULO). Tell not me. When the butt is out, we will drink water; not a
   drop before. Therefore bear up and board 'em: servant-monster, drink to me.
TRINCULO. Servant-monster! The folly of this island! They say there's but five upon this
   isle: we are three of them; if th' other two be brained like us, the state totters.
STEPHANO. Drink, servant-monster, when I bid thee. Thy eyes are almost set in thy
   head.
TRINCULO. Where should they be set else? He were a brave monster indeed if they
   were set in his tail!
STEPHANO. My man-monster hath drowned his tongue in sack. For my part, the sea
10   cannot drown me: I swam, ere I could recover the shore, five and thirty leagues off
   and on, by this light. Thou shalt be my lieutenant-monster, or my standard.
TRINCULO. Your lieutenant if you list; he's no standard.
STEPHANO. We'll not run, Monsieur Monster.
TRINCULO. Nor go neither; but you'll lie like dogs, and yet say nothing neither.
STEPHANO. Mooncalf, speak once in thy life, if thou beest a good mooncalf.
CALIBAN. How does thy honour? Let me lick thy shoe. I'll not serve him, he is not
   valiant.

---

88 willing desirous.   **89–90 my hand . . . in't** 'With heart and hand' is proverbial.   **91 thousand-thousand**
i.e. a million.   **93 surprised** both astonished and caught unawares.
3.2.1 Tell not me Trinculo has been trying to moderate their drinking;   **butt is out** cask is finished.   **2 bear
up** sail up (to an enemy ship): the naval order here means 'drink up.'   **3 folly** absurdity.   **4 be brained like
us** i.e. are no more intelligent than we are.   **5 set** fixed (drunkenly).   **10 five and thirty leagues** A league
was a variable measure, usually about 3 miles; hence Stephano is claiming to have swum over 100 miles.
10–11 off and on either one way and another, or intermittently.   **12 standard** standard bearer;   **he's no
standard** i.e. he can't stand up.   **13 run** i.e. from the enemy.   **14 go walk.** Tilley cites 'He may ill run that
cannot go';   **lie** (a) lie down; (b) tell lies.

TRINCULO. Thou liest, most ignorant monster: I am in case to jostle a constable. Why
thou debauched fish, thou, was there ever man a coward that hath drunk so much sack
20   as I today? Wilt thou tell a monstrous lie, being but half a fish and half a monster?
CALIBAN. Lo, how he mocks me! Wilt thou let him, my lord?
TRINCULO. 'Lord', quoth he? That a monster should be such a natural!
CALIBAN. Lo, lo again! Bite him to death, I prithee.
STEPHANO. Trinculo, keep a good tongue in your head. If you prove a mutineer, the
next tree! The poor monster's my subject, and he shall not suffer indignity.
CALIBAN. I thank my noble lord. Wilt thou be pleased to hearken once again to the suit
I made to thee?
STEPHANO. Marry, will I. Kneel and repeat it. I will stand, and so shall Trinculo.

Enter ARIEL, *invisible*

CALIBAN. As I told thee before, I am subject to a tyrant, a sorcerer that by his cunning
30   hath cheated me of the island.
ARIEL. Thou liest.
CALIBAN (*to* TRINCULO). Thou liest, thou jesting monkey, thou! I would my valiant
master would destroy thee! I do not lie.
STEPHANO. Trinculo, if you trouble him any more in's tale, by this hand, I will supplant
some of your teeth.
TRINCULO. Why, I said nothing.
STEPHANO. Mum, then, and no more.—Proceed.
CALIBAN.
I say by sorcery he got this isle;
From me he got it. If thy greatness will
40   Revenge it on him—for I know thou dar'st,
But this thing dare not—
STEPHANO. That's most certain.
CALIBAN. Thou shalt be lord of it, and I'll serve thee.
STEPHANO. How now shall this be compassed? Canst thou bring me to the party?
CALIBAN.
Yea, yea, my lord. I'll yield him thee asleep,
Where thou mayst knock a nail into his head.
ARIEL. Thou liest, thou canst not.
CALIBAN.
What a pied ninny's this! Thou scurvy patch!
I do beseech thy greatness, give him blows,
50   And take his bottle from him. When that's gone,

---

18 in case prepared (i.e. drunk, and hence valiant).   **22 natural** idiot; the point of the quibble is that a
monster is by definition unnatural.   **25 the next tree** i.e. to serve as a gallows.   **34 supplant** uproot.
36–9 nothing. | Mum proverbial: 'I will say nothing but mum.'   **46 knock . . . head** on the biblical model of
Jael's murder of the sleeping Sisera (Judges 4:21).   **48 pied** Caliban alludes to Trinculo's particoloured jester's
costume;   **patch** jester, fool. The word is probably cognate with Italian *pazzo* (fool), but Shakespeare seems to
have associated it with the jester's particoloured garments.

He shall drink naught but brine, for I'll not show him
Where the quick freshes are.

STEPHANO. Trinculo, run into no further danger. Interrupt the monster one word further, and by this hand, I'll turn my mercy out o' doors and make a stockfish of thee.

TRINCULO. Why, what did I? I did nothing! I'll go farther off.

STEPHANO. Didst thou not say he lied?

ARIEL. Thou liest.

STEPHANO. Do I so? Take thou that! (*Beats* TRINCULO) As you like this, give me the lie
another time!

60   TRINCULO. I did not give the lie! Out o' your wits and hearing too? A pox o' your bottle!
This can sack and drinking do. A murrain on your monster, and the devil take your
fingers!

CALIBAN. Ha, ha, ha!

STEPHANO. Now forward with your tale. (*To* TRINCULO)
Prithee, stand further off.

CALIBAN.
Beat him enough. After a little time
I'll beat him too.

STEPHANO. Stand farther.—Come, proceed.

CALIBAN.
Why, as I told thee, 'tis a custom with him

70   I' th' afternoon to sleep. There thou mayst brain him,
Having first seized his books; or with a log
Batter his skull, or paunch him with a stake,
Or cut his weasand with thy knife. Remember
First to possess his books; for without them
He's but a sot, as I am, nor hath not
One spirit to command—they all do hate him
As rootedly as I. Burn but his books.
He has brave utensils, for so he calls them,
Which when he has a house, he'll deck withal.

80   And that most deeply to consider is
The beauty of his daughter. He himself
Calls her a nonpareil. I never saw a woman
But only Sycorax, my dam, and she;
But she as far surpasseth Sycorax
As great'st does least.

STEPHANO.   Is it so brave a lass?

---

54 stockfish dried and salted cod, beaten to tenderize it before cooking.   **58 give me the lie** call me a lair.
61 murrain plague.   **65 stand further off** i.e. further than Trinculo himself has offered to stand, l. 55.
70 There then.   **72 paunch him** stab him in the belly.   **75 sot** fool.   **78 utensils** either magical parapher-
nalia or simply household goods: l. 79 would admit of either meaning. The word was accented on the first syllable until the mid-eighteenth century.   **85 brave** good looking.

CALIBAN.
     Ay, lord, she will become thy bed, I warrant,
     And bring thee forth brave brood.
STEPHANO. Monster, I will kill this man. His daughter and I will be king and queen—
     save our graces!—and Trinculo and thyself shall be viceroys. Dost thou like the plot,
90   Trinculo?
TRINCULO. Excellent.
STEPHANO. Give me thy hand. I am sorry I beat thee. But while thou liv'st keep a good
     tongue in thy head.
CALIBAN.
     Within this half hour will he be asleep.
     Wilt thou destroy him then?
STEPHANO.   Ay, on mine honour.
ARIEL. This will I tell my master.
CALIBAN.
     Thou mak'st me merry. I am full of pleasure;
     Let us be jocund. Will you troll the catch
     You taught me but whilere?
STEPHANO.
100   At thy request, monster, I will do reason, any reason.
     Come on, Trinculo, let us sing.

          They sing

               Flout 'em and cout 'em
               And scout 'em and flout 'em,
                    Thought is free.
CALIBAN. That's not the tune.

          ARIEL *plays the tune on a tabor and pipe*

STEPHANO. What is this same?
TRINCULO. This is the tune of our catch, played by the picture of Nobody.
STEPHANO. If thou beest a man, show thyself in thy likeness.
     If thou beest a devil, take't as thou list.
110 TRINCULO. O, forgive me my sins!
STEPHANO. He that dies pays all debts. I defy thee! Mercy upon us!
CALIBAN. Art thou afeard?
STEPHANO. No, monster, not I.

---

98 troll the catch sing the round.   **99 but whilere** a little while ago.   **100 reason, any reason** anything reasonable.   **102 cout** The word must, like *flout* and *scout,* imply ridicule.   **103 scout** mock, deride. **105.1 *tabor and pipe*** A tabor is a drum that hangs at one's side, and the pipe is a tabor-pipe, designed to be played with one hand. The combination was associated with rustic dances and popular merry-making. **107 the picture of Nobody** This would, of course, be invisible. The personification of Nobody has a long history, beginning with the Cyclops episode in the *Odyssey.*   **111 Mercy upon us** Stephano's bravado collapses.

CALIBAN.
 Be not afeard, the isle is full of noises,
 Sounds, and sweet airs, that give delight and hurt not.
 Sometimes a thousand twangling instruments
 Will hum about mine ears; and sometime voices,
 That if I then had waked after long sleep,
 Will make me sleep again, and then in dreaming
120 The clouds methought would open and show riches
 Ready to drop upon me, that when I waked
 I cried to dream again.
STEPHANO. This will prove a brave kingdom to me, where I shall have my music for
 nothing.
CALIBAN. When Prospero is destroyed.
STEPHANO. That shall be by and by. I remember the story.
TRINCULO. The sound is going away. Let's follow it, and after do our work.
STEPHANO. Lead, monster, we'll follow. I would I could see this taborer; he lays on it.
TRINCULO (*to* CALIBAN). Wilt come? I'll follow Stephano.   *Exeunt*

3.3 *Enter* ALONSO, SEBASTIAN, ANTONIO, GONZALO, ADRIAN, FRANCISCO

GONZALO (*to* ALONSO).
 By'r lakin, I can go no further, sir,
 My old bones aches. Here's a maze trod indeed
 Through forth-rights and meanders! By your patience,
 I needs must rest me.
ALONSO.   Old lord, I cannot blame thee,
 Who am myself attached with weariness
 To th' dulling of my spirits. Sit down and rest.
 Even here I will put off my hope, and keep it
 No longer for my flatterer. He is drowned
 Whom thus we stray to find, and the sea mocks
10 Our frustrate search on land. Well, let him go.
ANTONIO (*aside to* SEBASTIAN).
 I am right glad that he's so out of hope.
 Do not for one repulse forgo the purpose
 That you resolved t' effect.
SEBASTIAN (*aside to* ANTONIO). The next advantage
 Will we take throughly.
ANTONIO (*aside to* SEBASTIAN). Let it be tonight;

---

116 twangling 'Describing a resonant sound of the nature of a twang, but thinner and continuous or repeated.'
The word is usually used pejoratively. **128 lays it on** i.e. bangs his drum.
3.3.1 By'r lakin by our ladykin, a mild form of 'by our Lady.' **3 forth-rights and meanders** paths that are
sometimes straight and sometimes winding. **5 attached** seized; a legal metaphor. **6 To . . . spirits** to the
point at which my spirits are dulled. **10 frustrate** vain. **14 throughly** thoroughly.

For now they are oppressed with travail, they
Will not nor cannot use such vigilance
As when they are fresh.

SEBASTIAN (*aside to* ANTONIO).   I say tonight. No more.

Solemn and strange music, and PROSPERO *on the top, invisible*

ALONSO.
What harmony is this? My good friends, hark!

GONZALO.   Marvellous sweet music!

Enter several strange shapes bringing in a banquet, and dance about it with gentle actions of salutations; and inviting the King, etc., to eat, they depart

ALONSO.
20   Give us kind keepers, heavens! What were these?

SEBASTIAN.
A living drollery! Now I will believe
That there are unicorns; that in Arabia
There is one tree, the phoenix' throne, one phoenix
At this hour reigning there.

ANTONIO.   I'll believe both;
And what does else want credit, come to me,
And I'll be sworn 'tis true. Travellers ne'er did lie,
Though fools at home condemn 'em.

GONZALO.   If in Naples
I should report this now, would they believe me?
If I should say I saw such islanders—
30   For certes these are people of the island—
Who though they are of monstrous shape, yet note
Their manners are more gentle-kind than of
Our human generation you shall find
Many, nay almost any.

PROSPERO (*aside*).   Honest lord,
Thou hast said well; for some of you there present
Are worse than devils.

ALONSO.   I cannot too much muse
Such shapes, such gesture, and such sound expressing,

---

20 keepers guardian angels.   **21 A living drollery** either a comic play in real life, or a living caricature. The relevant senses of *drollery* are 'comic entertainment,' 'comic picture or caricature,' and 'puppet show.' **23 phoenix** a mythical Arabian bird, said to exist only one at a time, to nest in a single tree, and to reproduce by expiring in flame and then resurrecting itself from its own ashes. Shakespeare made it the subject of an elegant and elusive allegorical poem, *The Phoenix and the Turtle,* published in 1601.   **25 what . . . credit** anything else unbelievable.   **30 certes** certainly; by Shakespeare's time the word was archaic and exclusively literary.   **32 gentle-kind** either having the graciousness of nobility or noble-mannered.   **36 muse** marvel at.

Although they want the use of tongue, a kind
Of excellent dumb discourse.

PROSPERO (*aside*). Praise in departing.

FRANCISCO.

They vanished strangely.

40 SEBASTIAN. No matter, since
They have left their viands behind; for we have stomachs.
Will't please you taste of what is here?

ALONSO. Not I.

GONZALO.

Faith, sir, you need not fear. When we were boys,
Who would believe that there were mountaineers
Dewlapped like bulls, whose throats had hanging at 'em
Wallets of flesh?—or that there were such men
Whose heads stood in their breasts?—which now we find
Each putter-out of five for one will bring us
Good warrant of.

ALONSO. I will stand to, and feed,
50 Although my last—no matter, since I feel
The best is past. Brother, my lord the Duke,
Stand to and do as we.

     Thunder and lightning.

     Enter ARIEL, *like a harpy, claps his wings upon the table, and with a quaint device the banquet vanishes*

ARIEL.

You are three men of sin, whom Destiny,
That hath to instrument this lower world
And what is in't, the never-surfeited sea
Hath caused to belch up you, and on this island,

---

41 viands food; **stomachs** good appetites. **44 mountaineers** mountain-dwellers. **46 Wallets** wattles.
46–7 men | Whose heads stood in their breasts alluded to also in *Othello* 1.3.144–5: 'The anthropophagi,
and men whose heads | Do grow beneath their shoulders.' **48 putter-out of five for one** London brokers
provided a form of insurance to allow travellers to recoup their expenses: the traveller deposited a sum of
money with the broker before departing, which was repaid fivefold if he returned with proof that he had
reached his destination, but failing that was forfeited to the broker. The 'putter-out,' then, is either the traveller,
who invests his money at the rate of five to one, or the broker, who pays at that rate and reports the traveller's
tales. **49 stand to** 'To set to work, fall to; *esp.* to begin eating.' **52.2 Ariel . . . harpy** The episode is based
on *Aeneid* iii. 225 ff. Harpies had the faces and breasts of young women, the wings and bodies of birds, and
talons for hands. *Enter . . . like a harpy* may imply that Ariel enters flying. **52.3 with a quaint device** by
means of an ingenious mechanism (which probably whisked the banquet down through a hole in the table, perhaps with the assistance of a stagehand hidden beneath it). **54 to instrument** as its instrument.

Where man doth not inhabit—you 'mongst men
Being most unfit to live. I have made you mad;
And even with such-like valour men hang and drown
Their proper selves.

    ALONSO, SEBASTIAN, *etc. draw their swords*

60   You fools! I and my fellows
Are ministers of Fate—the elements
Of whom your swords are tempered may as well
Wound the loud winds, or with bemocked-at stabs
Kill the still-closing waters, as diminish
One dowl that's in my plume. My fellow ministers
Are like invulnerable. If you could hurt,
Your swords are now too massy for your strengths,
And will not be uplifted. But remember—
For that's my business to you—that you three
70 From Milan did supplant good Prospero,
Exposed unto the sea, which hath requit it,
Him and his innocent child; for which foul deed,
The powers delaying, not forgetting, have
Incensed the seas and shores, yea all the creatures
Against your peace. Thee of thy son, Alonso,
They have bereft; and do pronounce by me
Ling'ring perdition, worse than any death
Can be at once, shall step by step attend
You and your ways; whose wraths to guard you from,
80 Which here, in this most desolate isle, else falls
Upon your heads, is nothing but heart's sorrow,
And a clear life ensuing.

    He vanishes in thunder. Then, to soft music, enter the shapes again, and dance with
    mocks and mows, and carrying out the table [they depart]

PROSPERO.
  Bravely the figure of this harpy hast thou
  Performed, my Ariel; a grace it had, devouring.

---

59 such-like valour insane courage, as opposed to true heroism.   **61–4 elements . . . waters** The swords are forged by the action of fire on metal refined from earth; these elements are ineffective against the other two elements, the air of winds and 'the still-closing waters.'   **64 still-closing** that close as soon as they are parted. **65 dowl** the filament of a feather; the smallest feather.   **66 like** alike.   **67 massy** heavy.   **71 Exposed** The object of the verb is 'Him and his innocent child.'   **77 Ling'ring perdition** slow and continuous destruction; a protracted hell-on-earth. The threat has been exemplified in the emblem of the disappearing banquet, tantalizing, but promising only slow starvation.   **81 is nothing** there is no alternative.   **82 clear** blameless.

Of my instruction hast thou nothing bated
In what thou hadst to say; so with good life
And observation strange my meaner ministers
Their several kinds have done. My high charms work,
And these, mine enemies, are all knit up
90   In their distractions. They now are in my power;
And in these fits I leave them, while I visit
Young Ferdinand, whom they suppose is drowned,
And his and mine loved darling.   *Exit above*

GONZALO.
I' th' name of something holy, sir, why stand you
In this strange stare?

ALONSO.   O, it is monstrous, monstrous!
Methought the billows spoke and told me of it,
The winds did sing it to me; and the thunder,
That deep and dreadful organ-pipe, pronounced
The name of Prosper: it did bass my trespass.
100   Therefore my son i' th' ooze is bedded; and
I'll seek him deeper than e'er plummet sounded,
And with him there lie mudded.   *Exit*

SEBASTIAN.   But one fiend at a time,
I'll fight their legions o'er.

ANTONIO.   I'll be thy second.

Exeunt SEBASTIAN *and* ANTONIO

GONZALO.
All three of them are desperate: their great guilt,
Like poison given to work a great time after,
Now 'gins to bite the spirits. I do beseech you
That are of suppler joints, follow them swiftly,
And hinder them from what this ecstasy
May now provoke them to.

ADRIAN.   Follow, I pray you.

All exeunt

---

85 bated omitted.   **86 so** in the same way.   **with good life** Prospero praises the spirits for both vitality and naturalness in their performance.   **87 observation strange** wonderful attentiveness (to Prospero's commands).   **88 Their several kinds have done** have performed their various roles.   **95 stare** 'A condition of amazement, horror, admiration.   **99 bass my trespass** (a) sing out my guilt in a bass voice; in the harmonic image, the thunder takes the bass while the winds of l. 97 sing the higher parts; (b) provide a (musical) ground or basis for the revelation of my guilt; (c) with a play on 'utter the baseness of my guilt.' Alonso hears Ariel's speech as the assertion of retributive justice through the harmony of nature.   **100 Therefore** for that.   **103 o'er** one after another.   **104 desperate** (a) in despair; (b) dangerously reckless.   **106 spirits** vital powers.   **108 ecstasy** madness.

4.1 *Enter* Prospero, Ferdinand, *and* Miranda

Prospero (*to* Ferdinand).
　　If I have too austerely punished you
　　Your compensation makes amends, for I
　　Have given you here a third of mine own life,
　　Or that for which I live; who once again
　　I tender to thy hand. All thy vexations
　　Were but my trials of thy love, and thou
　　Hast strangely stood the test. Here, afore heaven,
　　I ratify this my rich gift. O Ferdinand,
　　Do not smile at me that I boast of her,
10　　For thou shalt find she will outstrip all praise,
　　And make it halt behind her.
Ferdinand.　　　　　　　　　　I do believe it
　　Against an oracle.
Prospero.
　　Then as my gift, and thine own acquisition
　　Worthily purchased, take my daughter. But
　　If thou dost break her virgin-knot before
　　All sanctimonious ceremonies may
　　With full and holy rite be ministered,
　　No sweet aspersion shall the heavens let fall
　　To make this contract grow; but barren hate,
20　　Sour-eyed disdain, and discord shall bestrew
　　The union of your bed with weeds so loathly
　　That you shall hate it both. Therefore take heed,
　　As Hymen's lamps shall light you.
Ferdinand.　　　　　　　　　　As I hope
　　For quiet days, fair issue, and long life,
　　With such love as 'tis now, the murkiest den,

4.1.1 austerely harshly, rigorously; **punished** Prospero in l. 6 explains his actions as constituting 'trials of thy love,' but punishment implies crimes to be atoned for, and the choice of words here recalls his baseless charges against Ferdinand at 1.2.454 ff. **3–4 a third . . . live** The simplest explanation is that a third merely signifies a very important part, as it clearly does in Prospero's later declaration that 'Every third thought shall be my grave' (5.1.308). Alternatively, we may take it to mean that for a third of his life Miranda has been the centre of his existence (this would put Prospero's age at 45). **7 strangely** wonderfully; compare 'by observation strange,' 3.3.87. **11 halt** limp. **12 Against an oracle** though an oracle should contradict it—an ambiguous assurance. **14 purchased** won. **15 break . . . knot** Probably alluding to Catullus iii. 27, 'Zonam soluere virgineam,' to untie the virgin's girdle. **16 sanctimonious** sacred. **18 aspersion** literally, sprinkling; the heavenly rain that nourishes fruition. Compare 3.1.75–6: 'Heavens rain grace | On that which breeds between 'em!' **21 bed** with an overtone of 'seed-bed'; **weeds** The marriage bed was customarily strewn with flowers; **loathly** loathsome: 'rare in the seventeenth and eighteenth centuries.' **23 Hymen's lamps** Hymen was god of marriage, and his lamps are the wedding torches. These were regarded as good omens if they burned clear, bad if they were smoky. **25 den** originally the lair of a wild beast, and by extension any enclosed hiding place, generally with dangerous or unsavoury overtones.

The most opportune place, the strong'st suggestion
Our worser genius can, shall never melt
Mine honour into lust, to take away
The edge of that day's celebration
30   When I shall think or Phoebus' steeds are foundered,
Or night kept chained below.

PROSPERO.   Fairly spoke.
Sit then and talk with her, she is thine own.
What, Ariel! My industrious servant Ariel!

        Enter ARIEL

ARIEL.
What would my potent master? Here I am.
PROSPERO.
Thou and thy meaner fellows your last service
Did worthily perform, and I must use you
In such another trick. Go, bring the rabble
O'er whom I give thee pow'r here to this place.
Incite them to quick motion, for I must
40   Bestow upon the eyes of this young couple
Some vanity of mine art: it is my promise,
And they expect it from me.
ARIEL.   Presently?
PROSPERO.   Ay, with a twink.
ARIEL.   Before you can say 'come' and 'go',
              And breathe twice, and cry 'so, so',
              Each one, tripping on his toe,
              Will be here with mop and mow.
              Do you love me, master? No?
PROSPERO.
Dearly, my delicate Ariel. Do not approach

---

26 opportune accented on the second syllable suggestion temptation.   **27 genius** 'The tutelary god or attendant spirit allotted to every person at his birth, to govern his fortunes and determine his character, and finally to conduct him out of the world,' and from this, a person's good and evil genius, 'the two mutually opposed spirits (in Christian language *angels*) by whom every person was supposed to be attended throughout his life';   **can** can make.   **28 to** so as to.   **29 edge** ardour, with explicit sexual connotations.   **29–30 that day's celebration | When** the celebration of that day on which   **30–1 Or . . . below** either that the sun's horses have collapsed through overriding (so that the wedding night will never come) or that night is forcibly prevented from arriving.   **33 What** now then.   **35 meaner fellows** the 'meaner ministers' of 3.3.87.   **37 trick** ingenious artifice; here, with *perform* (l. 36), including specifically theatrical implications;   **rabble** the 'meaner fellows'; the word is invariably pejorative.   **39 motion** 'Perhaps with a trace of the sense "puppet show."'   **41 vanity** a trifling display, as opposed to the raising of the storm and Ariel's portentous performance on the beach.   **42 Presently** immediately.   **43 with a twink** in the twinkling of an eye (literally, the time it takes to wink).   **47 mop and mow** Both words mean grimace.

Till thou dost hear me call.

50 ARIEL.   Well, I conceive.   *Exit*

PROSPERO (*to* FERDINAND).

Look thou be true; do not give dalliance
Too much the rein. The strongest oaths are straw
To th' fire i' th' blood. Be more abstemious,
Or else good night your vow.

FERDINAND.   I warrant you, sir,
The white cold virgin snow upon my heart
Abates the ardour of my liver.

PROSPERO.   Well.
Now come, my Ariel. Being a corollary,
Rather than want a spirit. Appear, and pertly!

Soft music

No tongue! All eyes! Be silent!

Enter IRIS

IRIS.

60 Ceres, most bounteous lady, thy rich leas
Of wheat, rye, barley, vetches, oats, and peas;
Thy turfy mountains, where live nibbling sheep,
And flat meads thatched with stover them to keep;
Thy banks with pionèd and twillèd brims,
Which spongy April at thy hest betrims
To make cold nymphs chaste crowns; and thy broom groves,
Whose shadow the dismissèd bachelor loves,
Being lass-lorn; thy poll-clipped vineyard,
And thy sea-marge sterile and rocky-hard,

---

50 conceive understand.   **51 true** faithful to your word: Prospero returns to the question of Ferdinand's chastity;   **dalliance** originally simply conversation; by Chaucer's time the primary sense was 'flirtation, amorous toying.'   **53 Be more abstemious** This implies some kind of intense commerce between Ferdinand and Miranda. Most editors assume that when Prospero turns his attention to the lovers, they are embracing; but given the hyperbolic nature of Prospero's fears, they may merely be holding hands, deep in conversation, or looking adoringly into each other's eyes. How a director chooses to stage the moment will depend on the extent to which he sees Prospero's libidinous apprehensions as justified.   **55 The . . . heart** either the thought of Miranda enshrined in his heart, or his own chaste love for her. 'As chaste as ice' was proverbial.   **56 liver** in the old physiology, the seat of physical love and violent passion.   **57 a corollary** one too many, 'a surplussage.'   **58 want** lack.   **pertly** smartly, briskly.   **59 No tongue** 'Those who are present at incantations are obliged to be strictly silent, "else," as we are afterwards told, "the spell is marr'd."'   **59.1 Enter Iris** Iris is the messenger of the gods, and goddess of the rainbow. The masque she introduces is a bethrothal masque, a concept that is apparently Shakespeare's invention.   **60 Ceres** goddess of earth and patroness of agriculture;   **leas** meadows. **61 vetches** tares, grown for fodder.   **63 stover** winter forage.   **66 broom groves** Editorial opinion since the mid-eighteenth century has found a problem here: broom, which is a shrub, not a tree, cannot be said to grow in groves.   **67 dismissèd bachelor** rejected suitor.   **68 poll-clipped** pollarded or pruned: this seems a more likely reading than 'pole-clipped,' hedged with poles.

70 Where thou thyself dost air: the Queen o' th' sky,
Whose watery arch and messenger am I,
Bids thee leave these, and with her sovereign grace,
Here on this grass-plot, in this very place,
To come and sport. Her peacocks fly amain.

[JUNO's *chariot appears suspended above the stage*]

Approach, rich Ceres, her to entertain.

Enter [ARIEL *as*] CERES

CERES.
Hail, many-coloured messenger, that ne'er
Dost disobey the wife of Jupiter;
Who with thy saffron wings upon my flowers
Diffusest honey-drops, refreshing showers;
80 And with each end of thy blue bow dost crown
My bosky acres and my unshrubbed down,
Rich scarf to my proud earth: why hath thy queen
Summoned me hither to this short-grassed green?
IRIS.
A contract of true love to celebrate,
And some donation freely to estate
On the blessed lovers.
CERES.   Tell me, heavenly bow,
If Venus or her son, as thou dost know,
Do now attend the Queen? Since they did plot
The means that dusky Dis my daughter got,
90 Her and her blind boy's scandalled company
I have forsworn.
IRIS.   Of her society
Be not afraid. I met her deity
Cutting the clouds towards Paphos, and her son

---

70 Queen o' th' sky Juno.   **71 watery arch** Iris as the rainbow.   **72 these** 'thy rich leas' and the other places just described.   **74 peacocks** sacred to Juno, and here conceived as drawing her chariot;   **amain** at full speed.   **75 entertain** receive as a guest.   **81 bosky** covered with bushes;   **unshrubbed down** bare plains.   **83 short-grassed green** The masque takes place on a well-tended lawn, as opposed to the wild nature of the island.   **85 estate** bestow.   **86 bow** rainbow.   **87 as** so far as.   **88–9 Since . . . got** In Ovid's account, Venus and Cupid, in order to extend their dominion to the underworld, inspired in Pluto the love that prompted him to abduct Proserpine. See "The Myth of Cupid and Psyche," p. 000.   **89 dusky** both dark and melancholy. Ovid calls Pluto *'niger'* (black);   **Dis** The name means 'wealth': Pluto as god of the underworld was also god of riches. Dis is the Latin translation of the Greek name, a shortened form of *Dives*, wealth.   **90 blind** Cupid was traditionally represented as blindfolded (hence 'love is blind');   **scandalled** scandalous.   **92 her deity** jocular usage, on the model of 'his worship,' 'her majesty,' etc.   **93 Paphos** in Cyprus, the centre of Venus' cult.

Dove-drawn with her. Here thought they to have done
Some wanton charm upon this man and maid,
Whose vows are that no bed-right shall be paid
Till Hymen's torch be lighted; but in vain.
Mars's hot minion is returned again;
Her waspish-headed son has broke his arrows,
100   Swears he will shoot no more, but play with sparrows,
And be a boy right out.
CERES.   Highest Queen of state,
Great Juno comes; I know her by her gait.

[JUNO's *chariot descends to the stage*]

JUNO.
How does my bounteous sister? Go with me
To bless this twain, that they may prosperous be,
And honoured in their issue.

[CERES *joins Juno in the chariot, which rises and hovers above the stage.*] *They sing*

JUNO.
Honour, riches, marriage-blessing,
Long continuance, and increasing,
Hourly joys be still upon you!
Juno sings her blessings on you.
CERES.
110   Earth's increase, foison plenty,
Barns and garners never empty,
Vines with clust'ring bunches growing,
Plants with goodly burden bowing;

---

94 Dove-drawn Doves were sacred to Venus, and drew her chariot. At the end of *Venus and Adonis*, the goddess.   Yokes her silver doves, by whose swift aid

Their mistress mounted through the empty skies
In her light chariot quickly is conveyed,
Holding their course to Paphos, where their queen
Means to immure herself, and not be seen. (1190–94)

94–5 to . . . charm to inspire them with lust, as they did to Dis.   **96 bed-right shall be paid** The bed-right involves the payment of a debt of homage to Hymen.   **97 Till . . . lighted** till the marriage ceremony is performed.   **98 Mars's hot minion** the lustful Venus, whose illicit passion for Mars was discovered and revealed by her husband Vulcan (*Metamorphoses*). *Minion* = darling, mistress (French, *mignon*).   **99 waspish-headed** irascible; and his arrows sting.   **100 sparrows** emblematic of lechery and associated with Venus. **101 be . . . out** simply be a boy, give up his status as the god of love.   **110 foison** abundance (used by Gonzalo at 2.1.161).   **111 garners** granaries.

Spring come to you at the farthest,
In the very end of harvest!
Scarcity and want shall shun you;
Ceres' blessing so is on you.

FERDINAND.
This is a most majestic vision, and
Harmonious charmingly. May I be bold
To think these spirits?

120   PROSPERO.   Spirits, which by mine art
I have from their confines called to enact
My present fancies.

FERDINAND.   Let me live here ever.
So rare a wondered father and a wife
Makes this place paradise.

>   JUNO *and* CERES *whisper, and send* IRIS *on employment*

PROSPERO.   Sweet, now, silence!
Juno and Ceres whisper seriously.
There's something else to do. Hush, and be mute,
Or else our spell is marred.

IRIS.
You nymphs called naiads of the windring brooks,
With your sedged crowns, and ever harmless looks,

130   Leave your crisp channels, and on this green land
Answer your summons, Juno does command.
Come, temperate nymphs, and help to celebrate
A contract of true love. Be not too late.

>   *Enter certain nymphs*

You sunburned sickle-men, of August weary,
Come hither from the furrow and be merry;
Make holiday; your rye-straw hats put on,

114–15 i.e., after autumn, may spring return at once, and your years have no winter. The benediction undoes the effects of Ceres' allusion to the rape of Proserpine (ll. 88–9), which is responsible for the fact that winter exists in nature: Proserpine spends six months on earth and six in the underworld, and during the latter period Ceres, in mourning for her daughter, allows no crops to grow.   **119 Harmonious charmingly** 'Charming' has a double etymology, from Latin *carmen*, a song, and Anglo-Saxon *cierm*, a spell, reflected in the traditional association of music with magic.   **122 fancies** the same word as 'fantasies,' and originally simply a shortened spelling. By Shakespeare's time 'fancy' had overtones of the light, arbitrary, and capricious: Prospero here recalls the tone of his characterization of the masque as 'some vanity of mine art' (l. 41).   **123 wondered** wonderful, endowed with wonders—possibly also alluding to Miranda's name.   **124 Sweet** The epithet could be used between men.   **128 naiads** mermaids;   **windring** the only citation for this word in the *OED*, which considers it a misprint for 'winding.'   **129 sedged crowns** garlands of sedge, a river plant. See Keats's "LaBelle Dame san Merci," p. 000;   **harmless** literally translating 'innocent.'   **130 crisp** rippling.   **132 temperate nymphs** Nymphs were associated with chaste Diana.   **134 of August weary** because this is the time of harvest.

And these fresh nymphs encounter every one
In country footing.

*Enter certain reapers, properly habited. They join with the nymphs in a graceful
dance, towards the end whereof* PROSPERO *starts suddenly and speaks, after which, to
a strange hollow and confused noise, they heavily vanish*

PROSPERO (*aside*).
I had forgot that foul conspiracy
140   Of the beast Caliban and his confederates
Against my life. The minute of their plot
Is almost come. (*To the spirits*)—Well done, avoid. No more.

[JUNO *and* CERES *ascend in their chariot and the reapers exeunt*]

FERDINAND.
This is strange. Your father's in some passion
That works him strongly.
MIRANDA.   Never till this day
Saw I him touched with anger, so distempered.
PROSPERO (*to* FERDINAND).
You do look, my son, in a moved sort,
As if you were dismayed. Be cheerful, sir;
Our revels now are ended. These our actors,
As I foretold you, were all spirits, and
150   Are melted into air, into thin air,
And, like the baseless fabric of this vision,
The cloud-capped towers, the gorgeous palaces,
The solemn temples, the great globe itself,
Yea, all which it inherit, shall dissolve,
And, like this insubstantial pageant faded,
Leave not a rack behind. We are such stuff

---

137 encounter join.   **138 country footing** rustic dancing.   **138.1** *properly* appropriately.
138.3 *strange . . . noise* The harmony of the dance music dissolves in discord.   *Hollow* = not full-toned,
sepulchral.   **142 avoid** begone.   **144–5 Never . . . distempered** Prospero's sudden rage has been anticipated earlier in the day in Act 1, Scene 2, in his account of his brother's usurpation and in his behaviour to
Ferdinand; his actions here are clearly related to the complex feelings expressed in both those instances.
145 distempered literally, having the temper, or proportion, of the bodily humours disturbed. The term implies a physiological basis for vexation.   **146–7 You . . . dismayed** Critics have been puzzled at Prospero's
need to comfort Ferdinand, when it is Prospero who is distressed. But Ferdinand is witnessing a return of the
irrational behaviour of 1.2.443 ff., when he was accused of treason, paralysed, threatened with imprisonment,
and forced to carry logs; and his dismay at Prospero's disruption of what seemed a happy ending to his trials is
dramatically perfectly coherent.   **146 sort** condition.   **148 revels** entertainment, with an overtone from the
technical language of the masque, in which the term is used for the final dance between masquers and spectators, the physical assertion of social harmony and aristocratic community.   **154 which it inherit** who subsequently possess it; succeeding generations.   **155 pageant** another technical term, like 'revels.' The basic
meanings are 'scene acted upon the stage,' 'stage on which scenes are performed,' 'stage machine,' 'tableau or allegorical device'; when extended into the moral sphere the word implied deception, trickery, specious or empty
show.   **156 rack** cloud or mist driven by the wind, perhaps also with a suggestion of the cloud effects of
masque scenery.

As dreams are made on, and our little life
Is rounded with a sleep. Sir, I am vexed.
Bear with my weakness, my old brain is troubled.
160 Be not disturbed with my infirmity.
If you be pleased, retire into my cell,
And there repose. A turn or two I'll walk
To still my beating mind.
FERDINAND *and* MIRANDA.   We wish your peace.   *Exeunt*
PROSPERO.
Come with a thought!—I thank thee.—Ariel, come!

    Enter ARIEL

ARIEL.
Thy thoughts I cleave to. What's thy pleasure?
PROSPERO.
Spirit, we must prepare to meet with Caliban.
ARIEL.
Ay, my commander. When I presented Ceres
I thought to have told thee of it, but I feared
Lest I might anger thee.
PROSPERO.
170 Say again, where didst thou leave these varlets?
ARIEL.
I told you, sir, they were red-hot with drinking,
So full of valour that they smote the air
For breathing in their faces, beat the ground
For kissing of their feet; yet always bending
Towards their project. Then I beat my tabor,
At which like unbacked colts they pricked their ears,
Advanced their eyelids, lifted up their noses
As they smelt music. So I charmed their ears
That calf-like they my lowing followed through
180 Toothed briars, sharp furzes, pricking gorse, and thorns,
Which entered their frail shins. At last I left them
I' th' filthy-mantled pool beyond your cell,
There dancing up to th' chins, that the foul lake

---

157 **on** of.   158 **rounded** either surrounded—our little life then being a brief awaking from an eternal sleep—or rounded off, i.e. completed. Prospero is not conceiving of death as the reward or high point of life, but as its largest condition.   160 **with** by.   163 **beating** throbbing, agitated.   164 **I thank thee** addressed to the parting Ferdinand and Miranda.   167 **When I presented Ceres** most likely, 'when I played the role of Ceres in the masque'; alternatively, 'when I produced the masque of Ceres.'   170 **varlets** clearly pejorative here, though the original meaning, servants or menials, was still current in Shakespeare's time.   174 **bending** aiming.   175 **tabor** Ariel's side-drum (see 3.2.122.1).   176 **unbacked** never ridden, and hence unbroken. 177 **Advanced** raised.   180 **furzes, gorse** forms of the same plant.   182 **filthy-mantled** covered with filthy scum. *Mantle* is both 'the green vegetable coating on standing water' and 'the foam that covers the surface of liquor'—the latter sense is especially appropriate to the situation of the drunken conspirators.

O'er-stunk their feet.

PROSPERO.   This was well done, my bird.

Thy shape invisible retain thou still.

The trumpery in my house, go bring it hither,

For stale to catch these thieves.

ARIEL.   I go, I go.   *Exit*

PROSPERO.

A devil, a born devil, on whose nature

Nurture can never stick; on whom my pains,

190   Humanely taken, all, all lost, quite lost;

And as with age his body uglier grows,

So his mind cankers. I will plague them all,

Even to roaring.

> *Enter* ARIEL, *loaden with glistering apparel, etc.*

Come, hang them on this line.

> PROSPERO *and* ARIEL *remain, invisible.*

> *Enter* CALIBAN, STEPHANO, *and* TRINCULO, *all wet*

CALIBAN. Pray you tread softly, that the blind mole may not hear a footfall. We now are
near his cell.

STEPHANO. Monster, your fairy, which you say is a harmless fairy, has done little better

200   than played the jack with us.

TRINCULO. Monster, I do smell all horse-piss, at which my nose is in great indignation.

STEPHANO. So is mine. Do you hear, monster? If I should take a displeasure against
you, look you—

TRINCULO. Thou wert but a lost monster.

CALIBAN.

Good my lord, give me thy favour still.

Be patient, for the prize I'll bring thee to

Shall hoodwink this mischance; therefore speak softly,

All's hushed as midnight yet.

TRINCULO. Ay, but to lose our bottles in the pool!

---

184 bird youngster; Prospero at 5.1.313 calls Ariel 'chick.'   **186 trumpery** attractive trash, the 'glistering apparel' of l. 193.1. Prospero, suiting his art to its audience, produces carnival costumes from his cell.   **187 stale** decoy.   **188–9 nature | Nurture** The question of the relation between these was a Renaissance *topos*, and the ability of nurture—training, education—to transform nature in any essential way was an ongoing subject of debate. Proverbial wisdom taught that 'Nature passes nurture'; Prospero analogously assumes that his education has succeeded with Miranda and failed with Caliban not through any defect in the teaching methods but because his pupils are respectively good and bad by nature.   **191–2 as . . . cankers** The charge may be less straightforward than it appears: Prospero has just become conscious of his own advancing age, and has expressed fears for his own mind.   **193 line** a variant form of lind, the lime-tree or linden. Although *line* could mean a string, there are no contemporary references to clothes-lines, and it is more likely that the reference is to a stage-property tree.   **197 jack** knave (as in the deck of cards).   **203 prize** booty.   **204 hoodwink this mischance** render this mischance harmless. To hoodwink is to cover the eyes with a hood, or to blindfold.

STEPHANO. There is not only disgrace and dishonour in that, monster, but an infinite loss.

TRINCULO. That's more to me than my wetting; yet this is your harmless fairy, monster!

210   STEPHANO. I will fetch off my bottle, though I be o'er ears for my labour.

CALIBAN.

> Prithee, my kind, be quiet. Seest thou here,
> This is the mouth o' th' cell. No noise, and enter.
> Do that good mischief which may make this island
> Thine own forever, and I, thy Caliban,
> For aye thy foot-licker.

STEPHANO. Give me thy hand. I do begin to have bloody thoughts.

TRINCULO. O King Stephano! O peer! O worthy Stephano—look what a wardrobe here is for thee!

CALIBAN. Let it alone, thou fool, it is but trash.

220   TRINCULO. O ho, monster! We know what belongs to a frippery.

He takes a robe from the tree and puts it on

> O King Stephano!

STEPHANO. Put off that gown, Trinculo. (*Reaches for it*) By this hand, I'll have that gown.

TRINCULO. Thy grace shall have it.

CALIBAN.

> The dropsy drown this fool! What do you mean
> To dote thus on such luggage? Let't alone,
> And do the murder first. If he awake,
> From toe to crown he'll fill our skins with pinches,
> Make us strange stuff.

230   STEPHANO. Be you quiet, monster. Mistress line, is not this my jerkin? (*Removes it from the tree*) Now is the jerkin under the line. Now, jerkin, you are like to lose your hair, and prove a bald jerkin.

TRINCULO. Do, do; we steal by line and level, an't like your grace.

STEPHANO. I thank thee for that jest: here's a garment for't.

He takes a garment from the tree and gives it to TRINCULO

> Wit shall not go unrewarded while I am king of this country. 'Steal by line and level' is an excellent pass of pate.

He takes another garment and gives it to him

> There's another garment for't.

---

210 fetch off either rescue or drink up;   **o'er ears** i.e. drowned.   **220 frippery** second-hand clothing shop, i.e. this is *not* trash.   **222 Put off** take off.   **225 dropsy** The disease is characterized by an excessive accumulation of fluid in the bodily tissues, and hence was used figuratively for an insatiable thirst or craving. **226 luggage** encumbrances (literally, what must be lugged about).   **229 stuff** referring both to the 'luggage' of l. 226 and the fabric of the 'glistering apparel.'   **231 Now . . . line** The literal sense is that Stephano has taken the jerkin off the tree.   **236 pass of pate** skillful thrust; *pass* is a fencing metaphor, *of pate* refers to 'the head as the seat of the intellect; hence put for skill, cleverness.'

TRINCULO. Monster, come put some lime on your fingers, and away with the rest.

CALIBAN.

240
> I will have none on't. We shall lose our time,
> And all be turned to barnacles, or to apes
> With foreheads villainous low.

STEPHANO. Monster, lay to your fingers. Help to bear this away where my hogshead of wine is, or I'll turn you out of my kingdom. Go to, carry this.

TRINCULO. And this.

STEPHANO. Ay, and this.

> *They give* CALIBAN *the remaining garments. A noise of hunters heard. Enter divers spirits in shape of dogs and hounds, hunting them about,* PROSPERO *and* ARIEL *setting them on*

PROSPERO. Hey, Mountain, hey!

ARIEL. Silver! There it goes, Silver!

PROSPERO. Fury, Fury! There Tyrant, there! Hark, hark!

> CALIBAN, STEPHANO, *and* TRINCULO *are driven out*

250
> Go charge my goblins that they grind their joints
> With dry convulsions, shorten up their sinews
> With agèd cramps, and more pinch-spotted make them
> Than pard of cat o' mountain.

ARIEL.   Hark, they roar.

PROSPERO.

> Let them be hunted soundly. At this hour
> Lies at my mercy all mine enemies.
> Shortly shall all my labours end, and thou
> Shalt have the air at freedom. For a little,
> Follow, and do me service.   *Exeunt*

5.1   *Enter* PROSPERO *in his magic robes, and* ARIEL

PROSPERO.

> Now does my project gather to a head.
> My charms crack not, my spirits obey, and Time
> Goes upright with his carriage. How's the day?

ARIEL.

> On the sixth hour, at which time, my lord,
> You said our work should cease.

PROSPERO.   I did say so

---

238 lime birdlime, a sticky substance painted on trees to catch birds. Thieves are said to have sticky fingers; Tilly records 'His fingers are lime twigs.'   **241 villainous** vilely.   **242 lay to** apply;   **this** the clothing from the lime-tree.   **252 pard, cat o' mountain** Both terms applied to the leopard or panther, and the latter in addition to various kinds of wild-cat. Of these animals, however, only the leopard is spotted.
2 crack fail.   **3 Goes . . . carriage** walks without stooping because his burden (*carriage* = what he carries) is no longer heavy.

When first I raised the tempest. Say, my spirit,
How fares the King and's followers?

ARIEL.   Confined together
In the same fashion as you gave in charge,
Just as you left them; all prisoners, sir,
10   In the line-grove which weather-fends your cell;
They cannot budge till your release. The King,
His brother, and yours, abide all three distracted,
And the remainder mourning over them,
Brimful of sorrow and dismay; but chiefly
Him that you termed, sir, the good old Lord Gonzalo,
His tears runs down his beard like winter's drops
From eaves of reeds. Your charm so strongly works 'em
That if you now beheld them, your affections
Would become tender.

PROSPERO.   Dost thou think so, spirit?

ARIEL.
Mine would, sir, were I human.

20   PROSPERO.   And mine shall.
Hast thou, which art but air, a touch, a feeling
Of their afflictions, and shall not myself,
One of their kind, that relish all as sharply
Passion as they, be kindlier moved than thou art?
Though with their high wrongs I am struck to th' quick,
Yet with my nobler reason 'gainst my fury
Do I take part. The rarer action is
In virtue than in vengeance. They being penitent,
The sole drift of my purpose doth extend
30   Not a frown further. Go, release them, Ariel.
My charms I'll break, their senses I'll restore,
And they shall be themselves.

ARIEL.   I'll fetch them, sir.   *Exit*

[PROSPERO *traces a magic circle on the stage with his staff*]

PROSPERO.
Ye elves of hills, brooks, standing lakes, and groves,
And ye that on the sands with printless foot
Do chase the ebbing Neptune, and do fly him

---

17 eaves of reeds thatched roofs.   **18 affections** feelings.   **21 touch** delicate perception.   **24 kindlier** both more generously and more humanly, in accordance with my kind.   **25 quick** the tenderest or most vital part.   **28 virtue** a much broader concept than the expected 'forgiveness.' *Virtue* is parallel with and a logical extension of *reason* in l. 26. The classical *virtus* implied both heroic magnanimity and the stoic ability to remain unmoved by suffering.   **32.1 *Prospero traces a magic circle*** F at l. 57.5 has the shipwreck victims 'all enter the circle which Prospero had made,' but gives no indication of when he makes it. Either here or when he begins his 'airy charm' at l. 52 would be appropriate points.

When he comes back; you demi-puppets that
By moonshine do the green sour ringlets make,
Whereof the ewe not bites; and you whose pastime
Is to make midnight mushrooms, that rejoice
40 To hear the solemn curfew, by whose aid—
Weak masters though ye be—I have bedimmed
The noontide sun, called forth the mutinous winds,
And 'twixt the green sea and the azured vault
Set roaring war; to the dread rattling thunder
Have I given fire, and rifted Jove's stout oak
With his own bolt; the strong-based promontory
Have I made shake, and by the spurs plucked up
The pine and cedar. Graves at my command
Have waked their sleepers, oped, and let 'em forth
50 By my so potent art. But this rough magic
I here abjure; and when I have required
Some heavenly music—which even now I do—
To work mine end upon their senses that
This airy charm is for, I'll break my staff,
Bury it certain fathoms in the earth,
And deeper than did ever plummet sound
I'll drown my book.

Solemn music.

Here enters ARIEL *before; then* ALONSO, *with a frantic gesture, attended by* GONZALO; SEBASTIAN *and* ANTONIO *in like manner, attended by* ADRIAN *and* FRANCISCO. *They all enter the circle which* PROSPERO *has made, and there stand charmed; which* PROSPERO *observing, speaks*

---

36 demi-puppets because they are partially subject to Prospero's will, or because they are diminutive dolls; in either case, with a theatrical overtone.   **37 green sour ringlets** fairy rings, small circles of sour grass near, and caused by the roots of, toadstools. They were said to be caused by fairies dancing.   **39 midnight mushrooms** mushrooms that appear overnight.   **40 curfew** the evening bell, rung at nine o'clock in Shakespeare's time, originally as a signal to extinguish all household fires, but by the sixteenth century merely marking the hour. Spirits were said to be free to walk either then or at midnight.   **41 masters** ministers or instruments.   **45 rifted** split;   **Jove's . . . oak** The tree was sacred to Jove because of its hardness and endurance.   **47 spurs** roots.   **50 rough magic** The renunciation of the *potent art* is manifest in Prospero's language. Barton argues that the phrase suggests a new awareness of the limitations of Prospero's powers: he can raise storms, but cannot enforce penitence or changes of heart (Introduction, p. 29). Kermode's explanation, 'unsubtle by comparison with the next degree of the mage's enlightenment,' requires the dubious assumption that Prospero is pursuing a systematic Neoplatonic ascent.   **54 airy** in the air, with an overtone of the musical sense of *air*, 'song-like music, melody.'   **57.4–5 Prospero . . . speaks** Prospero is invisible and inaudible to the assembled company until he reveals himself at l. 106.

A solemn air, and the best comforter
To an unsettled fancy, cure thy brains,
60 Now useless, boil within thy skull. There stand,
For you are spell-stopped.
Holy Gonzalo, honourable man,
Mine eyes, ev'n sociable to the show of thine,
Fall fellowly drops. The charm dissolves apace,
And as the morning steals upon the night,
Melting the darkness, so their rising senses
Begin to chase the ignorant fumes that mantle
Their clearer reason. O good Gonzalo,
My true preserver, and a loyal sir
70 To him thou follow'st, I will pay thy graces
Home both in word and deed! Most cruelly
Didst thou, Alonso, use me and my daughter.
Thy brother was a furtherer in the act—
Thou art pinched for't now, Sebastian! Flesh and blood,
You, brother mine, that entertained ambition,
Expelled remorse and nature, whom, with Sebastian—
Whose inward pinches therefore are most strong—
Would here have killed your king, I do forgive thee,
Unnatural though thou art.—Their understanding
80 Begins to swell, and the approaching tide
Will shortly fill the reasonable shore,
That now lies foul and muddy. Not one of them
That yet looks on me, or would know me. Ariel,
Fetch me the hat and rapier in my cell.

    Exit ARIEL *and returns immediately*

I will discase me, and myself present
As I was sometime Milan. Quickly, spirit!
Thou shalt ere long be free.

    ARIEL *sings, and helps to attire him*

58–9 A solemn . . . fancy Musical therapy had been in use since ancient times as a way of adjusting the distempered harmony of the human system. **59 unsettled fancy** disturbed imagination, here with implications of delusion and insanity. **59–60 thy . . . thy** Prospero begins his address to Alonso as leader of the party. **63 sociable** humanly sympathetic; **show** appearance (Gonzalo is weeping). **64 Fall** let fall. **67 ignorant . . . mantle** fogs that keep in ignorance. **74 pinched** tortured, punished. The metaphor is literalized in Prospero's threats to Caliban: 'Thou shalt be pinched | As thick as honeycomb,' 1.2.328–9. **79–82 understanding . . . muddy** The metaphor elaborates the notion of their minds returning to reason: understanding is conceived as the sea and the uncomprehending reason as the shore at low tide, which will be cleared of its obscuring scum and mud (compare 'the ignorant fumes' of l. 67) as the tide turns. **81 reasonable shore** shore of reason. **84 hat and rapier** These are essential elements of aristocratic dress. **85 discase me** take off my magic robes. *Disease* (for 'undress') is used only by Shakespeare, though 'uncase' is common in this sense. **86 sometime Milan** formerly, when Duke of Milan.

ARIEL.

　　Where the bee sucks, there suck I,

　　In a cowslip's bell I lie;

90　There I couch when owls do cry;

　　On the bat's back I do fly

　　After summer merrily.

　　Merrily, merrily shall I live now

　　Under the blossom that hangs on the bough.

PROSPERO.

　　Why, that's my dainty Ariel! I shall miss thee,

　　But yet thou shalt have freedom. (*Arranging his attire*)

　　　　　　　　　　　　So, so, so.

　　To the King's ship, invisible as thou art;

　　There shalt thou find the mariners asleep

　　Under the hatches. The master and the boatswain

100　Being awake, enforce them to this place,

　　And presently, I prithee.

ARIEL.

　　I drink the air before me, and return

　　Or ere your pulse twice beat.　　　　　　　　　　　　　　　*Exit*

GONZALO.

　　All torment, trouble, wonder, and amazement

　　Inhabits here. Some heavenly power guide us

　　Out of this fearful country!

PROSPERO.　　　　　　　　Behold, sir King,

　　The wrongèd Duke of Milan, Prospero.

　　For more assurance that a living prince

　　Does now speak to thee, I embrace thy body,

　　Embraces ALONSO

110　And to thee and thy company I bid

　　A hearty welcome.

ALONSO.　　　　　　Whe'er thou beest he or no,

　　Or some enchanted trifle to abuse me,

　　As late I have been, I not know. Thy pulse

　　Beats as of flesh and blood; and since I saw thee,

　　Th'affliction of my mind amends, with which

　　I fear a madness held me. This must crave,

　　An if this be at all, a most strange story.

88–94 The song is Ariel's proleptic celebration of freedom.　**92 After summer** pursuing summer, as birds migrate when the weather grows cold. Ariel anticipates a life of everlasting summer, as Prospero's masque had promised the lovers a world without winter.　**98–9 There . . . hatches** Prospero reports to Ariel information he has had from Ariel in the first place: see 1.2.230.　**102 I drink the air** The Latinism is *viam vorare,* to devour the road.　**112 enchanted trifle** insubstantial apparition produced by magic; **abuse** both delude and maltreat.　**116 crave** call for.

Thy dukedom I resign, and do entreat
Thou pardon me my wrongs. But how should Prospero
Be living, and be here?

120 PROSPERO (*to* GONZALO). First, noble friend,
Let me embrace thine age, whose honour cannot
Be measured or confined.

> *Embraces* GONZALO

GONZALO.   Whether this be,
Or be not, I'll not swear.
PROSPERO.   You do yet taste
Some subtleties o'th' isle, that will not let you
Believe things certain. Welcome, my friends all!
(*Aside to* SEBASTIAN *and* ANTONIO) But you, my brace of lords, were I so minded,
I here could pluck his highness' frown upon you,
And justify you traitors. At this time
I will tell no tales.
SEBASTIAN (*aside*). The devil speaks in him!
PROSPERO.   No.
130 For you, most wicked sir, whom to call brother
Would even infect my mouth, I do forgive
Thy rankest fault—all of them—and require
My dukedom of thee, which perforce I know
Thou must restore.
ALONSO.   If thou beest Prospero,
Give us particulars of thy preservation,
How thou hast met us here, whom three hours since
Were wrecked upon this shore, where I have lost—
How sharp the point of this remembrance is!—
My dear son Ferdinand.
PROSPERO.   I am woe for't, sir.
ALONSO.
140 Irreparable is the loss, and patience
Says it is past her cure.
PROSPERO.   I rather think
You have not sought her help, of whose soft grace
For the like loss I have her sovereign aid,
And rest myself content.
ALONSO.   You the like loss?
PROSPERO.
As great to me, as late; and supportable
To make the dear loss, have I means much weaker

---

119 my wrongs the wrongs I have done you.   **124 subtleties** deceptions, illusions, and with 'taste,' punning on the sense of elaborate ornamental sugar confections arranged as a pageant and served at the conclusion of a banquet.   **126 brace** pair.   **128 justify** prove.   **139 woe** sorry.   **145 late** recent.   **146 dear** grievous.

Than you may call to comfort you, for I
Have lost my daughter.

ALONSO.   A daughter?
O heavens, that they were living both in Naples,
150 The king and queen there! That they were, I wish
Myself were mudded in that oozy bed
Where my son lies. When did you lose your daughter?

PROSPERO.
In this last tempest. I perceive these lords
At this encounter do so much admire
That they devour their reason, and scarce think
Their eyes do offices of truth, their words
Are natural breath; but howsoe'er you have
Been jostled from your senses, know for certain
That I am Prospero, and that very Duke
160 Which was thrust forth of Milan, who most strangely
Upon this shore, where you were wrecked, was landed
To be the lord on't. No more yet of this,
For 'tis a chronicle of day by day,
Not a relation for a breakfast, nor
Befitting this first meeting. Welcome, sir;
This cell's my court. Here have I few attendants,
And subjects none abroad. Pray you look in.
My dukedom since you have given me again,
I will requite you with as good a thing,
170 At least bring forth a wonder to content ye
As much as me my dukedom.

> *Here* PROSPERO *discovers* FERDINAND *and* MIRANDA *playing at chess*

MIRANDA.
Sweet lord, you play me false.

FERDINAND.   No, my dearest love,
I would not for the world.

---

151 mudded buried in mud.   **154 encounter** meeting;   **admire** wonder.   **156 do offices of truth** function accurately.   **160 strangely** wonderfully.   **163 of day by day** to be told over many days.   **164 relation** story.   **167 abroad** elsewhere, beyond what is right here.   **170 bring forth a wonder** Prospero, punning on Miranda's name, seems to promise another illusion.   **171.1 *discovers*** reveals (by pulling aside a curtain). If the discovery place is Prospero's cell—into which the Neapolitans have just been invited to look—Ferdinand and Miranda must be concealed elsewhere, possibly in a small portable pavilion placed on stage only for this scene. Alternatively, if they are in the discovery place, one of the stage doors may be doing service for Prospero's cell, which would be established as such by his entrance through it in his magic robes at the opening of the scene;   ***playing at chess*** The territorial ambitions of their elders are transformed by Ferdinand and Miranda into the stratagems of chess. The game was an aristocratic pastime associated especially with lovers, often with illicit sexual overtones, and also served as a frequent allegory of politics.   **172 You play me false** Though most editors have resisted the idea, Miranda is clearly accusing Ferdinand of cheating here, and in ll. 174–5 declares her willing complicity in the act (see the Introduction, pp. 29–30). The remark is an affectionate echo of Prospero's earlier charge of treason against Ferdinand (1.2.454 ff.).

MIRANDA.
  Yes, for a score of kingdoms you should wrangle,
  And I would call it fair play.
ALONSO.   If this prove
  A vision of the island, one dear son
  Shall I twice lose.
SEBASTIAN.   A most high miracle!
FERDINAND (*Coming forward*).
  Though the seas threaten, they are merciful.
  I have cursed them without cause.

    He kneels before ALONSO

ALONSO.   Now all the blessings
180 Of a glad father compass thee about!
  Arise, and say how thou cam'st here.

    FERDINAND *rises*

MIRANDA.   O wonder!
  How many goodly creatures are there here!
  How beauteous mankind is! O brave new world
  That has such people in't!
PROSPERO.   'Tis new to thee.
ALONSO.
  What is this maid with whom thou wast at play?
  Your eld'st acquaintance cannot be three hours.
  Is she the goddess that hath severed us,
  And brought us thus together?
FERDINAND.   Sir, she is mortal;
  But by immortal providence, she's mine.
190 I chose her when I could not ask my father
  For his advice—nor thought I had one. She
  Is daughter to this famous Duke of Milan,
  Of whom so often I have heard renown,
  But never saw before; of whom I have
  Received a second life; and second father
  This lady makes him to me.
ALONSO.   I am hers.
  But O, how oddly will it sound that I

---

174 wrangle contend with me, be my adversary. The word has no necessary imputation of dishonest dealing, but it is here presented as an antithesis to *fair play* (l. 175), and dishonesty must be implied. The stake in the larger context of their 'wrangling' is, of course, Milan, the realm he has played for and won. **177 A . . . miracle** Sebastian is either for once impressed, or merely being characteristically sarcastic. **183 mankind** presumably humanity; but, other than Miranda, there are only men present. **186 eld'st** longest. **187 Is she the goddess** Compare Ferdinand's response to his first sight of Miranda, 1.2.422. **196 I am hers** I am her servant; my respects to her.

Must ask my child forgiveness!

PROSPERO.   There, sir, stop.

Let us not burden our remembrances with

A heaviness that's gone.

200 GONZALO.   I have inly wept,

Or should have spoke ere this: look down, you gods,

And on this couple drop a blessèd crown;

For it is you that have chalked forth the way

Which brought us hither.

ALONSO.   I say 'amen', Gonzalo.

GONZALO.

Was Milan thrust from Milan that his issue

Should become kings of Naples? O rejoice

Beyond a common joy, and set it down

With gold on lasting pillars! In one voyage

Did Claribel her husband find at Tunis,

210 And Ferdinand, her brother, found a wife

Where he himself was lost, Prospero his dukedom

In a poor isle, and all of us ourselves

When no man was his own.

ALONSO (*to* FERDINAND *and* MIRANDA).

                    Give me your hands.

Let grief and sorrow still embrace his heart

That doth not wish you joy!

GONZALO.   Be it so, amen.

    Enter ARIEL, *with the* MASTER *and* BOATSWAIN *amazedly following*

O look, sir, look, sir, here is more of us!

I prophesied if a gallows were on land

This fellow could not drown. (*To* BOATSWAIN) Now, blasphemy,

That swear'st grace o'erboard, not an oath on shore?

220 Hast thou no mouth by land? What is the news?

BOATSWAIN.

The best news is that we have safely found

Our king and company; the next, our ship,

---

200 heaviness grief. **203 chalked forth the way** marked the true path as with a chalk line. **205 Milan . . . Milan** the Duke of Milan . . . the realm. **208 on lasting pillars** There may be an allusion here to the imperial emblem of Charles V, the pillars of Hercules, familiar from the triumphal iconography of the Holy Roman and the Spanish Empires, and subsequently adapted by monarchs throughout Europe, as well as by Elizabeth I after the defeat of the Armada. **213 When . . . own** when we had lost our senses. Gonzalo's characteristically optimistic summary ignores the unregeneracy of Antonio and Sebastian. **214 still** forever. **218 blasphemy** quintessential blasphemer, the embodiment of blasphemy. **219 swear'st grace o'erboard** drivest God's grace from the ship by swearing. Kermode, citing R. R. Cawley, notes that 'Ralegh ordered his captains to "take especial care that God be not blasphemed in your ship."'

Which but three glasses since we gave out split,
Is tight and yare and bravely rigged as when
We first put out to sea.
ARIEL (*aside to* PROSPERO).   Sir, all this service
Have I done since I went.
PROSPERO (*aside to* ARIEL).   My tricksy spirit!
ALONSO.
These are not natural events, they strengthen
From strange to stranger. Say, how came you hither?
BOATSWAIN.
If I did think, sir, I were well awake,
230 I'd strive to tell you. We were dead of sleep,
And—how we know not—all clapped under hatches,
Where but even now with strange and several noises
Of roaring, shrieking, howling, jingling chains,
And more diversity of sounds, all horrible,
We were awaked, straightway at liberty,
Where we, in all our trim, freshly beheld
Our royal, good, and gallant ship; our master
Cap'ring to eye her—on a trice, so please you,
Even in a dream, were we divided from them,
And were brought moping hither.
240 ARIEL (*aside to* PROSPERO).   Was't well done?
PROSPERO (*aside to* ARIEL).
Bravely, my diligence. Thou shalt be free.
ALONSO.
This is as strange a maze as e'er men trod,
And there is in this business more than nature
Was ever conduct of. Some oracle
Must rectify our knowledge.
PROSPERO.   Sir, my liege,
Do not infest your mind with beating on
The strangeness of this business. At picked leisure,
Which shall be shortly single, I'll resolve you,
Which to you shall seem probable, of every
250 These happened accidents; till when, be cheerful
And think of each thing well. (*Aside to* ARIEL) Come hither, spirit.
Set Caliban and his companions free;

---

223 three glasses since three hours ago; see l. 186 and 1.2.240;   **gave out** declared.   **224 yare** trim,
seaworthy.   **226 tricksy** playful, sportive; also ingenious. Onions suggests 'full of devices, resourceful.'
227 strengthen increase.   **236–7 our trim . . . ship** i.e. our garments, like our ship, were undamaged.
238 Cap'ring dancing for joy.   **240 moping** bewildered.   **242 maze** Compare Gonzalo's characterization
of the island: 'Here's a maze trod indeed,' 3.3.2.   **244 conduct** director.   **246 infest** trouble; **beating**
hammering, insistently thinking.

Untie the spell.   *Exit* ARIEL
         How fares my gracious sir?
There are yet missing of your company
Some few odd lads that you remember not.

    Enter ARIEL, *driving in* CALIBAN, STEPHANO, *and* TRINCULO *in their stolen apparel*

STEPHANO. Every man shift for all the rest, and let no man take care of himself, for all
     is but fortune. Coraggio, bully-monster, coraggio!
TRINCULO. If these be true spies which I wear in my head, here's a goodly sight.
CALIBAN.
     O Setebos, these be brave spirits indeed.
260   How fine my master is! I am afraid
     He will chastise me.
SEBASTIAN.   Ha, ha!
     What things are these, my lord Antonio?
     Will money buy 'em?
ANTONIO.   Very like. One of them
     Is a plain fish, and no doubt marketable.
PROSPERO.
     Mark but the badges of these men, my lords,
     Then say if they be true. This misshapen knave,
     His mother was a witch, and one so strong
     That could control the moon, make flows and ebbs,
     And deal in her command without her power.
270   These three have robbed me, and this demi-devil—
     For he's a bastard one—had plotted with them
     To take my life. Two of these fellows you
     Must know and own; this thing of darkness I
     Acknowledge mine.
CALIBAN.   I shall be pinched to death!
ALONSO. Is not this Stephano, my drunken butler?
SEBASTIAN. He is drunk now—where had he wine?
ALONSO.
     And Trinculo is reeling-ripe! Where should they

---

253 Untie the spell Enchanted characters are regularly described in the play as 'knit up' (Alonso, Sebastian, etc., 3.3.89) or 'bound' (Ferdinand, 1.2.487). **257 Coraggio** courage (Italian); possibly an affected usage, or perhaps a little Neapolitan local colour; **bully** 'A term of endearment and familiarity . . . implying friendly admiration. . . . Often prefixed as a sort of title to the name or designation of the person addressed, as in "bully Bottom," "bully doctor."' **259 Setebos** Caliban's god: see 1.2.372; **brave** handsome, impressive. **260 fine** splendidly dressed: Prospero is in his ducal garments (see ll. 85–6). **264 fish** recalling Trinculo's doubt about whether Caliban was more like a man or a fish: see 2.2.22 ff. **265 badges** heraldic devices worn as identification by the servants of great houses. The point is that, though they are Alonso's servants, their 'livery' has been stolen from Prospero. **266 true** honest. **269 without** beyond the reach of. **270 demi-devil** recalling the charge that Caliban was 'got by the devil himself | Upon thy wicked dam' (1.2.319–20). Both may be mere invective, as Othello calls Iago a demi-devil, 5.2.300. **277 reeling-ripe** ready (i.e. drunk enough) for reeling.

Find this grand liquor that hath gilded 'em?
How cam'st thou in this pickle?

280 TRINCULO. I have been in such a pickle since I saw you last that I fear me will never
out of my bones. I shall not fear fly-blowing.

SEBASTIAN. Why, how now, Stephano?

STEPHANO.
O, touch me not; I am not Stephano, but a cramp.

PROSPERO.
You'd be king o' the isle, sirrah?

STEPHANO.
I should have been a sore one then.

ALONSO (*indicating* CALIBAN).
This is a strange thing as e'er I looked on.

PROSPERO.
He is as disproportioned in his manners
As in his shape. Go, sirrah, to my cell;
Take with you your companions. As you look
290   To have my pardon, trim it handsomely.

CALIBAN.
Ay, that I will; and I'll be wise hereafter,
And seek for grace. What a thrice-double ass
Was I to take this drunkard for a god,
And worship this dull fool!

PROSPERO.   Go to, away.

ALONSO.
Hence, and bestow your luggage where you found it.

SEBASTIAN. Or stole it, rather.

Exeunt CALIBAN, STEPHANO, *and* TRINCULO

PROSPERO.
Sir, I invite your highness and your train
To my poor cell, where you shall take your rest
For this one night, which part of it I'll waste
300   With such discourse as I not doubt shall make it
Go quick away: the story of my life,
And the particular accidents gone by
Since I came to this isle; and in the morn
I'll bring you to your ship, and so to Naples,
Where I have hope to see the nuptial

---

278 gilded flushed their faces.   **279 pickle** both 'preserving liquor' and 'predicament.'   **284 sirrah** The
term expresses 'contempt, reprimand, or assumption of authority on the part of the speaker.'   **285 sore** (a)
sorry, inept; in pain. The sense 'oppressive, severe' does not seem relevant here.   **287 manners** both 'forms of
behaviour' and 'moral character.'   **290 trim** prepare, with implications of both 'make neat' and 'decorate.'
292 grace forgiveness, favour.   **295 luggage** the stolen garments; the term is contemptuous, as in 4.1.231.
299 waste pass, occupy (with no pejorative connotation).   **302 accidents** events.

Of these our dear-belov'd solemnizèd,
And thence retire me to my Milan, where
Every third thought shall be my grave.
ALONSO.   I long
To hear the story of your life, which must
310   Take the ear strangely.
PROSPERO.   I'll deliver all,
And promise you calm seas, auspicious gales,
And sail so expeditious that shall catch
Your royal fleet far off. My Ariel, chick,
That is thy charge. Then to the elements
Be free, and fare thou well.—Please you draw near.

Exeunt all

Epilogue *spoken by* PROSPERO
       Now my charms are all o'erthrown,
       And what strength I have's mine own,
       Which is most faint. Now 'tis true
       I must be here confined by you,
320   Or sent to Naples. Let me not,
       Since I have my dukedom got,
       And pardoned the deceiver, dwell
       In this bare island by your spell,
       But release me from my bands
       With the help of your good hands.
       Gentle breath of yours my sails
       Must fill, or else my project fails,
       Which was to please. Now I want
       Spirits to enforce, art to enchant;
330   And my ending is despair
       Unless I be relieved by prayer,
       Which pierces so that it assaults
       Mercy itself, and frees all faults.
       As you from crimes would pardoned be,
       Let your indulgence set me free.

Exit

(1611)

---

310 strangely wonderfully; **deliver** relate.   **316 Epilogue** Prospero's epilogue is unique in the Shakespeare canon in that its speaker declares himself not an actor in a play but a character in a fiction. The release he craves of the audience is the freedom to continue his history.   **320–4** Prospero puts himself in the position of Ariel, Caliban, Ferdinand, and the other shipwreck victims throughout the play, threatened with confinement, pleading for release from bondage; and his magical powers are now invested in the audience.   **325 your good hands** Sudden noises, and especially the clapping of hands, were thought to dissolve spells.   **326 Gentle breath** kind words (i.e. about the performance).   **326–7 breath . . . fill** This had been Ariel's charge at 314–17: the audience is now master and servant.   **333 Mercy** 'God's pitiful forbearance towards His creatures and forgiveness of their offences,' and hence a synecdoche for God.   **335 indulgence** playing on the technical sense of remission of the punishment for sin.

QUESTIONS

1. Identify the various roles that Prospero assumes in *The Tempest,* and then explain how each role demonstrates a specific power or relationship. In which role is Prospero most successful and least successful?

2. Explain the nature of Ariel's relationship to Prospero and why he is so beholden to him.

3. What do you think Shakespeare is suggesting about the nature of humanity through his creation of Caliban? Explain what you think Caliban's role is in *The Tempest.*

4. In what way is music so important to the play?

5. Characterize the father-daughter relationship between Prospero and Miranda. How does it compare to the father-son relationship between King Alonso and Prince Ferdinand? Which of the two fathers would you prefer for your own?

6. Why are Antonio and Sebastian so ready to betray their brothers?

7. Why do you think Prospero chooses to forgive his enemies, despite the cruel treatment he and his daughter have received? Why does he even go so far as to unite his daughter with the son of his enemy?

8. What role does magic play in *The Tempest?*

Writing Topics for Drama

1. Discuss the choice that children in Shakespeare's *The Tempest* have in accepting or rejecting the legacy of their parents. How does this choice shape their personalities and motivate Miranda and Ferdinand to fulfill their destinies?

2. Describe the special powers of Prospero in Shakespeare's *The Tempest.* How does his ability to see more than the others play an important role in the drama?

3. How does Prospero bear his fate and what drives him to seek to change it in Shakespeare's *The Tempest?*

4. Analyze the role of setting—weather, place, time of day or night—as it affects the plot of *The Tempest.*

PART 1: PARENTS AND CHILDREN
CROSS-GENRE DISCUSSION AND WRITING TOPICS

1. Compare the behavior and character of the mother in Hong Kingston's essay "The Woman Warrior" and the mother in Yamamoto's short story "Seventeen Syllables." How does the narrator's point of view shape the way each mother is perceived?

2. Compare the portraits of the stepmothers in the Grimms's fairy tale "Snow White" and Levine Keating's poem "The Envious Heart." Why do you think Levine Keating has transformed the original "Snow White"? In your comparison, consider how Gilbert and

Gubar's essay "Snow White and Her Wicked Stepmother" illuminates each version of the fairy tale.

3. Analyze how each narrator's reflections on the past affect the present in Yamamoto's story "Seventeen Syllables," Olds's poem "I Go Back to May 1937," Walker's short story "Everyday Use," and Kunitz's poem "The Portrait."

4. Compare Demeter's feelings for her daughter in "The Myth of Demeter and Persephone" with the feelings of Boland's speaker for her daughter in her poem "The Pomegranate."

5. Compare Daedalus's feelings for his son in "The Myth of Daedalus and Icarus" with the feelings of the speaker for his son in Reid's poem "Daedalus."

6. Discuss the common thread demonstrating the relationship between father and son in two of the following: "The Myth of Daedalus and Icarus," "The Parable of the Prodigal Son," Achebe's story "Marriage Is a Private Affair," Bly's poem "The Prodigal Son," and Gordimer's story "The Moment Before the Gun Went Off."

7. Various selections in this part focus on the theme of guilt, either from the parent's or the child's point of view. Analyze the reasons for guilt in Merwin's poem "Yesterday," Olsen's story "I Stand Here Ironing," Gordimer's story "The Moment Before the Gun Went Off," or Kunitz's poem "The Portrait" and discuss whether you think the guilt is justified.

8. Olsen's story "I Stand Here Ironing" and Levine Keating's poem "The Envious Heart" both deal with the children of marriages that have ended. Compare the experiences of the speaker in each work, as well as the emotions each expresses. Show how time and place and time of life have much to do with how a person shows love, understanding, and compassion.

9. "The Myth of Demeter and Persephone," Glück's poem "Pomegranate," Boland's poem "The Pomegranate, "Yamamoto's short story "Seventeen Syllables," and Walker's short story "Everyday Use" all focus on maturing daughters and the theme of separating from each other. What event has each of these writers chosen to illustrate this process of separation? Explain how these events can be construed as representing female initiation into adulthood.

10. Compare Plath's poem "Daddy," Rukeyser's poem "Ms. Lot," and Alvarez's essay "El Doctor." What imagery and tone of voice does each speaker or narrator use to convey her parent's power over her?

11. Examine the theme of the quest, for example, the quest for freedom, independence, identity, and so on, as demonstrated in Olds's poem "I Go Back to May 1937," "The Myth of Daedalus and Icarus," and Lessing's story "Throught the Tunnel." What makes a quest successful? Why do some quests fail?

12. Based on your reading of Shakespeare's play *The Tempest*, Hughes's poem "Mother to Son," Hayden's poem "Those Winter Sundays," and Walker's story "Everyday Use," in what ways can a parent prepare his or her child for life?

Etching from *The Book of Adam to Moses* by Lore Segal; illustrations by
Leonard Baskin. New York: Knopf, © 1987. Leonard Baskin (b. 1922). *Cain
and Abel* (1987) Etching. R. Michelson Galleries.

PART 2

SISTERS AND BROTHERS

For many of us, our first peers, our first best friends, and our first taste of rivalry come from having siblings. Whatever our gender or theirs, whether we are the oldest or the youngest or somewhere in between, to have or be a sibling colors us forever. Feelings about our siblings tend to accompany us well into adulthood, as numerous writers reveal by choosing the sibling relationship as their theme. The following selections reveal the breadth and variety of sibling relationships: sisters and brothers can love you, torment you, teach you, and kill you.

Jorge Luis Borges's short stories "Legend" and "In Memoriam, J.F.K.," Rainer Maria Rilke's poem "I am not. The Brother did something to me," and Demetrios Capetanakis's poem "Abel" all retell this famous story, shedding new light on the mystery of Cain and Abel's relationship. Sometimes a sibling's jealousy inadvertently causes her sister's death, as in Cynthia Ozick's short story "The Shawl." In the folktales "Cinderella" and "Vasilisa the Beautiful," a young woman is exploited by her stepsisters and stepmother. Alice Munro's "Boys and Girls" shows how rivalry between a brother and a sister can be caused by birth order and gender.

Sibling relationships are often contrasted, with a division of siblings into opposites: good and bad, beautiful and ugly, rich and poor, intelligent and stupid. Sylvia Plath's poem "Two Sisters of Persephone" contrasts two sisters, one happy, the other sad. Tobias Wolff retells the story of Cain and Abel with less drastic results from a modern standpoint. His title "The Rich Brother" suggests the inherent difficulty when the values of brothers conflict, and one embraces materialism and the other the spiritual life. In an unusual turn of events, Robert Coover's story "The Brother" portrays the traditionally "good" biblical figure of Noah as the one who will not save his brother as the land around them begins to flood, while in Cynthia Ozick's story "The Shawl," envy on the part of an older sister brings great harm to her innocent younger sister.

Sibling relationships may be among the most loving. Some of the deepest bonds exist between siblings, yet trying to help a sibling is not always successful, as Tennessee Williams's play *The Glass Menagerie* reveals. In the folktale "Hansel and Gretel," a sister does save her brother from death, but one's life may never be the same again, as Louise Glück's poem "Gretel in Darkness" shows. Seamus Heaney's poem "Mid-Term Break," Diane Keating's poem "Far Summers," and Catullus's "Poem 101" all attempt to come to terms with the death of a beloved sibling.

Myths, Parables, and Folktales

GENESIS 4:1–26*

The Story of Cain and Abel

And Adam knew Eve his wife; and she conceived, and bare Cain, and said, I have gotten a man from the LORD. And she again bare his brother Abel. And Abel was a keeper of sheep, but Cain was a tiller of the ground. And in process of time it came to pass, that Cain brought of the fruit of the ground an offering unto the LORD. And Abel, he also brought of the firstlings of his flock and of the fat thereof. And the LORD had respect unto Abel and to his offering: But unto Cain and to his offering he had not respect. And Cain was very wroth, and his countenance fell. And the LORD said unto Cain, Why art thou wroth? and why is thy countenance fallen? If thou doest well, shalt thou not be accepted? and if thou doest not well, sin lieth at the door: and unto thee *shall be* his desire, and thou shalt rule over him. And Cain talked with Abel his brother: and it came to pass, when they were in the field, that Cain rose up against Abel his brother, and slew him. (1–8)

And the LORD said unto Cain, Where is Abel thy brother? And he said, I know not: *Am* I my brother's keeper? And he said, What hast thou done? the voice of thy brother's blood crieth unto me from the ground. And now *art* thou cursed from the earth, which hath opened her mouth to receive thy brother's blood from thy hand. When thou tillest the ground, it shall not henceforth yield unto thee her strength; a fugitive and a vagabond shalt thou be in the earth. And Cain said unto the LORD, My punishment *is* greater than I can bear. Behold, thou hast driven me out this day from the face of the earth; and from thy face shall I be hid; and I shall be a fugitive and a vagabond in the earth; and it shall come to pass, *that* every one that findeth me shall slay me. And the LORD said unto him, Therefore whosoever slayeth Cain, vengeance shall be taken on him sevenfold. And the LORD set a mark upon Cain, lest any finding him should kill him. (9–15)

---

* King James Version of the Bible.

And Cain went out from the presence of the LORD, and dwelt in the land of Nod, on the east of Ē'den. And Cain knew his wife; and she conceived, and bare Enoch: and he builded a city, and called the name of the city, after the name of his son, Enoch. And unto Enoch was born I'răd: and I'răd begat Mē-hū'jā-ĕl: and Mē-hū'jā-ĕl begat Mē-thū'sā-ĕl: and Mē-thū'sā-ĕl begat Lā'mĕch. (16–18)

And Lā'mĕch took unto him two wives: the name of the one *was* Ā'dáh, and the name of the other Zil'láh. And Ā'dáh bare Jā'băl: he was the father of such as dwell in tents, and of *such as have* cattle. And his brother's name *was* Jubal: he was the father of all such as handle the harp and organ. And Zil'láh, she also bare Tū'băl-cāin, an instructor of every artificer in brass and iron: and the sister of Tū'băl-cāin *was* Nā'á-máh. And Lā'mĕch said unto his wives, Ā'dáh and Zil'láh, hear my voice; ye wives of Lā'mĕch, hearken unto my speech: for I have slain a man to my wounding, and a young man to my hurt. If Cain shall be avenged sevenfold, truly Lā'mĕch seventy and sevenfold. (19–24)

And Adam knew his wife again; and she bare a son, and called his name Seth: For God, *said she,* hath appointed me another seed instead of Abel, whom Cain slew. And to Seth, to him also there was born a son; and he called his name Ē'nŏs: then began men to call upon the name of the LORD. (25–26)

(C. 350 B.C.E.)

QUESTIONS

1. Why does God favor Abel?

2. Why is Cain so angry with his brother? Is his anger justified?

3. Do you think that Cain's punishment is fair? What purpose does this story serve in the Bible?

Jacob Grimm (1785–1863) and
Wilhelm Grimm (1786–1859)

Hansel and Gretel

Translated by Lucy Crane

Near a great forest there lived a poor woodcutter and his wife, and his two children; the boy's name was Hansel and the girl's Gretel. They had very little to bite or to sup, and once, when there was great dearth in the land, the man could not even gain the daily bread. As he lay in bed one night thinking of this, and turning and tossing, he sighed heavily, and said to his wife,

"What will become of us? we cannot even feed our children; there is nothing left for ourselves."

"I will tell you what, husband," answered the wife; "we will take the children early in the morning into the forest, where it is thickest; we will make them a fire, and we will give each of them a piece of bread, then we will go to our work and leave them alone; they will never find the way home again, and we shall be quit of them."

"No, wife," said the man, "I cannot do that; I cannot find in my heart to take my children into the forest and to leave them alone; the wild animals would soon come and devour them."

"O you fool," said she, "then we will all four starve; you had better get the coffins ready,"—and she left him no peace until he consented.

"But I really pity the poor children," said the man.

The two children had not been able to sleep for hunger, and had heard what their step-mother had said to their father. Gretel wept bitterly, and said to Hansel.

"It is all over with us."

"Do be quiet, Gretel," said Hansel, "and do not fret; I will manage something." And when the parents had gone to sleep he got up, put on his little coat, opened the back door, and slipped out. The moon was shining brightly, and the white flints that lay in front of the house glistened like pieces of silver. Hansel stooped and filled the little pockets of his coat. Then he went back again, and said to Gretel,

"Be easy, dear little sister, and go to sleep quietly; God will not forsake us," and laid himself down again in his bed.

When the day was breaking, and before the sun had risen, the wife came and awakened the two children, saying,

"Get up, you lazy bones; we are going into the forest to cut wood."

Then she gave each of them a piece of bread, and said,

"That is for dinner, and you must not eat it before then, for you will get no more."

Gretel carried the bread under her apron, for Hansel had his pockets full of the flints. Then they set off all together on their way to the forest. When they had gone a little way Hansel stood still and looked back towards the house, and this he did again and again, till his father said to him,

"Hansel, what are you looking at? take care not to forget your legs."

"O father," said Hansel, "I am looking at my little white kitten, who is sitting up on the roof to bid me good-bye."

"You young fool," said the woman, "that is not your kitten, but the sunshine on the chimney-pot."

Of course Hansel had not been looking at his kitten, but had been taking every now and then a flint from his pocket and dropping it on the road.

When they reached the middle of the forest the father told the children to collect wood to make a fire to keep them warm; and Hansel and Gretel gathered brushwood enough for a little mountain; and it was set on fire, and when the flame was burning quite high the wife said,

"Now lie down by the fire and rest yourselves, you children, and we will go and cut wood; and when we are ready we will come and fetch you."

So Hansel and Gretel sat by the fire, and at noon they each ate their pieces of bread. They thought their father was in the wood all the time, as they seemed to hear the strokes of the axe: but really it was only a dry branch hanging to a withered tree that the wind moved to and fro. So when they had stayed there a long time their eyelids closed with weariness, and they fell fast asleep. When at last they woke it was night, and Gretel began to cry, and said,

"How shall we ever get out of this wood?" But Hansel comforted her, saying,

"Wait a little while longer, until the moon rises, and then we can easily find the way home."

And when the full moon got up Hansel took his little sister by the hand, and followed the way where the flint stones shone like silver, and showed them the road. They walked on the whole night through, and at the break of day they came to their father's house. They knocked at the door, and when the wife opened it and saw that it was Hansel and Gretel she said,

"You naughty children, why did you sleep so long in the wood? We thought you were never coming home again!"

But the father was glad, for it had gone to his heart to leave them both in the woods alone.

Not very long after that there was again great scarcity in those parts, and the children heard their mother say at night in bed to their father,

"Everything is finished up; we have only half a loaf, and after that the tale comes to an end. The children must be off; we will take them farther into the wood this time, so that they shall not be able to find the way back again; there is no other way to manage."

The man felt sad at heart, and he thought,

"It would be better to share one's last morsel with one's children."

But the wife would listen to nothing that he said, but scolded and reproached him. He who says A must say B too, and when a man has given in once he has to do it a second time.

But the children were not asleep, and had heard all the talk. When the parents had gone to sleep Hansel got up to go out and get more flint stones, as he did before, but the wife had locked the door, and Hansel could not get out; but he comforted his little sister, and said,

"Don't cry, Gretel, and go to sleep quietly, and God will help us."

Early the next morning the wife came and pulled the children out of bed. She gave them each a little piece of bread—less than before; and on the way to the wood Hansel crumbled the bread in his pocket, and often stopped to throw a crumb on the ground.

"Hansel, what are you stopping behind and staring for?" said the father.

"I am looking at my little pigeon sitting on the roof, to say good-bye to me," answered Hansel.

"You fool," said the wife, "that is no pigeon, but the morning sun shining on the chimney pots."

Hansel went on as before, and strewed bread crumbs all along the road.

The woman led the children far into the wood, where they had never been before in all their lives. And again there was a large fire made, and the mother said,

"Sit still there, you children, and when you are tired you can go to sleep; we are going into the forest to cut wood, and in the evening, when we are ready to go home we will come and fetch you."

So when noon came Gretel shared her bread with Hansel, who had strewed his along the road. Then they went to sleep, and the evening passed, and no one came for the poor children. When they awoke it was dark night, and Hansel comforted his little sister, and said,

"Wait a little, Gretel, until the moon gets up, then we shall be able to see the way home by the crumbs of bread that I have scattered along it."

So when the moon rose they got up, but they could find no crumbs of bread, for the birds of the woods and of the fields had come and picked them up. Hansel thought they might find the way all the same, but they could not. They went on all that night, and the next day from the morning until the evening, but they could not find the way out of the wood, and they were very hungry, for they had nothing to eat but the few berries they could pick up. And when they were so tired that they could no longer drag themselves along, they lay down under a tree and fell asleep.

It was now the third morning since they had left their father's house. They were always trying to get back to it, but instead of that they only found themselves further in the wood, and if help had not soon come they would have been starved. About noon they saw a pretty snow-white bird sitting on a bough, and singing so sweetly that they stopped to listen. And when he had finished the bird spread his wings and flew before them, and they followed after him until they came to a little house, and the bird perched on the roof, and when they came nearer they saw that the house was built of bread, and roofed with cakes; and the window was of transparent sugar.

"We will have some of this," said Hansel, "and make a fine meal. I will eat a piece of the roof, Gretel, and you can have some of the window—that will taste sweet."

So Hansel reached up and broke off a bit of the roof, just to see how it tasted, and Gretel stood by the window and gnawed at it. Then they heard a thin voice call out from inside,

"Nibble, nibble, like a mouse,
Who is nibbling at my house?"

And the children answered,

> "Never mind,
> It is the wind."

And they went on eating, never disturbing themselves. Hansel, who found that the roof tasted very nice, took down a great piece of it, and Gretel pulled out a large round windowpane, and sat her down and began upon it. Then the door opened, and an aged woman came out, leaning upon a crutch. Hansel and Gretel felt very frightened, and let fall what they had in their hands. The old woman, however, nodded her head, and said,

"Ah, my dear children, how come you here? you must come indoors and stay with me, you will be no trouble."

So she took them each by the hand, and led them into her little house. And there they found a good meal laid out, of milk and pancakes, with sugar, apples, and nuts. After that she showed them two little white beds, and Hansel and Gretel laid themselves down on them, and thought they were in heaven.

The old woman, although her behavior was so kind, was a wicked witch, who lay in wait for children, and had built the little house on purpose to entice them. When they were once inside she used to kill them, cook them, and eat them, and then it was a feast-day with her. The witch's eyes were red, and she could not see very far, but she had a keen scent, like the beasts, and knew very well when human creatures were near. When she knew that Hansel and Gretel were coming, she gave a spiteful laugh, and said triumphantly,

"I have them, and they shall not escape me!"

Early in the morning, before the children were awake, she got up to look at them, and as they lay sleeping so peacefully with round rosy cheeks, she said to herself,

"What a fine feast I shall have!"

Then she grasped Hansel with her withered hand, and led him into a little stable, and shut him up behind a grating; and call and scream as he might, it was no good. Then she went back to Gretel and shook her, crying,

"Get up, lazy bones; fetch water, and cook something nice for your brother; he is outside in the stable, and must be fattened up. And when he is fat enough I will eat him."

Gretel began to weep bitterly, but it was of no use, she had to do what the wicked witch bade her.

And so the best kind of victuals was cooked for poor Hansel, while Gretel got nothing but crab-shells. Each morning the old woman visited the little stable, and cried,

"Hansel, stretch out your finger, and I may tell if you will soon be fat enough."

Hansel, however, used to hold out a little bone, and the old woman, who had weak eyes, could not see what it was, and supposing it to be Hansel's finger, wondered very much that it was not getting fatter. When four weeks had passed and Hansel seemed to remain so thin, she lost patience and could wait no longer.

"Now then, Gretel," cried she to the little girl; "be quick and draw water; be Hansel fat or be he lean, to-morrow I must kill and cook him."

Oh what a grief for the poor little sister to have to fetch water, and how the tears flowed down over her cheeks!

"Dear God, pray help us!" cried she; "if we had been devoured by wild beasts in the wood at least we should have died together."

"Spare me your lamentations," said the old woman; "they are of no avail."

Early next morning Gretel had to get up, make the fire, and fill the kettle.

"First we will do the baking," said the old woman; "I have heated the oven already, and kneaded the dough."

She pushed poor Gretel towards the oven, out of which the flames were already shining.

"Creep in," said the witch, "and see if it is properly hot, so that the bread may be baked."

And Gretel once in, she meant to shut the door upon her and let her be baked, and then she would have eaten her. But Gretel perceived her intention, and said,

"I don't know how to do it: how shall I get in?"

"Stupid goose," said the old woman, "the opening is big enough, do you see? I could get in myself!" and she stooped down and put her head in the oven's mouth. Then Gretel gave her a push, so that she went in further, and she shut the iron door upon her, and put up the bar. Oh how frightfully she howled! but Gretel ran away, and left the wicked witch to burn miserably. Gretel went straight to Hansel, opened the stable-door, and cried,

"Hansel, we are free! the old witch is dead!"

Then out flew Hansel like a bird from its cage as soon as the door is opened. How rejoiced they both were! how they fell each on the other's neck! and danced about, and kissed each other! And as they had nothing more to fear they went over all the old witch's house, and in every corner there stood chests of pearls and precious stones.

"This is something better than flint stones," said Hansel, as he filled his pockets, and Gretel, thinking she also would like to carry something home with her, filled her apron full.

"Now, away we go," said Hansel;—"if we only can get out of the witch's wood."

When they had journeyed a few hours they came to a great piece of water.

"We can never get across this," said Hansel, "I see no stepping-stones and no bridge."

"And there is no boat either," said Gretel; "but here comes a white duck; as I ask her she will help us over." So she cried,

> "Duck, duck, here we stand,
> Hansel and Gretel, on the land,
> Stepping-stones and bridge we lack,
> Carry us over on your nice white back."

And the duck came accordingly, and Hansel got upon her and told his sister to come too.

"No," answered Gretel, "that would be too hard upon the duck; we can go separately, one after the other."

And that was how it was managed, and after that they went on happily, until they came to the wood, and the way grew more and more familiar, till at last they saw in the distance their father's house. Then they ran till they came up to it, rushed in at the door, and fell on their father's neck. The man had not had a quiet hour since he left his children in the wood; but the wife was dead. And when Gretel opened her apron the pearls and precious stones were scattered all over the room, and Hansel took one handful after another out of his pocket. Then was all care at an end, and they all lived happily ever after.

(1812)

QUESTIONS

1. Why are the parents so willing to sacrifice their children? Why is it important that the children overhear their parents' conversation?

2. How does Hansel contrive to return to the house the first day? What happens the second time Hansel and Gretel are abandoned? What do you make of the refrain that "the good God will help us"?

3. In what way does Gretel prove a heroine and save Hansel? Can you think of any other folktales where a sister saves a brother or a female saves a male?

4. Explain the implicit connection between the stepmother and the old witch.

CHARLES PERRAULT (1628–1703)

Cinderella

or, The Little Glass Slipper

Translated by Robert Samber

There was once upon a time, a gentleman who married for his second wife the proudest and most haughty woman that ever was known. She had been a widow, and had by her former husband two daughters of her own humour, who were exactly like her in all things. He had also by a former wife a young daughter, but of an unparalleled goodness and sweetness of temper, which she took from her mother, who was the best creature in the world.

No sooner were the ceremonies of the wedding over, but the mother-in-law began to display her ill humour; she could not bear the good qualities of this pretty girl; and the less, because they made her own daughters so much the more hated and despised. She employed her in the meanest work of the house, she cleaned the dishes and stands, and rubbed Madam's chamber, and those of the young Madams her daughters: she lay on the top of the house in a garret, upon a wretched straw bed, while her sisters lay in fine rooms, with floors all inlaid, upon beds of the newst fashion, and where they had looking-glasses so large, that they might see themselves at their full length, from head to foot. The poor girl bore all patiently, and dared not tell her father, who would have rattled her off; for his wife governed him entirely. When she had done her work, she used to go into the chimney corner, and sit down upon the cinders, which made her commonly be called in the house *Cinderbreech:* but the youngest, who was not so rude and uncivil as the eldest, called her *Cinderella.* However, *Cinderella,* notwithstanding her poor clothes, was a hundred times handsomer than her sisters, though they wore the most magnificent apparel.

Now, it happened that the King's son gave a ball, and invited all persons of quality to it: our young ladies were also invited; for they made a very great figure. They were very well pleased thereat, and were very busy in choosing out such gowns, petticoats, and head-clothes as might become them best. This was a new trouble to *Cinderella;* for it was she that ironed her sisters linen, and plaited their ruffles; they talked all day long of nothing but how they should be dress'd. For my part, said the eldest, I'll wear my red velvet suit, with French trimming. And I, said the youngest, will have my common petticoat; but then, to make amends for that, I'll put on my gold flowered manteau,[1] and my diamond stomacher,[2] which is not the most indifferent in the world. They sent for the best tirewoman they could get, to dress their heads, and adjust their double pinners, and they had their red brushes and patches from Mrs. *De la poche.*

---

[1] manteau: loose cloak or mantle.
[2] stomacher: a heavily embroidered or jeweled garment worn by a woman over the chest and stomach.

Cinderella advised them the best in the world, and offered herself to dress their heads; which they were very willing she should do. As she was doing this, they said to her, *Cinderella,* would you not be glad to go to the ball? Ah! said she, you only banter me; it is not for such as I am to go thither. You are in the right of it, said they, it would make the people laugh to see a *Cinderbreech* at a ball. Any one but *Cinderella* would have dress'd their heads awry; but she was very good, and dress'd them perfectly well. They were almost two days without eating, so much were they transported with joy: they broke above a dozen of laces in trying to be laced up close, that they might have a fine slender shape, and they were continually at their looking-glass. At last the happy day came; they went to court, and *Cinderella* followed them with her eyes as long as she could, and when she had lost sight of them, she fell a crying.

Her godmother, who saw her all in tears, asked her what was the matter? I wish I could——, I wish I could——; she could not speak the rest, her tears interrupting her. Her godmother, who was a Fairy, said to her, Thou wishest thou could'st go to the ball, is it not so? Y——es, said *Cinderella,* with a great Sob. Well, said her godmother, be but a good girl, and I'll contrive thou shalt go. Then she took her into her chamber, and said to her, go into the garden, and bring me a pompion,[3] *Cinderella* went immediately to gather the finest she could get, and brought it to her godmother, not being able to imagine how this pompion could make her go to the ball: her godmother scooped out all the inside of it, having left nothing but the rind; she struck it with her wand, and the pompion immediately was turned into a fine coach, gilt all over with gold. After that, she went to look into her mouse-trap, where she found six mice all alive; she ordered *Cinderella* to lift up a little the trap door, and she gave every mouse that went out a stroke with her wand, and the mouse was that moment turned into a fine horse, which all together made a very fine set of six horses, of a beautiful mouse-coloured dapple grey. As she was at a loss for a coach-man, I'll go and see, says *Cinderella,* if there be never a rat in the rat-trap, we'll make a coach-man of him. You are in the right, said her godmother, go and see. *Cinderella* brought the trap to her, and in it there were three huge rats: the Fairy made choice of one of the three, which had the largest beard, and having touched him with her wand, he was turned into a fat jolly coach-man, that had the finest whiskers as ever were seen.

After that, she said to her, Go into the garden, and you will find six Lizards behind the watering-pot, bring them to me; she had no sooner done so, but her godmother turned them into six footmen, who skipped up immediately behind the coach, with their liveries all bedaubed with gold and silver, and clung so close behind one another, as if they had done nothing else all their lives. The Fairy then said to *Cinderella,* Well, you see here an equipage fit to go to the Ball with; are you not pleased with it? O yes, said she, but must I go thither as I am, with these ugly nasty clothes? Her godmother only just touched her with her wand, and at the same instant her clothes were turned into cloth of gold and silver, all beset with jewels: after this, she gave her a pair of Glass Slippers, the finest in the world. Being thus dress'd out she got into her coach; but her godmother, above all things, commanded her not to stay beyond twelve a clock at night;

---

[3] pompion: pumpkin.

telling her at the same time, that if she stay'd at the ball one moment longer, her coach would be a pompion again, her horses mice, her footmen lizards, and her clothes resume their old form.

She promised her godmother she would not fail of leaving the ball before midnight, and then departed not a little joyful at her good fortune. The King's son, who was informed that a great Princess, whom they did not know, was come, ran out to receive her; he gave her his hand as she alighted out of the coach, and led her into the hall where the company was: there was a great silence; they left off dancing, and the violins ceased to play, so attentive was every body to contemplate the extraordinary beauties of this unknown person: there was heard nothing but a confused noise of ha! how handsome she is, ha! how handsome she is. The King himself, as old as he was, could not help looking at her, and telling the Queen in a low voice, that it was a long time since that he had seen so beautiful and lovely a creature. All the ladies were busied in considering her clothes and head-dress, that they might have some made the next day after the same pattern, supposing they might get such fine materials, and as able hands to make them.

The King's son shewed her to the most honourable place, and afterwards took her out to dance with him: she danced with so much gracefulness, that they more and more admired her. A fine collation was served up, of which the young Prince ate nothing, so much was he taken up in looking upon her. She went and set herself down by her sisters, and showed them a thousand civilities: she gave them some of the oranges and lemons that the Prince had presented her with; which very much surprised them; for they did not know her. While the company was thus employed, *Cinderella* heard the clock go eleven and three quarters; upon which she immediately made a courtesy to the company, and went away as fast as she could.

As soon as she came home, she went to find out her godmother, and after having thanked her, she told her, she could not but heartily wish to go the next day to the ball, because the King's son had desired her. As she was busy in telling her godmother everything that had passed at the ball, her two sisters knock'd at the door, *Cinderella* went and opened it. You have stay'd a long while, said she, gaping, rubbing her eyes, and stretching herself as if she had been just awaked out of her sleep; she had however no manner of inclination to sleep since they went from home. If thou hadst been at the ball, said one of her sisters, thou would'st not have been tired with it: there came thither the most beautiful Princess, the most beautiful that ever was seen; she showed us a thousand civilities, and gave us oranges and lemons. *Cinderella* seem'd indifferent; she asked them the name of that Princess; but they told her they did not know it, and that the King's son was very uneasy on her account, and would give all the world to know where she was. At this *Cinderella* smiled, and said, she must then be very handsome indeed; Lord how happy have you been, could not I see her? Ah! good Madam *Charlotte,* lend me your yellow suit of clothes that you wear every day. Undoubtedly, said Madam *Charlotte,* lend my clothes to such a Cinderbreech as you are, who is fool then? *Cinderella* was very glad of the refusal, for she would have been sadly put to it, if her sister had lent her her clothes.

The next day the two sisters were at the ball, and so was *Cinderella,* but dressed more richly than she was at first. The King's son was always by her, and saying abundance of tender things to her; the young lady was no ways tired, and forgot what her godmother had recommended to her, so that she heard the clock begin to strike twelve, when she thought it was only eleven, she then rose up and fled as nimble as a deer: the Prince followed her, but could not catch hold of her; she dropt one of her Glass Slippers, which the Prince took up very carefully; *Cinderella* came home quite out of breath, without coach or footmen, and in her old ugly clothes; she had nothing left her of all her finery, but one of the little Slippers, fellow to that she drop'd. The guards at the palace-gate were asked if they had not seen a Princess go out, who said, they had seen no body go out, but a young woman very badly dress'd, and who had more the air of a poor country wench than a lady.

When the two sisters returned from the ball, *Cinderella* asked them, if they had been well diverted, and if the fine lady had been there; they told her, Yes, but that she flew away as soon as it had struck twelve a clock, and with so much haste, that she drop'd one of her little Glass Slippers, the prettiest in the world, and which the King's son had taken up, that he did nothing but look at her all the time of the ball, and that certainly he was very much in love with the beautiful person who owned the little Slipper. What they said was very true; for a few days after, the King's son caused it to be proclaimed by sound of trumpet, that he would marry her whose foot this Slipper would just fit. They began to try it on upon the princesses, then the dutchesses, and all the court, but in vain; it was brought to the two sisters, who did all they possibly could to thrust their foot into the Slipper, but they could not effect it. *Cinderella,* who saw all this, and knew the Slipper, said to them laughing, Let me see if it will not fit me; her sisters burst out a laughing, and began to banter her. The gentleman who was sent to try the Slipper, looked earnestly at *Cinderella* and finding her very handsome, said, it was but just that she should try, and that he had orders to let every body do so. He made *Cinderella* sit down, and putting the Slipper to her foot, he found it went in very easily, and fitted her, as if it had been made of wax. The astonishment her two sisters were in, was very great; but much greater, when *Cinderella* pulled out of her pocket the other Slipper, and put it upon her foot. Upon this her godmother came in, who having touch'd with her wand *Cinderella's* clothes, made them more rich and magnificent than ever they were before.

And now, her two sisters found her to be that fine beautiful lady that they had seen at the ball. They threw themselves at her feet, to beg pardon for all the ill treatment they had made her undergo. *Cinderella* took them up, and told them, as she embraced them, that she forgave them with all her heart, and desired them always to love her. She was conducted to the young Prince dress'd as she was: he thought her more beautiful then ever, and a few days after married her. *Cinderella,* who was as good as handsome, gave her two sisters lodgings in the palace, and married them the same day to two great lords of the court.

(1697)

QUESTIONS

1. Explain the connection between Cinderella's fairy godmother and Cinderella's "perfect" dead mother.

2. What is the folktale's moral? How might this moral apply more to young girls than it does to boys, or can it be argued that it transcends gender?

3. What is the prince's role in Cinderella's salvation?

4. Identify the roles of Cinderella's father and stepmother in this story. Why does Cinderella's father allow her to be treated so badly?

5. Why are the stepsisters rewarded by Cinderella, but not her father or stepmother?

6. Since "Cinderella" is probably the most popular of all folktales, explain which of its qualities have caused its success.

ALEKSANDR AFANAS'EV (1826–1871)

Vasilisa the Beautiful

Translated by Norbert Guterman

In a certain kingdom there lived a merchant. Although he had been married for twelve years, he had only one daughter, called Vasilisa the Beautiful. When the girl was eight years old, her mother died. On her deathbed the merchant's wife called her daughter, took a doll from under her coverlet, gave it to the girl, and said: "Listen, Vasilisushka. Remember and heed my last words. I am dying, and together with my maternal blessing I leave you this doll. Always keep it with you and do not show it to anyone; if you get into trouble, give the doll food, and ask its advice. When it has eaten, it will tell you what to do in your trouble." Then the mother kissed her child and died.

After his wife's death the merchant mourned as is proper, and then began to think of marrying again. He was a handsome man and had no difficulty in finding a bride, but he liked best a certain widow. Because she was elderly and had two daughters of her own, of almost the same age as Vasilisa, he thought that she was an experienced housewife and mother. So he married her, but was deceived, for she did not turn out to be a good mother for his Vasilisa. Vasilisa was the most beautiful girl in the village; her stepmother and stepsisters were jealous of her beauty and tormented her by giving her all kinds of work to do, hoping that she would grow thin from toil and tanned from exposure to the wind and sun; in truth, she had a most miserable life. But Vasilisa bore all this without complaint and became lovelier and more buxom, every day, while the stepmother and her daughters grew thin and ugly from spite, although they always sat with folded hands, like ladies.

How did all this come about? Vasilisa was helped by her doll. Without its aid the girl could never have managed all that work. In return, Vasilisa sometimes did not eat, but kept the choicest morsels for her doll. And at night, when everyone was asleep, she would lock herself in the little room in which she lived, and would give the doll a treat, saying: "Now, little doll, eat, and listen to my troubles. I live in my father's house but am deprived of all joy; a wicked stepmother is driving me from the white world. Tell me how I should live and what I should do." The doll would eat, then would give her advice and comfort her in her trouble, and in the morning, she would perform all the chores for Vasilisa, who rested in the shade and picked flowers while the flower beds were weeded, the cabbage sprayed, the water brought in, and the stove fired. The doll even showed Vasilisa an herb that would protect her from sunburn. She led an easy life, thanks to her doll.

Several years went by. Vasilisa grew up and reached the marriage age. She was wooed by all the young men in the village, but no one would even look at the stepmother's daughters. The stepmother was more spiteful than ever, and her answer to all the suitors was: "I will not give the youngest in marriage before the elder ones." And each time she sent a suitor away, she vented her anger on Vasilisa in cruel blows.

One day the merchant had to leave home for a long time in order to trade in distant lands. The stepmother moved to another house; near that house was a thick forest, and in a glade of that forest there stood a hut, and in the hut lived Baba Yaga.[1] She never allowed anyone to come near her and ate human beings as if they were chickens. Having moved into the new house, the merchant's wife, hating Vasilisa, repeatedly sent the girl to the woods for one thing or another; but each time Vasilisa returned home safe and sound: her doll had showed her the way and kept her far from Baba Yaga's hut.

Autumn came. The stepmother gave evening work to all three maidens: the oldest had to make lace, the second had to knit stockings, and Vasilisa had to spin; and each one had to finish her task. The stepmother put out the lights all over the house, leaving only one candle in the room where the girls worked, and went to bed. The girls worked. The candle began to smoke; one of the stepsisters took up a scissors to trim it, but instead, following her mother's order, she snuffed it out, as though inadvertently. "What shall we do now?" said the girls. "There is no light in the house and our tasks are not finished. Someone must run to Baba Yaga and get some light." "The pins on my lace give me light," said the one who was making lace. "I shall not go." "I shall not go either," said the one who was knitting stockings, "my knitting needles give me light." "Then you must go," both of them cried to their stepsister. "Go to Baba Yaga!" And they pushed Vasilisa out of the room. She went into her own little room, put the supper she had prepared before her doll, and said: "Now dolly, eat, and aid me in my need. They are sending me to Baba Yaga for a light, and she will eat me up." The doll ate the supper and its eyes gleamed like two candles. "Fear not, Vasilisushka," it said. "Go where you are sent, only keep me with you all the time. With me in your pocket you will suffer no harm from Baba Yaga." Vasilisa made ready, put her doll in her pocket, and, having made the sign of the cross, went into the deep forest.

She walked in fear and trembling. Suddenly a horseman galloped past her: his face was white, he was dressed in white, his horse was white, and his horse's trappings were white—daybreak came to the woods.

She walked on farther, and a second horseman galloped past her: he was all red, he was dressed in red, and his horse was red—the sun began to rise.

Vasilisa walked the whole night and the whole day, and only on the following evening did she come to the glade where Baba Yaga's hut stood. The fence around the hut was made of human bones, and on the spikes were human skulls with staring eyes; the doors had human legs for doorposts, human hands for bolts, and a mouth with sharp teeth in place of a lock. Vasilisa was numb with horror and stood rooted to the spot. Suddenly another horseman rode by. He was all black, he was dressed in black, and his horse was black. He galloped up to Baba Yaga's door and vanished, as though the earth had swallowed him up—night came. But the darkness did not last long. The eyes of all the skulls on the fence began to gleam and the glade was as bright as day. Vasilisa shuddered with fear, but not knowing where to run, remained on the spot.

Soon a terrible noise resounded through the woods; the trees crackled, the dry leaves rustled; from the woods Baba Yaga drove out in a mortar, prodding it on with a

---

[1] Baba Yaga: bony-legged wild woman or witch of Russian folktales.

pestle, and sweeping her traces with a broom. She rode up to the gate, stopped, and sniffing the air around her, cried: "Fie, fie! I smell a Russian smell! Who is here?" Vasilisa came up to the old witch and, trembling with fear, bowed low to her and said: "It is I, grandmother. My stepsisters sent me to get some light." "Very well," said Baba Yaga. "I know them, but before I give you the light you must live with me and work for me; if not, I will eat you up." Then she turned to the gate and cried: "Hey, my strong bolts, unlock! Open up, my wide gate!" The gate opened, and Baba Yaga drove in whistling. Vasilisa followed her, and then everything closed again.

Having entered the room, Baba Yaga stretched herself out in her chair and said to Vasilisa: "Serve me what is in the stove; I am hungry." Vasilisa lit a torch from the skulls on the fence and began to serve Yaga the food from the stove—and enough food had been prepared for ten people. She brought kvass, mead, beer, and wine from the cellar. The old witch ate and drank everything, leaving for Vasilisa only a little cabbage soup, a crust of bread, and a piece of pork. Then Baba Yaga made ready to go to bed and said: "Tomorrow after I go, see to it that you sweep the yard, clean the hut, cook the dinner, wash the linen, and go to the cornbin and sort out a bushel of wheat. And let everything be done, or I will eat you up!" Having given these orders, Baba Yaga began to snore. Vasilisa set the remnants of the old witch's supper before her doll, wept bitter tears, and said: "Here dolly, eat, and aid me in my need! Baba Yaga has given me a hard task to do and threatens to eat me up if I do not do it all. Help me!" The doll answered: "Fear not, Vasilisa the Beautiful! Eat your supper, say your prayers, and go to sleep; the morning is wiser than the evening."

Very early next morning Vasilisa awoke, after Baba Yaga had arisen, and looked out of the window. The eyes of the skulls were going out; then the white horseman flashed by, and it was daybreak. Baba Yaga went out into the yard, whistled, and the mortar, pestle, and broom appeared before her. The red horseman flashed by, and the sun rose. Baba Yaga sat in the mortar, prodded it on with the pestle, and swept her traces with the broom. Vasilisa remained alone, looked about Baba Yaga's hut, was amazed at the abundance of everything, and stopped wondering which work she should do first. For lo and behold, all the work was done; the doll was picking the last shreds of chaff from the wheat. "Ah my savior," said Vasilisa to her doll, "you have delivered me from death." "All you have to do," answered the doll, creeping into Vasilisa's pocket, "is to cook the dinner; cook it with the help of God and then rest, for your health's sake."

When evening came Vasilisa sat the table and waited for Baba Yaga. Dusk began to fall, the black horseman flashed by the gate, and night came; only the skulls' eyes were shining. The trees crackled, the leaves rustled; Baba Yaga was coming. Vasilisa met her. "Is everything done?" asked Yaga. "Please see for yourself, grandmother," said Vasilisa. Baba Yaga looked at everything, was annoyed that there was nothing she could complain about, and said: "Very well, then." Then she cried: "My faithful servants, my dear friends, grind my wheat!" Three pairs of hands appeared, took the wheat, and carried it out of sight. Baba Yaga ate her fill, made ready to go to sleep, and again gave her orders to Vasilisa. "Tomorrow," she commanded, "do the same work you have done today, and in addition take the poppy seed from the bin and get rid of the dust, grain by grain; someone threw dust into the bins out of spite." Having said this, the old witch turned to the wall and began to snore, and Vasilisa set about feeding her doll. The doll ate, and spoke as she had spoken the day before: "Pray to God and go to sleep; the morning is wiser than the evening. Everything will be done, Vasilisushka."

Next morning Baba Yaga again left the yard in her mortar, and Vasilisa and the doll soon had all the work done. The old witch came back, looked at everything, and cried: "My faithful servants, my dear friends, press the oil out of the poppy seed!" Three pairs of hands appeared, took the poppy seed, and carried it out of sight. Baba Yaga sat down to dine; she ate, and Vasilisa stood silent. "Why do you not speak to me?" said Baba Yaga. "You stand there as though you were dumb." "I did not dare to speak," said Vasilisa, "but if you'll give me leave, I'd like to ask you something." "Go ahead. But not every question has a good answer; if you know too much, you will soon grow old." "I want to ask you, grandmother, only about what I have seen. As I was on my way to you, a horseman on a white horse, all white himself and dressed in white, overtook me. Who is he?" "He is my bright day," said Baba Yaga. "Then another horseman overtook me; he had a red horse, was red himself, and was dressed in red. Who is he?" "He is my red sun." "And who is the black horseman whom I met at your very gate, grandmother?" "He is my dark night—and all of them are my faithful servants."

Vasilisa remembered the three pairs of hands, but kept silent. "Why don't you ask me more?" said Baba Yaga. "That will be enough," Vasilisa replied. "You said yourself, grandmother, that one who knows too much will grow old soon." "It is well," said Baba Yaga, "that you ask only about what you have seen outside my house, not inside my house; I do not like to have my dirty linen washed in public, and I eat the overcurious. Now I shall ask you something. How do you manage to do the work I set for you?" "I am helped by the blessing of my mother," said Vasilisa. "So that is what it is," shrieked Baba Yaga. "Get you gone, blessed daughter! I want no blessed ones in my house!" She dragged Vasilisa out of the room and pushed her outside the gate, took a skull with burning eyes from the fence, stuck it on a stick, and gave it to the girl, saying: "Here is your light for your stepsisters. Take it; that is what they sent you for."

Vasilisa ran homeward by the light of the skull, which went out only at daybreak, and by nightfall of the following day she reached the house. As she approached the gate, she was about to throw the skull away, thinking that surely they no longer needed a light in the house. But suddenly a dull voice came from the skull, saying: "Do not throw me away, take me to your stepmother." She looked at the stepmother's house and, seeing that there was no light in the windows, decided to enter with her skull. For the first time she was received kindly. Her stepmother and stepsisters told her that since she had left they had had no fire in the house; they were unable to strike a flame themselves, and whatever light was brought by the neighbors went out the moment it was brought into the house. "Perhaps your fire will last," said the stepmother. The skull was brought into the room, and its eyes kept staring at the stepmother and her daughters, and burned them. They tried to hide, but wherever they went the eyes followed them. By morning they were all burned to ashes; only Vasilisa remained untouched by the fire.

In the morning Vasilisa buried the skull in the ground, locked up the house, and went to the town. A certain childless old woman gave her shelter, and there she lived, waiting for her father's return. One day she said to the woman: "I am weary of sitting without work, grandmother. Buy me some flax, the best you can get; at least I shall be spinning." The old woman bought good flax and Vasilisa set to work. She spun as fast as lightning and her threads were even and thin as a hair. She spun a great deal of yarn; it was time to start weaving it, but no comb fine enough for Vasilisa's yarn could be found, and no one would undertake to make one. Vasilisa asked her doll for aid. The doll said: "Bring me an old comb, an old shuttle, and a horse's mane; I will make a loom for you." Vasilisa got everything that was required and went to sleep, and during the night the doll made a wonderful loom for her.

By the end of the winter the linen was woven, and it was so fine that it could be passed through a needle like a thread. In the spring the linen was bleached, and Vasilisa said to the old woman: "Grandmother, sell this linen and keep the money for yourself." The old woman looked at the linen and gasped: "No, my child! No one can wear such linen except the tsar; I shall take it to the palace." The old woman went to the tsar's palace and walked back and forth beneath the windows. The tsar saw her and asked: "What do you want, old woman?" "Your Majesty," she answered, "I have brought rare merchandise; I do not want to show it to anyone but you." The tsar ordered her to be brought before him, and when he saw the linen he was amazed. "What do you want for it?" asked the tsar. "It has no price, little father tsar! I have brought it as a gift to you." The tsar thanked her and rewarded her with gifts.

The tsar ordered shirts to be made of the linen. It was cut, but nowhere could they find a seamstress who was willing to sew them. For a long time they tried to find one, but in the end the tsar summoned the old woman and said: "You have known how to spin and weave such linen, you must know how to sew shirts of it." "It was not I that spun and wove this linen, Your Majesty," said the old woman. "This is the work of a maiden to whom I give shelter." "Then let her sew the shirts," ordered the tsar.

The old woman returned home and told everything to Vasilisa. "I knew all the time," said Vasilisa to her, "that I would have to do this work." She locked herself in her room and set to work; she sewed without rest and soon a dozen shirts were ready. The old woman took them to the tsar, and Vasilisa washed herself, combed her hair, dressed in her finest clothes, and sat at the window. She sat there waiting to see what would happen. She saw a servant of the tsar entering the courtyard. The messenger came into the room and said: "The tsar wishes to see the needlewoman who made his shirts, and wishes to reward her with his own hands." Vasilisa appeared before the tsar. When the tsar saw Vasilisa the Beautiful he fell madly in love with her. "No, my beauty," he said, "I will not separate from you; you shall be my wife." He took Vasilisa by her white hands, seated her by his side, and the wedding was celebrated at once. Soon Vasilisa's father returned, was overjoyed at her good fortune, and came to live in his daughter's house. Vasilisa took the old woman into her home too, and carried her doll in her pocket till the end of her life.

(AFTER 1866)

QUESTIONS

1. What does the doll represent and what are the sources of its magical powers?

2. How might Baba Yaga be perceived by a child? What does an adult seem to have in mind when telling a child about a character such as Baba Yaga, a wicked crone who eats human flesh? Why doesn't she eat Vasilisa, letting her go instead?

3. Explain the references to light and dark imagery that appear throughout the tale.

Writing Topics for Myths, Parables, and Folktales

1. What are the strategies for dealing with sibling rivalry as depicted in the biblical "The Story of Cain and Abel" and the folktale "Cinderella"? In what ways are they successful or problematic?

2. Why do you think the Bible presents the occasion of the first murder as the result of sibling rivalry? Why do you think Cain's punishment is exile, not death?

3. Explain the similarities between the sibling relationships in "Vasilisa the Beautiful" and "Cinderella." What do these similarities reveal about the themes, values, and purpose of folktales?

4. What role do wealth and poverty play in determining the actions of each of the characters in the folktales "Hansel and Gretel," "Vasilisa the Beautiful," and "Cinderella"?

5. How does the folktale "Hansel and Gretel" grapple with Cain's haunting question in "The Story of Cain and Abel," "Am I my brother's keeper?"

Essays

BRUNO BETTELHEIM (1903–1990)

Cinderella*

By all accounts, "Cinderella" is the best-known fairy tale, and probably also the best-liked. It is quite an old story; when first written down in China during the ninth century A.D., it already had a history. The unrivaled tiny foot size as a mark of extraordinary virtue, distinction, and beauty, and the slipper made of precious material are facets which point to an Eastern, if not necessarily Chinese, origin.[1] The modern hearer does not connect sexual attractiveness and beauty in general with extreme smallness of the foot, as the ancient Chinese did, in accordance with their practice of binding women's feet.

"Cinderella," as we know it, is experienced as a story about the agonies and hopes which form the essential content of sibling rivalry; and about the degraded heroine winning out over her siblings who abused her. Long before Perrault gave "Cinderella" the form in which it is now widely known, "having to live among the ashes" was a symbol of being debased in comparison to one's siblings, irrespective of sex. In Germany, for example, there were stories in which such an ash-boy later becomes king, which parallels Cinderella's fate. "Aschenputtel" is the title of the Brothers Grimm's version of the tale. The term originally designated a lowly, dirty kitchenmaid who must tend to the fireplace ashes.

There are many examples in the German language of how being forced to dwell among the ashes was a symbol not just of degradation, but also of sibling rivalry, and of the sibling who finally surpasses the brother or brothers who have debased him. Martin Luther[2] in his *Table Talks* speaks about Cain as the God-forsaken evildoer who is

---

* This selection is from *The Uses of Enchantment: The Meaning and Importance of Fairy Tales* (New York: Alfred A. Knopf, Inc.) 1976.

[1] Artistically made slippers of precious material were reported in Egypt from the third century on. The Roman emperor Diocletian in a decree of 301 set maximum prices for different kinds of footwear, including slippers made of fine Babylonian leather, dyed purple or scarlet, and gilded slippers for women. (Bettelheim.)

[2] Martin Luther (1483–1546): German leader of the Protestant Reformation and Lutheranism, a sect of Christianity.

powerful, while pious Abel is forced to be his ash-brother (*Aschebrüdel*), a mere nothing, subject to Cain; in one of Luther's sermons he says that Esau was forced into the role of Jacob's ash-brother. Cain and Abel, Jacob and Esau are Biblical examples of one brother being suppressed or destroyed by the other.

The fairy tale replaces sibling relations with relations between step-siblings—perhaps a device to explain and make acceptable an animosity which one wishes would not exist among true siblings. Although sibling rivalry is universal and "natural" in the sense that it is the negative consequence of being a sibling, this same relation also generates equally as much positive feeling between siblings, highlighted in fairy tales such as "Brother and Sister."

No other fairy tale renders so well as the "Cinderella" stories the inner experiences of the young child in the throes of sibling rivalry, when he feels hopelessly outclassed by his brothers and sisters. Cinderella is pushed down and degraded by her stepsisters; her interests are sacrificed to theirs by her (step)mother; she is expected to do the dirtiest work and although she performs it well, she receives no credit for it; only more is demanded of her. This is how the child feels when devastated by the miseries of sibling rivalry. Exaggerated though Cinderella's tribulations and degradations may seem to the adult, the child carried away by sibling rivalry feels, "That's me; that's how they mistreat me, or would want to; that's how little they think of me." And there are moments—often long time periods—when for inner reasons a child feels this way even when his position among his siblings may seem to give him no cause for it.

When a story corresponds to how the child feels deep down—as no realistic narrative is likely to do—it attains an emotional quality of "truth" for the child. The events of "Cinderella" offer him vivid images that give body to his overwhelming but nevertheless often vague and nondescript emotions; so these episodes seem more convincing to him than his life experiences.

The term "sibling rivalry" refers to a most complex constellation of feelings and their causes. With extremely rare exceptions, the emotions aroused in the person subject to sibling rivalry are far out of proportion to what his real situation with his sisters and brothers would justify, seen objectively. While all children at times suffer greatly from sibling rivalry, parents seldom sacrifice one of the children to the others, nor do they condone the other children's persecuting one of them. Difficult as objective judgments are for the young child—nearly impossible when his emotions are aroused—even he in his more rational moments "knows" that he is not treated as badly as Cinderella. But the child often feels mistreated, despite all his "knowledge" to the contrary. That is why he believes in the inherent truth of "Cinderella," and then he also comes to believe in her eventual deliverance and victory. From her triumph he gains the exaggerated hopes for his future which he needs to counteract the extreme misery he experiences when ravaged by sibling rivalry.

Despite the name "sibling rivalry," this miserable passion has only incidentally to do with a child's actual brothers and sisters. The real source of it is the child's feelings about his parents. When a child's older brother or sister is more competent than he, this arouses only temporary feelings of jealousy. Another child being given special attention becomes an insult only if the child fears that, in contrast, he is thought little of by his parents, or feels rejected by them. It is because of such an anxiety that one or all of a child's sisters or brothers may become a thorn in his flesh. Fearing that in comparison to them he cannot win his parents' love and esteem is what inflames sibling rivalry. This is indicated in stories by the fact that it matters little whether the siblings actually possess greater competence. The Biblical story of Joseph tells that it is jealousy of parental affection lavished on him which accounts for the destructive behavior of his brothers. Unlike Cinderella's, Joseph's parent does not participate in degrading him, and, on the contrary, prefers him to his other children. But Joseph, like Cinderella, is turned into a slave, and, like her, he miraculously escapes and ends by surpassing his siblings.

Telling a child who is devastated by sibling rivalry that he will grow up to do as well as his brothers and sisters offers little relief from his present feelings of dejection. Much as he would like to trust our assurances, most of the time he cannot. A child can see things only with subjective eyes, and comparing himself on this basis to his siblings, he has no confidence that he, on his own, will someday be able to fare as well as they. If he could believe more in himself, he would not feel destroyed by his siblings no matter what they might do to him, since then he could trust that time would bring about a desired reversal of fortune. But since the child cannot, on his own, look forward with confidence to some future day when things will turn out all right for him, he can gain relief only through fantasies of glory—a domination over his siblings—which he hopes will become reality through some fortunate event.

Whatever our position within the family, at certain times in our lives we are beset by sibling rivalry in some form or other. Even an only child feels that other children have some great advantages over him, and this makes him intensely jealous. Further, he may suffer from the anxious thought that if he did have a sibling, his parents would prefer this other child to him. "Cinderella" is a fairy tale which makes nearly as strong an appeal to boys as to girls, since children of both sexes suffer equally from sibling rivalry, and have the same desire to be rescued from their lowly position and surpass those who seem superior to them.

On the surface, "Cinderella" is as deceptively simple as the story of Little Red Riding Hood, with which it shares greatest popularity. "Cinderella" tells about the agonies of sibling rivalry, of wishes coming true, of the humble being elevated, of true merit being recognized even when hidden under rags, of virtue rewarded and evil punished—a straightforward story. But under this overt content is concealed a welter of complex and largely unconscious material, which details of the story allude to just enough to set our unconscious associations going. This makes a contrast between surface simplicity and underlying complexity which arouses deep interest in the story and explains its appeal to the millions over centuries. To begin gaining an understanding of these hidden meanings, we have to penetrate behind the obvious sources of sibling rivalry discussed so far.

As mentioned before, if the child could only believe that it is the infirmities of his age which account for his lowly position, he would not have to suffer so wretchedly from sibling rivalry, because he could trust the future to right matters. When he thinks that his degradation is deserved, he feels his plight is utterly hopeless. Djuna Barnes's perceptive statement about fairy tales—that the child knows something about them which he cannot tell (such as that he likes the idea of Little Red Riding Hood and the wolf being in bed together)—could be extended by dividing fairy tales into two groups: one group where the child responds only unconsciously to the inherent truth of the story and thus cannot tell about it; and another large number of tales where the child precon-sciously or even consciously knows what the "truth" of the story consists of and thus could tell about it, but does not want to let on that he knows. Some aspects of "Cinderella" fall into the latter category. Many children believe that Cinderella probably deserves her fate at the beginning of the story, as they feel they would, too; but they don't want anyone to know it. Despite this, she is worthy at the end to be exalted, as the child hopes he will be too, irrespective of his earlier shortcomings.

Every child believes at some period of his life—and this is not only at rare mo-ments—that because of his secret wishes, if not also his clandestine actions, he deserves to be degraded, banned from the presence of others, relegated to a netherworld of smut. He fears this may be so, irrespective of how fortunate his situation may be in re-ality. He hates and fears those others—such as his siblings—whom he believes to be en-tirely free of similar evilness, and he fears that they or his parents will discover what he is really like, and then demean him as Cinderella was by her family. Because he wants oth-ers—most of all, his parents—to believe in his innocence, he is delighted that "everybody" believes in Cinderella's. This is one of the great attractions of this fairy tale. Since people give credence to Cinderella's goodness, they will also believe in his, so the child hopes. And "Cinderella" nourishes this hope, which is one reason it is such a delightful story.

Another aspect which holds large appeal for the child is the vileness of the step-mother and stepsisters. Whatever the shortcomings of a child may be in his own eyes, these pale into insignificance when compared to the stepsisters' and stepmother's false-hood and nastiness. Further, what these stepsisters do to Cinderella justifies whatever nasty thoughts one may have about one's siblings: they are so vile that anything one may wish would happen to them is more than justified. Compared to their behavior, Cinderella is indeed innocent. So the child, on hearing her story, feels he need not feel guilty about his angry thoughts.

On a very different level—and reality considerations coexist easily with fantastic exaggerations in the child's mind—as badly as one's parents or siblings seem to treat one, and much as one thinks one suffers because of it, all this is nothing compared to Cinderella's fate. Her story reminds the child at the same time how lucky he is, and how much worse things could be. (Any anxiety about the latter possibility is relieved, as al-ways in fairy tales, by the happy ending.)

The behavior of a five-and-a-half-year-old girl, as reported by her father, may illus-trate how easily a child may feel that she is a "Cinderella." This little girl had a younger sister of whom she was very jealous. The girl was very fond of "Cinderella," since the story offered her material with which to act out her feelings, and because without the story's imagery she would have been hard pressed to comprehend and express them. This little girl had used to dress very neatly and liked pretty clothes, but she became un-kempt and dirty. One day when she was asked to fetch some salt, she said as she was doing so, "Why do you treat me like Cinderella?"

Almost speechless, her mother asked her, "Why do you think I treat you like Cinderella?"

"Because you make me do all the hardest work in the house!" was the little girl's answer. Having thus drawn her parents into her fantasies, she acted them out more openly, pretending to sweep up all the dirt, etc. She went even further, playing that she prepared her little sister for the ball. But she went the "Cinderella" story one better, based on her unconscious understanding of the contradictory emotions fused into the "Cinderella" role, because at another moment she told her mother and sister, "You shouldn't be jealous of me just because I am the most beautiful in the family."

This shows that behind the surface humility of Cinderella lies the conviction of her superiority to mother and sisters, as if she would think: "You can make me do all the dirty work, and I pretend that I am dirty, but within me I know that you treat me this way because you are jealous of me because I am so much better than you." This conviction is supported by the story's ending, which assures every "Cinderella" that eventually she will be discovered by her prince.

Why does the child believe deep within himself that Cinderella deserves her dejected state? This question takes us back to the child's state of mind at the end of the oedipal period. Before he is caught in oedipal entanglements, the child is convinced that he is lovable, and loved, if all is well within his family relationships. Psychoanalysis describes this stage of complete satisfaction with oneself as "primary narcissism." During this period the child feels certain that he is the center of the universe, so there is no reason to be jealous of anybody.

The oedipal disappointments which come at the end of this developmental stage cast deep shadows of doubt on the child's sense of his worthiness. He feels that if he were really as deserving of love as he had thought, then his parents would never be critical of him or disappoint him. The only explanation for parental criticism the child can think of is that there must be some serious flaw in him which accounts for what he experiences as rejection. If his desires remain unsatisfied and his parents disappoint him, there must be something wrong with him or his desires, or both. He cannot yet accept that reasons other than those residing within him could have an impact on his fate. In his oedipal jealousy, wanting to get rid of the parent of the same sex had seemed the most natural thing in the world, but now the child realizes that he cannot have his own way, and that maybe this is so because the desire was wrong. He is no longer so sure that he is preferred to his siblings, and he begins to suspect that this may be due to the fact that *they* are free of any bad thoughts or wrongdoing such as his.

All this happens as the child is gradually subjected to ever more critical attitudes as he is being socialized. He is asked to behave in ways which run counter to his natural desires, and he resents this. Still he must obey, which makes him very angry. This anger is directed against those who make demands, most likely his parents; and this is another reason to wish to get rid of them, and still another reason to feel guilty about such wishes. This is why the child also feels that he deserves to be chastised for his feelings, a punishment he believes he can escape only if nobody learns what he is thinking when he is angry. The feeling of being unworthy to be loved by his parents at a time when his desire for their love is very strong leads to the fear of rejection, even when in reality there is none. This rejection fear compounds the anxiety that others are preferred and also maybe preferable—the root of sibling rivalry.

(1976)

QUESTIONS

1. According to Bettelheim, what purpose is served by reading a folktale like "Cinderella"?

2. Explain why you agree or disagree with Bettelheim that Cinderella is more than just a story about a young woman struggling with her stepsisters and stepmother.

3. Why does a folktale like this require a happy ending? How would you react if the story ended unhappily?

SIGMUND FREUD (1856–1939)

The Theme of the Three Caskets[1]

Translated by C. J. M. Hubback

Two scenes from Shakespeare, one from a comedy and the other from a tragedy, have lately given me occasion for setting and solving a little problem.

The former scene is the suitors' choice between the three caskets in *The Merchant of Venice*. The fair and wise Portia, at her father's bidding, is bound to take for her husband only that one among her suitors who chooses the right casket from among the three before him. The three caskets are of gold, silver and lead: the right one is that containing her portrait. Two suitors have already withdrawn, unsuccessful: they have chosen gold and silver. Bassanio, the third, elects for the lead; he thereby wins the bride, whose affection was already his before the trial of fortune. Each of the suitors had given reasons for his choice in a speech in which he praised the metal he preferred, while depreciating the other two. The most difficult task thus fell to the share of the third fortunate suitor; what he finds to say in glorification of lead as against gold and silver is but little and has a forced ring about it. If in psychoanalytic practice we were confronted with such a speech, we should suspect concealed motives behind the unsatisfying argument.

Shakespeare did not invent this oracle of choosing a casket; he took it from a tale in the *Gesta Romanorum,* in which a girl undertakes the same choice to win the son of the Emperor.[2] Here too the third metal, the lead, is the bringer of fortune. It is not hard to guess that we have here an ancient theme, which requires to be interpreted and traced back to its origin. A preliminary conjecture about the meaning of this choice between gold, silver and lead is soon confirmed by a statement from E. Stucken,[3] who has made a study of the same material in far-reaching connections. He says, "The identity of the three suitors of Portia is clear from the choice: the Prince of Morocco chooses the gold casket: he is the sun; the Prince of Arragon chooses the silver casket: he is the moon; Bassanio chooses the leaden casket: he is the star youth." In support of this explanation he cites an episode from the Esthonian folk-epic "Kalewipoeg," in which the three suitors appear undisguisedly as the sun, moon and star youths ("the eldest son of the Pole star") and the bride again falls to the lot of the third.

Thus our little problem leads to an astral myth. The only pity is that with this explanation we have not got to the end of the matter. The question goes further, for we do not share the belief of many investigators that myths were read off direct from the heavens; we are more inclined to judge with Otto Rank[4] that they were projected on to the

---

[1] First published in *Imago,* 1913.
[2] G. Brandes, *William Shakespeare,* 1896. (Freud.)
[3] *Astralmythen,* p. 655. (Freud.)
[4] O. Rank, *Der Mythus von der Geburt des Helden* (Vienna, 1909), p. 8 *et seq.* (Freud.)

heavens after having arisen quite otherwise under purely human conditions. Now our interest is in this human content.

Let us glance once more at our material. In the Esthonian epic, as in the tale from the *Gesta Romanorum,* the subject is the choice of a maiden among three suitors; in the scene from *The Merchant of Venice* apparently the subject is the same, but at the same time in this last something in the nature of an inversion of the idea makes its appearance: a man chooses between three—caskets. If we had to do with a dream, it would at once occur to us that caskets are also women, symbols of the essential thing in woman, and therefore of a woman herself, like boxes, large or small, baskets, and so on. If we let ourselves assume the same symbolic substitution in the story, then the casket scene in *The Merchant of Venice* really becomes the inversion we suspected. With one wave of the hand, such as usually only happens in fairy-tales, we have stripped the astral garment from our theme; and now we see that the subject is an idea from human life, a man's choice between three women.

This same content, however, is to be found in another scene of Shakespeare's, in one of his most powerfully moving dramas; this time not the choice of a bride, yet linked by many mysterious resemblances to the casket-choice in *The Merchant of Venice.* The old King Lear resolves to divide his kingdom while he yet lives among his three daughters, according to the love they each in turn express for him. The two elder ones, Goneril and Regan, exhaust themselves in asseverations and glorifications of their love for him, the third, Cordelia, refuses to join in these. He should have recognized the unassuming, speechless love of the third and rewarded it, but he misinterprets it, banishes Cordelia, and divides the kingdom between the other two, to his own and the general ruin. Is not this once more a scene of choosing between three women, of whom the youngest is the best, the supreme one?

There immediately occur to us other scenes from myth, folktale and literature, with the same situation as their content: the shepherd Paris has to choose between three goddesses, of whom he declares the third to be the fairest. Cinderella[5] is another such youngest, and is preferred by the prince to the two elder sisters; Psyche[6] in the tale of Apuleius is the youngest and fairest of three sisters; on the one hand, she becomes human and is revered as Aphrodite, on the other, she is treated by the goddess as Cinderella was treated by her stepmother and has to sort a heap of mixed seeds, which she accomplishes with the help of little creatures (doves for Cinderella, ants for Psyche). Anyone who cared to look more closely into the material could undoubtedly discover other versions of the same idea in which the same essential features had been retained.

Let us content ourselves with Cordelia, Aphrodite, Cinderella and Psyche! The three women, of whom the third surpasses the other two, must surely be regarded as in some way alike if they are represented as sisters. It must not lead us astray if in *Lear* the three are the daughters of him who makes the choice; this means probably nothing more than that Lear has to be represented as an old man. An old man cannot very well choose between three women in any other way: thus they become his daughters.

---

[5] See p. 202.
[6] See p. 345.

But who are these three sisters and why must the choice fall on the third? If we could answer this question, we should be in possession of the solution we are seeking. We have once already availed ourselves of an application of psychoanalytic technique, in explaining the three caskets as symbolic of three women. If we have the courage to continue the process, we shall be setting foot on a path which leads us first to something unexpected and incomprehensible, but perhaps by a devious route to a goal.

It may strike us that this surpassing third one has in several instances certain peculiar qualities besides her beauty. They are qualities that seem to be tending towards some kind of unity; we certainly may not expect to find them equally well marked in every example. Cordelia masks her true self, becomes as unassuming as lead, she remains dumb, she "loves and is silent." Cinderella hides herself, so that she is not to be found. We may perhaps equate concealment and dumbness. These would of course be only two instances out of the five we have picked out. But there is an intimation of the same thing to be found, curiously enough, in two other cases. We have decided to compare Cordelia, with her obstinate refusal, to lead. In Bassanio's short speech during the choice of the caskets these are his words of the lead—properly speaking; without any connection:

> Thy paleness moves me more than eloquence
> ("Plainness," according to another reading)

Thus: Thy plainness moves me more than the blatant nature of the other two. Gold and silver are "loud"; lead is dumb, in effect like Cordelia, who "loves and is silent."[7]

In the ancient Greek tales of the Judgement of Paris, nothing is said of such a withholding of herself on the part of Aphrodite. Each of the three goddesses speaks to the youth and tries to win him by promises. But, curiously enough, in a quite modern handling of the same scene this characteristic of the third that has struck us makes its appearance again. In the libretto of Offenbach's *La Belle Hélène,* Paris, after telling of the solicitations of the other two goddesses, relates how Aphrodite bore herself in this contest for the prize of beauty:

> La troisième, ah! la troisième!
> La troisième ne dit rien,
> Elle eut le prix tout de même. . . .[8]

If we decide to regard the peculiarities of our "third one" as concentrated in the "dumbness," then psychoanalysis has to say that dumbness is in dreams a familiar representation of death.[9]

---

[7] In Schlegel's translation this allusion is quite lost; indeed, changed into the opposite meaning: *Dein schlichtes Wesen spricht beredt mich an.* (Thy plainness speaks to me with eloquence.) (Freud.)

[8] Translates as, "The third, ah! the third!
    The third says nothing,
        Yet wins the prize just the same. . . ."

[9] In Stekel's *Sprache des Traumes* (1911), dumbness is also mentioned among the "death" symbols (p. 351). (Freud.)

More than ten years ago a highly intelligent man told me a dream which he wanted to look upon as proof of the telepathic nature of dreams. He saw an absent friend from whom he had received no news for a very long time, and reproached him warmly for his silence. The friend made no reply. It then proved that he had met his death by suicide about the time of the dream. Let us leave the problem of telepathy on one side: there seems to be no doubt that here the dumbness in the dream represents death. Concealment, disappearance from view, too, which the prince in the fairy-tale of Cinderella has to experience three times, is in dreams an unmistakable symbol of death; and no less so is a striking pallor, of which the paleness of the lead in one reading of Shakespeare's text reminds us. The difficulty of translating these significations from the language of dreams into the mode of expression in the myth now occupying our attention is much lightened if we can show with any probability that dumbness must be interpreted as a sign of death in other productions that are not dreams.

I will single out at this point the ninth of Grimm's *Fairy Tales,* the one with the title "The Twelve Brothers." A king and a queen have twelve children, all boys. Thereupon the king says, "If the thirteenth child is a girl, the boys must die." In expectation of this birth he has twelve coffins made. The twelve sons flee with their mother's help into a secret wood, and swear death to every maiden they shall meet.

A girl-child is born, grows up, and learns one day from her mother that she had twelve brothers. She decides to seek them out, and finds the youngest in the wood; he recognizes her but wants to hide her on account of the brothers' oath. The sister says: "I will gladly die, if thereby I can save my twelve brothers." The brothers welcome her gladly, however, and she stays with them and looks after their house for them.

In a little garden near the house grow twelve lilies: the maiden plucks these to give one to each brother. At that moment the brothers are changed into ravens, and disappear, together with the house and garden. Ravens are spirit-birds, the killing of the twelve brothers by their sister is thus again represented by the plucking of the flowers, as at the beginning of the story by the coffins and the disappearance of the brothers. The maiden, who is once more ready to save her brothers from death, is now told that as a condition she is to be dumb for seven years, and not speak one single word. She submits to the test, by which she herself goes into danger, *i.e.* she herself dies for her brothers, as she promised before meeting with them. By remaining dumb she succeeds at last in delivering the ravens.

In the story of "The Six Swans" the brothers who are changed into birds are released in exactly the same way, *i.e.* restored to life by the dumbness of the sister. The maiden has taken the firm resolve to release her brothers, "an if it cost her life"; as the king's wife she again risks her own life because she will not relinquish her dumbness to defend herself against evil accusations.

Further proofs could undoubtedly be gathered from fairy-tales that dumbness is to be understood as representing death. If we follow these indications, then the third one of the sisters between whom the choice lies would be a dead woman. She may, however, be something else, namely, Death itself, the Goddess of Death. By virtue of a displacement that is not infrequent, the qualities that a deity imparts to men are ascribed to the deity himself. Such a displacement will astonish us least of all in relation to the Goddess of Death, since in modern thought and artistic representation, which would thus be anticipated in these stories, death itself is nothing but a dead man.

But if the third of the sisters is the Goddess of Death, we know the sisters. They are the Fates, the Moerae, the Parcae or the Norns, the third of whom is called Atropos, the inexorable.

2

Let us leave on one side for a while the task of inserting this new-found meaning into our myth, and let us hear what the mythologists have to say about the origin of and the part played by the Fates.[10]

The earliest Greek mythology only knows one Moera, personifying the inevitable doom (in Homer). The further development of this one Moera into a group of three sisters—goddesses—, less often two, probably came about in connection with other divine figures to which the Moerae are clearly related: the Graces and the Horae, the Hours.

The Hours are originally goddesses of the waters of the sky, dispensing rain and dew, and of the clouds from which rain falls; and since these clouds are conceived of as a kind of web it comes about that these goddesses are looked on as spinners, a character that then became attached to the Moerae. In the sun-favoured Mediterranean lands it is the rain on which the fertility of the soil depends, and thus the Hours become the goddesses of vegetation. The beauty of flowers and the abundance of fruit is their doing, and man endows them plentifully with charming and graceful traits. They become the divine representatives of the Seasons, and possibly in this connection acquire their triple number, if the sacred nature of the number three is not sufficient explanation of this. For these ancient peoples at first distinguished only three seasons: winter, spring, summer. Autumn was only added in late Graeco-Roman times, after which four Hours were often represented in art.

The relation to time remained attached to the Hours: later they presided over the time of day, as at first over the periods of the year: at last their name came to be merely a designation for the period of sixty minutes (hour, *heure, ora*). The Norns[11] of German mythology are akin to the Hours and the Moerae[12] and exhibit this time-signification in their names. The nature of these deities could not fail, however, to be apprehended more profoundly in time, so that the essential thing about them was shifted until it came to consist of the abiding law at work in the passage of time: the Hours thus became guardians of the law of Nature, and of the divine order of things whereby the constant recurrence of the same things in unalterable succession in the natural world takes place.

This knowledge of nature reacted on the conception of human life. The nature-myth changed into a myth of human life: the weather-goddesses became goddesses of destiny. But this aspect of the Hours only found expression in the Moerae, who watch over the needful ordering of human life as inexorably as do the Hours over the regular order of nature. The implacable severity of this law, the affinity of it with death and ruin,

---

[10] What follows is taken from Roscher's *Lexikon der griechischen und römischen Mythologie,* under the relevant headings. (Freud.)

[11] Norns: Norse or Germanic Fates who spin the web of life: past, present, and future.

[12] Moerae: the Greek Fates.

avoided in the winsome figures of the Hours, was now stamped upon the Moerae, as though mankind had only perceived the full solemnity of natural law when he had to submit his own personality to its working.

The names of the three spinners have been interpreted significantly by mythologists. Lachesis, the name of the second, seems to mean "the accidental within the decrees of destiny"—we might say "that which is experienced"—while Atropos means "the inevitable"—Death—, and then for Clotho there remains "the fateful tendencies each one of us brings into the world."

And now it is time to return to the idea contained in the choice between the three sisters, which we are endeavouring to interpret. It is with deep dissatisfaction that we find how unintelligible insertion of the new interpretation makes the situations we are considering and what contradictions of the apparent content then result. The third of the sisters should be the Goddess of Death, nay, Death itself; in the Judgment of Paris she is the Goddess of Love, in the tale of Apuleius[13] one comparable to the goddess for her beauty, in *The Merchant of Venice* the fairest and wisest of women, in *Lear* the one faithful daughter. Can a contradiction be more complete? Yet perhaps close at hand there lies even this, improbable as it is—the acme of contradiction. It is certainly forthcoming if every time in this theme of ours there occurs a free choice between the women, and if the choice is thereupon to fall on death—that which no man chooses, to which by destiny alone man falls a victim.

However, contradictions of a certain kind, replacements by the exact opposite, offer no serious difficulty to analytic interpretation. We shall not this time take our stand on the fact that contraries are constantly represented by one and the same element in the modes of expression used by the unconscious, such as dreams. But we shall remember that there are forces in mental life tending to bring about replacement by the opposite, such as the so-called reaction-formation, and it is just in the discovery of such hidden forces that we look for the reward of our labours. The Moerae were created as a result of a recognition which warns man that he too is a part of nature and therefore subject to the immutable law of death. Against this subjection something in man was bound to struggle, for it is only with extreme unwillingness that he gives up his claim to an exceptional position. We know that man makes use of his imaginative faculty (phantasy) to satisfy those wishes that reality does not satisfy. So his imagination rebelled against the recognition of the truth embodied in the myth of the Moerae, and constructed instead the myth derived from it, in which the Goddess of Death was replaced by the Goddess of Love and by that which most resembles her in human shape. The third of the sisters is no longer Death, she is the fairest, best, most desirable and the most lovable among women. Nor was this substitution in any way difficult: it was prepared for by an ancient ambivalence, it fulfilled itself along the lines of an ancient context which could at that time not long have been forgotten. The Goddess of Love herself, who now took the place of the Goddess of Death, had once been identical with her. Even the Greek Aphrodite had not wholly relinquished her connection with the underworld, although she had long surrendered her rôle of goddess of that region to other

---

[13] Lucius Apulieus (c.125–?): a lawyer and author who spent most of his life in Carthage. He is best known for his collection of tales entitled *Metamorphosis*, or *The Golden Ass.* See p. 345.

divine shapes, to Persephone, or to the tri-form Artemis-Hecate. The great Mother-goddesses of the oriental peoples, however, all seem to have been both founts of being and destroyers; goddesses of life and of fertility, and death-goddesses. Thus the replacement by the wish-opposite of which we have spoken in our theme is built upon an ancient identity.

The same consideration answers the question how the episode of a choice came into the myth of the three sisters. A wished-for reversal is again found here. Choice stands in the place of necessity, of destiny. Thus man overcomes death, which in thought he has acknowledged. No greater triumph of wish-fulfilment is conceivable. Just where in reality he obeys compulsion, he exercises choice; and that which he chooses is not a thing of horror, but the fairest and most desirable thing in life.

On a closer inspection we observe, to be sure, that the original myth is not so much disguised that traces of it do not show through and betray its presence. The free choice between the three sisters is, properly speaking, no free choice, for it must necessarily fall on the third if every kind of evil is not to come about, as in *Lear*. The fairest and the best, she who has stepped into the place of the Death-goddess, has kept certain characteristics that border on the uncanny, so that from them we might guess at what lay beneath.[14]

So far we have followed out the myth and its transformation, and trust that we have rightly indicated the hidden causes of this transformation. Now we may well be interested in the way in which the poet has made use of the idea. We gain the impression that in his mind a reduction to the original idea of the myth is going on, so that we once more perceive the original meaning containing all the power to move us that had been weakened by the distortion of the myth. It is by means of this undoing of the distortion and partial return to the original that the poet achieves his profound effect upon us.

To avoid misunderstandings, I wish to say that I have no intention of denying that the drama of *King Lear* inculcates the two prudent maxims: that one should not forgo one's possessions and privileges in one's lifetime and that one must guard against accepting flattery as genuine. These and similar warnings do undoubtedly arise from the play; but it seems to me quite impossible to explain the overpowering effect of *Lear* from the impression that such a train of thought would produce, or to assume that the poet's own creative instincts would not carry him further than the impulse to illustrate these maxims. Moreover, even though we are told that the poet's intention was to present the tragedy of ingratitude, the sting of which he probably felt in his own heart, and that the effect of the play depends on the purely formal element, its artistic trappings, it seems

---

[14] The Psyche of Apuleius' story has kept many traits that remind us of her kinship with death. Her wedding is celebrated like a funeral, she has to descend into the underworld, and afterwards sinks into a death-like sleep (Otto Rank).

On the significance of Psyche as goddess of the spring and as "Bride of Death," cf. A. Zinzow, *Psyche und Eros*.

In another of Grimm's Tales ("The Goose-girl at the Fountain") there is, as in "Cinderella," an alternation between the ugly and the beautiful aspect of the third sister, in which may be seen an indication of her double nature—before and after the substitution. This third one is repudiated by her father, after a test which nearly corresponds with that in *King Lear*. Like the other sisters, she has to say how dear she holds their father, and finds no expression for her love except the comparison of it with salt. (Kindly communicated by Dr. Hanns Sachs.) (Freud.)

to me that this information cannot compete with the comprehension that dawns upon us after our study of the theme of a choice between the three sisters.

Lear is an old man. We said before that this is why the three sisters appear as his daughters. The paternal relationship, out of which so many fruitful dramatic situations might arise, is not turned to further account in the drama. But Lear is not only an old man; he is a dying man. The extraordinary project of dividing the inheritance thus loses its strangeness. The doomed man is nevertheless not willing to renounce the love of women; he insists on hearing how much he is loved. Let us now recall that most moving last scene, one of the culminating points reached in modern tragic drama: "Enter Lear with Cordelia dead in his arms." Cordelia is Death. Reverse the situation and it becomes intelligible and familiar to us—the Death-goddess bearing away the dead hero from the place of battle, like the Valkyr[15] in German mythology. Eternal wisdom, in the garb of the primitive myth, bids the old man renounce love, choose death and make friends with the necessity of dying.

The poet brings us very near to the ancient idea by making the man who accomplishes the choice between the three sisters aged and dying. The regressive treatment he has thus undertaken with the myth, which was disguised by the reversal of the wish, allows its original meaning so far to appear that perhaps a superficial allegorical interpretation of the three female figures in the theme becomes possible as well. One might say that the three inevitable relations man has with woman are here represented: that with the mother who bears him, with the companion of his bed and board, and with the destroyer. Or it is the three forms taken on by the figure of the mother as life proceeds: the mother herself, the beloved who is chosen after her pattern, and finally the Mother Earth who receives him again. But it is in vain that the old man yearns after the love of woman as once he had it from his mother; the third of the Fates alone, the silent goddess of Death, will take him into her arms.

(1913)

QUESTIONS

1. What connection does Freud make between the choice of one of the three sisters in "Cupid and Psyche," "Cinderella," and *King Lear* and the choice of one of the three goddesses and three caskets in *The Merchant of Venice?*

2. Who are the Fates and what is their function? Who are the Graces and the Hours and what do they represent? Why are there always three of them?

3. Discuss whether you think that the link between love and death is far-fetched.

4. How does Freud explain the choice of the third—the youngest, prettiest, wisest, etc.? What does he theorize to be the meaning of the hidden and silent quality of this chosen third?

---

[15] Valkyr: in Germanic myth, warrior maidens who chose those who would die and those who would go to Valhalla (Paradise).

VIRGINIA WOOLF (1882–1941)

Shakespeare's Sister*

Be that as it may, I could not help thinking, as I looked at the works of Shakespeare on the shelf, that the bishop was right at least in this; it would have been impossible, completely and entirely, for any woman to have written the plays of Shakespeare in the age of Shakespeare. Let me imagine, since facts are so hard to come by, what would have happened had Shakespeare had a wonderfully gifted sister, called Judith, let us say. Shakespeare himself went, very probably—his mother was an heiress—to the grammar school, where he may have learnt Latin—Ovid, Virgil and Horace[1]—and the elements of grammar and logic. He was, it is well known, a wild boy who poached rabbits, perhaps shot a deer, and had, rather sooner than he should have done, to marry a woman in the neighbourhood, who bore him a child rather quicker than was right. That escapade sent him to seek his fortune in London. He had, it seemed, a taste for the theatre; he began by holding horses at the stage door. Very soon he got work in the theatre, became a successful actor, and lived at the hub of the universe, meeting everybody, knowing everybody, practising his art on the boards, exercising his wits in the streets, and even getting access to the palace of the queen. Meanwhile his extraordinarily gifted sister, let us suppose, remained at home. She was as adventurous, as imaginative, as agog to see the world as he was. But she was not sent to school. She had no chance of learning grammar and logic, let alone of reading Horace and Virgil. She picked up a book now and then, one of her brother's perhaps, and read a few pages. But then her parents came in and told her to mend the stockings or mind the stew and not moon about with books and papers. They would have spoken sharply but kindly, for they were substantial people who knew the conditions of life for a woman and loved their daughter—indeed, more likely than not she was the apple of her father's eye. Perhaps she scribbled some pages up in an apple loft on the sly, but was careful to hide them or set fire to them. Soon, however, before she was out of her teens, she was to be betrothed to the son of a neighbouring wool-stapler. She cried out that marriage was hateful to her, and for that she was severely beaten by her father. Then he ceased to scold her. He begged her instead not to hurt him, not to shame him in this matter of her marriage. He would give her a chain of beads or a fine petticoat, he said; and there were tears in his eyes. How could she disobey him? How could she break his heart? The force of her own gift alone drove her to it. She made up a small parcel of her belongings, let herself down by a rope one summer's night and took the road to London. She was not seventeen. The birds that sang in the hedge were not more musical than she was. She had the quickest fancy, a gift like her brother's, for the tune of words. Like him, she had a taste for the theatre. She stood at the stage door; she wanted to act, she said. Men laughed in her face. The

---

*This selection is an excerpt from *A Room of One's Own*.
[1] Ovid: Roman poet (43 B.C.E.–17 C.E.), famous for writing *The Metamorphosis* (see p. 352); Virgil (70–19 B.C.E.), Roman poet famous for writing the epic poem, *The Aeneid*; Horace (65-8 B.C.E.), Roman lyric poet and satirist.

manager—a fat, loose-lipped man—guffawed. He bellowed something about poodles dancing and women acting—no woman, he said, could possibly be an actress. He hinted—you can imagine what. She could get no training in her craft. Could she even seek her dinner in a tavern or roam the streets at midnight? Yet her genius was for fiction and lusted to feed abundantly upon the lives of men and women and the study of their ways. At last—for she was very young, oddly like Shakespeare the poet in her face, with the same grey eyes and rounded brows—at last Nick Greene the actor-manager took pity on her; she found herself with child by that gentleman and so—who shall measure the heat and violence of the poet's heart when caught and tangled in a woman's body?—killed herself one winter's night and lies buried at some cross-roads where the omnibuses now stop outside the Elephant and Castle.[2]

That, more or less, is how the story would run, I think, if a woman in Shakespeare's day had had Shakespeare's genius. But for my part, I agree with the deceased bishop, if such he was—it is unthinkable that any woman in Shakespeare's day should have had Shakespeare's genius. For genius like Shakespeare's is not born among labouring, uneducated, servile people. It was not born in England among the Saxons and the Britons. It is not born today among the working classes. How, then, could it have been born among women whose work began, according to Professor Trevelyan,[3] almost before they were out of the nursery, who were forced to it by their parents and held to it by all the power of law and custom? Yet genius of a sort must have existed among women as it must have existed among the working classes. Now and again an Emily Brontë or a Robert Burns[4] blazes out and proves its presence. But certainly it never got itself on to paper. When, however, one reads of a witch being ducked,[5] of a woman possessed by devils, of a wise woman selling herbs, or even of a very remarkable man who had a mother, then I think we are on the track of a lost novelist, a suppressed poet, of some mute and inglorious Jane Austen,[6] some Emily Brontë who dashed her brains out on the moor or mopped and mowed about the highways crazed with the torture that her gift had put her to. Indeed, I would venture to guess that Anon,[7] who wrote so many poems without signing them, was often a woman. It was a woman Edward Fitzgerald,[8] I think, suggested who made the ballads and the folk-songs, crooning them to her children, beguiling her spinning with them, or the length of the winter's night.

This may be true or it may be false—who can say?—but what is true in it, so it seemed to me, reviewing the story of Shakespeare's sister as I had made it, is that any woman born with a great gift in the sixteenth century would certainly have gone crazed,

---

[2] Elephant and Castle: typical name of an English pub where buses dropped off and picked up passengers.
[3] Professor Trevalyan (1876–1962): an English historian and professor of modern history at Cambridge University from 1927–1951.
[4] Emily Brontë (1818–1848): English author of *Wuthering Heights* and mystical poetry; Robert Burns (1759–1796), Scotch poet (see p. 436 and p. 811 for examples of his poetry).
[5] "witch being ducked": women believed to be witches were often held under water as punishment.
[6] Jane Austen (1775–1817): a highly acclaimed English novelist, author of works such as *Emma* and *Pride and Prejudice*.
[7] Anon: shortened form of Anonymous, which was how various authors signed their work when they wanted to hide their true identities.
[8] Edward Fitzgerald (1809–1883): an English translator and man of letters known for his translation of *The Rubaiyat of Omar Khayyam*.

shot herself, or ended her days in some lonely cottage outside the village, half witch, half wizard, feared and mocked at. For it needs little skill in psychology to be sure that a highly gifted girl who had tried to use her gift for poetry would have been so thwarted and hindered by other people, so tortured and pulled asunder by her own contrary instincts, that she must have lost her health and sanity to a certainty. No girl could have walked to London and stood at a stage door and forced her way into the presence of actor-managers without doing herself a violence and suffering an anguish which may have been irrational—for chastity may be a fetish invented by certain societies for unknown reasons—but were none the less inevitable. Chastity had then, it has even now, a religious importance in a woman's life, and has so wrapped itself round with nerves and instincts that to cut it free and bring it to the light of day demands courage of the rarest. To have lived a free life in London in the sixteenth century would have meant for a woman who was poet and playwright a nervous stress and dilemma which might well have killed her. Had she survived, whatever she had written would have been twisted and deformed, issuing from a strained and morbid imagination. And undoubtedly, I thought, looking at the shelf where there are no plays by women, her work would have gone unsigned.

(1927, 1928)

QUESTIONS

1. According to Woolf's depiction of her life, Shakespeare's fictional sister, "Judith," would never have been able to become the playwright that her brother was. Give at least three reasons why, which Woolf uses to support her thesis.

2. What is the point Woolf is trying to make in this excerpt from her longer essay, *A Room of One's Own,* regarding the answer to the question, "Why have there been no great women writers?"

3. Explain what you think has changed since Shakespeare's time that makes it possible today for a woman writer to be accomplished and successful.

Writing Topics for Essays

1. Compare Bettelheim's and Freud's psychoanalyses of "Cinderella." Explain whether you find these interpretations illuminating or shocking. Recalling some of your experiences with folktales when you were a child, explain whether you think that the joy of the folktale is enriched or diminished by subjecting it to psychological analysis.

2. Compare the issues that women faced in the fifteenth and sixteenth centuries in England as depicted by Woolf in "Shakespeare's Sister" with the issues women face today?

Short Stories

JORGE LUIS BORGES (1899–1986)

Legend

Translated by Andrew Hurley

Cain and Abel came upon each other after Abel's death. They were walking through the desert, and they recognized each other from afar, since both men were very tall. The two brothers sat on the ground, made a fire, and ate. They sat silently, as weary people do when dusk begins to fall. In the sky, a star glimmered, though it had not yet been given a name. In the light of the fire, Cain saw that Abel's forehead bore the mark of the stone, and he dropped the bread he was about to carry to his mouth and asked his brother to forgive him.

"Was it you that killed me, or did I kill you?" Abel answered. "I don't remember anymore; here we are, together, like before."

"Now I know that you have truly forgiven me," Cain said, "because forgetting is forgiving. I, too, will try to forget."

"Yes," said Abel slowly. "So long as remorse lasts, guilt lasts."

QUESTIONS

1. What is suggested about sibling rivalry and brotherly love in this retelling of the story of Cain and Abel? And what is signified by having Abel bear "the mark," rather than Cain?

2. What does "Legend" suggest about the personality of Abel? Does Cain's angry, rebellious nature seem to have changed over the years?

3. Explain whether or not you agree with the concept that "forgetting is forgiving."

4. What do you think that Abel means when he says, "So long as remorse lasts, guilt lasts"?

JORGE LUIS BORGES

In Memoriam, J.F.K.[1]

Translated by Andrew Hurley

This bullet is an old one.

In 1897, it was fired at the president of Uruguay by a young man from Montevideo, Avelino Arredondo, who had spent long weeks without seeing anyone so that the world might know that he acted alone. Thirty years earlier, Lincoln had been murdered by that same ball, by the criminal or magical hand of an actor transformed by the words of Shakespeare into Marcus Brutus, Cæsar's murderer.[2] In the mid-seventeenth century, vengeance had employed it for the assassination of Sweden's Gustavus Adolphus,[3] in the midst of the public hecatomb of a battle.

In earlier times, the bullet had been other things, because Pythagorean metempsychosis[4] is not reserved for humankind alone. It was the silken cord given to viziers in the East,[5] the rifles and bayonets that cut down the defenders of the Alamo,[6] the triangular blade that slit a queen's throat, the wood of the Cross and the dark nails that pierced the flesh of the Redeemer, the poison kept by the Carthaginian chief in an iron ring on his finger,[7] the serene goblet that Socrates drank down one evening.[8]

In the dawn of time it was the stone that Cain hurled at Abel, and in the future it shall be many things that we cannot even imagine today, but that will be able to put an end to men and their wondrous, fragile life.

---

[1] John Fitzgerald Kennedy (1917–1963): 35th president of the United States, shot and assassinated in Dallas, Texas, 1963.
[2] Abraham Lincoln (1809–1865): 16th president of the United States, assassinated by the actor John Wilkes Booth (1838–1865); Marcus Junius Brutus (85[?] B.C.E.–42 B.C.E.), Roman politician and general who conspired to assassinate Julius Caesar (100–44 B.C.E.), Roman general, statesman, historian, and dictator assassinated in 44 B.C.E. by a group led by Brutus and Cassius.
[3] Gustavus III (1746–1792): gifted, learned, and literary monarch assassinated by a noble at a masked ball.
[4] Reference to Hannibal (247–183 B.C.E.): Carthaginian general who fought Rome, was recalled to Carthage (near Tunis, North Africa), and committed suicide rather than be extradited to Rome.
[5] Viziers: high officers in the Muslim government of the Ottoman Empire (a vast Turkish sultanate extending through Southwest Asia, Northeast Africa, and Southeast Europe from the thirteenth century through World War I) who used a "silken cord" as a method of murder.
[6] Alamo: a fortified mission in Texas where, during the Texas rebellion against Mexico, all the defenders were killed in hand-to-hand combat by General Santa Anna's much larger Mexican army.
[7] Pythagoras: a sixth century B.C.E. Greek philosopher and mathematician, believed in the transmigration (metempsychosis or reincarnation) of souls.
[8] Socrates (C. 470–379 B.C.E.): Greek philosopher and teacher of wisdom, sentenced to death by the Athenians for impiety and corruption of youth, who drank the poison hemlock.

QUESTIONS

1. What do all of the deaths mentioned here have in common? And what is suggested about the dark side of human nature?

2. Explain what you think "the bullet" and "the stone" suggest.

3. Explain whether you agree with Borges's concept that all these deaths lead back to Cain's murder of Abel in "Genesis."

Tobias Wolff (b. 1945)

The Rich Brother

There were two brothers, Pete and Donald.

Pete, the older brother, was in real estate. He and his wife had a Century 21 franchise in Santa Cruz. Pete worked hard and made a lot of money, but not any more than he thought he deserved. He had two daughters, a sailboat, a house from which he could see a thin slice of the ocean, and friends doing well enough in their own lives not to wish bad luck on him. Donald, the younger brother, was still single. He lived alone, painted houses when he found the work, and got deeper in debt to Pete when he didn't.

No one would have taken them for brothers. Where Pete was stout and hearty and at home in the world, Donald was bony, grave, and obsessed with the fate of his soul. Over the years Donald had worn the images of two different Perfect Masters around his neck. Out of devotion to the second of these he entered an ashram in Berkeley, where he nearly died of undiagnosed hepatitis. By the time Pete finished paying the medical bills Donald had become a Christian. He drifted from church to church, then joined a pentecostal community that met somewhere in the Mission District to sing in tongues and swap prophecies.

Pete couldn't make sense of it. Their parents were both dead, but while they were alive neither of them had found it necessary to believe in anything. They managed to be decent people without making fools of themselves, and Pete had the same ambition. He thought that the whole thing was an excuse for Donald to take himself seriously.

The trouble was that Donald couldn't content himself with worrying about his own soul. He had to worry about everyone else's, and especially Pete's. He handed down his judgments in ways that he seemed to consider subtle: through significant silence, innuendo, looks of mild despair that said, *Brother, what have you come to?* What Pete had come to, as far as he could tell, was prosperity. That was the real issue between them. Pete prospered and Donald did not prosper.

At the age of forty Pete took up sky diving. He made his first jump with two friends who'd started only a few months earlier and were already doing stunts. They were both coked to the gills when they jumped but Pete wanted to do it straight, at least the first time, and he was glad that he did. He would never have used the word "mystical," but that was how Pete felt about the experience. Later he made the mistake of trying to describe it to Donald, who kept asking how much it cost and then acted appalled when Pete told him.

"At least I'm trying something new," Pete said. "At least I'm breaking the pattern."

Not long after that conversation Donald also broke the pattern, by going to live on a farm outside of Paso Robles. The farm was owned by several members of Donald's community, who had bought it and moved there with the idea of forming a family of faith. That was how Donald explained it in the first letter he sent. Every week Pete heard how happy Donald was, how "in the Lord." He told Pete that he was praying for him, he and the rest of Pete's brothers and sisters on the farm.

"I only have one brother," Pete wanted to answer, "and that's enough." But he kept this thought to himself.

In November the letters stopped. Pete didn't worry about this at first, but when he called Donald at Thanksgiving Donald was grim. He tried to sound upbeat but he didn't try hard enough to make it convincing. "Now listen," Pete said, "you don't have to stay in that place if you don't want to."

"I'll be all right," Donald answered.

"That's not the point. Being all right is not the point. If you don't like what's going on up there, then get out."

"I'm all right," Donald said again, more firmly. "I'm doing fine."

But he called Pete a week later and said that he was quitting the farm. When Pete asked him where he intended to go, Donald admitted that he had no plan. His car had been repossessed just before he left the city, and he was flat broke.

"I guess you'll have to stay with us," Pete said.

Donald put up a show of resistance. Then he gave in. "Just until I get my feet on the ground," he said.

"Right," Pete said. "Check out your options." He told Donald he'd send him money for a bus ticket, but as they were about to hang up Pete changed his mind. He knew that Donald would try hitchhiking to save the fare. Pete didn't want him out on the road all alone where some head case could pick him up, where anything could happen to him.

"Better yet," he said. "I'll come and get you."

"You don't have to do that. I didn't expect you to do that," Donald said. He added, "It's a pretty long drive."

"Just tell me how to get there."

But Donald wouldn't give him directions. He said that the farm was too depressing, that Pete wouldn't like it. Instead, he insisted on meeting Pete at a service station called Jonathan's Mechanical Emporium.

"You must be kidding," Pete said.

"It's close to the highway," Donald said. "I didn't name it."

"That's one for the collection," Pete said.

The day before he left to bring Donald home, Pete received a letter from a man who described himself as "head of household" at the farm where Donald had been living. From this letter Pete learned that Donald had not quit the farm, but had been asked to leave. The letter was written on the back of a mimeographed survey form asking people to record their response to a ceremony of some kind. The last question said:

What did you feel during the liturgy?

a) *Being*

b) *Becoming*

c) *Being and Becoming*

d) *None of the Above*

e) *All of the Above*

Pete tried to forget the letter. But of course he couldn't. Each time he thought of it he felt crowded and breathless, a feeling that came over him again when he drove into the service station and saw Donald sitting against a wall with his head on his knees. It was late afternoon. A paper cup tumbled slowly past Donald's feet, pushed by the damp wind.

Pete honked and Donald raised his head. He smiled at Pete, then stood and stretched. His arms were long and thin and white. He wore a red bandanna across his forehead, a T-shirt with a couple of words on the front. Pete couldn't read them because the letters were inverted.

"Grow up," Pete yelled. "Get a Mercedes."

Donald came up to the window. He bent down and said, "Thanks for coming. You must be totally whipped."

"I'll make it." Pete pointed at Donald's T-shirt. "What's that supposed to say?"

Donald looked down at his shirt front. "Try God. I guess I put it on backwards. Pete, could I borrow a couple of dollars? I owe these people for coffee and sandwiches."

Pete took five twenties from his wallet and held them out the window.

Donald stepped back as if horrified. "I don't need that much."

"I can't keep track of all these nickels and dimes," Pete said. "Just pay me back when your ship comes in." He waved the bills impatiently. "Go on—take it."

"Only for now." Donald took the money and went into the service station office. He came out carrying two orange sodas, one of which he gave to Pete as he got into the car. "My treat," he said.

"No bags?"

"Wow, thanks for reminding me," Donald said. He balanced his drink on the dashboard, but the slight rocking of the car as he got out tipped it onto the passenger's seat, where half its contents foamed over before Pete could snatch it up again. Donald looked on while Pete held the bottle out the window, soda running down his fingers.

"Wipe it up," Pete told him. "Quick!"

"With what?"

Pete stared at Donald. "That shirt. Use the shirt."

Donald pulled a long face but did as he was told, his pale skin puckering against the wind.

"Great, just great," Pete said. "We haven't even left the gas station yet."

Afterwards, on the highway, Donald said, "This is a new car, isn't it?"

"Yes. This is a new car."

"Is that why you're so upset about the seat?"

"Forget it, okay? Let's just forget about it."

"I said I was sorry."

Pete said, "I just wish you'd be more careful. These seats are made of leather. That stain won't come out, not to mention the smell. I don't see why I can't have leather seats that smell like leather instead of orange pop."

"What was wrong with the other car?"

Pete glanced over at Donald. Donald had raised the hood of the blue sweatshirt he'd put on. The peaked hood above his gaunt, watchful face gave him the look of an inquisitor.

"There wasn't anything wrong with it," Pete said. "I just happened to like this one better."

Donald nodded.

There was a long silence between them as Pete drove on and the day darkened toward evening. On either side of the road lay stubble-covered fields. A line of low hills ran along the horizon, topped here and there with trees black against the gray sky. In the approaching line of cars a driver turned on his headlights. Pete did the same.

"So what happened?" he asked. "Farm life not your bag?"

Donald took some time to answer, and at last he said, simply, "It was my fault."

"What was your fault?"

"The whole thing. Don't play dumb, Pete. I know they wrote to you." Donald looked at Pete, then stared out the windshield again.

"I'm not playing dumb."

Donald shrugged.

"All I really know is they asked you to leave," Pete went on. "I don't know any of the particulars."

"I blew it," Donald said. "Believe me, you don't want to hear the gory details."

"Sure I do," Pete said. He added, "Everybody likes the gory details."

"You mean everybody likes to hear how someone else messed up."

"Right," Pete said. "That's the way it is here on Spaceship Earth."

Donald bent one knee onto the front seat and leaned against the door so that he was facing Pete instead of the windshield. Pete was aware of Donald's scrutiny. He waited. Night was coming on in a rush now, filling the hollows of the land. Donald's long cheeks and deep-set eyes were dark with shadow. His brow was white. "Do you ever dream about me?" Donald asked.

"Do I ever dream about you? What kind of a question is that? Of course I don't dream about you." Pete said, untruthfully.

"What do you dream about?"

"Sex and money. Mostly money. A nightmare is when I dream I don't have any."

"You're just making that up," Donald said.

Pete smiled.

"Sometimes I wake up at night," Donald went on, "and I can tell you're dreaming about me."

"We were talking about the farm," Pete said. "Let's finish that conversation and then we can talk about our various out-of-body experiences and the interesting things we did during previous incarnations."

For a moment Donald looked like a grinning skull; then he turned serious again. "There's not that much to tell," he said. "I just didn't do anything right."

"That's a little vague," Pete said.

"Well, like the groceries. Whenever it was my turn to get the groceries I'd blow it somehow. I'd bring the groceries home and half of them would be missing, or I'd have all the wrong things, the wrong kind of flour or the wrong kind of chocolate or whatever. One time I gave them away. It's not funny, Pete."

Pete said, "Who did you give the groceries to?"

"Just some people I picked up on the way home. Some fieldworkers. They had about eight kids with them and they didn't even speak English—just nodded their heads. Still, I shouldn't have given away the groceries. Not all of them, anyway. I really learned my lesson about that. You have to be practical. You have to be fair to yourself." Donald leaned forward, and Pete could sense his excitement. "There's nothing actually wrong with being in business," he said. "As long as you're fair to other people you can still be fair to yourself. I'm thinking of going into business, Pete."

"We'll talk about it," Pete said. "So, that's the story? There isn't any more to it than that?"

"What did they tell you?" Donald asked.

"Nothing."

"They must have told you something."

Pete shook his head.

"They didn't tell you about the fire?" When Pete shook his head again Donald regarded him for a time, then said, "I don't know. It was stupid. I just completely lost it." He folded his arms across his chest and slumped back into the corner. "Everybody had to take turns cooking dinner. I usually did tuna casserole or spaghetti with garlic bread. But this one night I thought I'd do something different, something really interesting." Donald looked sharply at Pete. "It's all a big laugh to you, isn't it?"

"I'm sorry," Pete said.

"You don't know when to quit. You just keep hitting away."

"Tell me about the fire, Donald."

Donald kept watching him. "You have this compulsion to make me look foolish."

"Come off it, Donald. Don't make a big thing out of this."

"I know why you do it. It's because you don't have any purpose in life. You're afraid to relate to people who do, so you make fun of them."

"Relate," Pete said softly.

"You're basically a very frightened individual," Donald said. "Very threatened. You've always been like that. Do you remember when you used to try to kill me?"

"I don't have any compulsion to make you look foolish, Donald—You do it yourself. You're doing it right now."

"You can't tell me you don't remember," Donald said. "It was after my operation. You remember that."

"Sort of." Pete shrugged. "Not really."

"Oh, yes." Donald said. "Do you want to see the scar?"

"I remember you had an operation. I don't remember the specifics, that's all. And I sure as hell don't remember trying to kill you."

"Oh yes," Donald repeated, maddeningly. "You bet your life you did. All the time. The thing was, I couldn't have anything happen to me where they sewed me up because then my intestines would come apart again and poison me. That was a big issue, Pete. Mom was always in a state about me climbing trees and so on. And you used to hit me there every chance you got."

"Mom was in a state every time you burped," Pete said. "I don't know. Maybe I bumped into you accidentally once or twice. I never did it deliberately."

"Every chance you got," Donald said. "Like when the folks went out at night and left you to baby-sit. I'd hear them say good night, and then I'd hear the car start up, and when they were gone I'd lie there and listen. After a while I would hear you coming down the hall, and I would close my eyes and pretend to be asleep. There were nights when you would stand outside the door, just stand there, and then go away again. But most nights you'd open the door and I would hear you in the room with me, breathing. You'd come over and sit next to me on the bed—you remember, Pete, you have to—you'd sit next to me on the bed and pull the sheets back. If I was on my stomach you'd roll me over. Then you would lift up my pajama shirt and start hitting me on my stitches. You'd hit me as hard as you could, over and over. And I would just keep lying there with my eyes closed. I was afraid that you'd get mad if you knew I was awake. Is that strange or what? I was afraid that you'd get mad if you found out that I knew you were trying to kill me." Donald laughed. "Come on, you can't tell me you don't remember that."

"It might have happened once or twice. Kids do those things. I can't get all excited about something I maybe did twenty-five years ago."

"No maybe about it. You did it."

Pete said. "You're wearing me out with this stuff. We've got a long drive ahead of us and if you don't back off pretty soon we aren't going to make it. You aren't anyway."

Donald turned away.

"I'm doing my best," Pete said. The self-pity in his own voice made the words sound like a lie. But they weren't a lie! He was doing his best.

The car topped a rise. In the distance Pete saw a cluster of lights that blinked out when he started downhill. There was no moon. The sky was low and black.

"Come to think of it," Pete said, "I did have a dream about you the other night." Then he added, impatiently, as if Donald were badgering him. "A couple of other nights too. I'm getting hungry," he said.

"The same dream?"

"Different dreams. I only remember one of them well. There was something wrong with me, and you were helping out. Taking care of me. Just the two of us. I don't know where everyone else was supposed to be."

Pete left it that. He didn't tell Donald that in this dream he was blind.

"I wonder if that was when I woke up," Donald said. He added, "I'm sorry I got into that thing about my scar. I keep trying to forget it but I guess I never will. Not really. It was pretty strange, having someone around all the time who wanted to get rid of me."

"Kid stuff," Pete said. "Ancient history."

They ate dinner at a Denny's on the other side of King City. As Pete was paying the check he heard a man behind him say, "Excuse me, but I wonder if I might ask which way you're going?" and Donald answer, "Santa Cruz."

"Perfect," the man said.

Pete could see him in the fish-eye mirror above the cash register: a red blazer with some kind of crest on the pocket, little black mustache, glossy black hair combed down on his forehead like a Roman emperor's. A rug, Pete thought. Definitely a rug.

Pete got his change and turned. "Why is that perfect?" he asked.

The man looked at Pete. He had a soft ruddy face that was doing its best to express pleasant surprise, as if this new wrinkle were all he could have wished for, but the eyes behind the aviator glasses showed signs of regret. His lips were moist and shiny. "I take it you're together," he said.

"You got it," Pete told him.

"All the better, then," the man went on. "It so happens I'm going to Santa Cruz myself. Had a spot of car trouble down the road. The old Caddy let me down."

"What kind of trouble?" Pete asked.

"Engine trouble," the man said. "I'm afraid it's a bit urgent. My daughter is sick. Urgently sick. I've got a telegram here." He patted the breast pocket of his blazer.

Pete grinned. Amazing, he thought, the old sick daughter ploy, but before he could say anything Donald got into the act again. "No problem," Donald said. "We've got tons of room."

"Not that much room," Pete said.

Donald nodded. "I'll put my things in the trunk."

"The trunk's full," Pete told him.

"It so happens I'm traveling light," the man said. "This leg of the trip anyway. In fact I don't have any luggage at this particular time."

Pete said, "Left it in the old Caddy, did you?"

"Exactly," the man said.

"No problem," Donald repeated. He walked outside and the man went with him. Together they strolled across the parking lot, Pete following at a distance. When they reached Pete's car Donald raised his face to the sky, and the man did the same. They stood there looking up. "Dark night," Donald said.

"Stygian," the man said.[1]

Pete still had it in mind to brush him off, but he didn't do that. Instead he unlocked the door for him. He wanted to see what would happen. It was an adventure, but not a dangerous adventure. The man might steal Pete's ashtrays but he wouldn't kill him. If Pete got killed on the road it would be by some spiritual person in a sweatsuit, someone with his eyes on the far horizon and a wet Try God T-shirt in his duffel bag.

As soon as they left the parking lot the man lit a cigar. He blew a cloud of smoke over Pete's shoulder and sighed with pleasure. "Put it out," Pete told him.

"Of course," the man said. Pete looked into the rear-view mirror and saw the man take another long puff before dropping the cigar out the window. "Forgive me," he said. "I should have asked. Name's Webster, by the way."

Donald turned and looked back at him. "First name or last?"

The man hesitated. "Last," he said finally.

"I know a Webster," Donald said. "Mick Webster."

"There are many of us," Webster said.

"Big fellow, wooden leg," Pete said.

Donald gave Pete a look.

Webster shook his head. "Doesn't ring a bell. Still, I wouldn't deny the connection. Might be one of the cousinry."

---

[1] Stygian: pertaining to the River Styx in Classical mythology; meaning gloomy, hellish, or infernal.

"What's your daughter got?" Pete asked.

"That isn't clear," Webster answered. "It appears to be a female complaint of some nature. Then again it may be tropical." He was quiet for a moment, and then added: "If indeed it is tropical, I will have to assume some of the blame myself. It was my own vaulting ambition that first led us to the tropics and kept us in the tropics all those many years, exposed to every evil. Truly I have much to answer for. I left my wife there."

Donald said quietly, "You mean she died?"

"I buried her with these hands. The earth will be repaid, gold for gold."

"Which tropics?" Pete asked.

"The tropics of Peru."

"What part of Peru are they in?"

"The lowlands," Webster said.

Pete nodded. "What's it like down there?"

"Another world," Webster said. His tone was sepulchral. "A world better imagined than described."

"Far out," Pete said.

The three men rode in silence for a time. A line of trucks went past in the other direction, trailers festooned with running lights, engines roaring.

"Yes," Webster said at last, "I have much to answer for."

Pete smiled at Donald, but Donald had turned in his seat again and was gazing at Webster. "I'm sorry about your wife," Donald said.

"What did she die of?" Pete asked.

"A wasting illness," Webster said. "The doctors have no name for it, but I do." He leaned forward and said, fiercely, *"Greed."* Then he slumped back against his seat. "My greed, not hers. She wanted no part of it."

Pete bit his lip. Webster was a find and Pete didn't want to scare him off by hooting at him. In a voice low and innocent of knowingness, he asked, "What took you there?"

"It's difficult for me to talk about."

"Try," Pete told him.

"A cigar would make it easier."

Donald turned to Pete and said, "It's okay with me."

"All right," Pete said. "Go ahead. Just keep the window rolled down."

"Much obliged." A match flared. There were eager sucking sounds.

"Let's hear it," Pete said.

"I am by training an engineer," Webster began. "My work has exposed me to all but one of the continents, to desert and alp and forest, to every terrain and season of the earth. Some years ago I was hired by the Peruvian government to search for tungsten in the tropics. My wife and daughter accompanied me. We were the only white people for a thousand miles in any direction, and we had no choice but to live as the Indians lived—to share their food and drink and even their culture."

Pete said. "You knew the lingo, did you?"

"We picked it up." The ember of the cigar bobbed up and down. "We were used to learning as necessity decreed. At any rate, it became evident after a couple of years that there was no tungsten to be found. My wife had fallen ill and was pleading to be taken home. But I was deaf to her pleas, because by then I was on the trail of another metal—a metal far more valuable than tungsten."

"Let me guess," Pete said, "Gold?"

Donald looked at Pete, then back at Webster.

"Gold," Webster said. "A vein of gold greater than the Mother Lode itself. After I found the first traces of it nothing could tear me away from my search—not the sickness of my wife nor anything else. I was determined to uncover the vein, and so I did—but not before I laid my wife to rest. As I say, the earth will be repaid."

Webster was quiet. Then he said, "But life must go on. In the years since my wife's death I have been making the arrangements necessary to open the mine. I could have done it immediately, of course, enriching myself beyond measure, but I knew what that would mean—the exploitation of our beloved Indians, the brutal destruction of their environment. I felt I had too much to atone for already." Webster paused, and when he spoke again his voice was dull and rushed, as if he had used up all the interest he had in his own words. "Instead I drew up a program for returning the bulk of the wealth to the Indians themselves. A kind of trust fund. The interest alone will allow them to secure their ancient lands and rights in perpetuity. At the same time, our investors will be rewarded a thousandfold. Two-thousandfold. Everyone will prosper together."

"That's great," Donald said. "That's the way it ought to be."

Pete said, "I'm willing to bet that you just happen to have a few shares left. Am I right?"

Webster made no reply.

"Well?" Pete knew that Webster was on to him now, but he didn't care. The story had bored him. He'd expected something different, something original, and Webster had let him down. He hadn't even tried. Pete felt sour and stale. His eyes burned from cigar smoke and the high beams of road-hogging truckers. "Douse the stogie," he said to Webster. "I told you to keep the window down."

"Got a little nippy back there."

Donald said. "Hey, Pete. Lighten up."

"Douse it!"

Webster sighed. He got rid of the cigar.

"I'm a wreck," Pete said to Donald. "You want to drive for a while?"

Donald nodded.

Pete pulled over and they changed places.

Webster kept his counsel in the back seat. Donald hummed while he drove, until Pete told him to stop. Then everything was quiet.

Donald was humming again when Pete woke up. Pete stared sullenly at the road, at the white lines sliding past the car. After a few moments of this he turned and said, "How long have I been out?"

Donald glanced at him. "Twenty, twenty-five minutes."

Pete looked behind him and saw that Webster was gone. "Where's our friend?"

"You just missed him. He got out in Soledad. He told me to say thanks and goodbye."

"Soledad? What about his sick daughter? How did he explain her away?" Pete leaned over the seat. Both ashtrays were still in place. Floor mats. Door handles.

"He has a brother living there. He's going to borrow a car from him and drive the rest of the way in the morning."

"I'll bet his brother's living there," Pete said. "Doing fifty concurrent life sentences. His brother and his sister and his mom and his dad."

"I kind of liked him," Donald said.

"I'm sure you did," Pete said wearily.

"He was interesting. He'd been places."

"His cigars had been places, I'll give you that."

"Come on, Pete."

"Come on yourself. What a phony."

"You don't know that."

"Sure I do."

"How? How do you know?"

Pete stretched. "Brother, there are some things you're just born knowing. What's the gas situation?"

"We're a little low."

"Then why didn't you get some more?"

"I wish you wouldn't snap at me like that," Donald said.

"Then why don't you use your head? What if we run out?"

"We'll make it," Donald said. "I'm pretty sure we've got enough to make it. You didn't have to be so rude to him," Donald added.

Pete took a deep breath. "I don't feel like running out of gas tonight, okay?"

Donald pulled in at the next station they came to and filled the tank while Pete went to the men's room. When Pete came back, Donald was sitting in the passenger's seat. The attendant came up to the driver's window as Pete got in behind the wheel. He bent down and said, "Twenty-two fifty-five."

"You heard the man," Pete said to Donald.

Donald looked straight ahead. He didn't move.

"Cough up," Pete said. "This trip's on you."

Donald said, softly, "I can't."

"Sure you can. Break out that wad."

Donald glanced up at the attendant, then at Pete. "Please," he said. "Pete, I don't have it anymore."

Pete took this in. He nodded, and paid the attendant.

Donald began to speak when they left the station but Pete cut him off. He said, "I don't want to hear from you right now. You just keep quiet or I swear to God I won't be responsible."

They left the fields and entered a tunnel of tall trees. The trees went on and on. "Let me get this straight," Pete said at last. "You don't have the money I gave you."

"You treated him like a bug or something," Donald said.

"You don't have the money," Pete said again.

Donald shook his head.

"Since I bought dinner, and since we didn't stop anywhere in between, I assume you gave it to Webster. Is that right? Is that what you did with it?"

"Yes."

Pete looked at Donald. His face was dark under the hood but he still managed to convey a sense of remove, as if none of this had anything to do with him.

"Why?" Pete asked. "Why did you give it to him?" When Donald didn't answer, Pete said, "A hundred dollars. Gone. Just like that. I *worked* for that money, Donald."

"I know, I know," Donald said.

"You don't know! How could you? You get money by holding out your hand."

"I work too," Donald said.

"You work too. Don't kid yourself, brother."

Donald leaned toward Pete, about to say something, but Pete cut him off again.

"You're not the only one on the payroll, Donald. I don't think you understand that. I have a family."

"Pete, I'll pay you back."

"Like hell you will. A hundred dollars!" Pete hit the steering wheel with the palm of his hand. "Just because you think I hurt some goofball's feelings. Jesus, Donald."

"That's not the reason," Donald said. "And I didn't just *give* him the money."

"What do you call it, then? What do you call what you did?"

"I *invested* it. I wanted a share, Pete." When Pete looked over at him Donald nodded and said again, "I wanted a share."

Pete said, "I take it you're referring to the gold mine in Peru."

"Yes," Donald said.

"You believe that such a gold mine exists?"

Donald looked at Pete, and Pete could see him just beginning to catch on. "You'll believe anything," Pete said. "Won't you? You really will believe anything at all."

"I'm sorry," Donald said, and turned away.

Pete drove on between the trees and considered the truth of what he had just said—that Donald would believe anything at all. And it came to him that it would be just like this unfair life for Donald to come out ahead in the end, by believing in some outrageous promise that would turn out to be true and that he, Pete, would reject out of hand because he was too wised up to listen to anybody's pitch anymore except for laughs. What a joke. What a joke if there really was a blessing to be had, and the blessing didn't come to the one who deserved it, the one who did all the work, but to the other.

And as if this had already happened Pete felt a shadow move upon him, darkening his thoughts. After a time he said, "I can see where all this is going, Donald."

"I'll pay you back," Donald said.

"No," Pete said. "You won't pay me back. You can't. You don't know how. All you've ever done is take. All your life."

Donald shook his head.

"I see exactly where this is going," Pete went on. "You can't work, you can't take care of yourself, you believe anything anyone tells you. I'm stuck with you, aren't I?" He looked over at Donald. "I've got you on my hands for good."

Donald pressed his fingers against the dashboard as if to brace himself. "I'll get out," he said.

Pete kept driving.

"Let me out," Donald said. "I mean it, Pete."

"Do you?"

Donald hesitated. "Yes," he said.

"Be sure," Pete told him. "This is it. This is for keeps."

"I mean it."

"All right. You made the choice." Pete braked the car sharply and swung it to the shoulder of the road. He turned off the engine and got out. Trees loomed on both sides, shutting out the sky. The air was cold and musty. Pete took Donald's duffel bag from the back seat and set it down behind the car. He stood there, facing Donald in the red glow of the taillights. "It's better this way." Pete said.

Donald just looked at him.

"Better for you," Pete said.

Donald hugged himself. He was shaking. "You don't have to say all that," he told Pete. "I don't blame you."

"Blame me? What the hell are you talking about? Blame me for what?"

"For anything," Donald said.

"I want to know what you mean by blame me."

"Nothing. Nothing, Pete. You'd better get going. God bless you."

"That's it," Pete said. He dropped to one knee, searching the packed dirt with his hands. He didn't know what he was looking for; his hands would know when they found it.

Donald touched Pete's shoulder. "You'd better go," he said.

Somewhere in the trees Pete heard a branch snap. He stood up. He looked at Donald, then went back to the car and drove away. He drove fast, hunched over the wheel, conscious of the way he was hunched and the shallowness of his breathing, refusing to look at the mirror above his head until there was nothing behind him but darkness.

Then he said, "A hundred dollars," as if there were someone to hear.

The trees gave way to fields. Metal fences ran beside the road, plastered with windblown scraps of paper. Tule fog hung above the ditches, spilling into the road, dimming the ghostly halogen lights that burned in the yards of the farms Pete passed. The fog left beads of water rolling up the windshield.

Pete rummaged among his cassettes. He found Pachelbel's *Canon*[2] and pushed it into the tape deck. When the violins began to play he leaned back and assumed an attentive expression as if he were really listening to them. He smiled to himself like a man at liberty to enjoy music, a man who has finished his work and settled his debts, done all things meet and due.

And in this way, smiling, nodding to the music, he went another mile or so and pretended that he was not already slowing down, that he was not going to turn back, that he would be able to drive on like this, alone, and have the right answer when his wife stood before him in the doorway of his home and asked, Where is he? Where is your brother?

(1985)

---

[2] Johann Pachelbel (1653–1706): an organist and composer known for his *Canon in D* (c. 1700).

QUESTIONS

1. What understanding can you formulate about Pete's values and how they account for his attitudes towards people and things?

2. What does Donald's recollection of Pete's attempt to kill him tell you about his character and sense of brotherhood?

3. If Pete loves Donald, why does he drive so far to pick up Donald, only to leave him by the side of the road once again?

4. How is conflict resolved in this story? Do you think that it is resolved once and for all?

ROBERT COOVER (B. 1932)

The Brother

right there right there in the middle of the damn field he says he wants to put that thing together him and his buggy ideas and so me I says "how the hell you gonna get it down to the water?" but he just focuses me out sweepin the blue his eyes rollin like they do when he gets het on some new lunatic notion and he says not to worry none about that just would I help him for God's sake and because he don't know how he can get it done in time otherwise and though you'd have to be loonier than him to say yes I says I will of course I always would crazy as my brother is I've done little else since I was born and my wife she says "I can't figure it out I can't see why you always have to be babyin that old fool he ain't never done nothin for you God knows and you got enough to do here fields need plowin it's a bad enough year already my God and now that red-eyed brother of yours wingin around like a damn cloud and not knowin what in the world he's doin buildin a damn boat in the country my God what next? you're a damn fool I tell you" but packs me some sandwiches just the same and some sandwiches for my brother Lord knows *his* wife don't have no truck with him no more says he can go starve for all she cares she's fed up ever since the time he made her sit out on a hillside for three whole days rain and everything because he said she'd see God and she didn't see nothin and in fact she like to die from hunger nothin but berries and his boys too they ain't so bright neither but at least they come to help him out with his damn boat so it ain't just the two of us thank God for *that* and it ain't no goddamn fishin boat he wants to put up neither in fact it's the biggest damn thing I ever heard of and for weeks *weeks* I'm tellin you we ain't doin nothin but cuttin down pine trees and haulin them out to his field which is really pretty high up a hill and my God *that's* work lemme tell you and my wife she sighs and says I am really crazy r-e-a-l-l-y crazy and her four months with a child and tryin to do my work and hers too and still when I come home from haulin timbers around all day she's got enough left to rub my shoulders and the small of my back and fix a hot meal her long black hair pulled to a knot behind her head and hangin marvelously down her back her eyes gentle but very tired my God and I says to my brother I says "look I got a lotta work to do buddy you'll have to finish this idiot thing yourself I wanna help you all I can you know that but" and he looks off and he says "it don't matter none your work" and I says "the hell it don't how you think me and my wife we're gonna eat I mean where do you think this food comes from you been puttin away man? you can't eat this goddamn boat out here ready to rot in that bastard sun" and he just sighs long and says "no it just don't matter" and he sits him down on a rock kinda tired like and stares off and looks like he might even for God's sake cry and so I go back to bringin wood up to him and he's already started on the keel and frame God knows how *he* ever found out to build a damn boat lost in *his* fog where he is Lord he was twenty when I was born and the first thing I remember was having to lead him around so he didn't get kicked by a damn mule him who couldn't never do nothin in a normal way just a huge oversize fuzzyface boy so anyway I take to gettin up a few hours earlier ever day to do my farmin my wife apt to lose the baby if she should keep pullin around like she was doin then I go to work on the boat until sundown and on and on the days hot and dry and my wife keepin good food in me or else I'd of dropped sure and no matter what I say to try and get out of it my brother he says "you come and help now the rest don't matter" and we just keep hammerin away and my God the damn thing is big enough for a hundred people and at least I think at *least* it's a place to live and not too bad at that at least it's good for somethin but my wife she just sighs and says no good will come of it and runs her hands through my hair but she don't ask me to stop helpin no more because she knows it won't do no good and she's kinda turned into herself now these days and gettin herself all ready and still we keep workin on that damn thing that damn boat and the days pass and my brother he says we gotta work harder we ain't got much time and from time to time he gets a coupla neighbors to come over and give a hand them sucked in by the size and the novelty of the thing makin jokes some but they don't stay around more than a day or two and they go away shakin their heads and swearin under their breath and disgusted they got weaseled into the thing in the first place and me I only get about half my place planted and see to my stock as much as I can my wife she takes more care of them than I can but at least we won't starve we say if we just get some rain and finally we get the damn thing done all finished by God and we cover it in and out with pitch and put a kinda fancy roof on it and I come home on that last day and I ain't never goin back ain't *never* gonna let him talk me into nothin again and I'm all smellin of tar and my wife she cries and cries and I says to her not to worry no more I'll be home all the time and me I'm crying a little too though she don't notice just thinkin how she's had it so lonely and hard and all and for one whole day I just sleep the whole damn day and the rest of the week I work around the farm and one day I get an idea and I go over to my brother's place and get some pieces of wood left over and whaddya know? they are all livin on that damn boat there in the middle of nowhere him and his boys and some women and my brother's wife she's there too but she's madder than hell and carpin at him to get outa that damn boat and come home and he says she's got just one more day and then he's gonna drug her on the boat but he don't say it like a threat or nothin more like a fact a plain fact tomorrow he's gonna drug her on the boat well I ain't one to get mixed up in domestic quarrels God knows so I grab up the wood and beat it back to my farm and that evenin I make a little cradle a kinda fancy one with little animal figures cut in it and polished down and after supper I give it to my wife as a surprise and she cries and cries and holds me tight and says don't never go away again and stay close by her and all and I feel so damn good and warm about it all and glad the boat thing is over and we get out a little wine and we decide the baby's name is gonna be either Nathaniel or Anna and so we drink an extra cup to Nathaniel's health and we laugh and we sigh and drink one to Anna and my wife she gently fingers the little animal figures and says they're beautiful and really they ain't I ain't much good at that sorta thing but I know what she means and then she says "where did you get the wood?" and I says "it's left over from the boat" and she don't say nothin for a moment and then she says "you been over there again today?" and I says "yes just to get the wood" and she says "what's he doin now he's got the boat done?" and I says "funny thing they're all living in the damn thing all except the old lady she's over there hollerin at him how he's gettin senile and where does he think he's sailin to and how if he ain't afraid of runnin into a octypuss on the way he oughta get back home and him sayin she's a nut there ain't no water and her sayin that's what *she's* been tellin *him* for six months" and my wife she laughs and it's the happiest laugh I've heard from her in half a year and I laugh and we both have another cup of wine and my wife she says "so he's just livin on that big thing all by hisself ?" and I says "no he's got his boys on there and some young women who are maybe wives of the boys or somethin I don't know I ain't never seen them before and all kindsa damn animals and birds and things I ain't never seen the likes" and my wife she says "animals? what animals?" and I says "oh all kinds I don't know a whole damn menagerie all clutterin and stinkin up the boat *God* what a mess" and my wife laughs again and she's a little silly with the wine and she says "I bet he ain't got no pigs" and "oh yes I seen them" I says and we laugh thinkin about pigs rootin around in that big tub and she says "I bet he ain't got no jackdaws" and I says "yes I seen a couple of them too or mostly I heard them you couldn't hardly hear nothin else" and we laugh again thinkin about them crows and his old lady and the pigs and all and my wife she says "*I* know what he ain't got I bet he ain't got no lice" and we both laugh like crazy and when I can I says "oh yes he does less he's took a bath" and we both laugh till we're cryin and we finish off the wine and my wife says "look now I *know* what he ain't got he ain't got no termites" and I says "you're right I don't recollect no termites maybe we oughta make him a present" and my wife she holds me close quiet all of a sudden and says "he's really movin Nathaniel's really movin' and she puts my hand down on her round belly and the little fella is kickin up a terrific storm and I says kinda anxious "does it hurt? do you think that—?" and "no" she says "it's good" she says and so I says with my hand on her belly "here's to you Nathaniel" and we drain what's left in the bottom of our cups and the next day we wake up in each other's arms and it's rainin and *thank God* we say and since it's rainin real good we stay inside and do things around the place and we're happy because the rain has come just in time and in the evenin things smell green and fresh and delicious and it's still raining a little but not too hard so I decide to take a walk and I wander over by my brother's place thinkin I'll ask him if he's like to take on some pet termites to go with his collection and there by God is his wife on the boat and I don't know if he drug her on or if she just finally come by herself but she ain't sayin nothing which is damn unusual and the boys they ain't sayin nothin neither and my brother he ain't sayin nothin they're just all standin up there on top and gazin off and I holler up at them "nice rain ain't it?" and my brother he looks down at me standin there in the rain and still he don't say nothin but he raises his hand kinda funny like and then puts it back on the rail and I decide not to say nothin about the termites and it's startin to rain a little harder again so I turn away and go back home and I tell my wife about what happened and my wife she just laughs and says "they're *all* crazy he's finally got them *all* crazy" and she's cooked me up a special pastry with fresh meat and so we forget about them but by God the next day the rain's still comin down harder than ever and water's beginnin to stand around in places and after a week of rain I can see the crops is pretty well ruined and I'm havin trouble keepin my stock fed and my wife she's cryin and talkin about our bad luck that we might as well of built a damn boat as plant all them crops and still we don't figure things out I mean it just don't come to our minds not even when the rain keeps spillin down like a ocean dumped upsidedown and now water is beginnin to stand around in big pools really big ones and water up to the ankles around the house and leakin in and pretty soon the whole damn house is gettin fulla water and I keep sayin maybe we oughta go use my brother's boat till this blows over but my wife she says "never" and then she starts in cryin again so finally I says to her I says "we can't be so proud I'll go ask him" and so I set out in the storm and I can hardly see where I'm goin and I slip up to my neck in places and finally I get to where the boat is and I holler up and my brother he comes out he looks down at where I am and he don't say nothin that bastard he just looks at me and I shout up at him I says "hey is it all right for me and my wife to come over until this thing blows over?" and still he don't say a damn word he just raises his hand in that same sillyass way and I holler "hey you stupid sonuvabitch I'm soakin wet goddamn it and my house is fulla water and my wife she's about to have a kid and she's apt to get sick all wet and cold to the bone and all I'm askin you—" and right then right while I'm still talkin he turns around and he goes back in the boat and I can't hardly believe it me his brother but he don't come back out and I push up under the boat and I beat on it with my fists and scream at him and call him every name I can think up and I shout for his boys and for his wife and for anybody inside and nobody comes out "GOD*damn* YOU" I cry out at the top of my lungs and half sobbin and sick and then feelin too beat out to do anythin more I turn around and head back for home but the rain is thunderin down like mad now and in places I gotta swim and I can't make it no further and I recollect a hill nearby and I head for it and when I get to it I climb up on top of it and it feels good to be on land again even if it is soggy and greasy and I vomit and retch there awhile and move further up and the next thing I know I'm wakin up the rain still in my face and the water halfway up the hill toward me and I look out and I can see my brother's boat is floatin and I wave at it but I don't see nobody wave back and then I quick look out towards my own place and all I can see is the top of it and of a sudden I'm scared scared about my wife and I go tearin for the house swimmin most all the way and cryin and shoutin and the rain still comin down like crazy and so now well now I'm back here on the hill again what little there is left of it and I'm figurin maybe I got a day left if the rain keeps comin and it don't show no signs of stoppin and I can't see my brother's boat no more gone just water how *how* did he know? that bastard and yet I gotta hand it to him it's not hard to see who's crazy around here I can't see my house no more I just left my wife inside where I found her I couldn't hardly stand to look at her the way she was

(1969)

QUESTIONS

1. In the biblical story of The Flood, Noah is supposed to be a good man. How does Coover change the story? Explain the paradox of a good man letting his brother die.

2. What does the narrator's relationship with his brother demonstrate about the power of older brothers, personal obligation, and family ties?

3. What is the effect of Coover's omission of all punctuation from the story?

ALICE MUNRO (B. 1931)

Boys and Girls

My father was a fox farmer. That is, he raised silver foxes, in pens; and in the fall and early winter, when their fur was prime, he killed them and skinned them and sold their pelts to the Hudson's Bay Company or the Montreal Fur Traders. These companies supplied us with heroic calendars to hang, one on each side of the kitchen door. Against a background of cold blue sky and black pine forests and treacherous northern rivers, plumed adventurers planted the flags of England or of France; magnificent savages bent their backs to the portage.

For several weeks before Christmas, my father worked after supper in the cellar of our house. The cellar was whitewashed, and lit by a hundred-watt bulb over the worktable. My brother Laird and I sat on the top step and watched. My father removed the pelt inside-out from the body of the fox, which looked surprisingly small, mean and rat-like, deprived of its arrogant weight of fur. The naked, slippery bodies were collected in a sack and buried at the dump. One time the hired man, Henry Bailey, had taken a swipe at me with this sack, saying, "Christmas present!" My mother thought that was not funny. In fact she disliked the whole pelting operation—that was what the killing, skinning, and preparation of the furs was called—and wished it did not have to take place in the house. There was the smell. After the pelt had been stretched inside-out on a long board my father scraped away delicately, removing the little clotted webs of blood vessels, the bubbles of fat; the smell of blood and animal fat, with the strong primitive odor of the fox itself, penetrated all parts of the house. I found it reassuringly seasonal, like the smell of oranges and pine needles.

Henry Bailey suffered from bronchial troubles. He would cough and cough until his narrow face turned scarlet, and his light blue, derisive eyes filled up with tears; then he took the lid off the stove, and, standing well back, shot out a great clot of phlegm—hsss—straight into the heart of the flames. We admired him for this performance and for his ability to make his stomach growl at will, and for his laughter, which was full of high whistlings and gurglings and involved the whole faulty machinery of his chest. It was sometimes hard to tell what he was laughing at, and always possible that it might be us.

After we had been sent to bed we could still smell fox and still hear Henry's laugh, but these things, reminders of the warm, safe, brightly lit downstairs world, seemed lost and diminished, floating on the stale cold air upstairs. We were afraid at night in the winter. We were not afraid of *outside* though this was the time of year when snowdrifts curled around our house like sleeping whales and the wind harassed us all night, coming up from the buried fields, the frozen swamp, with its old bugbear chorus of threats and misery. We were afraid of *inside,* the room where we slept. At this time the upstairs of our house was not finished. A brick chimney went up one wall. In the middle of the floor was a square hole, with a wooden railing around it; that was where the stairs came up. On the other side of the stairwell were the things that nobody had any use for any more—a soldiery roll of linoleum, standing on end, a wicker baby carriage, a fern basket, china jugs and basins with cracks in them, a picture of the Battle of Balaclava, very sad to look at. I had told Laird, as soon as he was old enough to understand such things, that bats and skeletons lived over there; whenever a man escaped from the county jail, twenty miles away, I imagined that he had somehow let himself in the window and was hiding behind the linoleum. But we had rules to keep us safe. When the light was on, we were safe as long as we did not step off the square of worn carpet which defined our bedroom-space; when the light was off no place was safe but the beds themselves. I had to turn out the light kneeling on the end of my bed, and stretching as far as I could to reach the cord.

In the dark we lay on our beds, our narrow life rafts, and fixed our eyes on the faint light coming up the stairwell, and sang songs. Laird sang "Jingle Bells," which he would sing any time, whether it was Christmas or not, and I sang "Danny Boy." I loved the sound of my own voice, frail and supplicating, rising in the dark. We could make out the tall frosted shapes of the windows now, gloomy and white. When I came to the part, *When I am dead, as dead I well may be*—a fit of shivering caused not by the cold sheets but by pleasurable emotion almost silenced me. *You'll kneel and say, an Ave there above me*—What was an Ave? Every day I forgot to find out.

Laird went straight from singing to sleep. I could hear his long, satisfied, bubbly breaths. Now for the time that remained to me, the most perfectly private and perhaps the best time of the whole day, I arranged myself tightly under the covers and went on with one of the stories I was telling myself from night to night. These stories were about myself, when I had grown a little older; they took place in a world that was recognizably mine, yet one that presented opportunities for courage, boldness and self-sacrifice, as mine never did. I rescued people from a bombed building (it discouraged me that the real war had gone on so far away from Jubilee). I shot two rabid wolves who were menacing the schoolyard (the teachers cowered terrified at my back). I rode a fine horse spiritedly down the main street of Jubilee, acknowledging the townspeople's gratitude for some yet-to-be-worked-out piece of heroism (nobody ever rode a horse there, except King Billy in the Orangemen's Day parade).[1] There was always riding and shooting in these stories, though I had only been on a horse twice—bareback because we did not own a saddle—and the second time I had slid right around and dropped under the horse's feet; it had stepped placidly over me. I really was learning to shoot, but I could not hit anything yet, not even tin cans on fence posts.

Alive, the foxes inhabited a world my father made for them. It was surrounded by a high guard fence, like a medieval town, with a gate that was padlocked at night. Along the streets of this town were ranged large, sturdy pens. Each of them had a real door that a man could go through, a wooden ramp along the wire, for the foxes to run up and down on, and a kennel—something like a clothes chest with airholes—where they slept and stayed in winter and had their young. There were feeding and watering dishes attached to the wire in such a way that they could be emptied and cleaned from the outside. The

---

[1] July 12: the Protestant counterpart of St. Patrick's Day, celebrating the Battle of Boyne in which William of Orange (1650–1702) was victorious. William was joint ruler of England with Mary II from 1689 to 1702.

dishes were made of old tin cans, and the ramps and kennels of odds and ends of old lumber. Everything was tidy and ingenious; my father was tirelessly inventive and his favorite book in the world was *Robinson Crusoe*. He had fitted a tin drum on a wheelbarrow, for bringing water down to the pens. This was my job in summer, when the foxes had to have water twice a day. Between nine and ten o'clock in the morning, and again after supper, I filled the drum at the pump and trundled it down through the barnyard to the pens, where I parked it, and filled my watering can and went along the streets. Laird came to, with his little cream and green gardening can, filled too full and knocking against his legs and slopping water on his canvas shoes. I had the real watering can, my father's, though I could only carry it three-quarters full.

The foxes all had names, which were printed on a tin plate and hung beside their doors. They were not named when they were born, but when they survived the first year's pelting and were added to the breeding stock. Those my father had named were called names like Prince, Bob, Wally and Betty. Those I had named were called Star or Turk, or Maureen or Diana. Laird named one Maud after a hired girl we had when he was little, one Harold after a boy at school, and one Mexico, he did not say why.

Naming them did not make pets out of them, or anything like it. Nobody but my father ever went into the pens, and he had twice had blood-poisoning from bites. When I was bringing them their water they prowled up and down on the paths they had made inside their pens, barking seldom—they saved that for nighttime, when they might get up a chorus of community frenzy—but always watching me, their eyes burning, clear gold, in their pointed, malevolent faces. They were beautiful for their delicate legs and heavy, aristocratic tails and the bright fur sprinkled on dark down their backs—which gave them their name—but especially for their faces, drawn exquisitely sharp in pure hostility, and their golden eyes.

Besides carrying water I helped my father when he cut the long grass, and the lamb's quarter and flowering money-musk, that grew between the pens. He cut with the scythe and I raked into piles. Then he took a pitchfork and threw fresh-cut grass all over the top of the pens, to keep the foxes cooler and shade their coats, which were browned by too much sun. My father did not talk to me unless it was about the job we were doing. In this he was quite different from my mother, who, if she was feeling cheerful, would tell me all sorts of things—the name of a dog she had had when she was a little girl, the name of boys she had gone out with later on when she was grown up, and what certain dresses of hers had looked like—she could not imagine now what had become of them. Whatever thoughts and stories my father had were private, and I was shy of him and would never ask him questions. Nevertheless I worked willingly under his eyes, and with a feeling of pride. One time a feed salesman came down into the pens to talk to him and my father said, "Like to have you meet my new hired man." I turned away and raked furiously, red in the face with pleasure.

"Could of fooled me," said the salesman. "I thought it was only a girl."

After the grass was cut, it seemed suddenly much later in the year. I walked on stubble in the earlier evening, aware of the reddening skies, the entering silences, of fall. When I wheeled the tank out of the gate and put the padlock on, it was almost dark. One night at this time I saw my mother and father standing talking on the little rise of ground we called the gangway, in front of the barn. My father had just come from the meathouse; he had his stiff bloody apron on, and a pail of cut-up meat in his hand.

It was an odd thing to see my mother down at the barn. She did not often come out of the house unless it was to do something—hang out the wash or dig potatoes in the garden. She looked out of place, with her bare lumpy legs, not touched by the sun, her apron still on and damp across the stomach from the supper dishes. Her hair was tied up in a kerchief, wisps of it falling out. She would tie her hair up like this in the morning, saying she did not have time to do it properly, and it would stay tied up all day. It was true, too; she really did not have time. These days our back porch was piled with baskets of peaches and grapes and pears, bought in town, and onions and tomatoes and cucumbers grown at home, all waiting to be made into jelly and jam and preserves, pickles and chili sauce. In the kitchen there was a fire in the stove all day, jars clinked in boiling water, sometimes a cheesecloth bag was strung on a pole between two chairs straining blue-black grape pulp for jelly. I was given jobs to do and I would sit at the table peeling peaches that had been soaked in the hot water, or cutting up onions, my eyes smarting and streaming. As soon as I was done I ran out of the house, trying to get out of earshot before my mother thought of what she wanted me to do next. I hated the hot dark kitchen in summer, the green blinds and the flypapers, the same old oilcloth table and wavy mirror and bumpy linoleum. My mother was too tired and preoccupied to talk to me, she had no heart to tell about the Normal School Graduation Dance; sweat trickled over her face and she was always counting under her breath, pointing at jars, dumping cups of sugar. It seemed to me that work in the house was endless, dreary and peculiarly depressing; work done out of doors, and in my father's service, was ritualistically important.

I wheeled the tank up to the barn, where it was kept, and I heard my mother saying, "Wait till Laird gets a little bigger, then you'll have a real help."

What my father said I did not hear. I was pleased by the way he stood listening, politely as he would to a salesman or a stranger, but with an air of wanting to get on with his real work. I felt my mother had no business down here and I wanted him to feel the same way. What did she mean about Laird? He was no help to anybody. Where was he now? Swinging himself sick on the swing, going around in circles, or trying to catch caterpillars. He never once stayed with me till I was finished.

"And then I can use her more in the house," I heard my mother say. She had a dead-quiet, regretful way of talking about me that always made me uneasy. "I just get my back turned and she runs off. It's not like I had a girl in the family at all."

I went and sat on a feed bag in the corner of the barn, not wanting to appear when this conversation was going on. My mother, I felt, was not to be trusted. She was kinder than my father and more easily fooled, but you could not depend on her, and the real reasons for the things she said and did were not to be known. She loved me, and she sat up late at night making a dress of the difficult style I wanted, for me to wear when school started, but she was also my enemy. She was always plotting. She was plotting now to get me to stay in the house more, although she knew I hated it (*because* she knew I hated it) and keep me from working for my father. It seemed to me she would do this simply out of perversity, and to try her power. It did not occur to me that she could be lonely, or jealous. No grown-up could be; they were too fortunate. I sat and kicked my heels monotonously against a feed bag, raising dust, and did not come out till she was gone.

At any rate, I did not expect my father to pay any attention to what she said. Who could imagine Laird doing my work—Laird remembering the padlock and cleaning out the watering dishes with a leaf on the end of a stick, or even wheeling the tank without it tumbling over? It showed how little my mother knew about the way things really were.

I have forgotten to say what the foxes were fed. My father's bloody apron reminded me. They were fed horsemeat. At this time most farmers still kept horses, and when a horse got too old to work, or broke a leg or got down and would not get up, as they sometimes did, the owner would call my father, and he and Henry went out to the farm in the truck. Usually they shot and butchered the horse there, paying the farmer from five to twelve dollars. If they had already too much meat on hand, they would bring the horse back alive, and keep it for a few days or weeks in our stable, until the meat was needed. After the war the farmers were buying tractors and gradually getting rid of horses altogether, so it sometimes happened that we got a good healthy horse, that there was just no use for any more. If this happened in the winter we might keep the horse in our stable till spring, for we had plenty of hay and if there was a lot of snow—and the plow did not always get our road cleared—it was convenient to be able to go to town with a horse and cutter.

The winter I was eleven years old we had two horses in the stable. We did not know what names they had had before, so we called them Mack and Flora. Mack was an old black workhorse, sooty and indifferent. Flora was a sorrel mare, a driver. We took them both out in the cutter. Mack was slow and easy to handle. Flora was given to fits of violent alarm, veering at cars and even at other horses, but we loved her speed and high-stepping, her general air of gallantry and abandon. On Saturdays we went down to the stable and as soon as we opened the door on its cosy, animal-smelling darkness Flora threw up her head, rolled her eyes, whinnied despairingly and pulled herself through a crisis of nerves on the spot. It was not safe to go into her stall; she would kick.

This winter also I began to hear a great deal more on the theme my mother had sounded when she had been talking in front of the barn. I no longer felt safe. It seemed that in the minds of the people around me there was a steady undercurrent of thought, not to be deflected, on this one subject. The word *girl* had formerly seemed to me innocent and unburdened, like the word *child*; now it appeared that it was no such thing. A girl was not, as I had supposed, simply what I was; it was what I had to become. It was a definition, always touched with emphasis, with reproach and disappointment. Also it was a joke on me. Once Laird and I were fighting, and for the first time ever I had to use all my strength against him; even so, he caught and pinned my arm for a moment, really hurting me. Henry saw this, and laughed, saying, "Oh, that there Laird's gonna show you, one of these days!" Laird was getting a lot bigger. But I was getting bigger too.

My grandmother came to stay with us for a few weeks and I heard other things. "Girls don't slam doors like that." "Girls keep their knees together when they sit down." And worse still, when I asked some questions, "That's none of girls' business." I continued to slam the doors and sit as awkwardly as possible, thinking that by such measures I kept myself free.

When spring came, the horses were let out in the barnyard. Mack stood against the barn wall trying to scratch his neck and haunches, but Flora trotted up and down and reared at the fences, clattering her hooves against the rails. Snow drifts dwindled quickly, revealing the hard gray and brown earth, the familiar rise and fall of the ground, plain and bare after the fantastic landscape of winter. There was a great feeling of opening-out, of release. We just wore rubbers now, over our shoes; our feet felt ridiculously light. One Saturday we went out to the stable and found all the doors open, letting in the unaccustomed sunlight and fresh air. Henry was there, just idling around looking at his collection of calendars which were tacked up behind the stalls in a part of the stable my mother had probably never seen.

"Come to say goodbye to your old friend Mack?" Henry said. "Here, you give him a taste of oats." He poured some oats into Laird's cupped hands and Laird went to feed Mack. Mack's teeth were in bad shape. He ate very slowly, patiently shifting the oats around in his mouth, trying to find a stump of a molar to grind it on. "Poor old Mack," said Henry mournfully. "When a horse's teeth's gone, he's gone. That's about the way."

"Are you going to shoot him today?" I said. Mack and Flora had been in the stable so long I had almost forgotten they were going to be shot.

Henry didn't answer me. Instead he started to sing in a high, trembly, mocking-sorrowful voice, *Oh, there's no more work, for poor Uncle Ned, he's gone where the good darkies go.* Mack's thick, blackish tongue worked diligently at Laird's hand. I went out before the song was ended and sat down on the gangway.

I had never seen them shoot a horse, but I knew where it was done. Last summer Laird and I had come upon a horse's entrails before they were buried. We had thought it was a big black snake, coiled up in the sun. That was around in the field that ran up beside the barn. I thought that if we went inside the barn, and found a wide crack or a knothole to look through, we would be able to see them do it. It was not something I wanted to see; just the same, if a thing really happened, it was better to see it, and know.

My father came down from the house, carrying the gun.

"What are you doing here?" he said.

"Nothing."

"Go on up and play around the house."

He sent Laird out of the stable. I said to Laird, "Do you want to see them shoot Mack?" and without waiting for an answer led him around to the front door of the barn, opened it carefully, and went in. "Be quiet or they'll hear us," I said. We could hear Henry and my father talking in the stable, then the heavy, shuffling steps of Mack being backed out of his stall.

In the loft it was cold and dark. Thin, crisscrossed beams of sunlight fell through the cracks. The hay was low. It was a rolling country, hills and hollows, slipping under our feet. About four feet up was a beam going around the walls. We piled hay up in one corner and I boosted Laird up and hoisted myself. The beam was not very wide; we crept along it with our hands flat on the barn walls. There were plenty of knotholes, and I found one that gave me the view I wanted—a corner of the barnyard, the gate, part of the field. Laird did not have a knothole and began to complain.

I showed him a widened crack between two boards. "Be quiet and wait. If they hear you you'll get us in trouble."

My father came in sight carrying the gun. Henry was leading Mack by the halter. He dropped it and took out his cigarette papers and tobacco; he rolled cigarettes for my father and himself. While this was going on Mack nosed around in the old, dead grass along the fence. Then my father opened the gate and they took Mack through. Henry led Mack away from the path to a patch of ground and they talked together, not loud enough for us to hear. Mack again began searching for a mouthful of fresh grass, which was not to be found. My father walked away in a straight line, and stopped short at a distance which seemed to suit him. Henry was walking away from Mack too, but sideways, still negligently holding on to the halter. My father raised the gun and Mack looked up as if he had noticed something and my father shot him.

Mack did not collapse at once but swayed, lurched sideways and fell, first on his side; then he rolled over on his back and, amazingly, kicked his legs for a few seconds in the air. At this Henry laughed, as if Mack had done a trick for him. Laird, who had drawn a long, groaning breath of surprise when the shot was fired, said out loud, "He's not dead." And it seemed to me it might be true. But his legs stopped, he rolled on his side again, his muscles quivered and sank. The two men walked over and looked at him in a businesslike way; they bent down and examined his forehead where the bullet had gone in, and now I saw his blood on the brown grass.

"Now they just skin him and cut him up," I said. "Let's go." My legs were a little shaky and I jumped gratefully down into the hay. "Now you've seen how they shoot a horse," I said in a congratulatory way, as if I had seen it many times before. "Let's see if any barn cat's had kittens in the hay." Laird jumped. He seemed young and obedient again. Suddenly I remembered how, when he was little, I had brought him into the barn and told him to climb the ladder to the top beam. That was in the spring, too, when the hay was low. I had done it out of a need for excitement, a desire for something to happen so that I could tell about it. He was wearing a little bulky brown and white checked coat, made down from one of mine. He went all the way up just as I told him, and sat down on the top beam with the hay far below him on one side, and the barn floor and some old machinery on the other. Then I ran screaming to my father, "Laird's up on the top beam!" My father came, my mother came, my father went up the ladder talking very quietly and brought Laird down under his arm, at which my mother leaned against the ladder and began to cry. They said to me, "Why weren't you watching him?" but nobody ever knew the truth. Laird did not know enough to tell. But whenever I saw the brown and white checked coat hanging in the closet, or at the bottom of the rag bag, which was where it ended up, I felt a weight in my stomach, the sadness of unexorcised guilt.

I looked at Laird, who did not even remember this, and I did not like the look on this thin, winter-pale face. His expression was not frightened or upset, but remote, concentrating. "Listen," I said, in an unusually bright and friendly voice, "you aren't going to tell, are you?"

"No," he said absently.

"Promise."

"Promise," he said. I grabbed the hand behind his back to make sure he was not crossing his fingers. Even so, he might have a nightmare; it might come out that way. I decided I had better work hard to get all thoughts of what he had seen out of his mind—which, it seemed to me, could not hold very many things at a time. I got some money I had saved and that afternoon we went into Jubilee and saw a show, with Judy Canova,[2] at which we both laughed a great deal. After that I thought it would be all right.

Two weeks later I knew they were going to shoot Flora. I knew from the night before, when I heard my mother ask if the hay was holding out all right, and my father said, "Well, after tomorrow there'll just be the cow, and we should be able to put her out to grass in another week." So I knew it was Flora's turn in the morning.

This time I didn't think of watching it. That was something to see just one time. I had not thought about it very often since, but sometimes when I was busy, working at school, or standing in front of the mirror combing my hair and wondering if I would be pretty when I grew up, the whole scene would flash into my mind: I would see the easy, practiced way my father raised the gun, and hear Henry laughing when Mack kicked his legs in the air. I did not have any great feeling of horror and opposition, such as a city child might have had; I was too used to seeing the death of animals as a necessity by which we lived. Yet I felt a little ashamed, and there was a new wariness, a sense of holding-off, in my attitude to my father and his work.

It was a fine day, and we were going around the yard picking up tree branches that had been torn off in winter storms. This was something we had been told to do and also we wanted to use them to make a teepee. We heard Flora whinny, and then my father's voice and Henry's shouting, and we ran down to the barnyard to see what was going on.

The stable door was open. Henry had just brought Flora out, and she had broken away from him. She was running free in the barnyard, from one end to the other. We climbed up on the fence. It was exciting to see her running, whinnying, going up on her hind legs, prancing and threatening like a horse in a Western movie, an unbroken ranch horse, though she was just an old driver, an old sorrel mare. My father and Henry ran after her and tried to grab the dangling halter. They tried to work her into a corner, and they had almost succeeded when she made a run between them, wild-eyed, and disappeared around the corner of the barn. We heard the rails clatter down as she got over the fence, and Henry yelled, "She's into the field now!"

That meant she was in the long L-shaped field that ran up by the house. If she got around the center, heading toward the lane, the gate was open; the truck had been driven into the field this morning. My father shouted to me, because I was on the other side of the fence, nearest the lane, "Go shut the gate!"

I could run very fast. I ran across the garden, past the tree where our swing was hung, and jumped across a ditch into the lane. There was the open gate. She had not got out, I could not see her up on the road; she must have run to the other end of the field. The gate was heavy. I lifted it out of the gravel and carried it across the roadway. I had it halfway across when she came in sight, galloping straight towards me. There was just time to get the chain on. Laird came scrambling through the ditch to help me.

Instead of shutting the gate, I opened it as wide as I could. I did not make any decision to do this, it was just what I did. Flora never slowed down; she galloped straight

---

[2] Judy Canova: a Hollywood comic actress.

past me, and Laird jumped up and down, yelling, "Shut it, shut it!" even after it was too late. My father and Henry appeared in the field a moment too late to see what I had done. They only saw Flora heading for the township road. They would think I had not got there in time.

They did not waste any time asking about it. They went back to the barn and got the gun and the knives they used, and put these in the truck; then they turned the truck around and came bouncing up the field toward us. Laird called to them, "Let me go too, let me go too!" and Henry stopped the truck and they took him in. I shut the gate after they were all gone.

I supposed Laird would tell. I wondered what would happen to me. I had never disobeyed my father before, and I could not understand why I had done it. Flora would not really get away. They would catch up with her in the truck. Or if they did not catch her this morning somebody would see her and telephone us this afternoon or tomorrow. There was no wild country here for her to run to, only farms. What was more, my father had paid for her, we needed the meat to feed the foxes, we needed the foxes to make our living. All I had done was make more work for my father who worked hard enough already. And when my father found out about it he was not going to trust me any more; he would know that I was not entirely on his side. I was on Flora's side, and that made me no use to anybody, not even to her. Just the same, I did not regret it; when she came running at me and I held the gate open, that was the only thing I could do.

I went back to the house, and my mother said, "What's all the commotion?" I told her that Flora had kicked down the fence and got away. "Your poor father," she said, "now he'll have to go chasing over the countryside. Well, there isn't any use planning dinner before one." She put up the ironing board. I wanted to tell her, but thought better of it and went upstairs and sat on my bed.

Lately I had been trying to make my part of the room fancy, spreading the bed with old lace curtains, and fixing myself a dressing table with some leftovers of cretonne for a skirt. I planned to put up some kind of barricade between my bed and Laird's, to keep my section separate from his. In the sunlight, the lace curtains were just dusty rags. We did not sing at night any more. One night when I was singing Laird said, "You sound silly," and I went right on but the next night I did not start. There was not so much need to anyway, we were no longer afraid. We knew it was just old furniture over there, old jumble and confusion. We did not keep to the rules. I still stayed awake after Laird was asleep and told myself stories, but even in these stories something different was happening, mysterious alterations took place. A story might start off in the old way, with a spectacular danger, a fire or wild animals, and for a while I might rescue people; then things would change around, and instead, somebody would be rescuing me. It might be a boy from our class at school, or even Mr. Campbell, our teacher, who tickled girls under the arms. And at this point the story concerned itself at great length with what I looked like—how long my hair was, and what kind of dress I had on; by the time I had these details worked out the real excitement of the story was lost.

It was later than one o'clock when the truck came back. The tarpaulin was over the back, which meant there was meat in it. My mother had to heat dinner up all over again. Henry and my father had changed from their bloody overalls into ordinary working overalls in the barn, and they washed their arms and necks and faces at the sink, and splashed water on their hair and combed it. Laird lifted his arm to show off a streak of blood. "We shot old Flora," he said, "and cut her up in fifty pieces."

"Well I don't want to hear about it," my mother said. "And don't come to my table like that."

My father made him go and wash the blood off.

We sat down and my father said grace and Henry pasted his chewing gum on the end of his fork, the way he always did; when he took if off he would have us admire the pattern. We began to pass the bowls of steaming, overcooked vegetables. Laird looked across the table at me and said proudly, distinctly, "Anyway it was her fault Flora got away."

"What?" my father said.

"She could of shut the gate and she didn't. She just open' it up and Flora run out."

"Is that right?" my father said.

Everybody at the table was looking at me. I nodded, swallowing food with great difficulty. To my shame, tears flooded my eyes.

My father made a curt sound of disgust. "What did you do that for?"

I did not answer. I put down my fork and waited to be sent from the table, still not looking up.

But this did not happen. For some time nobody said anything, then Laird said matter-of-factly, "She's crying."

"Never mind," my father said. He spoke with resignation, even good humor, the words which absolved and dismissed me for good. "She's only a girl," he said.

I didn't protest that, even in my heart. Maybe it was true.

(1968)

QUESTIONS

1. How does the narrator view her younger brother, Laird, her mother, and her father? Why does she open the gate for Flora?

2. What do the terms "inside" and "outside" symbolize to the narrator?

3. Why does Laird tell on his sister? Explain the significance of the narrator's final remark: "Maybe it was true."

4. How would you describe the theme of this story?

ERNEST HEMINGWAY (1899–1961)

Soldier's Home

Krebs went to the war from a Methodist college in Kansas. There is a picture which shows him among his fraternity brothers, all of them wearing exactly the same height and style collar. He enlisted in the Marines in 1917 and did not return to the United States until the second division returned from the Rhine in the summer of 1919.

There is a picture which shows him on the Rhine with two German girls and another corporal. Krebs and the corporal look too big for their uniforms. The German girls are not beautiful. The Rhine does not show in the picture.

By the time Krebs returned to his home town in Oklahoma the greeting of heroes was over. He came back much too late. The men from the town who had been drafted had all been welcomed elaborately on their return. There had been a great deal of hysteria. Now the reaction had set in. People seemed to think it was rather ridiculous for Krebs to be getting back so late, years after the war was over.

At first Krebs, who had been at Belleau Wood, Soissons, the Champagne, St. Mihiel and in the Argonne[1] did not want to talk about the war at all. Later he felt the need to talk but no one wanted to hear about it. His town had heard too many atrocity stories to be thrilled by actualities. Krebs found that to be listened to at all he had to lie, and after he had done this twice he, too, had a reaction against the war and against talking about it. A distaste for everything that had happened to him in the war set in because of the lies he had told. All of the times that had been able to make him feel cool and clear inside himself when he thought of them; the times so long back when he had done the one thing, the only thing for a man to do, easily and naturally, when he might have done something else, now lost their cool, valuable quality and then were lost themselves.

His lies were quite unimportant lies and consisted in attributing to himself things other men had seen, done or heard of, and stating as facts certain apocryphal incidents familiar to all soldiers. Even his lies were not sensational at the pool room. His acquaintances, who had heard detailed accounts of German women found chained to machine guns in the Argonne forest and who could not comprehend, or were barred by their patriotism from interest in, any German machine gunners who were not chained, were not thrilled by his stories.

Krebs acquired the nausea in regard to experience that is the result of untruth or exaggeration, and when he occasionally met another man who had really been a soldier and they talked a few minutes in the dressing room at a dance he fell into the easy pose of the old soldier among other soldiers: that he had been badly, sickeningly frightened all the time. In this way he lost everything.

During this time, it was late summer, he was sleeping late in bed, getting up to walk down town to the library to get a book, eating lunch at home, reading on the front

---

[1] Argonne: locations in Normandy, northeast France, where major World War I battles were fought.

porch until he became bored and then walking down through the town to spend the hottest hours of the day in the cool dark of the pool room. He loved to play pool.

In the evening he practised on his clarinet, strolled down town, read and went to bed. He was still a hero to his two young sisters. His mother would have given him breakfast in bed if he had wanted it. She often came in when he was in bed and asked him to tell her about the war, but her attention always wandered. His father was non-committal.

Before Krebs went away to the war he had never been allowed to drive the family motor car. His father was in the real estate business and always wanted the car to be at his command when he required it to take clients out into the country to show them a piece of farm property. The car always stood outside the First National Bank building where his father had an office on the second floor. Now, after the war, it was still the same car.

Nothing was changed in the town except that the young girls had grown up. But they lived in such a complicated world of already defined alliances and shifting feuds that Krebs did not feel the energy or the courage to break into it. He liked to look at them, though. There were so many good-looking young girls. Most of them had their hair cut short. When he went away only little girls wore their hair like that or girls that were fast. They all wore sweaters and shirt waists with round Dutch collars. It was a pattern. He liked to look at them from the front porch as they walked on the other side of the street. He liked to watch them walking under the shake of the trees. He like the round Dutch collars above their sweaters. He liked their silk stockings and flat shoes. He liked their bobbed hair and the way they walked.

When he was in town their appeal to him was not very strong. He did not like them when he saw them in the Greek's ice cream parlor. He did not want them themselves really. They were too complicated. There was something else. Vaguely he wanted a girl but he did not want to have to work to get her. He would have liked to have a girl but he did not want to have to spend a long time getting her. He did not want to get into the intrigue and the politics. He did not want to have to do any courting. He did not want to tell any more lies. It wasn't worth it.

He did not want any consequences. He did not want any consequences ever again. He wanted to live along without consequences. Besides he did not really need a girl. The army had taught him that. It was all right to pose as though you had to have a girl. Nearly everybody did that. But it wasn't true. You did not need a girl. That was the funny thing. First a fellow boasted how girls mean nothing to him, that he never thought of them, that they could not touch him. Then a fellow boasted that he could not get along without girls, that he had to have them all the time, that he could not go to sleep without them.

That was all a lie. It was all a lie both ways. You did not need a girl unless you thought about them. He learned that in the army. Then sooner or later you always got one. When you were really ripe for a girl you always got one. You did not have to think about it. Sooner or later it would come. He had learned that in the army.

Now he would have liked a girl if she had come to him and not wanted to talk. But here at home it was all too complicated. He knew he could never get through it all again. It was not worth the trouble. That was the thing about French girls and German girls. There was not all this talking. You couldn't talk much and you did not need to talk.

It was simple and you were friends. He thought about France and then be began to think about Germany. On the whole he had liked Germany better. He did not want to leave Germany. He did not want to come home. Still, he had come home. He sat on the front porch.

He liked the girls that were walking along the other side of the street. He liked the look of them much better than the French girls or the German girls. But the world they were in was not the world he was in. He would like to have one of them. But it was not worth it. They were such a nice pattern. He liked the pattern. It was exciting. But he would not go through all the talking. He did not want one badly enough. He liked to look at them all, though. It was not worth it. Not now when things were getting good again.

He sat there on the porch reading a book on the war. It was a history and he was reading about all the engagements he had been in. It was the most interesting reading he had ever done. He wished there were more maps. He looked forward with a good feeling to reading all the really good histories when they would come out with good detail maps. Now he was really learning about the war. He had been a good soldier. That made a difference.

One morning after he had been home about a month his mother came into his bedroom and sat on the bed. She smoothed her apron.

"I had a talk with your father last night, Harold," she said, "and he is willing for you to take the car out in the evenings."

"Yeah?" said Krebs, who was not fully awake. "Take the car out? Yeah?"

"Yes. Your father has felt for some time that you should be able to take the car out in the evenings whenever you wished but we only talked it over last night."

"I'll bet you made him," Krebs said.

"No. It was your father's suggestion that we talk the matter over."

"Yeah. I'll bet you made him," Krebs sat up in bed.

"Will you come down to breakfast, Harold?" his mother said.

"As soon as I get my clothes on," Krebs said.

His mother went out of the room and he could hear her frying something downstairs while he washed, shaved and dressed to go down into the dining-room for breakfast. While he was eating breakfast his sister brought in the mail.

"Well, Hare," she said. "You old sleepy-head. What do you ever get up for?"

Krebs looked at her. He liked her. She was his best sister.

"Have you got the paper?" he asked.

She handed him *The Kansas City Star* and he shucked off its brown wrapper and opened it to the sporting page. He folded *The Star* open and propped it against the water pitcher with his cereal dish to steady it, so he could read while he ate.

"Harold," his mother stood in the kitchen doorway, "Harold, please don't muss up the paper. Your father can't read his *Star* if it's been mussed."

"I won't muss it," Krebs said.

His sister sat down at the table and watched him while he read.

"We're playing indoor over at school this afternoon," she said. "I'm going to pitch."

"Good," said Krebs. "How's the old wing?"

"I can pitch better than lots of the boys. I tell them all you taught me. The other girls aren't much good."

"Yeah?" said Krebs.

"I tell them all you're my beau. Aren't you my beau, Hare?"

"You bet."

"Couldn't your brother really be your beau just because he's your brother?"

"I don't know."

"Sure you know. Couldn't you be my beau, Hare, if I was old enough and if you wanted to?"

"Sure. You're my girl now."

"Am I really your girl?"

"Sure."

"Do you love me?"

"Uh, huh."

"Will you love me always?"

"Sure."

"Will you come over and watch me play indoor?"

"Maybe."

"Aw, Hare, you don't love me. If you loved me, you'd want to come over and watch me play indoor."

Krebs's mother came into the dining-room from the kitchen. She carried a plate with two fried eggs and some crisp bacon on it and a plate of buckwheat cakes.

"You run along, Helen," she said. "I want to talk to Harold."

She put the eggs and bacon down in front of him and brought in a jug of maple syrup for the buckwheat cakes. Then she sat down across the table from Krebs.

"I wish you'd put down the paper a minute, Harold," she said.

Krebs took down the paper and folded it.

"Have you decided what you are going to do yet, Harold?" his mother said, taking off her glasses.

"No," said Krebs.

"Don't you think it's about time?" His mother did not say this in a mean way. She seemed worried.

"I hadn't thought about it," Krebs said.

"God has some work for every one to do," his mother said. "There can be no idle hands in His Kingdom."

"I'm not in His Kingdom," Krebs said.

"We are all of us in His Kingdom."

Krebs felt embarrassed and resentful as always.

"I've worried about you so much, Harold," his mother went on. "I know the temptations you must have been exposed to. I know how weak men are. I know what your own dear grandfather, my own father, told us about the Civil War and I have prayed for you. I pray for you all day long, Harold."

Krebs looked at the bacon fat hardening on his plate.

"Your father is worried, too," his mother went on. "He thinks you have lost your ambition, that you haven't got a definite aim in life. Charley Simmons, who is just your age, has a good job and is going to be married. The boys are all settling down; they're all determined to get somewhere; you can see that boys like Charley Simmons are on their way to being really a credit to the community."

Krebs said nothing.

"Don't look that way, Harold," his mother said. "You know we love you and I want to tell you for your own good how matters stand. Your father does not want to hamper your freedom. He thinks you should be allowed to drive the car. If you want to take some of the nice girls out riding with you, we are only too pleased. We want you to enjoy yourself. But you are going to have to settle down to work, Harold. Your father doesn't care what you start in at. All work is honorable as he says. But you've got to make a start at something. He asked me to speak to you this morning and then you can stop in and see him at his office."

"Is that all?" Krebs said.

"Yes. Don't you love your mother, dear boy?"

"No," Krebs said.

His mother looked at him across the table. Her eyes were shiny. She started crying.

"I don't love anybody," Krebs said.

It wasn't any good. He couldn't tell her, he couldn't make her see it. It was silly to have said it. He had only hurt her. He went over and took hold of her arm. She was crying with her head in her hands.

"I didn't mean it," he said. "I was just angry at something. I didn't mean I didn't love you."

His mother went on crying. Krebs put his arm on her shoulder.

"Can't you believe me, mother?"

His mother shook her head.

"Please, please, mother. Please believe me."

"All right," his mother said chokily. She looked up at him. "I believe you, Harold."

Krebs kissed her hair. She put her face up to him.

"I'm your mother," she said. "I held you next to my heart when you were a tiny baby."

Krebs felt sick and vaguely nauseated.

"I know, Mummy," he said. "I'll try and be a good boy for you."

"Would you kneel and pray with me, Harold?" his mother asked.

They knelt down beside the dining-room table and Krebs's mother prayed.

"Now, you pray, Harold," she said.

"I can't," Krebs said.

"Try, Harold."

"I can't."

"Do you want me to pray for you?"

"Yes."

So his mother prayed for him and then they stood up and Krebs kissed his mother and went out of the house. He had tried so to keep his life from being complicated. Still, none of it had touched him. He had felt sorry for his mother and she had made him lie. He would go to Kansas City and get a job and she would feel all right about it. There would be one more scene maybe before he got away. He would not go down to his father's office. He would miss that one. He wanted his life to go smoothly. It had just gotten going that way. Well, that was all over now, anyway. He would go over to the schoolyard and watch Helen play indoor baseball.

(1925)

QUESTIONS

1. Why is it significant that Krebs returns home from World War I later than many of the other soldiers?

2. Explain why you think Krebs is so lacking in energy for wooing girls or even enjoying himself.

3. Discuss the reasons for Krebs's connection to his sister Helen and distance from his mother and father.

4. What comment do you think Hemingway is making in this story about the nature of the truth and lying? How is the question of truth related to Krebs's alienation?

CYNTHIA OZICK (B. 1928)

The Shawl

Stella, cold, cold, the coldness of hell. How they walked on the roads together, Rosa with Magda curled up between sore breasts, Magda wound up in the shawl. Sometimes Stella carried Magda. But she was jealous of Magda. A thin girl of fourteen, too small, with thin breasts of her own, Stella wanted to be wrapped in a shawl, hidden away, asleep, rocked by the march, a baby, a round infant in arms. Magda took Rosa's nipple, and Rosa never stopped walking, a walking cradle. There was not enough milk; sometimes Magda sucked air; then she screamed. Stella was ravenous. Her knees were tumors on sticks, her elbows chicken bones.

Rosa did not feel hunger; she felt light, not like someone walking but like someone in a faint, in trance, arrested in a fit, someone who is already a floating angel, alert and seeing everything, but in the air, not there, not touching the road. As if teetering on the tips of her fingernails. She looked into Magda's face through a gap in the shawl: a squirrel in a nest, safe, no one could reach her inside the little house of the shawl's windings. The face, very round, a pocket mirror of a face: but it was not Rosa's bleak complexion, dark like cholera,[1] it was another kind of face altogether, eyes blue as air, smooth feathers of hair nearly as yellow as the Star sewn into Rosa's coat.[2] You could think she was one of *their* babies.

Rosa, floating, dreamed of giving Magda away in one of the villages. She could leave the line for a minute and push Magda into the hands of any woman on the side of the road. But if she moved out of line they might shoot. And even if she fled the line for half a second and pushed the shawl-bundle at a stranger, would the woman take it? She might be surprised, or afraid; she might drop the shawl, and Magda would fall out and strike her head and die. The little round head. Such a good child, she gave up screaming, and sucked now only for the taste of the drying nipple itself. The neat grip of the tiny gums. One mite of a tooth tip sticking up in the bottom gum, how shining, an elfin tombstone of white marble gleaming there. Without complaining, Magda relinquished Rosa's teats, first the left, then the right; both were cracked, not a sniff of milk. The duct-crevice extinct, a dead volcano, blind eye, chill hole, so Magda took the corner of the shawl and milked it instead. She sucked and sucked, flooding the threads with wetness. The shawl's good flavor, milk of linen.

It was a magic shawl, it could nourish an infant for three days and three nights. Magda did not die, she stayed alive, although very quiet. A peculiar smell, of cinnamon and almonds, lifted out of her mouth. She held her eyes open every moment, forgetting how to blink or nap, and Rosa and sometimes Stella studied their blueness. On the road they raised one burden of a leg after another and studied Magda's face. "Aryan,"[3] Stella

---

[1] cholera: acute, often fatal infectious disease of the small intestine.
[2] "yellow as the star sewn into Rosa's coat": reference to the yellow cloth six-pointed "Jewish" stars European Jews under the Hitler regime were required to wear sewn on the sleeve of their coats.
[3] Aryan: name used during Nazism for a Caucasian gentile.

said, in a voice grown as thin as a string; and Rosa thought how Stella gazed at Magda like a young cannibal. And the time that Stella said "Aryan," it sounded to Rosa as if Stella had really said "Let us devour her."

But Magda lived to walk. She lived that long, but she did not walk very well, partly because she was only fifteen months old, and partly because the spindles of her legs could not hold up her fat belly. It was fat with air, full and round. Rosa gave almost all her food to Magda, Stella gave nothing; Stella was ravenous, a growing child herself, but not growing much. Stella did not menstruate. Rosa did not menstruate. Rosa was ravenous, but also not; she learned from Magda how to drink the taste of a finger in one's mouth. They were in a place without pity, all pity was annihilated in Rosa, she looked at Stella's bones without pity. She was sure that Stella was waiting for Magda to die so she could put her teeth into the little thighs.

Rosa knew Magda was going to die very soon; she should have been dead already, but she had been buried away deep inside the magic shawl, mistaken there for the shivering mound of Rosa's breasts; Rosa clung to the shawl as if it covered only herself. No one took it away from her. Magda was mute. She never cried. Rosa hid her in the barracks, under the shawl, but she knew that one day someone would inform; or one day someone, not even Stella, would steal Magda to eat her. When Magda began to walk Rosa knew that Magda was going to die very soon, something would happen. She was afraid to fall asleep; she slept with the weight of her thigh on Magda's body; she was afraid she would smother Magda under her thigh. The weight of Rosa was becoming less and less; Rosa and Stella were slowly turning into air.

Magda was quiet, but her eyes were horribly alive, like blue tigers. She watched. Sometimes she laughed—it seemed a laugh, but how could it be? Magda had never seen anyone laugh. Still, Magda laughed at her shawl when the wind blew its corners, the bad wind with pieces of black in it, that made Stella's and Rosa's eyes tear. Magda's eyes were always clear and tearless. She watched like a tiger. She guarded her shawl. No one could touch it; only Rosa could touch it. Stella was not allowed. The shawl was Magda's own baby, her pet, her little sister. She tangled herself up it in and sucked on one of the corners when she wanted to be very still.

Then Stella took the shawl away and made Magda die.

Afterward Stella said: "I was cold."

And afterward she was always cold, always. The cold went into her heart: Rosa saw that Stella's heart was cold. Magda flopped onward with her little pencil legs scribbling this way and that, in search of the shawl; the pencils faltered at the barracks opening, where the light began. Rosa saw and pursued. But already Magda was in the square outside the barracks, in the jolly light. It was the roll-call arena. Every morning Rosa had to conceal Magda under the shawl against a wall of the barracks and go out and stand in the arena with Stella and hundreds of others, sometimes for hours, and Magda, deserted, was quiet under the shawl, sucking on her corner. Every day Magda was silent, and so she did not die. Rosa saw that today Magda was going to die, and at the same time a fearful joy ran in Rosa's two palms, her fingers were on fire, she was astonished, febrile: Magda, in the sunlight, swaying on her pencil legs, was howling. Ever since the drying up of Rosa's nipples, ever since Magda's last scream on the road, Magda had been devoid of any syllable; Magda was a mute. Rosa believed that something had gone wrong with her vocal cords, with her windpipe, with the cave of her larynx; Magda was defective, without a voice; perhaps she was deaf; there might be something amiss with her intelligence; Magda was dumb. Even the laugh that came when the ash-stippled wind[4] made a clown out of Magda's shawl was only the air-blown showing of her teeth. Even when the lice, head lice and body lice, crazed her so that she became as wild as one of the big rats that plundered the barracks at daybreak looking for carrion, she rubbed and scratched and kicked and bit and rolled without a whimper. But now Magda's mouth was spilling a long viscous rope of clamor.

"Maaaa—"

It was the first noise Magda had ever sent out from her throat since the drying up of Rosa's nipples.

"Maaaa . . . aaa!"

Again! Magda was wavering in the perilous sunlight of the arena, scribbling on such pitiful little bent shins. Rosa saw. She saw that Magda was grieving for the loss of her shawl, she saw that Magda was going to die. A tide of commands hammered in Rosa's nipples: Fetch, get, bring! But she did not know which to go after first, Magda or the shawl. If she jumped out into the arena to snatch Magda up, the howling would not stop, because Magda would still not have the shawl; but if she ran back into the barracks to find the shawl, and if she found it, and if she came after Magda holding it and shaking it, then she would get Magda back, Magda would put the shawl in her mouth and turn dumb again.

Rosa entered the dark. It was easy to discover the shawl. Stella was heaped under it, asleep in her thin bones. Rosa tore the shawl free and flew—she could fly, she was only air—into the arena. The sunheat murmured of another life, of butterflies in summer. The light was placid, mellow. On the other side of the steel fence, far away, there were green meadows speckled with dandelions and deep-colored violets; beyond them, even farther, innocent tiger lilies, tall, lifting their orange bonnets. In the barracks they spoke of "flowers," of "rain": excrement, thick turd-braids, and the slow stinking maroon waterfall that slunk down from the upper bunks, the stink mixed with a bitter fatty floating smoke that greased Rosa's skin. She stood for an instant at the margin of the arena. Sometimes the electricity inside the fence would seem to hum; even Stella said it was only an imagining, but Rosa heard real sounds in the wire; grainy sad voices. The farther she was from the fence, the more clearly the voices crowded at her. The lamenting voices strummed so convincingly, so passionately, it was impossible to suspect them of being phantoms. The voices told her to hold up the shawl, high; the voices told her to shake it, to whip with it, to unfurl it like a flag. Rosa lifted, shook, whipped, unfurled. Far off, very far, Magda leaned across her air-fed belly, reaching out with the rods of her arms. She was high up, elevated, riding someone's shoulder. But the shoulder that carried Magda was not coming toward Rosa and the shawl, it was drifting away, the speck of Magda was moving more and more into the smoky distance. Above the shoulder a helmet glinted. The light tapped the helmet and sparkled it into a goblet. Below the helmet a black body

---

[4] "ash-stippled wind": allusion to the ashes blown from the ovens where victims of Nazi concentration camps were cremated during World War II.

like a domino and a pair of black boots hurled themselves in the direction of the electrified fence. The electric voices began to chatter wildly. "Maamaa, maaa-maaa," they all hummed together. How far Magda was from Rosa now, across the whole square, past a dozen barracks, all the way on the other side! She was no bigger than a moth.

All at once Magda was swimming through the air. The whole of Magda traveled through loftiness. She looked like a butterfly touching a silver vine. And the moment Magda's feathered round head and her pencil legs and balloonish belly and zigzag arms splashed against the fence, the steel voices went mad in their growling, urging Rosa to run and run to the spot where Magda had fallen from her flight against the electrified fence; but of course Rosa did not obey them. She only stood, because if she ran they would shoot, and if she tried to pick up the sticks of Magda's body they would shoot, and if she let the wolf's screech ascending now through the ladder of her skeleton break out, they would shoot; so she took Magda's shawl and filled her own mouth with it, stuffed it in and stuffed it in, until she was swallowing up the wolf's screech and tasting the cinnamon and almond depth of Magda's saliva; and Rosa drank Magda's shawl until it dried.

(1980)

QUESTIONS

1. What do you think the shawl symbolizes for Rosa, the mother; Magda, the baby; and Stella, the older sister? Why do you think the shawl has "magical" qualities?

2. How does the presence of the magical quilt fit into the awful realism of the Nazi concentration camp?

3. What do you think the sources of jealousy are that make Stella want to "devour" her sister?

4. Explain why it is so important to Rosa that Magda is no longer "mute."

Writing Topics for Short Stories

1. Identify the moral questions concerning sibling rivalry that are raised in Borges's "Legend," Ozick's "The Shawl," Wolff's "The Rich Brother," and Coover's "The Brother." In what ways are these stories commentaries on Cain's statement "Am I my brother's keeper?"

2. Analyze the conflict between individuality and conformity in Munro's "Boys and Girls."

3. Compare the adolescent and young adult struggles of the main characters of Hemingway's "Soldier's Home" and Munro's "Boys and Girls." What frightens them about the gender role expectations that confront them?

4. Explain the function of setting (place, time, weather) and its relationship to understanding character in Hemingway's "Soldier's Home," Wolff's "The Rich Brother," and Coover's "The Brother."

5. Analyze the journey "home" as experienced by Krebs, by Pete during his journey by automobile in the desert in "The Rich Brother," and by the narrator as he awaits imminent destruction in the deluge in "The Brother."

6. Discuss the connotation of the word *boys* and the word *girls* for each of the characters in Munro's "Boys and Girls." What do you think these connotations reveal about the narrator's society and our society?

7. Explain the ways in which Ozick's "The Shawl" evokes the intense pain caused by the Holocaust and the destruction of Jewish civilization in Europe. Your essay may require that you do some research on this topic.

8. Compare the effects of war on the behavior and mental state of individuals, especially toward their siblings, as seen in Hemingway's "Soldier's Home" and Ozick's "The Shawl." How does Borges's "In Memoriam, J.F.K." illuminate Hemingway's and Ozick's themes?

Poems

RAINER MARIA RILKE (1875–1926)

I Am Not. The Brother
Did Something to Me

Translated by Anita Barrows and Joanna Macy

Ich bin nicht. Der Bruder hat mir was getan

(Abel speaks)

I am not. The brother did something to me
that my eyes didn't see.
He veiled the light.
He hid my face with his face.
Now he is alone.
I think he must still exist,
for no one does to him what he did to me.
All have gone the same way:
all are met with his rage,
10   beside him all are lost.

I sense my older brother lies awake
as if accused.
Night offers itself to me,
not to him.

I, 10

(1899)

QUESTIONS

1. Who is the speaker, what is his tone of voice, and where is he when he speaks?

2. What kind of life does Cain lead as depicted by Abel?

3. Is it ironic that Abel sees himself as better off than Cain? What does this reveal about Abel and about Cain's sibling rivalry with him?

4. How does Rilke's version of the story of Cain and Abel compare with the version in "Genesis" (p. 194)?

DEMETRIOS CAPETANAKIS (1912–1944)

Abel

My brother Cain,[1] the wounded, liked to sit
Brushing my shoulder, by the staring water
Of life, or death, in cinemas half-lit
By scenes of peace that always turned to slaughter.

He liked to talk to me. His eager voice
Whispered the puzzle of his bleeding thirst,
Or prayed me not to make my final choice,
Unless we had a chat about it first.

And then he chose the final pain for me.
10   I do not blame his nature: he's my brother;
Nor what you call the times: our love was free,
Would be the same at any time; but rather

The ageless ambiguity of things
Which makes our life mean death, our love be hate.
My blood that streams across the bedroom sings:
"I am my brother opening the gate!"

(1943)

QUESTIONS

1. How does the title help you to better understand the poem's purpose? What emotions does Abel's tone of voice reveal?

---

[1] Cain: an allusion to "The Story of Cain and Abel." (See p. 194.)

2. Does Capetanakis portray Cain in the manner in which he is drawn in the Bible? (See "The Story of Cain and Abel," p. 194.)

3. What anachronisms in the poem make the story contemporary?

SYLVIA PLATH (1932–1963)

Two Sisters of Persephone[1]

Two girls there are: within the house
One sits; the other, without.
Daylong a duet of shade and light
Plays between these.

In her dark wainscoted room
The first works problems on
A mathematical machine.
Dry ticks mark time

As she calculates each sum.
10   At this barren enterprise
Rat-shrewd go her squint eyes,
Root-pale her meager frame.

Bronzed as earth, the second lies,
Hearing ticks blown gold
Like pollen on bright air. Lulled
Near a bed of poppies,

She sees how their red silk flare
Of petaled blood
Burns open to sun's blade.
20   On that green altar

Freely become sun's bride, the latter
Grows quick with seed.
Grass-couched in her labor's pride,
She bears a king. Turned bitter

And sallow as any lemon,
The other, wry virgin to the last,
Goes graveward with flesh laid waste,
Worm-husbanded, yet no woman.

(1956)

---

[1] Persephone: a daughter of Demeter and Zeus, who was abducted by Hades. (See "The Myth of Demeter and Persephone," p. 3.)

Questions

1. What imagery characterizes the difference between these two sisters?

2. Which sister seems to be better off, and how does the poem's imagery support your opinion?

3. How are these two sisters connected to the character of Persephone in the Greek myth? (See p. 3.)

Anne Sexton (1928–1974)

Hansel and Gretel

Little plum,
said the mother to her son,
I want to bite,
I want to chew,
I will eat you up.
Little child,
little nubkin,
sweet as fudge,
you are my blitz.
10   I will spit on you for luck
for you are better than money.
Your neck as smooth
as a hard-boiled egg;
soft cheeks, my pears,
let me buzz you on the neck
and take a bite.
I have a pan that will fit you.
Just pull up your knees like a game hen.
Let me take your pulse
20   and set the oven for 350.
Come, my pretender, my fritter,
my bubbler, my chicken biddy!
Oh succulent one,
it is but one turn in the road
and I would be a cannibal!

Hansel and Gretel
and their parents
had come upon evil times.

They had cooked the dog
30 and served him up like lamb chops.
There was only a loaf of bread left.
The final solution,
their mother told their father,
was to lose the children in the forest.
We have enough bread for ourselves
but none for them.
Hansel heard this
and took pebbles with him
into the forest.
40 He dropped a pebble every fifth step
and later, after their parents had left them,
they followed the pebbles home.
The next day their mother gave them
each a hunk of bread
like a page out of the Bible
and sent them out again.
This time Hansel dropped bits of bread.
The birds, however, ate the bread
and they were lost at last.
50 They were blind as worms.
They turned like ants in a glove
not knowing which direction to take.
The sun was in Leo
and water spouted from the lion's head
but still they did not know their way.
So they walked for twenty days
and twenty nights
and came upon a rococo house
made all of food from its windows
60 to its chocolate chimney.
A witch lived in that house
and she took them in.
She gave them a large supper
to fatten them up
and then they slept,
z's buzzing from their mouths like flies.
Then she took Hansel,
the smarter, the bigger,
the juicier, into the barn
70 and locked him up.
Each day she fed him goose liver
so that he would fatten,
so that he would be as larded

as a plump coachman,
that knight of the whip.
She was planning to cook him
and then gobble him up
as in a feast
after a holy war.

80   She spoke to Gretel
and told her how her brother
would be better than mutton;
how a thrill would go through her
as she smelled him cooking;
how she would lay the table
and sharpen the knives
and neglect none of the refinements.
Gretel
who had said nothing so far
90   nodded her head and wept.
She who neither dropped pebbles or bread
bided her time.
The witch looked upon her
with new eyes and thought:
Why not this saucy lass
for an hors d'oeuvre?
She explained to Gretel
that she must climb into the oven
to see if she would fit.
100   Gretel spoke at last:
Ja, Fräulein, show me how it can be done.
The witch thought this fair
and climbed in to show the way.
It was a matter of gymnastics.
Gretel,
seeing her moment in history,
shut fast the oven,
locked fast the door,
fast as Houdini,
110   and turned the oven on to bake.
The witch turned as red
as the Jap flag.
Her blood began to boil up
like Coca-Cola.
Her eyes began to melt.
She was done for.
Altogether a memorable incident.

As for Hansel and Gretel,
they escaped and went home to their father.
120   Their mother,
you'll be glad to hear, was dead.
Only at suppertime
while eating a chicken leg
did our children remember
the woe of the oven,
the smell of the cooking witch,
a little like mutton,
to be served only with burgundy
and fine white linen
130   like something religious.

(1971)

QUESTIONS

1. What tone of voice does the speaker use to portray the mother's desires in the opening stanza of the poem?

2. Whose mother do you think the speaker of the poem is referring to: all mothers, some mothers, Hansel's mother, or the witch?

3. How is there intended irony in what mothers mean when they affectionately say to their small children, "I could eat you up"? How does the speaker allude to this in the poem?

4. What do the phrases "final solution," "Ja, Fraulein," and "red as the Jap flag" allude to? What is the speaker's purpose in using them?

5. Since the speaker describes Hansel as being "the smarter" of the two children, what is implied by the fact that Gretel is the one who outwits the witch and saves them both?

LOUISE GLÜCK (B. 1943)

Gretel in Darkness[1]

This is the world we wanted.
All who would have seen us dead
are dead. I hear the witch's cry
break in the moonlight through a sheet

---

[1] Gretel in Darkness: an allusion to the story of "Hansel and Gretel." (See p. 196.)

of sugar: God rewards.
Her tongue shrivels into gas. . . .

        Now, far from women's arms
and memory of women, in our father's hut
we sleep, are never hungry.
10   Why do I not forget?
My father bars the door, bars harm
from this house, and it is years.

No one remembers. Even you, my brother,
summer afternoons you look at me as though
you meant to leave,
as though it never happened.
But I killed for you. I see armed firs,
the spires of that gleaming kiln—

Nights I turn to you to hold me
20   but you are not there.
Am I alone? Spies
hiss in the stillness, Hansel,
we are there still and it is real, real,
that black forest and the fire in earnest.

                       (1975)

QUESTIONS

1. What has changed in the time that has elapsed between the end of the folktale and the time Gretel speaks?

2. How do the images Gretel uses describe the quality of her life since she killed the witch? Why is the poem's title significant?

3. What is Gretel's tone of voice in the poem? How can the point Glück is making about Gretel's relationship with Hansel be applied to any set of siblings? Why is it significant that a sister has saved a brother?

ANNE SEXTON (1928–1974)

Cinderella

You always read about it:
the plumber with twelve children
who wins the Irish Sweepstakes.
From toilets to riches.
That story.

Or the nursemaid,
some luscious sweet from Denmark
who captures the oldest son's heart.
From diapers to Dior.
10 That story.

Or a milkman who serves the wealthy,
eggs, cream, butter, yogurt, milk,
the white truck like an ambulance
who goes into real estate
and makes a pile.
From homogenized to martinis at lunch.

Or the charwoman
who is on the bus when it cracks up
and collects enough from the insurance.
20 From mops to Bonwit Teller.
That story.

Once
the wife of a rich man was on her deathbed
and she said to her daughter Cinderella:
Be devout. Be good. Then I will smile
down from heaven in the seam of a cloud.
The man took another wife who had
two daughters, pretty enough
but with hearts like blackjacks.
30 Cinderella was their maid.
She slept on the sooty hearth each night
and walked around looking like Al Jolson.
Her father brought presents home from town,
jewels and gowns for the other women
but the twig of a tree for Cinderella.
She planted that twig on her mother's grave
and it grew to a three where a white dove sat.

Whenever she wished for anything the dove
would drop it like an egg upon the ground.
40 The bird is important, my dears, so heed him.

Next came the ball, as you all know.
It was a marriage market.
The prince was looking for a wife.
All but Cinderella were preparing
and gussying up for the big event.
Cinderella begged to go too.
Her stepmother threw a dish of lentils
into the cinders and said: Pick them
up in an hour and you shall go.
50 The white dove brought all his friends;
all the warm wings of the fatherland came,
and picked up the lentils in a jiffy.
No, Cinderella, said the stepmother,
you have no clothes and cannot dance.
That's the way with stepmothers.

Cinderella went to the tree at the grave
and cried forth like a gospel singer:
Mama! Mama! My turtledove,
send me to the prince's ball!
60 The bird dropped down a golden dress
and delicate little gold slippers.
Rather a large package for a simple bird.
So she went. Which is no surprise.
Her stepmother and sisters didn't
recognize her without her cinder face
and the prince took her hand on the spot
and danced with no other the whole day.

As nightfall came she thought she'd better
get home. The prince walked her home
70 and she disappeared into the pigeon house
and although the prince took an axe and broke
it open she was gone. Back to her cinders.
These events repeated themselves for three days.
However on the third day the prince
covered the palace steps with cobbler's wax
and Cinderella's gold shoe stuck upon it.

Now he would find whom the shoe fit
and find his strange dancing girl for keeps.
He went to their house and the two sisters
80 were delighted because they had lovely feet.
The eldest went into a room to try the slipper on

but her big toe got in the way so she simply
sliced it off and put on the slipper.
The prince rode away with her until the white dove
told him to look at the blood pouring forth.
That is the way with amputations.
They don't just heal up like a wish.
The other sister cut off her heel
but the blood told as blood will.

90   The prince was getting tired.
He began to feel like a shoe salesman.
But he gave it one last try.
This time Cinderella fit into the shoe
like a love letter into its envelope.

At the wedding ceremony
the two sisters came to curry favor
and the white dove pecked their eyes out.
Two hollow spots were left
like soup spoons.

100   Cinderella and the prince
lived, they say, happily ever after,
like two dolls in a museum case
never bothered by diapers or dust,
never arguing over the timing of an egg,
never telling the same story twice,
never getting a middle-aged spread,
their darling smiles pasted on for eternity.
Regular Bobbsey Twins.[1]
That story.

(1971)

QUESTIONS

1. Explain the purpose of the first four stanzas of the poem and how they frame the rest of the poem.

2. How do the speaker's ironic tone of voice and choice of diction convey a message about "Cinderella" as a contemporary icon of femininity?

3. What does this transformation of the folktale "Cinderella" convey about Sexton's view of folktales?

4. Do you think that this retelling of Cinderella improves on Perrault's seventeenth-century telling of the story (p. 202)?

---

[1] Bobbsey Twins: popular series of books for children in the 1920s–1950s, focussing on the adventures of Bert, Nan, Flossie, and Freddie Bobbsey, two sets of twins in one family.

Seamus Heaney (b. 1939)

Mid-Term Break

I sat all morning in the college sick bay
Counting bells knelling classes to a close.
At two o'clock our neighbours drove me home.

In the porch I met my father crying—
He had always taken funerals in his stride—
And Big Jim Evans saying it was a hard blow.

The baby cooed and laughed and rocked the pram
When I came in, and I was embarrassed
By old men standing up to shake my hand

10   And tell me they were 'sorry for my trouble',
Whispers informed strangers I was the eldest,
Away at school, as my mother held my hand

In hers and coughed out angry tearless sighs.
At ten o'clock the ambulance arrived
With the corpse, stanched and bandaged by the nurses.

Next morning I went up into the room. Snowdrops
And candles soothed the bedside; I saw him
For the first time in six weeks. Paler now,

Wearing a poppy bruise on his left temple,
20   He lay in the four foot box as in his cot.
No gaudy scars, the bumper knocked him clear.

A four foot box, a foot for every year.

(1980)

Questions

1. What details in the poem communicate the fact that this is an unusual occasion?

2. What is the speaker's relationship with the person in the box? Why doesn't he ever mention who this person is? Which images serve as clues to the cause of death?

3. After writing the whole poem in stanzas of triplets, Heaney makes the last line of the poem a singlet. What effect is created by ending the poem this way?

DIANE KEATING (B. 1944)

Far Summers

Benediction

Dusk, driving
through a landscape
wide and flat
as a dreamless sleep,
my sister and I
are curled
in the back seat
while alone
on the horizon
10   a house stared
out its windows.
That solitary
glimmer! For
the first time
I saw night,
felt the dark
dimensions
of the heart.

Sticks and Stones

Even birds paused under the fierce gaze
of noon. Nothing to do

we hid in the deepest thicket; nuzzled
and tickled, peeled sticks into snakes

sleeking their cool lengths along our thighs.
Here and there the round white

stones were fallen stars
we turned over—damp underparts

mysterious as our own. When the heat
10   broke we crept into time again.

On the path home we looked unthinking
at a hawk poised in the air. Yes

it was a far summer. You are dead.
Sticks are sticks and stones, stones.

Tonight at my desk I turn over ideas,
peel words, looking for something unsaid

that keeps on growing . . . seeds in the blood,
wood in the bone.

(1984)

QUESTIONS

1. What event is alluded to in the sections "Benediction" and "Sticks and Stones"?

2. Why is the time shift between the two sections significant, and how is it ironic?

3. What images capture the relationship between the sisters, as children and now?

CATULLUS (87–54? B.C.E.)

Poem 101 (Hail and Farewell)

Translated by William A. Clary

Carried through many nations and over many seas,
    I come, brother, with these poor offerings
To honor you at last with gifts appointed for the dead
    And address in vain your unresponding ashes,
Since Fate has deprived me of you yourself—
    Alas, poor brother unjustly taken from me.
Accept, now, these things which by ancient custom of our fathers
    Have been handed down as the sad gifts for final offerings,
Things flowing heavily with a brother's tears.
10   And so, for all eternity, brother, hail and farewell.

(58 B.C.E.)

QUESTIONS

1. What features of the poem seem most important for illustrating the speaker's feelings for his brother?

2. Why are rituals performed over a person's remains when he or she dies? How is this elegy a ritual?

3. Have you ever written or spoken an elegy for a person you loved who died? What traits or incidents were called to mind? Did they commemorate your feelings or give the best image of the person who died?

Writing Topics for Poems

1. What point does Plath's "Two Sisters of Persephone" make about personal and family relationships and obligations as well as the sacrifices a woman writer or artist must make? Is the speaker's judgment about family and artists ironic or unexpected? If the praise in our society is usually reserved for the person who tries to advance him- or herself, why does Plath reverse this order?

2. The death of a sibling is central to the following poems: Heaney's "Mid-Term Break," Keating's "Far Summers," and Catullus's "Poem 101 (Hail and Farewell)." Explain how death and its effect on the speaker of each poem is illustrated through imagery, figures of speech, tone of voice, and sound.

3. Select one poem from the selections in Part 2: Sisters and Brothers and demonstrate how working out the impact and finality of death seems to be cathartic for the speaker.

4. Capetanakis in "Abel" and Rilke in "I Am Not. The Brother Did Something to Me" use the technique of the persona to develop Abel's point of view if he were to have the opportunity to comment on his brother Cain. Explain whether you find Capetanakis's and Rilke's portrayals of Abel believeable.

5. Working from the point of view that childhood memories are captured through imagery, simile, and metaphor, consider how these memories remain private, yet manage to make us recall our own memories. Base your discussion on Heaney's "Mid-Term Break" and Keating's "Far Summers."

6. Compare the points of view expressed in Sexton's "Hansel and Gretel" and Glück's "Gretel in Darkness." How does the focus of each poem reflect a somewhat different vision of the sibling relationship from the folktale "Hansel and Gretel"?

Drama

TENNESSEE WILLIAMS (1911–1983)

The Glass Menagerie

Nobody, not even the rain, has such small hands.
—e.e. cummings[1]

THE CHARACTERS

AMANDA WINGFIELD, *the mother*
  A little woman of great but confused vitality clinging frantically to another time and place. Her characterization must be carefully created, not copied from type. She is not paranoiac, but her life is paranoia. There is much to admire in AMANDA, and as much to love and pity as there is to laugh at. Certainly she has endurance and a kind of heroism, and though her foolishness makes her unwittingly cruel at times, there is tenderness in her slight person.

LAURA WINGFIELD, *her daughter*
  AMANDA, having failed to establish contact with reality, continues to live vitally in her illusions, but LAURA's situation is even graver. A childhood illness has left her crippled, one leg slightly shorter than the other, and held in a brace. This defect need not be more than suggested on the stage. Stemming from this, LAURA's separation increases till she is like a piece of her own glass collection, too exquisitely fragile to move from the shelf.

TOM WINGFIELD, *her son*
  And the narrator of the play. A poet with a job in a warehouse. His nature is not remorseless, but to escape from a trap he has to act without pity.

JIM O'CONNOR, *the gentleman caller*
  A nice, ordinary, young man.

---

[1] Last line of e.e. cummings's poem "somewhere I have never travelled."

Scene: An Alley in St. Louis

PART I. *Preparation for a Gentleman Caller.*
PART II. *The Gentleman calls.*

Time: Now and the Past.

PRODUCTION NOTES

Being a "memory play," *The Glass Menagerie* can be presented with unusual freedom of convention. Because of its considerably delicate or tenuous material, atmospheric touches and subtleties of direction play a particularly important part. Expressionism[2] and all other unconventional techniques in drama have only one valid aim, and that is a closer approach to truth. When a play employs unconventional techniques, it is not, or certainly shouldn't be, trying to escape its responsibility of dealing with reality, or interpreting experience, but is actually or should be attempting to find a closer approach, a more penetrating and vivid expression of things as they are. The straight realistic play with its genuine Frigidaire and authentic ice-cubes, its characters who speak exactly as its audience speaks, corresponds to the academic landscape and has the same virtue of a photographic likeness. Everyone should know nowadays the unimportance of the photographic in art: that truth, life, or reality is an organic thing which the poetic imagination can represent or suggest, in essence, only through transformation, through changing into other forms that those which were merely present in appearance.

These remarks are not meant as a preface only to this particular play. They have to do with a conception of a new, plastic theatre which must take the place of the exhausted theatre of realistic conventions if the theatre is to resume vitality as a part of our culture.

THE SCREEN DEVICE. There is *only one important difference between the original and the acting version of the play* and that is the *omission* in the latter of the device that I tentatively included in my *original* script. This device was the use of a screen on which were projected magic-lantern slides bearing images or titles. I do not regret the omission of this device from the original Broadway production. The extraordinary power of Miss Taylor's performance made it suitable to have the utmost simplicity in the physical production. But I think it may be interesting to some readers to see how this device was conceived. So I am putting it into the published manuscript. These images and legends, projected from behind, were cast on a section of wall between the front-room and dining-room areas, which should be indistinguishable from the rest of when not in use.

The purpose of this will probably be apparent. It is to give accent to certain values in each scene. Each scene contains a particular point (or several) which is structurally the most important. In an episodic play, such as this, the basic structure or narrative line may be obscured from the audience; the effect may seem fragmentary rather

---

[2] Expressionism: an early twentieth-century movement in the arts that emphasized subjective expression of the artist's inner experiences.

than architectural. This may not be the fault of the play so much as a lack of attention in the audience. The legend or image upon the screen will strengthen the effect of what is merely allusion in the writing and allow the primary point to be made more simply and lightly than if the entire responsibility were on the spoken lines. Aside from this structural value, I think the screen will have a definite emotional appeal, less definable but just as important. An imaginative producer or director may invent many other uses for this device than those indicated in the present script. In fact the possibilities of the device seem much larger to me than the instance of this play can possibly utilize.

THE MUSIC. Another extra-literary accent in this play is provided by the use of music. A single recurring tune, "The Glass Menagerie," is used to give emotional emphasis to suitable passages. This tune is like circus music, not when you are on the grounds or in the immediate vicinity of the parade, but when you are at some distance and very likely thinking of something else. It seems under those circumstances to continue almost interminably and it weaves in and out of your preoccupied consciousness; then it is the lightest, most delicate music in the world and perhaps the saddest. It expresses the surface vivacity of life with the underlying strain of immutable and inexpressible sorrow. When you look at a piece of delicately spun glass you think of two things: how beautiful it is and how easily it can be broken. Both of those ideas should be woven into the recurring tune, which dips in and out of the play as if it were carried on a wind that changes. It serves as a thread of connection and allusion between the narrator with his separate point in time and space and the subject of his story. Between each episode it returns as reference to the emotion, nostalgia, which is the first condition of the play. It is primarily Laura's music and therefore comes out most clearly when the play focuses upon her and the lovely fragility of glass which is her image.

THE LIGHTING. The lighting in the play is not realistic. In keeping with the atmosphere of memory, the stage is dim. Shafts of light are focused on selected areas or actors, sometimes in contradistinction to what is the apparent center. For instance, in the quarrel scene between Tom and Amanda, in which Laura has no active part, the clearest pool of light is on her figure. This is also true of the supper scene, when her silent figure on the sofa should remain the visual center. The light upon Laura should be distinct from the others, having a peculiar pristine clarity such as light used in early religious portraits of female saints or madonnas. A certain correspondence to light in religious paintings, such as El Greco's, where the figures are radiant in atmosphere that is relatively dusky, could be effectively used throughout the play. (It will also permit a more effective use of the screen.) A free, imaginative use of light can be of enormous value in giving a mobile, plastic quality to plays of a more or less static nature.

Tennessee Williams

SCENE 1

The Wingfield apartment is in the rear of the building, one of those vast hive-like conglomerations of cellular living-units that flower as warty growths in overcrowded urban centers of lower middle-class population and are symptomatic of the impulse of this largest and fundamentally enslaved section of American society to avoid fluidity and differentiation and to exist and function as one interfused mass of automatism.

The apartment faces an alley and is entered by a fire escape, a structure whose name is a touch of accidental poetic truth, for all of these huge buildings are always burning with the slow and implacable fires of human desperation. The fire escape is part of what we see— that is, the landing of it and steps descending from it.

The scene is memory and is therefore nonrealistic. Memory takes a lot of poetic license. It omits some details; others are exaggerated, according to the emotional value of the articles it touches, for memory is seated predominantly in the heart. The interior is therefore rather dim and poetic.

At the rise of the curtain, the audience is faced with the dark, grim rear wall of the Wingfield tenement. This building is flanked on both sides by dark, narrow alleys which run into murky canyons of tangled clotheslines, garbage cans, and the sinister latticework of neighboring fire escapes. It is up and down these side alleys that exterior entrances and exits are made during the play. At the end of TOM's *opening commentary, the dark tenement wall slowly becomes transparent and reveals the interior of the groundfloor Wingfield apartment.*

Nearest the audience is the living room, which also serves as a sleeping room for LAURA, *the sofa unfolding to make her bed. Just beyond, separated from the living room by a wide arch or second proscenium with transparent faded portieres (or second curtain), is the dining room. In an old-fashioned whatnot in the living room are seen scores of transparent glass animals. A blown-up photograph of the father hangs on the wall of the living room, to the left of the archway. It is the face of a very handsome young man in a doughboy's First World War cap.[3] He is gallantly smiling, ineluctably smiling, as if to say "I will be smiling forever."*

Also hanging on the wall, near the photograph, are a typewriter keyboard chart and a Gregg shorthand diagram.[4] An upright typewriter on a small table stands beneath the charts.

The audience hears and sees the opening scene in the dining room through both the transparent fourth wall of the building and the transparent gauze portieres of the dining-room arch. It is during this revealing scene that the fourth wall slowly ascends, out of sight. This transparent exterior wall is not brought down again until the very end of the play, during TOM's *final speech.*

The narrator is an undisguised convention of the play. He takes whatever license with dramatic convention is convenient to his purposes.

TOM *enters, dressed as a merchant sailor, and strolls across to the fire escape. There he stops and lights a cigarette. He addresses the audience.*

TOM. Yes, I have tricks in my pocket, I have things up my sleeve. But I am the opposite of a stage magician. He gives you illusion that has the appearance of truth. I give you truth in the pleasant disguise of illusion.

To begin with, I turn back time. I reverse it to that quaint period, the thirties, when the huge middle class of America was matriculating in a school for the blind. Their eyes

---

[3] "Doughboy's First World War cap": cap worn by American World War I infantrymen.
[4] "Gregg shorthand diagram": chart used to present the symbols for words, phrases, and letters used in shorthand, a system of rapid handwriting.

had failed them, or they had failed their eyes, and so they were having their fingers pressed forcibly down on the fiery Braille alphabet of a dissolving economy.

In Spain there was revolution. Here there was only shouting and confusion. In Spain there was Guernica.[5] Here there were disturbances of labor, sometimes pretty violent, in otherwise peaceful cities such as Chicago, Cleveland, Saint Louis . . .

This is the social background of the play.

[*Music begins to play.*]

The play is memory. Being a memory play, it is dimly lighted, it is sentimental, it is not realistic. In memory everything seems to happen to music. This explains the fiddle in the wings.

I am the narrator of the play, and also a character in it. The other characters are my mother, Amanda, my sister, Laura, and a gentleman caller who appears in the final scenes. He is the most realistic character in the play, being an emissary from a world of reality that we were somehow set apart from. But since I have a poet's weakness for symbols, I am using this character also as a symbol; he is the long-delayed but always expected something that we live for.

There is a fifth character in the play who doesn't appear except in this larger-than-life-size photograph over the mantel. This is our father who left us a long time ago. He was a telephone man who fell in love with long distances; he gave up his job with the telephone company and skipped the light fantastic out of town . . .

The last we heard of him was a picture postcard from Mazatlan, on the Pacific coast of Mexico, containing a message of two words: "Hello—Goodbye!" and no address.

I think the rest of the play will explain itself. . . .

[AMANDA'*s voice becomes audible through the portieres.*]

[*Legend on screen:* "Ou sont les neiges."]

[TOM *divides the portieres and enters the dining room.* AMANDA *and* LAURA *are seated at a drop-leaf table. Eating is indicated by gestures without food or utensils.* AMANDA *faces the audience.* TOM *and* LAURA *are seated in profile. The interior has lit up softly and through the scrim we see* AMANDA *and* LAURA *seated at the table.*]

AMANDA [*calling*]. Tom?
TOM. Yes, Mother.
AMANDA. We can't say grace until you come to the table.
TOM. Coming, Mother. [*He bows slightly and withdraws, reappearing a few moments later in his place at the table.*]

---

[5] Guernica: a Basque town of north central Spain bombed in April 1937 by German planes during the Spanish Civil War.

AMANDA [*to her son*]. Honey, don't *push* with your *fingers.* If you have to push with something, the thing to push with is a crust of bread. And chew—chew! Animals have secretions in their stomachs which enable them to digest food without mastication, but human beings are supposed to chew their food before they swallow it down. Eat food leisurely, son, and really enjoy it. A well-cooked meal has lots of delicate flavors that have to be held in the mouth for appreciation. So chew your food and give your salivary glands a chance to function!

[TOM *deliberately lays his imaginary fork down and pushes his chair back from the table.*]

TOM. I haven't enjoyed one bite of this dinner because of your constant directions on
40   how to eat it. It's you that make me rush through meals with your hawklike attention to every bite I take. Sickening—spoils my appetite—all this discussion of—animals' secretion—salivary glands—mastication!
AMANDA [*lightly*]. Temperament like a Metropolitan star!

[TOM *rises and walks toward the living room.*]

You're not excused from the table.
TOM. I'm getting a cigarette.
AMANDA. You smoke too much.

[LAURA *rises.*]

LAURA. I'll bring in the blanc mange.[6]

[TOM *remains standing with his cigarette by the portieres.*]

AMANDA [*rising*]. No, sister, no, sister—you be the lady this time and I'll be the darky.[7]
LAURA. I'm already up.
50   Amanda. Resume your seat, little sister—I want you to stay fresh and pretty—for gentlemen callers!
LAURA [*sitting down*]. I'm not expecting any gentlemen callers.
AMANDA [*crossing out to the kitchenette, airily*]. Sometimes they come when they are least expected! Why, I remember one Sunday afternoon in Blue Mountain—

[*She enters the kitchenette.*]

TOM. I know what's coming!
LAURA. Yes. But let her tell it.
TOM. Again?
LAURA. She loves to tell it.

[AMANDA *returns with a bowl of dessert.*]

AMANDA. One Sunday afternoon in Blue Mountain—your mother received
60   *seventeen!*—gentlemen callers! Why, sometimes there weren't chairs enough to

---

[6] blanc mange: a flavored and sweetened thick milk pudding.
[7] darky: a term used in the American South before and after the Civil War to refer to an African American.

accommodate them all. We had to send the nigger over to bring in folding chairs from the parish house.

TOM [*remaining at the portieres*]. How did you entertain those gentlemen callers?

AMANDA. I understood the art of conversation!

TOM. I bet you could talk.

AMANDA. Girls in those days *knew* how to talk, I can tell you.

TOM. Yes?

[*Image on screen:* AMANDA *as a girl on a porch, greeting callers.*]

AMANDA. They knew how to entertain their gentlemen callers. It wasn't enough for a girl to be possessed of a pretty face and a graceful figure—although I wasn't slighted in either respect. She also needed to have a nimble wit and a tongue to meet all occasions.

TOM. What did you talk about?

AMANDA. Things of importance going on in the world! Never anything coarse or common or vulgar.

[*She addresses* TOM *as though he were seated in the vacant chair at the table though he remains by the portieres. He plays this scene as though reading from a script.*]

My callers were gentlemen—all! Among my callers were some of the most prominent young planters of the Mississippi Delta—planters and sons of planters!

[TOM *motions for music and a spot of light on* AMANDA. *Her eyes lift, her face glows, her voice becomes rich and elegiac.*]

[*Screen legend:* "Où sont les neiges d'antan?"][8]

There was young Champ Laughlin who later became vice-president of the Delta Planters Bank. Hadley Stevenson who was drowned in Moon Lake and left his widow one hundred and fifty thousand in Government bonds. There were the Cutrere brothers, Wesley and Bates. Bates was one of my bright particular beaux! He got in a quarrel with that wild Wainwright boy. They shot it out on the floor of Moon Lake Casino. Bates was shot through the stomach. Died in the ambulance on his way to Memphis. His widow was also well provided-for, came into eight or ten thousand acres, that's all. She married him on the rebound—never loved her—carried my picture on him the night he died! And there was that boy that every girl in the Delta had set her cap for! That beautiful, brilliant young Fitzhugh boy from Greene Country!

TOM. What did he leave his widow?

AMANDA. He never married! Gracious, you talk as though all of my old admirers had turned up their toes to the daisies!

TOM. Isn't this the first you've mentioned that still survives?

AMANDA. That Fitzhugh boy went North and made a fortune—came to be known as the Wolf of Wall Street! He had the Midas touch, whatever he touched turned to

---

[8]"Où sont les neiges d'antan?": "Where are the snows of yesteryear?"

gold! And I could have been Mrs. Duncan J. Fitzhugh, mind you! But—I picked your *father!*

LAURA [*rising*]. Mother, let me clear the table.

AMANDA. No, dear, you go in front and study your typewriter chart. Or practice your shorthand a little. Stay fresh and pretty!—It's almost time for our gentlemen callers to start arriving. [*She flounces girlishly toward the kitchenette.*] How many do you suppose we're going to entertain this afternoon?

[TOM *throws down the paper and jumps up with a groan.*]

100   LAURA [*alone in the dining room*]. I don't believe we're going to receive any, Mother.

AMANDA [*reappearing, airily*]. What? No one—not one? You must be joking!

[LAURA *nervously echoes her laugh. She slips in a fugitive manner through the half-open portieres and draws them gently behind her. A shaft of very clear light is thrown on her face against the faded tapestry of the curtains. Faintly the music of "The Glass Menagerie" is heard as she continues, lightly.*]

Not one gentleman caller? It can't be true! There must be a flood, there must have been a tornado!

LAURA. It isn't a flood, it's not a tornado, Mother. I'm just not popular like you were in Blue Mountain. . . .

[TOM *utters another groan.* LAURA *glances at him with a faint, apologetic smile. Her voice catches a little:*]

Mother's afraid I'm going to be an old maid.

[*The scene dims out with the "Glass Menagerie" music.*]

SCENE 2

On the dark stage the screen is lighted with the image of blue roses. Gradually LAURA's *figure becomes apparent and the screen goes out. The music subsides.*

LAURA *is seated in the delicate ivory chair at the small claw-foot table. She wears a dress of soft violet material for a kimono—her hair is tied back from her forehead with a ribbon. She is washing and polishing her collection of glass.* AMANDA *appears on the fire escape steps. At the sound of her ascent,* LAURA *catches her breath, thrusts the bowl of ornaments away, and seats herself stiffly before the diagram of the typewriter keyboard as though it held her spellbound. Something has happened to* AMANDA. *It is written in her face as she climbs to the landing: a look that is grim and hopeless and a little absurd. She has on one of those cheap or imitation velvety-looking cloth coats with imitation fur collar. Her hat is five or six years old, one of those dreadful cloche hats that were worn in the late Twenties, and she is clutching an enormous black patent-leather pocketbook with nickel clasps and initials. This is her full-dress out-fit, the one she usually wears to the D.A.R. Before entering she looks through the door. She purses her lips, opens her eyes very wide, rolls them upward and shakes her head. Then she slowly lets herself in the door. Seeing her mother's expression* LAURA *touches her lips with a nervous gesture.*

LAURA. Hello, Mother, I was—[*She makes a nervous gesture toward the chart on the wall.* AMANDA *leans against the shut door and stares at* LAURA *with a martyred look.*]

AMANDA. Deception? Deception? [*She slowly removes her hat and gloves, continuing the sweet suffering stare. She lets the hat and gloves fall on the floor—a bit of acting.*]

LAURA [*shakily*]. How was the D.A.R. meeting?[9]

[AMANDA *slowly opens her purse and removes a dainty white handkerchief which she shakes out delicately and delicately touches to her lips and nostrils.*]

Didn't you go to the D.A.R. meeting, Mother?

AMANDA [*faintly, almost inaudibly*]. —No.—No. [*Then more forcibly.*] I did not have the strength—to go to the D.A.R. In fact, I did not have the courage! I wanted to find a hole in the ground and hide myself in it forever! [*She crosses slowly to the wall and removes the diagram of the typewriter keyboard. She holds it in front of her for a second, staring at it sweetly and sorrowfully—then bites her lips and tears it in two pieces.*]

LAURA [*faintly*]. Why did you do that, Mother?

[AMANDA *repeats the same procedure with the chart of the Gregg Alphabet.*]

Why are you—

10 AMANDA. Why? Why? How old are you, Laura?

LAURA. Mother, you know my age.

AMANDA. I thought that you were an adult; it seems that I was mistaken. [*She crosses slowly to the sofa and sinks down and stares at* LAURA.]

LAURA. Please don't stare at me, Mother.

[AMANDA *closes her eyes and lowers her head. There is a ten-second pause.*]

AMANDA. What are we going to do, what is going to become of us, what is the future?

[*There is another pause.*]

LAURA. Has something happened, Mother?

[AMANDA *draws a long breath, takes out the handkerchief again, goes through the dabbing process.*]

Mother, has—something happened?

AMANDA. I'll be all right in a minute, I'm just bewildered— [*She hesitates.*] —by life. . . .

LAURA. Mother, I wish that you would tell me what's happened!

20 AMANDA. As you know, I was supposed to be inducted into my office at the D.A.R. this afternoon.

[*Screen image:* A swarm of typewriters.]

---

[9] D.A.R. meeting: a gathering of the Daughters of the American Revolution.

But I stopped off at Rubicam's Business College to speak to your teachers about your having a cold and ask them what progress they thought you were making down there.

LAURA. Oh. . . .

AMANDA. I went to the typing instructor and introduced myself as your mother. She didn't know who you were. "Wingfield," she said, "We don't have any such student enrolled at the school!" I assured her she did, that you had been going to classes since early in January.

30   "I wonder," she said, "If you could be talking about that terribly shy little girl who dropped out of school after only a few days' attendance?"

"No," I said, "Laura, my daughter, has been going to school every day for the past six weeks!"

"Excuse me," she said. She took the attendance book out and there was your name, unmistakably printed, and all the dates you were absent until they decided that you had dropped out of school. I still said, "No, there must have been some mistake! There must have been some mix-up in the records!"

And she said, "No—I remember her perfectly now. Her hands shook so that she couldn't hit the right keys! The first time we gave a speed test, she broke down completely—was sick at the stomach and almost had to be carried into the wash room! Af-

40   ter that morning she never showed up any more. We phoned the house but never got any answer"—While I was working at Famous-Barr, I suppose, demonstrating those—

[*She indicates a brassiere with her hands.*]

Oh! I felt so weak I could barely keep on my feet! I had to sit down while they got me a glass of water! Fifty dollars' tuition, all of our plans—my hopes and ambitions for you—just gone up the spout, just gone up the spout like that.

[LAURA *draws a long breath and gets awkwardly to her feet. She crosses to the Victrola and winds it up.*]

What are your doing?

LAURA. Oh! [*She releases the handle and returns to her seat.*]

AMANDA. Laura, where have you been going when you've gone out pretending that you were going to business college?

LAURA. I've just been going out walking.

50   AMANDA. That's not true.

LAURA. It is. I just went walking.

AMANDA. Walking? Walking? In winter? Deliberately courting pneumonia in that light coat? Where did you walk to, Laura?

LAURA. All sorts of places—mostly in the park.

AMANDA. Even after you'd started catching that cold?

LAURA. It was the lesser of two evils, Mother.

[*Screen image:* Winter scene in a park.]

I couldn't go back there. I—threw up—on the floor!

AMANDA. From half past seven till after five every day you mean to tell me you walked
around in the park, because you wanted to make me think that you were still going to
60   Rubicam's Business College?

LAURA. It wasn't as bad as it sounds. I went inside places to get warmed up.

AMANDA. Inside where?

LAURA. I went in the art museum and the bird houses at the Zoo. I visited the penguins
every day! Sometimes I did without lunch and went to the movies. Lately I've been
spending most of my afternoons in the Jewel Box, that big glass house where they
raise the tropical flowers.

AMANDA. You did all this to deceive me, just for deception? [LAURA *looks down.*] Why?

LAURA. Mother, when you're disappointed, you get that awful suffering look on your
face, like the picture of Jesus' mother in the museum!

70   AMANDA. Hush!

LAURA. I couldn't face it.

> [*There is a pause. A whisper of strings is heard. Legend on screen:* "The Crust of
> Humility."]

Amanda [*hopelessly fingering the huge pocketbook*]. So what are we going to do the rest
of our lives? Stay home and watch the parades go by? Amuse ourselves with the glass
menagerie, darling? Eternally play those worn-out phonograph records your father left
as a painful reminder of him? We won't have a business career—we've given that up
because it gave us nervous indigestion! [*She laughs wearily.*] What is there left but de-
pendency all our lives? I know so well what becomes of unmarried women who aren't
prepared to occupy a position. I've seen such pitiful cases in the South—barely toler-
ated spinsters living upon the grudging patronage of sister's husband or brother's
80   wife!—stuck away in some little mousetrap of a room—encouraged by one in-law to
visit another—little birdlike women without any nest—eating the crust of humility all
their life!

> Is that the future that we've mapped out for ourselves? I swear it's the only alter-
native I can think of! [*She pauses.*] It isn't a very pleasant alternative, is it? [*She pauses
again.*] Of course—some girls *do* marry.

> [LAURA *twists her hands nervously.*]

> Haven't you every liked some boy?

LAURA. Yes. I liked one once. [*She rises.*] I came across his picture a while ago.

AMANDA [*with some interest*]. He gave you his picture?

LAURA. No, it's in the yearbook.

90   AMANDA [*disappointed*]. Oh—a high school boy.

> [*Screen image:* JIM *as the high school hero bearing a silver cup.*]

LAURA. Yes. His name was Jim. [*She lifts the heavy annual from the claw-foot table.*]
Here he is in *The Pirates of Penzance.*

AMANDA [*absently*]. The what?

LAURA. The operetta the senior class put on. He had a wonderful voice and we sat
across the aisle from each other Mondays, Wednesdays and Fridays in the Aud. Here
he is with the silver cup for debating! See his grin?

AMANDA [*absently*]. He must have had a jolly disposition.

LAURA. He used to call me—Blue Roses.

[*Screen image:* Blue roses.]

AMANDA. Why did he call you such a name as that?

100 LAURA. When I had that attack of pleurosis[10]—he asked me what was the matter when I came back. I said pleurosis—he thought that I said Blue Roses! So that's what he always called me after that. Whenever he saw me, he'd hollar, "Hello, Blue Roses!" I didn't care for the girl that he went out with. Emily Meisenbach. Emily was the best-dressed girl at Soldan. She never struck me, though, as being sincere . . . It says in the Personal Section—they're engaged. That's—six years ago! They must be married by now.

AMANDA. Girls that aren't cut out for business careers usually wind up married to some nice man. [*She gets up with a spark of revival.*] Sister, that's what you'll do!

[LAURA *utters a startled, doubtful laugh. She reaches quickly for a piece of glass.*]

LAURA. But, Mother—

110 AMANDA. Yes? [*She goes over to the photograph.*]

LAURA [*in a tone of frightened apology*]. I'm—crippled!

AMANDA. Nonsense! Laura, I've told you never, never to use that word. Why, you're not crippled, you just have a little defect—hardly noticeable, even! When people have some slight disadvantage like that, they cultivate other things to make up for it—develop charm—and vivacity—and—*charm!* That's all you have to do! [*She turns again to the photograph.*] One thing your father had *plenty of*—was *charm!*

[*The scene fades out with music.*]

SCENE 3

Legend on screen: "After the fiasco—"

TOM *speaks from the fire escape landing.*

TOM. After the fiasco at Rubicam's Business College, the idea of getting a gentleman caller for Laura began to play a more and more important part in Mother's calculations. It became an obsession. Like some archetype of the universal unconscious, the image of the gentleman caller haunted our small apartment. . . .

[*Screen image:* A young man at the door of a house with flowers.]

An evening at home rarely passed without some allusion to this image, this specter, this hope. . . . Even when he wasn't mentioned, his presence hung in Mother's preoccupied look and in my sister's frightened, apologetic manner—hung like a sentence passed upon the Wingfields!

---

[10]pleurosis: inflammation of the lungs occurring as a complication of pneumonia.

Mother was a woman of action as well as words. She began to take logical steps in the planned direction. Late that winter and in the early spring—realizing that extra money would be needed to properly feather the nest and plume the bird—she conducted a vigorous campaign on the telephone, roping in subscribers to one of those magazines for matrons called *The Homemaker's Companion,* the type of journal that features the serialized sublimations of ladies of letters who think in terms of delicate cuplike breasts, slim, tapering waists, rich, creamy thighs, eyes like wood smoke in autumn, fingers that soothe and caress like strains of music, bodies as powerful as Etruscan sculpture.

[*Screen image:* The cover of a glamor magazine.]

[AMANDA *enters with the telephone on a long extension cord. She is spotlighted in the dim stage.*]

AMANDA. Ida Scott? This is Amanda Wingfield! We *missed* you at the D.A.R. last Monday! I said to myself: She's probably suffering with that sinus condition! How is that sinus condition?

Horrors! Heaven have mercy!—You're a Christian martyr, yes, that's what you are, a Christian martyr!

Well, I just now happened to notice that your subscription to the *Companion*'s about to expire! Yes, it expires with the next issue, honey!—just when that wonderful new serial by Bessie Mae Hopper is getting off to such an exciting start. Oh, honey, it's something that you can't miss! You remember how *Gone with the Wind* took everybody by storm? You simply couldn't go out if you hadn't read it. All everybody *talked* was Scarlett O'Hara. Well, this is a book that critics already compare to *Gone with the Wind*. It's the *Gone with the Wind* of the post-World-War generation!—What? Burning?—Oh, honey, don't let them burn, go take a look in the oven and I'll hold the wire! Heavens—I think she's hung up!

[*The scene dims out.*]

[*Legend on screen:* "You think I'm in love with Continental Shoemakers?"]

[*Before the lights come up again, the violent voices of* TOM *and* AMANDA *are heard. They are quarreling behind the portieres. In front of them stands* LAURA *with clenched hands and panicky expression. A clear pool of light is on her figure throughout this scene.*]

TOM. What in Christ's name am I—
AMANDA [*shrilly*]. Don't you use that—
TOM. —supposed to do!
AMANDA. —expression! Not in my—
TOM. Ohhh!
AMANDA. —presence! Have you gone out of your senses?
TOM. I have, that's true, *driven* out!
AMANDA. What is the matter with you, you—big—big—IDIOT!
TOM. Look!—I've got *no thing,* no single thing—

AMANDA. Lower your voice!

TOM. —in my life here that I can call my OWN! Everything is—

AMANDA. Stop that shouting!

TOM. Yesterday you confiscated my books! You had the nerve to—

AMANDA. I took that horrible novel back to the library—yes! That hideous book by that insane Mr. Lawrence.[11]

[TOM *laughs wildly.*]

I cannot control the output of diseased minds or people who cater to them—

[TOM *laughs still more wildly.*]

BUT I WON'T ALLOW SUCH FILTH BROUGHT INTO MY HOUSE! No, no, no, no, no!

TOM. House, house! Who pays rent on it, who makes a slave of himself to—

50 AMANDA [*fairly screeching*]. Don't you DARE to—

TOM. No, no, I mustn't say things! *I've* got to just—

AMANDA. Let me tell you—

TOM. I don't want to hear any more!

[*He tears the portieres open. The dining-room area is lit with a turgid smokey red glow. Now we see* AMANDA; *her hair is in metal curlers and she is wearing a very old bathrobe, much too large for her slight figure, a relic of the faithless Mr. Wingfield. The upright typewriter now stands on the drop-leaf table, along with a wild disarray of manuscripts. The quarrel was probably precipitated by* AMANDA'S *interruption of* TOM'S *creative labor. A chair lies overthrown on the floor. Their gesticulating shadows are cast on the ceiling by the fiery glow.*]

AMANDA. You *will* hear more, you—

TOM. No, I won't hear more, I'm going out!

AMANDA. You come right back in—

TOM. Out, out, out! Because I'm—

AMANDA. Come back here, Tom Wingfield! I'm not through talking to you!

TOM. Oh, go—

60 LAURA [*desperately*]. —TOM!

AMANDA. You're going to listen, and no more insolence from you! I'm at the end of my patience!

[*He comes back toward her.*]

TOM. What do you think I'm at? Aren't I supposed to have any patience to reach the end of, Mother? I know, I know. It seems unimportant to you, what I'm *doing*—what I *want* to do—having a little *difference* between them! You don't think that—

AMANDA. I think you've been doing things that you're ashamed of. That's why you act like this. I don't believe that you go every night to the movies. Nobody goes to the movies night after night. Nobody in their right minds goes to the movies as often as

---

[11] "insane Mr. Lawrence": reference to D. H. Lawrence (1885–1930), British writer made famous when his 1928 novel *Lady Chatterley's Lover* was banned (see p. 388 and p. 940).

you pretend to. People don't go to the movies at nearly midnight, and movies don't let
70   out at two A.M. Come in stumbling. Muttering to yourself like a maniac! You get three
hours' sleep and then go to work. Oh, I can picture the way you're doing down there.
Moping, doping, because you're in no condition!

TOM [*wildly*]. No, I'm in no condition!

AMANDA. What right have you got to jeopardize your job? Jeopardize the security of us
all? How do you think we'd manage if you were—

TOM. Listen! You think I'm crazy about the *warehouse?* [*He bends fiercely toward her
slight figure.*] You think I'm in love with the Continental Shoemakers? You think I
want to spend fifty-five *years* down there in that—*celotex interior!*—with—
fluorescent—tubes! Look! I'd rather somebody picked up a crowbar and battered out
80   my brains—than go back mornings! I *go!* Every time you come in yelling that Goddamn *"Rise and Shine!"* *"Rise and Shine!"* I say to myself, "How *lucky dead* people are!"
But I get up. I *go!* For sixty-five dollars a month I give up all that I dream of doing and
being *ever!* And you say self—*self's* all I ever think of. Why, listen, if self is what I
thought of, Mother, I'd be where he is—GONE! [*He points to his father's picture.*] As
far as the system of transportation reaches! [*He starts past her. She grabs his arm.*]
Don't grab at me, Mother!

AMANDA. Where are you going?

TOM. I'm going to the *movies!*

AMANDA. I don't believe that lie!

[TOM *crouches toward her, overtowering her tiny figure. She backs away, gasping.*]

90   TOM. I'm going to opium dens! Yes, opium dens, dens of vice and criminals' hangouts,
Mother. I've joined the Hogan Gang, I'm a hired assassin, I carry a tommy gun in a violin case! I run a string of cat houses in the Valley! They call me Killer, Killer Wingfield, I'm leading a double-life, a simple, honest warehouse worker by day, by night a
dynamic *czar* of the *underworld, Mother.* I go to gambling casinos, I spin away fortunes on the roulette table! I wear a patch over one eye and a false mustache, sometimes I put on green whiskers. On those occasions they call me—*El Diablo!*[12] Oh, I
could tell you many things to make you sleepless! My enemies plan to dynamite this
place. They're going to blow us all sky-high some night! I'll be glad, very happy, and so
will you! You'll go up, up on a broomstick, over Blue Mountain with seventeen gentl
100   men callers! You ugly—babbling old—*witch*. . . .

[*He goes through a series of violent, clumsy movements, seizing his overcoat, lunging to
the door, pulling it fiercely open. The women watch him, aghast. His arm catches in the
sleeve of the coat as he struggles to pull it on. For a moment he is pinioned by the bulky
garment. With an outraged groan he tears the coat off again, splitting the shoulder of it,
and hurls it across the room. It strikes against the shelf of LAURA's glass collection, and
there is a tinkle of shattering glass. LAURA cries out as if wounded.*]

[*Music.*]

---

[12] "El Diablo": Spanish for the devil.

[*Screen legend:* "The Glass Menagerie."]

LAURA [*shrilly*]. My glass!—menagerie . . . [*She covers her face and turns away.*]

[*But* AMANDA *is still stunned and stupefied by the "ugly witch" so that she barely notices this occurrence. Now she recovers her speech.*]

AMANDA [*in an awful voice*]. I won't speak to you—until you apologize!

[*She crosses through the portieres and draws them together behind her.* TOM *is left with* LAURA. LAURA *clings weakly to the mantel with her face averted.* TOM *stares at her stupidly for a moment. Then he crosses to the shelf. He drops awkwardly on his knees to collect the fallen glass, glancing at* LAURA *as if he would speak but couldn't.*]

[*"The Glass Menagerie" music steals in as the scene dims out.*]

SCENE 4

The interior of the apartment is dark. There is a faint light in the alley. A deep-voiced bell in a church is tolling the hour of five.]

TOM *appears at the top of the alley. After each solemn boom of the bell in the tower, he shakes a little noisemaker or rattle as if to express the tiny spasm of man in contrast to the sustained power and dignity of the Almighty. This and the unsteadiness of his advance make it evident that he has been drinking. As he climbs the few steps to the fire escape landing light steals up inside.* LAURA *appears in the front room in a nightdress. She notices that* TOM's *bed is empty.* TOM *fishes in his pockets for his door key, removing a motley assortment of articles in the search, including a shower of movie ticket stubs and an empty bottle. At last he finds the key, but just as he is about to insert it, it slips from his fingers. He strikes a match and crouches below the door.*

TOM [*bitterly*]. One crack—and it falls through!

[LAURA *opens the door.*]

LAURA. Tom! Tom, what are you doing?
TOM. Looking for a door key.
LAURA. Where have you been all this time?
TOM. I have been to the movies.
LAURA. All this time at the movies?
TOM. There was a very long program. There was a Garbo[13] picture and a Mickey Mouse and a travelogue and a newsreel and a preview of coming attractions. And there was an organ solo and a collection for the Milk Fund—simultaneously—which ended up in a terrible fight between a fat lady and an usher!
LAURA [*innocently*]. Did you have to stay through everything?

10

---

[13] Garbo: allusion to Greta Garbo (1905–1990), the elusive, beautiful, Swedish-born American actress.

TOM. Of course! And, oh, I forgot! There was a big stage show! The headliner on this stage show was Malvolio the Magician. He performed wonderful tricks, many of them, such as pouring water back and forth between pitchers. First it turned to wine and then it turned to beer and then it turned to whisky. I know it was whisky it finally turned into because he needed somebody to come up out of the audience to help him, and I came up—both shows! It was Kentucky Straight Bourbon. A very generous fellow, he gave souvenirs. [*He pulls from his back pocket a shimmering rainbow-colored scarf.*] He gave me this. This is his magic scarf. You can have it, Laura. You wave it

20   over a canary cage and you get a bowl of goldfish. You wave it over the goldfish bowl and they fly away canaries. . . . But the wonderfullest trick of all was the coffin trick. We nailed him into a coffin and he got out of the coffin without removing one nail. [*He has come inside.*] There is a trick that would come in handy for me—get me out of this two-by-four situation! [*He flops onto the bed and starts removing his shoes.*]

LAURA. Tom—shhh!

TOM. What're you shushing me for?

LAURA. You'll wake up Mother.

TOM. Goody, goody! Pay 'er back for all those "Rise an' Shines." [*He lies down, groaning.*] You know it don't take much intelligence to get yourself into a nailed-up

30   coffin, Laura. But who in hell ever got himself out of one without removing one nail?

[*As if in answer, the father's grinning photograph lights up. The scene dims out.*]

[*Immediately following, the church bell is heard striking six. At the sixth stroke the alarm clock goes off in AMANDA's room, and after a few moments we hear her calling: "Rise and Shine! Rise and Shine! LAURA, go tell your brother to rise and shine!"*]

TOM [*sitting up slowly*]. I'll rise—but I won't shine.

[*The light increases.*]

AMANDA. Laura, tell your brother his coffee is ready.

[LAURA *slips into the front room.*]

LAURA. Tom!—It's nearly seven. Don't make Mother nervous.

[*He stares at her stupidly.*]

[*beseechingly*] Tom, speak to Mother this morning. Make up with her, apologize, speak to her!

TOM. She won't to me. It's her that started not speaking.

LAURA. If you just say you're sorry she'll start speaking.

TOM. Her not speaking—is that such a tragedy?

LAURA. Please—please!

40 AMANDA [*calling from the kitchenette*]. Laura, are you going to do what I asked you to do, or do I have to get dressed and go out myself?

LAURA. Going, going—soon as I get on my coat!

[*She pulls on a shapeless felt hat with a nervous, jerky movement, pleadingly glancing at* TOM. *She rushes awkwardly for her coat. The coat is one of* AMANDA's, *inaccurately made-over, the sleeves too short for* LAURA.]

Butter and what else?

AMANDA [*entering from the kitchenette*]. Just butter. Tell them to charge it.

LAURA. Mother, they make such faces when I do that.

AMANDA. Sticks and stones can break our bones, but the expression on Mr. Garfinkel's face won't harm us! Tell your brother his coffee is getting cold.

LAURA [*at the door*]. Do what I asked you, will you, will you, Tom?

[*He looks sullenly away.*]

AMANDA. Laura, go now or just don't go at all!

50 LAURA [*rushing out*]. Going—going!

[*A second later she cries out. TOM springs up and crosses to the door. TOM opens the door.*]

TOM. Laura?

LAURA. I'm all right. I slipped, but I'm all right.

AMANDA [*peering anxiously after her*]. If anyone breaks a leg on those fire-escape steps, the landlord ought to be sued for every cent he possesses! [*She shuts the door. Now she remembers she isn't speaking to TOM and returns to the other room.*]

[*As TOM comes listlessly for his coffee, she turns her back to him and stands rigidly facing the window on the gloomy gray vault of the areaway. Its light on her face with its aged but childish features is cruelly sharp, satirical as a Daumier print.*]

[*The music of "Ave Maria," is heard softly.*]

[*TOM glances sheepishly but sullenly at her averted figure and slumps at the table. The coffee is scalding hot; he sips it and gasps and spits it back in the cup. At his gasp, AMANDA catches her breath and half turns. Then she catches herself and turns back to the window. TOM blows on his coffee, glancing sidewise at his mother. She clears her throat. TOM clears his. He starts to rise, sinks back down again, scratches his head, clears his throat again. AMANDA coughs. TOM raises his cup in both hands to blow on it, his eyes staring over the rim of it at his mother for several moments. Then he slowly sets the cup down and awkwardly and hesitantly rises from the chair.*]

TOM [*hoarsely*]. Mother. I—I apologize, Mother.

[*AMANDA draws a quick, shuddering breath. Her face works grotesquely. She breaks into childlike tears.*]

I'm sorry for what I said, for everything that I said, I didn't mean it.

AMANDA [*sobbingly*]. My devotion has made me a witch and so I make myself hateful to my children!

TOM. *No,* you *don't.*

60 AMANDA. I worry so much, don't sleep, it makes me nervous!

TOM [*gently*]. I understand that.

AMANDA. I've had to put up a solitary battle all these years. But you're my right-hand bower! Don't fall down, don't fail!

TOM [*gently*]. I try, Mother.

AMANDA [*with great enthusiasm*]. Try and you will *succeed!* [*The notion makes her breathless.*] Why, you—you're just *full* of natural endowments! Both of my children—they're *unusual* children! Don't you think I know it? I'm so—*proud!* Happy and—feel I've—so much to be thankful for but—promise me one thing, son!

TOM. What, Mother?

70 AMANDA. Promise, son, you'll—never be a drunkard!

TOM [*turns to her grinning*]. I will never be a drunkard, Mother.

AMANDA. That's what frightened me so, that you'd be drinking! Eat a bowl of Purina!

TOM. Just coffee, Mother.

AMANDA. Shredded wheat biscuit?

80 TOM. No. No, Mother, just coffee.

AMANDA. You can't put in a day's work on an empty stomach. You've got ten minutes—don't gulp! Drinking too hot liquids makes cancer of the stomach. . . . Put cream in.

TOM. No, thank you.

AMANDA. To cool it.

TOM. No! No, thank you, I want it black.

AMANDA. I know, but it's not good for you. We have to do all that we can to build ourselves up. In these trying times we live in, all that we have to cling to is—each other. . . . That's why it's so important to—Tom, I—I sent out your sister so I could discuss something with you. If you hadn't spoken I would have spoken to you. [*She sits down.*]

TOM [*gently*]. What is it, Mother, that you want to discuss?

AMANDA. *Laura!*

[TOM *puts his cup down slowly.*]

[*Legend on screen: "Laura" Music: "The Glass Menagerie."*]

TOM. —Oh.—Laura . . .

AMANDA [*touching his sleeve*]. You know how Laura is. So quiet but—still water runs deep! She notices things and I think she—broods about them.

[TOM *looks up.*]

90 A few days ago I came in and she was crying.

TOM. What about?

AMANDA. You.

TOM. Me?

AMANDA. She has an idea that you're not happy here.

TOM. What gave her that idea?

AMANDA. What gives her any idea? However, you do act strangely. I—I'm not criticizing, understand *that!* I know your ambitions do not lie in the warehouse, that like everybody in the whole wide world—you've had to—make sacrifices, but—Tom—Tom—life's not easy, it calls for—Spartan endurance! There's so many things in my

100 heart that I cannot describe to you! I've never told you but I—*loved* your father. . . .

TOM [*gently*]. I know that, Mother.

AMANDA. And you—when I see you taking after his ways! Staying out late—and—well, you *had* been drinking the night you were in that—terrifying condition! Laura says that you hate the apartment and that you go out nights to get away from it! Is that true, Tom?

TOM. No. You say there's so much in your heart that you can't describe to me. That's true of me, too. There's so much in my heart that I can't describe to *you!* So let's respect each other's—

AMANDA. But, why—*why,* Tom—are you always so *restless?* Where do you *go* to, nights?

110   TOM. I—go to the movies.

AMANDA. Why do you go to the movies so much, Tom?

TOM. I go to the movies because—I like adventure. Adventure is something I don't have much of at work, so I go to the movies.

AMANDA. But, Tom, you go to the movies *entirely* too *much!*

TOM. I like a lot of adventure.

[AMANDA *looks baffled, then hurt. As the familiar inquisition resumes,* TOM *becomes hard and impatient again.* AMANDA *slips back into her querulous attitude toward him.*]

[*Image on screen:* A sailing vessel with Jolly Roger.]

AMANDA. Most young men find adventure in their careers.

TOM. Then most young men are not employed in a warehouse.

AMANDA. The world is full of young men employed in warehouses and offices and factories.

120   TOM. Do all of them find adventure in their careers?

AMANDA. They do or they do without it! Not everybody has a craze for adventure.

TOM. Man is by instinct a lover, a hunter, a fighter, and none of those instincts are given much play at the warehouse!

AMANDA. Man is by instinct! Don't quote instinct to me! Instinct is something that people have got away from! It belongs to animals! Christian adults don't want it!

TOM. What do Christian adults want, then, Mother?

AMANDA. Superior things! Things of the mind and the spirit! Only animals have to satisfy instincts! Surely your aims are somewhat higher than theirs! Than monkeys— pigs—

130   TOM. I reckon they're not.

AMANDA. You're joking. However, that isn't what I wanted to discuss.

TOM [*rising*]. I haven't much time.

AMANDA [*pushing his shoulders*]. Sit down.

TOM. You want me to punch in red at the warehouse, Mother?

AMANDA. You have five minutes. I want to talk about Laura.

[*Screen legend:* "Plans and Provisions."]

TOM. All right! What about Laura?

AMANDA. We have to be making some plans and provisions for her. She's older than you, two years, and nothing has happened. She just drifts along doing nothing. It frightens me terribly how she just drifts along.

140   TOM. I guess she's the type that people call home girls.

AMANDA. There's no such type, and if there is, it's a pity! That is unless the home is hers, with a husband!

TOM. What?

AMANDA. Oh, I can see the handwriting on the wall as plain as I see the nose in front of my face! It's terrifying! More and more you remind me of your father! He was out all hours without explanation!—Then *left! Goodbye!* And me with the bag to hold. I saw that letter you got from the Merchant Marine. I know what you're dreaming of. I'm not standing here blindfolded. [*She pauses.*] Very well, then. Then *do* it! But not till there's somebody to take your place.

150   TOM. What do you mean?

AMANDA. I mean that as soon as Laura has got somebody to take care of her, married, a home of her own, independent—why, then you'll be free to go wherever you please, on land, on sea, whichever way the wind blows you! But until that time you've got to look out for your sister. I don't say me because I'm old and don't matter! I say for your sister because she's young and dependent.

I put her in business college—a dismal failure! Frightened her so it made her sick at the stomach. I took her over to the Young People's League at the church. Another fiasco. She spoke to nobody, nobody spoke to her. Now all she does is fool with those pieces of glass and play those worn-out records. What kind of a life is that for a girl to

160   lead?

TOM. What can I do about it?

AMANDA. Overcome selfishness! Self, self, self is all that you ever think of!

[TOM *springs up and crosses to get his coat. It is ugly and bulky. He pulls on a cap with earmuffs.*]

Where is your muffler? Put your wool muffler on!

[*He snatches it angrily from the closet, tosses it around his neck and pulls both ends tight.*]

Tom! I haven't said what I had in mind to ask you.

TOM. I'm too late to—

AMANDA [*catching his arm—very importunately; then shyly*]. Down at the warehouse, aren't there some—nice young men?

TOM. No!

AMANDA. There *must* be—*some* . . .

170   TOM. Mother—[*He gestures.*]

AMANDA. Find out one that's clean-living—doesn't drink and ask him out for sister!

TOM. What?

AMANDA. For *sister!* To *meet!* Get *acquainted!*

TOM [*stamping to the door*]. Oh, my go-osh!

AMANDA. Will you?

[*He opens the door. She says, imploringly:*]

Will you?

[*He starts down the fire escape.*]

Will you? *Will* you, dear?

TOM [*calling back*]. *Yes!*

[AMANDA *closes the door hesitantly and with a troubled but faintly hopeful expression.*]

[*Screen image:* The cover of a glamor magazine.]

[*The spotlight picks up* AMANDA *at the phone.*]

AMANDA. Ella Cartwright? This is Amanda Wingfield! How are you, honey? How is that kidney condition?

[*There is a five-second pause.*]

Horrors!

[*There is another pause.*]

You're a Christian martyr, yes, honey, that's what you are, a Christian martyr! Well, I just now happened to notice in my little red book that your subscription to the *Companion* has just run out! I knew that you wouldn't want to miss out on the wonderful serial starting in this new issue. It's by Bessie Mae Hopper, the first thing she's written since *Honeymoon for Three.* Wasn't that a strange and interesting story? Well, this one is even lovelier, I believe. It has a sophisticated, society background. It's all about the horsey set on Long Island!

[*The light fades out.*]

SCENE 5

Legend on the screen: "Annunciation."

> *Music is heard as the light slowly comes on.*

> *It is early dusk of a spring evening. Supper has just been finished in the Wingfield apartment.* AMANDA *and* LAURA, *in light-colored dresses, are removing dishes from the table in the dining room, which is shadowy, their movements formalized almost as a dance or ritual, their moving forms as pale and silent as moths.* TOM *in white shirt and trousers, rises from the table and crosses toward the fire escape.*

AMANDA [*as he passes her*]. Son, will you do me a favor?
TOM. What?
AMANDA. Comb your hair! You look so pretty when your hair is combed!

[TOM *slouches on the sofa with the evening paper. Its enormous headline reads: "Franco Triumphs."*]

There is only one respect in which I would like you to emulate your father.
TOM. What respect is that?
AMANDA. The care he always took of his appearance. He never allowed himself to look untidy.

[*He throws down the paper and crosses to the fire escape.*]

Where are you going?

TOM. I'm going out to smoke.

10   AMANDA. You smoke too much. A pack a day at fifteen cents a pack. How much would that amount to in a month? Thirty times fifteen is how much, Tom? Figure it out and you will be astounded at what you could save. Enough to give you a night-school course in accounting at Washington U.! Just think what a wonderful thing that would be for you, son!

[TOM *is unmoved by the thought.*]

TOM. I'd rather smoke. [*He steps out on the landing, letting the screen door slam.*]

AMANDA [*sharply*]. I know! That's the tragedy of it. . . . [*Alone, she turns to look at her husband's picture.*]

[*Dance music: "The World Is Waiting for the Sunrise!"*]

TOM [*to the audience*]. Across the alley from us was the Paradise Dance Hall. On evenings in spring the windows and doors were open and the music came outdoors. Sometimes the lights were turned out except for a large glass sphere that hung from

20   the ceiling. It would turn slowly about and filter the dusk with delicate rainbow colors. Then the orchestra played a waltz or a tango, something that had a slow and sensuous rhythm. Couples would come outside, to the relative privacy of the alley. You could see them kissing behind ash pits and telephone poles. This was the compensation for lives that passed like mine, without any change or adventure. Adventure and change were imminent in this year. They were waiting around the corner for all these kids. Suspended in the mist over Berchtesgaden, caught in the folds of Chamberlain's umbrella.[14] In Spain there was Guernica! But here there was only hot swing music and liquor, dance halls, bars, and movies, and sex that hung in the gloom like a chandelier and flooded the world with brief, deceptive rainbows. . . . All the world was

30   waiting for bombardments!

[AMANDA *turns from the picture and comes outside.*]

AMANDA [*sighing*]. A fire escape landing's a poor excuse for a porch. [*She spreads a newspaper on a step and sits down, gracefully and demurely as if she were settling into a swing on a Mississippi veranda.*] What are you looking at?

TOM. The moon.

AMANDA. Is there a moon this evening?

TOM. It's rising over Garfinkel's Delicatessen.

AMANDA. So it is! A little silver slipper of a moon. Have you made a wish on it yet?

TOM. Um-hum.

---

[14] Berchtesgaden: southeast town in the Bavarian Alps on a peak above which Adolf Hitler's wartime villa was situated; Chamberlain's umbrella: reference to the conservative prime minister of England from 1937–1940 who made a pact with Hitler in Munich in 1938 and was blamed for delivering Czechoslovakia to the Nazis.

AMANDA. What did you wish for?

TOM. That's a secret.

40   AMANDA. A secret, huh? Well, I won't tell mine either. I will be just as mysterious as you.

TOM. I bet I can guess what yours is.

AMANDA. Is my head so transparent?

TOM. You're not a sphinx.

AMANDA. No, I don't have secrets. I'll tell you what I wished for on the moon. Success and happiness for my precious children! I wish for that whenever there's a moon, and when there isn't a moon, I wish for it, too.

TOM. I thought perhaps you wished for a gentleman caller.

AMANDA. Why do you say that?

50   TOM. Don't you remember asking me to fetch one?

AMANDA. I remember suggesting that it would be nice for your sister if you brought home some nice young man from the warehouse. I think that I've made that suggestion more than once.

TOM. Yes, you have made it repeatedly.

AMANDA. Well?

TOM. We are going to have one.

AMANDA. *What?*

TOM. A gentleman caller!

[*The annunciation is celebrated with music.*]

[AMANDA *rises.*]

[*Image on screen:* A caller with a bouquet.]

AMANDA. You mean you have asked some nice young man to come over?

60   TOM. Yep. I've asked him to dinner.

AMANDA. You really did?

TOM. I did!

AMANDA. You did, and did he—*accept?*

TOM. He did!

AMANDA. Well, well—well, well! That's—lovely!

TOM. I thought that you would be pleased.

AMANDA. It's definite then?

TOM. Very definite.

AMANDA. Soon?

70   TOM. Very Soon.

AMANDA. For heaven's sake, stop putting on and tell me some things, will you?

TOM. What things do you want me to tell you?

AMANDA. *Naturally* I would like to know when he's *coming!*

TOM. He's coming tomorrow.

AMANDA. *Tomorrow?*

TOM. Yep. Tomorrow.

AMANDA. But, Tom!

TOM. Yes, Mother?

AMANDA. Tomorrow gives me no time!

80 TOM. Time for what?

AMANDA. Preparations! Why didn't you phone me at once, as soon as you asked him, the minute that he accepted? Then, don't you see, I could have been getting ready!

TOM. You don't have to make any fuss.

AMANDA. Oh, Tom, Tom, Tom, of course I have to make a fuss! I want things nice, not sloppy! Not thrown together. I'll certainly have to do some fast thinking, won't I?

TOM. I don't see why you have to think at all.

AMANDA. You just don't know. We can't have a gentleman caller in a pigsty! All my wedding silver has to be polished, the monogrammed table linen ought to be laundered! The windows have to be washed and fresh curtains put up. And how about clothes?

90 We have to *wear* something, don't we?

TOM. Mother, this boy is no one to make a fuss over!

AMANDA. Do you realize he's the first young man we've introduced to your sister? It's terrible, dreadful, disgraceful that poor little sister has never received a single gentleman caller! Tom, come inside! [*She opens the screen door.*]

TOM. What for?

AMANDA. I want to ask you some things.

TOM. If you're going to make such a fuss, I'll call it off, I'll tell him not to come!

AMANDA. You certainly won't do anything of the kind. Nothing offends people worse than broken engagements. It simply means I'll have to work like a Turk! We won't be

100 brilliant, but we will pass inspection. Come on inside.

[TOM *follows her inside, groaning.*]

Sit down.

TOM. Any particular place you would like me to sit?

AMANDA. Thank heavens I've got that new sofa! I'm also making payments on a floor lamp I'll have sent out! And put the chintz covers on, they'll brighten things up! Of course I'd hoped to have these walls re-papered. . . . What is the young man's name?

TOM. His name is O'Connor.

AMANDA. That, of course, means fish—tomorrow is Friday! I'll have that salmon loaf— with Durkee's dressing! What does he do? He works at the warehouse?

TOM. Of course! How else would I—

110 AMANDA. Tom, he—doesn't drink?

TOM. Why do you ask me that?

AMANDA. Your father *did!*

TOM. Don't get started on that!

AMANDA. He *does* drink, then?

TOM. Not that I know of!

AMANDA. Make sure, be certain! The last thing I want for my daughter's a boy who drinks!

TOM. Aren't you being a little bit premature? Mr. O'Connor has not yet appeared on the scene!

120   AMANDA. But will tomorrow. To meet your sister, and what do I know about his character? Nothing! Old maids are better off than wives of drunkards!

TOM. Oh, my God!

AMANDA. Be still!

TOM [*leaning forward to whisper*]. Lots of fellows meet girls whom they don't marry!

AMANDA. Oh, talk sensibly, Tom—and don't be sarcastic! [*She has gotten a hairbrush.*]

TOM. What are you doing?

AMANDA. I'm brushing that cowlick down! [*She attacks his hair with the brush.*] What is
this young man's position at the warehouse?

TOM [*submitting grimly to the brush and the interrogation*]. This young man's position is
130   that of a shipping clerk, Mother.

AMANDA. Sounds to me like a fairly responsible job, the sort of a job *you* would be in if
you just had more *get-up*. What is his salary? Have you any idea?

TOM. I would judge it to be approximately eighty-five dollars a month.

AMANDA. Well—not princely, but—

TOM. Twenty more than I make.

AMANDA. Yes, how well I know! But for a family man, eighty-five dollars a month is not
much more than you can just get by on. . . .

TOM. Yes, but Mr. O'Connor is not a family man.

AMANDA. He might be, mightn't he? Some time in the future?

140   TOM. I see. Plans and provisions.

AMANDA. You are the only young man that I know of who ignores the fact that the future becomes the present, the present the past, and the past turns into everlasting regret if you don't plan for it!

TOM. I will think that over and see what I can make of it.

AMANDA. Don't be supercilious with your mother! Tell me some more about this—what
do you call him?

TOM. James D. O'Connor. The D. is for Delaney.

AMANDA. Irish on *both* sides! *Gracious!* And doesn't drink?

TOM. Shall I call him up and ask him right this minute?

150   AMANDA. The only way to find out about those things is to make discreet inquiries at
the proper moment. When I was a girl in Blue Mountain and it was suspected that a
young man drank, the girl whose attentions he had been receiving, if any girl *was*,
would sometimes speak to the minister of his church, or rather her father would if her
father was living, and sort of feel him out on the young man's character. That is the
way such things are discreetly handled to keep a young woman from making a tragic
mistake!

TOM. Then how did you happen to make a tragic mistake?

AMANDA. That innocent look of your father's had everyone fooled! He *smiled*—the
world was *enchanted!* No girl can do worse than put herself at the mercy of a hand-
160   some appearance! I hope that Mr. O'Connor is not too good-looking.

TOM. No, he's not too good-looking. He's covered with freckles and hasn't too much of
a nose.

AMANDA. He's not right-down homely, though?

TOM. Not right-down homely. Just medium homely, I'd say.

AMANDA. Character's what to look for in a man.

TOM. That's what I've always said, Mother.

AMANDA. You've never said anything of the kind and I suspect you would never give it a thought.

TOM. Don't be so suspicious of me.

AMANDA. At least I hope he's the type that's up and coming.

170 TOM. I think he really goes in for self-improvement.

AMANDA. What reason have you to think so?

TOM. He goes to night school.

AMANDA [*beaming*]. Splendid! What does he do, I mean study?

TOM. Radio engineering and public speaking!

AMANDA. Then he has visions of being advanced in the world! Any young man who studies public speaking is aiming to have an executive job some day! And radio engineering? A thing for the future! Both of these facts are very illuminating. Those are the sort of things that a mother should know concerning any young man who comes

180 to call on her daughter. Seriously or—not.

TOM. One little warning. He doesn't know about Laura. I didn't let on that we had dark ulterior motives. I just said, why don't you come and have dinner with us? He said okay and that was the whole conversation.

AMANDA. I bet it was! You're eloquent as an oyster. However, he'll know about Laura when he gets here. When he sees how lovely and sweet and pretty she is, he'll thank his lucky stars he was asked to dinner.

TOM. Mother, you mustn't expect too much of Laura.

AMANDA. What do you mean?

TOM. Laura seems all those things to you and me because she's ours and we love her.

190 We don't even notice she's crippled any more.

AMANDA. Don't say crippled! You know that I never allow that word to be used!

TOM. But face facts, Mother. She is and—that's not all—

AMANDA. What do you mean "not all"?

TOM. Laura is very different from other girls.

AMANDA. I think the difference is all to her advantage.

TOM. Not quite all—in the eyes of others—strangers—she's terribly shy and lives in a world of her own and those things make her seem a little peculiar to people outside the house.

AMANDA. Don't say peculiar.

200 TOM. Face the facts. She is.

[*The dance hall music changes to a tango that has a minor and somewhat ominous tone.*]

AMANDA. In what way is she peculiar—may I ask?

TOM [*gently*]. She lives in a world of her own—a world of little glass ornaments, Mother. . . .

[*He gets up.* AMANDA *remains holding the brush, looking at him, troubled.*]

She plays old phonograph records and—that's about all— [*He glances at himself in the mirror and crosses to the door.*]

AMANDA [*sharply*]. Where are you going?

TOM. I'm going to the movies. [*He goes out the screen door.*]

AMANDA. Not to the movies, every night to the movies! [*She follows quickly to the screen door.*] I don't believe you always go to the movies!

[*He is gone.* AMANDA *looks worriedly after him for a moment. Then vitality and optimism return and she turns from the door, crossing to the portieres.*]

Laura! Laura!

[LAURA *answers from the kitchenette.*]

210 LAURA. Yes, Mother.

AMANDA. Let those dishes go and come in front!

[LAURA *appears with a dish towel.* AMANDA *speaks to her gaily.*]

Laura, come here and make a wish on the moon!

[*Screen image:* The Moon.]

LAURA [*entering*]. Moon—moon?

AMANDA. A little silver slipper of a moon. Look over your left shoulder, Laura, and make a wish!

[LAURA *looks faintly puzzled as if called out of sleep.* AMANDA *seizes her shoulders and turns her at an angle by the door.*]

Now! Now, darling, *wish!*

LAURA. What shall I wish for, Mother?

AMANDA [*her voice trembling and her eyes suddenly filling with tears*]. Happiness! Good fortune!

[*The sound of the violin rises and the stage dims out.*]

SCENE 6

The light comes up on the fire escape landing. TOM *is leaning against the grill, smoking.*

[*Screen image:* The high school hero.]

TOM. And so the following evening I brought Jim home to dinner. I had known Jim slightly in high school. In high school Jim was a hero. He had tremendous Irish good nature and vitality with the scrubbed and polished look of white chinaware. He seemed to move in a continual spotlight. He was a star in basketball, captain of the debating club, president of the senior class and the glee club, and he sang the male lead in the annual light operas. He was always running or bounding, never just walking. He seemed always at the point of defeating the law of gravity. He was shooting with such velocity through his adolescence that you would logically expect him to

arrive at nothing short of the White House by the time he was thirty. But Jim apparently
ran into more interference after his graduation from Soldan. His speed had definitely
slowed. Six years after he left high school he was holding a job that wasn't much better than mine.

[*Screen image:* The Clerk.]

He was the only one at the warehouse with whom I was on friendly terms. I was
valuable to him as someone who could remember his former glory, who had seen him
win basketball games and the silver cup in debating. He knew of my secret practice of
retiring to a cabinet of the washroom to work on poems when business was slack in
the warehouse. He called me Shakespeare. And while the other boys in the warehouse regarded me with suspicious hostility, Jim took a humorous attitude toward me.
Gradually his attitude affected the others, their hostility wore off and they also began
to smile at me as people smile at an oddly fashioned dog who trots across their path at
some distance.

I knew that Jim and Laura had known each other at Soldan, and I had heard
Laura speak admiringly of his voice. I didn't know if Jim remembered her or not. In
high school Laura had been as unobtrusive as Jim has been astonishing. If he did remember Laura, it was not as my sister, for when I asked him to dinner, he grinned
and said, "You know, Shakespeare, I never thought of you as having folks!"

He was about to discover that I did . . .

[*Legend on screen:* "The accent of a coming foot."]

[*The light dims out on* TOM *and comes up in the Wingfield living room—a delicate
lemony light. It is about five on a Friday evening of late spring which comes "scattering
poems in the sky."*]

[AMANDA *has worked like a Turk in preparation for the gentleman caller. The results are
astonishing. The new floor lamp with its rose silk shade is in place, a colored paper
lantern conceals the broken light fixture in the ceiling, new billowing white curtains are
at the windows, chintz covers are on the chairs and sofa, a pair of new sofa pillows make
their initial appearance. Open boxes and tissue paper are scattered on the floor.*]

[LAURA *stands in the middle of the room with lifted arms while* AMANDA *crouches before
her, adjusting the hem of a new dress, devout and ritualistic. The dress is colored and designed by memory. The arrangement of* LAURA's *hair is changed; it is softer and more becoming. A fragile, unearthly prettiness has come out in* LAURA: *she is like a piece of
translucent glass touched by light, given a momentary radiance, not actual, not lasting.*]

AMANDA [*impatiently*]. Why are you trembling?
LAURA. Mother, you've made me so nervous!
AMANDA. How have I made you nervous?
LAURA. By all this fuss! You make it seem so important!
AMANDA. I don't understand you, Laura. You couldn't be satisfied with just sitting
home, and yet whenever I try to arrange something for you, you seem to resist it. [*She
gets up.*] Now take a look at yourself. No, wait! Wait just a moment—I have an idea!

LAURA. What is it now?

[AMANDA *produces two powder puffs which she wraps in handkerchiefs and stuffs in* LAURA's *bosom.*]

LAURA. Mother, what are you doing?
AMANDA. They call them "Gay Deceivers"!
LAURA. I won't wear them!
AMANDA. You will!
40   Laura. Why should I?
AMANDA. Because, to be painfully honest, your chest is flat.
LAURA. You make it seem like we were setting a trap.
AMANDA. All pretty girls are a trap, a pretty trap, and men expect them to be.

[*Legend on screen:* "A pretty trap."]

Now look at yourself, young lady. This is the prettiest you will ever be! [*She stands back to admire* LAURA.] I've got to fix myself now! You're going to be surprised by your mother's appearance!

[AMANDA *crosses through the portieres, humming gaily.* LAURA *moves slowly to the long mirror and stares solemnly at herself. A wind blows the white curtains inward in a slow, graceful motion and with a faint, sorrowful sighing.*]

AMANDA [*from somewhere behind the portieres*]. It isn't dark enough yet.

[LAURA *turns slowly before the mirror with a troubled look.*]

[*Legend on screen:* "This is my sister: Celebrate her with strings!" *Music plays.*]

AMANDA [*laughing, still not visible*]. I'm going to show you something. I'm going to make a spectacular appearance!
50   LAURA. What is it, Mother?
AMANDA. Possess your soul in patience—you will see! Something I've resurrected from that old trunk! Styles haven't changed so terribly much after all. . . . [*She parts the portieres.*] Now just look at your mother! [*She wears a girlish frock of yellowed voile with a blue silk sash. She carries a bunch of jonquils—the legend of her youth is nearly revived. Now she speaks feverishly.*] This is the dress in which I led the cotillion. Won the cakewalk twice at Sunset Hill, wore one Spring to the Governor's Ball in Jackson! See how I sashayed around the ballroom, Laura? [*She raises her skirt and does a mincing step around the room.*] I wore it on Sundays for my gentlemen callers! I had it on the day I met your father. . . . I had malaria fever all that Spring. The change of climate from East Tennessee to the Delta—weakened resistance. I had a little tempera-
60   ture all the time—not enough to be serious—just enough to make me restless and giddy! Invitations poured in—parties all over the Delta! "Stay in bed," said Mother, "you have a fever!"—but I just wouldn't. I took quinine but kept on going, going! Evenings, dances! Afternoons, long, long rides! Picnics—lovely! So lovely, that country in May—all lacy with dogwood, literally flooded with jonquils! That was the spring I had the craze for jonquils. Jonquils became an absolute obsession. Mother said,

"Honey, there's no more room for jonquils." And still I kept on bringing in more jonquils. Whenever, wherever I saw them, I'd say, "Stop! Stop! I see jonquils!" I made the young men help me gather the jonquils! It was a joke, Amanda and her jonquils. Finally there were no more vases to hold them, every available space was filled with jonquils. No vases to hold them? All right, I'll hold them myself! And then I— [*She stops in front of the picture. Music plays.*] met your father! Malaria fever and jonquils and then—this—boy.... [*She switches on the rose-colored lamp.*] I hope they get here before it starts to rain. [*She crosses the room and places the jonquils in a bowl on the table.*] I gave your brother a little extra change so he and Mr. O'Connor could take the service car home.

LAURA [*with an altered look*]. What did you say his name was?

AMANDA. O'Connor.

LAURA. What is his first name?

AMANDA. I don't remember. Oh, yes, I do. It was—Jim!

[LAURA *sways slightly and catches hold of a chair.*]

[*Legend on screen:* "Not Jim!"]

LAURA [*faintly*]. Not—Jim!

AMANDA. Yes, that was it, it was Jim! I've never known a Jim that wasn't nice!

[*The music becomes ominous.*]

LAURA. Are you sure his name is Jim O'Connor?

AMANDA. Yes. Why?

LAURA. Is he the one that Tom used to know in high school?

AMANDA. He didn't say so. I think he just got to know him at the warehouse.

LAURA. There was a Jim O'Connor we both knew in high school— [*Then, with effort.*] If that is the one that Tom is bringing to dinner—you'll have to excuse me, I won't come to the table.

AMANDA. What sort of nonsense is this?

LAURA. You asked me once if I'd ever liked a boy. Don't you remember I showed you this boy's picture?

AMANDA. You mean the boy you showed me in the yearbook?

LAURA. Yes, that boy.

AMANDA. Laura, Laura, were you in love with that boy?

LAURA. I don't know, Mother. All I know is I couldn't sit at the table if it was him!

AMANDA. It won't be him! It isn't the least bit likely. But whether it is or not, you will come to the table. You will not be excused.

LAURA. I'll have to be, Mother.

AMANDA. I don't intend to humor your silliness, Laura. I've had too much from you and your brother, both! So just sit down and compose yourself till they come. Tom has forgotten his key so you'll have to let them in, when they arrive.

LAURA [*panicky*]. Oh, Mother—*you* answer the door!

AMANDA [*lightly*]. I'll be in the kitchen—busy!

LAURA. Oh, Mother, please answer the door, don't make me do it!

AMANDA [*crossing into the kitchenette*]. I've got to fix the dressing for the salmon. Fuss, fuss—silliness!—over a gentleman caller!

[*The door swings shut.* LAURA *is left alone.*]

[*Legend on screen:* "Terror!"]

[*She utters a low moan and turns off the lamp—sits stiffly on the edge of the sofa, knotting her fingers together.*]

[*Legend on screen:* "The Opening of a Door!"]

[TOM *and* JIM *appear on the fire escape steps and climb to the landing. Hearing them approach,* LAURA *rises with a panicky gesture. She retreats to the portieres. The doorbell rings.* LAURA *catches her breath and touches her throat. Low drums sound.*]

AMANDA [*calling*]. Laura, sweetheart! The door!

[LAURA *stares at it without moving.*]

JIM. I think we just beat the rain.

TOM. Uh-huh. [*He rings again, nervously.* JIM *whistles and fishes for a cigarette.*]

110 AMANDA [*very, very gaily*]. Laura, this is your brother and Mr. O'Connor! Will you let them in, darling?

[LAURA *crosses toward the kitchenette door.*]

LAURA [*breathlessly*]. Mother—you go to the door!

[AMANDA *steps out of the kitchenette and s tares furiously at* LAURA. *She points imperiously at the door.*]

LAURA. Please, please!

AMANDA [*in a fierce whisper*]. What is the matter with you, you silly thing?

LAURA [*desperately*]. Please, you answer it, *please!*

AMANDA. I told you I wasn't going to humor you, Laura. Why have you chosen this moment to lose your mind?

LAURA. Please, please, please, you go!

AMANDA. You'll have to go to the door because I can't!

120 LAURA [*despairingly*]. I can't either!

AMANDA. *Why?*

LAURA. I'm *sick!*

AMANDA. I'm sick, too—of your nonsense! Why can't you and your brother be normal people? Fantastic whims and behavior!

[TOM *gives a long ring.*]

Preposterous goings on! Can you give me one reason— [*She calls out lyrically.*] Coming! Just one second!—why you should be afraid to open a door? Now you answer it, Laura!

LAURA. Oh, oh, oh . . . [*She returns through the portieres, darts to the Victrola, winds it frantically and turns it on.*]

AMANDA. Laura Wingfield, you march right to that door!

130   LAURA. *Yes—yes, Mother!*

[*A faraway, scratchy rendition of "Dardanella" softens the air and gives her strength to move through it. She slips to the door and draws it cautiously open.* TOM *enters with the caller,* JIM O'CONNOR.]

TOM. Laura, this is Jim. Jim, this is my sister, Laura.

JIM [*stepping inside*]. I didn't know that Shakespeare had a sister!

LAURA [*retreating, stiff and trembling, from the door*]. How—how do you do?

JIM [*heartily, extending his hand*]. Okay!

[LAURA *touches it hesitantly with hers.*]

JIM. Your hand's *cold,* Laura!

LAURA. Yes, well—I've been playing the Victrola. . . .

JIM. Must have been playing classical music on it! You ought to play a little hot swing music to warm you up!

LAURA. Excuse me—I haven't finished playing the Victrola. . . . [*She turns awkwardly and hurries into the front room. She pauses a second by the Victrola. Then she catches her breath and darts through the portieres like a frightened deer.*]

140   JIM [*grinning*]. What was the matter?

TOM. Oh—with Laura? Laura is—terribly shy.

JIM. Shy, huh? It's unusual to meet a shy girl nowadays. I don't believe you ever mentioned you had a sister.

TOM. Well, now you know. I have one. Here is the *Post Dispatch.* You want a piece of it?

JIM. Uh-huh.

TOM. What piece? The comics?

JIM. Sports! [*He glances at it.*] Ole Dizzy Dean is on his bad behavior.

TOM [*uninterested*]. Yeah? [*He lights a cigarette and goes over to the fire-escape door.*]

JIM. Where are *you* going?

150   TOM. I'm going out on the terrace.

JIM [*going after him*]. You know, Shakespeare—I'm going to sell you a bill of goods!

TOM. What goods?

JIM. A course I'm taking.

TOM. Huh?

JIM. In public speaking! You and me, we're not the warehouse type.

TOM. Thanks—that's good news. But what has public speaking got to do with it?

JIM. It fits you for—executive positions!

TOM. Awww.

JIM. I tell you it's done a helluva lot for me.

[*Image on screen:* Executive at his desk.]

160   TOM. In what respect?

JIM. In every! Ask yourself what is the difference between you an' me and men in the office down front? Brains?—No!—Ability?—No! Then what? Just one little thing—

TOM. What is that one little thing?

JIM. Primarily it amounts to—social poise! Being able to square up to people and hold your own on any social level!

AMANDA [*from the kitchenette*]. Tom?

TOM. Yes, Mother?

AMANDA. Is that you and Mr. O'Connor?

TOM. Yes, Mother.

170 AMANDA. Well, you just make yourselves comfortable in there.

TOM. Yes, Mother.

AMANDA. Ask Mr. O'Connor if he would like to wash his hands.

JIM. Aw, no—no—thank you—I took care of that at the warehouse. Tom—

TOM. Yes?

JIM. Mr. Mendoza was speaking to me about you.

TOM. Favorably?

JIM. What do you think?

TOM. Well—

JIM. You're going to be out of a job if you don't wake up.

180 TOM. I am waking up—

JIM. You show no signs—

TOM. The signs are interior.

[*Image on screen:* The sailing vessel with the Jolly Roger again.]

TOM. I'm planning to change. [*He leans over the fire-escape rail, speaking with quiet exhilaration. The incandescent marquees and signs of the first-run movie houses light his face from across the alley. He looks like a voyager.*] I'm right at the point of committing myself to a future that doesn't include the warehouse and Mr. Mendoza or even a night-school course in public speaking.

JIM. What are you gassing about?

TOM. I'm tired of the movies.

JIM. Movies!

190 TOM. Yes, movies! Look at them— [*A wave toward the marvels of Grand Avenue.*] All of those glamorous people—having adventures—hogging it all, gobbling the whole thing up! You know what happens? People go to the *movies* instead of *moving!* Hollywood characters are supposed to have all the adventures for everybody in America, while everybody in America sits in a dark room and watches them have them! Yes, until there's a war. That's when adventure becomes available to the masses! *Everyone's* dish, not only Gable's![15] Then the people in the dark room come out of the dark room to have some adventures themselves—goody, goody! It's our turn now, to go to the South

---

[15] Gable's: reference to American actor Clark Gable (1901–1960).

Sea Island—to make a safari—to be exotic, far-off! But I'm not patient. I don't want to wait till then. I'm tired of the *movies* and I am *about* to *move!*

200   JIM [*incredulously*]. Move?

TOM. Yes.

JIM. When?

TOM. Soon!

JIM. Where? Where?

[*The music seems to answer the question, while* TOM *thinks it over. He searches in his pockets.*]

TOM. I'm starting to boil inside. I know I seem dreamy, but inside—well, I'm boiling! Whenever I pick up a shoe, I shudder a little thinking how short life is and what I am doing! Whatever that means, I know it doesn't mean shoes—except as something to wear on a traveler's feet! [*He finds what he has been searching for in his pockets and holds out a paper to* JIM.] Look—

210   JIM. What?

TOM. I'm a member.

JIM [*reading*]. The Union of Merchant Seamen.

TOM. I paid my dues this month, instead of the light bill.

JIM. You will regret it when they turn the lights off.

TOM. I won't be here.

JIM. How about your mother?

TOM. I'm like my father. The bastard son of a bastard! Did you notice how he's grinning in his picture in there? And he's been absent going on sixteen years!

JIM. You're just talking, you drip. How does your mother feel about it?

220   TOM. Shhh! Here comes Mother! Mother is not acquainted with my plans!

AMANDA [*coming through the portieres*]. Where are you all?

TOM. On the terrace, Mother.

[*They start inside. She advances to them.* TOM *is distinctly shocked at her appearance. Even* JIM *blinks a little. He is making his first contact with girlish Southern vivacity and in spite of the night-school course in public speaking is somewhat thrown off the beam by the unexpected outlay of social charm. Certain responses are attempted by* JIM *but are swept aside by* AMANDA's *gay laughter and chatter.* TOM *is embarrassed but after the first shock* JIM *reacts very warmly. He grins and chuckles, is altogether won over.*]

[*Image on screen:* Amanda as a girl.]

AMANDA [*coyly smiling, shaking her girlish ringlets*]. Well, well, well, so this is Mr. O'Connor. Introductions entirely unnecessary. I've heard so much about you from my boy. I finally said to him, Tom—good gracious!—why don't you bring this paragon to supper? I'd like to meet this nice young man at the warehouse!—instead of just hearing him sing your praises so much! I don't know why my son is so stand-offish—that's not Southern behavior!

Let's sit down and—I think we could stand a little more air in here! Tom, leave the
230   door open. I felt a nice fresh breeze a moment ago. Where has it gone to? Mmm, so

warm already! And not quite summer, even. We're going to burn up when summer really gets started. However, we're having—we're having a very light supper. I think light things are better fo' this time of year. The same as light clothes are. Light clothes an' light food are what warm weather calls fo'. You know our blood gets so thick during th' winter—it takes a whole fo' us to *adjust* ou'selves!—when the season changes . . . It's come so quick this year. I wasn't prepared. All of a sudden—heavens! Already summer! I ran to the trunk an' pulled out this light dress—terribly old! Historical almost! But feels so good—so good an' co-ol, y' know. . . .

TOM. Mother—

240 AMANDA. Yes, honey?

TOM. How about—supper?

AMANDA. Honey, you go ask Sister if supper is ready! You know that Sister is in full charge of supper! Tell her you hungry boys are waiting for it. [*To* JIM.] Have you met Laura?

JIM. She—

AMANDA. Let you in? Oh, good, you've met already! It's rare for a girl as sweet an' pretty as Laura to be domestic! But Laura is, thank heavens, not only pretty but also very domestic. I'm not at all. I never was a bit. I never could make a thing but angel-food cake. Well, in the South we had so many servants. Gone, gone, gone. All vestige of 250 gracious living! Gone completely! I wasn't prepared for what the future brought me. All of my gentlemen callers were sons of planters and so of course I assumed that I would be married to one and raise my family on a large piece of land with plenty of servants. But man proposes—and woman accepts the proposal! To vary that old, old saying a little bit—I married no planter! I married a man who worked for the telephone company! That gallantly smiling gentleman over there! [*She points to the picture.*] A telephone man who—fell in love with long-distance! Now he travels and I don't even know where! But what am I going on for about my—tribulations? Tell me yours—I hope you don't have any! Tom?

TOM [*returning*]. Yes, Mother?

260 AMANDA. Is supper nearly ready?

TOM. It looks to me like supper is on the table.

AMANDA. Let me look— [*She rises prettily and looks through the portieres.*] Oh, lovely! But where is Sister?

TOM. Laura is not feeling well and she says that she thinks she'd better not come to the table.

AMANDA. What? Nonsense! Laura? Oh, Laura!

LAURA [*from the kitchenette, faintly*]. Yes, Mother.

AMANDA. You really must come to the table. We won't be seated until you come to the table! Come in, Mr. O'Connor. You sit over there, and I'll . . . Laura? Laura Wingfield! 270 You're keeping us waiting, honey! We can't say grace until you come to the table!

[*The kitchenette door is pushed weakly open and* LAURA *comes in. She is obviously quite faint, her lips trembling, her eyes wide and staring. She moves unsteadily toward the table.*]

[*Screen legend:* "Terror!"]

[*Outside a summer storm is coming on abruptly. The white curtains billow inward at the windows and there is a sorrowful murmur from the deep blue dusk.*]

[LAURA *suddenly stumbles; she catches at a chair with a faint moan.*]

TOM. Laura!
AMANDA. Laura!

[*There is a clap of thunder.*]

[*Screen legend:* "Ah!"]

[*despairingly.*] Why, Laura, you *are* ill, darling! Tom, help your sister into the living room, dear! Sit in the living room, Laura—rest on the sofa. Well! [*To* JIM *as* TOM *helps his sister to the sofa in the living room.*] Standing over the hot stove made her ill! I told her that it was just too warm this evening, but—

[TOM *comes back to the table.*]

Is Laura all right now?
TOM. Yes.
AMANDA. What *is* that? Rain? A nice cool rain has come up! [*She gives* JIM *a frightened look.*] I think we may—have grace—now . . .
[TOM *looks at her stupidly.*] Tom, honey—you say grace!
TOM. Oh . . . "For these and all thy mercies—"

[*They bow their heads,* AMANDA *stealing a nervous glance at* JIM. *In the living room* LAURA, *stretched on the sofa, clenches her hand to her lips, to hold back a shuddering sob.*]

God's Holy Name be praised—

[*The scene dims out.*]

SCENE 7

It is half an hour later. Dinner is just being finished in the dining room, LAURA *is still huddled upon the sofa, her feet drawn under her, her head resting on a pale blue pillow, her eyes wide and mysteriously watchful. The new floor lamp with its shade of rose-colored silk gives a soft, becoming light to her face, bringing out the fragile, unearthly prettiness which usually escapes attention. From outside there is a steady murmur of rain, but it is slackening and soon stops; the air outside becomes pale and luminous as the moon breaks through the clouds. A moment after the curtain rises, the lights in both rooms flicker and go out.*

JIM. Hey, there, Mr. Light Bulb!

[AMANDA *laughs nervously.*]

[*Legend on screen:* "Suspension of a public service."]

AMANDA. Where was Moses when the lights went out? Ha-ha. Do you know the answer to that one, Mr. O'Connor?

JIM. No, Ma'am, what's the answer?

AMANDA. In the dark!

[JIM *laughs appreciatively.*]

Everybody sit still. I'll light the candles. Isn't it lucky we have them on the table? Where's a match? Which of you gentlemen can provide a match?

JIM. Here.

AMANDA. Thank you, Sir.

10   JIM. Not at all, Ma'am!

AMANDA [*as she lights the candles*]. I guess the fuse has burnt out. Mr. O'Connor, can you tell a burnt-out fuse? I know I can't and Tom is a total loss when it comes to mechanics.

[*They rise from the table and go into the kitchenette, from where their voices are heard.*]

Oh, be careful you don't bump into something. We don't want our gentleman caller to break his neck. Now wouldn't that be a fine howdy-do?

JIM. Ha-ha! Where is the fuse-box?

AMANDA. Right here next to the stove. Can you see anything?

JIM. Just a minute.

AMANDA. Isn't electricity a mysterious thing? Wasn't it Benjamin Franklin who tied a

20   key to a kite? We live in such a mysterious universe, don't we? Some people say that science clears up all the mysteries for us. In my opinion it only creates more! Have you found it yet?

JIM. No, Ma'am. All these fuses look okay to me.

AMANDA. Tom!

TOM. Yes, Mother?

AMANDA. That light bill I give you several days ago. The one I told you we got the notices about?

[*Legend on screen:* "Ha!"]

TOM. Oh—yeah.

AMANDA. You didn't neglect to pay it by any chance?

30   TOM. Why, I—

AMANDA. Didn't! I might have known it!

JIM. Shakespeare probably wrote a poem on that light bill, Mrs. Wingfield.

AMANDA. I might have known better than to trust him with it! There's such a high price for negligence in this world!

JIM. Maybe the poem will win a ten-dollar prize.

AMANDA. We'll just have to spend the remainder of the evening in the nineteenth century, before Mr. Edison made the Mazda lamp!

JIM. Candlelight is my favorite kind of light.

AMANDA. That shows you're romantic! But that's no excuse for Tom. Well, we got

40   through dinner. Very considerate of them to let us get through dinner before they plunged us into everlasting darkness, wasn't it, Mr. O'Connor?

JIM. Ha-ha!

AMANDA. Tom, as a penalty for your carelessness you can help me with the dishes.

JIM. Let me give you a hand.

AMANDA. Indeed you will not!

JIM. I ought to be good for something.

AMANDA. Good for something? [*Her tone is rhapsodic.*] You? Why, Mr. O'Connor, no-body, *nobody's* given me this much entertainment in years—as you have!

JIM. Aw, now, Mrs. Wingfield!

50   AMANDA. I'm not exaggerating, not one bit! But Sister is all by her lonesome. You go keep her company in the parlor! I'll give you this lovely old candelabrum that used to be on the altar at the Church of the Heavenly Rest. It was melted a little out of shape when the church burnt down. Lightning struck it one spring. Gypsy Jones was hold-ing a revival at the time and he intimated that the church was destroyed because the Episcopalians gave card parties.

JIM. Ha-ha.

AMANDA. And how about you coaxing Sister to drink a little wine? I think it would be good for her! Can you carry both at once?

JIM. Sure. I'm Superman!

60   AMANDA. Now, Thomas, get into this apron!

[JIM *comes into the dining room, carrying the candelabrum, its candles lighted, in one hand and a glass of wine in the other. The door of the kitchenette swings closed on* AMANDA's *gay laughter; the flickering light approaches the portieres.* LAURA *sits up nerv-ously as* JIM *enters. She can hardly speak from the almost intolerable strain of being alone with a stranger.*]

[*Screen legend: "I don't suppose you remember me at all!"*]

[*At first, before* JIM's *warmth overcomes her paralyzing shyness,* LAURA's *voice is thin and breathless, as though she had just run up a steep flight of stairs.* JIM's *attitude is gently humorous. While the incident is apparently unimportant, it is to* LAURA *the climax of her secret life.*]

JIM. Hello there, Laura.

LAURA [*faintly*]. Hello.

[*She clears her throat.*]

JIM. How are you feeling now? Better?

LAURA. Yes. Yes, thank you.

JIM. This is for you. A little dandelion wine. [*He extends the glass toward her with extrav-agant gallantry.*]

LAURA. Thank you.

JIM. Drink it—but don't get drunk!

[*He laughs heartily.* LAURA *takes the glass uncertainly; she laughs shyly.*]

Where shall I set the candles?

LAURA. Oh—oh, anywhere . . .

70   JIM. How about here on the floor? Any objections?

LAURA. No.

JIM. I'll spread a newspaper under to catch the drippings. I like to sit on the floor. Mind if I do?

LAURA. Oh, no.

JIM. Give me a pillow?

LAURA. What?

JIM. A pillow!

LAURA. Oh . . . [*She hands him one quickly.*]

JIM. How about you? Don't you like to sit on the floor?

80   LAURA. Oh—yes.

JIM. Why don't you, then?

LAURA. I—will.

JIM. Take a pillow!

[LAURA *does. She sits on the floor on the other side of the candelabrum.* JIM *crosses his legs and smiles engagingly at her.*] I can't hardly see you sitting way over there.

LAURA. I can—see you.

JIM. I know, but that's not fair, I'm in the limelight.

[LAURA *moves her pillow closer.*]

Good! Now I can see you! Comfortable?

LAURA. Yes.

JIM. So am I. Comfortable as a cow! Will you have some gum?

LAURA. No, thank you.

90   JIM. I think that I will indulge, with your permission. [*He musingly unwraps a stick of gum and holds it up.*] Think of the fortune made by the guy that invented the first piece of chewing gum. Amazing, huh? The Wrigley Building is one of the sights of Chicago—I saw it when I went up to the Century of Progress. Did you take in the Century of Progress?

LAURA. No, I didn't.

JIM. Well, it was quite a wonderful exposition. What impressed me most was the Hall of Science. Gives you an idea of what the future will be in America, even more wonderful than the present time is! [*There is a pause.* JIM *smiles at her.*] Your brother tells me you're shy. Is that right, Laura?

100   LAURA. I—don't know.

JIM. I judge you to be an old-fashioned type of girl. Well, I think that's a pretty good type to be. Hope you don't think I'm being too personal—do you?

LAURA [*hastily, out of embarrassment*]. I believe I *will* take a piece of gum, if you—don't mind. [*Clearing her throat.*] Mr. O'Connor, have you—kept up with your singing?

JIM. Singing? Me?

LAURA. Yes. I remember what a beautiful voice you had.

JIM. When did you hear me sing?

[LAURA *does not answer, and in the long pause which follows a man's voice is heard singing offstage.*]

VOICE.
> O blow, ye winds, heigh-ho,
> A-roving I will go!
110   I'm off to my love
>   With a boxing glove—
> Ten thousand miles away!

JIM. You say you've heard me sing?

LAURA. Oh, yes! Yes, very often . . . I—don't suppose—you remember me—at all?

JIM [*smiling doubtfully*]. You know I have an idea I've seen you before. I had that idea soon as you opened the door. It seemed almost like I was about to remember your name. But the name that I started to call you—wasn't a name! And so I stopped my-self before I said it.

LAURA. Wasn't it—Blue Roses?

120 JIM [*springing up, grinning*]. Blue Roses! My gosh, yes—Blue Roses! That's what I had on my tongue when you opened the door! Isn't it funny what tricks your memory plays? I didn't connect you with high school somehow or other. But that's where it was; it was high school. I didn't even know you were Shakespeare's sister! Gosh, I'm sorry.

LAURA. I didn't expect you to. You—barely knew me!

JIM. But we did have a speaking acquaintance, huh?

LAURA. Yes, we—spoke to each other.

JIM. When did you recognize me?

LAURA. Oh, right away!

130 JIM. Soon as I came in the door?

LAURA. When I heard your name I thought it was probably you. I knew that Tom used to know you a little in high school. So when you came in the door—well, then I was—sure.

JIM. Why didn't you *say* something, then?

LAURA [*breathlessly*]. I didn't know what to say, I was—too surprised!

JIM. For goodness' sakes! You know, this sure is funny!

LAURA. Yes! Yes, isn't it, though . . .

JIM. Didn't we have a class in something together?

LAURA. Yes, we did.

140 JIM. What class was that?

LAURA. It was—singing—chorus!

JIM. Aw!

LAURA. I sat across the aisle from you in the Aud.

JIM. Aw.

LAURA. Mondays, Wednesdays, and Fridays.

JIM. Now I remember—you always came in late.

LAURA. Yes, it was so hard for me, getting upstairs. I had that brace on my leg—it clumped so loud!

JIM. I never heard any clumping.

150 LAURA [*wincing at the recollection*]. To me it sounded like—thunder!

JIM. Well, well, well, I never even noticed.

LAURA. And everybody was seated before I came in. I had to walk in front of all those people. My seat was in the back row. I had to go clumping all the way up the aisle with everyone watching!

JIM. You shouldn't have been self-conscious.

LAURA. I know, but I was. It was always such a relief when the singing started.

JIM. Aw, yes, I've placed you now! I used to call you Blue Roses. How was it that I got started calling you that?

LAURA. I was out of school a little while with pleurosis. When I came back you asked
160   me what was the matter. I said I had pleurosis—you thought I said *Blue Roses.* That's what you always called me after that!

JIM. I hope you didn't mind.

LAURA. Oh, no—I liked it. You see, I wasn't acquainted with many—people. . . .

JIM. As I remember you sort of stuck by yourself.

LAURA. I—I—never have had much luck at—making friends.

JIM. I don't see why you wouldn't.

LAURA. Well, I—started out badly.

JIM. You mean being—

LAURA. Yes, it sort of—stood between me—
170 JIM. You shouldn't have let it!

LAURA. I know, but it did, and—

JIM. You were shy with people!

LAURA. I tried not to be but never could—

JIM. Overcome it?

LAURA. No, I—I never could!

JIM. I guess being shy is something you have to work out of kind of gradually.

LAURA [*sorrowfully*]. Yes—I guess it—

JIM. Takes time!

LAURA. Yes—
180 JIM. People are not so dreadful when you know them. That's what you have to remember! And everybody has problems, not just you, but practically everybody has got some problems. You think of yourself as having the only problems, as being the only one who is disappointed. But just look around you and you will see lots of people as disappointed as you are. For instance, I hoped when I was going to high school that I would be further along at this time, six years later, than I am now. You remember that wonderful write-up I had in *The Torch?*

LAURA. Yes! [*She rises and crosses to the table.*]

JIM. It said I was bound to succeed in anything I went into!

[LAURA *returns with the high school yearbook.*]

Holy Jeez! *The Torch!*

[*He accepts it reverently. They smile across the book with mutual wonder.* LAURA *crouches beside him and they begin to turn the pages.* LAURA's *shyness is dissolving in his warmth.*]

190   LAURA. Here you are in *The Pirates of Penzance!*

JIM [*wistfully*]. I sang the baritone lead in that operetta.

LAURA [*raptly*]. So—*beautifully!*

JIM [*protesting*]. Aw—

LAURA. Yes, yes—beautifully—beautifully!

JIM. You heard me?

LAURA. All three times!

JIM. No!

LAURA. Yes!

JIM. All three performances?

200   LAURA [*looking down*]. Yes.

JIM. Why?

LAURA. I—wanted to ask you to—autograph my program. [*She takes the program from the back of the yearbook and shows it to him.*]

JIM. Why didn't you ask me to?

LAURA. You were always surrounded by your own friends so much that I never had a chance to.

JIM. You should have just—

LAURA. Well, I—thought you might think I was—

JIM. Thought I might think you was—what?

LAURA. Oh—

210   JIM [*with reflective relish*]. I was beleaguered by females in those days.

LAURA. You were terribly popular!

JIM. Yeah—

LAURA. You had such a—friendly way—

JIM. I was spoiled in high school.

LAURA. Everybody—liked you!

JIM. Including you?

LAURA. I—yes, I—did, too— [*She gently closes the book in her lap.*]

JIM. Well, well, well! Give me that program, Laura.

[*She hands it to him. He signs it with a flourish.*]

There you are—better late than never!

220   LAURA. Oh, I—what a—surprise!

JIM. My signature isn't worth very much right now. But some day—maybe—it will increase in value! Being disappointed is one thing and being discouraged is something else. I am disappointed but I am not discouraged. I'm twenty-three years old. How old are you?

LAURA. I'll be twenty-four in June.

JIM. That's not old age!

LAURA. No, but—

JIM. You finished high school?

LAURA [*with difficulty*]. I didn't go back.

230   JIM. You mean you dropped out?

LAURA. I made bad grades in my final examinations. [*She rises and replaces the book and the program on the table. Her voice is strained.*] How is—Emily Meisenbach getting along?

JIM. Oh, that kraut-head![16]

LAURA. Why do you call her that?

JIM. That's what she was.

LAURA. You're not still—going with her?

JIM. I never see her.

LAURA. It said the "Personal" section that you were—engaged!

240   JIM. I know, but I wasn't impressed by that—propaganda!

LAURA. It wasn't—the truth?

JIM. Only in Emily's optimistic opinion!

LAURA. Oh—

[*Legend:* "What have you done since high school?"]

[JIM *lights a cigarette and leans indolently back on his elbows smiling at* LAURA *with a warmth and charm which lights her inwardly with altar candles. She remains by the table, picks up a piece from the glass menagerie collection, and turns it in her hands to cover her tumult.*]

JIM [*after several reflective puffs on his cigarette*]. What have you done since high school?

[*She seems not to hear him.*]

Huh?

[LAURA *looks up.*]

I said what have you done since high school, Laura?

LAURA. Nothing much.

JIM. You must have been doing something these six long years.

LAURA. Yes.

250   JIM. Well, then, such as what?

LAURA. I took a business course at business college—

JIM. How did that work out?

LAURA. Well, not very—well—I had to drop out, it gave me—indigestion—

[JIM *laughs gently.*]

JIM. What are you doing now?

LAURA. I don't do anything—much. Oh, please don't think I sit around doing nothing! My glass collection takes up a good deal of time. Glass is something you have to take good care of.

JIM. What did you say—about glass?

---

[16] "Kraut-head": disparaging term for a German.

LAURA. Collection I said—I have one— [*She clears her throat and turns away again, acutely shy.*]

260   JIM [*abruptly*]. You know what I judge to be the trouble with you? Inferiority complex! Know what that is? That's what they call it when someone low-rates himself! I understand it because I had it, too. Although my case was not so aggravated as yours seems to be. I had it until I took up public speaking, developed my voice, and learned that I had an aptitude for science. Before that time I never thought of myself as being outstanding in any way whatsoever! Now I've never made a regular study of it, but I have a friend who says I can analyze people better than doctors that make a profession of it. I don't claim that to be necessarily true, but I can sure guess a person's psychology, Laura! [*He takes out his gum.*] Excuse me, Laura. I always take it out when the flavor is gone. I'll use this scrap of paper to wrap it in. I know how it is to get it stuck on a

270   shoe. [*He wraps the gum in paper and puts it in his pocket.*] Yep—that's what I judge to be your principal trouble. A lack of confidence in yourself as a person. You don't have the proper amount of faith in yourself. I'm basing that fact on a number of your remarks and also on certain observations I've made. For instance that clumping you thought was so awful in high school. You say that you even dreaded to walk into class. You see what you did? You dropped out of school, you gave up an education because of a clump, which as far as I know was practically non-existent! A little physical defect is what you have. Hardly noticeable even! Magnified thousands of times by imagination! You know what my strong advice to you is? Think of yourself *superior* in some way!

280   LAURA. In what way would I think?

JIM. Why, man alive, Laura! Just look about you a little. What do you see? A world full of common people! All of 'em born and all of 'em going to die! Which of them has one-tenth of your good points! Or mine! Or anyone else's, as far as that goes—gosh! Everybody excels in some one thing. Some in many! [*He unconsciously glances at himself in the mirror.*] All you've got to do is discover in *what*! Take me, for instance. [*He adjusts his tie at the mirror.*] My interest happens to lie in electro-dynamics. I'm taking a course in radio engineering at night school, Laura, on top of a fairly responsible job at the warehouse. I'm taking that course and studying public speaking.

LAURA. Ohhhh.

290   JIM. Because I believe in the future of television! [*Turning his back to her.*] I wish to be ready to go up right along with it. Therefore I'm planning to get in on the ground floor. In fact I've already made the right connections and all that remains is for the industry itself to get under way! Full steam— [*His eyes are starry.*] Knowledge—Zzzzzp! Money—Zzzzzp!—Power! That's the cycle democracy is built on!

[*His attitude is convincingly dynamic. LAURA stares at him, even her shyness eclipsed in her absolute wonder. He suddenly grins.*]

I guess you think I think a lot of myself!

LAURA. No—o-o-o, I—

JIM. Now how about you? Isn't there something you take more interest in than anything else?

LAURA. Well, I do—as I said—have my—glass collection—

[*A peal of girlish laughter rings from the kitchenette.*]

300 JIM. I'm not right sure I know what you're talking about. What kind of glass is it?

LAURA. Little articles of it, they're ornaments mostly! Most of them are little animals made out of glass, the tiniest little animals in the world. Mother calls them a glass menagerie! Here's an example of one, if you'd like to see it! This one is one of the oldest. It's nearly thirteen.

[*Music:* "The Glass Menagerie."]

[*He stretches out his hand.*]

Oh, be careful—if you breathe, it breaks!

JIM. I'd better not take it. I'm pretty clumsy with things.

LAURA. Go on, I trust you with him! [*She places the piece in his palm.*] There now—you're holding him gently! Hold him over the light, he loves the light! You see how the light shines through him?

310 JIM. It sure does shine!

LAURA. I shouldn't be partial, but he is my favorite one.

JIM. What kind of a thing is this one supposed to be?

LAURA. Haven't you noticed the single horn on his forehead?

JIM. A unicorn, huh?

LAURA. Mmmm-hmmm!

JIM. Unicorns—aren't they extinct in the modern world?

LAURA. I know!

JIM. Poor little fellow, he must feel sort of lonesome.

LAURA [*smiling*]. Well, if he does, he doesn't complain about it. He stays on a shelf with
320 some horses that don't have horns and all of them seem to get along nicely together.

JIM. How do you know?

LAURA [*lightly*]. I haven't heard any arguments among them!

JIM [*grinning*]. No arguments, huh? Well, that's a pretty good sign! Where shall I set him?

LAURA. Put him on the table. They all like a change of scenery once in a while!

JIM. Well, well, well, well— [*He places the glass piece on the table, then raises his arms and stretches.*] Look how big my shadow is when I stretch!

LAURA. Oh, oh, yes—it stretches across the ceiling!

JIM [*crossing to the door*]. I think it's stopped raining. [*He opens the fire-escape door and
330 the background music changes to a dance tune.*] Where does the music come from?

LAURA. From the Paradise Dance Hall across the alley.

JIM. How about cutting the rug a little, Miss Wingfield?

LAURA. Oh, I—

JIM. Or is your program filled up? Let me have a look at it. [*He grasps an imaginary card.*] Why, every dance is taken! I'll just have to scratch some out.

[*Waltz music:* "La Golondrina."]

Ahhh, a waltz! [*He executes some sweeping turns by himself, then holds his arms toward* LAURA.]

LAURA [*breathlessly*]. I—can't dance!

JIM. There you go, that inferiority stuff!

LAURA. I've never danced in my life!

340　JIM. Come on, try!

LAURA. Oh, but I'd step on you!

JIM. I'm not made out of glass.

LAURA. How—how—how do we start?

JIM. Just leave it to me. You hold your arms out a little.

LAURA. Like this?

JIM [*taking her in his arms*]. A little bit higher. Right. Now don't tighten up, that's the main thing about it—relax.

LAURA [*laughing breathlessly*]. It's hard not to.

JIM. Okay.

350　LAURA. I'm afraid you can't budge me.

JIM. What do you bet I can't? [*He swings her into motion.*]

LAURA. Goodness, yes, you can!

JIM. Let yourself go, now, Laura, just let yourself go.

LAURA. I'm—

JIM. Come on!

LAURA. —trying!

JIM. Not so stiff—easy does it!

LAURA. I know but I'm—

JIM. Loosen th' backbone! There now, that's a lot better.

360　LAURA. Am I?

JIM. Lots, lots better! [*He moves her about the room in a clumsy waltz.*]

LAURA. Oh, my!

JIM. Ha-ha!

LAURA. Oh, my goodness!

JIM. Ha-ha-ha!

[*They suddenly bump into the table, and the glass piece on it falls to the floor.* JIM *stops the dance.*]

　　What did we hit on?

LAURA. Table.

JIM. Did something fall off it? I think—

LAURA. Yes.

370　JIM. I hope that it wasn't the little glass horse with the horn!

LAURA. Yes. [*She stoops to pick it up.*]

JIM. Aw, aw, aw. Is it broken?

LAURA. Now it is just like all the other horses.

JIM. It's lost its—

LAURA. Horn! It doesn't matter. Maybe it's a blessing in disguise.

JIM. You'll never forgive me. I bet that that was your favorite piece of glass.

LAURA. I don't have favorites much. It's no tragedy, Freckles. Glass breaks so easily. No matter how careful you are. The traffic jars the shelves and things fall off them.

JIM. Still I'm awfully sorry that I was the cause.

380 LAURA [*smiling*]. I'll just imagine he had an operation. The horn was removed to make him feel less—freakish!

[*They both laugh.*]

Now he will feel more at home with the other horses, the ones that don't have horns. . . .

JIM. Ha-ha, that's very funny! [*Suddenly he is serious.*] I'm glad to see that you have a sense of humor. You know—you're—well—very different! Surprisingly different from anyone else I know! [*His voice becomes soft and hesitant with a genuine feeling.*] Do you mind me telling you that?

[LAURA *is abashed beyond speech.*]

I mean it in a nice way—

[LAURA *nods shyly, looking away.*]

You make me feel sort of—I don't know how to put it! I'm usually pretty good at ex-
390 pressing things, but—this is something that I don't know how to say!

[LAURA *touches her throat and clears it—turns the broken unicorn in her hands. His voice becomes softer.*]

Has anyone ever told you that you were pretty?

[*There is a pause, and the music rises slightly.* LAURA *looks up slowly, with wonder, and shakes her head.*]

Well, you are! In a very different way from anyone else. And all the nicer because of the difference, too.

[*His voice becomes low and husky.* LAURA *turns away, nearly faint with the novelty of her emotions.*]

I wish that you were my sister. I'd teach you to have some confidence in yourself. The different people are not like other people, but being different is nothing to be ashamed of. Because other people are not such wonderful people. They're one hundred times one thousand. You're one times one! They walk all over the earth. You just stay here. They're common as—weeds, but—you—well, you're—*Blue Roses!*

[*Image on screen:* Blue Roses.]

[*The music changes.*]

LAURA. But blue is wrong for—roses. . . .
400 JIM. It's right for you! You're—pretty!

LAURA. In what respect am I pretty?

JIM. In all respects—believe me! Your eyes—your hair—are pretty! Your hands are pretty! [*He catches hold of her hand.*] You think I'm making this up because I'm invited to dinner and have to be nice. Oh, I could do that! I could put on an act for you,

Laura, and say lots of things without being very sincere. But this time I am. I'm talking to you sincerely. I happened to notice you had this inferiority complex that keeps you from feeling comfortable with people. Somebody needs to build your confidence up and make you proud instead of shy and turning away and—blushing. Somebody—ought to—*kiss you, Laura!*

[*His hand slips slowly up her arm to her shoulder as the music swells tumultuously. He suddenly turns her about and kisses her on the lips. When he releases her,* LAURA *sinks on the sofa with a bright, dazed look.* JIM *backs away and fishes in his pocket for a cigarette.*]

[*Legend on screen: "A souvenir."*]

410   Stumblejohn!

[*He lights the cigarette, avoiding her look. There is a peal of girlish laughter from* AMANDA *in the kitchenette.* LAURA *slowly raises and opens her hand. It still contains the little broken glass animal. She looks at it with a tender, bewildered expression.*]

Stumblejohn! I shouldn't have done that—that was way off the beam. You don't smoke, do you?

[*She looks up, smiling, not hearing the question. He sits beside her rather gingerly. She looks at him speechlessly—waiting. He coughs decorously and moves a little farther aside as he considers the situation and senses her feelings, dimly, with perturbation. He speaks gently.*]

Would you—care for a—mint?

[*She doesn't seem to hear him but her look grows brighter even.*]

Peppermint? Life Saver? My pocket's a regular drugstore—wherever I go. . . . [*He pops a mint in his mouth. Then he gulps and decides to make a clean breast of it. He speaks slowly and gingerly.*] Laura, you know, if I had a sister like you, I'd do the same thing as Tom. I'd bring out fellows and—introduce her to them. The right type of boys—of a type to—appreciate her. Only—well—he made a mistake about me. Maybe I've got no call to be saying this. That may not have been the idea in having me over. But what

420   if it was? There's nothing wrong about that. The only trouble is that in my case—I'm not in a situation to—do the right thing. I can't take down your number and say I'll phone. I can't call up next week and—ask for a date. I thought I had better explain the situation in case you—misunderstood it and—I hurt your feelings. . . .

[*There is a pause. Slowly, very slowly,* LAURA'S *look changes, her eyes returning slowly from his to the glass figure in her palm.* AMANDA *utters another gay laugh in the kitchenette.*]

LAURA [*faintly*]. You—won't—call again?

JIM. No, Laura, I can't. [*He rises from the sofa.*] As I was just explaining, I've—got strings on me. Laura, I've—been going steady! I go out all the time with a girl named Betty. She's a home-girl like you, and Catholic, and Irish, and in a great many ways we—get along fine. I met her last summer on a moon-light boat trip up the river to Alton, on the *Majestic*. Well—right away from the start it was—love!

[*Legend:* Love!]

[LAURA *sways slightly forward and grips the arm of the sofa. He fails to notice, now enrapt in his own comfortable being.*]

430   Being in love has made a new man of me!

[*Leaning stiffly forward, clutching the arm of the sofa,* LAURA *struggles visibly with her storm. But* JIM *is oblivious; she is a long way off.*]

The power of love is really pretty tremendous! Love is something that—changes the whole world, Laura!

[*The storm abates a little and* LAURA *leans back. He notices her again.*]

It happened that Betty's aunt took sick, she got a wire and had to go to Centralia. So Tom—when he asked me to dinner—I naturally just accepted the invitation, not knowing that you—that he—that I—[*He stops awkwardly.*] Huh—I'm a stumblejohn!

[*He flops back on the sofa. The holy candles on the altar of* LAURA's *face have been snuffed out. There is a look of almost infinite desolation.* JIM *glances at her uneasily.*]

I wish that you would—say something.

[*She bites her lip which was trembling and then bravely smiles. She opens her hand again on the broken glass figure. Then she gently takes his hand and raises it level with her own. She carefully places the unicorn in the palm of his hand, then pushes his finger closed upon it.*]

What are you—doing that for? You want me to have him? Laura?

[*She nods.*]

What for?

LAURA. A—souvenir. . . .

[*She rises unsteadily and crouches beside the Victrola to wind it up.*]

[*Legend on screen:* "Things have a way of turning out so badly!" *Or image:* "Gentleman caller waving goodbye—gaily."]

[*At the moment* AMANDA *rushes brightly back into the living room. She bears a pitcher of fruit punch in an old-fashioned cut-glass pitcher, and a plate of macaroons. The plate has a gold border and poppies painted on it.*]

440   AMANDA. Well, well, well! Isn't the air delightful after the shower? I've made you children a little liquid refreshment.

[*She turns gaily to* JIM.] Jim, do you know that song about lemonade?

"Lemonade, lemonade
Made in the shade and stirred with a spade—
Good enough for any old maid!"

JIM [*uneasily*]. Ha-ha! No—I never heard it.

AMANDA. Why, Laura! You look so serious!

JIM. We were having a serious conversation.

AMANDA. Good! Now you're better acquainted!

JIM [*uncertainly*]. Ha-ha! Yes.

450   AMANDA. You modern young people are much more serious-minded than my generation. I was so gay as a girl!

JIM. You haven't changed, Mrs. Wingfield.

AMANDA. Tonight I'm rejuvenated! The gaiety of the occasion, Mr. O'Connor! [*She tosses her head with a peal of laughter, spilling some lemonade.*] Oooo! I'm baptizing myself!

JIM. Here—let me—

AMANDA [*setting the pitcher down*]. There now. I discovered we had some maraschino cherries. I dumped them in, juice and all!

JIM. You shouldn't have gone to that trouble, Mrs. Wingfield.

460   AMANDA. Trouble, trouble? Why, it was loads of fun! Didn't you hear me cutting up in the kitchen? I bet your ears were burning! I told Tom how outdone with him I was for keeping you to himself so long a time! He should have brought you over much, much sooner! Well, now that you've found your way, I want you to be a very frequent caller! Not just occasional but all the time. Oh, we're going to have a lot of gay times together! I see them coming! Mmm, just breathe that air! So fresh, and the moon's so pretty! I'll skip back out—I know where my place is when young folks are having a—serious conversation!

JIM. Oh, don't go out, Mrs. Wingfield. The fact of the matter is I've got to be going.

AMANDA. Going, now? You're joking! Why, it's only the shank of the evening, Mr.
470   O'Connor!

JIM. Well, you know how it is.

AMANDA. You mean you're a young workingman and have to keep workingmen's hours. We'll let you off early tonight. But only on the condition that next time you stay later. What's the best night for you? Isn't Saturday night the best night for you workingmen?

JIM. I have a couple of time-clocks to punch, Mrs. Wingfield. One at morning, another one at night!

AMANDA. My, but you *are* ambitious! You work at night, too?

JIM. No, Ma'am, not work but—Betty!

[*He crosses deliberately to pick up his hat. The band at the Paradise Dance Hall goes into a tender waltz.*]

AMANDA. Betty? Betty? Who's—Betty?

[*There is an ominous cracking sound in the sky.*]

480   JIM. Oh, just a girl. The girl I go steady with!

[*He smiles charmingly. The sky falls.*]

[*Legend:* "The Sky Falls."]

AMANDA [*a long-drawn exhalation*]. Ohhhh . . . Is it a serious romance, Mr. O'Connor?

JIM. We're going to be married the second Sunday in June.

AMANDA. Ohhhh—how nice! Tom didn't mention that you were engaged to be married.

JIM. The cat's not out of the bag at the warehouse yet. You know how they are. They call you Romeo and stuff like that. [*He stops at the oval mirror to put on his hat. He carefully shapes the brim and the crown to give a discreetly dashing effect.*] It's been a wonderful evening, Mrs. Wingfield. I guess this is what they meant by Southern hospitality.

AMANDA. It really wasn't anything at all.

490   JIM. I hope it don't seem like I'm rushing off. But I promised Betty I'd pick her up at the Wabash depot, an' by the time I get my jalopy down there her train'll be in. Some women are pretty upset if you keep 'em waiting.

AMANDA. Yes, I know—the tyranny of women! [*She extends her hand.*] Goodbye, Mr. O'Connor. I wish you luck—and happiness—and success! All three of them, and so does Laura. Don't you, Laura?

LAURA. Yes!

JIM [*taking* LAURA'S *hand*]. Goodbye, Laura. I'm certainly going to treasure that souvenir. And don't you forget the good advice I gave you. [*He raises his voice to a cheery shout.*] So long, Shakespeare! Thanks again, ladies. Good night!

[*He grins and ducks jauntily out. Still bravely grimacing,* AMANDA *closes the door on the gentleman caller. Then she turns back to the room with a puzzled expression. She and* LAURA *don't dare to face each other.* LAURA *crouches beside the Victrola to wind it.*]

500   AMANDA [*faintly*]. Things have a way of turning out so badly. I don't believe that I would play the Victrola. Well, well—well! Our gentleman caller was engaged to be married! [*She raises her voice.*] Tom!

TOM [*from the kitchenette*]. Yes, Mother?

AMANDA. Come in here a minute. I want to tell you something awfully funny.

TOM [*entering with a macaroon and a glass of the lemonade*]. Has the gentleman caller gotten away already?

AMANDA. The gentleman caller has made an early departure. What a wonderful joke you played on us!

TOM. How do you mean?

510   AMANDA. You didn't mention that he was engaged to be married.

JIM. Jim? Engaged?

AMANDA. That's what he just informed us.

TOM. I'll be jiggered! I didn't know about that.

AMANDA. That seems very peculiar.

TOM. What's peculiar about it?

AMANDA. Didn't you call him your best friend down at the warehouse?

TOM. He is, but how did I know?

AMANDA. It seems extremely peculiar that you wouldn't know your best friend was going to be married!

520 TOM. The warehouse is where I work, not where I know things about people!

AMANDA. You don't know things anywhere! You live in a dream; you manufacture illusions!

[*He crosses to the door.*]

Where are you going?

TOM. I'm going to the movies.

AMANDA. That's right, now that you've had us make such fools of ourselves. The effort, the preparations, all the expense! The new floor lamp, the rug, the clothes for Laura! All for what? To entertain some other girl's fiancé! Go to the movies, go! Don't think about us, a mother deserted, an unmarried sister who's crippled and has no job! Don't let anything interfere with your selfish pleasure! Just go, go, go—to the movies!

530 TOM. All right, I will! The more you shout about my selfishness to me the quicker I'll go, and I won't go to the movies!

AMANDA. Go, then! Go to the moon—you selfish dreamer!

[TOM *smashes his glass on the floor. He plunges out on the fire-escape, slamming the door.* LAURA *screams in fright. The dance-hall music becomes louder.* TOM *stands on the fire escape, gripping the rail. The moon breaks through the storm clouds, illuminating his face.*]

[*Legend on screen:* "And so goodbye . . ."]

[TOM's *closing speech is timed with what is happening inside the house. We see, as though through soundproof glass, that* AMANDA *appears to be making a comforting speech to* LAURA, *who is huddled upon the sofa. Now that we cannot hear the mother's speech, her silliness is gone and she has dignity and tragic beauty.* LAURA's *hair hides her face until, at the end of the speech, she lifts her head to smile at her mother.* AMANDA's *gestures are slow and graceful, almost dancelike, as she comforts her daughter. At the end of her speech she glances a moment at the father's picture—then withdraws through the portieres. At the close of* TOM's *speech,* LAURA *blows out the candles, ending the play.*]

TOM. I didn't go to the moon, I went much further—for time is the longest distance between two places. Not long after that I was fired for writing a poem on the lid of a shoe-box. I left Saint Louis. I descended the steps of this fire escape for a last time and followed, from then on, in my father's footsteps, attempting to find in motion what was lost in space. I traveled around a great deal. The cities swept about me like dead leaves, leaves that were brightly colored but torn away from the branches. I would have stopped, but I was pursued by something. It always came upon me un-

540 awares, taking me altogether by surprise. Perhaps it was a familiar bit of music. Perhaps it was only a piece of transparent glass. Perhaps I am walking along a street at night, in some strange city, before I have found companions. I pass the lighted window of a shop where perfume is sold. The window is filled with pieces of colored glass, tiny transparent bottles in delicate colors, like bits of a shattered rainbow. Then all at once my sister touches my shoulder. I turn around and look into her eyes. Oh,

Laura, Laura, I tried to leave you behind me, but I am more faithful than I intended to be! I reach for a cigarette, I cross the street, I run into the movies or a bar, I buy a drink, I speak to the nearest stranger—anything that can blow your candles out!

[LAURA *bends over the candles.*]

For nowadays the world is lit by lightning! Blow out your candles, Laura—and so goodbye. . . .

550

[*She blows the candles out.*]

(1944)

QUESTIONS

1. Williams called this "a memory play" since it is told by Tom long after the events have taken place. With this in mind, how trustworthy is Tom's version of the events depicted in the play? And is he correct in his decision to leave home?

2. If Tom really cares for Laura, why do you think that he is so careless in dealing with her feelings?

3. Describe the character of Laura and her relationship with Amanda and Tom. What prevents Laura from confiding in her brother Tom and her mother Amanda?

4. What does the menagerie of glass animals, especially the unicorn, reveal about Laura?

5. How does Amanda see her role as a wife and mother, and how has her point of view and value system shaped her children's lives?

6. Indicate several ways that Laura's life can be seen to parallel her brother Tom's life.

7. Why does Jim call Laura "Blue Roses"? How is this name for Laura so significant?

8. Discuss whether you believe Tom feels any remorse for abandoning Laura at the end of the play.

Writing Topics for Drama

1. Some critics argue that Amanda is a monster; some argue that she is a well-meaning mother who just gets carried away with feeling for her children. Take a position one way or the other, contrasting Amanda's flaws with her good qualities.

2. Discuss Tom's relationship with Laura. What is suggested in the final scene when Tom says, "Laura, Laura, I tried to leave you behind me, but I am more faithful than I intended to be!"

3. Analyze Tom's motives for bringing home Jim to meet Laura and Amanda. Is Tom naive or callous? Is he really trying to help ameliorate an unhappy situation or just unconsciously adding to its severity?

4. Amanda and Laura are defined by their lack of a male partner. Discuss what role Tom must play as a result.

5. Discuss Laura's case as a young woman trapped in a family with an overbearing mother and a callow brother.

6. Explain how the play's setting as described in the opening notes contributes to our understanding of the characters' actions and aspirations for a better future.

PART 2: SISTERS AND BROTHERS
CROSS-GENRE DISCUSSION AND WRITING TOPICS

1. Discuss the ways that biblical stories have been transformed by modern authors in Capetanakis's poem "Abel," Rolke's poem "I Am Not. The Brother Did Something to Me," Borges's short story "Legend," Wolff's short story "The Rich Brother," and Coover's short story "The Brother." Explain what part of the story each author selects to focus on, and then speculate on what you think might have motivated them to use these stories.

2. Contrast the relationship between the sisters in Perrault's folktale "Cinderella," Afans'ev's folktale "Vasilisa the Beautiful," Ozick's short story "The Shawl," and Sexton's poem "Cinderella." How is the conflict resolved for each? Explain why the resolution of each selection is so different.

3. Order of birth seems to play an important role in the way characters treat each other. Explain why birth order is so significant in Williams's play *The Glass Menagerie,* Hayslip's memoir "Sisters and Brothers," Heaney's poem "Mid-Term Break," Coover's short story "The Brother," Munro's short story "Girls and Boys," and Wolff's short story "The Rich Brother."

4. Write a memoir in which you consider your place in the sibling pecking order. You might provide experiences in which you shared pleasure and pain.

5. The narrator in Munro's short story "Girls and Boys," the narrator/character Tom in Williams's play *The Glass Menagerie,* and the speaker in Glück's poem "Gretel in Darkness" experience conflict regarding their relationships with siblings. Compare the traumatic events these figures in each poem share, and how their attitudes toward family and self lead them to deal with the consequences of their actions.

6. Analyze the way sisters or brothers seem to be opposites of each other in Wolff's short story "The Rich Brother," and Plath's poem "Two Sisters of Persephone." What conflicts are caused by this? It may be helpful to review Bettelheim's discussion of such relationships in his essay "Cinderella."

7. Analyze the choices open to women in Williams's play *The Glass Menagerie,* Munro's short story "Boys and Girls," and Plath's poem "Two Sisters of Persephone," considering the particular time and culture of each selection and the consequences these choices may generate. Explain whether or not you believe that these selections offer negative points of view of how a girl or woman was supposed to behave and whether these expectations of female behavior still exist today.

8. Contrast Glück's poem "Gretel in Darkness" and Sexton's poem "Hansel and Gretel" with the original story as told by the Grimm Brothers. What do you think the contemporary social significance is for Glück's and Sexton's revisions of the Grimms's "Hansel and Gretel"?

9. Examine how threatening circumstances can generate positive sibling relationships. Use the Grimms's folktale "Hansel and Gretel" and Hemingway's "Soldier's Home" to develop your thesis.

10. Some sisters and brothers seem luckier and more privileged in terms of looks, personality, health, wealth, or good fortune than their less fortunate siblings. Examine the best ways for dealing with these discrepancies, drawing on the selections in this section and on your own experience.

Sir Frank Dicksee (1853-1928), *La Belle Dame Sans Merci*. Exh. 1902 (oil on canvas). Bristol City Museum and Art Gallery. UK/Bridgeman Art Library.

PART 3

PEOPLE IN LOVE

One of life's great mysteries centers on the act of falling in love. We have no way of knowing when, why, and with whom we will fall in love or what the outcome will be. Romantic love evades rational choice, no matter how often family or friends might advise us to choose carefully. Love does not necessarily pay attention to age, race, class, or gender. It follows its own rules and can grow or diminish of its own accord. Because it is so unpredictable and elusive, romantic love has long been a favorite theme of writers.

Love can be passionate and overwhelming, catching us off our guard. In his essay "Romantic Love," Robert Solomon defines romantic love as "sexual in origin and motivation," "spontaneous and voluntary," and "appropriate only between equals." D. H. Lawrence's story "The Horse-Dealer's Daughter" evokes the mystery of love when it suddenly and overwhelmingly strikes. Lucius Apuleius embedded "The Myth of Cupid and Psyche" in his second-century "novel," *The Golden Ass,* to show how love is strong even in darkness and how truth in loving wins out over duplicity and jealousy. The story is about Psyche (which means "butterfly"), who is loved by Cupid, a god. Though it is improper for a god to love a mortal, the marriage of Cupid and Psyche does not end in despair. Because she perseveres and demonstrates her love, Psyche is elevated to the stature of a goddess. It is a story of the triumph of love and will over adversity. As the Chinese folktale "Faithful Even in Death" and Becky Birtha's story "In the Life" illustrate, love can even bloom in old age and continue after death.

At times love can turn dangerous, either physically, emotionally, or both. John Keats's poem "La Belle Dame sans Merci" depicts a knight forlornly waiting for his fairy princess to return and love him, and Anton Chekhov's story "The Lady with the Dog" shows how love can arise in inappropriate circumstances. Elizabeth Bishop's poem "One Art" subtly portrays the pain of loss when love has ended, and Katherine Mansfield's story "A Dill Pickle" suggests how differently two lovers view their romance long after it is over. Robert Browning's poem "Porphyria's Lover," Alfred, Lord Tennyson's poem "The Lady of Shalott," Ted Hughes's poem "Lovesong," and Arthur Miller's *A View from the Bridge* are about the destructive force of obsessive love.

Love may be humorous as in Andrew Marvell's poem "To His Coy Mistress," which offers a witty and persuasive argument for not postponing love. Love may be ironic as in William Shakespeare's sonnet "My Mistress' Eyes Are Nothing Like the Sun," in which the beautiful and the ugly are compared to his mistress's advantage. It may also be lighthearted and surreal, as in André Breton's poem "Free Union," where the speaker's love for his woman is described in bizarre and unexpected ways.

There are many ways of loving, as Elizabeth Barrett Browning's poem "How Do I Love Thee?" counts. Despite Barrett Browning's list, the experience of love remains elusive, mysterious, irrational, overpowering, and ineffable. Although writers are driven to find ways to put love into words, love is such an intense emotion that it can often be expressed only by comparing it to something else, as W. S. Merwin's poem "When You Go Away" and Robert Burns's poem "A Red, Red Rose" show. What is certain about love is that it is an emotion and an experience capable of plunging you into despair or lifting you up until you soar.

Myths, Parables, and Folktales

LUCIUS APULEIUS (FL. 125)

The Myth of Cupid and Psyche*

Edited by Thomas Bulfinch (1796–1867)

A certain king and queen had three daughters. The charms of the two elder were more than common, but the beauty of the youngest was so wonderful that the poverty of language is unable to express its due praise. The fame of her beauty was so great that strangers from neighboring countries came in crowds to enjoy the sight, and looked on her with amazement paying her that homage which is due only to Venus herself. In fact Venus[1] found her altars deserted, while men turned their devotion to this young virgin. As she passed along, the people sang her praises, and strewed her way with chaplets and flowers.

This perversion of homage due only to the immortal powers to the exaltation of a mortal gave great offence to the real Venus. Shaking her ambrosial locks with indignation, she exclaimed, "Am I then to be eclipsed in my honors by a mortal girl? In vain then did that royal shepherd, whose judgment was approved by Jove himself, give me the palm of beauty over my illustrious rivals, Pallas and Juno.[2] But she shall not so quietly usurp my honors. I will give her cause to repent of so unlawful a beauty."

Thereupon she calls her winged son Cupid,[3] mischievous enough in his own nature, and rouses and provokes him yet more by her complaints. She points out Psyche to him and says, "My dear son, punish that contumacious beauty; give thy mother a revenge as sweet as her injuries are great; infuse into the bosom of that haughty girl a

---

[1] Cupid: Roman name for Aphrodite, the Greek goddess of love.
[2] Jove: Roman name for Zeus, mightiest of the Greek gods; Pallas: name for Athena, Greek goddess of war and justice; Juno: Roman name for Hera, Greek goddess who is Zeus' wife and sister.
[3] Cupid: Roman name for Eros, a Greek Olympian who is a personification of Love. Eros' parents are said to be Aphrodite (Venus) and Hermes (Mercury).

passion for some low, mean, unworthy being, so that she may reap a mortification as great as her present exultation and triumph."

Cupid prepared to obey the commands of his mother. There are two fountains in Venus's garden, one of sweet waters, the other of bitter. Cupid filled two amber vases, one from each fountain, and suspending them from the top of his quiver, hastened to the chamber of Psyche, whom he found asleep. He shed a few drops from the bitter fountain over her lips, though the sight of her almost moved him to pity; then touched her side with the point of his arrow. At the touch she awoke, and opened eyes upon Cupid (himself invisible), which so startled him that in his confusion he wounded himself with his own arrow. Heedless of his wound, his whole thought now was to repair the mischief he had done, and he poured the balmy drops of joy over all her silken ringlets.

Psyche, henceforth frowned upon by Venus, derived no benefit from all her charms. True, all eyes were cast eagerly upon her, and every mouth spoke her praises; but neither king, royal youth, nor plebeian presented himself to demand her in marriage. Her two elder sisters of moderate charms had now long been married to two royal princes; but Psyche, in her lonely apartment, deplored her solitude, sick of that beauty which, while it procured abundance of flattery, had failed to awaken love.

Her parents, afraid that they had unwittingly incurred the anger of the gods, consulted the oracle of Apollo, and received this answer: "The virgin is destined for the bride of no mortal lover. Her future husband awaits her on the top of the mountain. He is a monster whom neither gods nor men can resist."

This dreadful decree of the oracle filled all the people with dismay, and her parents abandoned themselves to grief. But Psyche said, "Why, my dear parents, do you now lament me? You should rather have grieved when the people showered upon me undeserved honors, and with one voice called me a Venus. I now perceive that I am a victim to that name. I submit. Lead me to that rock to which my unhappy fate has destined me." Accordingly, all things being prepared, the royal maid took her place in the procession, which more resembled a funeral than a nuptial pomp, and with her parents, amid the lamentations of the people, ascended the mountain, on the summit of which they left her alone, and with sorrowful hearts returned home.

While Psyche stood on the ridge of the mountain, panting with fear and with eyes full of tears, the gentle Zephyr[4] raised her from the earth and bore her with an easy motion into a flowery dale. By degrees her mind became composed, and she laid herself down on the grassy bank to sleep. When she awoke refreshed with sleep, she looked around and beheld near by a pleasant grove of tall and stately trees. She entered it, and in the midst discovered a fountain, sending forth clear and crystal waters, and fast by, a magnificent palace whose august front impressed the spectator that it was not the work of mortal hands, but the happy retreat of some god. Drawn by admiration and wonder, she approached the building and ventured to enter. Every object she met filled her with pleasure and amazement. Golden pillars supported the vaulted roof, and the walls were enriched with carvings and paintings representing beasts of the chase and rural scenes, adapted to delight the eye of the beholder. Proceeding onward, she perceived

---

[4]Zephyr: also known as Zepherus, the god of the soft and gentle west wind.

that besides the apartments of state there were others filled with all manner and treasures, and beautiful and precious productions of nature and art.

While her eyes were thus occupied, a voice addressed her, though she saw no one, uttering these words: "Sovereign lady, all that you see is yours. We whose voices you hear are your servants and shall obey all your commands with our utmost care and diligence. Retire, therefore, to your chamber and repose on your bed of down, and when you see fit repair to the bath. Supper awaits you in the adjoining alcove when it pleases you to take your seat there."

Psyche gave ear to the admonitions of her vocal attendants, and after repose and the refreshment of the bath, seated herself in the alcove, where a table immediately presented itself, without any visible aid from waiters or servants, and covered with the greatest delicacies of food and the most nectareous wines. Her ears too were feasted with music from invisible performers; of whom one sang, another played on the flute, and all closed in the wonderful harmony of a full chorus.

She had not yet seen her destined husband. He came only in the hours of the darkness and fled before the dawn of morning, but his accents were full of love, and inspired a like passion in her. She often begged him to stay and let her behold him, but he would not consent. On the contrary he charged her to make no attempt to see him, for it was his pleasure, for the best of reasons, to keep concealed. "Why should you wish to behold me?" he said; "have you any doubt of my love? have you any wish ungratified? If you saw me, perhaps you would fear me, perhaps adore me, but all I ask of you is to love me. I would rather you would love me as an equal than adore me as a god."

This reasoning somewhat quieted Psyche for a time, and while the novelty lasted she felt quite happy. But at length the thought of her parents, left in ignorance of her fate, and of her sisters, precluded from sharing with her the delights of her situation, preyed on her mind and made her begin to feel her palace as but a splendid prison. When her husband came one night, she told him her distress, and at last drew from him an unwilling consent that her sisters should be brought to see her.

So, calling Zephyr, she acquainted him with her husband's commands, and he, promptly obedient, soon brought them across the mountain down to their sister's valley. They embraced her and she returned their caresses. "Come," said Psyche, "enter with me my house and refresh yourselves with whatever your sister has to offer." Then taking their hands she led them into her golden palace, and committed them to the care of her numerous train of attendant voices, to refresh them in her baths and at her table, and to show them all her treasures. The view of these celestial delights caused envy to enter their bosoms, at seeing their young sister possessed of such state and splendor, so much exceeding their own.

They asked her numberless questions, among others what sort of a person her husband was. Psyche replied that he was a beautiful youth, who generally spent the daytime in hunting upon the mountains. The sisters, not satisfied with this reply, soon made her confess that she had never seen him. Then they proceeded to fill her bosom with dark suspicions. "Call to mind," they said, "the Pythian oracle that declared you destined to marry a direful and tremendous monster. The inhabitants of this valley say that your husband is a terrible and monstrous serpent, who nourishes you for a while with dainties that he may by and by devour you. Take our advice. Provide yourself with a lamp and a sharp knife; put them in concealment that your husband may not discover them, and when he is sound asleep, slip out of bed, bring forth your lamp, and see for yourself whether what they say is true or not. If it is, hesitate not to cut off the monster's head, and thereby recover your liberty."

Psyche resisted these persuasions as well as she could, but they did not fail to have their effect on her mind, and when her sisters were gone, their words and her own curiosity were too strong for her to resist. So she prepared her lamp and a sharp knife, and hid them out of sight of her husband. When he had fallen into his first sleep, she silently rose and uncovering her lamp beheld not a hideous monster, but the most beautiful and charming of the gods, with his golden ringlets wandering over his snowy neck and crimson cheek, with two dewy wings on his shoulders, whiter than snow, and with shining feathers like the tender blossoms of spring. As she leaned the lamp over to have a nearer view of his face a drop of burning oil fell on the shoulder of the god, startled with which he opened his eyes and fixed them full upon her; then, without saying one word, he spread his white wings and flew out of the window. Psyche, in vain endeavoring to follow him, fell from the window to the ground. Cupid, beholding her as she lay in the dust, stopped his flight for an instant and said, "O foolish Psyche, is it thus you repay my love? After having disobeyed my mother's commands and made you my wife, will you think me a monster and cut off my head? But go; return to your sisters, whose advice you seem to think preferable to mine. I inflict no other punishment on you than to leave you forever. Love cannot dwell with suspicion." So saying, he fled away, leaving poor Psyche prostrate on the ground, filling the place with mournful lamentations.

When she had recovered some degree of composure she looked around her, but the palace and gardens had vanished, and she found herself in the open field not far from the city where her sisters dwelt. She repaired thither and told them the whole story of her misfortunes, at which, pretending to grieve, those spiteful creatures inwardly rejoiced. "For now," said they, "he will perhaps choose one of us." With this idea, without saying a word of her intentions, each of them rose early the next morning and ascended the mountains, and having reached the top, called upon Zephyr to receive her and bear her to his lord; then leaping up, and not being sustained by Zephyr, fell down the precipice and was dashed to pieces.

Psyche meanwhile wandered day and night, without food or repose, in search of her husband. Casting her eyes on a lofty mountain having on its brow a magnificent temple, she sighed and said to herself, "Perhaps my love, my lord, inhabits there," and directed her steps thither.

She had no sooner entered than she saw heaps of corn, some in loose ears and some in sheaves, with mingled ears of barley. Scattered about, lay sickles and rakes, and all the instruments of harvest, without order, as if thrown carelessly out of the weary reapers' hands in the sultry hours of the day.

This unseemly confusion the pious Psyche put an end to, by separating and sorting everything to its proper place and kind, believing that she ought to neglect none of the gods, but endeavor by her piety to engage them all in her behalf. The holy Ceres,[5]

---

[5] Ceres: the Roman name for Demeter, the goddess of agriculture and fertility.

whose temple it was, finding her so religiously employed, thus spoke to her: "O Psyche, truly worthy of our pity, though I cannot shield you from the frowns of Venus, yet I can teach you how best to allay her displeasure. Go, then, and voluntarily surrender yourself to your lady and sovereign, and try by modesty and submission to win her forgiveness, and perhaps her favor will restore you the husband you have lost."

Psyche obeyed the commands of Ceres and took her way to the temple of Venus, endeavoring to fortify her mind and ruminating on what she should say and how best propitiate the angry goddess, feeling that the issue was doubtful and perhaps fatal.

Venus received her with angry countenance. "Most undutiful and faithless of servants," said she, "do you at last remember that you really have a mistress? Or have you rather come to see your sick husband, yet laid up of the wound given him by his loving wife? You are so ill-favored and disagreeable that the only way you can merit your lover must be by dint of industry and diligence. I will make trial of your housewifery." Then she ordered Psyche to be led to the storehouse of her temple, where was laid up a great quantity of wheat, barley, millet, vetches, beans, and lentils prepared for food for her pigeons, and said, "Take and separate all these grains, putting all of the same kind in a parcel by themselves, and see that you get it done before evening." Then Venus departed and left her to her task.

But Psyche, in a perfect consternation at the enormous work, sat stupid and silent, without moving a finger to the inextricable heap.

While she sat despairing, Cupid stirred up the little ant, a native of the fields, to take compassion on her. The leader of the ant hill, followed by whole hosts of his six-legged subjects, approached the heap, and with the utmost diligence, taking grain by grain, they separated the pile, sorting each kind to its parcel; and when it was all done, they vanished out of sight in a moment.

Venus at the approach of twilight returned from the banquet of the gods, breathing odors and crowned with roses. Seeing the task done, she exclaimed, "This is no work of yours, wicked one, but his, whom to your own and his misfortune you have enticed." So saying, she threw her a piece of black bread for her supper and went away.

Next morning Venus ordered Psyche to be called and said to her, "Behold yonder grove which stretches along the margin of the water. There you will find sheep feeding without a shepherd, with golden-shining fleeces on their backs. Go, fetch me a sample of that precious wool gathered from every one of their fleeces."

Psyche obediently went to the riverside, prepared to do her best to execute the command. But the river god inspired the reeds with harmonious murmurs, which seemed to say, "O maiden, severely tried, tempt not the dangerous flood, nor venture among the formidable rams on the other side, for as long as they are under the influence of the rising sun, they burn with a cruel rage to destroy mortals with their sharp horns or rude teeth. But when the noontide sun has driven the cattle to the shade, and the serene spirit of the flood has lulled them to rest, you may then cross in safety, and you will find the woolly gold sticking to the bushes and the trunks of the trees."

Thus the compassionate river god gave Psyche instructions how to accomplish her task, and by observing his directions she soon returned to Venus with her arms full of golden fleece; but she received not the approbation of her implacable mistress, who said, "I know very well it is by none of your own doings that you have succeeded in this task, and I am not satisfied yet that you have any capacity to make yourself useful. But I have another task for you. Here, take this box and go your way to the infernal shades, and give this box to Proserpine[6] and say, 'My mistress Venus desires you to send her a little of your beauty, for in tending her sick son she has lost some of her own.' Be not too long on your errand, for I must paint myself with it to appear at the circle of the gods and goddesses this evening."

Psyche was now satisfied that her destruction was at hand, being obliged to go with her own feet directly down to Erebus.[7] Wherefore, to make no delay of what was not to be avoided, she goes to the top of a high tower to precipitate herself headlong, thus to descend the shortest way to the shades below. But a voice from the tower said to her, "Why, poor unlucky girl, dost thou design to put an end to thy days in so dreadful a manner? And what cowardice makes thee sink under this last danger who hast been so miraculously supported in all thy former?" Then the voice told her how by a certain cave she might reach the realms of Pluto, and how to avoid all the dangers of the road, to pass by Cerberus,[8] the three-headed dog, and prevail on Charon,[9] the ferryman, to take her across the black river and bring her back again. But the voice added, "When Proserpine has given you the box filled with her beauty, of all things this is chiefly to be observed by you, that you never once open or look into the box nor allow your curiosity to pry into the treasure of the beauty of the goddesses."

Psyche, encouraged by this advice, obeyed it in all things, and taking heed to her ways travelled safely to the kingdom of Pluto.[10] She was admitted to the palace of Proserpine, and without accepting the delicate seat or delicious banquet that was offered her, but contented with coarse bread for her food, she delivered her message from Venus. Presently the box was returned to her, shut and filled with the precious commodity. Then she returned the way she came, and glad was she to come out once more into the light of day.

But having got so far successfully through her dangerous task, a longing desire seized her to examine the contents of the box. "What," said she, "shall I, the carrier of this divine beauty, not take the least bit to put on my cheeks to appear to more advantage in the eyes of my beloved husband!" So she carefully opened the box, but found nothing there of any beauty at all, but an infernal and truly Stygian[11] sleep, which being thus set free from its prison, took possession of her, and she fell down in the midst of the road, a sleepy corpse without sense or motion.

But Cupid, being now recovered from his wound, and not able longer to bear the absence of his beloved Psyche, slipping through the smallest crack of the window of his chamber which happened to be left open, flew to the spot where Psyche lay, and

---

[6] Proserpine: the Roman name for Persephone, daughter of Demeter, wife of Hades, and queen of the Underworld.

[7] Erebus: a place of extreme darkness through which souls passed on the way to Hades, the Underworld; also personified as a "shade," or dweller in the Underworld.

[8] Cerberus: the watchdog of Hades, the Underworld, who forbade living people from entering. He had three dog's heads, a serpent's tail, and a back covered with the heads of snakes.

[9] Charon: the ferryman who carries the dead over the marshes of the Underworld and across the river Styx.

[10] Pluto: also called Hades, the Greek god of the Underworld. The Romans renamed him as Dis.

[11] Stygian: from the River Styx, meaning dark, gloomy, and binding.

gathering up the sleep from her body closed it again in the box, and waked Psyche with a light touch of one of his arrows. "Again," said he, "hast thou almost perished by the same curiosity. But now perform exactly the task imposed on you by my mother, and I will take care of the rest."

Then Cupid, as swift as lightning penetrating the heights of heaven, presented himself before Jupiter with his supplication. Jupiter lent a favoring ear, and pleaded the cause of the lovers so earnestly with Venus that he won her consent. On this he sent Mercury[12] to bring Psyche up to the heavenly assembly, and when she arrived, handing her a cup of ambrosia, he said, "Drink this, Psyche, and be immortal; nor shall Cupid ever break away from the knot in which he is tied, but these nuptials shall be perpetual."

Thus Psyche became at last united to Cupid, and in due time they had a daughter born to them whose name was Pleasure.

Commentary by Bulfinch

The fable of Cupid and Psyche is usually considered allegorical. The Greek name for a *butterfly* is Psyche, and the same word means the *soul*. There is no illustration of the immortality of the soul so striking and beautiful as the butterfly, bursting on brilliant wings from the tomb in which it has lain, after a dull, grovelling, caterpillar existence, to flutter in the blaze of day and feed on the most fragrant and delicate productions of the spring. Psyche, then, is the human soul, which is purified by sufferings and misfortunes, and is thus prepared for the enjoyment of true and pure happiness.

In works of art Psyche is represented as a maiden with the wings of a butterfly, along with Cupid, in the different situations described in the allegory.

(2ND CENTURY)

QUESTIONS

1. Why must Cupid remain invisible to Psyche, and their love be subject to darkness?

2. Why does Psyche give in to the demands of her jealous sisters and break her pledge? What trials must Psyche successfully complete in order to prove that she is worthy of Cupid's love, and what is her reward?

3. What do the names Cupid and Psyche mean, and how does their marriage symbolize wholeness?

---

[12] Mercury: the Roman name for Hermes, the messenger of Jupiter (Zeus). Hermes invented the lyre and pipes; he is a protector of heroes, a god of travel and commerce. Hermes usually is seen wearing distinctive winged shoes and a broad-brimmed hat, and carrying a winged staff.

Ovid (43 b.c.e.–17 c.e.)

The Myth of Pygmalion

Translated by Mary M. Inness

When Pygmalion[1] saw these women, living such wicked lives, he was revolted by the many faults which nature has implanted in the female sex, and long lived a bachelor existence, without any wife to share his home. But meanwhile, with marvellous artistry, he skillfully carved a snowy ivory statue. He made it lovelier than any woman born, and fell in love with his own creation. The statue had all the appearance of a real girl, so that it seemed to be alive, to want to move, did not modesty forbid. So cleverly did his art conceal its art. Pygmalion gazed in wonder, and in his heart there rose a passionate love for this image of a human form. Often he ran his hands over the work, feeling it to see whether it was flesh or ivory, and would not yet admit that ivory was all it was. He kissed the statue, and imagined that it kissed him back, spoke to it and embraced it, and thought he felt his fingers sink into the limbs he touched, so that he was afraid lest a bruise appear where he had pressed the flesh. Sometimes he addressed it in flattering speeches, sometimes brought the kind of presents that girls enjoy: shells and polished pebbles, little birds and flowers of a thousand hues, lilies and painted balls, and drops of amber which fall from the trees that were once Phaethon's sisters.[2] He dressed the limbs of his statue in woman's robes, and put rings on its fingers, long necklaces round its neck. Pearls hung from its ears, and chains were looped upon its breast. All this finery became the image well, but it was no less lovely unadorned. Pygmalion then placed the statue on a couch that was covered with cloths of Tyrian purple, laid its head to rest on soft down pillows, as if it could appreciate them, and called it his bedfellow.

The festival of Venus,[3] which is celebrated with the greatest pomp all through Cyprus, was now in progress, and heifers, their crooked horns gilded for the occasion, had fallen at the altar as the axe struck their snowy necks. Smoke was rising from the incense, when Pygmalion, having made his offering, stood by the altar and timidly prayed, saying: "If you gods can give all things, may I have as my wife, I pray—" he did not dare to say: "the ivory maiden," but finished: "one like the ivory maid." However, golden Venus, present at her festival in person, understood what his prayers meant, and as a sign that the gods were kindly disposed, the flames burned up three times, shooting a tongue of fire into the air. When Pygmalion returned home, he made straight for the statue of the girl he loved, leaned over the couch, and kissed her. She seemed warm: he laid his lips on hers again, and touched her breast with his hands—at his touch the ivory lost its hardness, and grew soft: his fingers made an imprint on the yielding surface, just

---

[1] Pygmalian: the king of Cyprus.
[2] Phaeton's sisters wept so piteously at his death that they were transformed into poplar trees and their tears into amber.
[3] Venus: the Roman name for Aphrodite, goddess of love.

as wax of Hymettus melts in the sun and, worked by men's fingers, is fashioned into many different shapes, and made fit for use by being used. The lover stood, amazed, afraid of being mistaken, his joy tempered with doubt, and again and again stroked the object of his prayers. It was indeed a human body! The veins throbbed as he pressed them with his thumb. Then Pygmalion of Paphos[4] was eloquent in his thanks to Venus. At long last, he pressed his lips upon living lips, and the girl felt the kisses he gave her, and blushed. Timidly raising her eyes, she saw her lover and the light of day together. The goddess Venus was present at the marriage she had arranged and, when the moon's horns had nine times been rounded into a full circle, Pygmalion's bride[5] bore a child, Paphos, from whom the island takes its name.

(c. 8)

Questions

1. Why does Pygmalion find solace with only a make-believe woman?
2. What is the point of Aphrodite's compassion for Pygmalion?
3. Discuss whether the happy ending of this myth is necessary to convey its message.

---

[4] Paphos: an ancient city in southwest Cyprus.
[5] Pygmalion's bride: Galatea.

Faithful Even in Death*

Translated by Wolfram Eberhard

The village of the Liang family and that of the Chu family were close together. The inhabitants were well-to-do and content. Old excellency Liang and old excellency Chu were good friends. A son was born to the Liang family, who was given the name Hsienpo. Being an unusually quick and clever child, he was sent to the school in the town.

At the same time a daughter was born to the Chu family, who, besides being very clever, was particularly beautiful. As a child she loved to read and study, and only needed to glance at a book to know a whole sentence by heart. Old Chu simply doted on her. When she grew up, she wanted to go away and study. Her father tried in vain to dissuade her, but eventually he arranged for her to dress as a boy and study with Hsienpo.

The two lived together, worked together, argued together, and were the best of friends. The eager and zealous Hsienpo did not notice that Yingt'ai was really a girl, and therefore he did not fall in love with her. Yingt'ai studied so hard and was so wrapped up in her work that her fellow students paid no attention to her. Being very modest, and never taking part in the children's jokes, she exercised a calming influence over even the most impudent. When she slept with Hsienpo, each lay on one side of the bed, and between them stood a bowl of water. They had arranged that whoever knocked over the bowl must pay a fine; but the serious little Hsienpo never touched it.

When Yingt'ai changed her clothes, she never stood about naked but pulled on her clean clothes under the old ones, which she then took off and finished dressing. Her fellow students could not understand why she did this, and asked her the reason. "Only peasants expose the body they have received from their parents," she said; "it should not be done." Then the boys began to copy her, not knowing her real reason was to prevent their noticing that she was a girl.

Then her father died, and her sister-in-law, who did not approve of Yingt'ai's studying, ordered her to come home and learn housework. But Yingt'ai refused and continued to study.

The sister-in-law, fearing that Yingt'ai had fallen in love with Hsienpo, used to send her from time to time babies' things, swaddling clothes, children's clothes and covers, and many other things. The students became curious when they saw the things, and Yingt'ai could tell them only that they were the things she herself had used as a child, which her sister-in-law was now sending her to keep.

---

* Also known as "The Butterfly Lover."

The time passed quickly. Soon Yingt'ai and Hsienpo were grown up. Yingt'ai still dressed as a man, and being a well-brought-up girl, she did not dare to ask Hsienpo to marry her; but when she looked at him, her heart was filled with love. His delicate manner attracted her irresistibly, and she swore to marry him and none other.

She proposed the marriage to her sister-in-law, who did not consider it suitable, because after her father's death they had lost all their money. Against Yingt'ai's will the sister-in-law arranged a match with a Dr. Ma, of a newly rich family in the village. Yingt'ai objected strongly, but she could do nothing about it. Day after day she had to listen to complaints: she was without filial piety, she was a shameless, decadent girl, a disgrace to the family. Her sister-in-law still feared she might secretly marry Hsienpo, and she urged the Ma family to appoint a day for the wedding. Then she cut off Yingt'ai's school money, which forced her to return home.

Yingt'ai was obliged to hide her misery. Weeping bitterly, she said good-bye to Hsienpo, who accompanied her part of the way home. As they separated, Yingt'ai sang a song which revealed that she was a girl and that she wanted to marry him. But the good, dense Hsienpo did not understand her hints. He did not see into Yingt'ai's heart, and tried to comfort her by telling her that one must return home some time and that they would soon meet again. Yingt'ai saw that everything was hopeless, and went home in tears.

Hsienpo felt very lonely without his companion, with whom he had lived day and night for many years. He kept on writing letters to Yingt'ai, begging her to come back to school, but he never received a reply.

Finally he could bear it no longer, and went to visit her. "Is Mr. Yingt'ai at home?" he asked. "Please tell him his school friend, Hsienpo, has come and wants to see him."

The servant looked at him curiously, and then said curtly, "There is no Mr. Yingt'ai here—only a Miss Yingt'ai. She is to be married soon, and naturally she can't leave her room. How could she speak to a man? Please go away, sir, for if the master discovers you, he will make a complaint against you for improper behavior."

Suddenly everything was clear to Hsienpo. In a state of collapse he crept home. There he found, under Yingt'ai's books, a bundle of letters and essays which showed him clearly how deeply Yingt'ai loved him and also that she did not want to marry any other man. Through his own stupidity, his lack of understanding, the dream had come to nought.

Overcome by remorse, he spent the days lost in tears. Yingt'ai was always before his eyes, and in his dreams he called her name, or cursed her sister-in-law and Dr. Ma, himself, and all the ways of society. Because he ceased to eat or drink, he fell ill and gradually sank into the grave.

Yingt'ai heard the sad news. Now she had nothing more to live for. If she had not been so carefully watched, she would have done herself some injury. In this state of despair the wedding day arrived. Listlessly she allowed herself to be pushed into the red bridal chair and set off for the house of her bridegroom, Dr. Ma. But when they passed the grave of Hsienpo, she begged her attendants to let her get out and visit it, to thank him for all his kindness. On the grave, overcome by grief, she flung herself down and sobbed. Her attendants urged her to return to her chair, but she refused. Finally, after great persuasion, she got up, dried her tears, and, bowing several times in front of the grave, she prayed as follows: "You are Hsienpo, and I am Yingt'ai. If we were really intended to be man and wife, open your grave three feet wide."

Scarcely had she spoken when there came a clap like thunder and the grave opened. Yingt'ai leaped into the opening, which closed again before the maids could catch hold of her, leaving only two bits of her dress in their hands. When they let these go, they changed into two butterflies which flew up into the air.

Dr. Ma was furious when he heard that his wife had jumped into the grave of Hsienpo. He had the grave opened, but the coffin was empty except for two white stones. No one knew where Hsienpo and Yingt'ai had gone. In a rage the grave violators flung the two stones onto the road, where immediately a bamboo with two stems shot up. They were shimmering green, and swayed in the wind. The grave robbers knew that this was the result of magic, and cut down the bamboo with a knife; but as soon as they had cut down one, another shot up, until finally several people cut down the two stems at the same time. Then these flew up to heaven and became rainbows.

Now the two lovers have become immortals. If they ever want to be together, undisturbed and unseen, so that no one on earth can see them or even talk about them, they wait until it is raining and the clouds are hiding the sky. The red in the rainbow is Hsienpo, and the blue is Yingt'ai.

(C. 1368 OR EARLIER)

QUESTIONS

1. Can you explain why no one notices that Yingt'ai is a woman? Why is Hsienpo so dense?

2. What elements in this folktale give it an air of unreality and make it seem a fairy tale? What is the importance of the role of magic in resolving the grief of the lovers?

3. What does this folktale suggest about the social and cultural obligations of men and women in Chinese culture?

4. Explain the symbolism of the bamboo, butterflies, and rainbow.

JEANNE-MARIE LE PRINCE DE BEAUMONT (1711–1780)

Beauty and the Beast

Translated by Dinah Maria Muluck Craik

There was once a very rich merchant, who had six children, three boys and three girls. As he was himself a man of great sense, he spared no expense for their education. The three daughters were all handsome, but particularly the youngest; indeed, she was so very beautiful, that in her childhood everyone called her the Little Beauty; and being equally lovely when she was grown up, nobody called her by any other name, which made her sisters very jealous of her. This youngest daughter was not only more handsome than her sisters, but also was better tempered. The two eldest were vain of their wealth and position. They gave themselves a thousand airs, and refused to visit other merchants' daughters; nor would they condescend to be seen except with persons of quality.

They went every day to balls, plays, and public walks, and always made game of their youngest sister for spending her time in reading and other useful employments. As it was well known that these young ladies would have large fortunes, many great merchants wished to get them for wives; but the two eldest always answered, that, for their parts, they had no thoughts of marrying anyone below a duke or an earl at least. Beauty had quite as many offers as her sisters, but she always answered, with the greatest civility, that though she was obliged to her lovers, she would rather live some years longer with her father, as she thought herself too young to marry.

It happened that, by some unlucky accident, the merchant suddenly lost all his fortune, and had nothing left but a small cottage in the country. Upon this he said to his daughters, while the tears ran down his cheeks, "My children, we must now go and dwell in the cottage, and try to get a living by labor, for we have no other means of support." The two eldest replied that they did not know how to work, and would not leave town; for they had lovers enough who would be glad to marry them, though they had no longer any fortune. But in this they were mistaken; for when the lovers heard what had happened, they said: "The girls were so proud and ill-tempered, that all we wanted was their fortune; we are not sorry at all to see their pride brought down; let them show off their airs to their cows and sheep." But everybody pitied poor Beauty, because she was so sweet-tempered and kind to all, and several gentlemen offered to marry her, though she had not a penny; but Beauty still refused, and said she could not think of leaving her poor father in this trouble. At first Beauty could not help sometimes crying in secret for the hardships she was now obliged to suffer; but in a very short time she said to herself, "All the crying in the world will do me no good, so I will try to be happy without a fortune."

When they had removed to their cottage, the merchant and his three sons employed themselves in plowing and sowing the fields, and working in the garden. Beauty also did her part, for she rose by four o'clock every morning, lighted the fires, cleaned the house, and got ready the breakfast for the whole family. At first she found all this very hard; but she soon grew quite used to it, and thought it no hardship; indeed, the work greatly benefited her health. When she had done, she used to amuse herself with reading, playing her music, or singing while she spun. But her two sisters were at a loss what to do to pass the time away; they had their breakfast in bed, and did not rise till ten o'clock. Then they commonly walked out, but always found themselves very soon tired; when they would often sit down under a shady tree, and grieve for the loss of their carriage and fine clothes, and say to each other, "What a mean-spirited, poor stupid creature our young sister is, to be so content with this low way of life!" But their father thought differently; and loved and admired his youngest child more than ever.

After they had lived in this manner about a year the merchant received a letter, which informed him that one of his richest ships, which he thought was lost, had just come into port. This news made the two eldest sisters almost mad with joy; for they thought they should now leave the cottage, and have all their finery again. When they found that their father must take a journey to the ship, the two eldest begged he would not fail to bring them back some new gowns, caps, rings, and all sorts of trinkets. But Beauty asked for nothing; for she thought in herself that all the ship was worth would hardly buy everything her sisters wished for. "Beauty," said the merchant, "you ask for nothing: what can I bring you, my child?"

"Since you are so kind as to think of me, dear father," she answered, "I should be glad if you would bring me a rose, for we have none in our garden." Now Beauty did not indeed wish for a rose, nor anything else, but she only said this that she might not affront her sisters; otherwise they would have said she wanted her father to praise her for desiring nothing. The merchant took his leave of them, and set out on his journey; but when he got to the ship, some persons went to law with him about the cargo, and after a deal of trouble he came back to his cottage as poor as he had left it. When he was within thirty miles of his home, and thinking of the joy of again meeting his children, he lost his way in the midst of a dense forest. It rained and snowed very hard, and besides, the wind was so high as to throw him twice from his horse. Night came on, and he feared he should die of cold and hunger, or be torn to pieces by the wolves that he heard howling around him. All at once, he cast his eyes toward a long avenue, and saw at the end a light, but it seemed a great way off. He made the best of his way toward it, and found that it came from a splendid palace, the windows of which were all blazing with light. It had great bronze gates, standing wide open, and fine courtyards, through which the merchant passed; but not a living soul was to be seen. There were stables, too, which his poor, starved horse, less scrupulous than himself, entered at once, and took a good meal of oats and hay. His master then tied him up, and walked toward the entrance hall, but still without seeing a single creature. He went on to a large dining parlor, where he found a good fire, and a table covered with some very nice dishes, but only one plate with a knife and fork. As the snow and rain had wetted him to the skin, he went up to the fire to dry himself. "I hope," said he, "the master of the house or his servants will excuse me, for it surely will not be long now before I see them." He waited some time, but still nobody came: at last the clock struck eleven, and the merchant, being quite faint for the want of food, helped himself to a chicken, and to a few glasses of wine, yet all the time trembling with fear. He sat till the clock struck twelve, and then, taking courage, began to think he might as well look about him: so he opened a door at the end of the hall, and went through it into a very grand room, in which there was a fine bed; and as he was feeling very weary, he shut the door, took off his clothes, and got into it.

It was ten o'clock in the morning before he awoke, when he was amazed to see a handsome new suit of clothes laid ready for him, instead of his own, which were all torn and spoiled. "To be sure," said he to himself, "this place belongs to some good fairy, who has taken pity on my ill luck." He looked out of the window, and instead of the snow-covered wood, where he had lost himself the previous night, he saw the most charming arbors covered with all kinds of flowers. Returning to the hall where he had supper, he found a breakfast table, ready prepared. "Indeed, my good fairy," said the merchant aloud, "I am vastly obliged to you for your kind care of me." He then made a hearty breakfast, took his hat, and was going to the stable to pay his horse a visit; but as he passed under one of the arbors, which was loaded with roses, he thought of what Beauty had asked him to bring back to her, and so he took a bunch of roses to carry home. At the same moment he heard a loud noise, and saw coming toward him a beast, so frightful to look at that he was ready to faint with fear. "Ungrateful man!" said the beast in a terrible voice. "I have saved your life by admitting you into my palace, and in return you steal my roses, which I value more than anything I possess. But you shall atone for your fault—die in a quarter of an hour."

The merchant fell on his knees, and clasping his hands, said, "Sir, I humbly beg your pardon: I did not think it would offend you to gather a rose for one of my daughters, who had entreated me to bring her one home. Do not kill me, my lord!"

"I am not a lord, but a beast," replied the monster. "I hate false compliments: so do not fancy that you can coax me by any such ways. You tell me that you have daughters; now I will suffer you to escape, if one of them will come and die in your stead. If not, promise you will yourself return in three months, to be dealt with as I may choose."

The tender-hearted merchant had no thoughts of letting any one of his daughters die for his sake; but he knew that if he seemed to accept the beast's terms, he should at least have the pleasure of seeing them once again. So he gave his promise, and was told that he might then set off as soon as he liked. "But," said the beast, "I do not wish you to go back empty-handed. Go to the room you slept in, and you will find a chest there; fill it with whatsoever you like best, and I will have it taken to your own house for you."

When the beast said this, he went away. The good merchant, left to himself, began to consider that, as he must die—for he had no thought of breaking a promise, made even to a beast—he might as well have the comfort of leaving his children provided for. He returned to the room he had slept in, and found there heaps of gold pieces lying about. He filled the chest with them to the very brim, locked it, and, mounting his horse, left the palace as sorrowful as he had been glad when he first beheld it. The horse took a path across the forest of his own accord, and in a few hours they reached the merchant's house. His children came running round him, but, instead of kissing them with joy, he could not help weeping as he looked at them. He held in his hand the bunch of roses, which he gave to Beauty, saying, "Take these roses, Beauty; but little do you think how dear they have cost your poor father"; and then he gave them an account of all that he had seen or heard in the palace of the beast.

The two eldest sisters now began to shed tears, and to lay the blame upon Beauty, who, they said, would be cause of her father's death. "See," said they, "what happens from the pride of the little wretch; why did not she ask for such things as we did? But, to be sure, Miss must not be like other people; and though she will be the cause of her father's death, yet she does not shed a tear."

"It would be useless," replied Beauty, "for my father shall not die. As the beast will accept one of his daughters, I will give myself up, and be only too happy to prove my love for the best of fathers."

"No, sister," said the three brothers with one voice, "that cannot be; we will go in search of this monster, and either he or we will perish."

"Do not hope to kill him," said the merchant, "his power is far too great. But Beauty's young life shall not be sacrificed; I am old, and cannot expect to live much longer; so I shall but give up a few years of my life, and shall only grieve for the sake of my children."

"Never, father," cried Beauty; "if you go back to the palace, you cannot hinder my going after you! Though young, I am not over-fond of life; and I would much rather be eaten up by the monster, than die of grief for your loss."

The merchant in vain tried to reason with Beauty who still obstinately kept to her purpose; which, in truth, made her two sisters glad, for they were jealous of her, because everybody loved her.

The merchant was so grieved at the thought of losing his child, that he never once thought of the chest filled with gold, but at night, to his great surprise, he found it standing by his bedside. He said nothing about his riches to his eldest daughters, for he knew very well it would at once make them want to return to town; but he told Beauty his secret, and she then said, that while he was away, two gentlemen had been on a visit at her cottage, who had fallen in love with her two sisters. She entreated her father to marry them without delay, for she was so sweet-natured she only wished them to be happy.

Three months went by, only too fast, and then the merchant and Beauty got ready to set out for the palace of the beast. Upon this, the two sisters rubbed their eyes with an onion, to make believe they were crying; both the merchant and his sons cried in earnest. Only Beauty shed no tears. They reached the palace in a very few hours, and the horse, without bidding, went into the stable as before. The merchant and Beauty walked toward the large hall, where they found a table covered with every dainty and two plates laid already. The merchant had very little appetite; but Beauty, that she might the better hide her grief, placed herself at the table, and helped her father; she then began to eat herself, and thought all the time that, to be sure, the beast had a mind to fatten her before he ate her up, since he had provided such good cheer for her. When they had done their supper, they heard a great noise, and the good old man began to bid his poor child farewell, for he knew that it was the beast coming to them. When Beauty first saw that frightful form, she was very much terrified, but tried to hide her fear. The creature walked up to her, and eyed her all over—then asked her in a dreadful voice if she had come quite of her own accord.

"Yes," said Beauty.

"Then you are a good girl, and I am very much obliged to you."

This was such an astonishingly civil answer that Beauty's courage rose: but it sank again when the beast, addressing the merchant, desired him to leave the palace next morning, and never return to it again. "And so good night, merchant. And good night, Beauty."

"Good night, beast," she answered, as the monster shuffled out.

"Ah! my dear child," said the merchant, kissing his daughter, "I am half dead already, at the thought of leaving you with this dreadful beast; you shall go back and let me stay in your place."

"No," said Beauty, boldly, "I will never agree to that; you must go home tomorrow morning."

They then wished each other good night, and went to bed, both of them thinking they should not be able to close their eyes; but as soon as ever they had lain down, they fell in to a deep sleep, and did not awake till morning. Beauty dreamed that a lady came up to her, who said, "I am very much pleased, Beauty, with the goodness you have shown, in being willing to give your life to save that of your father. Do not be afraid of anything; you shall not go without a reward."

As soon as Beauty awoke she told her father this dream; but though it gave him some comfort, he was a long time before he could be persuaded to leave the palace. At last Beauty succeeded in getting him safely away.

When her father was out of sight, poor Beauty began to weep sorely; still, having naturally a courageous spirit, she soon resolved not to make her sad case still worse by sorrow, which she knew was vain, but to wait and be patient. She walked about to take a view of all the palace, and the elegance of every part of it much charmed her.

But what was her surprise, when she came to a door on which was written, BEAUTY'S ROOM! She opened it in haste, and her eyes were dazzled by the splendor and taste of the apartment. What made her wonder more than all the rest, was a large library filled with books, a harpsichord, and many pieces of music. "The beast surely does not mean to eat me up immediately," said she, "since he takes care I shall not be at loss how to amuse myself." She opened the library and saw these verses written in letters of gold in the back of one of the books:

"Beauteous lady, dry your tears,
Here's no cause for sighs or fears.
Command as freely as you may,
For you command and I obey."

"Alas!" said she, sighing: "I wish I could only command a sight of my poor father, and to know what he is doing at this moment." Just then, by chance, she cast her eyes upon a looking-glass that stood near her, and in it she saw a picture of her old home, and her father riding mournfully up to the door. Her sisters came out to meet him, and although they tried to look sorry, it was easy to see that in their hearts they were very glad. In a short time all this picture disappeared, but it caused Beauty to think that the beast, besides being very powerful, was also very kind. About the middle of the day she found a table laid ready for her, and a sweet concert of music played all the time she was dining, without her seeing anybody. But at supper, when she was going to seat herself at table, she heard the noise of the beast, and could not help trembling with fear.

"Beauty," said he, "will you give me leave to see you sup?"

"That is as you please," answered she, very much afraid.

"Not in the least," said the beast. "You alone command in this place. If you should not like my company, you need only say so, and I will leave you that moment. But tell me, Beauty, do you not think me very ugly?"

"Why, yes," said she, "for I cannot tell a falsehood; but then I think you are very good."

"Am I?" sadly replied the beast. "Yet, besides being ugly, I am also very stupid; I know well enough that I am but a beast."

"Stupid people," said Beauty, "are never aware of it themselves."

At which kindly speech the beast looked pleased, and replied, not without an awkward sort of politeness. "Pray do not let me detain you from supper, and be sure that you are well served. All you see is your own, and I should be deeply grieved if you wanted for anything."

"You are very kind—so kind that I almost forgot you are so ugly," said Beauty, earnestly.

"Ah! yes," answered the beast, with a great sigh; "I hope I am good-tempered, but still I am only a monster."

"There is many a monster who wears the form of a man; it is better of the two to have the heart of a man and the form of a monster."

"I would thank you, Beauty, for this speech, but I am too senseless to say anything that would please you," returned the beast in a melancholy voice; and altogether he seemed so gentle and so unhappy that Beauty, who had the tenderest heart in the world, felt her fear of him gradually vanish.

She ate her supper with a good appetite, and conversed in her own sensible and charming way, till at last, when the beast rose to depart, he terrified her more than ever by saying abruptly, in his gruff voice, "Beauty, will you marry me?"

Now Beauty, frightened as she was, would speak only the exact truth; besides her father had told her that the beast liked only to have the truth spoken to him. So she answered, in a very firm tone, "No, beast."

He did not get into a passion, but sighed deeply and departed.

When Beauty found herself alone, she began to feel pity for the poor beast. "Oh," she said, "what a sad thing it is that he should be so very frightful, since he is so good-tempered!"

Beauty lived three months in this palace very well pleased. The beast came to see her every night, and talked with her while she supped; and though what he said was not very clever, yet, as she saw in him every day some new goodness, instead of dreading the time of his coming, she soon began continually looking at her watch, to see if it were nine o'clock; for that was the hour when he never failed to visit her. One thing only vexed her, which was that every night before he went away, he always made it a rule to ask her if she would be his wife, and seemed very much grieved at her steadfastly replying "No." At last, one night, she said to him, "You wound me greatly, beast, by forcing me to refuse you so often; I wish I could take such a liking to you as to agree to marry you; but I must tell you plainly that I do not think it will ever happen. I shall always be your friend; so try to let that content you."

"I must," sighed the beast, "for I know well enough how frightful I am; but I love you better than myself. Yet I think I am very lucky in your being pleased to stay with me; now promise, Beauty, that you will never leave me."

Beauty would almost have agreed to this, so sorry was she for him, but she had that day seen in her magic glass, which she looked at constantly, that her father was dying of grief for her sake.

"Alas!" she said. "I long so much to see my father, that if you do not give me leave to visit him, I shall break my heart."

"I would rather break mine, Beauty," answered the beast; "I will send you to your father's cottage: you shall stay there, and your poor beast shall die of sorrow."

"No," said Beauty, crying, "I love you too well to be the cause of your death; I promise to return in a week. You have shown me that my sisters are married, and my brothers are gone for soldiers, so that my father is left all alone. Let me stay a week with him."

"You shall find yourself with him tomorrow morning," replied the beast; "but mind, do not forget your promise. When you wish to return, you have nothing to do but to put your ring on a table when you go to bed. Good-bye, Beauty!" The beast sighed as he said these words, and Beauty went to bed very sorry to see him so much grieved. When she awoke in the morning, she found herself in her father's cottage. She rang a bell that was at her bedside, and a servant entered; but as soon as she saw Beauty, the woman gave a loud shriek; upon which the merchant ran upstairs, and when he beheld his daughter he ran to her, and kissed her a hundred times. At last Beauty began to remember that she had brought no clothes with her to put on; but the servant told her she had just found in the next room a large chest full of dresses, trimmed all over with gold, and adorned with pearls and diamonds.

Beauty, in her own mind, thanked the beast for his kindness, and put on the plainest gown she could find among them all. She then desired the servant to lay the rest aside, for she intended to give them to her sisters; but, as soon as she had spoken these words, the chest was gone out of sight in a moment. Her father then suggested, perhaps the beast chose for her to keep them all for herself: and as soon as he had said this, they saw the chest standing again in the same place. While Beauty was dressing herself, a servant brought word to her that her sisters were come with their husbands to pay her a visit. They both lived unhappily with the gentlemen they had married. The husband of the eldest was very handsome, but was so proud of this that he thought of nothing else from morning till night, and did not care a pin for the beauty of his wife. The second had married a man of great learning; but he made no use of it, except to torment and affront all his friends, and his wife more than any of them. The two sisters were ready to burst with spite when they saw Beauty dressed like a princess, and looking so very charming. All the kindness that she showed them was of no use; for they were vexed more than ever when she told them how happy she lived at the palace of the beast. The spiteful creatures went by themselves into the garden, where they cried to think of her good fortune.

"Why should the little wretch be better off than we?" said they. "We are much handsomer than she is."

"Sister," said the eldest, "a thought has just come into my head; let us try to keep her here longer than the week for which the beast gave her leave; and then he will be so angry that perhaps when she goes back to him he will eat her up in a moment."

"That is well thought of," answered the other, "but to do this, we must pretend to be very kind."

They then went to join her in the cottage, where they showed her so much false love that Beauty could not help crying for joy.

When the week was ended, the two sisters began to pretend such grief at the thought of her leaving them that she agreed to stay a week more; but all that time Beauty could not help fretting for the sorrow that she knew her absence would give her poor beast; for she tenderly loved him, and much wished for his company again. Among all the grand and clever people she saw, she found nobody who was half so sensible, so affectionate, so thoughtful, or so kind. The tenth night of her being at the cottage, she dreamed she was in the garden of the palace, that the beast lay dying on a grass plot, and with his last breath put her in mind of her promise, and laid his death to her forsaking him. Beauty awoke in a great fright, and she burst into tears. "Am not I wicked," said she, "to behave so ill to a beast who has shown me so much kindness? Why will I not marry him? I am sure I should be more happy with him than my sisters are with their husbands. He shall not be wretched any longer on my account; for I should do nothing but blame myself all the rest of my life."

She then rose, put her ring on the table, got into bed again, and soon fell asleep. In the morning she with joy found herself in the palace of the beast. She dressed herself very carefully, that she might please him the better, and thought she had never known a day pass away so slowly. At last the clock struck nine, but the beast did not come. Beauty, dreading lest she might truly have caused his death, ran from room to room, calling out: "Beast, dear beast"; but there was no answer. At last she remembered her dream, rushed to the grass plot, and there saw him lying apparently dead beside the fountain. Forgetting all his ugliness, she threw herself upon his body, and finding his heart still beating, she fetched some water and sprinkled it over him, weeping and sobbing the while.

The beast opened his eyes. "You forgot your promise, Beauty, and so I determined to die; for I could not live without you. I have starved myself to death, but I shall die content since I have seen your face once more."

"No, dear beast," cried Beauty, passionately, "you shall not die; you shall live to be my husband. I thought it was only friendship I felt for you, but now I know it was love."

The moment Beauty had spoken these words, the palace was suddenly lighted up, and all kinds of rejoicings were heard around them, none of which she noticed, but hung over her dear beast with the utmost tenderness. At last, unable to restrain herself, she dropped her head over her hands, covered her eyes, and cried for joy; and, when she looked up again, the beast was gone. In his stead she saw at her feet a handsome, graceful young prince, who thanked her with the tenderest expressions for having freed him from enchantment.

"But where is my poor beast? I only want him and nobody else," sobbed Beauty.

"I am he," replied the prince. "A wicked fairy condemned me to this form, and forbade me to show that I had any wit or sense, till a beautiful lady should consent to marry me. You alone, dearest Beauty, judged me neither by my looks nor by my talents, but by my heart alone. Take it then, and all that I have besides, for all is yours."

Beauty, full of surprise, but very happy, suffered the prince to lead her to his palace, where she found her father and sisters, who had been brought there by the fairy lady whom she had seen in a dream the first night she came.

"Beauty," said the fairy, "you have chosen well, and you have your reward, for a true heart is better than either good looks or clever brains. As for you, ladies," and she turned to the two elder sisters, "I know all your ill deeds, but I have no worse punishment for you than to see your sister happy. You shall stand as statues at the door of her palace, and when you repent of and have amended your faults, you shall become women again. But, to tell you the truth, I very much fear you will remain statues forever."

(1756)

QUESTIONS

1. What social and moral qualities make Beauty a model young woman and provide for her rewards?

2. Why are her sisters turned into statues, and how can this punishment be seen to fit their crime?

3. What role does magic play in this tale, and why does Beauty merit the intervention of the grand fairy?

4. What does this tale suggest about the ambiguity of beauty and ugliness? What change of heart prompts Beauty to fall in love with the Beast as he is, and why does she seem somewhat disappointed when the Beast turns into a handsome prince? What do you think this reveals about her?

5. Who seems to be the primary audience for this tale? What is the moral of this tale?

The Lady of Shalott

Edited by Thomas Bulfinch (1796–1867)

King Arthur proclaimed a solemn tournament to be held at Winchester. The king, not less impatient than his knights for this festival, set off some days before to superintend the preparations, leaving the queen with her court at Camelot. Sir Launcelot, under pretence of indisposition, remained behind also. His intention was to attend the tournament in disguise; and having communicated his project to Guenever, he mounted his horse, set off without any attendant, and, counterfeiting the feebleness of age, took the most unfrequented road to Winchester, and passed unnoticed as an old knight who was going to be a spectator of the sports. Even Arthur and Gawain, who happened to behold him from the windows of a castle under which he passed, were the dupes of his disguise. But an accident betrayed him. His horse happened to stumble, and the hero, forgetting for a moment his assumed character, recovered the animal with a strength and agility so peculiar to himself that they instantly recognized the inimitable Launcelot. They suffered him, however, to proceed on his journey without interruption, convinced that his extraordinary feats of arms must discover him at the approaching festival.

In the evening, Launcelot was magnificently entertained as a stranger knight at the neighboring castle of Shalott. The lord of this castle had a daughter of exquisite beauty and two sons lately received into the order of knighthood, one of whom was at that time ill in bed and thereby prevented from attending the tournament, for which both brothers had long made preparations. Launcelot offered to attend the other, if he were permitted to borrow the armor of the invalid, and the lord of Shalott, without knowing the name of his guest, being satisfied from his appearance that his son could not have a better assistant in arms, most thankfully accepted the offer. In the meantime the young lady, who had been much struck by the first appearance of the stranger knight, continued to survey him with increased attention, and, before the conclusion of supper, became so deeply enamored of him that, after frequent changes of color and other symptoms which Sir Launcelot could not possibly mistake, she was obliged to retire to her chamber and seek relief in tears. Sir Launcelot hastened to convey to her, by means of her brother, the information that his heart was already disposed of, but that it would be his pride and pleasure to act as her knight at the approaching tournament. The lady, obliged to be satisfied with that courtesy, presented him her scarf to be worn at the tournament.

Launcelot set off in the morning with the young knight, who, on their approaching Winchester, carried him to the castle of a lady, sister to the lord of Shalott, by whom they were hospitably entertained. The next day they put on their armor, which was perfectly plain, and without any device, as was usual to youths during the first year of knighthood, their shields being only painted red, as some color was necessary to enable them to be recognized by their attendants. Launcelot wore on his crest the scarf of the maid of Shalott, and, thus equipped, proceeded to the tournament, where the knights were divided into two companies, the one commanded by Sir Gallehaut,[1] the other by King Arthur. Having surveyed the combat for a short time from without the lists and observed that Sir Gallehaut's party began to give way, they joined the press and attacked the royal knights, the young man choosing such adversaries as were suited to his strength, while his companion selected the principal champions of the Round Table and successively overthrew Gawain, Bohort, and Lionel. The astonishment of the spectators were extreme, for it was thought that no one but Launcelot could possess such invincible force; yet the favor on his crest seemed to preclude the possibility of his being thus disguised, for Launcelot had never been known to wear the badge of any but his sovereign lady. At length, Sir Hector, Launcelot's brother, engaged him and, after a dreadful combat, wounded him dangerously in the head, but was himself completely stunned by a blow on the helmet and felled to the ground, after which the conqueror rode off at full speed, attended by his companion.

They returned to the castle of Shalott, where Launcelot was attended with the greatest care by the good earl, by his two sons, and, above all, by his fair daughter, whose medical skill probably much hastened the period of his recovery. His health was almost completely restored when Sir Hector, Sir Bohort, and Sir Lionel, who, after the return of the court to Camelot, had undertaken the quest of their relation, discovered him walking on the walls of the castle. Their meeting was very joyful; they passed three days in the castle amidst constant festivities and bantered each other on the events of the tournament. Launcelot, though he began by vowing vengeance against the author of his wound, yet ended by declaring that he felt rewarded for the pain by the pride he took in witnessing his brother's extraordinary prowess. He then dismissed them with a message to the queen, promising to follow immediately, it being necessary that he should first take a formal leave of his kind hosts, as well as of the fair maid of Shalott.

The young lady, after vainly attempting to detain him by her tears and solicitations, saw him depart without leaving her any ground for hope.

It was early summer when the tournament took place; but some months had passed since Launcelot's departure, and winter was now near at hand. The health and strength of the Lady of Shalott had gradually sunk, and she felt that she could not live apart from the object of her affections. She left the castle and, descending to the river's brink, placed herself in a boat, which she loosed from its moorings and suffered to bear her down the current towards Camelot.

One morning, as Arthur and Sir Lionel looked from the window of the tower, the walls of which were washed by a river, they descried a boat, richly ornamented and covered with an awning of cloth of gold, which appeared to be floating down the stream without any human guidance. It struck the shore while they watched it, and they hastened down to examine it. Beneath the awning they discovered the dead body of a beautiful woman, in whose features Sir Lionel easily recognized the lovely maid of Shalott. Pursuing their search, they discovered a purse richly embroidered with gold and jewels, and within the purse a letter, which Arthur opened, and found addressed to himself and all the knights of the Round Table, stating that Launcelot of the Lake, the most accomplished of

---

[1] Gallehaut: more often spelled Gallahad.

knights and most beautiful of men, but at the same time the most cruel and inflexible, had by his rigor produced the death of the wretched maiden, whose love was no less invincible than his cruelty. The king immediately gave orders for the interment of the lady, with all the honors suited to her rank, at the same time explaining to the knights the history of her affection for Launcelot, which moved the compassion and regret of all.

Tennyson[2] has chosen the story of the Lady of Shalott for the subject of a poem. The catastrophe is told thus:

> Under tower and balcony,
> By garden-wall and gallery,
> A gleaming shape she floated by,
> A corse between the houses high,
>   Silent into Camelot.
> Out upon the wharfs they came,
> Knight and burgher, lord and dame,
> And round the prow they read her name,
>   "The Lady of Shalott."
>
> Who is this? and what is here?
> And in the lighted palace near
> Died the sound of royal cheer;
> And they crossed themselves for fear,
>   All the knights at Camelot.
> But Launcelot mused a little space;
> He said, "She has a lovely face;
> God in his mercy lend her grace,
>   The Lady of Shalott."

QUESTIONS

1. What is the impulse that attracts the Lady of Shalott to Sir Launcelot, especially since he is disguised as an old man?

2. Explain how this folktale depicts the myth of "knight in shining armor." How, in particular, does it portray the character of Sir Launcelot of the Lake?

3. What does the extreme outcome of "The Lady of Shalott" suggest about the power of romantic and/or unrequited love?

---

[2] See Alfred, Lord Tennyson, "The Lady of Shalott" p. 451.

JALAL AL-DIN RUMI (1207–1273)

The lover and the letter, on complete absorption*

A Sufi Parable, translated by A. J. Arberry

A Lover, being admitted to sit beside his beloved, thereupon drew out a letter and read it to her. The letter, which was in verse, told over her praises together with much lamentation, misery and supplication.

'If all this is for my sake,' said the beloved, 'to read this now you are with me is a sheer waste of time. Here I am beside you, and you read a letter! This is certainly not the sign of a true lover.'

'True, you are here with me,' the lover replied. 'All the same, I am not enjoying myself as well as I should. Though we are united now, I am not experiencing what I did last year on your account. I have drunk limpid water from this fountain, I have refreshed my eyes and my heart. I still see the fountain, but there is no water; perchance some foot-pad has cut off my water!'

'Then,' said his lady, 'I am not your beloved. I am in Tartary,[1] while your desire is in Cathay.[2] You are in love with me and with a certain emotion together, and the emotion eludes your grasp, young man. So I am not the entire object of your quest; at this moment I am only a part of your aim. I am the dwelling-place of the beloved, not the beloved herself. True love is fixed on the gold and not on the coffer.'

(C. 1256–1273)

QUESTIONS

1. Explain what seems to be wrong with the lover's method of wooing, according to his beloved.

2. What is the lover's complaint? What does the water symbolize for him?

3. What is paradoxical about the lady's statement, "I am the dwelling place of the beloved, not the beloved herself"?

4. Discuss your opinion of the effect that the lady's coolness has on her lover.

Writing Topics for Myths, Parables, and Folktales

1. Discuss the similarities of plot, character, and morality in de Beaumont's "Beauty and the Beast" and Apuleius's "The Myth of Cupid and Psyche."

---

*This selection is from *Tales from the Masnavi*.
[1] Tartary: a region in Eastern Europe and Central Asia ruled by the Tartars during the Middle Ages.
[2] Cathay: another name for China, no longer used.

2. Compare Bulfinch's "Lady of Shalott" and Psyche of Apuleius's "The Myth of Cupid and Psyche." What differences in their roles account for the differences in their circumstances at the end of each story? How can the portrayal of each woman be seen as exemplifying the male point of view of each type of woman?

3. Secrets, disguises, and transformation often seem to be ingredients in love stories. What role do they play in Apuleius's "The Myth of Cupid and Psyche," Ovid's "The Myth of Pygmalion," de Beaumont's "Beauty and the Beast," and the Chinese folktale "Faithful Even in Death"?

4. In what ways does Freud's essay "The Theme of the Three Caskets" (see p. 219) illuminate Apuleius's "The Myth of Cupid and Psyche" and de Beaumont's "Beauty and the Beast"? What other meanings might be derived from this myth and folktale?

5. What insights about the state of being in love does Rumi's "The Lover and the letter, on complete absorption" reveal? Can you make any connections between this parable and the folktales in this section?

Essays

ANDREA HOPKINS (N.D.)

The Marriage of True Minds*

A furious debate raged in the Middle Ages about the nature of love. Could true love exist within marriage? This is not without relevance today when for many couples matrimony can herald the end of romance. In a sense the whole idea of courtly love developed in response to social circumstances in which marriage was often likely to be loveless—when it was arranged for political or economic considerations. But marriages of affection were not unknown, even in the twelfth century, and for some writers marriage seemed the natural outcome of successful love. Some writers however, saw romantic love as different in kind from the affection between married people.

In the first two books of his treatise Andreas Capellanus[1] maintained his stance on the incompatibility of true love and marriage. In one of his dialogues which details a conversation between a nobleman and a gentlewoman, the lady advances the argument that she ought not to grant him her love because she has a very good and noble husband who loves her with all his heart, and whom she loves in return. This leads to an extended discussion of the possibility and propriety of true love within marriage. The nobleman argues that the affection between husband and wife is not the same thing as true love; while the gentlewoman disagrees with him.

Perceiving that they will never agree, the two of them refer the dispute to the arbitration of the great Countess Marie of Champagne,[2] whose definitive decision is as follows:

> We state and consider as firmly established, that love cannot exert its powers between two married people. For lovers give everything to one another freely, not by

---

*This is an excerpt from *The Book of Courtly Love: The Passionate Code of the Troubadours* (1994).
[1] Andreas Capellanus (flourished in the 1180s): best known for his book *De Arte Honeste Amandi* (also called *De Amore*, the Book of Love).
[2] Countess Marie de Champagne (1100–1100): the patron of Andreas Capellanus.

reason of force or necessity. Married people, on the other hand, have to obey each other's wishes out of duty, and can deny nothing of themselves to one another. Besides, how does it increase a husband's honor, if he enjoys his wife's embraces like a lover, since neither of them will be improved in worth and virtue by this, and they seem to possess nothing but what they have always had a right to? And we shall assert yet another reason: for a precept of love informs us, that no woman, even a married woman, can be crowned with the prize of the King of Love unless she is perceived to be enlisted in love's service outside the bonds of matrimony. And indeed another rule of love teaches that no one can be wounded by love for two men. Therefore, Love cannot rightly acknowledge that he has any rights between married people.

(Andreas Capellanus, *De Arte,* Book I, chapter VI, dialogue 7)

The examples of alleged real-life cases submitted to the judgment of certain eminent ladies also unequivocally support the argument that love is not possible between married people. Andreas cites three: in the first case, a lady who had a perfectly good lover was subsequently married, through no fault of her own, to someone else, and as a result she avoided her lover and refused to see him anymore. The lover appealed for judgment to the Countess Ermengard of Narbonne, whose verdict, in accordance with the first of Andreas' rules of love, was that the lady's marriage did not constitute an acceptable reason for terminating her love affair:

Entering into a new union of marriage does not by rights exclude a previous love, unless the woman gives up making time for love altogether, is disposed to love no one at all any more.

(Andreas Capellanus, *De Arte,* Book II, chapter VII, decision 8)

In the second instance the same noble lady was invited to pronounce on whether the greatest affection existed between married people or between lovers. She gave a masterly response, according to the style of scholarly dispute, that it was not possible to make valid comparisons between things that differ in kind, thus claiming of course that these are two things differing in kind, and saving herself from having to advance an argument in support of that proposition.

The third example is the most outrageous of all:

A certain knight was bound by love to a woman who was tied to the love of another man, but from her he got this much hope of her love: that, if at some time she happened to be deprived of the love of her lover, then without a doubt she would grant her love to this knight.

A short time later, this same woman and her lover were married. The knight then demanded to be shown the fruition of the hope she had given him; the woman however absolutely refused, saying that she had not lost her beloved's love. In this case, the Queen responded as follows: "We do not dare to set ourselves against the opinion of the Countess of Champagne, who set down as her judgment that love cannot exert any power between husband and wife. Therefore we recommend that the lady should make good her promise of love."

Though we can probably agree that the affection of married people is a different sort of things from passionate love, this is clearly absurd.

In addition, Andreas Capellanus wrote in the third book of his treatise a retraction of everything he said in the first two volumes. Here he confirms that it is really wicked to pursue love outside marriage, for many good reasons: it is disobedient to God's law, it injures your neighbor to sleep with his wife, it leads to selfishness and alienates all your friends; it causes you to suffer the terrible agonies of jealousy; it makes a man into a slave because he has to be obedient to the whims of his beloved; it makes lovers poor because of the requirement of generosity; it leads to loss of reputation, and to all sorts of serious crimes; and most of all, because it is a mortal sin and leads to eternal damnation. He particularly condemns love for being the frequent cause of broken marriages, and for leading men to kill their wives. He then goes on to speak of the great advantages of a good marriage:

> For a man ought not to love anything in this life as much as the wife to whom he is rightfully and legitimately joined, for God has declared that a wife is one flesh with her husband, and he commanded her, forsaking all others, to cleave to him. . . Besides, we overcome our lust without sin with a wife, and we remove the incentives to rank excess without staining our souls; and we recognize legitimate offspring by our wives, who will offer us suitable comforts both living and dying, and in them God will be able to perceive our fruit.

> (Andreas Capellanus, *De Arte,* Book III)

Which of these completely opposite views are we to take as Andreas' real opinion? Probably Book III, which expresses the genuine disapproval of the medieval churchman for a phenomenon opposed to the laws of the Church, and of the member of an ordered society for something chaotic, powerful, and potentially destructive. His treatise was popular among medieval readers for it was a parody of courtly love pushed to the limits. But Andreas was parodying something real, and there is plenty of evidence from other sources to suggest that his nonsensical arguments about love being impossible within marriage were based on the poetry of the troubadours, and other medieval love literature. In the poems of the troubadours, all the ladies who were the objects of their affections were married, and most were of a higher rank than their lover; and the most famous of lovers from medieval romance, Lancelot and Guinevere, and Tristan and Isolt, were all in the same classic circumstances, in which a young man has fallen in love with the wife of his overlord. Other romances in which love takes place outside marriage include *Lanval, Flamenca,* and *Troilus and Criseyde.*[3] In *Flamenca,* too, the lady is a married woman and the knight is a bachelor. In these circumstances the love affair must be adulterous because the lovers cannot marry one another. This is not the case however in *Troilus and Criseyde,* where the hero is a bachelor and the heroine a widow. There is no

---

[3] *Troilus and Criseyde*: the longest complete poem by Geoffrey Chaucer (c. 1340–1400).

obvious reason why Troilus and Criseyde should not simply get married to one another, but it never seems to occur to them to do this—they just take it for granted that a love affair and not a marriage is the natural sequel to the pains of love. There were nevertheless several romances in which the goal of the lovers was clearly marriage; for example in *Cligès*,[4] *Yvain, Perceval, Les Deuz Amanz, Guy of Warwick, Floris and Blanchefleur, Aucassin and Nicolette, The Knight's Tale,* and the very interesting *Franklin's Tale,*[5] in which a married lady is approached by a young bachelor knight, but wishes to remain faithful to the husband she loves. The most important of these as a contributor to the debate is *Cligès,* which seems to have been written partly to refute the idea that love within marriage is inappropriate and to provide a specific counter to the popular tale of *Tristan and Yseult.*[6] In *Cligès,* the heroine Fenice has fallen in love with Cligès, but is betrothed to his uncle, the Emperor Alis. Miserably unhappy at the prospect of marriage to a man she detests, she confides in her nurse Thessala, and accounts for her sorrow:

> I would rather be torn limb from limb than that the love of we two should be remembered like the love of Tristan and Yseult, of which so much nonsense is talked that I am ashamed to speak of it. I could not agree to the life Yseult led. Love was too cheapened in her, who gave her whole heart to one man, while two enjoyed the favors of her body. Thus she spent her life, and never refused them both. That love was not rational, but mine shall be constant forever, for nothing will ever cause my heart to go one way and my body another. My body will never be a whore, and two men will never share it. He who has my heart shall have my body; all others I reject.

> (Chrétien de Troyes, *Cligès,* ll 3098–3124)

This is a very determined rejection of those precepts of courtly love which dictate that love can only be experienced as something separate from marriage. The same contradiction preoccupies us today. There is nothing so wonderful as to be overpowered by the sweep of romantic love, but everyone acknowledges that after several years of marriage this usually simmers down to a calmer, and ideally more enduring , affection and respect. Thereafter the perilous delights of passion can only be had outside marriage; yet we have been conditioned by our culture to expect that people who are in love with one another will get married, and "live happily ever after" in some effortless way. It is not really very surprising that the middle and upper classes of medieval Europe, untutored in the idea that it is wicked to marry someone you do not love, came up with a system in which marriage was more of a business partnership and nothing whatever to do with love; it is more surprising that we should recognize in so many of the stories in medieval love literature the urge felt by lovers to marry, to celebrate their love in a union blessed by society, and set hopefully forward on a life together.

---

[4] Chrétien de Troyes (flourished 1170–1190): regarded as the greatest writer of courtly romance. *Cligès, Yvain, Perceval* are among his most famous romances.
[5] "The Knight's Tale" and "The Franklin's Tale" are included in Chaucer's most important work, *The Canterbury Tales* (1387–1400).
[6] *Tristan and Yseult* (also called Isoud): a popular courtly romance perhaps written by Chrétien de Troyes.

Romantic Love After the Middle Ages

The Occitan culture that had nurtured the troubadours was destroyed in the first half of the thirteenth century. In 1209 Pope Innocent III proclaimed a crusade against certain heretical sects who were based throughout the south of France. For the next thirty years war was enthusiastically waged against the people of rich Occitania by the overpopulated and impoverished North; in 1244 the last stronghold of the heretics, the mountain fortress of Monségur, was taken; everyone inside perished. The society, laws, language, and culture of Occitania were smashed forever, and the poetry of the troubadours, which the Church found particularly offensive, was silenced.

But by then it was too late to stop the spread of the religion of love. The troubadours had given voice to something essential, fundamental, deeply rooted. Their view of romantic love had already spread over the whole of western Europe, and it was never to be absent from its literature or from its living consciousness again. The concept of love as obsessive, as a source of insecurity, fear and pain, but yet as potentially yielding the greatest happiness obtainable by human beings in this life, of love as a power for good which refines and ennobles its practitioners, and as something which triumphs over all obstacles—these ideas have become so central to our thought and culture that they seem natural. We scarcely question them or think of them as the direct inheritance of a distant set of historical circumstances; novels and films are still being written and made, nineteen to the dozen, celebrating romantic love.

It seems that people clung to this ideal through all the changes and developments of the succeeding centuries. For, when the Middle Ages faded and were superseded by the sparkling triumphs of the Renaissance, their cultural achievements were thoroughly despised. The cold clear light of classical Roman and Greek civilization with its reason, philosophy, law, art and architecture, led people to condemn the Middle Ages as a time of barbarism, superstition, and ignorance. Speaking of Sir Thomas Malory's great masterpiece *Le Morte d'Arthur*,[7] the Elizabethan theorist Roger Ascham memorably commented:

> . . . the whole of which booke standeth in two speciall poyntes, in open mans slaughter and bold bawdrye: In which booke these be counted the noblest knightes, that do kill most men without any quarell, and commit foulest adulteries by subtlest shiftes.[8]

In the Middle Ages people had inherited a view of their own culture as the poor remains of a more glorious past; thus the splendors of the Roman world were remembered with loving nostalgia in the Dark Ages and beyond. But in the Renaissance people began to look forward with energy and pride, and to see their culture as better than what had gone before, and in a state of calm but continual improvement—an attitude that

---

[7] *Le Morte d'Arthur* (1470): the most famous telling of the story of King Arthur completed by Sir Thomas Malory shortly before his death in 1471.

[8] Roger Ascham (1515–1568): an English classical scholar and essayist.

still prevails today. From the worst excesses of courtly love this new consciousness shrank, appalled. Why should a man make himself the slave of a woman, when he was clearly the superior creature? Why would anyone allow themselves to be dominated by a hopeless, unrequited passion? Why would anyone bring on themselves the misery and guilt of an adulterous love affair? But romantic love, the enduring myth that had sprung from the troubadours and matured in medieval romance, continued to inspire poetry and influence behavior. Even at the height of the Age of Reason, with its distrust of passion and excess, Love was, if not as busy as in the twelfth century, never successfully banished. Men still wooed women courteously, respectfully; they continued to feel that they would be rewarded by her love only after demonstrating their devotion. Literary lovers still found themselves suffering for love, struck by love's darts, slain by beautiful eyes, though they expressed their feelings in new and exciting ways and used the old clichés of medieval romance with tongue in cheek.

But in the final decades of the eighteenth century there was a revolt against reason. The Romantic movement wanted passion, cultivated sensibility, rejected cold logic. At the same time there was a renewal of interest in medieval art and literature, which developed in the first half of the nineteenth century into the great Victorian obsession with medieval culture. Painters like the Pre-Raphaelite Brotherhood[9] strove to obtain the massively detailed realism and jewel-like brilliance and clarity of late medieval art; splendidly elaborate neo-Gothic architecture appeared; books commending the medieval ideal of chivalry reinterpreted for modern times were a great success; the great poets and novelists, notably Scott, Keats, Browning, Tennyson,[10] took medieval subjects for some of their major works. But the Victorians created their own version of medieval ideas. It is principally through the rose-tinted and slightly distorting lenses of Victorian perception that we are familiar today with the concepts of chivalry and courtly love. They brought the nineteenth century's agonized moral consciousness to their subjects, and were far more judgmental than any medieval source. Here, for example, is Tennyson's account of what King Arthur said to Guinevere in their final interview together, after the destruction of the Round Table Fellowship:

> I made them lay their hands in mine and swear
> To reverence their King, as if he were their conscience,
>   and their conscience as their King,
> To break the heathen and uphold the Christ,
> To ride abroad addressing human wrongs,
> To speak no slander, no, nor listen to it,
> To honor his own word as if his God's,
> To lead sweet lives in purest chastity,
> To love one maiden only, cleave to her
> And worship her by years of noble deeds,

---

[9] Pre-Raphaelite Brotherhood: a group of English artists, poets, and writers formed about 1848 whose works were greatly influenced by Raphael (1483–1520) and the style of fifteenth-century Italy.
[10] Sir Walter Scott (1771–1832), John Keats (1798–1824), Robert Browning (1812–1889), and Alfred, Lord Tennyson (1809–1892).

Until they won her; for indeed I knew
Of no more subtle master under heaven
Than is the maiden passion for a maid,
Not only to keep down the base in man,
But teach high thought, and amiable words
And courtliness, and the desire of fame,
And love of truth, and all that makes a man . . .
And all this throve before I wedded thee,
Believing, "Lo, mine helpmate, one to feel
My purpose and rejoicing in my joy."
Then came thy shameful sin with Lancelot;
Then came the sin of Tristan and Isolt;
Then others, following these my mightiest knights,
And drawing foul ensample from fair names,
Sinned also, til the loathesome opposite
Of all my heart had destined did obtain,
And all thro' thee!

(Tennyson, "Morte d'Arthur," *Idylls of the King*)

Medieval authors too had fully appreciated the destructive potential of romantic love, but no medieval person would ever insist on the conjunction of love with chastity and purity.

And so romantic love has come down to us in the final years of the twentieth century, as a consummation devoutly to be wished, and yet fearsomely difficult to obtain. We are brought up from birth with the idea that love makes life worthwhile, that it seductively promises the intensest happiness of personal fulfillment, and that although there may be other reasons for marrying, it is hopelessly wicked to marry without affection. Yet the various pains of disappointment, rejection, jealousy and betrayal are the other side of the coin and cause untold suffering to those unlucky in love. Is romantic love merely an artistic sublimation of sexual attraction? Or is it the expression of something much deeper in the human soul? Is it all an elaborate game, or the true business of life? We leave the judgment in the hands of the reader.

(1994)

Questions

1. Explain how Hopkins defines the way "romantic love" was regarded during the Middle Ages. What were some of the requirements for it to exist?

2. What role did the troubadours play in encouraging "romantic love"?

3. How does Hopkins's essay depict the differences between "romantic love" and "marital love"? Do you think these distinctions still exist?

ROBERT SOLOMON (B. 1942)

About Love*

I Love You

What we call "love" is a social invention, a construction of concepts that serve a very special function in our society. What we call "love" is not a universal phenomenon but a culture-specific interpretation of the universal phenomena of sexual attraction and its complications. Love may begin in biology, but it is essentially a set of ideas, ideas that may even turn against the biological impulses that are their source. The history of romantic love is the history of a special set of attitudes toward sex, even where sex is never mentioned, and if love seems so elusive that is in part because sex is so obviously tangible. Love is, as Willard Gaylin keeps telling us, "so much more" than sex, but it is that "so much more" that is so elusive, and the reason is that it is our own doing and it changes even as we are looking at it.

"Love" is first of all a word, a word we are taught to honor, a word that we are urged to use. It is not long after "dating" that one feels compelled, as one has been taught, to describe what one feels as love. The timing is essential: unless you are exceedingly confident and/or resistant to humiliation, one does not proclaim love at a first meeting. One should be cautious about first saying it during sex; it may not be taken seriously. Waiting too long does not increase the impact but reduces it, like the climax of a movie gone on too long. But it is our saying "love"—not feeling it—that is responsible for the existence and importance of love in our society. How many people would be in love, wrote the writer and aphorist La Rochefoucauld[1] two centuries ago, if they had never heard the word? The answer is "none of us," for to love is not to experience a natural sensation but rather to participate in one of the great ongoing innovations of modern Western culture.

It should not surprise us then that the definitive moment in love is not the moment of meeting, the first longing look or the initial touch or caress. It is not making love or the feeling of love but the word "love"—or rather "three little words," one referring to self, the third to the other and the verb tying the two together in a novel and perhaps terrifying complex of intentions, obligations, and social expectations. To be sure, love involves desire and feeling, but if love were just a desire or a feeling, there would be no need to announce it or even put a name on it, much less identify it as the most important event of our lives. We would not worry about the possibility of getting it wrong or wonder about whether or not it was "true." We would not feel so compelled to write poetry about it. There would be little cause for anxiety or embarrassment, much less sleepless nights and endless confusion. If love were, as the cynics say, nothing but

---

*This selection is an excerpt from *About Love* © 1988 by Robert Solomon.
[1] François, duc de La Rochefoucauld (1613–1680): a French author whose fame rests on *Maxims* (1665), a collection of moral maxims expressing a pessimistic view of the world.

"ignorance and deprivation" (Kingsley Amis in *Lucky Jim*)[2] or "lust plus the ordeal of civility" (Freud), it would be hard to imagine why it should be so important, why it should matter so much *whom* one loved, much less whether one is loved in return, why it would be anything more than an itch in need of a scratch easily satisfied or forgotten. It would not be clear why the desire for love to last—not for a while but "forever"—should be so essential to the emotion, nor would it be at all evident why the emotion should be so desirable in the first place.

To say "I love you" is not to report a feeling and it is not just the expression of a feeling. It is an aggressive, creative, socially definitive act, which among other things places the other person in an unexpected and very vulnerable position. The question may involve a long period of deliberation and shy hesitation. We might just blurt it out without any preparation at all, surprising even ourselves. It may follow months of passion and companionship or it might come immediately upon meeting, following a strangely long, hypnotic "hello." It is not so terrible, of course, if he or she is willing and ready with the one acceptable response, namely, "I love you too." But nothing else will do. No excuses are appropriate. One cannot say "How interesting" or "How curious, I'm in love with someone too." "You'll get over it" is outright cruelty, and silence isn't much better. But from that moment on, nothing will ever be the same. From that moment on, there is no going back. (Imagine saying "I love you" to someone by mistake, and then trying to explain how it was that you "didn't mean it.") From that moment on, there will be the need to keep saying it, day after day, year after year.

Why is the phrase so significant? Because it signifies a decision and presents an invitation, perhaps a dilemma, which may well change the whole of one's life. The phrase, like the emotion, is at its very heart *reciprocal,* not that it cannot be rebuffed (it often is) but in that it is essentially a plea, even a demand, for a response in kind. It is the signal that changes a delightful friendship or a casual relationship into something much more—or, if it misfires, something much less. "I love you" is not just a phrase or an expression. It is not a description of how one feels. It is the opening to an unknown future, an invitation to a new way of life.

"I love you" does not always have the same meaning, and this, too, should tell us something about the elusive nature of love. The first time it is always a surprise, an invasion, an aggressive act, but once said, "I love you" can only be repeated. It is unthinkable that it should not be said again, and again, and again. When one has not said it for a while, this may itself precipitate a crisis. ("Now why haven't you said that in all of these months!") On the other hand, "I love you" can also serve as a threat ("Don't push me on this; you might lose me"), emotional blackmail ("I've said it, now you have to respond in kind"), a warning ("It's only because I love you that I'm willing to put up with this"), an apology ("I could not possibly have meant what I just said to you, *to you* of all people"). It can be an instrument—more effective than the loudest noise—to interrupt a dull or painful conversation. It can be a cry, a plea, a verbal flag ("Pay attention to me!") or it can be an excuse ("It's only because I love you . . ."). It can be a disguise ("I love you," he whispered, looking awkwardly askance at the open door). It can be an attack ("How can

---

[2] *Lucky Jim* (1954): a comic novel about a man whose mistakes help him get the woman he loves.

you do this to me?") or even an end ("So that's that. With regrets, goodbye"). If this single phrase has so many meanings, how varied and variable must be the emotion.

But "I love you" is not a universal language. There is nothing like it in most societies, and so no emotion quite to compare with it. Some sort of sexual desire might be universal, but the set of ideas, demands, rituals and expectations that are synthesized in the words "I love you" are very special and, anthropologically speaking, quite rare. Love is elusive because we are trying to define a creative act in the making, trying to catch fully formed that which can be ours only in time, insisting on proof and assurances when it is in fact up to us whether "I love you" has any meaning at all. . . .

Romantic Love

"I do think," he said, "that the world is only held together by the mystic conjunction, the ultimate unison between people—a bond. And the immediate bond is between man and woman."

—D. H. Lawrence, *Women in Love*

We are getting closer to our goal of pinning love down, removing the "mystery" and in its place supplying some concrete understanding of what love is, how it works and how it can last. We began, innocently enough, by removing two prevalent obstacles to understanding—the honorable but nevertheless misleading temptation to think of love as a general attitude of loving instead of a particular passion that focuses—necessarily—on an individual person, and the mistaken idea that love is some form of admiration or desire, which treats the lover as an object rather than as a subject who might return one's affection. But this much is true of all forms of personal love, mother for a child, a brother for a brother, a friend for a friend. Romantic love is a certain kind of love, inappropriate or perverse between mother and child or between brothers, and it is quite distinct from friendship too. Our traditional paradigm of romantic love is a young, single man and woman "falling in love." But it is certainly not essential that they be young, or single, or be a man and a woman, or for that matter "fall" into anything.

Romantic love, unlike any form of family love, is distinguished by three features: (1) It is sexual in origin and motivation, no matter how otherwise inhibited, chaste or sublimated; (2) it is spontaneous and voluntary, a matter of will and not just circumstances; and (3) it is an emotion appropriate only between equals, Cinderella[3] and Lady Chatterley[4] notwithstanding.

The first essential structure of romantic emotions is sex. Romantic love isn't *about* sex (a common fallacy) but it depends upon sex, thrives upon sex, utilizes sex as its medium, its language and often its primary content. Whatever else it may be, romantic love begins with the inspiration and exhilaration of sexual attraction (sexual performance is secondary and in many cases actually a distraction). Sexual attraction is not "just physical," of course, and it is not to be confused with the bodily fetishism and

---

[3] Cinderella: an allusion to "Cinderella." (See p. 202.)
[4] Lady Chatterley: the heroine of D. H. Lawrence's novel *Lady Chatterley's Lover* (1931).

Hollywood charms that we too often confuse with attractiveness. But whatever else it may be, sex is bodily and sexual desire engages us as embodied creatures for whom "looks" and the blessings of nature are at least as important as the egalitarian insistence that we are all, "deep down," essentially the same. This suggestion has often offended the Foggers, with their idealized notion of spiritual love, and throughout the history of the subject theologians have struggled for an idealized concept of love that dispenses with sex altogether. (In just the last century American philosopher Ralph Waldo Emerson speaks rhapsodically of "a love that knows no sex," a refrain to be found over and over again since the beginning of the last millennium.) But as we have degraded friendship in favor of love, so, too, have we degraded sexuality. Sex is a spiritual impulse as well as a physical one. Sex, too, is part of the self, even the soul. One's true self-identity is something more than the honors, success and status that are conferred fully-clothed in society: It is rather to be found in our emotional nakedness. Nietzsche[5] remarks, sarcastically, "The body has the audacity to act as if it's *real!*" and, indeed, that is where our reality is to be found. There can be romance without "consummation," of course, for a dozen moral and medical reasons. But the fact is that romantic emotion is as intrinsically sexual as gourmet sensibilities are tied to food. "Man ist was Man isst" writes Feuerbach ("We are what we eat").[6] So, too, what we are is revealed by desire.

The second essential feature is the centrality of personal *choice* in love. On the one hand this is obvious, but at the same time it is so remarkable that only with a bit of distance from ourselves can we fully appreciate how much it sets us off from most of the world. To understand romantic love is to appreciate that peculiar sense of time and spontaneity that makes "love at first sight" and love between strangers possible. In societies where marriages are arranged, or, less formally, marriage is dictated within an established framework of social, religious and economic expectations, there is very limited room for choice and, consequently, very little room for romantic love. Most forms of love, we should note, are "prescribed," set by one's situation. One does not choose one's (literal) brother or sister; one finds oneself in a family and makes the emotional best of it. Brotherly and sisterly love take years to develop. Motherly love, on the other hand, may begin at the child's birth, but it, too, has been gestating for nine months or much more, and the mother in any case (except in adoption) does not *choose* the recipient of her motherly affection. But we *look for* romantic love, or it "finds us" in the most unexpected of places. Love in general takes time, but romantic love can begin all at once. And though romantic love may "deepen" and become enriched over time, it need not—as we all know too well—increase in either intensity or significance. It is sometimes most intense *before* it has had time to develop, and some authors deny that old, established love can still be "romantic" at all, just because it is no longer a matter of choice. Social significance, knowledge and the long habits of domesticity have their undisputed value, but it has been said that they are more antagonistic than compatible with romantic love just because they are not spontaneous, not exciting, *not new*. In our

---

[5] Friedrich Nietzsche (1844–1900): a German philosopher who advocated a heroic morality that affirms life. His most famous work is *Thus Spake Zarathustra* (1883–1891).
[6] Ludwig Andreas Feuerbach (1804–1872): a German philosopher who believed that mankind is the proper study of philosophy. His major work is *The Essence of Christianity* (1841).

culture, the tie between romantic love and marriage is virtually sacred, but if love is to last it must remain a matter of choice, a continuous decision. Love is the justification of marriage, not the other way around. In other cultures, love between a married man and woman may be possible and even desirable, but it is not the sine qua non of the relationship. In such societies, romantic love holds a low priority—if it is permissible or intelligible at all. Where choice is not available, romantic love will appear only as an aberration, even as a crime, in certain circumstances and societies.

The third, often neglected (or rejected) structure of romantic love is a powerful form of egalitarianism, not as a social or a political concept but concerning equality between two individuals. It is often remarked that love is a great "leveling" device, bringing the powerful down to the ordinary and raising the otherwise down if not out up to acceptable if not exceptional status. Romantic love not only requires equals, it, as the French Romantic Stendhal[7] tells us, *"creates"* them, whether it be the scullery maid Cinderella becoming Prince Charming's Princess or Lady Chatterley visiting the gardener's hut. Indeed, it is for this reason that romantic love, originally a distinctively aristocratic emotion, now finds its greatest popularity in self-consciously egalitarian societies, an antidote to, a conspiracy against, class stratifications. The heroes of Harlequins[8] may still be nobility, but romantic love itself is unabashedly bourgeois.

And yet it is often charged that romantic love is a structurally inegalitarian emotion, casting the woman in a subservient role. This has been asserted as a right by certain macho males (represented somewhat paradoxically by George Gilder in *Sexual Suicide*) and as an offense and an outrage by a good many feminists. This, I want to argue, is an abuse and a misunderstanding of the nature of romantic love. Equality is a complex business in most love relationships and, in Orwellian[9] phraseology, we might well point out that at any given time "some lovers are more equal than others." To insist that romantic love requires equality is not to deny that there are still gross injustices and institutionalized inequalities between the sexes; it is rather to point out that love presupposes a radical conception of privacy in which the public dimension is suspended, in which personal choice is definitive, in which equality is determined by two individuals and not by a structure that encloses them. Love is a democratic emotion, despite its aristocratic origins. It is clearly to be distinguished, in any case, from those brands of love in which domination or authority of one partner is essential, as in parent over child, as in beloved country over dutiful citizen, as in lover of pâté over pâté. Love of God, no matter how personal, is certainly not love of equals. (The very suggestion is what the Greeks called "hubris.") Romance is the vehicle, not obstacle, for equality. Cinderella could not remain a scullary maid once she had met her prince.

These three features begin to account not only for the differences between romantic love and other forms of personal love; they also give us some preliminary explanation of why romantic love should be such a powerful and celebrated emotion in our society. The sexuality of romance is already explosive, especially when it is forbidden, abused or

---

[7] Stendahl, pseudonym of Marie Henri Beyle (1783–1842): a French author, most famous for his novel *The Red and the Black* (1831), a romantic, passionate love story. Stendahl's typical hero pursues happiness through love or power.

[8] Harlequins: an allusion to the popular series of romantic novels.

[9] Orwellian: refers to George Orwell (1903–1950), pseudonym of Eric Blair, a writer most famous for his novel *1984*.

denied. The egalitarianism of love assures a continuing struggle for equal shares and status, a constant tension between demands, expectations, and sacrifices, not to mention the creation of a fertile field for envy and resentment. But most of all, the drama of love, the drama *in* love, is the result of spontaneity. Love appears unannounced, suddenly, often inappropriately, even disastrously. It is an emotion that is curiously severed from and even antithetical to our ordinary civil routines. It is an emotion—coupled with our vanity, pride and obstinacy—that thrives on opposition and implausibility. But spontaneity does not mean passivity, and suddenness does not mean unpreparedness. We are never mere victims of love. It is always our choice, our vanity, our achievement, our embarrassment, our tragedy or our comedy. Romantic love is essentially a decision—or a series of decisions—no matter how hard and arbitrary it seems to "hit" us. What's more, it is an emotion that has been publicly cultivated and encouraged—obsessively so—for the entirety of our lives, just so that—suddenly—it may seem to come out of nowhere.

Do we now have a "definition" of love? We are not even close. We have not yet said anything about the caring that is so essential to love, or the companionship, the compassion, the good times together. We have not said anything about time—the time love demands, the time it takes to let love grow. But most of all, we have not truly addressed what makes love *love,* as opposed to sex and friendship and companionship and caring and living together and shared interests and all of the other things that are familiar in but wholly possible without love. That central, definitive characteristic, I want to show, is a special conception of personal identity, a redefining of ourselves in terms of another. To make things more complicated, the terms of this redefinition vary enormously. Love is a historical emotion, a product of particular cultures and a special set of cultural circumstances. It is not a phenomenon that can be defined as such but rather a process that gets redefined and reinvented in every culture. There is no cross-cultural definition of love. Rather love is defined by a narrative, a culturally defined story (or set of stories) that weave our culture's sense of individual choice and autonomy, our natural sexuality and our political and personal sense of equality into the familiar process of "falling in love" and its consequences. What sets romance off from all other love is—as the very word tells us—the sense of drama and plot development, the way in which, no matter how unique our love, we are following in the footsteps of millions of lovers before us who also thought their passion utterly unique and individual. To understand love is to understand this narrative of shared selfhood and how peculiar as well as exciting it is.

Perhaps the very special and peculiar role of romantic love in our lives may be summarized in a recent response of the thirteen-year-old daughter of two of my friends. During a conversation concerning the possibility of her dating one of the boys in her class, she replied, shocked, "Not Jimmy! He's a *friend!*" That reply seemed to cut so deep into the fabric of emotions and judgments that define our ideas about love that I call it, after the young theorist in question, Becky's Theorem. It shows how naive we are when we cozily collapse love, friendship, familiarity and even marriage into the same gentle stew. Becky's Theorem makes explicit our strange obsession with an emotion that conscientiously severs itself from assurances, knowledge and the comforts of established relationships and then proceeds to define much of what we think of ourselves. It is a kind of love dramatically different from all other affections.

(1988)

QUESTIONS

1. In what ways does Solomon distinguish between love as a social invention and love as an emotion?

2. What does Solomon suggest that the sentence *I love you* means?

3. Explain whether or not you agree with Solomon that the word *love* has to be applied carefully and appropriately if it is to have any meaning at all in interpersonal relationships?

4. Explain what you think Solomon means when he says that "Love is a justification of marriage, not the other way around."

ROLLO MAY (1909–1994)

Love and Death*

*The confrontation with death—and the reprieve from it—
makes everything look so precious, so sacred, so beautiful that
I feel more strongly than ever the impulse to love it, to embrace it, and to let myself be overwhelmed by it. My river has
never looked so beautiful. . . . Death, and its ever present
possibility makes love, passionate love, more possible. I wonder if we could love passionately, if ecstasy would be possible
at all, if we knew we'd never die.*

—From a letter by Abraham Maslow, written
while recuperating from a heart attack.

We now confront one of the most profound and meaningful paradoxes of love.
This is the intensified openness to love which the awareness of death gives us and, simultaneously, the increased sense of death which love brings with it. We recall that even
the arrows with which Eros creates—these life-giving shafts he shoots into the cold
bosom of the earth to make the arid surface spring up with luxuriant green verdure—are
poisoned. Here lie the anxiety-creating elements of human love. For the shafts in Eros'
bow pierce "brutal as well as gentle hearts, to their death or to their healing in delight."[1]
Death and delight, anguish and joy, anxiety and the wonder of birth—these are the warp
and woof of which the fabric of human love is woven.

It is Eros who "breaks the limbs' strength," who, "in all gods, in all human beings,
overpowers the intelligence in the breast and all their shrewd planning."[2] Thus speaks
Hesiod in his *Theogony*. He was writing in that powerfully creative archaic period
(c. 750 B.C.) when Greece was filled with the ferment which marked the birth of the
city-states and the new Greek individual of self-consciousness and dignity. The "overpowering" of the rational functions is thus directly connected with the power of Eros to
create. How could we be told more eloquently that the act of creating form and life out
of chaos and bringing vitality to man requires a passion which transcends the intelligence and "calculated planning": Eros *"breaks the limbs' strength . . . in all gods, in all human beings!"* Eros destroys as he creates.[3]

---

*This selection is an excerpt from *Love and Will*.
[1] Joseph Campbell, *Occidental Mythology*, vol. III from *The Masks of God* (New York: Viking Press) 1964,
p. 67.
[2] Hesiod, *Theogony*, lines 120–122, trans. Richmond Lattimore (Ann Arbor: University of Michigan Press)
1961, quoted by Joseph Campbell, III, p. 234.
[3] *Ibid.*

LOVE AS THE INTIMATION OF MORTALITY

To love means to open ourselves to the negative as well as the positive—to grief, sorrow, and disappointment as well as to joy, fulfillment, and an intensity of consciousness we did not know was possible before. I shall first describe this phenomenologically, in its ideal form as a paradigm.

When we "fall" in love, as the expressive verb puts it, the world shakes and changes around us, not only in the way it looks but in our whole experience of what we are doing in the world. Generally, the shaking is consciously felt in its positive aspects—as the wonderful new heaven and earth which love with its miracle and mystery has suddenly produced. Love is the answer, we sing. Aside from the banality of such reassurances, our Western culture seems to be engaged in a romantic—albeit desperate—conspiracy to enforce the illusion that that is *all* there is to eros. The very strength of the effort to support that illusion betrays the presence of the repressed, opposing pole.

This opposing element is the consciousness of death. For death is always in the shadow of the delight of love. In faint adumbration there is present the dread, haunting question, Will this new relationship destroy us? When we love, we give up the center of ourselves. We are thrown from our previous state of existence into a void; and though we hope to attain a new world, a new existence, we can never be sure. Nothing looks the same, and may well never look the same again. The world is annihilated; how can we know whether it will ever be built up again? We give, and give *up*, our own center; how shall we know that we will get it back? We wake up to find the whole world shaking: where or when will it come to rest?

The most excruciating joy is accompanied by the consciousness of the imminence of death—and with the same intensity. And it seems that one is not possible without the other.

This experience of annihilation is an inward one and, as the myth rightly puts it, is essentially what *eros* does to us. It is not simply what the other person does to us. To love completely carries with it the threat of the annihilation of everything. This intensity of consciousness has something in common with the ecstasy of the mystic in his union with God: just as he can never be *sure* God is there, so love carries us to that intensity of consciousness in which we no longer have any guarantee of security.

This razor's edge, this dizzy balance of anxiety and joy, has much to do with the exciting quality of love. The dread joy is not just the question of whether the love will be returned in kind. Indeed, the real dialectic is within the person himself and the anxiety is not essentially quieted if the loved one *does* respond. Paradoxically, the lover is sometimes *more* anxious when the love is returned than when not. For if one loves unrequitedly, which is even an aim in some love writing, or from a safe distance, like Dante and the whole Stylist movement in Italian literature, he can at least go on about his customary daily tasks, writing his *Divine Comedy* or his sonnets or novels. It is when the love *is* realized that eros may literally "break the limb's strength," as with Anthony and Cleopatra, or Paris and Helen, or Héloise and Abelard. Hence, human beings are afraid of love. And, all the saccharine books to the contrary, there is reason to be afraid.

In common human experience, this relationship between death and love is perhaps most clear to people when they have children. A man may have thought very little about death—and prided himself on his "bravery"—until he becomes a father. Then he finds in his love for his child an experience of vulnerability to death: the Cruel Imposter can at any time take away the child, the object of his love. In this sense love is an experience of greater vulnerability.

Love is also a reminder of our own mortality. When a friend or member of our family dies, we are vividly impressed by the fact that life is evanescent and irretrievable. But there is also a deeper sense of its meaningful possibilities and an impetus to risk ourselves in taking the leap. Some—perhaps most—human beings never know deep love until they experience, at someone's death, the preciousness of friendship, devotion, loyalty. Abraham Maslow is profoundly right when he wonders whether we could love passionately if we knew we'd never die.

This is one of the reasons, mythologically speaking, why the love affairs among the immortal gods on Mt. Olympus are so insipid and boring. The loves of Zeus and Juno are completely uninteresting until they involve a mortal. Love has the power to change the course of history only when Zeus comes down to Leda or Io and falls in love with this mortal woman who can yearn to have a child because she knows she will not live forever. *Love is not only enriched by our sense of mortality but constituted by it.* Love is the cross-fertilization of mortality and immortality. This is why the daimon Eros is described as midway between gods and men and partakes of the nature of both.

(1969)

QUESTIONS

1. In what ways does May suggest that love is dependent on the recognition of our mortality?

2. How is Eros depicted by May? How does this depiction relate to Apuleius's "The Myth of Cupid and Psyche," (p. 345)?

3. How does May see the way different types of love are connected with death?

Writing Topics for Essays

1. Drawing on Solomon's essay "I Love You," explain why saying "I Love You" is far more perilous than it would seem at first.

2. Using your own experience, write an essay agreeing or disagreeing with Solomon's definitions of love in "Romantic Love."

3. Do you agree with May in his essay "Love and Death" that in order to experience love we must be aware of our mortality? Explain the significance of the connection between love and death that May makes.

4. How do Hopkins's essays "The Marriage of True Minds" and "Romantic Love After the Middle Ages" trace the historical evolution of "romantic love"? Compare the points she makes with those Solomon makes in his essay "Romantic Love."

Short Stories

D. H. LAWRENCE (1885–1930)

The Horse-Dealer's Daughter

"Well, Mabel, and what are you going to do with yourself?" asked Joe, with foolish flippancy. He felt quite safe himself. Without listening for an answer, he turned aside, worked a grain of tobacco to the tip of his tongue and spat it out. He did not care about anything, since he felt safe himself.

The three brothers and the sister sat round the desolate breakfast table, attempting some sort of desultory consultation. The morning's post had given the final tap to the family fortune, and all was over. The dreary dining room itself, with its heavy mahogany furniture, looked as if it were waiting to be done away with.

But the consultation amounted to nothing. There was a strange air of ineffectuality about the three men, as they sprawled at table, smoking and reflecting vaguely on their own condition. The girl was alone, a rather short, sullen-looking young woman of twenty-seven. She did not share the same life as her brothers. She would have been goodlooking, save for the impassive fixity of her face, "bull-dog," as her brothers called it.

There was a confused tramping of horses' feet outside. The three men all sprawled round in their chairs to watch. Beyond the dark holly bushes that separated the strip of lawn from the highroad, they could see a cavalcade of shire horses swinging out of their own yard, being taken for exercise. This was the last time. These were the last horses that would go through their hands. The young men watched with critical, callous look. They were all frightened at the collapse of their lives, and the sense of disaster in which they were involved left them no inner freedom.

Yet they were three fine, well-set fellows enough. Joe, the eldest, was a man of thirty-three, broad and handsome in a hot, flushed way. His face was red, he twisted his black moustache over a thick finger, his eyes were shallow and restless. He had a sensual way of uncovering his teeth when he laughed, and his bearing was stupid. Now he watched the horses with a glazed look of helplessness in his eyes, a certain stupor of downfall.

The great draught-horses swung past. They were tied head to tail, four of them, and they heaved along to where a lane branched off from the highroad, planting their great hoofs floutingly in the fine black mud, swinging their great rounded haunches sumptuously, and trotting a few sudden steps as they were led into the lane, round the corner. Every movement showed a massive, slumbrous strength, and a stupidity which held them in subjection. The groom at the head looked back, jerking the leading rope. And the cavalcade moved out of sight up the lane, the tail of the last horse, bobbed up tight and stiff, held out taut from the swinging great haunches as they rocked behind the hedges in a motion-like sleep.

Joe watched with glazed hopeless eyes. The horses were almost like his own body to him. He felt he was done for now. Luckily he was engaged to a woman as old as himself, and therefore her father, who was steward of a neighboring estate, would provide him with a job. He would marry and go into harness. His life was over, he would be a subject animal now.

He turned uneasily aside, the retreating steps of the horses echoing in his ears. Then, with foolish restlessness, he reached for the scraps of bacon rind from the plates, and making a faint whistling sound, flung them to the terrier that lay against the fender. He watched the dog swallow them, and waited till the creature looked into his eyes. Then a faint grin came on his face, and in a high, foolish voice he said:

"You won't get much more bacon, shall you, you little bitch?"

The dog faintly and dismally wagged its tail, then lowered its haunches, circled round, and lay down again.

The was another helpless silence at the table. Joe sprawled uneasily in his seat, not willing to go till the family conclave was dissolved. Fred Henry, the second brother, was erect, clean-limbed, alert. He had watched the passing of the horses with more sang-froid. If he was an animal, like Joe, he was an animal which controls, not one which is controlled. He was master of any horse, and he carried himself with a well-tempered air of mastery. But he was not master of the situations of life. He pushed his coarse brown moustache upwards, off his lip, and glanced irritably at his sister, who sat impassive and inscrutable.

"You'll go and stop with Lucy for a bit, shan't you?" he asked. The girl did not answer.

"I don't see what else you can do," persisted Fred Henry.

"Go as a skivvy," Joe interpolated laconically.[1]

The girl did not move a muscle.

"If I was her, I should go in for training for a nurse," said Malcolm, the youngest of them all. He was the baby of the family, a young man of twenty-two, with a fresh, jaunty *museau*.[2]

But Mabel did not take any notice of him. They had talked at her and round her for so many years, that she hardly heard them at all.

---

[1] skivvy: servant.
[2] *museau*: face, French slang.

The marble clock on the mantlepiece softly chimed the half-hour, the dog rose uneasily from the hearthrug and looked at the party at the breakfast table. But still they sat on in ineffectual conclave.

"Oh, all right," said Joe suddenly, apropos of nothing. "I'll get a move on."

He pushed back his chair, straddled his knees with a downward jerk, to get them free, in horsey fashion, and went to the fire. Still he did not go out of the room; he was curious to know what the others would do or say. He began to charge his pipe, looking down at the dog and saying, in a high, affected voice:

"Going wi' me? Going wi' me are ter? Tha'rt goin' further tha that counts on just now, dost hear?"

The dog faintly wagged its tail, the man stuck out his jaw and covered his pipe with his hands, and puffed intently, losing himself in the tobacco, looking down all the while at the dog with an absent brown eye. The dog looked at him in mournful distrust. Joe stood with his knees stuck out, in real horsey fashion.

"Have you had a letter from Lucy?" Fred Henry asked of his sister.

"Last week," came the neutral reply.

"And what does she say?"

There was no answer.

"Does she *ask* you to go and stop there?" persisted Fred Henry.

"She says I can if I like."

"Well, then, you'd better. Tell her you'll come on Monday."

This was received in silence.

"That's what you'll do then, is it?" said Fred Henry, in some exasperation.

But she made no answer. There was a silence of futility and irritation in the room. Malcolm grinned fatuously.

"You'll have to make up your mind between now and next Wednesday," said Joe loudly, "or else find yourself lodgings on the curbstone."

The face of the young woman darkened, but she sat on immutable.

"Here's Jack Fergusson!" exclaimed Malcolm, who was looking aimlessly out of the window.

"Where?" exclaimed Joe, loudly.

"Just gone past."

"Coming in?"

Malcolm craned his neck to see the gate.

"Yes," he said.

There was a silence. Mabel sat on like one condemned, at the head of the table. Then a whistle was heard from the kitchen. The dog got up and barked sharply. Joe opened the door and shouted:

"Come on."

After a moment a young man entered. He was muffled up in overcoat and a purple woolen scarf, and his tweed cap, which he did not remove, was pulled down on his head. He was of medium height, his face was rather long and pale, his eyes looked tired.

"Hello, Jack! Well, Jack!" exclaimed Malcolm and Joe. Fred Henry merely said, "Jack."

"What's doing?" asked the newcomer, evidently addressing Fred Henry.

"Same. We've got to be out by Wednesday. Got a cold?"

"I have—got it bad, too."

"Why don't you stop in?"

"*Me* stop in? When I can't stand on my legs, perhaps I shall have a chance." The young man spoke huskily. He had a slight Scotch accent.

"It's a knock-out, isn't it," said Joe, boisterously, "if a doctor goes round croaking with a cold. Looks bad for the patients, doesn't it?"

The young doctor looked at him slowly.

"Anything the matter with *you*, then?" he asked sarcastically.

"Not as I know of. Damn your eyes, I hope not. Why?"

"I thought you were very concerned about the patients, wondered if you might be one yourself."

"Damn it, no, I've never been patient to no flaming doctor, and hope I never shall be," returned Joe.

At this point Mabel rose from the table, and they all seemed to become aware of her existence. She began putting the dishes together. The young doctor looked at her, but did not address her. He had not greeted her. She went out of the room with the tray, her face impassive and unchanged.

"When are you off then, all of you?" asked the doctor.

"I'm catching the eleven-forty," replied Malcolm. "Are you goin' down wi' th' trap, Joe?"

"Yes, I've told you I'm going down wi' th' trap, haven't I?"

"We'd better be getting her in then. So long, Jack, if I don't see you before I go," said Malcolm, shaking hands.

He went out, followed by Joe, who seemed to have his tail between his legs.

"Well, this is the devil's own," exclaimed the doctor, when he was left alone with Fred Henry. "Going before Wednesday, are you?"

"That's the orders," replied the other.

"Where, to Northampton?"

"That's it."

"The devil!" exclaimed Fergusson, with quiet chagrin.

And there was silence between the two.

"All settled up, are you?" asked Fergusson.

"About."

There was another pause.

"Well, I shall miss yer, Freddy, boy," said the young doctor.

"And I shall miss thee, Jack," returned the other.

"Miss you like hell," mused the doctor.

Fred Henry turned aside. There was nothing to say. Mabel came in again, to finish clearing the table.

"What are *you* going to do, then, Miss Pervin?" asked Fergusson. "Going to your sister's, are you?"

Mabel looked at him with her steady, dangerous eyes, that always made him uncomfortable, unsettling his superficial ease.

"No," she said.

"Well, what in the name of fortune *are* you going to do? Say what you mean to do," cried Fred Henry, with futile intensity.

But she only averted her head, and continued her work. She folded the white table-cloth, and put on the chenille cloth.

"The sulkiest bitch that ever trod!" muttered her brother.

But she finished her task with perfectly impassive face, the young doctor watching her interestedly all the while. Then she went out.

Fred Henry stared after her, clenching his lips, his blue eyes fixing in sharp antagonism, as he made a grimace of sour exasperation.

"You could bray her into bits, and that's all you'd get out of her," he said in a small, narrowed tone.

The doctor smiled faintly.

"What's she *going* to do, then?" he asked.

"Strike me if *I* know!" returned the other.

There was a pause. Then the doctor stirred.

"I'll be seeing you to-night, shall I?" he said to his friend.

"Ay—where's it to be? Are we going over to Jessdale?"

"I don't know. I've got such a cold on me. I'll come round to the Moon and Stars, anyway."

"Let Lizzie and May miss their night for once, eh?"

"That's it—if I feel as I do now."

"All's one—"

The two young men went through the passage and down to the back door together. The house was large, but it was servantless now, and desolate. At the back was a small bricked house-yard, and beyond that a big square, graveled fine and red, and having stables on two sides. Sloping, dank, winter-dark fields stretched away on the open sides.

But the stables were empty. Joseph Pervin, the father of the family, had been a man of no education, who had become a fairly large horse dealer. The stables had been full of horses, there was a great turmoil and come-and-go of horses and of dealers and grooms. Then the kitchen was full of servants. But of late things had declined. The old man had married a second time, to retrieve his fortunes. Now he was dead and everything was gone to the dogs, there was nothing but debt and threatening.

For months, Mabel had been servantless in the big house, keeping the home together in penury for her ineffectual brothers. She had kept house for ten years. But previously it was with unstinted means. Then, however brutal and coarse everything was, the sense of money had kept her proud, confident. The men might be foul-mouthed, the women in the kitchen might have bad reputations, her brothers might have illegitimate children. But so long as there was money, the girl felt herself established, and brutally proud, reserved.

No company came to the house, save dealers and coarse men. Mabel had no associates of her own sex, after her sister went away. But she did not mind. She went regularly to church, she attended to her father. And she lived in the memory of her mother, who had died when she was fourteen, and whom she had loved. She had loved her father, too, in a different way, depending upon him, and feeling secure in him, until at the age of fifty-four he married again. And then she had set hard against him. Now he had died and left them all hopelessly in debt.

She had suffered badly during the period of poverty. Nothing, however, could shake the curious sullen, animal pride that dominated each member of the family. Now, for Mabel, the end had come. Still she would not cast about her. She would follow her own way just the same. She would always hold the keys of her own situation. Mindless and persistent, she endured from day to day. Why should she think? Why should she answer anybody? It was enough that this was the end, and there was no way out. She need not pass any more darkly along the main street of the small town, avoiding every eye. She need not demean herself any more, going into the shops and buying the cheapest food. This was at an end. She thought of nobody, not even of herself. Mindless and persistent, she seemed in a sort of ecstasy to be coming nearer to her fulfillment, her own glorification, approaching her dead mother, who was glorified.

In the afternoon she took a little bag, with shears and sponge and a small scrubbing brush, and went out. It was a gray, wintry day, with saddened, dark green fields and an atmosphere blackened by the smoke of foundries not far off. She went quickly, darkly along the causeway, heeding nobody, through the town to the churchyard.

There she always felt secure, as if no one could see her, although as a matter of fact she was exposed to the stare of every one who passed along under the churchyard wall. Nevertheless, once under the shadow of the great looming church, among the graves, she felt immune from the world, reserved within the thick churchyard wall as in another country.

Carefully she clipped the grass from the grave, and arranged the pinky white, small chrysanthemums in the tin cross. When this was done, she took an empty jar from a neighboring grave, brought water, and carefully, most scrupulously sponged the marble headstone and the coping-stone.

It gave her sincere satisfaction to do this. She felt in immediate contact with the world of her mother. She took minute pains, went through the park in a state bordering on pure happiness, as if in performing this task she came into a subtle, intimate connection with her mother. For the life she followed here in the world was far less real than the world of death she inherited from her mother.

The doctor's house was just by the church. Fergusson, being a mere hired assistant, was slave to the countryside. As he hurried now to attend to the outpatients in the surgery, glancing across the graveyard with his quick eyes, he saw the girl at her task at the grave. She seemed so intent and remote, it was like looking into another world. Some mystical element was touched in him. He slowed down as he walked, watching her as if spellbound.

She lifted her eyes, feeling him looking. Their eyes met. And each looked away again at once, each feeling, in some way, found out by the other. He lifted his cap and passed on down the road. There remained distinct in his consciousness, like a vision, the memory of her face, lifted from the tombstone in the churchyard, and looking at him with slow, large, portentous eyes. It *was* portentous, her face. It seemed to mesmerize him. There was a heavy power in her eyes which laid hold of his whole being, as if he had drunk some powerful drug. He had been feeling weak and done before. Now the life came back into him, he felt delivered from his own fretted, daily self.

He finished his duties at the surgery[3] as quickly as might be, hastily filling up the bottle of the waiting people with cheap drugs. Then, in perpetual haste, he set off again to visit several cases in another part of his round, before teatime. At all times he preferred to walk if he could, but particularly when he was not well. He fancied the motion restored him.

The afternoon was falling. It was gray, deadened, and wintry, with a slow, moist, heavy coldness sinking in and deadening all the faculties. But why should he think or notice? He hastily climbed the hill and turned across the dark green fields, following the black cindertrack. In the distance, across a shallow dip in the country, the small town was clustered like smouldering ash, a tower, a spire, a heap of low, raw, extinct houses. And on the nearest fringe of the town, sloping into the dip, was Oldmeadow, the Pervins' house. He could see the stables and the outbuildings distinctly, as they lay towards him on the slope. Well, he would not go there many more times! Another resource would be lost to him, another place gone: the only company he cared for in the alien, ugly little town he was losing. Nothing but work, drudgery, constant hastening from dwelling to dwelling among the colliers[4] and the iron-workers. It wore him out, but at the same time he had a craving for it. It was a stimulant to him to be in the homes of the working people, moving as it were through the innermost body of their life. His nerves were excited and gratified. He could come so near, into the very lives of the rough, inarticulate, powerfully emotional men and women. He grumbled, he said he hated the hellish hole. But as a matter of fact it excited him, the contact with the rough, strongly-feeling people was a stimulant applied direct to his nerves.

Below Oldmeadow, in the green, shallow, soddened hollow of fields, lay a square, deep pond. Roving across the landscape, the doctor's quick eye detected a figure in black passing through the gate of the field, down towards the pond. He looked again. It would be Mabel Pervin. His mind suddenly became alive and attentive.

Why was she going down there? He pulled up on the path on the slope above, and stood staring. He could just make sure of the small black figure moving in the hollow of the failing day. He seemed to see her in the midst of such obscurity, that he was like a clairvoyant, seeing rather with the mind's eye than with ordinary sight. Yet he could see her positively enough, while he kept his eye attentive. He felt, if he looked away from her, in the thick, ugly falling dusk, he would lose her altogether.

He followed her minutely as she moved, direct and intent, like something transmitted rather than stirring in voluntary activity, straight down the field towards the pond. There she stood on the bank for a moment. She never raised her head. Then she waded slowly into the water.

He stood motionless as the small black figure walked slowly and deliberately towards the center of the pond, very slowly, gradually moving deeper into the motionless water, and still moving forward as the water got up to her breast. Then he could see her no more in the dusk of the dead afternoon.

"There!" he exclaimed, "Would you believe it?"

---

[3] surgery: doctor's office.
[4] colliers: coal miners.

And he hastened straight down, running over the wet, soddened fields, pushing through the hedges, down into the depression of callous wintry obscurity. It took him several minutes to come to the pond. He stood on the bank, breathing heavily. He could see nothing. His eyes seemed to penetrate the dead water. Yes, perhaps that was the dark shadow of her black clothing beneath the surface of the water.

He slowly ventured into the pond. The bottom was deep, soft clay, he sank in, and the water clasped dead cold round his legs. As he stirred he could smell the cold, rotten clay that fouled up into the water. It was objectionable in his lungs. Still, repelled and yet not heeding, he moved deeper into the pond. The cold water rose over this thighs, over his loins, upon his abdomen. The lower part of his body was all sunk in the hideous cold element. And the bottom was so deeply soft and uncertain he was afraid of pitching with his mouth underneath. He could not swim, and was afraid.

He crouched a little, spreading his hands under the water and moving them round, trying to feel for her. The dead cold pond swayed upon his chest. He moved again, a little deeper, and again, with his hands underneath, he felt all around under the water. And he touched her clothing. But it evaded his fingers. He made a desperate effort to grasp it.

And so doing he lost his balance and went under, horribly, suffocating in the foul earthy water, struggling madly for a few moments. At last, after what seemed an eternity, he got his footing, rose again into the air and looked around. He gasped, and knew he was in the world. Then he looked at the water. She had risen near him. He grasped her clothing, and drawing her nearer, turned to take his way to land again.

He went very slowly, carefully, absorbed in the slow progress. He rose higher, climbing out of the pond. The water was now only about his legs; he was thankful, full of relief to be out of the clutches of the pond. He lifted her and staggered on to the bank, out of the horror of wet, gray clay.

He laid her down on the bank. She was quite unconscious and running with water. He made the water come from her mouth, he worked to restore her. He did not have to work very long before he could feel the breathing begin again in her; she was breathing naturally. He worked a little longer. He could feel her live beneath his hands; she was coming back. He wiped her face, wrapped her in his overcoat, looked round into the dim, dark gray world, then lifted her and staggered down the bank and across the fields.

It seemed an unthinkably long way, and his burden so heavy he felt he would never get to the house. But at last he was in the stableyard, and then in the house-yard. He opened the door and went into the house. In the kitchen he laid her down on the hearthrug, and called. The house was empty. But the fire was burning in the grate.

Then again he kneeled to attend to her. She was breathing regularly, her eyes were wide open and as if conscious, but there seemed something missing in her look. She was conscious in herself, but unconscious of her surroundings.

He ran upstairs, took blankets from a bed, and put them before the fire to warm. Then he removed her saturated, earthy-smelling clothing, rubbed her dry with a towel, and wrapped her naked in the blankets. Then he went into the dining-room, to look for spirits. There was a little whisky. He drank a gulp himself, and put some into her mouth.

The effect was instantaneous. She looked full into his face, as if she had been seeing him for some time, and yet had only just become conscious of him.

"Dr. Fergusson?" she said.

"What?" he answered.

He was divesting himself of his coat, intending to find some dry clothing upstairs. He could not bear the smell of the dead, clayey water, and he was mortally afraid of his own health.

"What did I do?" she asked.

"Walked into the pond," he replied. He had begun to shudder like one sick, and could hardly attend to her. Her eyes remained full on him, he seemed to be going dark in his mind, looking back at her helplessly. The shuddering became quieter in him, his life came back in him, dark and unknowing, but strong again.

"Was I out of my mind?" she asked, while her eyes were fixed on him all the time.

"Maybe, for the moment," he replied. He felt quiet, because his strength came back. The strange fretful strain had left him.

"Am I out of my mind now?" she asked.

"Are you?" he reflected a moment. "No," he answered truthfully. "I don't see that you are." He turned his face aside. He was afraid now, because he felt dazed, and felt dimly that her power was stronger than his, in this issue. And she continued to look at him fixedly all the time. "Can you tell me where I shall find some dry things to put on?" he asked.

"Did you dive into the pond for me?" she asked.

"No," he answered. "I walked in. But I went in overhead as well."

There was silence for a moment. He hesitated. He very much wanted to go upstairs to get into dry clothing. But there was another desire in him. And she seemed to hold him. His will seemed to have gone to sleep, and left him, standing there slack before her. But he felt warm inside himself. He did not shudder at all, though his clothes were sodden on him.

"Why did you?" she asked.

"Because I didn't want you to do such a foolish thing," he said.

"It wasn't foolish," she said, still gazing at him as she lay on the floor, with a sofa cushion under her head. "It was the right thing to do. *I* knew best, then."

"I'll go and shift these wet things," he said. But still he had not the power to move out of her presence, until she sent him. It was as if she had the life of his body in her hands, and he could not extricate himself. Or perhaps he did not want to.

Suddenly she sat up. Then she became aware of her own immediate condition. She felt the blankets about her, she knew her own limbs. For a moment it seemed as if her reason were going. She looked round, with wild eye, as if seeking something. He stood still with fear. She saw her clothing lying scattered.

"Who undressed me?" she asked, her eyes resting full and inevitable on his face.

"I did," he replied, "to bring you round."

For some moments she sat and gazed at him awfully, her lips parted.

"Do you love me, then?" she asked.

He only stood and stared at her, fascinated. His soul seemed to melt.

She shuffled forward on her knees, and put her arms round him, round his legs, as he stood there, pressing her breasts against his knees and thighs, clutching him with strange, convulsive certainty, pressing his thighs against her, drawing him to her face, her throat, as she looked up at him with flaring, humble eyes of transfiguration, triumphant in first possession.

"You love me," she murmured, in strange transport, yearning and triumphant and confident. "You love me. I know you love me, I know."

And she was passionately kissing his knees, through the wet clothing, passionately and indiscriminately kissing his knees, his legs, as if unaware of everything.

He looked down at the tangled wet hair, the wild, bare, animal shoulders. He was amazed, bewildered, and afraid. He had never thought of loving her. He had never wanted to love her. When he rescued her and restored her, he was a doctor, and she was a patient. He had had no single personal thought of her. Nay, this introduction of the personal element was very distasteful to him, a violation of his professional honor. It was horrible to have her there embracing his knees. It was horrible. He revolted from it, violently. And yet—and yet—he had not the power to break away.

She looked at him again, with the same supplication of powerful love, and that same transcendent, frightening light of triumph. In view of the delicate flame which seemed to come from her face like a light, he was powerless. And yet he had never intended to love her. He had never intended. And something stubborn in him could not give way.

"You love me," she repeated, in a murmur of deep, rhapsodic assurance. "You love me."

Her hands were drawing him, drawing him down to her. He was afraid, even a little horrified. For he had, really, no intention of loving her. Yet her hands were drawing him towards her. He put out his hand quickly to steady himself, and grasped her bare shoulder. A flame seemed to burn the hand that grasped her soft shoulder. He had no intention of loving her: his whole will was against his yielding. It was horrible. And yet wonderful was the touch of her shoulders, beautiful the shining of her face. Was she perhaps mad? He had a horror of yielding to her. Yet something in him ached also.

He had been staring away at the door, away from her. But his hand remained on her shoulder. She had gone suddenly very still. He looked down at her. Her eyes were now wide with fear, with doubt, the light was dying from her face, a shadow of terrible grayness was returning. He could not bear the touch of her eyes' question upon him, and the look of death behind the question.

With an inward groan he gave way, and let his heart yield towards her. A sudden gentle smile came on his face. And her eyes, which never left his face, slowly, slowly filled with tears. He watched the strange water rise in her eyes, like some slow fountain coming up. And his heart seemed to burn and melt away in his breast.

He could not bear to look at her any more. He dropped on his knees and caught her head with his arms and pressed her face against his throat. She was very still. His heart, which seemed to have broken, was burning with a kind of agony in his breast. And he felt her slow, hot tears wetting his throat. But he could not move.

He felt the hot tears wet his neck and the hollows of his neck, and he remained motionless, suspended through one of man's eternities. Only now it had become indispensable to him to have her face pressed close to him; he could never let her go again. He could never let her head go away from the close clutch of his arm. He wanted to remain like that for ever, with his heart hurting him in a pain that was also life to him. Without knowing, he was looking down on her damp, soft brown hair.

Then, as it were suddenly, he smelt the horrid stagnant smell of that water. And at the same moment she drew away from him and looked at him. Her eyes were wistful and unfathomable. He was afraid of them, and he fell to kissing her, not knowing what he was doing. He wanted her eyes not to have that terrible, wistful, unfathomable look.

When she turned her face to him again, a faint delicate flush was glowing, and there was again dawning that terrible shining of joy in her eyes, which really terrified him, and yet which he now wanted to see, because he feared the look of doubt still more.

"You love me?" she said, rather faltering.

"Yes." The word cost him a painful effort. Not because it wasn't true. But because it was too newly true, the *saying* seemed to tear open again his newly torn heart. And he hardly wanted it to be true, even now.

She lifted her face to him, and he bent forward and kissed her on the mouth, gently, with the one kiss that is an eternal pledge. And as he kissed her his heart strained again in his breast. He never intended to love her. But now it was over. He had crossed over the gulf to her, and all that he had left behind had shriveled and become void.

After the kiss, her eyes again slowly filled with tears. She sat still, away from him, with her face drooped aside, and her hands folded in her lap. The tears fell very slowly. There was complete silence. He too sat there motionless and silent on the hearthrug. The strange pain of his heart that was broken seemed to consume him. That he should love her? That this was love! That he should be ripped open in this way! Him, a doctor! How they would all jeer if they knew! It was agony to him to think they might know.

In the curious naked pain of the thought he looked again to her. She was sitting there drooped into a muse. He saw a tear fall, and his heart flared hot. He saw for the first time that one of her shoulders was quite uncovered, one arm bare, he could see one of her small breasts; dimly, because it had become almost dark in the room.

"Why are you crying?" he asked, in an altered voice.

She looked up at him, and behind her tears the consciousness of her situation for the first time brought a dark look of shame to her eyes.

"I'm not crying, really," she said, watching him half frightened.

He reached his hand, and softly closed it on her bare arm.

"I love you! I love you!" he said in a soft, low vibrating voice, unlike himself.

She shrank, and dropped her head. The soft, penetrating grip of his hand on her arm distressed her. She looked up at him.

"I want to go," she said. "I want to go and get you some dry things."

"Why?" he said. "I'm all right."

"But I want to go," she said. "And I want you to change your things."

He released her arm, and she wrapped herself in the blanket, looking at him rather frightened. And still she did not rise.

"Kiss me," she said wistfully.

He kissed her, but briefly, half in anger.

Then, after a second, she rose nervously, all mixed up in the blanket. He watched her in her confusion, as she tried to extricate herself and wrap herself up so that she could walk. He watched her relentlessly, as she knew. And as she went, the blanket trailing, and as he saw a glimpse of her feet and her white leg, he tried to remember her as she was when he had wrapped her in the blanket. But then he didn't want to remember, because she had been nothing to him then, and his nature revolted from remembering her as she was when she was nothing to him.

A tumbling, muffled noise from within the dark house startled him. Then he heard her voice:—"There are clothes." He rose and went to the foot of the stairs, and gathered up the garments she had thrown down. Then he came back to the fire, to rub himself down and dress. He grinned at his own appearance when he had finished.

The fire was sinking, so he put on coal. The house was now quite dark, save for the light of a street-lamp that shone in faintly from beyond the holly trees. He lit the gas with matches he found on the mantelpiece. Then he emptied the pockets of his own clothes, and threw all his wet things in a heap into the scullery.[5] After which he gathered up her sodden clothes, gently, and put them in a separate heap on the copper-top in the scullery.

It was six o'clock on the clock. His own watch had stopped. He ought to go back to the surgery. He waited, and still she did not come down. So he went to the foot of the stairs and called:

"I shall have to go."

Almost immediately he heard her coming down. She had on her best dress of black voile, and her hair was tidy, but still damp. She looked at him—and in spite of herself, smiled.

"I don't like you in those clothes," she said.

"Do I look a sight?" he answered.

They were shy of one another.

"I'll make you some tea," she said.

"No, I must go."

"Must you?" And she looked at him again with the wide, strained, doubtful eyes. And again, from the pain of his breast, he knew how he loved her. He went and bent to kiss her, gently, passionately, with his heart's painful kiss.

"And my hair smells so horrible," she murmured in distraction. "And I'm so awful, I'm so awful! Oh, no, I'm too awful." And she broke into bitter, heartbroken sobbing. "You can't want to love me, I'm horrible."

"Don't be silly, don't be silly," he said, trying to comfort her, kissing her, holding her in his arms. "I want you, I want to marry you, we're going to be married, quickly, quickly—tomorrow if I can."

But she only sobbed terribly, and cried:

"I feel awful. I feel awful. I feel I'm horrible to you."

"No, I want you, I want you," was all he answered, blindly, with that terrible intonation which frightened her almost more than her horror lest he should *not* want her.

(1922)

---

[5] scullery: a small room off a kitchen used for storing and washing utensils.

QUESTIONS

1. According to her brothers, what character traits does Mabel possess? Are these the same character traits she reveals in her encounter with Dr. Fergusson?

2. Why does Mabel go first to the graveyard and then to the pond?

3. How is it that Dr. Fergusson notices her activities? What makes him follow her?

4. When she realizes that Fergusson has undressed her, why does Mabel instantly assume that he loves her?

5. From whose point of view is the story told? How does the choice of narrator influence the way each of the characters is perceived?

6. How do language and imagery provide the mood and tone of this story?

7. What foreshadowing—if any—prepares you for the story's resolution?

ANTON CHEKHOV (1860–1904)

The Lady with the Dog

Translated by Constance Garnett

1

It was said that a new person had appeared on the sea-front: a lady with a little dog. Dmitri Dmitritch Gurov, who had by then been a fortnight at Yalta,[1] and so was fairly at home there, had begun to take an interest in new arrivals. Sitting in Verney's pavilion, he saw, walking on the sea-front, a fair-haired young lady of medium height, wearing a *béret;* a white Pomeranian dog was running behind her.

And afterwards he met her in the public gardens and in the square several times a day. She was walking alone, always wearing the same *béret,* and always with the same white dog; no one knew who she was, and every one called her simply "the lady with the dog."

"If she is here alone without a husband or friends, it wouldn't be amiss to make her acquaintance," Gurov reflected.

He was under forty, but he had a daughter already twelve years old, and two sons at school. He had been married young, when he was a student in his second year, and by now his wife seemed half as old again as he. She was a tall, erect woman with dark eyebrows, staid and dignified, and, as she said of herself, intellectual. She read a great deal, used phonetic spelling, called her husband, not Dmitri, but Dimitri, and he secretly considered her unintelligent, narrow, inelegant, was afraid of her, and did not like to be at home. He had begun being unfaithful to her long ago—had been unfaithful to her often, and, probably on that account, almost always spoke ill of women, and when they were talked about in his presence, used to call them "the lower race."

It seemed to him that he had been so schooled by bitter experience that he might call them what he liked, and yet he could not get on for two days together without "the lower race." In the society of men he was bored and not himself, with them he was cold and uncommunicative; but when he was in the company of women he felt free, and knew what to say to them and how to behave; and he was at ease with them even when he was silent. In his appearance, in his character, in his whole nature, there was something attractive and elusive which allured women and disposed them in his favour; he knew that, and some force seemed to draw him, too, to them.

Experience often repeated, truly bitter experience, had taught him long ago that with decent people, especially Moscow[2] people—always slow to move and irresolute—every intimacy, which at first so agreeably diversifies life and appears a light and charming adventure, inevitably grows into a regular problem of extreme intricacy, and in the

---

[1] Yalta: a resort town in the Crimea, Ukraine, on the Black Sea.
[2] Moscow: the largest city and capital of Russia.

long run the situation becomes unbearable. But at every fresh meeting with an interesting woman this experience seemed to slip out of his memory, and he was eager for life, and everything seemed simple and amusing.

One evening he was dining in the gardens, and the lady in the *béret* came up slowly to take the next table. Her expression, her gait, her dress, and the way she did her hair told him that she was a lady, that she was married, that she was in Yalta for the first time and alone, and that she was dull there. . . . The stories told of the immorality in such places as Yalta are to a great extent untrue; he despised them, and knew that such stories were for the most part made up by persons who would themselves have been glad to sin if they had been able; but when the lady sat down at the next table three paces from him, he remembered these tales of easy conquests, of trips to the mountains, and the tempting thought of a swift, fleeting love affair, a romance with an unknown woman, whose name he did not know, suddenly took possession of him.

He beckoned coaxingly to the Pomeranian, and when the dog came up to him he shook his finger at it. The Pomeranian growled: Gurov shook his finger at it again.

The lady looked at him and at once dropped her eyes.

"He doesn't bite," she said, and blushed.

"May I give him a bone?" he asked; and when she nodded he asked courteously, "Have you been long in Yalta?"

"Five days."

"And I have already dragged out a fortnight here."

There was a brief silence.

"Time goes fast, and yet it is so dull here!" she said, not looking at him.

"That's only the fashion to say it is dull here. A provincial will live in Belyov or Zhidra and not be dull, and when he comes here it's 'Oh, the dullness! Oh, the dust!' One would think he came from Grenada."

She laughed. Then both continued eating in silence, like strangers, but after dinner they walked side by side; and there sprang up between them the light jesting conversation of people who are free and satisfied, to whom it does not matter where they go or what they talk about. They walked and talked of the strange light on the sea: the water was of a soft warm lilac hue, and there was a golden streak from the moon upon it. They talked of how sultry it was after a hot day. Gurov told her that he came from Moscow, that he had taken his degree in Arts, but had a post in a bank; that he had trained as an opera-singer, but had given it up, that he owned two houses in Moscow. . . . And from her he learnt that she had grown up in Petersburg, but had lived in S— since her marriage two years before, that she was staying another month in Yalta, and that her husband, who needed a holiday too, might perhaps come and fetch her. She was not sure whether her husband had a post in a Crown Department or under the Provincial Council—and was amused by her own ignorance. And Gurov learnt, too, that she was called Anna Sergeyevna.

Afterwards he thought about her in his room at the hotel—thought she would certainly meet him next day; it would be sure to happen. As he got into bed he thought how lately she had been a girl at school, doing lessons like his own daughter; he recalled the diffidence, the angularity, that was still manifest in her laugh and her manner of talking with a stranger. This must have been the first time in her life she had been alone in surroundings in which she was followed, looked at, and spoken to merely from a secret motive which she could hardly fail to guess. He recalled her slender, delicate neck, her lovely grey eyes.

"There's something pathetic about her, anyway," he thought, and fell asleep.

2

A week had passed since they had made acquaintance. It was a holiday. It was sultry indoors, while in the street the wind whirled the dust round and round, and blew people's hats off. It was a thirsty day, and Gurov often went into the pavilion, and pressed Anna Sergeyevna to have syrup and water or an ice. One did not know what to do with oneself.

In the evening when the wind had dropped a little, they went out on the groyne[3] to see the steamer come in. There were a great many people walking about the harbour; they had gathered to welcome some one, bringing bouquets. And two peculiarities of a well-dressed Yalta crowd were very conspicuous: the elderly ladies were dressed like young ones, and there were great numbers of generals.

Owing to the roughness of the sea, the steamer arrived late, after the sun had set, and it was a long time turning about before it reached the groyne. Anna Sergeyevna looked through her lorgnette[4] at the steamer and the passengers as though looking for acquaintances, and when she turned to Gurov her eyes were shining. She talked a great deal and asked disconnected questions, forgetting next moment what she had asked; then she dropped her lorgnette in the crush.

The festive crowd began to disperse; it was too dark to see people's faces. The wind had completely dropped, but Gurov and Anna Sergeyevna still stood as though waiting to see some one else come from the steamer. Anna Sergeyevna was silent now, and sniffed the flowers without looking at Gurov.

"The weather is better this evening," he said. "Where shall we go now? Shall we drive somewhere?"

She made no answer.

Then he looked at her intently, and all at once put his arm round her and kissed her on the lips, and breathed in the moisture and the fragrance of the flowers; and he immediately looked round him, anxiously wondering whether any one had seen them.

"Let us go to your hotel," he said softly. And both walked quickly.

The room was close and smelt of the scent she had bought at the Japanese shop. Gurov looked at her and thought: "What different people one meets in the world!" From the past he preserved memories of careless, good-natured women, who loved cheerfully and were grateful to him for the happiness he gave them, however brief it might be; and of women like his wife who loved without any genuine feeling, with superfluous phrases, affectedly, hysterically, with an expression that suggested that it was not love nor passion, but something more significant; and of two or three others, very beautiful, cold

---

[3] groyne (also groin): a strong low sea wall.
[4] lorgnette: a pair of eyeglasses attached to a handle.

women, on whose faces he had caught a glimpse of a rapacious expression—an obstinate desire to snatch from life more than it could give, and these were capricious, unreflecting, domineering, unintelligent women not in their first youth, and when Gurov grew cold to them their beauty excited his hatred, and the lace on their linen seemed to him like scales.

But in this case there was still the diffidence, the angularity of inexperienced youth, an awkward feeling; and there was a sense of consternation as though some one had suddenly knocked at the door. The attitude of Anna Sergeyevna—"the lady with the dog"—to what had happened was somehow peculiar, very grave, as though it were her fall—so it seemed, and it was strange and inappropriate. Her face dropped and faded, and on both sides of it her long hair hung down mournfully; she mused in a dejected attitude like "the woman who was a sinner" in an old-fashioned picture.

"It's wrong," she said. "You will be the first to despise me now."

There was a water-melon on the table. Gurov cut himself a slice and began eating it without haste. There followed at least half an hour of silence.

Anna Sergeyevna was touching; there was about her the purity of a good, simple woman who had seen little of life. The solitary candle burning on the table threw a faint light on her face, yet it was clear that she was very unhappy.

"How could I despise you?" asked Gurov. "You don't know what you are saying."

"God forgive me," she said, and her eyes filled with tears. "It's awful."

"You seem to feel you need to be forgiven."

"Forgiven? No. I am a bad, low woman; I despise myself and I don't attempt to justify myself. It's not my husband but myself I have deceived. And not only just now; I have been deceiving myself for a long time. My husband may be a good, honest man, but he is a flunkey! I don't know what he does there, what his work is, but I know he is a flunkey! I was twenty when I was married to him. I have been tormented by curiosity; I wanted something better. 'There must be a different sort of life,' I said to myself. I wanted to live! To live, to live! . . . I was fired by curiosity . . . you don't understand it, but, I swear to God, I could not control myself; something happened to me: I could not be restrained. I told my husband I was ill, and came here. . . . And here I have been walking about as though I were dazed, like a mad creature; . . . and now I have become a vulgar, contemptible woman whom any one may despise."

Gurov felt bored already, listening to her. He was irritated by the naive tone, by this remorse, so unexpected and inopportune; but for the tears in her eyes, he might have thought she was jesting or playing a part.

"I don't understand," he said softly. "What is it you want?"

She hid her face on his breast and pressed close to him.

"Believe me, believe me, I beseech you . . ." she said. "I love a pure, honest life, and sin is loathsome to me. I don't know what I am doing. Simple people say: 'The Evil One has beguiled me.' And I may say of myself now that the Evil One has beguiled me."

"Hush, hush! . . ." he muttered.

He looked at her fixed, scared eyes, kissed her, talked softly and affectionately, and by degrees she was comforted, and her gaiety returned; they both began laughing.

Afterwards when they went out there was not a soul on the sea-front. The town with its cypresses had quite a deathlike air, but the sea still broke noisily on the shore; a single barge was rocking on the waves, and a lantern was blinking sleepily on it.

They found a cab and drove to Oreanda.

"I found out your surname in the hall just now: it was written on the board—Von Diderits," said Gurov. "Is your husband a German?"

"No, I believe his grandfather was a German, but he is an Orthodox Russian himself."

At Oreanda they sat on a seat not far from the church, looked down at the sea, and were silent. Yalta was hardly visible through the morning mist; white clouds stood motionless on the mountain-tops. The leaves did not stir on the trees, grasshoppers chirruped, and the monotonous hollow sound of the sea rising up from below, spoke of the peace, of the eternal sleep awaiting us. So it must have sounded when there was no Yalta, no Oreanda here; so it sounds now, and it will sound as indifferently and monotonously when we are all no more. And in this constancy, in this complete indifference to the life and death of each of us, there lies hid, perhaps, a pledge of our eternal salvation, of the unceasing movement of life upon earth, of unceasing progress towards perfection. Sitting beside a young woman who in the dawn seemed so lovely, soothed and spellbound in these magical surroundings—the sea, mountains, clouds, the open sky— Gurov thought how in reality everything is beautiful in this world when one reflects: everything except what we think or do ourselves when we forget our human dignity and the higher aims of our existence.

A man walked up to them—probably a keeper—looked at them and walked away. And this detail seemed mysterious and beautiful, too. They saw a steamer come from Theodosia, with its lights out in the glow of dawn.

"There is dew on the grass," said Anna Sergeyevna, after a silence.

"Yes. It's time to go home."

They went back to the town.

Then they met every day at twelve o'clock on the sea-front, lunched and dined together, went for walks, admired the sea. She complained that she slept badly, that her heart throbbed violently; asked the same questions, troubled now by jealousy and now by the fear that he did not respect her sufficiently. And often in the square or gardens, when there was no one near them, he suddenly drew her to him and kissed her passionately. Complete idleness, these kisses in broad daylight while he looked round in dread of some one's seeing them, the heat, the smell of the sea, and the continual passing to and fro before him of idle, well-dressed, well-fed people, made a new man of him; he told Anna Sergeyevna how beautiful she was, how fascinating. He was impatiently passionate, he would not move a step away from her, while she was often pensive and continually urged him to confess that he did not respect her, did not love her in the least, and thought of her as nothing but a common woman. Rather late almost every evening they drove somewhere out of town, to Oreanda or to the waterfall; and the expedition was always a success, the scenery invariably impressed them as grand and beautiful.

They were expecting her husband to come, but a letter came from him, saying that there was something wrong with his eyes, and he entreated his wife to come home as quickly as possible. Anna Sergeyevna made haste to go.

"It's a good thing I am going away," she said to Gurov. "It's the finger of destiny!"

She went by coach and he went with her. They were driving the whole day. When she had got into a compartment of the express, and when the second bell had rung, she said:

"Let me look at you once more . . . look at you once again. That's right."

She did not shed tears, but was so sad that she seemed ill, and her face was quivering.

"I shall remember you . . . think of you," she said. "God be with you; be happy. Don't remember evil against me. We are parting forever—it must be so, for we ought never to have met. Well, God be with you."

The train moved off rapidly, its lights soon vanished from sight, and a minute later there was no sound of it, as though everything had conspired together to end as quickly as possible that sweet delirium, that madness. Left alone on the platform, and gazing into the dark distance, Gurov listened to the chirrup of the grasshoppers and the hum of the telegraph wires, feeling as though he had only just waked up. And he thought, musing, that there had been another episode or adventure in his life, and it, too, was at an end, and nothing was left of it but a memory. . . . He was moved, sad, and conscious of a slight remorse. This young woman whom he would never meet again had not been happy with him; he was genuinely warm and affectionate with her, but yet in his manner, his tone, and his caresses there had been a shade of light irony, the coarse condescension of a happy man who was, besides, almost twice her age. All the time she had called him kind, exceptional, lofty; obviously he had seemed to her different from what he really was, so he had unintentionally deceived her. . . .

Here at the station was already a scent of autumn; it was a cold evening.

"It's time for me to go north," thought Gurov as he left the platform. "High time!"

3

At home in Moscow everything was in its winter routine; the stoves were heated, and in the morning it was still dark when the children were having breakfast and getting ready for school, and the nurse would light the lamp for a short time. The frosts had begun already. When the first snow has fallen, on the first day of sledge-driving it is pleasant to see the white earth, the white roofs, to draw soft, delicious breath, and the season brings back the days of one's youth. The old limes and birches, white with hoar-frost, have a good-natured expression; they are nearer to one's heart than cypresses and palms, and near them one doesn't want to be thinking of the sea and the mountains.

Gurov was Moscow born; he arrived in Moscow on a fine frosty day, and when he put on his fur coat and warm gloves, and walked along Petrovka, and when on Saturday evening he heard the ringing of the bells, his recent trip and the places he had seen lost all charm for him. Little by little he became absorbed in Moscow life, greedily read three newspapers a day, and declared he did not read the Moscow papers on principle! He already felt a longing to go to restaurants, clubs, dinner-parties, anniversary celebrations and he felt flattered at entertaining distinguished lawyers and artists, and at playing cards with a professor at the doctors' club. He could already eat a whole plateful of salt fish and cabbage. . . .

In another month, he fancied, the image of Anna Sergeyevna would be shrouded in a mist in his memory, and only from time to time would visit him in his dreams with a touching smile as others did. But more than a month passed, real winter had come, and everything was still clear in his memory as though he had parted with Anna Sergeyevna only the day before. And his memories glowed more and more vividly. When in the evening stillness he heard from his study the voices of his children, preparing their lessons, or when he listened to a song or the organ at the restaurant, or the storm howled in the chimney, suddenly everything would rise up in his memory: what had happened on the groyne, and the early morning with the mist on the mountains, and the steamer coming from Theodosia and the kisses. He would pace a long time about his room, remembering it all and smiling; then his memories passed into dreams, and in his fancy the past was mingled with what was to come. Anna Sergeyevna did not visit him in dreams, but followed him about everywhere like a shadow and haunted him. When he shut his eyes he saw her as though she were living before him, and she seemed to him lovelier, younger, tenderer than she was; and he imagined himself finer than he had been in Yalta. In the evenings she peeped out at him from the bookcase, from the fireplace, from the corner—he heard her breathing, the caressing rustle of her dress. In the street he watched the women, looking for some one like her.

He was tormented by an intense desire to confide his memories to some one. But in his home it was impossible to talk of his love, and he had no one outside; he could not talk to his tenants nor to any one at the bank. And what had he to talk of? Had he been in love, then? Had there been anything beautiful, poetical, or edifying or simply interesting in his relations with Anna Sergeyevna? And there was nothing for him but to talk vaguely of love, of woman, and no one guessed what it meant; only his wife twitched her black eyebrows, and said: "The part of a lady-killer does not suit you at all, Dimitri."

One evening, coming out of the doctors' club with an official with whom he had been playing cards, he could not resist saying:

"If only you knew what a fascinating woman I made the acquaintance of in Yalta!"

The official got into his sledge and was driving away, but turned suddenly and shouted:

"Dmitri Dmitritch!"

"What?"

"You were right this evening: the sturgeon was a bit too strong!"

These words, so ordinary, for some reason moved Gurov to indignation, and struck him as degrading and unclean. What savage manners, what people! What senseless nights, what uninteresting, uneventful days! The rage for card-playing, the gluttony, the drunkenness, the continual talk always about the same thing. Useless pursuits and conversations always about the same things absorb the better part of one's time, the better part of one's strength, and in the end there is left a life grovelling and curtailed, worthless and trivial, and there is no escaping or getting away from it—just as though one were in a madhouse or a prison.

Gurov did not sleep all night, and was filled with indignation. And he had a headache all next day. And the next night he slept badly; he sat up in bed, thinking, or paced up and down his room. He was sick of his children, sick of the bank; he had no desire to go anywhere or to talk of anything.

In the holidays in December he prepared for a journey, and told his wife he was going to Petersburg to do something in the interests of a young friend—and he set off for S—. What for? He did not very well know himself. He wanted to see Anna Sergeyevna and to talk with her—to arrange a meeting, if possible.

He reached S— in the morning, and took the best room at the hotel, in which the floor was covered with grey army cloth, and on the table was an inkstand, grey with dust and adorned with a figure on horseback, with its hat and its hand and its head broken off. The hotel porter gave him the necessary information; Von Diderits lived in a house of his own in Old Gontcharny Street—it was not far from the hotel: he was rich and lived in good style, and had his own horses; every one in town knew him. The porter pronounced the name "Dridirits."

Gurov went without haste to Old Gontcharny Street and found the house. Just opposite the house stretched a long grey fence adorned with nails.

"One would run away from a fence like that," thought Gurov, looking from the fence to the windows of the house and back again.

He considered: to-day was a holiday, and the husband would probably be at home. And in any case it would be tactless to go into the house and upset her. If he were to send her a note it might fall into her husband's hands, and then it might ruin everything. The best thing was to trust to chance. And he kept walking up and down the street by the fence, waiting for the chance. He saw a beggar go in at the gate and dogs fly at him; then an hour later he heard a piano, and the sounds were faint and indistinct. Probably it was Anna Sergeyevna playing. The front door suddenly opened, and an old woman came out, followed by the familiar white Pomeranian. Gurov was on the point of calling to the dog, but his heart began beating violently, and in his excitement he could not remember the dog's name.

He walked up and down, and loathed the grey fence more and more, and by now he thought irritably that Anna Sergeyevna had forgotten him, and was perhaps already amusing herself with some one else, and that that was very natural in a young woman who had nothing to look at from morning till night but that confounded fence. He went back to his hotel room and sat for a long while on the sofa, not knowing what to do, then he had dinner and a long nap.

"How stupid and worrying it is!" he thought when he woke and looked at the dark windows: it was already evening. "Here I've had a good sleep for some reason. What shall I do in the night?"

He sat on the bed, which was covered by a cheap grey blanket, such as one sees in hospitals, and he taunted himself in his vexation:

"So much for the lady with the dog . . . so much for the adventure. . . . You're in a nice fix. . . ."

That morning at the station a poster in large letters had caught his eye. "The Geisha" was to be performed for the first time. He thought of this and went to the theater.

"It's quite possible she may go to the first performance," he thought.

The theatre was full. As in all provincial theatres, there was a fog above the chandelier, the gallery was noisy and restless; in the front row the local dandies were standing up before the beginning of the performance, with their hands behind them; in the Governor's box the Governor's daughter, wearing a boa, was sitting in the front seat, while the Governor himself lurked modestly behind the curtain with only his hands visible;

the orchestra was a long time tuning up; the stage curtain swayed. All the time the audience were coming in and taking their seats Gurov looked at them eagerly.

Anna Sergeyevna, too, came in. She sat down in the third row, and when Gurov looked at her his heart contracted, and he understood clearly that for him there was in the whole world no creature so near, so precious, and so important to him; she, this little woman, in no way remarkable, lost in a provincial crowd, with a vulgar lorgnette in her hand, filled his whole life now, was his sorrow and his joy, the one happiness that he now desired for himself, and to the sounds of the inferior orchestra, of the wretched provincial violins, he thought how lovely she was. He thought and dreamed.

A young man with small side-whiskers, tall and stooping, came in with Anna Sergeyevna, and sat down beside her; he bent his head at every step and seemed to be continually bowing. Most likely this was the husband whom at Yalta, in a rush of bitter feeling, she had called a flunkey. And there really was in his long figure, his side-whiskers, and the small bald patch on his head, something of the flunkey's obsequiousness; his smile was sugary, and in his buttonhole there was some badge of distinction like the number on a waiter.

During the first interval the husband went away to smoke; she remained alone in her stall. Gurov, who was sitting in the stalls, too, went up to her and said in a trembling voice, with a forced smile:

"Good-evening."

She glanced at him and turned pale, then glanced again with horror, unable to believe her eyes, and tightly gripped her fan and the lorgnette in her hands, evidently struggling with herself not to faint. Both were silent. She was sitting, he was standing, frightened by her confusion and not venturing to sit down beside her. The violins and the flute began tuning up. He felt suddenly frightened; it seemed as though all the people in the boxes were looking at them. She got up and went quickly to the door; he followed her, and both walked senselessly along passages, and up and down stairs, and figures in legal, scholastic, and civil service uniforms, all wearing badges, flitted before their eyes. They caught glimpses of ladies, of fur coats hanging on pegs; the draughts blew on them, bringing a smell of stale tobacco. And Gurov, whose heart was beating violently, thought:

"Oh, heavens! Why are these people here and this orchestra! . . ."

And at that instant he recalled how when he had seen Anna Sergeyevna off at the station he had thought that everything was over and they would never meet again. But how far they were still from the end!

On the narrow, gloomy staircase over which was written "To the Amphitheatre," she stopped.

"How you have frightened me!" she said, breathing hard, still pale and overwhelmed. "Oh, how you have frightened me! I am half dead. Why have you come? Why?"

"But do understand, Anna, do understand . . ." he said hastily in a low voice. "I entreat you to understand. . . ."

She looked at him with dread, with entreaty, with love; she looked at him intently, to keep his features more distinctly in her memory.

"I am so unhappy," she went on, not heeding him. "I have thought of nothing but you all the time; I live only in the thought of you. And I wanted to forget, to forget you; but why, oh, why, have you come?"

On the landing above them two schoolboys were smoking and looking down, but that was nothing to Gurov; he drew Anna Sergeyevna to him, and began kissing her face, her cheeks, and her hands.

"What are you doing, what are you doing!" she cried in horror, pushing him away. "We are mad. Go away to-day; go away at once. . . . I beseech you by all that is sacred, I implore you. . . . There are people coming this way!"

Some one was coming up the stairs.

"You must go away," Anna Sergeyevna went on in a whisper. "Do you hear, Dmitri Dmitritch? I will come and see you in Moscow. I have never been happy; I am miserable now, and I never, never shall be happy, never! Don't make me suffer still more! I swear I'll come to Moscow. But now let us part. My precious, good, dear one, we must part!"

She pressed his hand and began rapidly going downstairs, looking round at him, and from her eyes he could see that she really was unhappy. Gurov stood for a little while, listened, then, when all sound had died away, he found his coat and left the theatre.

4

And Anna Sergeyevna began coming to see him in Moscow. Once in two or three months she left S——, telling her husband that she was going to consult a doctor about an internal complaint—and her husband believed her, and did not believe her. In Moscow she stayed at the Slaviansky Bazaar hotel, and at once sent a man in a red cap to Gurov. Gurov went to see her, and no one in Moscow knew of it.

Once he was going to see her in this way on a winter morning (the messenger had come the evening before when he was out). With him walked his daughter, whom he wanted to take to school: it was on the way. Snow was falling in big wet flakes.

"It's three degrees above freezing-point, and yet it is snowing," said Gurov to his daughter. "The thaw is only on the surface of the earth; there is quite a different temperature at a greater height in the atmosphere."

"And why are there no thunderstorms in the winter, father?"

He explained that, too. He talked, thinking all the while that he was going to see *her,* and no living soul knew of it, and probably never would know. He had two lives: one, open, seen and known by all who cared to know, full of relative truth and of relative falsehood, exactly like the lives of his friends and acquaintances; and another life running its course in secret. And through some strange, perhaps accidental, conjunction of circumstances, everything that was essential, of interest and of value to him, everything in which he was sincere and did not deceive himself, everything that made the kernel of his life, was hidden from other people; and all that was false in him, the sheath in which he hid himself to conceal the truth—such, for instance, as his work in the bank, his discussions at the club, his "lower race," his presence with his wife at anniversary festivities—all that was open. And he judged of others by himself, not believing in what he saw, and always believing that every man had his real, most interesting life under the cover of secrecy and under the cover of night. All personal life rested on secrecy, and possibly it was partly on that account that civilised man was so nervously anxious that personal privacy should be respected.

After leaving his daughter at school, Gurov went on to the Slaviansky Bazaar. He took off his fur coat below, went upstairs, and softly knocked at the door. Anna Sergeyevna, wearing his favourite grey dress, exhausted by the journey and the suspense, had been expecting him since the evening before. She was pale; she looked at him, and did not smile, and he had hardly come in when she fell on his breast. Their kiss was slow and prolonged, as though they had not met for two years.

"Well, how are you getting on there?" he asked. "What news?"

"Wait; I'll tell you directly. . . . I can't talk."

She could not speak; she was crying. She turned away from him, and pressed her handkerchief to her eyes.

"Let her have her cry out. I'll sit down and wait," he thought, and he sat down in an arm-chair.

Then he rang and asked for tea to be brought him, and while he drank his tea she remained standing at the window with her back to him. She was crying from emotion, from the miserable consciousness that their life was so hard for them; they could only meet in secret, hiding themselves from people, like thieves! Was not their life shattered?

"Come, do stop!" he said.

It was evident to him that this love of theirs would not soon be over, that he could not see the end of it. Anna Sergeyevna grew more and more attached to him. She adored him, and it was unthinkable to say to her that it was bound to have an end some day; besides, she would not have believed it!

He went up to her and took her by the shoulders to say something affectionate and cheering, and at that moment he saw himself in the looking-glass.

His hair was already beginning to turn grey. And it seemed strange to him that he had grown so much older, so much plainer during the last few years. The shoulders on which his hands rested were warm and quivering. He felt compassion for this life, still so warm and lovely, but probably already not far from beginning to fade and wither like his own. Why did she love him so much? He always seemed to women different from what he was, and they loved in him not himself, but the man created by their imagination, whom they had been eagerly seeking all their lives; and afterwards, when they noticed their mistake, they loved him all the same. And not one of them had been happy with him. Time passed, he had made their acquaintance, got on with them, parted, but he had never once loved; it was anything you like, but not love.

And only now when his head was grey he had fallen properly, really in love—for the first time in his life.

Anna Sergeyevna and he loved each other like people very close and akin, like husband and wife, like tender friends; it seemed to them that fate itself had meant them for one another, and they could not understand why he had a wife and she a husband; and it was as though they were a pair of birds of passage, caught and forced to live in different cages. They forgave each other for what they were ashamed of in their past, they forgave everything in the present, and felt that this love of theirs had changed them both.

In moments of depression in the past he had comforted himself with any arguments that came into his mind, but now he no longer cared for arguments; he felt profound compassion, he wanted to be sincere and tender. . . .

"Don't cry, my darling," he said. "You've had your cry; that's enough. . . . Let us talk now, let us think of some plan."

Then they spent a long while taking counsel together, talked of how to avoid the necessity for secrecy, for deception, for living in different towns and not seeing each other for long at a time. How could they be free from this intolerable bondage?

"How? How?" he asked, clutching his head. "How?"

And it seemed as though in a little while the solution would be found, and then a new and splendid life would begin; and it was clear to both of them that they had still a long, long road before them, and that the most complicated and difficult part of it was only just beginning.

(1898)

QUESTIONS

1. What draws Gurov and Anna together, despite their marriages?

2. What stages does their relationship go through? What makes Gurov leave Moscow to see Anna once again?

3. What evidence is there at the end of the story that Gurov and Anna will arrange their lives so they can be together? What is the point of the story in view of Chekhov's ending?

4. What role does setting play in "The Lady with the Dog"?

KATE CHOPIN (1851–1904)

The Storm

A Sequel to "At the 'Cadian Ball"

I

The leaves were so still that even Bibi thought it was going to rain. Bobinôt, who was accustomed to converse on terms of perfect equality with his little son, called the child's attention to certain sombre clouds that were rolling with sinister intention from the west, accompanied by a sullen, threatening roar. They were at Friedheimer's store and decided to remain there till the storm had passed. They sat within the door on two empty kegs. Bibi was four years old and looked very wise.

"Mama'll be 'fraid, yes," he suggested with blinking eyes.

"She'll shut the house. Maybe she got Sylvie helpin' her this evenin'," Bobinôt responded reassuringly.

"No; she ent got Sylvie. Sylvie was helpin' her yistiday," piped Bibi.

Bobinôt arose and going across to the counter purchased a can of shrimps, of which Calixta was very fond. Then he returned to his perch on the keg and sat stolidly holding the can of shrimps while the storm burst. It shook the wooden store and seemed to be ripping great furrows in the distant field. Bibi laid his little hand on his father's knee and was not afraid.

II

Calixta, at home, felt no uneasiness for their safety. She sat at a side window sewing furiously on a sewing machine. She was greatly occupied and did not notice the approaching storm. But she felt very warm and often stopped to mop her face on which the perspiration gathered in beads. She unfastened her white sacque at the throat. It began to grow dark, and suddenly realizing the situation she got up hurriedly and went about closing windows and doors.

Out on the small front gallery she had hung Bobinôt's Sunday clothes to air and she hastened out to gather them before the rain fell. As she stepped outside, Alcée Laballière rode in at the gate. She had not seen him very often since her marriage, and never alone. She stood there with Bobinôt's coat in her hands, and the big rain drops began to fall. Alcée rode his horse under the shelter of a side projection where the chickens had huddled and there were plows and a harrow piled up in the corner.

"May I come and wait on your gallery till the storm is over, Calixta?" he asked.

"Come 'long in, M'sieur Alcée."

His voice and her own startled her as if from a trance, and she seized Bobinôt's vest. Alcée, mounting to the porch, grabbed the trousers and snatched Bibi's braided jacket that was about to be carried away by a sudden gust of wind. He expressed an intention to remain outside, but it was soon apparent that he might as well have been out in the open: the water beat in upon the boards in driving sheets, and he went inside, closing the door after him. It was necessary to put something beneath the door to keep the water out.

"My! what a rain! It's good two years sence it rain' like that," exclaimed Calixta as she rolled up a piece of bagging and Alcée helped her to thrust it beneath the crack.

She was a little fuller of figure than five years before when she married; but she had lost nothing of her vivacity. Her blue eyes still retained their melting quality; and her yellow hair, dishevelled by the wind and rain, kinked more stubbornly than ever about her ears and temples.

The rain beat upon the low, shingled roof with a force and clatter that threatened to break an entrance and deluge them there. They were in the dining room—the sitting room—the general utility room. Adjoining was her bed room, with Bibi's couch along side her own. The door stood open, and the room with its white, monumental bed, its closed shutters, looked dim and mysterious.

Alcée flung himself into a rocker and Calixta nervously began to gather up from the floor the lengths of a cotton sheet which she had been sewing.

"If this keeps up, *Dieu sait*[1] if the levees goin' to stan' it!" she exclaimed.

"What have you got to do with the levees?"

"I got enough to do! An' there's Bobinôt with Bibi out in that storm—if he only didn' left Friedheimer's!"

"Let us hope, Calixta, that Bobinôt's got sense enough to come in out of a cyclone."

She went and stood at the window with a greatly disturbed look on her face. She wiped the frame that was clouded with moisture. It was stiflingly hot. Alcée got up and joined her at the window, looking over her shoulder. The rain was coming down in sheets obscuring the view of far-off cabins and enveloping the distant wood in a gray mist. The playing of the lightning was incessant. A bolt struck a tall chinaberry tree at the edge of the field. It filled all visible space with a blinding glare and the crash seemed to invade the very boards they stood upon.

Calixta put her hands to her eyes, and with a cry, staggered backward. Alcée's arm encircled her, and for an instant he drew her close and spasmodically to him.

"*Bonté!*"[2] she cried, releasing herself from his encircling arm and retreating from the window, "the house'll go next! If I only knew w'ere Bibi was!" She would not compose herself; she would not be seated. Alcée clasped her shoulders and looked into her face. The contact of her warm, palpitating body when he had unthinkingly drawn her into his arms, had aroused all the old-time infatuation and desire for her flesh.

"Calixta," he said, "don't be frightened. Nothing can happen. The house is too low to be struck, with so many tall trees standing about. There! aren't you going to be quiet? say, aren't you?" He pushed her hair back from her face that was warm and steaming. Her lips were as red and moist as pomegranate seed. Her white neck and a glimpse of her full, firm bosom disturbed him powerfully. As she glanced up at him the fear in her

---

[1] *Dieu sait:* French for "God knows."
[2] *Bonté!:* French for "Goodness!"

liquid blue eyes had given place to a drowsy gleam that unconsciously betrayed a sensuous desire. He looked down into her eyes and there was nothing for him to do but to gather her lips in a kiss. It reminded him of Assumption.

"Do you remember—in Assumption, Calixta?" he asked in a low voice broken by passion. Oh! she remembered; for in Assumption he had kissed her and kissed and kissed her; until his senses would well nigh fail, and to save her he would resort to a desperate flight. If she was not an immaculate dove in those days, she was still inviolate; a passionate creature whose very defenselessness had made her defense, against which his honor forbade him to prevail. Now—well, now—her lips seemed in a manner free to be tasted, as well as her round, white throat and her whiter breasts.

They did not heed the crashing torrents, and the roar of the elements made her laugh as she lay in his arms. She was a revelation in that dim, mysterious chamber; as white as the couch she lay upon. Her firm, elastic flesh that was knowing for the first time its birthright, was like a creamy lily that the sun invites to contribute its breath and perfume to the undying life of the world.

The generous abundance of her passion, without guile or trickery, was like a white flame which penetrated and found response in depths of his own sensuous nature that had never yet been reached.

When he touched her breasts they gave themselves up in quivering ecstasy, inviting his lips. Her mouth was a fountain of delight. And when he possessed her, they seemed to swoon together at the very borderland of life's mystery.

He stayed cushioned upon her, breathless, dazed, enervated, with his heart beating like a hammer upon her. With one hand she clasped his head, her lips lightly touching his forehead. The other hand stroked with a soothing rhythm his muscular shoulders.

The growl of the thunder was distant and passing away. The rain beat softly upon the shingles, inviting them to drowsiness and sleep. But they dared not yield.

The rain was over; and the sun was turning the glistening green world into a palace of gems. Calixta, on the gallery, watched Alcée ride away. He turned and smiled at her with a beaming face; and she lifted her pretty chin in the air and laughed aloud.

III

Bobinôt and Bibi, trudging home, stopped without at the cistern to make themselves presentable.

"My! Bibi, w'at will yo' mama say! You ought to be ashame'. You oughtn' put on those good pants. Look at 'em! An' that mud on yo' collar! How you got that mud on yo' collar, Bibi? I never saw such a boy!" Bibi was the picture of pathetic resignation. Bobinôt was the embodiment of serious solicitude as he strove to remove from his own person and his son's the signs of their tramp over heavy roads and through wet fields. He scraped the mud off Bibi's bare legs and feet with a stick and carefully removed all traces from his heavy brogans. Then, prepared for the worst—the meeting with an over-scrupulous housewife, they entered cautiously at the back door.

Calixta was preparing supper. She had set the table and was dripping coffee at the hearth. She sprang up as they came in.

"Oh, Bobinôt! You back! My! but I was uneasy. W'ere you been during the rain? An' Bibi? he ain't wet? he ain't hurt?" She had clasped Bibi and was kissing him effusively. Bobinôt's explanations and apologies which he had been composing all along the way, died on his lips as Calixta felt him to see if he were dry, and seemed to express nothing but satisfaction at their safe return.

"I brought you some shrimps, Calixta," offered Bobinôt, hauling the can from his ample side pocket and laying it on the table.

"Shrimps! Oh, Bobinôt! you too good fo' anything!" and she gave him a smacking kiss on the cheek that resounded. "*J'vous réponds,*[3] we'll have a feas' to night! umph-umph!"

Bobinôt and Bibi began to relax and enjoy themselves, and when the three seated themselves at table they laughed much and so loud that anyone might have heard them as far away as Laballière's.

IV

Alcée Laballière wrote to his wife, Clarisse, that night. It was a loving letter, full of tender solicitude. He told her not to hurry back, but if she and the babies liked it at Biloxi, to stay a month longer. He was getting on nicely; and though he missed them, he was willing to bear the separation a while longer—realizing that their health and pleasure were the first things to be considered.

V

As for Clarisse, she was charmed upon receiving her husband's letter. She and the babies were doing well. The society was agreeable; many of her old friends and acquaintances were at the bay. And the first free breath since her marriage seemed to restore the pleasant liberty of her maiden days. Devoted as she was to her husband, their intimate conjugal life was something which she was more than willing to forego for a while.

So the storm passed and every one was happy.

(1898)

QUESTIONS

1. What is the significance of the storm as metaphor?

2. How does Calixta and Alcée's past history influence their present actions? In what way can their behavior be viewed as understandable and justifiable?

3. How does the brief affair between Calixta and Alcée affect their marriages?

4. What comment do you think Chopin is making about the nature of love vs. marriage?

---

[3] *J'vous réponds:* French for "I tell you."

Becky Birtha (b. 1948)

In The Life[1]

Grace come to me in my sleep last night. I feel somebody presence, in the room with me, then I catch the scent of Posner's Bergamot Pressing Oil, and that cocoa butter grease she use on her skin. I know she standing at the bedside, right over me, and then she call my name.

"Pearl."

My Christian name Pearl Irene Jenkins, but don't nobody ever call me that no more. I been Jinx to the world for longer than I care to specify. Since my mother passed away, Grace the only one ever use my given name.

"Pearl," she say again. "I'm just gone down to the garden awhile. I be back."

I'm so deep asleep I have to fight my way awake, and when I do be fully woke, Grace is gone. I ease my tired bones up and drag em down the stairs, cross the kitchen in the dark, and out the back screen door onto the porch. I guess I'm half expecting Gracie to be there waiting for me, but there ain't another soul stirring tonight. Not a sound but singing crickets, and nothing staring back at me but that old weather-beaten fence I ought to painted this summer, and still ain't made time for. I lower myself down into the porch swing, where Gracie and I have sat so many still summer nights and watched the moon rising up over Old Mister Thompson's field.

I never had time to paint that fence back then, neither. But it didn't matter none, cause Gracie had it all covered up with her flowers. She used to sit right here on this swing at night, when a little breeze be blowing, and say she could tell all the different flowers apart, just by they smell. The wind pick up a scent, and Gracie say, "Smell that jasmine, Pearl?" Then a breeze come up from another direction, and she turn her head like somebody calling her and say, "Now that's my honeysuckle, now."

It used to tickle me, cause she knowed I couldn't tell all them flowers of hers apart when I was looking square at em in broad daylight. So how I'm gonna do it by smell in the middle of the night? I just laugh and rock the swing a little, and watch her enjoying herself in the soft moonlight.

I could never get enough of watching her. I always did think that Grace Simmons was the prettiest woman north of the Mason-Dixon line. Now I've lived enough years to know it's true. There's been other women in my life besides Grace, and I guess I loved them all, one way or another, but she was something special—Gracie was something else again.

She was a dark brownskin woman—the color of fresh gingerbread hot out the oven. In fact, I used to call her that—my gingerbread girl. She had plenty enough of that pretty brownskin flesh to fill your arms up with something substantial when you hugging her, and to make a nice background for them dimples in her cheeks and other places I won't go into detail about.

---

[1] In The Life: euphemism for living the life of a lesbian.

Gracie could be one elegant good looker when she set her mind to it. I'll never forget the picture she made, that time the New Year's Eve party was down at the Star Harbor Ballroom. That was the first year we was in The Club, and we was going to every event they had. Dressed to kill. Gracie had on that white silk dress that set off her complexion so perfect, with her hair done up in all them little curls. A single strand of pearls that could have fooled anybody. Long gloves. And a little fur stole. We was serious about our partying back then! I didn't look too bad myself, with that black velvet jacket I used to have, and the pleats in my slacks pressed so sharp you could cut yourself on em. I weighed quite a bit less than I do now, too. Right when you come in the door of the ballroom, they have a great big floor to ceiling gold frame mirror, and if I remember rightly, we didn't get past that for quite some time.

Everybody want to dance with Gracie that night. And that's fine with me. Along about the middle of the evening, the band is playing a real hot number, and here come Louie and Max over to me, all long-face serious, wanting to know how I can let my woman be out there shaking her behind with any stranger that wander in the door. Now they know good and well ain't no strangers here. The Cinnamon & Spice Club is a private club, and all events is by invitation only.

Of course, there's some thinks friends is more dangerous than strangers. But I never could be the jealous, overprotective type. And the fact is, I just love to watch the woman. I don't care if she out there shaking it with the Virgin Mary, long as she having a good time. And that's just what I told Max and Lou. I could lean up against that bar and watch her for hours.

You wouldn't know, to look at her, she done it all herself. Made all her own dresses and hats, and even took apart a old ratty fur coat that used to belong to my great aunt Malinda to make that cute little stole. She always did her own hair—every week or two. She used to do mine, too. Always be teasing me about let her make me some curls this time. I'd get right aggravated. Cause you can't have a proper argument with somebody when they standing over your head with a hot comb in they hand. You kinda at they mercy. I'm sitting fuming and cursing under them towels and stuff, with the sweat dripping all in my eyes in the steamy kitchen—and she just laughing. "Girl," I'm telling her, "you know won't no curls fit under my uniform cap. Less you want me to stay home this week and you gonna go work my job and your job too."

Both of us had to work, always, and we still ain't had much. Everybody always think Jinx and Grace doing all right, but we was scrimping and saving all along. Making stuff over and making do. Half of what we had to eat grew right here in this garden. Still and all, I guess we *was* doing all right. We had each other.

Now I finally got the damn house paid off, and she ain't even here to appreciate it with me. And Gracie's poor bedraggled garden is just struggling along on its last legs—kinda like me. I ain't the kind to complain about my lot, but truth to tell, I can't be down crawling around on my hands and knees no more—this body I got put up such a fuss and holler. Can't enjoy the garden at night proper nowadays, nohow. Since Mister Thompson's land was took over by the city and they built them housing projects where the field used to be, you can't even see the moon from here, till it get up past the fourteenth floor. Don't no moonlight come in my yard no more. And I guess I might as well pick my old self up and go on back to bed.

Sometimes I still ain't used to the fact that Grace is passed on. Not even after these thirteen years without her. She the only woman I ever lived with—and I lived with her more than half my life. This house her house, too, and she oughta be here in it with me.

I rise up by six o'clock most every day, same as I done all them years I worked driving for the C.T.C. If the weather ain't too bad, I take me a walk—and if I ain't careful, I'm liable to end up down at the Twelfth Street Depot, waiting to see what trolley they gonna give me this morning. There ain't a soul working in that office still remember me. And they don't even run a trolley on the Broadway line no more. They been running a bus for the past five years.

I forgets a lot of things these days. Last week, I had just took in the clean laundry off the line, and I'm up in the spare room fixing to iron my shirts, when I hear somebody pass through that squeaky side gate and go on around to the back yard. I ain't paid it no mind at all, cause that's the way Gracie most often do when she come home. Go see about her garden fore she even come in the house. I always be teasing her she care more about them collards and string beans than she do about me. I hear her moving around out there while I'm sprinkling the last shirt and plugging in the iron—hear leaves rustling, and a crate scraping along the walk.

While I'm waiting for the iron to heat up, I take a look out the window, and come to see it ain't Gracie at all, but two a them sassy little scoundrels from over the projects—one of em standing on a apple crate and holding up the other one, who is picking my ripe peaches off my tree, just as brazen as you please. Don't even blink a eyelash when I holler out the window. I have to go running down all them stairs and out on the back porch, waving the cord I done jerked out the iron—when Doctor Matthews has told me a hundred times I ain't supposed to be running or getting excited about nothing, with my pressure like it is. And I ain't even supposed to be *walking* up and down no stairs.

When they seen the ironing cord in my hand, them two little sneaks had a reaction all right. The one on the bottom drop the other one right on his padded quarters and lit out for the gate, hollering, "Look out, Timmy! Here come Old Lady Jenkins!"

When I think about it now, it was right funny, but at the time I was so mad it musta took me a whole half hour to cool off. I sat there on that apple crate just boiling.

Eventually, I begun to see how it wasn't even them two kids I was so mad at. I was mad at time. For playing tricks on me the way it done. So I don't even remember that Grace Simmons has been dead now for the past thirteen years. And mad at time just for passing—so fast. If I had my life to live over, I wouldn't trade in none of them years for nothing. I'd just slow em down.

The church sisters around here is always trying to get me to be thinking about dying, myself. They must figure, when you my age, that's the only excitement you got left to look forward to. Gladys Hawkins stopped out front this morning, while I was mending a patch in the top screen of the front door. She was grinning from ear to ear like she just spent the night with Jesus himself.

"Morning, Sister Jenkins. Right pretty day the good Lord seen fit to send us, ain't it?"

I ain't never known how to answer nobody who manages to bring the good Lord into every conversation. If I nod and say yes, she'll think I finally got religion. But if I disagree, she'll think I'm crazy, cause it truly is one pretty August morning. Fortunately, it don't matter to her whether I agree or not, cause she gone right on talking according to her own agenda anyway.

"You know, this Sunday is Women's Day over at Blessed Endurance. Reverend Solomon Moody is gonna be visiting, speaking on 'A Woman's Place In The Church.' Why don't you come and join us for worship? You'd be most welcome."

I'm tempted to tell her exactly what come to my mind—that I ain't never heard of no woman name Solomon. However, I'm polite enough to hold my tongue, which is more than I can say for Gladys.

She ain't waiting for no answer from me, just going right on. "I don't spose you need me to point it out to you, Sister Jenkins, but you know you ain't as young as you used to be." As if both of our ages wasn't common knowledge to each other, seeing as we been knowing one another since we was girls. "You reaching that time of life when you might wanna be giving a little more attention to the spiritual side of things than you been doing. . . ."

She referring, politely as she capable of, to the fact that I ain't been seen inside a church for thirty-five years.

". . . And you know what the good Lord say. 'Watch therefore, for ye know neither the day nor the hour . . .' But, 'He that believeth on the Son hath everlasting life . . .'"

It ain't no use to argue with her kind. The Lord is on they side in every little disagreement, and he don't never give up. So when she finally wind down and ask me again will she see me in church this Sunday, I just say I'll think about it.

Funny thing, I been thinking about it all day. But not the kinda thoughts she want me to think, I'm sure. Last time I went to church was on a Easter Sunday. We decided to go on accounta Gracie's old meddling cousin, who was always nagging us about how we unnatural and sinful and a disgrace to her family. Seem like she seen it as her one mission in life to get us two sinners inside a church. I guess she figure, once she get us in there, God gonna take over the job. So Grace and me finally conspires that the way to get her off our backs is to give her what she think she want.

Course, I ain't had on a skirt since before the war, and I ain't aiming to change my lifelong habits just to please Cousin Hattie. But I did take a lotta pains over my appearance that day. I'd had my best tailor-made suit pressed fresh, and slept in my stocking cap the night before so I'd have every hair in place. Even had one a Gracie's flowers stuck in my buttonhole. And a brand new narrow-brim dove gray Stetson hat. Gracie take one look at me when I'm ready and shake her head. "The good sisters is gonna have a hard time concentrating on the preacher today!"

We arrive at her cousin's church nice and early, but of course it's a big crowd inside already on accounta it being Easter Sunday. The organ music is wailing away, and the congregation is dazzling—decked out in nothing but the finest and doused with enough perfume to outsmell even the flowers up on the altar.

But as soon as we get in the door, this kinda sedate commotion break out—all them good Christian folks whispering and nudging each other and trying to turn around and get a good look. Well, Grace and me, we used to that. We just find us a nice seat in one of the empty pews near the back. But this busy buzzing keep up, even after we seated and more blended in with the crowd. And finally it come out that the point of contention ain't even the bottom half of my suit, but my new dove gray Stetson.

This old gentleman with a grizzled head, wearing glasses about a inch thick is turning around and leaning way over the back of the seat, whispering to Grace in a voice plenty loud enough for me to hear, "You better tell your beau to remove that hat, entering in Jesus' Holy Chapel."

Soon as I get my hat off, some old lady behind me is grumbling "I declare, some of these children haven't got no respect at all. Oughta know you sposed to keep your head covered, setting in the house of the Lord."

Seem like the congregation just can't make up its mind whether I'm supposed to wear my hat or I ain't.

I couldn't hardly keep a straight face all through the service. Every time I catch Gracie eye, or one or the other of us catch a sight of my hat, we off again. I couldn't wait to get outa that place. But it was worth it. Gracie and me was entertaining the gang with that story for weeks to come. And we ain't had no more problems with Cousin Hattie.

Far as life everlasting is concerned, I imagine I'll cross that bridge when I reach it. I don't see no reason to rush into things. Sure, I know Old Man Death is gonna be coming after me one of these days, same as he come for my mother and dad, and Gracie and, just last year, my old buddy Louie. But I ain't about to start nothing that might make him feel welcome. It might be different for Gladys Hawkins and the rest of them church sisters, but I got a whole lot left to live for. Including a mind fulla good time memories. When you in the life, one thing your days don't never be, and that's dull. Your nights neither. All these years I been in the life, I loved it. And you know Jinx ain't about to go off with no Old *Man* without no struggle, nohow.

To tell the truth, though, sometime I do get a funny feeling bout Old Death. Sometime I feel like he here already—been here. Waiting on me and watching me and biding his time. Paying attention when I have to stop on the landing of the stairs to catch my breath. Paying attention if I don't wake up till half past seven some morning, and my back is hurting me so bad it take me another half hour to pull myself together and get out the bed.

The same night after I been talking to Gladys in the morning, it take me a long time to fall asleep. I'm lying up in bed waiting for the aching in my back and my joints to ease off some, and I can swear I hear somebody else in the house. Seem like I hear em downstairs, maybe opening and shutting the icebox door, or switching off a light. Just when I finally manage to doze off, I hear somebody footsteps right here in the bedroom with me. Somebody tippy-toeing real quiet, creaking the floor boards between the bed and the dresser . . . over to the closet . . . back to the dresser again.

I'm almost scared to open my eyes. But it's only Gracie—in her old raggedy bathrobe and a silk handkerchief wrapped up around all them little braids in her head—putting her finger up to her lips to try and shush me so I won't wake up.

I can't help chuckling. "Hey Gingerbread Girl. Where you think you going in your house coat and bandana and it ain't even light out yet. Come on get back in this bed."

"You go on to sleep," she say. "I'm just going out back a spell."

It ain't no use me trying to make my voice sound angry, cause she so contrary when it come to that little piece of ground down there I can't help laughing. "What you think you gonna complish down there in the middle of the night? It ain't even no moon to watch tonight. The sky been filling up with clouds all evening, and the weather forecast say rain tomorrow."

"Just don't pay me no mind and go on back to sleep. It ain't the middle of the night. It's almost daybreak." She grinning like she up to something, and sure enough, she say, "This is the best time to pick off them black and yellow beetles been making mildew outa my cucumber vines. So I'm just fixing to turn the tables around a little bit. You gonna read in the papers tomorrow morning bout how the entire black and yellow beetle population of number Twenty-seven Bank Street been wiped off the face of the earth—while you was up here sleeping."

Both of us is laughing like we partners in a crime, and then she off down the hall, calling out, "I be back before you even know I'm gone."

But the full light of day is coming in the window, and she ain't back yet.

I'm over to the window with a mind to holler down to Grace to get her behind back in this house, when the sight of them housing projects hits me right in the face: stacks of dirt-colored bricks and little caged-in porches, heaped up into the sky blocking out what poor skimpy light this cloudy morning brung.

It's a awful funny feeling start to come over me. I mean to get my housecoat, and go down there anyway, just see what's what. But in the closet I can see it ain't but my own clothes hanging on the pole. All the shoes on the floor is mine. And I know I better go ahead and get washed, cause it's a whole lot I want to get done fore it rain, and that storm is coming in for sure. Better pick the rest of them ripe peaches and tomatoes. Maybe put in some peas for fall picking, if my knees'll allow me to get that close to the ground.

The rain finally catch up around noon time and slow me down a bit. I never could stand to be cooped up in no house in the rain. Always make me itchy. That's one reason I used to like driving a trolley for the C.T.C. Cause you get to be out every day, no matter what kinda weather coming down—get to see people and watch the world go by. And it ain't as if you exactly out in the weather, neither. You get to watch it all from behind that big picture window.

Not that I woulda minded being out in it. I used to want to get me a job with the post office, delivering mail. Black folks could made good money with the post office, even way back then. But they wouldn't out you on no mail route. Always stick em off in a back room someplace, where nobody can't see em and get upset cause some little colored girl making as much money as the white boy working next to her. So I stuck with the C.T.C. all them years, and got my pension to prove it.

The rain still coming down steady along about three o'clock, when Max call me up say do I want to come over to her and Yvonne's for dinner. Say they fried more chicken that they can eat, and anyway Yvonne all involved in some new project she want to talk to me about. And I'm glad for the chance to get out the house. Max and Yvonne got the place all picked up for company. I can smell that fried chicken soon as I get in the door.

Yvonne don't never miss a opportunity to dress up a bit. She got the front of her hair braided up, with beads hanging all in her eyes, and a kinda loose robe-like thing, in colors look like the fruit salad at a Independence Day picnic. Max her same old self in her slacks and loafers. She ain't changed in all the years I known her—cept we both got more wrinkles and gray hairs. Yvonne a whole lot younger than us two, but she hanging in there. Her and Max been together going on three years now.

Right away, Yvonne start to explain about this project she doing with her women's club. When I first heard about this club she in, I was kinda interested. But I come to find out it ain't no social club, like the Cinnamon & Spice Club used to be. It's more like a organization. Yvonne call it a collective. They never has no outings or parties or picnics or nothing—just meetings. And projects.

The project they working on right now, they all got tape recorders. And they going around tape-recording people story. Talking to people who been in the life for years and years, and asking em what it was like, back in the old days. I been in the life since before Yvonne born. But the second she stick that microphone in my face, I can't think of a blessed thing to say.

"Come on, Jinx, you always telling us all them funny old time stories."

Them little wheels is rolling round and round, and all that smooth, shiny brown tape is slipping off one reel and sliding onto the other, and I can't think of not one thing I remember.

"Tell how the Cinnamon & Spice Club got started," she say.

"I already told you about that before."

"Well tell how it ended, then. You never told me that."

"Ain't nothing to tell. Skip and Peaches broke up." Yvonne waiting, and the reels is rolling, but for the life of me I can't think of another word to say about it. And Max is sitting there grinning, like I'm the only one over thirty in the room and she don't remember a thing.

Yvonne finally give up and turn the thing off, and we go on and stuff ourselves on the chicken they fried and the greens I brung over from the garden. By the time we start in on the sweet potato pie, I have finally got to remembering. Telling Yvonne about when Skip and Peaches had they last big falling out, and they was both determine they was gonna stay in The Club—and couldn't be in the same room with one another for fifteen minutes. Both of em keep waiting on the other one to drop out, and both of em keep showing up, every time the gang get together. And none of the rest of us couldn't be in the same room with the two a them for even as long as they could stand each other. We'd be sneaking around, trying to hold a meeting without them finding out. But Peaches was the president and Skip was the treasurer, so you might say our hands was tied. Wouldn't neither one of em resign. They was both convince The Club couldn't go on without em, and by the time they was finished carrying on, they had done made sure it wouldn't.

Max is chiming in correcting all the details, every other breath come outa my mouth. And then when we all get up to go sit in the parlor again, it come out that Yvonne has sneaked that tape recording machine in here under that African poncho she got on, and has got down every word I said.

When time come to say good night, I'm thankful, for once, that Yvonne insist on driving me home—though it ain't even a whole mile. The rain ain't let up all evening, and is coming down in bucketfuls while we in the car. I'm half soaked just running from the car to the front door.

Yvonne is drove off down the street, and I'm halfway through the front door, when it hit me all of a sudden that the door ain't been locked. Now my mind may be getting a little threadbare in spots, but it ain't wore out yet. I know it's easy for me to slip back into doing things the way I done em twenty or thirty years ago, but I could swear I distinctly remember locking this door and hooking the key ring back on my belt loop, just fore Yvonne drove up in front. And now here's the door been open all this time.

Not a sign a nobody been here. Everything in its place, just like I left it. The slipcovers on the couch is smooth and neat. The candy dishes and ash trays and photographs is sitting just where they belong, on the end tables. Not even so much as a throw rug been moved a inch. I can feel my heart start to thumping like a blowout tire.

Must be, whoever come in here ain't left yet.

The idea of somebody got a nerve like that make me more mad than scared, and I know I'm gonna find out who it is broke in my house, even if it don't turn out to be nobody but them little peach-thieving rascals from round the block. Which I wouldn't be surprised if it ain't. I'm scooting from room to room, snatching open closet doors and whipping back curtains—tiptoeing down the hall and then flicking on the lights real sudden.

When I been in every room, I go back through everywhere I been, real slow, looking in all the drawers, and under the old glass doorstop in the hall, and in the back of the recipe box in the kitchen—and other places where I keep things. But it ain't nothing missing. No money—nothing.

In the end, ain't nothing left for me to do but go to bed. But I'm still feeling real uneasy. I know somebody or something done got in here while I was gone. And ain't left yet. I lay wake in the bed a long time, cause I ain't too particular about falling asleep tonight. Anyway, all this rain just make my joints swell up worse, and the pains in my knees just don't let up.

The next thing I know Gracie waking me up. She lying next to me and kissing me all over my face. I wake up laughing, and she say, "I never could see no use in shaking somebody I rather be kissing." I can feel the laughing running all through her body and mine, holding her up against my chest in the dark—knowing there must be a reason why she woke me up in the middle of the night, and pretty sure I can guess what it is. She kissing under my chin now, and starting to undo my buttons.

It seem like so long since we done this. My whole body is all a shimmer with this sweet, sweet craving. My blood is racing, singing, and her fingers is sliding inside my nightshirt. "Take it easy," I say in her ear. Cause I want this to take us a long, long time.

Outside, the sky is still wide open—the storm is throbbing and beating down on the roof over our heads, and pressing its wet self up against the window. I catch ahold of her fingers and bring em to my lips. Then I roll us both over so I can see her face. She smiling up at me through the dark, and her eyes is wide and shiny. And I run my fingers down along her breast, underneath her own nightgown. . . .

I wake up in the bed alone. It's still night. Like a flash I'm across the room, knowing I'm going after her, this time. The carpet treads is nubby and rough, flying past underneath my bare feet, and the kitchen linoleum cold and smooth. The back door standing wide open, and I push through the screen.

The storm is moved on. That fresh air feel good on my skin through the cotton nightshirt. Smell good, too, rising up outa the wet earth, and I can see the water sparkling on the leaves of the collards and kale, twinkling in the vines on the bean poles.

The moon is riding high up over Thompson's field, spilling moonlight all over the yard, and setting all them blossoms on the fence to shining pure white.

There ain't a leaf twitching and there ain't a sound. I ain't moving either. I'm just gonna stay right here on this back porch. And hold still. And listen close. Cause I know Gracie somewhere in this garden. And she waiting for me.

(1987)

QUESTIONS

1. What does the title of this story suggest? Is there a pun intended?

2. Given the length of time that Grace has been dead, why is Pearl (Jinx) still mourning her? What is the nature of their relationship?

3. What elements in this story belie the usual ingredients of middle-class life? Discuss the ways in which Pearl and Grace's relationship manages to endure.

4. Why does Pearl say that she is "mad at time"?

KATHERINE MANSFIELD (1888–1923)

A Dill Pickle

And then, after six years, she saw him again. He was seated at one of those little bamboo tables decorated with a Japanese vase of paper daffodils. There was a tall plate of fruit in front of him, and very carefully, in a way she recognized immediately as his "special" way, he was peeling an orange.

He must have felt that shock of recognition in her for he looked up and met her eyes. Incredible! He didn't know her! She smiled; he frowned. She came towards him. He closed his eyes an instant, but opening them his face lit up as though he had struck a match in a dark room. He laid down the orange and pushed back his chair, and she took her little warm hand out of her muff and gave it to him.

"Vera!" he exclaimed. "How strange. Really, for a moment I didn't know you. Won't you sit down? You've had lunch? Won't you have some coffee?"

She hesitated, but of course she meant to.

"Yes, I'd like some coffee." And she sat down opposite him.

"You've changed. You've changed very much," he said, staring at her with that eager, lighted look. "You look so well. I've never seen you look so well before."

"Really?" She raised her veil and unbuttoned her high fur collar. "I don't feel very well. I can't bear this weather, you know."

"Ah, no. You hate the cold. . . ."

"Loathe it." She shuddered. "And the worst of it is that the older one grows . . ."

He interrupted her. "Excuse me," and tapped on the table for the waitress. "Please bring some coffee and cream." To her: "You are sure you won't eat anything? Some fruit, perhaps. The fruit here is very good."

"No, thanks. Nothing."

"Then that's settled." And smiling just a hint too broadly he took up the orange again. "You were saying—the older one grows—"

"The colder," she laughed. But she was thinking how well she remembered that trick of his—the trick of interrupting her—and of how it used to exasperate her six years ago. She used to feel then as though he, quite suddenly, in the middle of what she was saying, put his hand over her lips, turned from her, attended to something different, and then took his hand away, and with just the same slightly too broad smile, gave her his attention again. . . . Now we are ready. That is settled.

"The colder!" He echoed her words, laughing too. "Ah, ah. You still say the same things. And there is another thing about you that is not changed at all—your beautiful voice—your beautiful way of speaking." Now he was very grave; he leaned towards her, and she smelled the warm, stinging scent of the orange peel. "You have only to say one word and I would know your voice among all other voices. I don't know what it is—I've often wondered—that makes your voice such a—haunting memory. . . . Do you remember that first afternoon we spent together at Kew Gardens? You were so surprised because I did not know the names of any flowers. I am still just as ignorant for all your telling me. But whenever it is very fine and warm, and I see some bright colours—it's awfully strange—I hear your voice saying: 'Geranium, marigold and verbena.' And I feel those three words are all I recall of some forgotten, heavenly language. . . . You remember that afternoon?"

"Oh, yes, very well." She drew a long, soft breath, as though the paper daffodils between them were almost too sweet to bear. Yet, what had remained in her mind of that particular afternoon was an absurd scene over the tea table. A great many people taking tea in a Chinese pagoda, and he behaving like a maniac about the wasps—waving them away, flapping at them with his straw hat, serious and infuriated out of all proportion to the occasion. How delighted the sniggering tea drinkers had been. And how she had suffered.

But now, as he spoke, that memory faded. His was the truer. Yes, it had been a wonderful afternoon, full of geranium and marigold and verbena, and—warm sunshine. Her thoughts lingered over the last two words as though she sang them.

In the warmth, as it were, another memory unfolded. She saw herself sitting on a lawn. He lay beside her, and suddenly, after a long silence, he rolled over and put his head in her lap.

"I wish," he said, in a low, troubled voice, "I wish that I had taken poison and were about to die—here now!"

At that moment a little girl in a white dress, holding a long, dripping water lily, dodged from behind a bush, stared at them, and dodged back again. But he did not see. She leaned over him.

"Ah, why do you say that? I could not say that."

But he gave a kind of soft moan, and taking her hand he held it to his cheek.

"Because I know I am going to love you too much—far too much. And I shall suffer so terribly, Vera, because you never, never will love me."

He was certainly far better looking now than he had been then. He had lost all that dreamy vagueness and indecision. Now he had the air of a man who has found his place in life, and fills it with a confidence and an assurance which was, to say the least, impressive. He must have made money, too. His clothes were admirable, and at that moment he pulled a Russian cigarette case out of his pocket.

"Won't you smoke?"

"Yes, I will." She hovered over them. "They look very good."

"I think they are. I get them made for me by a little man in St. James's Street. I don't smoke very much. I'm not like you—but when I do, they must be delicious, very fresh cigarettes. Smoking isn't a habit with me; it's a luxury—like perfume. Are you still so fond of perfumes? Ah, when I was in Russia . . ."

She broke in: "You've really been to Russia?"

"Oh, yes. I was there for over a year. Have you forgotten how we used to talk of going there?"

"No, I've not forgotten."

He gave a strange half laugh and leaned back in his chair. "Isn't it curious. I have really carried out all those journeys that we planned. Yes, I have been to all those places that we talked of, and stayed in them long enough to—as you used to say, 'air oneself' in them. In fact, I have spent the last three years of my life travelling all the time. Spain,

Corsica, Siberia, Russia, Egypt. The only country left is China, and I mean to go there, too, when the war is over."

As he spoke, so lightly, tapping the end of his cigarette against the ash-tray, she felt the strange beast that had slumbered so long within her bosom stir, stretch itself, yawn, prick up its ears, and suddenly bound to its feet, and fix its longing, hungry stare upon those far away places. But all she said was, smiling gently: "How I envy you."

He accepted that. "It has been," he said, "very wonderful—especially Russia. Russia was all that we had imagined, and far, far more. I even spent some days on a river boat on the Volga.[1] Do you remember that boatman's song that you used to play?"

"Yes." It began to play in her mind as she spoke.

"Do you ever play it now?"

"No, I've no piano."

He was amazed at that. "But what has become of your beautiful piano?"

She made a little grimace. "Sold. Ages ago."

"But you were so fond of music," he wondered.

"I've no time for it now," said she.

He let it go at that. "That river life," he went on, "is something quite special. After a day or two you cannot realize that you have ever known another. And it is not necessary to know the language—the life of the boat creates a bond between you and the people that's more than sufficient. You eat with them, pass the day with them, and in the evening there is that endless singing."

She shivered, hearing the boatman's song break out again loud and tragic, and seeing the boat floating on the darkening river with melancholy trees on either side. . . . "Yes, I should like that," said she, stroking her muff.

"You'd like almost everything about Russian life," he said warmly. "It's so informal, so impulsive, so free without question. And then the peasants are so splendid. They are such human beings—yes, that is it. Even the man who drives your carriage has—has some real part in what is happening. I remember the evening a party of us, two friends of mine and the wife of one of them, went for a picnic by the Black Sea. We took supper and champagne and ate and drank on the grass. And while we were eating the coachman came up. 'Have a dill pickle,' he said. He wanted to share with us. That seemed to me so right, so—you know what I mean?"

And she seemed at that moment to be sitting on the grass beside the mysteriously Black Sea, black as velvet, and rippling against the banks in silent, velvet waves. She saw the carriage drawn up to one side of the road, and the little group on the grass, their faces and hands white in the moonlight. She saw the pale dress of the woman outspread and her folded parasol, lying on the grass like a huge pearl crochet hook. Apart from them, with his supper in a cloth on his knees, sat the coachman. "Have a dill pickle," said he, and although she was not certain what a dill pickle was, she saw the greenish glass jar with a red chili like a parrot's beak glimmering through. She sucked in her cheeks; the dill pickle was terribly sour. . . .

---

[1] Volga: the longest river (2300 m.) in Europe located in western Russia and emptying into the Caspian Sea.

"Yes, I know perfectly what you mean," she said.

In the pause that followed they looked at each other. In the past when they had looked at each other like that they had felt such a boundless understanding between them that their souls had, as it were, put their arms round each other and dropped into the same sea, content to be drowned, like mournful lovers. But now, the surprising thing was that it was he who held back. He who said:

"What a marvellous listener you are. When you look at me with those wild eyes I feel that I could tell you things that I would never breathe to another human being."

Was there just a hint of mockery in his voice or was it her fancy? She could not be sure.

"Before I met you," he said, "I had never spoken of myself to anybody. How well I remember one night, the night that I brought you the little Christmas tree, telling you all about my childhood. And of how I was so miserable that I ran away and lived under a cart in our yard for two days without being discovered. And you listened, and your eyes shone, and I felt that you had even made the little Christmas tree listen too, as in a fairy story."

But of that evening she had remembered a little pot of caviare. It had cost seven and sixpence. He could not get over it. Think of it—a tiny jar like that costing seven and sixpence. While she ate it he watched her, delighted and shocked.

"No, really, that is eating money. You could not get seven shillings into a little pot that size. Only think of the profit they must make. . . . " And he had begun some immensely complicated calculations. . . . But now good-bye to the caviare. The Christmas tree was on the table, and the little boy lay under the cart with his head pillowed on the yard dog.

"The dog was called Bosun," she cried delightedly.

But he did not follow. "Which dog? Had you a dog? I don't remember a dog at all."

"No, no. I mean the yard dog when you were a little boy." He laughed and snapped the cigarette case to.

"Was he? Do you know I had forgotten that. It seems such ages ago. I cannot believe that it is only six years. After I had recognized you to-day—I had to take such a leap—I had to take a leap over my whole life to get back to that time. I was such a kid then." He drummed on the table. "I've often thought how I must have bored you. And now I understand so perfectly why you wrote to me as you did—although at the time that letter nearly finished my life. I found it again the other day, and I couldn't help laughing as I read it. It was so clever—such a true picture of me." He glanced up. "You're not going?"

She had buttoned her collar again and drawn down her veil.

"Yes, I am afraid I must," she said, and managed a smile. Now she knew that he had been mocking.

"Ah, no, please," he pleaded. "Don't go just for a moment," and he caught up one of her gloves from the table and clutched at it as if that would hold her. "I see so few people to talk to nowadays, that I have turned into a sort of barbarian," he said. "Have I said something to hurt you?"

"Not a bit," she lied. But as she watched him draw her glove through his fingers, gently, gently, her anger really did die down, and besides, at the moment he looked more like himself of six years ago. . . .

"What I really wanted then," he said softly, "was to be a sort of carpet—to make myself into a sort of carpet for you to walk on so that you need not be hurt by the sharp stones and the mud that you hated so. It was nothing more positive than that—nothing more selfish. Only I did desire, eventually, to turn into a magic carpet and carry you away to all those lands you longed to see."

As he spoke she lifted her head as though she drank something; the strange beast in her bosom began to purr. . . .

"I felt that you were more lonely than anybody else in the world," he went on, "and yet, perhaps, that you were the only person in the world who was really, truly alive. Born out of your time," he murmured, stroking the glove, "fated."

Ah, God! What had she done! How had she dared to throw away her happiness like this. This was the only man who had ever understood her. Was it too late? Could it be too late? *She* was that glove that he held in his fingers. . . .

"And then the fact that you had no friends and never had made friends with people. How I understood that, for neither had I. Is it just the same now?"

"Yes," she breathed. "Just the same. I am as alone as ever."

"So am I," he laughed gently, "just the same."

Suddenly with a quick gesture he handed her back the glove and scraped his chair on the floor. "But what seemed to me so mysterious then is perfectly plain to me now. And to you, too, of course. . . . It simply was that we were such egoists, so self-engrossed, so wrapped up in ourselves that we hadn't a corner in our hearts for anybody else. Do you know," he cried, naïve and hearty, and dreadfully like another side of that old self again, "I began studying a Mind System when I was in Russia, and I found that we were not peculiar at all. It's quite a well known form of . . ."

She had gone. He sat there, thunder-struck, astounded beyond words. . . . And then he asked the waitress for his bill.

"But the cream has not been touched," he said. "Please do no charge me for it."

(1920)

QUESTIONS

1. Explain who the narrator of "A Dill Pickle" is. From whose point of view is this story being told? Why is it significant that Vera's former lover remains unnamed throughout the story?

2. What is the "strange beast that had so long slumbered" within Vera? At what point in the conversation does it begin to awaken? Why? At what point does it "sour"?

3. What does this story suggest about Vera's and her lover's character traits? Has either one of them really changed very much after six years? What do you think Vera explained to her lover in the letter rejecting him?

4. Why does Vera leave so abruptly? What does the man's desire not to be charged for the cream say about him? Does this scene bear out Vera's perceptions?

5. What does the dill pickle symbolize in the context of this story? Why do you think Mansfield has chosen it as the story's title?

Writing Topics for Short Stories

1. Discuss how Chekhov's "The Lady with the Dog" and Lawrence's "The Horse-Dealer's Daughter" illustrate the "mystery" or irrationality of love.

2. Examine what you perceive as the prevailing attitudes in society toward older people in love. Do you know anyone whom you consider too old to be in love? Explain how you might act if you were the narrator or Jinx in Birtha's "In The Life."

3. Compare the way a love that is over is looked back on in Birtha's "In The Life" and Mansfield's "A Dill Pickle." What does each story suggest to you about the way we reconstruct the past?

4. Drawing on Chekhov's "The Lady with the Dog," Lawrence's "The Horse-Dealer's Daughter," Mansfield's "A Dill Pickle," and Chopin's "The Storm," analyze the role setting (time, place, season, weather) plays in when, where, why, and with whom people fall in love.

5. What is suggested in Mansfield's "A Dill Pickle" when the former lovers remember such different aspects of their shared experiences? What does this reveal about the nature of memory and shared moments?

6. Use the stories in Part 3: People in Love to discuss the ways that love can drive a character to behave in ways that are not sanctioned by family, society, or religion.

Poems

Western Wind

Western wind, when will thou blow,
  The small rain down can rain?
Christ, if my love were in my arms
  And I in my bed again!

(LATE 14TH OR EARLY 15TH CENTURY)

QUESTIONS

1. What situation and setting do you imagine for this speaker?
2. What symbolism or connotations can be connected with the western or west wind?

ROBERT BROWNING (1812–1889)

Meeting at Night

I

The grey sea and the long black land;
And the yellow half-moon large and low;
And the startled little waves that leap
In fiery ringlets from their sleep,
As I gain the cove with pushing prow,
And quench its speed i' the slushy sand.

II

Then a mile of warm sea-scented beach;
Three fields to cross till a farm appears;
A tap at the pane, the quick sharp scratch
10   And blue spurt of a lighted match,
And a voice less loud, thro' its joys and fears,
Than the two hearts beating each to each!

(1845)

ROBERT BROWNING (1812–1889)

Parting at Morning

Round the cape of a sudden came the sea,
And the sun looked over the mountain's rim:
And straight was a path of gold for him,
And the need of a world of men for me.

(1845)

QUESTIONS

1. What does the imagery in stanza one suggest about romantic love?

2. What seems to be the probable season of the year, and why is this appropriate to the relationship?

3. What does a night meeting suggest about the nature of this relationship?

4. What is it that calls the speaker so forcefully from his beloved?

5. What does this poem suggest about the nature of day as opposed to night?

6. What do these two poems suggest about the nature of romantic love?

ELIZABETH BARRETT BROWNING (1806–1861)

Sonnet XLIII: How Do I Love Thee? Let Me Count the Ways

How do I love thee? Let me count the ways.
I love thee to the depth and breadth and height
My soul can reach, when feeling out of sight
For the ends of Being and ideal Grace.
I love thee to the level of everyday's
Most quiet need, by sun and candle-light.
I love thee freely, as men strive for Right;
I love thee purely, as they turn from Praise.
I love thee with the passion put to use
10   In my old griefs, and with my childhood's faith.
I love thee with a love I seemed to lose
With my lost saints,—I love thee with the breath,
Smiles, tears, of all my life!—and, if God choose,
I shall but love thee better after death.

(1850)

QUESTIONS

1. What figures of speech are used to answer the question the speaker poses in the title of her sonnet? How many ways are given for loving?

2. What does the speaker mean when she says, "I love thee to the level of everyday's/ most quiet need"?

3. Is there an order or sequence or hierarchy for loving? Explain the paradox of how you can love someone better after death.

JOHN DONNE (1572–1631)

The Good-Morrow[1]

I wonder by my troth, what thou, and I
Did, till we lov'd? were we not wean'd till then?
But suck'd on country pleasures, childishly?
Or snorted we in the seven sleepers den?[2]
T'was so; But this, all pleasures fancies be.
If ever any beauty I did see,
Which I desir'd, and got, t'was but a dream of thee.

And now good morrow to our waking souls,
Which watch not one another out of fear;
10   For love, all love of other sights controls,
And makes one little room, an every where.
Let sea-discoverers to new worlds have gone,
Let Maps to other, worlds on worlds have shown,
Let us possess one world, each hath one, and is one.

My face in thine eye, thine in mine appears,
And true plain hearts do in the faces rest,
Where can we find two better hemispheres
Without sharp North, without declining West?
What ever dyes, was not mixt equally;
20   If our two loves be one, or, thou and I
Love so alike, that none do slacken, none can die.

(1633)

QUESTIONS

1. What does "good-morrow" mean and why is the poem titled "The Good-Morrow"?

2. What images and metaphors does the speaker use in each stanza to portray his love?

3. How does the description of life before they loved set in relief their present love? What is implied about their future love?

---

[1] Good-Morrow: good morning; a condensation of the phrase "God send you a good day."
[2] seven sleepers den: a legend of the seven Christians walled in a cave, who slept for 187 years in order to escape persecution.

ROBERT BURNS (1759–1796)

A Red, Red Rose

I

O, my luve is like a red, red rose,
  That's newly sprung in June.
O, my luve is like the melodie,
  That's sweetly play'd in tune.

II

As fair art thou, my bonnie lass,
  So deep in luve am I,
And I will luve thee still, my dear,
  Till a' the seas gang[1] dry.

III

Till a' the seas gang dry, my dear,
10   And the rocks melt wi' the sun!
And I will luve thee still, my dear,
  While the sands o' life shall run.

IV

And fare thee weel, my only luve,
  And fare thee weel a while;
And I will come again, my luve,
  Tho' it were ten thousand mile!

(1794)

QUESTIONS

1. What occasion seems to have prompted this poem?

2. What similes and metaphors does the speaker use to persuade his beloved of his love? What do these figures of speech suggest about the speaker's attitude toward his lover?

---

[1] gang: go.

3. How does the speaker use hyperbole as a persuasive device? Explain why you are or are not persuaded.

BHARTRIHARI (7TH CENTURY)

My Love Is Nothing Like the Moon

Translated by Tony Barnstone

My love is nothing like the moon,
her eyes are not two lotus blooms
and her shining flesh is not gold,
but listening to what poets say
even a sage will pray at the body's altar,
this sack of meat and bones.

(7TH CENTURY)

QUESTIONS

1. How does the speaker evoke his feelings for his beloved through the use of negation?

2. What is the mood of this poem? How are figurative language and imagery used to establish this mood?

WILLIAM SHAKESPEARE (1564–1616)

Sonnet CXXX: My Mistress' Eyes Are Nothing Like the Sun

My mistress' eyes are nothing like the sun,
Coral is far more red than her lips' red.
If snow be white, why then her breasts are dun,[1]
If hairs be wires, black wires grow on her head.
I have seen roses damasked,[2] red and white,

---

[1] dun: a dull grayish brown.
[2] damasked: ornately decorated or woven on fabric.

But no such roses see I in her cheeks.
And in some perfumes is there more delight
Than in the breath that from my mistress reeks.
I live to hear her speak, yet well I know
10   That music hath a far more pleasing sound.
I grant I never saw a goddess go,
My mistress, when she walks, treads on the ground.

And yet, by Heaven, I think my love as rare
As any she belied with false compare.

(1609)

QUESTIONS

1. What is the speaker's tone of voice? How does his tone of voice change in the last two lines?

2. What does the speaker reveal about his philosophy of love in his defiance of the typical expressions of love?

WILLIAM SHAKESPEARE (1564–1616)

Sonnet XVIII: Shall I Compare Thee to a Summer's Day?

Shall I compare thee to a summer's day?
Thou art more lovely and more temperate.
Rough winds do shake the darling buds of May,
And summer's lease hath all too short a date.
Sometime too hot the eye of heaven shines,
And often is his gold complexion dimmed.
And every fair[1] from fair sometime declines,
By chance or nature's changing course untrimmed.
But thy eternal summer shall not fade,
10   Nor lose possession of that fair thou owest,
Nor shall Death brag thou wander'st in his shade
When in eternal lines to time thou grow'st.
So long as men can breathe, or eyes can see,
So long lives this, and this gives life to thee.

(1609)

---

[1] fair: beautiful.

QUESTIONS

1. How does the description of summer differ from the usual associations of summer? What is the point of the difference?

2. Explain what makes this a sonnet, and how the ideas in the poem are organized into rhymed units.

TED HUGHES (1930–1999)

Song

O lady, when the tipped cup of the moon blessed you
You became soft fire with a cloud's grace;
The difficult stars swam for eyes in your face;
You stood, and your shadow was my place:
You turned, your shadow turned to ice,
    O my lady.

O lady, when the sea caressed you
You were a marble of foam, but dumb.
When will the stone open its tomb?
10   When will the waves give over their foam?
You will not die, nor come home,
    O my lady.

O lady, when the wind kissed you
You made him music, for you were a shaped shell.
I follow the waters and the wind still
Since my heart heard it and all to pieces fell
Which your lovers stole, meaning ill,
    O my lady.

O lady, consider when I shall have lost you
20   The moon's full hands, scattering waste,
The sea's hands, dark from the world's breast,
The world's decay where the wind's hands have passed,
And my head, worn out with love, at rest
In my hands, and my hands full of dust,
    O my lady.

(1957)

QUESTIONS

1. What qualities of the poem make the poet call it "Song"?

2. How can you tell what the speaker's feelings are for the "lady" whom he addresses? Is he expressing heart-felt admiration or do you think that he is being satirical?

3. How are metaphors and examples of personification used to enrich the meaning in this poem?

EDNA ST. VINCENT MILLAY (1892–1950)

Recuerdo[1]

We were very tired, we were very merry—
We had gone back and forth all night on the ferry.
It was bare and bright, and smelled like a stable—
But we looked into a fire, we leaned across a table,
We lay on a hill-top underneath the moon;
And the whistles kept blowing, and the dawn came soon.

We were very tired, we were very merry—
We had gone back and forth all night on the ferry;
And you ate an apple, and I ate a pear,
From a dozen of each we had bought somewhere;
And the sky went wan, and the wind came cold,
And the sun rose dripping, a bucketful of gold.

We were very tired, we were very merry,
We had gone back and forth all night on the ferry.
We hailed, "Good morrow, mother!" to a shawl-covered head,
And bought a morning paper, which neither of us read;
And she wept, "God bless you!" for the apples and pears,
And we gave her all our money but our subway fares.

(1920)

QUESTIONS

1. Explain what feelings "Recuerdo" conveys between the speaker and the person being addressed.

---

[1] Recuerdo: Spanish for memory.

2. What do you think induces the speaker and her companion to give all their money to the woman with the shawl-covered head?

3. What examples of synecdoche can you find in the poem? What effect do they have on the overall pleasure of reading this poem?

4. Describe how this poem's rhythm and rhyme develops a sense of the scene that is being described.

EMILY DICKINSON (1830–1886)

"Wild Nights–Wild Nights!"

(Poem 249)

Wild Nights—Wild Nights!
Were I with thee
Wild Nights should be
Our luxury!

Futile—the Winds—
To a Heart in port—
Done with the Compass—
Done with the Chart!

Rowing in Eden—
10 Ah, the Sea!
Might I but moor—Tonight—
In Thee!

(c. 1861, PUBLISHED 1891)

QUESTIONS

1. Explain how this poem captures the essential feeling of romantic love.

2. How does Dickinson convey mood and message through repetition and diction?

ANDRÉ BRETON (1896–1966)

Free Union

Translated by Daniel Galliduani

My woman with hair like wood fire
With hot lightning thoughts
With an hour-glass waist
My woman with an otter's waist between tiger's teeth
My woman with a cockade mouth and bouquet of stars of final grandeur
With teeth of white mouse imprints upon white earth
With an amber tongue and frosted glass
My woman with the tongue of a stabbed wafer
With the tongue of a doll who opens and closes her eyes
10   With a tongue of unbelievable stone
My woman with eyelashes of a child's handwritten lines
With eyebrows on the edge of a swallow's nest
My woman with temples of slate of a hothouse roof
And steam on window panes
My woman with shoulders of champagne
And a fountain of dolphins' heads under the ice
My woman with wrists of matches
My woman with fingers of fate and ace of hearts
With fingers of cut hay
20   My woman with armpits of martens and beech
Of the night of St. John
Of privet and a nest of sea mollusks
With arms of sea froth and flood gate
And with a mixture of wheat and mill
My woman with rocket legs
With the movement of a watch and despair
My woman with calves of elder tree sap
My woman with initialed feet
With feet of key rings with feet of drunken caulkers
30   My woman with a neck of iridescent barley
My woman with a golden vale throat
Of meeting in the stream bed itself
With breasts of night
My woman with breasts of an oceanic molehill
My woman with breasts of a ruby crucible
With breasts of the ghosts of the rose under dew

My woman with a belly like a fan unfolding day after day
With the belly of a giant claw
My woman with a bird's back flying vertically
40   With a quicksilver back
With a luminous back
With a nape of rolled stone and wet chalk
And a glass falling after one has just finished drinking
My woman with balloon basket hips
With lustrous hips and arrow feathers
And with stalks of white peacock feathers
Of insensible balance
My woman with a bottom of sandstone and asbestos
My woman with a bottom like a swan's back
50   My woman with a springtime bottom
With the sex of a gladiolus
My woman with the sex of gold dust and a platypus
My woman with the sex of seaweed and ancient candies
My woman with the sex of a mirror
My woman with eyes full of tears
With eyes of purple panoply and a magnetic needle
My woman with savannah eyes
My woman with eyes of water
My woman with eyes of water always under the axe
60   With eyes level with air, earth and fire

(1931)

QUESTIONS

1. Based on the extreme range of description in "Free Union," explain what you think Breton's reasons for writing this might be. Do you think this is a poem of great love?

2. What do the surreal imagery and metaphors of the poem suggest about the speaker's view of "his woman"?

3. Why do you think Breton chose the title "Free Union" ("L'Union Libre") for this poem?

4. What effect does the repetition of the phrase "My woman" have in evoking the speaker's feelings?

WILLIAM BUTLER YEATS (1865–1939)

No Second Troy

Why should I blame her that she filled my days
With misery, or that she would of late
Have taught to ignorant men most violent ways,
Or hurled the little streets upon the great,
Had they but courage equal to desire?
What could have made her peaceful with a mind
That nobleness made simple as a fire,
With beauty like a tightened bow, a kind
That is not natural in an age like this,
10   Being high and solitary and most stern?
Why, what could she have done, being what she is?
Was there another Troy[1] for her to burn?

(1910)

QUESTIONS

1. Why is the speaker asking these four questions? How and why does the speaker's tone change in each question?

2. What is the point of comparing a modern personal love affair with the ancient love affair of Helen and Paris and the destruction of Troy?

3. What is the speaker's explanation for his beloved's behavior? On what note does the poem end?

W. S. MERWIN (B. 1927)

When You Go Away

for Dido

When you go away the wind clicks around to the north
The painters work all day but at sundown the paint falls
Showing the black walls

---

[1] Troy: the city of the Trojans to which Paris, prince of Troy, took Helen, the wife of the Greek king Menelaus, an act which precipitated the Trojan War.

The clock goes back to striking the same hour
That has no place in the years

And at night wrapped in the bed of ashes
In one breath I wake
It is the time when the beards of the dead get their growth
I remember that I am falling
10   That I am the reason
And that my words are the garment of what I shall never be
Like the tucked sleeve of a one-armed boy

(1967)

QUESTIONS

1. What poetic devices, such as metaphor, simile, synecdoche, and hyperbole, does the speaker use to convey his feelings of loss?

2. Explain which of these adjectives, realistic or surreal, best characterize the imagery of the poem.

3. How would you describe the mood and tone of this poem? Do you consider it a testament of love?

4. What makes the final simile of the poem so unexpected? How does it evoke the speaker's feelings? What effect does it have on you as the audience?

ELIZABETH BISHOP (1911–1979)

One Art

The art of losing isn't hard to master;
so many things seem filled with the intent
to be lost that their loss is no disaster.

Lose something every day. Accept the fluster
of lost door keys, the hour badly spent.
The art of losing isn't hard to master.

Then practice losing farther, losing faster:
places, and names and where it was you meant
to travel. None of these will bring disaster.

10   I lost my mother's watch. And look! my last, or
next-to-last, of three loved houses went.
The art of losing isn't hard to master.

I lost two cities, lovely ones. And, vaster,
some realms I owned, two rivers, a continent.
I miss them, but it wasn't a disaster.

—Even losing you (the joking voice, a gesture
I love) I shan't have lied. It's evident
the art of losing's not too hard to master
though it may look like (*Write* it!) like disaster.

(1976)

QUESTIONS

1. What is the significance of the order of the various kinds of losses one is able to "master"?

2. Describe the tone of the poem. What evidence suggests the way the poem should be read? Why does the speaker say "(*Write* it!)" in the final line?

3. Explain how the use of end and slant rhyme and the rhyme scheme strengthen the meaning of the poem.

ANDREW MARVELL (1621–1678)

To His Coy Mistress

Had we but World enough, and Time,
This coyness Lady were no crime.
We would sit down, and think which way
To walk, and pass our long Loves Day.
Thou by the *Indian Ganges*[1] side
Should'st Rubies find: I by the Tide
Of *Humber*[2] would complain. I would
Love you ten years before the Flood:
And you should, if you please, refuse
10   Till the Conversion of the *Jews*.
My vegetable Love should grow
Vaster than Empires, and more slow.
An hundred years should go to praise
Thine Eyes, and on thy Forehead Gaze.
Two hundred to adore each Breast:

---

[1] Ganges: the chief river in India, flowing generally in the northeastern region for about 1500 miles. It is considered sacred by the Hindus.
[2] Humber: an estuary formed by two rivers emptying into the North Sea in northern England.

But thirty thousand to the rest.
An Age at least to every part,
And the last Age should show your Heart.
For Lady you deserve this State;
20   Nor would I love at lower rate.
    But at my back I alwaies hear
Times winged Charriot hurrying near:
And yonder all before us lye
Deserts of vast Eternity.
Thy Beauty shall no more be found;
Nor, in thy marble Vault, shall sound
My ecchoing Song: then Worms shall try
That long preserv'd Virginity:
And your quaint Honour turn to dust;
30   And into ashes all my Lust.
The Grave's a fine and private place,
But none I think do there embrace.
    Now therefore, while the youthful hew

Sits on thy skin like morning glew,[3]
And while thy willing Soul transpires
At every pore with instant Fires,
Now let us sport us while we may;
And now, like am'rous birds of prey,
Rather at once our Time devour,
40   Than languish in his slow-chapt pow'r.
Let us roll all our Strength, and all
Our sweetness, up into one Ball:
And tear our Pleasures with rough strife,
Thorough the Iron gates of Life.
Thus, though we cannot make our Sun
Stand still, yet we will make him run.

(1681)

QUESTIONS

1. What are the connotations of the word *coy* and the word *mistress*? What is the speaker trying to persuade his mistress to do and what does coyness have to do with the speaker's strategy for persuading her?

2. What new arguments are set forth in each stanza? Is there logic in his argument? Why does Marvell use hyperbolic images of time to support each argument?

3. Why does the poem allow for more than one level of reading? How can you determine whether or not the tone is serious, facetious, ironic, or playful?

---

[3] glew: dew.

MURIEL RUKEYSER (1913–1980)

Waiting for Icarus[1]

He said he would be back and we'd drink wine together
He said that everything would be better than before
He said we were on the edge of a new relation
He said he would never again cringe before his father
He said that he was going to invent full-time
He said he loved me that going into me
He said was going into the world and the sky
He said all the buckles were very firm
He said the wax was the best wax
10   He said Wait for me here on the beach
He said Just don't cry

I remember the gulls and the waves
I remember the islands going dark on the sea
I remember the girls laughing
I remember they said he only wanted to get away from me
I remember mother saying : Inventors are like poets,
                                    a trashy lot
I remember she told me those who try out inventions are worse
I remember she added : Women who love such are the worst of all

20   I have been waiting all day, or perhaps longer.
I would have liked to try those wings myself.
It would have been better than this.

(1973)

QUESTIONS

1. What point is Rukeyser trying to make by creating the persona of Icarus' girlfriend?

2. How is the poem a vehicle for commenting on our contemporary society?

3. What is the effect of the repetition used in this poem?

---

[1] An allusion to "The Myth of Dædelus and Icarus." (See p. 12.)

JOHN KEATS (1795–1821)

La Belle Dame sans Merci[1]

O what can ail thee, Knight at arms,
   Alone and palely loitering?
The sedge[2] has withered from the Lake
   And no birds sing!

O what can ail thee, Knight at arms,
   So haggard, and so woebegone?
The squirrel's granary is full
   And the harvest's done.

I see a lily on thy brow
10   With anguish moist and fever dew,
And on thy cheeks a fading rose
   Fast withereth too.

"I met a Lady in the Meads,[3]
   Full beautiful, a faery's child,
Her hair was long, her foot was light
   And her eyes were wild.

"I made a Garland for her head,
   And bracelets too, and fragrant Zone;
She looked at me as she did love
20   And made sweet moan.

"I set her on my pacing steed
   And nothing else saw all day long,
For sidelong would she bend and sing
   A faery's song.

"She found me roots of relish sweet,
   And honey wild, and manna dew,
And sure in language strange she said
   'I love thee true.'

"She took me to her elfin grot
30   And there she wept and sighed full sore,
And there I shut her wild wild eyes
   With kisses four.

---

[1] French: The Beautiful Lady without Pity.
[2] sedge: grasslike plants, growing in shallow water or marshy places.
[3] Meads: meadows.

"And there she lulléd me asleep,
    And there I dreamed, Ah Woe betide!
The latest dream I ever dreamt
    On the cold hill side.

"I saw pale Kings, and Princes too,
    Pale warriors, death-pale were they all;
They cried, 'La belle dame sans merci
40   Thee hath in thrall!'

"I saw their starved lips in the gloam⁴
    With horrid warning gapéd wide,
And I awoke, and found me here
    On the cold hill's side.

"And this is why I sojourn here,
    Alone and palely loitering;
Though the sedge is withered from the Lake
    And no birds sing."

(1819)

QUESTIONS

1. According to the knight, who is "La Belle Dame sans Merci," and why has she caused him to wander so aimlessly in a wasteland?

2. Who is speaking in the poem? How do the images differ, depending on the speaker?

3. Notice the rhythm and meter of the poem. What effect is achieved by Keats's alteration of the expected meter?

4. What elements of Keats's poem does Sir Frank Dicksee's painting *La Belle Dame Sans Merci* best illustrate? (See illustration, p. 342.)

---

⁴gloam: twilight.

ALFRED, LORD TENNYSON (1809–1892)

The Lady of Shalott

Part 1

On either side the river lie
Long fields of barley and of rye,
That clothe the wold[1] and meet the sky;
And through the field the road runs by
    To many-towered Camelot;
And up and down the people go,
Gazing where the lilies blow[2]
Round an island there below,
    The island of Shalott.

10 Willows whiten, aspens quiver,
Little breezes dusk and shiver
Through the wave that runs forever
By the island in the river
    Flowing down to Camelot.
Four gray walls, and four gray towers,
Overlook a space of flowers,
And the silent isle imbowers
    The Lady of Shalott.

By the margin, willow-veiled,
20 Slide the heavy barges trailed
By slow horses; and unhailed
The shallop[3] flitteth silken-sailed
    Skimming down to Camelot:

But who hath seen her wave her hand?
Or at the casement seen her stand?
Or is she known in all the land,
    The Lady of Shalott?

Only reapers, reaping early
In among the bearded barley,
30 Hear a song that echoes cheerly
From the river winding clearly,
    Down to towered Camelot;

---

[1] wold: a rolling plain.
[2] blow: bloom.
[3] shallop: a small open boat.

And by the moon the reaper weary,
Piling sheaves in uplands airy,
Listening, whispers "'Tis the fairy
    Lady of Shalott."

Part 2

There she weaves by night and day
A magic web with colors gay.
She has heard a whisper say,
40 A curse is on her if she stay
    To look down to Camelot.
She knows not what the curse may be,
And so she weaveth steadily,
And little other care hath she,
    The Lady of Shalott.

And moving through a mirror clear[4]
That hangs before her all the year,
Shadows of the world appear.
There she sees the highway near
50   Winding down to Camelot;
There the river eddy whirls,
And there the surly village churls,
And the red cloaks of market girls,
    Pass onward from Shalott.

Sometimes a troop of damsels glad,
An abbot on an ambling pad,[5]
Sometimes a curly shepherd lad,
Or long-haired page in crimson clad,
    Goes by to towered Camelot;
60 And sometimes through the mirror blue
The knights come riding two and two:
She hath no loyal knight and true,
    The Lady of Shalott.

But in her web she still delights
To weave the mirror's magic sights,
For often through the silent nights
A funeral, with plumes and lights
    And music, went to Camelot;

---

[4] mirror clear: Weavers often used a mirror placed over their looms to see their work in progress.
[5] ambling pad: a slow moving horse.

Or when the moon was overhead,
70   Came two young lovers lately wed:
"I am half sick of shadows," said
    The Lady of Shalott.

Part 3

A bowshot from her bower eaves,
He rode between the barley sheaves,
The sun came dazzling through the leaves,
And flamed upon the brazen greaves[6]
    Of bold Sir Lancelot.
A red-cross knight forever kneeled
To a lady in his shield,
80   That sparkled on the yellow field,
    Beside remote Shalott.

The gemmy bridle glittered free,
Like to some branch of stars we see
Hung in the golden Galaxy.
The bridle bells rang merrily
    As he rode down to Camelot;
And from his blazoned baldric[7] slung
A mighty silver bugle hung,
And as he rode his armor rung,
90   Beside remote Shalott.

All in the blue unclouded weather
Thick-jeweled shone the saddle leather,
The helmet and the helmet-feather
Burned like one burning flame together,
    As he rode down to Camelot;
As often through the purple night,
Below the starry clusters bright,
Some bearded meteor, trailing light,
    Moves over still Shalott.

100   His broad clear brow in sunlight glowed;
On burnished hooves his war horse trode;
From underneath his helmet flowed
His coal-black curls as on he rode,
    As he rode down to Camelot.

---

[6] greaves: protective armor covering the shins.
[7] Baldric: a sash worn diagonally across the body.

From the bank and from the river
He flashed into the crystal mirror,
"Tirra lirra," by the river
　　　Sang Sir Lancelot.

　　　She left the web, she left the loom,
110　She made three paces through the room,
She saw the water lily bloom,
She saw the helmet and the plume,
　　　She looked down to Camelot.
Out flew the web and floated wide;
The mirror cracked from side to side;
"The curse is come upon me," cried
　　　The Lady of Shalott.

Part 4

In the stormy east wind straining,
The pale yellow woods were waning,
120　The broad stream in his banks complaining,
Heavily the low sky raining
　　　Over towered Camelot;
Down she came and found a boat
Beneath a willow left afloat,
And round about the prow she wrote
　　　The Lady of Shalott.

And down the river's dim expanse
Like some bold seër in a trance,
Seeing all his own mischance—
130　With a glassy countenance
　　　Did she look to Camelot.
And at the closing of the day
She loosed the chain, and down she lay;
The broad steam bore her far away,
　　　The Lady of Shalott.

Lying, robed in snowy white
That loosely flew to left and right—
The leaves upon her falling light—
Through the noises of the night
140　　She floated down to Camelot;
And as the boat-head wound along
The willowy hills and fields among,
They heard her singing her last song,
　　　The Lady of Shalott.

Heard a carol, mournful, holy,
Chanted loudly, chanted lowly,
Till her blood was frozen slowly,
And her eyes were darkened wholly,
    Turned to towered Camelot.
150 For ere she reached upon the tide
The first house by the waterside,
Singing in her song she died,
    The Lady of Shalott.

Under tower and balcony,
By garden wall and gallery,
A gleaming shape she floated by,
Dead-pale between the houses high,
    Silent into Camelot.
Out upon the wharfs they came,
160 Knight and burgher, lord and dame,
And round the prow they read her name,
    The Lady of Shalott.

Who is this? and what is here?
And in the lighted palace near
Died the sound of royal cheer;
And they crossed themselves for fear,
    All the knights at Camelot:
But Lancelot mused a little space;
He said, "She has a lovely face;
170 God in his mercy lend her grace,
    The Lady of Shalott."

(1832, REVISED 1842)

QUESTIONS

1. Why do you think the reapers refer to the Lady as being a fairy?

2. What does the symbolism of the mirror suggest in the context of this poem?

3. What is the lady weaving?

4. Camelot is the city of King Arthur's Court, but what else might it represent?

5. What do you think is the real cause of the Lady's death? Do you agree that the risk she takes is worthwhile?

ROBERT BROWNING (1812–1889)

Porphyria's Lover

The rain set early in to-night,
    The sullen wind was soon awake,
It tore the elm-tops down for spite,
    And did its worse to vex the lake:
    I listened with heart fit to break.
When glided in Porphyria; straight
    She shut the cold out and the storm,
And kneeled and made the cheerless grate
    Blaze up, and all the cottage warm;
10   Which done, she rose, and from her form
Withdrew the dripping cloak and shawl,
    And laid her soiled gloves by, untied
Her hat and let the damp hair fall,
    And, last, she sat down by my side
    And called me. When no voice replied,
She put my arm about her waist,
    And made her smooth white shoulder bare,
And all her yellow hair displaced,
    And, stooping, made my cheek lie there,
20   And spread, o'er all, her yellow hair,
Murmuring how she loved me—she
    Too weak, for all her heart's endeavour,
To set its struggling passion free
    From pride, and vainer ties dissever,
    And give herself to me for ever.
But passion sometimes would prevail,
    Nor could to-night's gay feast restrain
A sudden thought of one so pale
    For love of her, and all in vain:
30   So, she was come through wind and rain.
Be sure I looked up at her eyes
    Happy and proud; at last I knew
Porphyria worshipped me; surprise
    Made my heart swell, and still it grew
    While I debated what to do.
That moment she was mine, mine, fair,
    Perfectly pure and good: I found
A thing to do, and all her hair
    In one long yellow string I wound
40   Three times her little throat around,

And strangled her. No pain felt she;
  I am quite sure she felt no pain.
As a shut bud that holds a bee,
  I warily oped her lids: again
  Laughed the blue eyes without a stain.
And I untightened next the tress
  About her neck; her cheek once more
Blushed bright beneath my burning kiss:
  I propped her head up as before,
50 Only, this time my shoulder bore
Her head, which droops upon it still:
  The smiling rosy little head,
So glad it has its utmost will,
  That all it scorned at once is fled,
  And I, its love, am gained instead!
Porphyria's love: she guessed not how
  Her darling one wish would be heard.
And thus we sit together now,
  And all night long we have not stirred,
60 And yet God has not said a word!

(1836)

QUESTIONS

1. What foreshadowing of events to come can be found in the way the speaker describes the setting before Porphyria enters?

2. How does Porphyria change the atmosphere once she enters and how does the speaker treat her in return? What reason does he give for his behavior?

3. What macabre hope does the speaker seek to achieve by killing her?

TED HUGHES (1927–1999)

Lovesong

He loved her and she loved him
His kisses sucked out her whole past and future or tried to
He had no other appetite
She bit him she gnawed him she sucked
She wanted him complete inside her
Safe and sure forever and ever
Their little cries fluttered into the curtains

Her eyes wanted nothing to get away
Her looks nailed down his hands his wrists his elbows
10   He gripped her hard so that life
Should not drag her from that moment
He wanted all future to cease
He wanted to topple with his arms round her
Off that moment's brink and into nothing
Or everlasting or whatever there was
Her embrace was an immense press
To print him into her bones
His smiles were the garrets of a fairy palace
Where the real world would never come
20   Her smiles were spider bites
So he would lie still till she felt hungry
His words were occupying armies
Her laughs were an assassin's attempts
His looks were bullets daggers of revenge
Her glances were ghosts in the corner with horrible secrets
His whispers were whips and jackboots
Her kisses were lawyers steadily writing
His caresses were the last hooks of a castaway
Her love-tricks were the grinding of locks
30   And their deep cries crawled over the floors
Like an animal dragging a great trap
His promises were the surgeon's gag
Her promises took the top off his skull
She would get a brooch made of it
His vows pulled out all her sinews
He showed her how to make a love-knot
Her vows put his eyes in formalin
At the back of her secret drawer
Their screams stuck in the wall

40   Their heads fell apart into sleep like the two halves
Of a lopped melon, but love is hard to stop

In their entwined sleep they exchanged arms and legs
In their dreams their brains took each other hostage

In the morning they wore each other's face

(1971)

Questions

1. Trace the points in the poem where the speaker's tone shifts. What do you think these shifts signify?

2. What do the metaphors and images of the poem suggest about the physical and psychological nature of the relationship?

3. Explain what seems to be happening to the lovers' relationship when their "little cries" become "deep cries" and then "screams."

4. What is the speaker suggesting about possessiveness in a love relationship when he says that "love is hard to stop"?

T. S. ELIOT (1888–1965)

The Love Song of J. Alfred Prufrock

S'io credessi che mia risposta fosse
A persona che mai tornasse al mondo,
Questa fiamma staria senza piá scosse.
Ma per co che giammai di questo fondo
Non tornò viva alcun, s'i'odo il vero,
Senza tema d'infamia ti rispondo.[1]

Let us go then, you and I,
When the evening is spread out against the sky
Like a patient etherised[2] upon a table;
Let us go, through certain half-deserted streets,
The muttering retreats
Of restless nights in one-night cheap hotels
And sawdust restaurants with oyster-shells:
Streets that follow like a tedious argument
Of insidious intent

10   To lead you to an overwhelming question . . .
Oh, do not ask, 'What is it?'
Let us go and make our visit.

In the room the women come and go
Talking of Michelangelo.[3]

The yellow fog that rubs its back upon the window-panes,
The yellow smoke that rubs its muzzle on the window-panes

---

[1] This epigraph is taken from Dante's *Inferno* (XXVII, 60–66). The occasion is a meeting between Dante (the character) and Guido Montefeltro, who is burning in the flames of Hell. Thinking that Dante is also a tormented soul, Montefeltro says, "If I thought my reply were to one who would ever return to the world, this flame would stop flickering. But since no man returns alive from this depth, if what I hear is true, I answer you without fear of infamy."
[2] etherised: to be in a deathlike trance. Ether is a gas used to induce unconsciousness and relieve pain.
[3] Michelangelo Buonarroti (1475–1564): Italian sculptor, painter, and poet.

Licked its tongue into the corners of the evening,
Lingered upon the pools that stand in drains,
Let fall upon its back the soot that falls from chimneys,
20   Slipped by the terrace, made a sudden leap,
And seeing that it was a soft October night,
Curled once about the house, and fell asleep.

And indeed there will be time
For the yellow smoke that slides along the street
Rubbing its back upon the window-panes;
There will be time, there will be time
To prepare a face to meet the faces that you meet;
There will be time to murder and create,
And time for all the works and days of hands
30   That lift and drop a question on your plate;
Time for you and time for me,
And time yet for a hundred indecisions,
And for a hundred visions and revisions,
Before the taking of a toast and tea.

In the room the women come and go
Talking of Michelangelo.

And indeed there will be time
To wonder, 'Do I dare?' and, 'Do I dare?'
Time to turn back and descend the stair,
40   With a bald spot in the middle of my hair—
[They will say: 'How his hair is growing thin!']
My morning coat,[4] my collar mounting firmly to the chin,
My necktie rich and modest, but asserted by a simple pin—
[They will say: 'But how his arms and legs are thin!']
Do I dare
Disturb the universe?
In a minute there is time
For decisions and revisions which a minute will reverse.

For I have known them all already, known them all—
50   Have known the evenings, mornings, afternoons,
I have measured out my life with coffee spoons;
I know the voices dying with a dying fall
Beneath the music from a farther room.
So how should I presume?

And I have known the eyes already, known them all—
The eyes that fix you in a formulated phrase,

---

[4] morning coat: a cutaway coat, formal daytime attire.

And when I am formulated, sprawling on a pin,
When I am pinned and wriggling on the wall,
Then how should I begin
60   To spit out all the butt-ends of my days and ways?
    And how should I presume?

    And I have known the arms already, known them all—
Arms that are braceleted and white and bare
[But in the lamplight, downed with light brown hair!]
Is it perfume from a dress
That makes me so digress?
Arms that lie along a table, or wrap about a shawl.
    And should I then presume?
    And how should I begin?

70   Shall I say, I have gone at dusk through narrow streets
And watched the smoke that rises from the pipes
Of lonely men in short-sleeves, leaning out of windows? . . .

    I should have been a pair of ragged claws
Scuttling across the floors of silent seas.

And the afternoon, the evening, sleeps so peacefully!
Smoothed by long fingers,
Asleep. . . .tired . . . or it malingers,
Stretched on the floor, here beside you and me.
Should I, after tea and cakes and ices,
80   Have the strength to force the moment to its crisis?
But though I have wept and fasted, wept and prayed,
Though I have seen my head [grown slightly bald] brought in upon a platter,[5]
I am no prophet—and here's no great matter;
I have seen the moment of my greatness flicker,
And I have seen the eternal Footman hold my coat, and snicker,
And in short, I was afraid.

    And would it have been worth it, after all,
After the cups, the marmalade, the tea,
Among the porcelain, among some talk of you and me,
90   Would it have been worth while,
To have bitten off the matter with a smile,
To have squeezed the universe into a ball[6]
To roll it toward some overwhelming question,
To say: 'I am Lazarus,[7] come from the dead,

---

[5] An allusion to John the Baptist, who was beheaded at the request of Salome. See Matthew 14:3–11.
[6] An allusion to Marvell's "To His Coy Mistress." (See p. 446.)
[7] Lazarus: a man raised from the dead by Jesus. See John 11:1–44.

Come back to tell you all, I shall tell you all'—
If one, settling a pillow by her head,
  Should say: 'That is not what I meant at all.
  That is not it, at all.'

  And would it have been worth it, after all,
100 Would it have been worth while,
After the sunsets and the dooryards and the sprinkled streets,
After the novels, after the teacups, after the skirts that trail along the floor—
And this, and so much more?—
It is impossible to say just what I mean!
But as if a magic lantern threw the nerves in patterns on a screen:
Would it have been worth while
If one, settling a pillow or throwing off a shawl,
And turning toward the window, should say:
  'That is not it at all,
110   That is not what I meant, at all.'

No! I am not Prince Hamlet,[8] nor was meant to be;
Am an attendant lord, one that will do
To swell a progress,[9] start a scene or two,
Advise the prince; no doubt, an easy tool,
Deferential, glad to be of use,
Politic, cautious, and meticulous;
Full of high sentence,[10] but a bit obtuse;
At times, indeed, almost ridiculous—
Almost, at times, the Fool.

120 I grow old . . . I grow old . . .
I shall wear the bottoms of my trousers rolled.
  Shall I part my hair behind? Do I dare to eat a peach?
I shall wear white flannel trousers, and walk upon the beach.
I have heard the mermaids singing, each to each.

  I do not think that they will sing to me.

  I have seen them riding seaward on the waves
Combing the white hair of the waves blown back
When the wind blows the water white and black.

  We have lingered in the chambers of the sea
130 By sea-girls wreathed with seaweed red and brown
Till human voices wake us, and we drown.

(1915)

---

[8] Prince Hamlet: the hero of Shakespeare's drama *The Tragedy of Hamlet, Prince of Denmark* (1601).
[9] progress: a royal procession.
[10] sentence: judgment or opinion.

QUESTIONS

1. According to Prufrock's description of himself, what is there in his personality that prevents him from experiencing fulfillment?

2. What does the poem's imagery of city, sky, clothing, food, and sea convey about Prufrock's relationship with women?

3. What is the importance of time in this poem? Why is there too much or too little time for Prufrock?

4. Why do you suppose that Eliot chose to call this a love song? Do you consider this a love poem at all? What kind of poem do you think it is?

Writing Topics for Poems

1. How is each love different from others yet the same as it is portrayed in Donne's "The Good Morrow," Browning's "How Do I Love Thee," Breton's "Free Union," and Burns's "A Red, Red Rose." How does hyperbole contribute to each poem?

2. Discuss Keats's "La Belle Dame sans Merci" and Tennyson's "The Lady of Shalott" as metaphors for male and female experiences of unrequited love. What similarities exist between The Lady's and the Knight's physical and mental states? What is the significance of the supernatural powers that affect each person?

3. Analyze the change in mood, setting, tone, and rhythm in Browning's "Meeting at Night" to "Parting at Morning."

4. Yeats's "No Second Troy" and Rukeyser's "Waiting for Icarus" make allusions to myths. Identify each myth and discuss its significance as it relates to the personal feelings and emotions of each speaker.

5. Marvell's "To His Coy Mistress" and Eliot's "The Love Song of J. Alfred Prufrock" are about unsuccessful lovers. What is the difference in tone between Marvell's speaker and Eliot's? What do these differences suggest about their characters?

6. Love can be dangerous enough to paralyze us, make us irrational, or cause us irreparable harm. Discuss the danger of love exemplified in Keats's "La Belle Dame sans Merci," Eliot's "The Love Song of J. Alfred Prufrock," Hughes's "Lovesong," Yeats's "No Second Troy," Rukeyser's "Waiting for Icarus," and Browning's "Porphyria's Lover."

7. Explain how each speaker copes with loss in Bishop's "One Art," Yeats's "No Second Troy," Merwin's "When You Go Away," and Rukeyser's "Waiting for Icarus."

8. Compare the use of the negative as a way of defining one's love in Bhartrihari's "My Love Is Nothing Like the Moon" and Shakespeare's "Sonnet CXXX" ("My Mistress' Eyes Are Nothing Like the Sun").

Drama

ARTHUR MILLER (B. 1915)

A View from the Bridge

CHARACTERS

LOUIS	RODOLPHO
MIKE	FIRST IMMIGRATION OFFICER
ALFIERI	SECOND IMMIGRATION OFFICER
EDDIE	MR. LIPARI
CATHERINE	MRS. LIPARI
BEATRICE	TWO "SUBMARINES"
MARCO	NEIGHBORS
TONY	

ACT ONE

The street and house front of a tenement building. The front is skeletal entirely. The main acting area is the living room–dining room of EDDIE'S apartment. It is a worker's flat, clean, sparse, homely. There is a rocker down front; a round dining table at center, with chairs; and a portable phonograph.

At back are a bedroom door and an opening to the kitchen; none of these interiors are seen.

At the right, forestage, a desk. This is MR. ALFIERI'S law office.

There is also a telephone booth. This is not used until the last scenes, so it may be covered or left in view.

A stairway leads up to the apartment, and then farther up to the next story, which is not seen.

Ramps, representing the street, run upstage and off to right and left.

As the curtain rises, LOUIS *and* MIKE, *longshoremen, are pitching coins against the building at left.*

A distant foghorn blows.

Enter ALFIERI, *a lawyer in his fifties turning gray; he is portly, good-humored, and thoughtful. The two pitchers nod to him as he passes. He crosses the stage to his desk, removes his hat, runs his fingers through his hair, and grinning, speaks to the audience.*

ALFIERI.[1] You wouldn't have known it, but something amusing has just happened. You see how uneasily they nod to me? That's because I am a lawyer. In this neighborhood to meet a lawyer or a priest on the street is unlucky. We're only thought of in connection with disasters, and they'd rather not get too close.

I often think that behind that suspicious little nod of theirs lie three thousand years of distrust. A lawyer means the law, and in Sicily, from where their fathers came, the law has not been a friendly idea since the Greeks were beaten.

I am inclined to notice the ruins in things, perhaps because I was born in Italy. . . . I only came here when I was twenty-five. In those days, Al Capone, the greatest
10   Carthaginian of all, was learning his trade on these pavements, and Frankie Yale himself was cut precisely in half by a machine gun on the corner of Union Street, two blocks away. Oh, there were many here who were justly shot by unjust men. Justice is very important here.

But this is Red Hook,[2] not Sicily. This is the slum that faces the bay on the seaward side of Brooklyn Bridge. This is the gullet of New York swallowing the tonnage of the world. And now we are quite civilized, quite American. Now we settle for half, and I like it better. I no longer keep a pistol in my filing cabinet.

And my practice is entirely unromantic.

My wife has warned me, so have my friends; they tell me the people in this
20   neighborhood lack elegance, glamour. After all, who have I dealt with in my life? Longshoremen and their wives, and fathers and grandfathers, compensation cases, evictions, family squabbles—the petty troubles of the poor—and yet . . . every few years there is still a case, and as the parties tell me what the trouble is, the flat air in my office suddenly washes in with the green scent of the sea, the dust in this air is blown away and the thought comes that in some Caesar's year, in Calabria perhaps or on the cliff at Syracuse,[3] another lawyer, quite differently dressed, heard the same complaint and set there as powerless as I, and watched it run its bloody course.

EDDIE *has appeared and has been pitching coins with the men and is highlighted among them. He is forty—a husky, slightly overweight longshoreman.*

---

[1] Allusion to Vittorio Alfieri (1749–1803): an Italian playwright who wrote nineteen tragedies, hated tyranny, and championed political and intellectual freedom.
[2] Red Hook: a waterfront section of the Borough of Brooklyn in New York City.
[3] Calabria and Syracuse: cities in Sicily.

This one's name was Eddie Carbone, a longshoreman working the docks from Brooklyn Bridge to the breakwater where the open sea begins.

ALFIERI *walks into darkness.*

30 EDDIE, *moving up steps into doorway.* Well, I'll see ya, fellas.

CATHERINE *enters from kitchen, crosses down to window, looks out.*

LOUIS. You workin' tomorrow?

EDDIE. Yeah, there's another day yet on that ship. See ya, Louis.

EDDIE *goes into the house, as light rises in the apartment.*

CATHERINE *is waving to* LOUIS *from the window and turns to him.*

CATHERINE. Hi, Eddie!

EDDIE *is pleased and therefore shy about it; he hangs up his cap and jacket.*

EDDIE. Where you goin' all dressed up?

CATHERINE, *running her hands over her skirt.* I just got it. You like it?

EDDIE. Yeah, it's nice. And what happened to your hair?

CATHERINE. You like it? I fixed it different. *Calling to kitchen:* He's here, B.!

EDDIE. Beautiful. Turn around, lemme see in the back. *She turns for him.* Oh, if your mother was alive to see you now! She wouldn't believe it.

40 CATHERINE. You like it, huh?

EDDIE. You look like one of them girls that went to college. Where you goin'?

CATHERINE, *taking his arm.* Wait'll B. comes in, I'll tell you something. Here, sit down. *She is walking him to the armchair. Calling offstage.* Hurry up, will you, B.?

EDDIE, *sitting.* What's goin' on?

CATHERINE. I'll get you a beer, all right?

EDDIE. Well, tell me what happened. Come over here, talk to me.

CATHERINE. I want to wait till B. comes in. *She sits on her heels beside him.* Guess how much we paid for the skirt.

EDDIE. I think it's too short, ain't it?

50 CATHERINE, *standing.* No! not when I stand up.

EDDIE. Yeah, but you gotta sit down sometimes.

CATHERINE. Eddie, it's the style now. *She walks to show him.* I mean, if you see me walkin' down the street—

EDDIE. Listen, you been givin' me the willies the way you walk down the street, I mean it.

CATHERINE. Why?

EDDIE. Catherine, I don't want to be a pest, but I'm tellin' you you're walkin' wavy.

CATHERINE. I'm walkin' wavy?

EDDIE. Now don't aggravate me, Katie, you are walkin' wavy! I don't like the looks they're givin' you in the candy store. And with them new high heels on the sidewalk

60 clack, clack, clack. The heads are turnin' like windmills.

CATHERINE. But those guys look at all the girls, you know that.

EDDIE. You ain't "all the girls."

CATHERINE, *almost in tears because he disapproves.* What do you want me to do? You want me to—

EDDIE. Now don't get mad, kid.

CATHERINE. Well, I don't know what you want from me.

EDDIE. Katie, I promised your mother on her deathbed. I'm responsible for you. You're a baby, you don't understand these things. I mean like when you stand here by the window, wavin' outside.

70   CATHERINE. I was wavin' to Louis!

EDDIE. Listen, I could tell you things about Louis which you wouldn't wave to him no more.

CATHERINE, *trying to joke him out of his warning.* Eddie, I wish there was one guy you couldn't tell me things about!

EDDIE. Catherine, do me a favor, will you? You're gettin' to be a big girl now, you gotta keep yourself more, you can't be so friendly, kid. *Calls.* Hey, B., what're you doin' in there? *To* CATHERINE. Get her in here, will you? I got news for her.

CATHERINE, *starting out.* What?

EDDIE. Her cousins landed.

80   CATHERINE, *clapping her hands together.* No! *She turns instantly and starts for the kitchen.* B.! Your cousins!

BEATRICE *enters, wiping her hands with a towel.*

BEATRICE, *in the face of* CATHERINE'S *shout.* What?

CATHERINE. Your cousins got in!

BEATRICE, *astounded, turns to* EDDIE. What are you talkin' about? Where?

EDDIE. I was just knockin' off work before and Tony Bereli come over to me; he says the ship is in the North River.[4]

BEATRICE—*her hands are clasped at her breast; she seems half in fear, half in unutterable joy.* They're all right?

EDDIE. He didn't see them yet, they're still on board. But as soon as they get off he'll
90   meet them. He figures about ten o'clock they'll be here.

BEATRICE *sits, almost weak from tension.* And they'll let them off the ship all right? That's fixed, heh?

EDDIE. Sure, they give them regular seamen papers and they walk off with the crew. Don't worry about it, B., there's nothin' to it. Couple of hours they'll be here.

BEATRICE. What happened? They wasn't supposed to be till next Thursday.

EDDIE. I don't know; they put them on any ship they can get them out on. Maybe the other ship they was supposed to take there was some danger— What you crying about?

BEATRICE, *astounded and afraid.* I'm— I just—I can't believe it! I didn't even buy a
100   new tablecloth; I was gonna wash the walls—

---

[4] North River: another name for the Hudson River.

EDDIE. Listen, they'll think it's a millionaire's house compared to the way they live. Don't worry about the walls. They'll be thankful. *To* CATHERINE. Whyn't you run down buy a tablecloth. Go ahead, here. *He is reaching into his pocket.*

CATHERINE. There's no stores open now.

EDDIE, *to* BEATRICE. You was gonna put a new cover on the chair.

BEATRICE. I know—well, I thought it was gonna be next week! I was gonna clean the walls, I was gonna wax the floors. *She stands disturbed.*

CATHERINE, *pointing upward.* Maybe Mrs. Dondero upstairs—

BEATRICE, *of the tablecloth.* No, hers is worse than this one. *Suddenly.* My God, I don't
110   even have nothin' to eat for them! *She starts for the kitchen.*

EDDIE, *reaching out and grabbing her arm.* Hey, hey! Take it easy.

BEATRICE. No, I'm just nervous, that's all. *To* CATHERINE. I'll make the fish.

EDDIE. You're savin' their lives, what're you worryin' about the tablecloth? They probably didn't see a tablecloth in their whole life where they come from.

BEATRICE, *looking into his eyes.* I'm just worried about you, that's all I'm worried.

EDDIE. Listen, as long as they know where they're gonna sleep.

BEATRICE. I told them in the letters. They're sleepin' on the floor.

EDDIE. Beatrice, all I'm worried about is you got such a heart that I'll end up on the floor with you, and they'll be in our bed.

120   BEATRICE. All right, stop it.

EDDIE. Because as soon as you see a tired relative, I end up on the floor.

BEATRICE. When did you end up on the floor?

EDDIE. When your father's house burned down I didn't end up on the floor?

BEATRICE. Well, their house burned down!

EDDIE. Yeah, but it didn't keep burnin' for two weeks!

BEATRICE. All right, look, I'll tell them to go someplace else. *She starts into the kitchen.*

EDDIE. Now wait a minute. Beatrice! *She halts. He goes to her.* I just don't want you bein' pushed around, that's all. You got too big a heart. *He touches her hand.* What're you so touchy?

130   BEATRICE. I'm just afraid if it don't turn out good you'll be mad at me.

EDDIE. Listen, if everybody keeps his mouth shut, nothin' can happen. They'll pay for their board.

BEATRICE. Oh, I told them.

EDDIE. Then what the hell. *Pause. He moves.* It's an honor, B. I mean it. I was just thinkin' before, comin' home, suppose my father didn't come to this country, and I was starvin' like them over there . . . and I had people in America could keep me a couple of months? The man would be honored to lend me a place to sleep.

BEATRICE—*there are tears in her eyes. She turns to* CATHERINE. You see what he is? *She turns and grabs* EDDIE's *face in her hands.* Mmm! You're an angel! God'll bless you. *He*
140   *is gratefully smiling.* You'll see, you'll get a blessing for this!

EDDIE, *laughing.* I'll settle for my own bed.

BEATRICE. Go, Baby, set the table.

CATHERINE. We didn't tell him about me yet.

BEATRICE. Let him eat first, then we'll tell him. Bring everything in. *She hurries* CATHERINE *out.*

EDDIE, *sitting at the table.* What's all that about? Where's she goin'?

BEATRICE. No place. It's very good news, Eddie. I want you to be happy.

EDDIE. What's goin' on?

CATHERINE *enters with plates, forks.*

BEATRICE. She's got a job.

Pause. EDDIE *looks at* CATHERINE, *then back to* BEATRICE.

EDDIE. What job? She's gonna finish school.

150 CATHERINE. Eddie, you won't believe it—

EDDIE. No—no, you gonna finish school. What kinda job, what do you mean? All of a sudden you—

CATHERINE. Listen a minute, it's wonderful.

EDDIE. It's not wonderful. You'll never get nowheres unless you finish school. You can't take no job. Why didn't you ask me before you take a job?

BEATRICE. She's askin' you now, she didn't take nothin' yet.

CATHERINE. Listen a minute! I came to school this morning and the principal called me out of the class, see? To go to his office.

EDDIE. Yeah?

160 CATHERINE. So I went in and he says to me he's got my records, y'know? And there's a company wants a girl right away. It ain't exactly a secretary, it's a stenographer first, but pretty soon you get to be secretary. And he says to me that I'm the best student in the whole class—

BEATRICE. You hear that?

EDDIE. Well why not? Sure she's the best.

CATHERINE. I'm the best student, he says, and if I want, I should take the job and the end of the year he'll let me take the examination and he'll give me the certificate. So I'll save practically a year!

EDDIE, *strangely nervous.* Where's the job? What company?

170 CATHERINE. It's a big plumbing company over Nostrand Avenue.

EDDIE. Nostrand Avenue and where?

CATHERINE. It's someplace by the Navy Yard.[5]

BEATRICE. Fifty dollars a week, Eddie.

EDDIE, *to* CATHERINE, *surprised.* Fifty?

CATHERINE. I SWEAR.

Pause.

EDDIE. What about all the stuff you wouldn't learn this year, though?

CATHERINE. There's nothin' more to learn, Eddie, I just gotta practice from now on. I know all the symbols and I know the keyboard. I'll just get faster, that's all. And when I'm workin' I'll keep gettin' better and better, you see?

180 BEATRICE. Work is the best practice anyway.

---

[5] The Brooklyn Navy Yard: a U.S. government shipyard, now defunct.

EDDIE. That ain't what I wanted, though.

CATHERINE. Why! It's a great big company—

EDDIE. I don't like that neighborhood over there.

CATHERINE. It's a block and half from the subway, he says.

EDDIE. Near the Navy Yard plenty can happen in a block and a half. And a plumbin' company! That's one step over the water front. They're practically longshoremen.

BEATRICE. Yeah, but she'll be in the office, Eddie.

EDDIE. I know she'll be in the office, but that ain't what I had in mind

BEATRICE. Listen, she's gotta go to work sometime.

190 EDDIE. Listen, B., she'll be with a lotta plumbers? And sailors up and down the street? So what did she go to school for?

CATHERINE. But it's fifty a week, Eddie.

EDDIE. Look, did I ask you for money? I supported you this long I support you a little more. Please, do me a favor, will ya? I want you to be with different kind of people. I want you to be in a nice office. Maybe a lawyer's office someplace in New York in one of them nice buildings. I mean if you're gonna get outa here then get out; don't go practically in the same kind of neighborhood.

Pause. CATHERINE *lowers her eyes.*

BEATRICE: Go, Baby, bring in the supper. CATHERINE *goes out.* Think about it a little bit, Eddie. Please. She's crazy to start work. It's not a little shop, it's a big company.

200 Some day she could be a secretary. They picked her out of the whole class. *He is silent, staring down at the tablecloth, fingering the pattern.* What are you worried about? She could take care of herself. She'll get out of the subway and be in the office in two minutes.

EDDIE, *somehow sickened.* I know that neighborhood, B., I don't like it.

BEATRICE. Listen, if nothin' happened to her in this neighborhood it ain't gonna happen noplace else. *She turns his face to her.* Look, you gotta get used to it, she's no baby no more. Tell her to take it. *He turns his head away.* You hear me? *She is angering.* I don't understand you; she's seventeen years old, you gonna keep her in the house all her life?

210 EDDIE, *insulted.* What kinda remark is that?

BEATRICE, *with sympathy but insistent force.* Well, I don't understand when it ends. First it was gonna be when she graduated high school, so she graduated high school. Then it was gonna be when she learned stenographer, so she learned stenographer. So what're we gonna wait for now? I mean it, Eddie, sometimes I don't understand you; they picked her out of the whole class, it's an honor for her.

CATHERINE *enters with food, which she silently sets on the table. After a moment of watching her face,* EDDIE *breaks into a smile, but it almost seems that tears will form in his eyes.*

EDDIE. With your hair that way you look like a madonna, you know that? You're the madonna type. *She doesn't look at him, but continues ladling out food onto the plates.* You wanna go to work, heh, Madonna?

CATHERINE, *softly.* Yeah.

220   EDDIE, *with a sense of her childhood, her babyhood, and the years.* All right, go to work. *She looks at him, then rushes and hugs him.* Hey, hey! Take it easy! *He holds her face away from him to look at her.* What're you cryin' about? *He is affected by her, but smiles his emotion away.*

CATHERINE, *sitting at her place.* I just— *Bursting out.* I'm gonna buy all new dishes with my first pay! *They laugh warmly.* I mean it. I'll fix up the whole house! I'll buy a rug!

EDDIE. And then you'll move away.

CATHERINE. No, Eddie!

EDDIE, *grinning.* Why not? That's life. And you'll come visit on Sundays, then once a month, then Christmas and New Year's, finally.

230   CATHERINE, *grasping his arm to reassure him and to erase the accusation.* No, please!

EDDIE, *smiling but hurt.* I only ask you one thing—don't trust nobody. You got a good aunt but she's got too big a heart, you learned bad from her. Believe me.

BEATRICE. Be the way you are, Katie, don't listen to him.

EDDIE, *to* BEATRICE—*strangely and quickly resentful.* You lived in a house all your life, what do you know about it? You never worked in your life.

BEATRICE. She likes people. What's wrong with that?

EDDIE. Because most people ain't people. She's goin' to work; plumbers; they'll chew her to pieces if she don't watch out. *To* CATHERINE. Believe me, Katie, the less you trust, the less you be sorry.

EDDIE *crosses himself and the women do the same, and they eat.*

240   CATHERINE. First thing I'll buy a rug, heh, B.?

BEATRICE. I don't mind. *To* EDDIE. I smelled coffee all day today. You unloadin' coffee today?

EDDIE. Yeah, a Brazil ship.

CATHERINE. I smelled it too. It smelled all over the neighborhood.

EDDIE. That's one time, boy, to be a longshoreman is a pleasure. I could work coffee ships twenty hours a day. You go down in the hold, y'know? It's like flowers, that smell. We'll bust a bag tomorrow, I'll bring you some.

BEATRICE. Just be sure there's no spiders in it, will ya? I mean it. *She directs this to* CATHERINE, *rolling her eyes upward.* I still remember that spider coming out of that

250   bag he brung home. I nearly died.

EDDIE. You call that a spider? You oughta see what comes outa the bananas sometimes.

BEATRICE. Don't talk about it!

EDDIE. I seen spiders could stop a Buick.

BEATRICE, *clapping her hands over her ears.* All right, shut up!

EDDIE, *laughing and taking a watch out of his pocket.* Well, who started with spiders?

BEATRICE. All right, I'm sorry, I didn't mean it. Just don't bring none home again. What time is it?

EDDIE. Quarter nine. *Puts watch back in his pocket. They continue eating in silence.*

CATHERINE. He's bringin' them ten o'clock, Tony?

EDDIE. Around, yeah. *He eats.*

260   CATHERINE. Eddie, suppose somebody asks if they're livin' here. *He looks at her as though already she had divulged something publicly. Defensively.* I mean if they ask.

EDDIE. Now look, Baby, I can see we're gettin' mixed up again here.

CATHERINE. No, I just mean . . . people'll see them goin' in and out.

EDDIE. I don't care who sees them goin' in and out as long as you don't see them goin' in and out. And this goes for you too, B. You don't see nothin' and you don't know nothin'.

BEATRICE. What do you mean? I understand.

EDDIE. You don't understand; you still think you can talk about this to somebody just a little bit. Now lemme say it once and for all, because you're makin' me nervous again,
270   both of you. I don't care if somebody comes in the house and sees them sleepin' on the floor, it never comes out of your mouth who they are or what they're doin' here.

BEATRICE. Yeah, but my mother'll know—

EDDIE. Sure she'll know, but just don't you be the one who told her, that's all. This is the United States government you're playin' with now, this is the Immigration Bureau. If you said it you knew it, if you didn't say it you didn't know it.

CATHERINE. Yeah, but Eddie, suppose somebody—

EDDIE. I don't care what question it is. You—don't—know—nothin'. They got stool pigeons all over this neighborhood they're payin' them every week for information, and you don't know who they are. It could be your best friend. You hear? *To* BEATRICE.
280   Like Vinny Bolzano, remember Vinny?

BEATRICE. Oh, yeah, God forbid.

EDDIE. Tell her about Vinny. *To* CATHERINE. You think I'm blowin' steam here? *To* BEATRICE. Go ahead, tell her. *To* CATHERINE. You was a baby then. There was a family lived next door to her mother, he was about sixteen—

BEATRICE. No, he was no more than fourteen, cause I was to his confirmation in Saint Agnes. But the family had an uncle that they were hidin' in the house, and he snitched to the Immigration.

CATHERINE. The kid snitched?

EDDIE. On his own uncle!

290   CATHERINE. What, was he crazy?

EDDIE. He was crazy after, I tell you that, boy.

BEATRICE. Oh, it was terrible. He had five brothers and the old father. And they grabbed him in the kitchen and pulled him down the stairs—three flights his head was bouncin' like a coconut. And they spit on him in the street, his own father and his brothers. The whole neighborhood was cryin'.

CATHERINE. Ts! So what happened to him?

BEATRICE. I think he went away. *To* EDDIE. I never seen him again, did you?

EDDIE *rises during this, taking out his watch.* Him? You'll never see him no more, a guy do a thing like that? How's he gonna show his face? *To* CATHERINE, *as he gets up un-*
300   *easily.* Just remember, kid, you can quicker get back a million dollars that was stole than a word that you gave away. *He is standing now, stretching his back.*

CATHERINE. Okay, I won't say a word to nobody, I swear.

EDDIE. Gonna rain tomorrow. We'll be slidin' all over the decks. Maybe you oughta put something on for them, they be here soon.

BEATRICE. I only got fish, I hate to spoil it if they ate already. I'll wait, it only takes a few minutes; I could broil it.

CATHERINE. What happens, Eddie, when that ship pulls and they ain't on it, though? Don't the captain say nothin'?

EDDIE, *slicing an apple with his pocket knife.* Captain's pieced off, what do you mean?

310   CATHERINE. Even the captain?

EDDIE. What's the matter, the captain don't have to live? Captain gets a piece, maybe one of the mates, piece for the guy in Italy who fixed the papers for them, Tony here'll get a little bite. . . .

BEATRICE. I just hope they get work here, that's all I hope.

EDDIE. Oh, the syndicate'll fix jobs for them; till they pay 'em off they'll get them work every day. It's after the pay-off, then they'll have to scramble like the rest of us.

BEATRICE. Well, it be better than they got there.

EDDIE. Oh sure, well, listen. So you gonna start Monday, heh, Madonna?

CATHERINE, *embarrassed.* I'm supposed to, yeah.

EDDIE *is standing facing the two seated women. First* BEATRICE *smiles, then* CATHERINE, *for a powerful emotion is on him, a childish one and a knowing fear, and the tears show in his eyes—and they are shy before the avowal.*

320   EDDIE, *sadly smiling, yet somehow proud of her.* Well . . . I hope you have good luck. I wish you the best. You know that, kid.

CATHERINE, *rising, trying to laugh.* You sound like I'm goin' a million miles!

EDDIE. I know. I guess I just never figured on one thing.

CATHERINE, *smiling.* What?

EDDIE. That you would ever grow up. *He utters a soundless laugh at himself, feeling his breast pocket of his shirt.* I left a cigar in my other coat, I think. *He starts for the bedroom.*

CATHERINE. Stay there! I'll get it for you.

She hurries out. There is a slight pause, and EDDIE *turns to* BEATRICE, *who has been avoiding his gaze.*

EDDIE. What are you mad at me lately?

BEATRICE. Who's mad? *She gets up, clearing the dishes.* I'm not mad. *She picks up the*
330   *dishes and turns to him.* You're the one is mad. *She turns and goes into the kitchen as* CATHERINE *enters from the bedroom with a cigar and a pack of matches.*

CATHERINE. Here! I'll light it for you! *She strikes a match and holds it to his cigar. He puffs. Quietly.* Don't worry about me, Eddie, heh?

EDDIE. Don't burn yourself. *Just in time she blows out the match.* You better go in help her with the dishes.

CATHERINE *turns quickly to the table, and, seeing the table cleared, she says, almost guiltily:* Oh! *She hurries into the kitchen, and as she exits there:* I'll do the dishes, B.!

Alone, EDDIE *stands looking toward the kitchen for a moment. Then he takes out his watch, glances at it, replaces it in his pocket, sits in the armchair, and stares at the smoke flowing out of his mouth.*

The lights go down, then come up on ALFIERI, *who has moved onto the forestage.*

ALFIERI. He was as good a man as he had to be in a life that was hard and even. He worked on the piers when there was work, he brought home his pay, and he lived. And toward ten o'clock of that night, after they had eaten, the cousins came.

The lights fade on ALFIERI *and rise on the street.*

Enter TONY, *escorting* MARCO *and* RODOLPHO, *each with a valise.* TONY *halts, indicates the house. They stand for a moment looking at it.*

MARCO—*he is a square-built peasant of thirty-two, suspicious, tender, and quiet-voiced.* Thank you.

340   TONY. You're on your own now. Just be careful, that's all. Ground floor.
MARCO. Thank you.
TONY, *indicating the house.* I'll see you on the pier tomorrow. You'll go to work.

    MARCO *nods.* TONY *continues on walking down the street.*

RODOLPHO. This will be the first house I ever walked into in America! Imagine! She said they were poor!
MARCO. Ssh! Come. *They go to door.*

    MARCO *knocks. The lights rise in the room.* EDDIE *goes and opens the door. Enter* MARCO *and* RODOLPHO, *removing their caps.* BEATRICE *and* CATHERINE *enter from the kitchen. The lights fade in the street.*

EDDIE. You Marco?
MARCO. Marco.
EDDIE. Come on in! *He shakes* MARCO's *hand.*
BEATRICE. Here, take the bags!
350   MARCO *nods, looks to the women and fixes on* BEATRICE. *Crosses to* BEATRICE. Are you my cousin?

    She nods. He kisses her hand.

BEATRICE, *above the table, touching her chest with her hand.* Beatrice. This is my husband, Eddie. *All nod.* Catherine, my sister Nancy's daughter. *The brothers nod.*
MARCO, *indicating* RODOLPHO. My brother. Rodolpho. RODOLPHO *nods.* MARCO *comes with a certain formal stiffness to* EDDIE. I want to tell you now Eddie—when you say go, we will go.
EDDIE. Oh, no . . . *Takes* MARCO's *bag.*
MARCO. I see it's a small house, but soon, maybe, we can have our own house.
EDDIE. You're welcome, Marco, we got plenty of room here. Katie, give them supper,
360   heh? *Exits into bedroom with their bags.*
CATHERINE. Come here, sit down. I'll get you some soup.

MARCO, *as they go to the table.* We ate on the ship. Thank you. *To* EDDIE, *calling off to bedroom.* Thank you.

BEATRICE. Get some coffee. We'll all have coffee. Come sit down.

RODOLPHO *and* MARCO *sit, at the table.*

CATHERINE, *wondrously.* How come he's so dark and you're so light, Rodolpho?

RODOLPHO, *ready to laugh.* I don't know. A thousand years ago, they say, the Danes invaded Sicily.

BEATRICE *kisses* RODOLPHO. *They laugh as* EDDIE *enters.*

CATHERINE, *to* BEATRICE. He's practically blond!

EDDIE. How's the coffee doin'?

370   CATHERINE, *brought up.* I'm gettin' it. *She hurries out to kitchen.*

EDDIE *sits on his rocker.* Yiz have a nice trip?

MARCO. The ocean is always rough. But we are good sailors.

EDDIE. No trouble gettin' here?

MARCO. No. The man brought us. Very nice man.

RODOLPHO, *to* EDDIE. He says we start to work tomorrow. Is he honest?

EDDIE, *laughing.* No. But as long as you owe them money, they'll get you plenty of work. *To* MARCO. Yiz ever work on the piers in Italy?

MARCO. Piers? Ts!—no.

RODOLPHO, *smiling at the smallness of his town.* In our town there are no piers, only the

380   beach, and little fishing boats.

BEATRICE. So what kind work did yiz do?

MARCO, *shrugging shyly, even embarrassed.* Whatever there is, anything.

RODOLPHO. Sometimes they build a house, or if they fix the bridge—Marco is a mason and I bring him the cement. *He laughs.* In harvest time we work in the fields . . . if there is work. Anything.

EDDIE. Still bad there, heh?

MARCO. Bad, yes.

RODOLPHO, *laughing.* It's terrible! We stand around all day in the piazza listening to the fountain like birds. Everybody waits only for the train.

390   BEATRICE. What's on the train?

RODOLPHO. Nothing. But if there are many passengers and you're lucky you make a few lire to push the taxi up the hill.

Enter CATHERINE; *she listens.*

BEATRICE. You gotta push a taxi?

RODOLPHO, *laughing.* Oh, sure! It's a feature in our town. The horses in our town are skinnier than goats. So if there are too many passengers we help to push the carriages up to the hotel. *He laughs.* In our town the horses are only for show.

CATHERINE. Why don't they have automobile taxis?

RODOLPHO. There is one. We push that too. *They laugh.* Everything in our town, you gotta push!

400   BEATRICE, *to* EDDIE. How do you like that!

EDDIE, *to* MARCO. So what're you wanna do, you gonna stay here in this country or you wanna go back?

MARCO, *surprised*. Go back?

EDDIE. Well, you're married, ain't you?

MARCO. Yes. I have three children.

BEATRICE. Three! I thought only one.

MARCO. Oh, no. I have three now. Four years, five years, six years.

BEATRICE. Ah . . . I bet they're cryin' for you already, heh?

410   MARCO. What can I do? The older one is sick in his chest. My wife—she feeds them from her own mouth. I tell you the truth, if I stay there they will never grow up. They eat the sunshine.

BEATRICE. My God. So how long you want to stay?

MARCO. With your permission, we will stay maybe a—

EDDIE. She don't mean in this house, she means in the country.

MARCO. Oh. Maybe four, five, six years, I think.

RODOLPHO, *smiling*. He trusts his wife.

BEATRICE. Yeah, but maybe you'll get enough, you'll be able to go back quicker.

MARCO. I hope. I don't know. *To* EDDIE. I understand it's not so good here either.

EDDIE. Oh, you guys'll be all right—till you pay them off, anyway. After that, you'll
420   have to scramble, that's all. But you'll make better here than you could there.

RODOLPHO. How much? We hear all kinds of figures. How much can a man make? We work hard, we'll work all day, all night—

MARCO *raises a hand to hush him.*

EDDIE—*he is coming more and more to address* MARCO *only*. On the average a whole year? Maybe—well, it's hard to say, see. Sometimes we lay off, there's no ships three four weeks.

MARCO. Three, four weeks!—Ts!

EDDIE. But I think you could probably—thirty, forty a week, over the whole twelve months of the year.

MARCO, *rises, crosses to* EDDIE. Dollars.

430   EDDIE. Sure dollars.

MARCO *puts an arm round* RODOLPHO *and they laugh.*

MARCO. If we stay here a few months, Beatrice—

BEATRICE. Listen, you're welcome, Marco—

MARCO. Because I could send them a little more if I stay here.

BEATRICE. As long as you want, we got plenty a room.

MARCO, *his eyes are showing tears*. My wife— *To* EDDIE. My wife—I want to send right away maybe twenty dollars—

EDDIE. You could send them something next week already.

MARCO—*he is near tears*. Eduardo . . . *He goes to* EDDIE, *offering his hand.*

EDDIE. Don't thank me. Listen, what the hell, it's no skin off me. *To* CATHERINE. What
440   happened to the coffee?

CATHERINE. I got it on. *To* RODOLPHO. You married too? No.

RODOLPHO *rises.* Oh, no . . .

BEATRICE, *to* CATHERINE. I told you he—

CATHERINE. I know, I just thought maybe he got married recently.

RODOLPHO. I have no money to get married. I have a nice face, but no money. *He laughs.*

CATHERINE, *to* BEATRICE. He's a real blond!

BEATRICE, *to* RODOLPHO. You want to stay here too, heh? For good?

RODOLPHO. Me? Yes, forever! Me, I want to be an American. And then I want to go back to Italy when I am rich, and I will buy a motorcycle. *He smiles.* MARCO *shakes him affectionately.*

450   CATHERINE. A motorcycle!

RODOLPHO. With a motorcycle in Italy you will never starve any more.

BEATRICE. I'll get you coffee. *She exits to the kitchen.*

EDDIE. What you do with a motorcycle?

MARCO. He dreams, he dreams.

RODOLPHO, *to* MARCO. Why? *To* EDDIE. Messages! The rich people in the hotel always need someone who will carry a message. But quickly, and with a great noise. With a blue motorcycle I would station myself in the courtyard of the hotel, and in a little while I would have messages.

MARCO. When you have no wife you have dreams.

460   EDDIE. Why can't you just walk, or take a trolley or sump'm?

Enter BEATRICE *with coffee.*

RODOLPHO. Oh, no, the machine, the machine is necessary. A man comes into a great hotel and says, I am a messenger. Who is this man? He disappears walking, there is no noise, nothing. Maybe he will never come back, maybe he will never deliver the message. But a man who rides up on a great machine, this man is responsible, this man exists. He will be given messages. *He helps* BEATRICE *set out the coffee things.* I am also a singer, though.

EDDIE. You mean a regular—?

RODOLPHO. Oh, yes. One night last year Andreola got sick. Baritone. And I took his place in the garden of the hotel. Three arias I sang without a mistake! Thousand-lire

470   notes they threw from the tables, money was falling like a storm in the treasury. It was magnificent. We lived six months on that night, eh, Marco?

MARCO *nods doubtfully.*

MARCO. Two months.

EDDIE *laughs.*

BEATRICE. Can't you get a job in that place?

RODOLPHO. Andreola got better. He's a baritone, very strong.

BEATRICE *laughs.*

MARCO, *regretfully, to* BEATRICE. He sang too loud.

RODOLPHO. Why too loud?

MARCO. Too loud. The guests in that hotel are all Englishmen. They don't like too loud.

RODOLPHO, *to* CATHERINE. Nobody ever said it was too loud!

MARCO. I say. It was too loud. *To* BEATRICE. I knew it as soon as he started to sing. Too
480   loud.

RODOLPHO. Then why did they throw so much money?

MARCO. They paid for your courage. The English like courage. But once is enough.

RODOLPHO, *to all but* MARCO. I never heard anybody say it was too loud.

CATHERINE. Did you ever hear of jazz?

RODOLPHO. Oh, sure! I *sing* jazz.

CATHERINE *rises.* You could sing jazz?

RODOLPHO. Oh, I sing Napolidan, jazz, bel canto—I sing "Paper Doll," you like "Paper
    Doll"?

CATHERINE. Oh, sure, I'm crazy for "Paper Doll." Go ahead, sing it.

> RODOLPHO *takes his stance after getting a nod of permission from* MARCO, *and with a
> high tenor voice begins singing:*

490   "I'll tell you boys it's tough to be alone,
    And it's tough to love a doll that's not your own.
    I'm through with all of them,
    I'll never fall again,
    Hey, boy, what you gonna do?
    I'm gonna buy a paper doll that I can call my own,
    A doll that other fellows cannot steal.

> EDDIE *rises and moves upstage.*

    And then those flirty, flirty guys
    With their flirty, flirty eyes
    Will have to flirt with dollies that are real—
500   EDDIE. Hey, kid—hey, wait a minute—

CATHERINE, *enthralled.* Leave him finish, it's beautiful! *To* BEATRICE. He's terrific! It's
    terrific, Rodolpho.

EDDIE. Look, kid; you don't want to be picked up, do ya?

MARCO. No—no! *He rises.*

EDDIE, *indicating the rest of the building.* Because we never had no singers here . . .
    and all of a sudden there's a singer in the house, y'know what I mean?

MARCO. Yes, yes. You'll be quiet, Rodolpho.

EDDIE—*he is flushed.* They got guys all over the place, Marco. I mean.

MARCO. Yes. He'll be quiet. *To* RODOLPHO. You'll be quiet.

> RODOLPHO *nods.*

> EDDIE *has risen, with iron control, even a smile. He moves to* CATHERINE.

510   EDDIE. What's the high heels for, Garbo?

CATHERINE. I figured for tonight—

EDDIE. Do me a favor, will you? Go ahead.

Embarrassed now, angered, CATHERINE *goes out into the bedroom.* BEATRICE *watches her go and gets up; in passing, she gives* EDDIE *a cold look, restrained only by the strangers, and goes to the table to pour coffee.*

EDDIE, *striving to laugh, and to* MARCO, *but directed as much to* BEATRICE. All actresses they want to be around here.

RODOLPHO, *happy about it.* In Italy too! All the girls.

CATHERINE *emerges from the bedroom in low-heel shoes, comes to the table.* RODOLPHO *is lifting a cup.*

EDDIE—*he is sizing up* RODOLPHO, *and there is a concealed suspicion.* Yeah, heh?

RODOLPHO. Yes! *Laughs, indicating* CATHERINE. Especially when they are so beautiful!

CATHERINE. You like sugar?

RODOLPHO. Sugar? Yes! I like sugar very much!

EDDIE *is downstage, watching as she pours a spoonful of sugar into his cup, his face puffed with trouble, and the room dies.*

Lights rise on ALFIERI.

520 ALFIERI. Who can ever know what will be discovered? Eddie Carbone had never expected to have a destiny. A man works, raises his family, goes bowling, eats, get old, and then he dies. Now, as the weeks passed, there was a future, there was a trouble that would not go away.

The lights fade on ALFIERI, *then rise on* EDDIE *standing at the doorway of the house.* BEATRICE *enters on the street. She sees* EDDIE, *smiles at him. He looks away.*

She starts to enter the house when EDDIE *speaks.*

EDDIE. It's after eight.

BEATRICE. Well, it's a long show at the Paramount.

EDDIE. They must've seen every picture in Brooklyn by now. He's supposed to stay in the house when he ain't working. He ain't supposed to go advertising himself.

BEATRICE. Well that's his trouble, what do you care? If they pick him up they pick him up, that's all. Come in the house.

530 EDDIE. What happened to the stenography? I don't see her practice no more.

BEATRICE. She'll get back to it. She's excited, Eddie.

EDDIE. She tell you anything?

BEATRICE, *comes to him, now the subject is opened.* What's the matter with you? He's a nice kid, what do you want from him?

EDDIE. That's a nice kid? He gives me the heeby-jeebies.

BEATRICE, *smiling.* Ah, go on, you're just jealous.

EDDIE. Of *him?* Boy, you don't think much of me.

BEATRICE. I don't understand you. What's so terrible about him?

EDDIE. You mean it's all right with you? That's gonna be her husband?

540 BEATRICE. Why? He's a nice fella, hard workin', he's a good-lookin' fella.

EDDIE. He sings on the ships, didja know that?

BEATRICE. What do you mean, he sings?

EDDIE. Just what I said, he sings. Right on the deck, all of a sudden, a whole song comes out of his mouth—with motions. You know what they're callin' him now? Paper Doll they're callin' him, Canary. He's like a weird. He comes out on the pier, one-two-three, it's a regular free show.

BEATRICE. Well, he's a kid; he don't know how to behave himself yet.

EDDIE. And with that wacky hair; he's like a chorus girl or sump'm.

BEATRICE. So he's blond, so—

550 EDDIE. I just hope that's his regular hair, that's all I hope.

BEATRICE. You crazy or sump'm? *She tries to turn him to her.*

EDDIE—*he keeps his head turned away.* What's so crazy? I don't like his whole way.

BEATRICE. Listen, you never seen a blond guy in your life? What about Whitey Balso?

EDDIE, *turning to her victoriously.* Sure, but Whitey don't sing; he don't do like that on the ships.

BEATRICE. Well, maybe that's the way they do in Italy.

EDDIE. Then why don't his brother sing? Marco goes around like a man; nobody kids Marco. *He moves from her, halts. She realizes there is a campaign solidified in him.* I tell you the truth I'm surprised I have to tell you all this. I mean I'm surprised, B.

560 BEATRICE—*she goes to him with purpose now.* Listen, you ain't gonna start nothin' here.

EDDIE. I ain't startin' nothin', but I ain't gonna stand around lookin' at that. For that character I didn't bring her up. I swear, B., I'm surprised at you; I sit there waitin' for you to wake up but everything is great with you.

BEATRICE. No, everything ain't great with me.

EDDIE. No?

BEATRICE. No. But I got other worries.

EDDIE. Yeah. *He is already weakening.*

BEATRICE. Yeah, you want me to tell you?

EDDIE, *in retreat.* Why? What worries you got?

570 BEATRICE. When am I gonna be a wife again, Eddie?

EDDIE. I ain't been feelin' good. They bother me since they came.

BEATRICE. It's almost three months you don't feel good; they're only here a couple of weeks. It's three months, Eddie.

EDDIE. I don't know, B. I don't want to talk about it.

BEATRICE. What's the matter, Eddie, you don't like me, heh?

EDDIE. What do you mean, I don't like you? I said I don't feel good, that's all.

BEATRICE. Well, tell me, am I doing something wrong? Talk to me.

EDDIE—*Pause. He can't speak, then.* I can't. I can't talk about it.

BEATRICE. Well tell me what—

580 EDDIE. I got nothin' to say about it!

She stands for a moment; he is looking off; she turns to go into the house.

EDDIE. I'll be all right, B.; just lay off me, will ya? I'm worried about her.

BEATRICE. The girl is gonna be eighteen years old, it's time already.

EDDIE. B., he's taking her for a ride!

BEATRICE. All right, that's her ride. What're you gonna stand over her till she's forty? Eddie, I want you to cut it out now, you hear me? I don't like it! Now come in the house.

EDDIE. I want to take a walk, I'll be in right away.

BEATRICE. They ain't goin' to come any quicker if you stand in the street. It ain't nice, Eddie.

590   EDDIE. I'll be in right away. Go ahead. *He walks off.*

She goes into the house. EDDIE *glances up the street, sees* LOUIS *and* MIKE *coming, and sits on an iron railing.* LOUIS *and* MIKE *enter.*

LOUIS. Wanna go bowlin' tonight?

EDDIE. I'm too tired. Goin' to sleep.

LOUIS. How's your two submarines?

EDDIE. They're okay.

LOUIS. I see they're gettin' work allatime.

EDDIE. Oh yeah, they're doin' all right.

MIKE. That's what we oughta do. We oughta leave the country and come in under the water. Then we get work.

EDDIE. You ain't kiddin'.

600   LOUIS. Well, what the hell. Y'know?

EDDIE. Sure.

LOUIS—*sits on railing beside* EDDIE. Believe me, Eddie, you got a lotta credit comin' to you.

EDDIE. Aah, they don't bother me, don't cost me nutt'n.

MIKE. That older one, boy, he's a regular bull. I seen him the other day liftin' coffee bags over the Matson Line. They leave him alone he woulda load the whole ship by himself.

EDDIE. Yeah, he's a strong guy, that guy. Their father was a regular giant, supposed to be.

610   LOUIS. Yeah, you could see. He's a regular slave.

MIKE, *grinning.* That blond one, though—EDDIE *looks at him.* He's got a sense of humor. LOUIS *snickers.*

EDDIE, *searchingly.* Yeah. He's funny—

MIKE, *starting to laugh.* Well he ain't exackly funny, but he's always like makin' remarks like, y'know? He comes around, everybody's laughin'. LOUIS *laughs.*

EDDIE, *uncomfortably, grinning.* Yeah, well . . . he's got a sense of humor.

MIKE, *laughing.* Yeah, I mean, he's always makin' like remarks, like, y'know?

EDDIE. Yeah, I know. But he's a kid yet, y'know? He—he's just a kid, that's all.

MIKE, *getting hysterical with* LOUIS. I know. You take one look at him—everybody's happy.

620   LOUIS *laughs.* I worked one day with him last week over the Moore-MacCormack Line, I'm tellin' you they was all hysterical. LOUIS *and he explode in laughter.*

EDDIE. Why? What'd he do?

MIKE. I don't know . . . he was just humorous. You never can remember what he says, y'know? But it's the way he says it. I mean he gives you a look sometimes and you start laughin'!

EDDIE. Yeah. *Troubled.* He's got a sense of humor.

MIKE, *gasping.* Yeah.

LOUIS, *rising.* Well, we see ya, Eddie.

EDDIE. Take it easy.

630　LOUIS. Yeah. See ya.

MIKE. If you wanna come bowlin' later we're goin' Flatbush Avenue.

> *Laughing, they move to exit, meeting* RODOLPHO *and* CATHERINE *entering on the street. Their laughter rises as they see* RODOLPHO, *who does not understand but joins in.* EDDIE *moves to enter the house as* LOUIS *and* MIKE *exit.* CATHERINE *stops him at the door.*

CATHERINE. Hey, Eddie—what a picture we saw! Did we laugh!

EDDIE—*he can't help smiling at sight of her.* Where'd you go?

CATHERINE. Paramount. It was with those two guys, y'know? That—

EDDIE. Brooklyn Paramount?

CATHERINE, *with an edge of anger, embarrassed before* RODOLPHO. Sure, the Brooklyn Paramount. I told you we wasn't goin' to New York.

EDDIE, *retreating before the threat of her anger.* All right, I only asked you. *To* RODOLPHO. I just don't want her hangin' around Times Square, see? It's full of

640　tramps over there.

RODOLPHO. I would like to go to Broadway once, Eddie. I would like to walk with her once where the theaters are and the opera. Since I was a boy I see pictures of those lights.

EDDIE, *his little patience waning.* I want to talk to her a minute, Rodolpho. Go inside, will you?

RODOLPHO. Eddie, we only walk together in the streets. She teaches me.

CATHERINE. You know what he can't get over? That there's no fountains in Brooklyn!

EDDIE, *smiling unwillingly.* Fountains? RODOLPHO *smiles at his own naïveté.*

CATHERINE. In Italy he says, every town's got fountains, and they meet there. And you

650　know what? They got oranges on the trees where he comes from, and lemons. Imag-ine—on the trees? I mean it's interesting. But he's crazy for New York.

RODOLPHO, *attempting familiarity.* Eddie, why can't we go once to Broadway—?

EDDIE. Look, I gotta tell her something—

RODOLPHO. Maybe you can come too. I want to see all those lights. *He sees no response in* EDDIE's *face. He glances at* CATHERINE. I'll walk by the river before I go to sleep. *He walks off down the street.*

CATHERINE. Why don't you talk to him, Eddie? He blesses you, and you don't talk to him hardly.

EDDIE, *enveloping her with his eyes.* I bless you and you don't talk to me. *He tries to smile.*

CATHERINE. *I* don't talk to you? *She hits his arm.* What do you mean?

660　EDDIE. I don't see you no more. I come home you're runnin' around someplace—

CATHERINE. Well, he wants to see everything, that's all, so we go. . . . You mad at me?

EDDIE. No. *He moves from her, smiling sadly.* It's just I used to come home, you was al-ways there. Now, I turn around, you're a big girl. I don't know how to talk to you.

CATHERINE. Why?

EDDIE. I don't know, you're runnin', you're runnin', Katie. I don't think you listening any more to me.

CATHERINE, *going to him.* Ah, Eddie, sure I am. What's the matter? You don't like him?

Slight pause.

EDDIE *turns to her.* You like him, Katie?

CATHERINE, *with a blush but holding her ground.* Yeah, I like him.

670 EDDIE—*his smiles goes.* You like him.

CATHERINE, *looking down.* Yeah. *Now she looks at him for the consequences, smiling but tense. He looks at her like a lost boy.* What're you got against him? I don't understand. He only blesses you.

EDDIE *turns away.* He don't bless me, Katie.

CATHERINE. He does! You're like a father to him!

EDDIE *turns to her.* Katie.

CATHERINE. What, Eddie?

EDDIE. You gonna marry him?

CATHERINE. I don't know. We just been . . . goin' around, that's all. *Turns to him.*

680 What're you got against him, Eddie? Please, tell me. What?

EDDIE. He don't respect you.

CATHERINE. Why?

EDDIE. Katie . . . if you wasn't an orphan, wouldn't he ask your father's permission before he run around with you like this?

CATHERINE. Oh, well, he didn't think you'd mind.

EDDIE. He knows I mind, but it don't bother him if I mind, don't you see that?

CATHERINE. No, Eddie, he's got all kinds of respect for me. And you too! We walk across the street he takes my arm—he almost bows to me! You got him all wrong, Eddie; I mean it, you—

690 EDDIE. Katie, he's only bowin' to his passport.

CATHERINE. His passport!

EDDIE. That's right. He marries you he's got the right to be an American citizen. That's what's goin' on here. *She is puzzled and surprised.* You understand what I'm tellin' you? The guy is lookin' for his break, that's all he's lookin' for.

CATHERINE, *pained.* Oh, no, Eddie, I don't think so.

EDDIE. You don't think so! Katie, you're gonna make me cry here. Is that a workin' man? What does he do with his first money? A snappy new jacket he buys, records, a pointy pair new shoes and his brother's kids are starvin' over there with tuberculosis? That's a hit-and-run guy, baby; he's got bright lights in his head, Broadway. Them guys don't

700 think of nobody but theirself! You marry him and the next time you see him it'll be for divorce!

CATHERINE *steps toward him.* Eddie, he never said a word about his papers or—

EDDIE. You mean he's supposed to tell you that?

CATHERINE. I don't think he's even thinking about it.

EDDIE. What's better for him to think about! He could be picked up any day here and he's back pushin' taxis up the hill!

CATHERINE. No, I don't believe it.

EDDIE. Katie, don't break my heart, listen to me.

CATHERINE. I don't want to hear it.

710 EDDIE. Katie, listen . . .

CATHERINE. He loves me!

EDDIE, *with deep alarm.* Don't say that, for God's sake! This is the oldest racket in the country—

CATHERINE, *desperately, as though he had made his imprint.* I don't believe it! *She rushes to the house.*

EDDIE, *following her.* They been pullin' this since the Immigration Law was put in! They grab a green kid that don't know nothin' and they—

CATHERINE, *sobbing.* I don't believe it and I wish to hell you'd stop it!

EDDIE. Katie!

They enter the apartment. The lights in the living room have risen and BEATRICE *is there. She looks past the sobbing* CATHERINE *at* EDDIE, *who in the presence of his wife, makes an awkward gesture of eroded command, indicating* CATHERINE.

EDDIE. Why don't you straighten her out?

720 BEATRICE, *inwardly angered at his flowing emotion, which in itself alarms her.* When are you going to leave her alone?

EDDIE. B., the guy is no good!

BEATRICE, *suddenly, with open fright and fury.* You going to leave her alone? Or you gonna drive me crazy? *He turns, striving to retain his dignity, but nevertheless in guilt walks out of the house, into the street and away.* CATHERINE *starts into a bedroom.* Listen, Catherine. CATHERINE *halts, turns to her sheepishly.* What are you going to do with yourself?

CATHERINE. I don't know.

BEATRICE. Don't tell me you don't know; you're not a baby any more, what are you go-
730 ing to do with yourself?

CATHERINE. He won't listen to me.

BEATRICE. I don't understand this. He's not your father, Catherine. I don't understand what's going on here.

CATHERINE, *as one who herself is trying to rationalize a buried impulse.* What am I going to do, just kick him in the face with it?

BEATRICE. Look, honey, you wanna get married, or don't you wanna get married? What are you worried about, Katie?

CATHERINE, *quietly, trembling.* I don't know B. It just seems wrong if he's against it so much.

740 BEATRICE, *never losing her aroused alarm.* Sit down, honey, I want to tell you something. Here, sit down. Was there ever any fella he liked for you? There wasn't, was there?

CATHERINE. But he says Rodolpho's just after his papers.

BEATRICE. Look, he'll say anything. What does he care what he says? If it was a prince came here for you it would be no different. You know that, don't you?

CATHERINE. Yeah, I guess.

BEATRICE. So what does that mean?

CATHERINE *slowly turns her head to* BEATRICE. What?

BEATRICE. It means you gotta be your own self more. You still think you're a little girl, honey. But nobody else can make up your mind for you any more, you understand? You gotta give him to understand that he can't give you orders no more.

CATHERINE. Yeah, but how am I going to do that? He thinks I'm a baby.

BEATRICE. Because *you* think you're a baby. I told you fifty times already, you can't act the way you act. You still walk around in front of him in your slip—

CATHERINE. Well I forgot.

BEATRICE. Well you can't do it. Or like you sit on the edge of the bathtub talkin' to him when he's shavin' in his underwear.

CATHERINE. When'd I do that?

BEATRICE. I seen you in there this morning.

CATHERINE. Oh . . . well, I wanted to tell him something and I—

BEATRICE. I know, honey. But if you act like a baby and he be treatin' you like a baby. Like when he come home sometimes you throw yourself at him like when you was twelve years old.

CATHERINE. Well I like to see him and I'm happy so I—

BEATRICE. Look, I'm not tellin' you what to do honey, but—

CATHERINE. No, you could tell me, B.! Gee, I'm all mixed up. See, I— He looks so sad now and it hurts me.

BEATRICE. Well look Katie, if it's goin' to hurt you so much you're gonna end up an old maid here.

CATHERINE. No!

BEATRICE. I'm tellin' you, I'm not makin' a joke. I tried to tell you a couple of times in the last year or so. That's why I was so happy you were going to go out and get work, you wouldn't be here so much, you'd be a little more independent. I mean it. It's wonderful for a whole family to love each other, but you're a grown woman and you're in the same house with a grown man. So you'll act different now, heh?

CATHERINE. Yeah, I will. I'll remember.

BEATRICE. Because it ain't only up to him, Katie, you understand? I told him the same thing already.

CATHERINE, *quickly.* What?

BEATRICE. That he should let you go. But, you see, if only I tell him, he thinks I'm just bawlin' him out, or maybe I'm jealous or somethin', you know?

CATHERINE, *astonished.* He said you was jealous?

BEATRICE. No, I'm just sayin' maybe that's what he thinks. *She reaches over to* CATHERINE's *hand; with a strained smile.* You think I'm jealous of you, honey?

CATHERINE. No! It's the first I thought of it.

BEATRICE, *with a quiet sad laugh.* Well you should have thought of it before . . . but I'm not. We'll be all right. Just give him to understand; you don't have to fight, you're just— You're a woman, that's all, and you got a nice boy, and now the time came when you said good-by. All right?

CATHERINE, *strangely moved at the prospect.* All right. . . . If I can.

790   BEATRICE. Honey . . . you gotta.

> CATHERINE, *sensing now an imperious demand, turns with some fear, with a discovery, to* BEATRICE. *She is at the edge of tears, as though a familiar world had shattered.*

CATHERINE. Okay.

> *Lights out on them and up on* ALFIERI, *seated behind his desk.*

ALFIERI. It was at this time that he first came to me. I had represented his father in an accident case some years before, and I was acquainted with the family in a casual way. I remember him now as he walked through my doorway—

> *Enter* EDDIE *down right ramp.*

His eyes were like tunnels; my first thought was that he had committed a crime,

> EDDIE *sits beside the desk, cap in hand, looking out.*

but soon I saw it was only a passion that had moved into his body, like a stranger. ALFIERI *pauses, looks down at his desk, then to* EDDIE *as though he were continuing a conversation with him.* I don't quite understand what I can do for you. Is there a question of law somewhere?

EDDIE. That's what I want to ask you.

800   ALFIERI. Because there's nothing illegal about a girl falling in love with an immigrant.

EDDIE. Yeah, but what about it if the only reason for it is to get his papers?

ALFIERI. First of all you don't know that.

EDDIE. I see it in his eyes; he's laughin' at her and he's laughin' at me.

ALFIERI. Eddie, I'm a lawyer. I can only deal in what's provable. You understand that, don't you? Can you prove that?

EDDIE. *I know what's in his mind, Mr. Alfieri!*

ALFIERI. Eddie, even if you could prove that—

EDDIE. Listen . . . will you listen to me a minute? My father always said you was a smart man. I want you to listen to me.

ALFIERI. I'm only a lawyer, Eddie.

810   EDDIE. Will you listen a minute? I'm talkin' about the law. Lemme just bring out what I mean. A man, which he comes into the country illegal, don't it stand to reason he's gonna take every penny and put it in the sock? Because they don't know from one day to another, right?

ALFIERI. All right.

EDDIE. He's spendin'. Records he buys now. Shoes. Jackets. Y'understand me? This guy ain't worried. This guy is *here*. So it must be that he's got it all laid out in his mind already—he's stayin'. Right?

ALFIERI. Well? What about it?

EDDIE. All right. *He glances at* ALFIERI, *then down to the floor.* I'm talking to you confi-
820   dential, ain't I?

ALFIERI. Certainly.

EDDIE. I mean it don't go no place but here. Because I don't like to say this about anybody. Even my wife I didn't exactly say this.

ALFIERI. What is it?

EDDIE *takes a breath and glances briefly over each shoulder.* This guy ain't right, Mr. Alfieri.

ALFIERI. What do you mean?

EDDIE. I mean he ain't right.

ALFIERI. I don't get you.

830 EDDIE *shifts to another position in the chair.* Dja ever get a look at him?

ALFIERI. Not that I know of, no.

EDDIE. He's a blond guy. Like . . . platinum. You know what I mean?

ALFIERI. No.

EDDIE. I mean if you close the paper fast—you could blow him over.

ALFIERI. Well that doesn't mean—

EDDIE. Wait a minute, I'm tellin' you sump'm. He sings, see. Which is— I mean it's all right, but sometimes he hits a note, see. I turn around. I mean—high. You know what I mean?

ALFIERI. Well, that's a tenor.

840 EDDIE. I know a tenor, Mr. Alfieri. This ain't no tenor. I mean if you came in the house and you didn't know who was singin', you wouldn't be lookin' for him you be lookin' for her.

ALFIERI. Yes, but that's not—

EDDIE. I'm tellin' you sump'm, wait a minute. Please, Mr. Alfieri. I'm tryin' to bring out my thoughts here. Couple of nights ago my niece brings out a dress which it's too small for her, because she shot up like a light this last year. He takes the dress, lays it on the table, he cuts it up; one-two-three, he makes a new dress. I mean he looked so sweet there, like an angel—you could kiss him he was so sweet.

ALFIERI. Now look, Eddie—

850 EDDIE. Mr. Alfieri, they're laughin' at him on the piers. I'm ashamed. Paper Doll they call him. Blondie now. His brother thinks it's because he's got a sense of humor, see—which he's got—but that ain't what they're laughin'. Which they're not goin' to come out with it because they know he's my relative, which they have to see me if they make a crack, y'know? But I know what they're laughin' at, and when I think of that guy layin' his hands on her I could—I mean it's eatin' me out, Mr. Alfieri, because I struggled for that girl. And now he comes in my house and—

ALFIERI. Eddie, look—I have my own children. I understand you. But the law is very specific. The law does not . . .

EDDIE, *with a fuller flow of indignation.* You mean to tell me there's no law that a guy
860 which he ain't right can go to work and marry a girl and—?

ALFIERI. You have no recourse in the law, Eddie.

EDDIE. Yeah, but if he ain't right, Mr. Alfieri, you mean to tell me—

ALFIERI. There is nothing you can do, Eddie, believe me.

EDDIE. Nothin'.

ALFIERI. Nothing at all. There's only one legal question here.

EDDIE. What?

ALFIERI. The manner in which they entered the country. But I don't think you want to do anything about that, do you?

EDDIE. You mean—?

870 ALFIERI. Well, they entered illegally.

EDDIE. Oh, Jesus, no, I wouldn't do nothin' about that, I mean—

ALFIERI. All right, then, let me talk now, eh?

EDDIE. Mr. Alfieri, I can't believe what you tell me. I mean there must be some kinda law which—

ALFIERI. Eddie, I want you to listen to me. *Pause.* You know, sometimes God mixes up the people. We all love somebody, the wife, the kids—every man's got somebody that he loves, heh? But sometimes . . . there's too much. You know? There's too much, and it goes where it mustn't. A man works hard, he brings up a child, sometimes it's a niece, sometimes even a daughter, and he never realizes it, but through the years—

880 there is too much love for the daughter, there is too much love for the niece. Do you understand what I'm saying to you?

EDDIE, *sardonically.* What do you mean, I shouldn't look out for her good?

ALFIERI. Yes, but these things have to end, Eddie, that's all. The child has to grow up and go away, and the man has to learn to forget. Because after all, Eddie—what other way can it end? *Pause.* Let her go. That's my advice. You did your job, now it's her life; wish her luck, and let her go. *Pause.* Will you do that? Because there's no law, Eddie; make up your mind to it; the law is not interested in this.

EDDIE. You mean to tell me, even if he's a punk? If he's—

ALFIERI. There's nothing you can do.

EDDIE *stands.*

890 EDDIE. Well, all right, thanks. Thanks very much.

ALFIERI. What are you going to do?

EDDIE, *with a helpless but ironic gesture.* What can I do? I'm a patsy, what can a patsy do? I worked like a dog twenty years so a punk could have her, so that's what I done. I mean, in the worst times, in the worst, when there wasn't a ship comin' in the harbor, I didn't stand around lookin' for relief—I hustled. When there was empty piers in Brooklyn I went to Hoboken, Staten Island, the West Side, Jersey, all over—because I made a promise. I took out of my own mouth to give to her. I took out of my wife's mouth. I walked hungry plenty days in this city! *It begins to break through.* And now I gotta sit in my own house and look at a son-of-a-bitch punk like that—which he

900 came out of nowhere! I give him my house to sleep! I take the blankets off my bed for him, and he takes and puts his dirty filthy hands on her like a goddam thief!

ALFIERI, *rising.* But, Eddie, she's a woman now.

EDDIE. He's stealing from me!

ALFIERI. She wants to get married, Eddie. She can't marry you, can she?

EDDIE, *furiously.* What're you talkin' about, marry me! I don't know what the hell you're talkin' about!

Pause.

ALFIERI. I gave you my advice, Eddie. That's it.

EDDIE *gathers himself. A pause.*

EDDIE. Well, thanks. Thanks very much. It just—it's breakin' my heart, y'know. I—

ALFIERI. I understand. Put it out of your mind. Can you do that?

910 EDDIE. I'm— *He feels the threat of sobs, and with a helpless wave.* I'll see you around. *He goes out up the right ramp.*

ALFIERI *sits on desk.* There are times when you want to spread an alarm, but nothing has happened. I knew, I knew then and there—I could have finished the whole story that afternoon. It wasn't as though there was a mystery to unravel. I could see every step coming, step after step, like a dark figure walking down a hall toward a certain door. I knew where he was heading for, I knew where he was going to end. And I sat here many afternoons asking myself why, being an intelligent man, I was so powerless to stop it. I even went to a certain old lady in the neighborhood, a very wise old woman, and I told her, and she only nodded, and said, "Pray for him . . ." And so I— waited here.

As lights go out on ALFIERI, *they rise in the apartment where all are finishing dinner.* BEATRICE *and* CATHERINE *are clearing the table.*

920 CATHERINE. You know where they went?

BEATRICE. Where?

CATHERINE. They went to Africa once. On a fishing boat. EDDIE *glances at her.* It's true, Eddie.

BEATRICE *exits into the kitchen with dishes.*

EDDIE. I didn't say nothin'. *He goes to his rocker, picks up a newspaper.*

CATHERINE. And I was never even in Staten Island.[6]

EDDIE, *sitting with the paper.* You didn't miss nothin'. *Pause.* CATHERINE *takes dishes out.* How long that take you, Marco—to get to Africa?

MARCO, *rising.* Oh . . . two days. We go all over.

RODOLPHO, *rising.* Once we went to Yugoslavia.

930 EDDIE, *to* MARCO. They pay all right on them boats?

BEATRICE *enters. She and* RODOLPHO *stack the remaining dishes.*

MARCO. If they catch fish they pay all right. *Sits on a stool.*

RODOLPHO. They're family boats, though. And nobody in our family owned one. So we only worked when one of the families was sick.

BEATRICE. Y'know, Marco, what I don't understand—there's an ocean full of fish and yiz are all starvin'.

EDDIE. They gotta have boats, nets, you need money.

CATHERINE *enters.*

BEATRICE. Yeah, but couldn't they like fish from the beach? You see them down Coney Island—

MARCO. Sardines.

---

[6] Staten Island: a borough of New York City, a short ferry ride from lower Manhattan. The Verrazano Narrows Bridge now connects Brooklyn and Staten Island; it was built after the publication of this play.

940   EDDIE. Sure. *Laughing.* How you gonna catch sardines on a hook?

BEATRICE. Oh, I didn't know they're sardines. *To* CATHERINE. They're sardines!

CATHERINE. Yeah, they follow them all over the ocean, Africa, Yugoslavia . . . *She sits and begins to look through a movie magazine.* RODOLPHO *joins her.*

BEATRICE, *to* EDDIE. It's funny, y'know. You never think of it, that sardines are swimming in the ocean! *She exits to kitchen with dishes.*

CATHERINE. I know. It's like oranges and lemons on a tree. *To* EDDIE. I mean you ever think of oranges and lemons on a tree?

EDDIE. Yeah, I know. It's funny. *To* MARCO. I heard that they paint the oranges to make them look orange.

BEATRICE *enters.*

MARCO—*he has been reading a letter.* Paint?

950   EDDIE. Yeah, I heard that they grow like green.

MARCO. No, in Italy the oranges are orange.

RODOLPHO. Lemons are green.

EDDIE, *resenting his instruction.* I know lemons are green, for Christ's sake, you see them in the store they're green sometimes. I said oranges they paint, I didn't say nothin' about lemons.

BEATRICE, *sitting; diverting their attention.* Your wife is gettin' the money all right, Marco?

MARCO. Oh, yes. She bought medicine for my boy.

BEATRICE. That's wonderful. You feel better, heh?

960   MARCO. Oh, yes! But I'm lonesome.

BEATRICE. I just hope you ain't gonna do like some of them around here. They're here twenty-five years, some men, and they didn't get enough together to go back twice.

MARCO. Oh, I know. We have many families in our town, the children never saw the father. But I will go home. Three, four years, I think.

BEATRICE. Maybe you should keep more here. Because maybe she thinks it comes so easy you'll never get ahead of yourself.

MARCO. Oh, no, she saves. I send everything. My wife is very lonesome. *He smiles shyly.*

BEATRICE. She must be nice. She pretty? I bet, heh?

MARCO, *blushing.* No, but she understand everything.

970   RODOLPHO. Oh, he's got a clever wife!

EDDIE. I betcha there's plenty surprises sometimes when those guys get back there, heh?

MARCO. Surprises?

EDDIE, *laughing.* I mean, you know—they count the kids and there's a couple extra than when they left?

MARCO. No—no . . . The women wait, Eddie. Most. Most. Very few surprises.

RODOLPHO. It's more strict in our town. EDDIE *looks at him now.* It's not so free.

EDDIE *rises, paces up and down.* It ain't so free here either, Rodolpho, like you think. I seen greenhorns sometimes get in trouble that way—they think just because a girl

980   don't go around with a shawl over her head that she ain't strict, y'know? Girl don't have to wear black dress to be strict. Know what I mean?

RODOLPHO. Well, I always have respect—

EDDIE. I know, but in your town you wouldn't just drag off some girl without permission, I mean. *He turns.* You know what I mean, Marco? It ain't that much different here.

MARCO, *cautiously.* Yes.

BEATRICE. Well, he didn't exactly drag her off though, Eddie.

EDDIE. I know, but I seen some of them get the wrong idea sometimes. *To* RODOLPHO. I mean it might be a little more free here but it's just as strict.

990   RODOLPHO. I have respect for her, Eddie. I do anything wrong?

EDDIE. Look, kid, I ain't her father, I'm only her uncle—

BEATRICE. Well then, be an uncle then. EDDIE *looks at her, aware of her criticizing force.* I *mean.*

MARCO. No, Beatrice, if he does wrong you must tell him. *To* EDDIE. What does he do wrong?

EDDIE. Well, Marco, till he came here she was never out on the street twelve o'clock at night.

MARCO, *to* RODOLPHO. You come home early now.

BEATRICE, *to* CATHERINE. Well, you said the movie ended late, didn't you?

1000   CATHERINE. Yeah.

BEATRICE. Well, tell him, honey. *To* EDDIE. The movie ended late.

EDDIE. Look, B., I'm just sayin'—he thinks she always stayed out like that.

MARCO. You come home early now, Rodolpho.

RODOLPHO, *embarrassed.* All right, sure. But I can't stay in the house all the time, Eddie.

EDDIE. Look, kid, I'm not only talkin' about her. The more you run around like that the more chance you're takin'. *To* BEATRICE. I mean suppose he gets hit by a car or something. *To* MARCO. Where's his papers, who is he? Know what I mean?

BEATRICE. Yeah, but who is he in the daytime, though? It's the same chance in the
1010   daytime.

EDDIE, *holding back a voice full of anger.* Yeah, but he don't have to go lookin' for it, Beatrice. If he's here to work, then he should work; if he's here for a good time then he could fool around! *To* MARCO. But I understood, Marco, that you was both comin' to make a livin' for your family. You understand me, don't you, Marco? *He goes to his rocker.*

MARCO. I beg your pardon, Eddie.

EDDIE. I mean, that's what I understood in the first place, see.

MARCO. Yes. That's why we came.

EDDIE *sits on his rocker.* Well, that's all I'm askin'.

EDDIE *reads his paper. There is a pause, an awkwardness. Now* CATHERINE *gets up and puts a record on the phonograph—"Paper Doll."*

CATHERINE, *flushed with revolt.* You wanna dance, Rodolpho?

EDDIE *freezes.*

1020   RODOLPHO, *in deference to* EDDIE. No, I—I'm tired.

BEATRICE. Go ahead, dance, Rodolpho.

CATHERINE. Ah, come on. They got a beautiful quartet, these guys. Come.

She has taken his hand and he stiffly rises, feeling EDDIE's *eyes on his back, and they dance.*

EDDIE, *to* CATHERINE. What's that, a new record?

CATHERINE. It's the same one. We bought it the other day.

BEATRICE, *to* EDDIE. They only bought three records. *She watches them dance;* EDDIE *turns his head away.* MARCO *just sits there, waiting. Now* BEATRICE *turns to* EDDIE. Must be nice to go all over in one of them fishin' boats. I would like that myself. See all them other countries?

EDDIE. Yeah.

1030 BEATRICE, *to* MARCO. But the women don't go along, I bet.

MARCO. No, not on the boats. Hard work.

BEATRICE. What're you got, a regular kitchen and everything?

MARCO. Yes, we eat very good on the boats—especially when Rodolpho comes along; everybody gets fat.

BEATRICE. Oh, he cooks?

MARCO. Sure, very good cook. Rice, pasta, fish, everything.

EDDIE *lowers his paper.*

EDDIE. He's a cook, too! *Looking at* RODOLPHO. He sings, he cooks . . .

RODOLPHO *smiles thankfully.*

BEATRICE. Well it's good, he could always make a living.

EDDIE. It's wonderful. He sings, he cooks, he could make dresses . . .

1040 CATHERINE. They get some high pay, them guys. The head chefs in all the big hotels are men. You read about them.

EDDIE. That's what I'm sayin'.

CATHERINE *and* RODOLPHO *continue dancing.*

CATHERINE. Yeah, well, I mean.

EDDIE, *to* BEATRICE. He's lucky, believe me. *Slight pause. He looks away, then back to* BEATRICE. That's why the water front is no place for him. *They stop dancing.* RODOLPHO *turns off phonograph.* I mean like me—I can't cook, I can't sing, I can't make dresses, so I'm on the water front. But if I could cook, if I could sing, if I could make dresses, I wouldn't be on the water front. *He has been unconsciously twisting the newspaper into a tight roll. They are all regarding him now; he senses he is exposing the issue and he is driven on.* I would be someplace else. I would be like in a dress store. *He has bent the rolled paper and it suddenly tears in two. He suddenly gets up and pulls* 1050 *his pants up over his belly and goes to* MARCO. What do you say, Marco, we go to the bouts next Saturday night. You never seen a fight, did you?

MARCO, *uneasily.* Only in the moving pictures.

EDDIE, *going to* RODOLPHO. I'll treat yiz. What do you say, Danish? You wanna come along? I'll buy the tickets.

RODOLPHO. Sure. I like to go.

CATHERINE *goes to* EDDIE; *nervously happy now.* I'll make some coffee, all right?

EDDIE. Go ahead, make some! Make it nice and strong. *Mystified, she smiles and exits to kitchen. He is weirdly elated, rubbing his fists into his palms. He strides to* MARCO. You wait, Marco, you see some real fights here. You ever do any boxing?

1060   MARCO. No, I never.

EDDIE, *to* RODOLPHO. Betcha you have done some, heh?

RODOLPHO. No.

EDDIE. Well, come on, I'll teach you.

BEATRICE. What's he got to learn that for?

EDDIE. Ya can't tell, one a these days somebody's liable to step on his foot or sump'm. Come on, Rodolpho, I show you a couple a passes. *He stands below table.*

BEATRICE. Go ahead, Rodolpho. He's a good boxer, he could teach you.

RODOLPHO, *embarrassed.* Well, I don't know how to— *He moves down to* EDDIE.

EDDIE. Just put your hands up. Like this, see? That's right. That's very good, keep your
1070   left up, because you lead with the left, see, like this. *He gently moves his left into* RODOLPHO'S *face.* See? Now what you gotta do is you gotta block me, so when I come in like that you— RODOLPHO *parries his left.* Hey, that's very good! RODOLPHO *laughs.* All right, now come into me. Come on.

RODOLPHO. I don't want to hit you, Eddie.

EDDIE. Don't pity me, come on. Throw it, I'll show you how to block it. RODOLPHO *jabs at him, laughing. The others join.* 'At's it. Come on again. For the jaw right here. RODOLPHO *jabs with more assurance.* Very good!

BEATRICE, *to* MARCO. He's very good!

EDDIE *crosses directly upstage of* RODOLPHO.

EDDIE. Sure, he's great! Come on, kid, put sump'm behind it, you can't hurt me.
1080   RODOLPHO, *more seriously, jabs at* EDDIE'S *jaw and grazes it.* Attaboy.

CATHERINE *comes from the kitchen, watches.*

Now I'm gonna hit you, so block me, see?

CATHERINE, *with beginning alarm.* What are they doin'?

They are lightly boxing now.

BEATRICE—*she senses only the comradeship in it now.* He's teachin' him; he's very good!

EDDIE. Sure, he's terrific! Look at him go! RODOLPHO *lands a blow.* 'At's it! Now, watch out, here I come, Danish! *He feints with his left hand and lands with his right. It mildly staggers* RODOLPHO. MARCO *rises.*

CATHERINE, *rushing to* RODOLPHO. Eddie!

EDDIE. Why? I didn't hurt him. Did I hurt you, kid? *He rubs the back of his hand across his mouth.*

RODOLPHO. No, no, he didn't hurt me. *To* EDDIE *with a certain gleam and a smile.* I was only surprised.

1090   BEATRICE, *pulling* EDDIE *down into the rocker.* That's enough, Eddie; he did pretty good, though.

EDDIE. Yeah. *Rubbing his fists together.* He could be very good, Marco. I'll teach him again.

MARCO *nods at him dubiously.*

RODOLPHO. Dance, Catherine. Come. *He takes her hand; they go to phonograph and start it. It plays "Paper Doll."*

RODOLPHO *takes her in his arms. They dance.* EDDIE *in thought sits in his chair, and* MARCO *takes a chair, places it in front of* EDDIE, *and looks down at it.* BEATRICE *and* EDDIE *watch him.*

MARCO. Can you lift this chair?

EDDIE. What do you mean?

MARCO. From here. *He gets on one knee with one hand behind his back, and grasps the bottom of one of the chair legs but does not raise it.*

EDDIE. Sure, why not? *He comes to the chair, kneels, grasps the leg, raises the chair one inch, but it leans over to the floor.* Gee, that's hard, I never knew that. *He tries again, and again fails.* It's on an angle, that's why, heh?

MARCO. Here. *He kneels, grasps, and with strain slowly raises the chair higher and higher, getting to his feet now.* RODOLPHO *and* CATHERINE *have stopped dancing as* MARCO *raises the chair over his head.*

MARCO *is face to face with* EDDIE, *a strained tension gripping his eyes and jaw, his neck stiff, the chair raised like a weapon over* EDDIE's *head—and he transforms what might appear like a glare of warning into a smile of triumph, and* EDDIE's *grin vanishes as he absorbs his look.*

CURTAIN

ACT TWO

Light rises on ALFIERI *at his desk.*

ALFIERI. On the twenty-third of that December a case of Scotch whisky slipped from a net while being unloaded—as a case of Scotch whisky is inclined to do on the twenty-third of December on Pier Forty-one. There was no snow, but it was cold, his wife was out shopping. Marco was still at work. The boy had not been hired that day; Catherine told me later that this was the first time they had been alone together in the house.

Light is rising on CATHERINE *in the apartment.* RODOLPHO *is watching as she arranges a paper pattern on cloth spread on the table.*

CATHERINE. You hungry?

RODOLPHO. Not for anything to eat. *Pause.* I have nearly three hundred dollars. Catherine?

10   CATHERINE. I heard you.

RODOLPHO. You don't like to talk about it any more?

CATHERINE. Sure, I don't mind talkin' about it.

RODOLPHO. What worries you, Catherine?

CATHERINE. I been wantin' to ask you about something. Could I?

RODOLPHO. All the answers are in my eyes, Catherine. But you don't look in my eyes lately. You're full of secrets. *She looks at him. She seems withdrawn.* What is the question?

CATHERINE. Suppose I wanted to live in Italy.

RODOLPHO, *smiling at the incongruity.* You going to marry somebody rich?

20   CATHERINE. No, I mean live there — you and me.

RODOLPHO, *his smile vanishing.* When?

CATHERINE. Well . . . when we get married.

RODOLPHO, *astonished.* You want to be an Italian?

CATHERINE. No, but I could live there without being Italian. Americans live there.

RODOLPHO. Forever?

CATHERINE. Yeah.

RODOLPHO *crosses to rocker.* You're fooling.

CATHERINE. No, I mean it.

RODOLPHO. Where do you get such an idea?

30   CATHERINE. Well, you're always saying it's so beautiful there, with the mountains and the ocean and all the —

RODOLPHO. You're fooling me.

CATHERINE. I mean it.

RODOLPHO *goes to her slowly.* Catherine, if I ever brought you home with no money, no business, nothing, they would call the priest and the doctor and they would say Rodolpho is crazy.

CATHERINE. I know, but I think we would be happier there.

RODOLPHO. Happier! What would you eat? You can't cook the view!

CATHERINE. Maybe you could be a singer, like in Rome or —

40   RODOLPHO. Rome! Rome is full of singers.

CATHERINE. Well, I could work then.

RODOLPHO. Where?

CATHERINE. God, there must be jobs somewhere!

RODOLPHO. There's nothing! Nothing, nothing, nothing. Now tell me what you're talking about. How can I bring you from a rich country to suffer in a poor country? What are you talking about? *She searches for words.* I would be a criminal stealing your face. In two years you would have an old, hungry face. When my brother's babies cry they give them water, water that boiled a bone. Don't you believe that?

CATHERINE, *quietly.* I'm afraid of Eddie here.

Slight pause.

50   RODOLPHO *steps closer to her.* We wouldn't live here. Once I am a citizen I could work anywhere and I would find better jobs and we would have a house, Catherine. If I were not afraid to be arrested I would start to be something wonderful here!

CATHERINE, *steeling herself.* Tell me something. I mean just tell me, Rodolpho—would you still want to do it if it turned out we had to go live in Italy? I mean just if it turned out that way.

RODOLPHO. This is your question or his question?

CATHERINE. I would like to know, Rodolpho. I mean it.

RODOLPHO. To go there with nothing.

CATHERINE. Yeah.

60   RODOLPHO. No. *She looks at him wide-eyed.* No.

CATHERINE. You wouldn't?

RODOLPHO. No; I will not marry you to live in Italy. I want you to be my wife, and I want to be a citizen. Tell him that, or I will. Yes. *He moves about angrily.* And tell him also, and tell yourself, please, that I am not a beggar, and you are not a horse, a gift, a favor for a poor immigrant.

CATHERINE. Well, don't get mad!

RODOLPHO. I am furious! *Goes to her.* Do you think I am so desperate? My brother is desperate, not me. You think I would carry on my back the rest of my life a woman I didn't love just to be an American? It's so wonderful? You think we have no tall build-

70   ings in Italy? Electric lights? No wide streets? No flags? No automobiles? Only work we don't have. I want to be an American so I can work, that is the only wonder here—work! How can you insult me, Catherine?

CATHERINE. I didn't mean that—

RODOLPHO. My heart dies to look at you. Why are you so afraid of him?

CATHERINE, *near tears.* I don't know!

RODOLPHO. Do you trust me, Catherine? You?

CATHERINE. It's only that I— He was good to me, Rodolpho. You don't know him; he was always the sweetest guy to me. Good. He razzes me all the time but he don't mean it. I know. I would—just feel ashamed if I made him sad. 'Cause I always

80   dreamt that when I got married he would be happy at the wedding, and laughin'—and now he's—mad all the time and nasty— *She is weeping.* Tell him you'd live in Italy—just tell him, and maybe he would start to trust you a little, see? Because I want him to be happy; I mean—I like him, Rodolpho—and I can't stand it!

RODOLPHO. Oh, Catherine—oh, little girl.

CATHERINE. I love you, Rodolpho, I love you.

RODOLPHO. Then why are you afraid? That he'll spank you?

CATHERINE. Don't, don't laugh at me! I've been here all my life. . . . Every day I saw him when he left in the morning and when he came home at night. You think it's so easy to turn around and say to a man he's nothin' to you no more?

90   RODOLPHO. I know, but—

CATHERINE. You don't know; nobody knows! I'm not a baby, I know a lot more than people think I know. Beatrice says to be a woman, but—

RODOLPHO. Yes.

CATHERINE. Then why don't she be a woman? If I was a wife I would make a man happy instead of goin' at him all the time. I can tell a block away when he's blue in his mind and just wants to talk to somebody quiet and nice. . . . I can tell when he's hungry or wants a beer before he even says anything. I know when his feet hurt him, I mean I *know* him and now I'm supposed to turn around and make a stranger out of him? I don't know why I have to do that, I mean.

100   RODOLPHO. Catherine. If I take in my hands a little bird. And she grows and wishes to fly. But I will not let her out of my hands because I love her so much, is that right for me to do? I don't say you must hate him; but anyway you must go, mustn't you? Catherine?

CATHERINE, *softly.* Hold me.

RODOLPHO, *clasping her to him.* Oh, my little girl.

CATHERINE. Teach me. *She is weeping.* I don't know anything, teach me, Rodolpho, hold me.

RODOLPHO. There's nobody here now. Come inside. Come. *He is leading her toward the bedrooms.* And don't cry any more.

Light rises on the street. In a moment EDDIE *appears. He is unsteady, drunk. He mounts the stairs. He enters the apartment, looks around, takes out a bottle from one pocket, puts it on the table. Then another bottle from another pocket, and a third from an inside pocket. He sees the pattern and cloth, goes over to it and touches it, and turns toward up-stage.*

110   EDDIE. Beatrice? *He goes to the open kitchen door and looks in.* Beatrice? Beatrice?

CATHERINE *enters from bedroom; under his gaze she adjusts her dress.*

CATHERINE. You got home early.

EDDIE. Knocked off for Christmas early. *Indicating the pattern.* Rodolpho makin' you a dress?

CATHERINE. No. I'm makin' a blouse.

RODOLPHO *appears in the bedroom doorway.* EDDIE *sees him and his arm jerks slightly in shock.* RODOLPHO *nods to him testingly.*

RODOLPHO. Beatrice went to buy presents for her mother.

Pause.

EDDIE. Pack it up. Go ahead. Get your stuff and get outa here. CATHERINE *instantly turns and walks toward the bedroom, and* EDDIE *grabs her arm.* Where you goin'?

CATHERINE, *trembling with fright.* I think I have to get out of here, Eddie.

EDDIE. No, you ain't goin' nowheres, he's the one.

120   CATHERINE. I think I can't stay here no more. *She frees her arm, steps back toward the bedroom.* I'm sorry, Eddie. *She sees the tears in his eyes.* Well, don't cry. I'll be around the neighborhood; I'll see you. I just can't stay here no more. You know I can't. *Her sobs of pity and love for him break her composure.* Don't you know I can't? You know that, don't you? *She goes to him.* Wish me luck. *She clasps her hands prayerfully.* Oh, Eddie, don't be like that!

EDDIE. You ain't goin' nowheres.

CATHERINE. Eddie, I'm not gonna be a baby any more! You—

He reaches out suddenly, draws her to him, and as she strives to free herself he kisses her on the mouth.

RODOLPHO. Don't! *He pulls on* EDDIE*'s arm.* Stop that! Have respect for her!

EDDIE, *spun round by* RODOLPHO. You want something?

130 RODOLPHO. Yes! She'll be my wife. That is what I want. My wife!

EDDIE. But what're you gonna be?

RODOLPHO. I show you what I be!

CATHERINE. Wait outside; don't argue with him!

EDDIE. Come on, show me! What're you gonna be? Show me!

RODOLPHO, *with tears of rage.* Don't say that to me!

> RODOLPHO *flies at him in attack.* EDDIE *pins his arms, laughing, and suddenly kisses him.*

CATHERINE. Eddie! Let go, ya hear me! I'll kill you! Leggo of him!

> *She tears at* EDDIE*'s face and* EDDIE *releases* RODOLPHO. EDDIE *stands there with tears rolling down his face as he laughs mockingly at* RODOLPHO. *She is staring at him in horror.* RODOLPHO *is rigid. They are like animals that have torn at one another and broken up without a decision, each waiting for the other's mood.*

EDDIE, *to* CATHERINE. You see? *To* RODOLPHO.   I give you till tomorrow, kid. Get outa here. Alone. You hear me? Alone.

CATHERINE. I'm going with him, Eddie. *She starts toward* RODOLPHO.

140 EDDIE, *indicating* RODOLPHO *with his head.* Not with that. *She halts, frightened. He sits, still panting for breath, and they watch him helplessly as he leans toward them over the table.* Don't make me do nuttin', Catherine. Watch your step, submarine.[7] By rights they oughta throw you back in the water. But I got pity for you. *He moves unsteadily toward the door, always facing* RODOLPHO. Just get outa here and don't lay another hand on her unless you wanna go out feet first. *He goes out of the apartment.*

> *The lights go down, as they rise on* ALFIERI.

ALFIERI. On December twenty-seventh I saw him next. I normally go home well before six, but that day I sat around looking out my window at the bay, and when I saw him walking through my doorway, I knew why I had waited. And if I seem to tell this like a dream, it was that way. Several moments arrived in the course of the two talks we had when it occurred to me how—almost transfixed I had come to feel. I had lost my

150 strength somewhere. EDDIE *enters, removing his cap, sits in the chair, looks thoughtfully out.* I looked in his eyes more than I listened—in fact, I can hardly remember the conversation. But I will never forget how dark the room became when he looked at me; his eyes were like tunnels. I kept wanting to call the police, but nothing had happened. Nothing at all had really happened. *He breaks off and looks down at the desk. Then he turns to* EDDIE. So in other words, he won't leave?

EDDIE. My wife is talkin' about renting a room upstairs for them. An old lady on the top floor is got an empty room.

---

[7]submarine: slang term indicating that Rodolpho is an illegal alien.

ALFIERI. What does Marco say?

EDDIE. He just sits there. Marco don't say much.

160   ALFIERI. I guess they didn't tell him, heh? What happened?

EDDIE. I don't know; Marco don't say much.

ALFIERI. What does your wife say?

EDDIE, *unwilling to pursue this.* Nobody's talkin' much in the house. So what about that?

ALFIERI. But you didn't prove anything about him. It sounds like he just wasn't strong enough to break your grip.

EDDIE. I'm tellin' you I know—he ain't right. Somebody that don't want it can break it. Even a mouse, if you catch a teeny mouse and you hold it in your hand, that mouse can give you the right kind of fight. He didn't give me the right kind of fight, I know

170   it, Mr. Alfieri, the guy ain't right.

ALFIERI. What did you do that for, Eddie?

EDDIE. To show her what he is! So she would see, once and for all! Her mother'll turn over in the grave! *He gathers himself almost peremptorily.* So what do I gotta do now? Tell me what to do.

ALFIERI. She actually said she's marrying him?

EDDIE. She told me, yeah. So what do I do?

Slight pause.

ALFIERI. This is my last word, Eddie, take it or not, that's your business. Morally and legally you have no rights, you cannot stop it; she is a free agent.

EDDIE, *angering.* Didn't you hear what I told you?

180   ALFIERI, *with a tougher tone.* I heard what you told me, and I'm telling you what the answer is. I'm not only telling you now, I'm warning you—the law is nature. The law is only a word for what has a right to happen. When the law is wrong it's because it's unnatural, but in this case it is natural and a river will drown you if you buck it now. Let her go. And bless her. *A phone booth begins to glow on the opposite side of the stage; a faint, lonely blue.* EDDIE *stands up, jaws clenched.* Somebody had to come for her, Eddie, sooner or later. EDDIE *starts turning to go and* ALFIERI *rises with new anxiety.* You won't have a friend in the world, Eddie! Even those who understand will turn against you, even the ones who feel the same will despise you! EDDIE *moves off.* Put it out of your mind! Eddie! *He follows into the darkness, calling desperately.*

EDDIE *is gone. The phone is glowing in light now. Light is out on* ALFIERI. EDDIE *has at the same time appeared beside the phone.*

190   EDDIE. Give me the number of the Immigration Bureau. Thanks. *He dials.* I want to report something. Illegal immigrants. Two of them. That's right. Four-forty-one Saxon Street, Brooklyn, yeah. Ground floor. Heh? *With greater difficulty.* I'm just around the neighborhood, that's all. Heh?

Evidently he is being questioned further, and he slowly hangs up. He leaves the phone just as LOUIS *and* MIKE *come down the street.*

LOUIS. Go bowlin', Eddie?

EDDIE. No, I'm due home.

LOUIS. Well, take it easy.

EDDIE. I'll see yiz.

> *They leave him, exiting right, and he watches them go. He glances about, then goes up into the house. The lights go on in the apartment.* BEATRICE *is taking down Christmas decorations and packing them in a box.*

EDDIE. Where is everybody? BEATRICE *does not answer.* I says where is everybody?

BEATRICE, *looking up at him, wearied with it, and concealing a fear of him.* I decided to
200   move them upstairs with Mrs. Dondero.

EDDIE. Oh, they're all moved up there already?

BEATRICE. Yeah.

EDDIE. Where's Catherine? She up there?

BEATRICE. Only to bring pillow cases.

EDDIE. She ain't movin' in with them.

BEATRICE. Look, I'm sick and tired of it. I'm sick and tired of it!

EDDIE. All right, all right, take it easy.

BEATRICE. I don't wanna hear no more about it, you understand? Nothin'!

EDDIE. What're you blowin' off about? Who brought them in here?

210   BEATRICE. All right, I'm sorry; I wish I'd a drop dead before I told them to come. In the
ground I wish I was.

EDDIE. Don't drop dead, just keep in mind who brought them in here, that's all. *He moves about restlessly.* I mean I got a couple of rights here. *He moves, wanting to beat down her evident disapproval of him.* This is my house here not their house.

BEATRICE. What do you want from me? They're moved out; what do you want now?

EDDIE. I want my respect!

BEATRICE. So I moved them out, what more do you want? You got your house now, you got your respect.

EDDIE—*he moves about biting his lip.* I don't like the way you talk to me, Beatrice.

220   BEATRICE. I'm just tellin' you I done what you want!

EDDIE. I don't like it! The way you talk to me and the way you look at me. This is my house. And she is my niece and I'm responsible for her.

BEATRICE. So that's why you done that to him?

EDDIE. I done what to him?

BEATRICE. What you done to him in front of her; you know what I'm talkin' about. She goes around shakin' all the time, she can't go to sleep! That's what you call responsible for her?

EDDIE, *quietly.* The guy ain't right, Beatrice. *She is silent.* Did you hear what I said?

BEATRICE. Look, I'm finished with it. That's all. *She resumes her work.*

230   EDDIE, *helping her to pack the tinsel.* I'm gonna have it out with you one of these days, Beatrice.

BEATRICE. Nothin' to have out with me, it's all settled. Now we gonna be like it never happened, that's all.

EDDIE. I want my respect, Beatrice, and you know what I'm talkin' about.

BEATRICE. What?

Pause.

EDDIE—*finally his resolution hardens.* What I feel like doin' in the bed and what I don't feel like doin'. I don't want no—

BEATRICE. When'd I say anything about that?

EDDIE. You said, you said, I ain't deaf. I don't want no more conversations about that, Beatrice. I do what I feel like doin' or what I don't feel like doin'.

BEATRICE. Okay.

Pause.

EDDIE. You used to be different, Beatrice. You had a whole different way.

BEATRICE. *I'm* no different.

EDDIE. You didn't used to jump me all the time about everything. The last year or two I come in the house I don't know what's gonna hit me. It's a shootin' gallery in here and I'm the pigeon.

BEATRICE. Okay, okay.

EDDIE. Don't tell me okay, okay, I'm tellin' you the truth. A wife is supposed to believe the husband. If I tell you that guy ain't right don't tell me he is right.

BEATRICE. But how do you know?

EDDIE. Because I know. I don't go around makin' accusations. He give me the heeby-jeebies the first minute I seen him. And I don't like you sayin' I don't want her marryin' anybody. I broke my back payin' her stenography lessons so she could go out and meet a better class of people. Would I do that if I didn't want her to get married? Sometimes you talk like I was a crazy man or sump'm.

BEATRICE. But she likes him.

EDDIE. Beatrice, she's a baby, how is she gonna know what she likes?

BEATRICE. Well, you kept her a baby, you wouldn't let her go out. I told you a hundred times.

Pause.

EDDIE. All right. Let her go out, then.

BEATRICE. She don't wanna go out now. It's too late, Eddie.

Pause.

EDDIE. Suppose I told her to go out. Suppose I—

BEATRICE. They're going to get married next week, Eddie.

EDDIE—*his head jerks around to her.* She said that?

BEATRICE. Eddie, if you want my advice, go to her and tell her good luck. I think maybe now that you had it out you learned better.

EDDIE. What's the hurry next week?

BEATRICE. Well, she's been worried about him bein' picked up; this way he could start to be a citizen. She loves him, Eddie. *He gets up, moves about uneasily, restlessly.* Why

270   don't you give her a good word? Because I still think she would like you to be a friend, y'know? *He is standing, looking at the floor.* I mean like if you told her you'd go to the wedding.

EDDIE. She asked you that?

BEATRICE. I know she would like it. I'd like to make a party here for her. I mean there oughta be some kinda send-off. Heh? I mean she'll have trouble enough in her life, let's start it off happy. What do you say? Cause in her heart she still loves you, Eddie. I know it. *He presses his fingers against his eyes.* What're you, cryin'? *She goes to him, holds his face.* Go . . . whyn't you go tell her you're sorry? CATHERINE *is seen on the upper landing of the stairway, and they hear her descending.* There . . . she's comin' down.

280   Come on, shake hands with her.

EDDIE, *moving with suppressed suddenness.* No, I can't, I can't talk to her.

BEATRICE. Eddie, give her a break; a wedding should be happy!

EDDIE. I'm goin', I'm goin' for a walk.

He goes upstage for his jacket. CATHERINE *enters and starts for the bedroom door.*

BEATRICE. Katie? . . . Eddie, don't go, wait a minute. *She embraces* EDDIE'S *arm with warmth.* Ask him, Katie. Come on, honey.

EDDIE. It's all right, I'm— *He starts to go and she holds him.*

BEATRICE. No, she wants to ask you. Come on, Katie, ask him. We'll have a party! What're we gonna do, hate each other? Come on!

CATHERINE. I'm gonna get married, Eddie. So if you wanna come, the wedding be on

290   Saturday.

Pause.

EDDIE. Okay. I only wanted the best for you, Katie. I hope you know that.

CATHERINE. Okay. *She starts out again.*

EDDIE. Catherine? *She turns to him.* I was just tellin' Beatrice . . . if you wanna go out, like . . . I mean I realize maybe I kept you home too much. Because he's the first guy you ever knew, y'know? I mean now that you got a job, you might meet some fellas, and you get a different idea, y'know? I mean you could always come back to him, you're still only kids, the both of yiz. What's the hurry? Maybe you'll get around a little bit, you grow up a little more, maybe you'll see different in a couple of months. I mean you be surprised, it don't have to be him.

300   CATHERINE. No, we made it up already.

EDDIE, *with increasing anxiety.* Katie, wait a minute.

CATHERINE. No, I made up my mind.

EDDIE. But you never knew no other fella, Katie! How could you make up your mind?

CATHERINE. Cause I did. I don't want nobody else.

EDDIE. But, Katie, suppose he gets picked up.

CATHERINE. That's why we gonna do it right away. Soon as we finish the wedding he's goin' right over and start to be a citizen. I made up my mind, Eddie. I'm sorry. *To* BEATRICE. Could I take two more pillow cases for the other guys?

BEATRICE. Sure, go ahead. Only don't let her forget where they came from.

CATHERINE *goes into a bedroom.*

310   EDDIE. She's got other boarders up there?

BEATRICE. Yeah, there's two guys that just came over.

EDDIE. What do you mean, came over?

BEATRICE. From Italy. Lipari the butcher—his nephew. They come from Bari,[8] they just got here yesterday. I didn't even know till Marco and Rodolpho moved up there before. CATHERINE *enters, going toward exit with two pillow cases.* It'll be nice, they could all talk together.

EDDIE. Catherine! *She halts near the exit door. He takes in* BEATRICE *too.* What're you, got no brains? You put them up there with two other submarines?

CATHERINE. Why?

320   EDDIE, *in a driving fright and anger.* Why! How do you know they're not trackin' these guys? They'll come up for them and find Marco and Rodolpho! Get them out of the house!

BEATRICE. But they been here so long already—

EDDIE. How do you know what enemies Lipari's got? Which they'd love to stab him in the back?

CATHERINE. Well what'll I do with them?

EDDIE. The neighborhood is full of rooms. Can't you stand to live a couple of blocks away from him? Get them out of the house!

CATHERINE. Well maybe tomorrow night I'll—

330   EDDIE. Not tomorrow, do it now. Catherine, you never mix yourself with somebody's else's family! These guys get picked up, Lipari's liable to blame you or me and we got his whole family on our head. They got a temper, that family.

Two men in overcoats appear outside, start into the house.

CATHERINE. How'm I gonna find a place tonight?

EDDIE. Will you stop arguin' with me and get them out! You think I'm always tryin' to fool you or sump'm? What's the matter with you, don't you believe I could think of your good? Did I ever ask sump'm for myself? You think I got no feelin's? I never told you nothin' in my life that wasn't for your good. Nothin'! And look at the way you talk to me! Like I was an enemy! Like I— *A knock on the door. His head swerves. They all stand motionless. Another knock.* EDDIE, *in a whisper, pointing upstage.* Go up the fire

340   escape, get them out over the back fence.

CATHERINE *stands motionless, uncomprehending.*

FIRST OFFICER, *in the hall.* Immigration! Open up in there!

EDDIE. Go, go. Hurry up! *She stands a moment staring at him in a realized horror.* Well, what're you lookin' at!

FIRST OFFICER. Open up!

---

[8] Bari: a city in southeast Italy on the Adriatic Sea.

EDDIE, *calling toward door.* Who's that there?

FIRST OFFICER. Immigration, open up.

> EDDIE *turns, looks at* BEATRICE. *She sits. Then he looks at* CATHERINE. *With a sob of fury* CATHERINE *streaks into a bedroom.*

> *Knock is repeated.*

EDDIE. All right, take it easy, take it easy. *He goes and opens the door. The* OFFICER *steps inside.* What's all this?

FIRST OFFICER. Where are they?

> SECOND OFFICER *sweeps past and, glancing about, goes into the kitchen.*

350   EDDIE. Where's who?

FIRST OFFICER. Come on, come on, where are they? *He hurries into the bedrooms.*

EDDIE. Who? We got nobody here. *He looks at* BEATRICE, *who turns her head away. Pugnaciously, furious, he steps toward* BEATRICE. What's the matter with *you?*

FIRST OFFICER *enters from the bedroom, calls to the kitchen.*

FIRST OFFICER. Dominick?

> *Enter* SECOND OFFICER *from kitchen.*

SECOND OFFICER. Maybe it's a different apartment.

FIRST OFFICER. There's only two more floors up there. I'll take the front, you go up the fire escape. I'll let you in. Watch your step up there.

SECOND OFFICER. Okay, right, Charley. FIRST OFFICER *goes out apartment door and runs up the stairs.* This is Four-forty-one, isn't it?

360   EDDIE. That's right.

> SECOND OFFICER *goes out into the kitchen.*

> EDDIE *turns to* BEATRICE. *She looks at him now and sees his terror.*

BEATRICE, *weakened with fear.* Oh, Jesus, Eddie.

EDDIE. What's the matter with *you?*

BEATRICE, *pressing her palms against her face.* Oh, my God, my God.

EDDIE. What're you, accusin' me?

BEATRICE—*her final thrust is to turn toward him instead of running from him.* My God, what did you do?

> *Many steps on the outer stair draw his attention. We see the* FIRST OFFICER *descending, with* MARCO, *behind him* RODOLPHO, *and* CATHERINE *and the two strange immigrants, followed by* SECOND OFFICER. BEATRICE *hurries to door.*

CATHERINE, *backing down stairs, fighting with* FIRST OFFICER; *as they appear on the stairs.* What do yiz want from them? They work, that's all. They're boarders upstairs, they work on the piers.

BEATRICE, *to* FIRST OFFICER. Ah, Mister, what do you want from them, who do they
370   hurt?

CATHERINE, *pointing to* RODOLPHO. They ain't no submarines, he was born in Philadelphia.

FIRST OFFICER. Step aside, lady.

CATHERINE. What do you mean? You can't just come in a house and—

FIRST OFFICER. All right, take it easy. *To* RODOLPHO. What street were you born in Philadelphia?

CATHERINE. What do you mean, what street? Could you tell me what street you were born?

FIRST OFFICER. Sure. Four blocks away, One-eleven Union Street. Let's go fellas.

380   CATHERINE, *fending him off* RODOLPHO. No, you can't! Now, get outa here!

FIRST OFFICER. Look, girlie, if they're all right they'll be out tomorrow. If they're illegal they go back where they came from. If you want, get yourself a lawyer, although I'm tellin' you now you're wasting your money. Let's get them in the car, Dom. *To the men.* Andiamo, Andiamo, let's go.

The men start, but MARCO *hangs back.*

BEATRICE, *from doorway.* Who're they hurtin', for God's sake, what do you want from them? They're starvin' over there, what do you want! Marco!

MARCO *suddenly breaks from the group and dashes into the room and faces* EDDIE; BEATRICE *and* FIRST OFFICER *rush in as* MARCO *spits into* EDDIE'*s face.*

CATHERINE *runs into hallway and throws herself into* RODOLPHO'*s arms.* EDDIE, *with an enraged cry, lunges for* MARCO.

EDDIE. Oh, you mother's—!

FIRST OFFICER *quickly intercedes and pushes* EDDIE *from* MARCO, *who stands there accusingly.*

FIRST OFFICER, *between them, pushing* EDDIE *from* MARCO. Cut it out!

EDDIE, *over the* FIRST OFFICER'*s shoulder, to* MARCO. I'll kill you for that, you son of a

390   bitch!

FIRST OFFICER. Hey! *Shakes him.* Stay in here now, don't come out, don't bother him. You hear me? Don't come out, fella.

For an instant there is silence. Then FIRST OFFICER *turns and takes* MARCO'*s arm and then gives a last, informative look at* EDDIE. *As he and* MARCO *are going out into the hall,* EDDIE *erupts.*

EDDIE. I don't forget that, Marco! You hear what I'm sayin'?

Out in the hall, FIRST OFFICER *and* MARCO *go down the stairs. Now, in the street,* LOUIS, MIKE, *and several neighbors including the butcher,* LIPARI—*a stout, intense, middle-aged man—are gathering around the stoop.*

LIPARI, *the butcher, walks over to the two strange men and kisses them. His wife, keening, goes and kisses their hands.* EDDIE *is emerging from the house shouting after* MARCO. BEATRICE *is trying to restrain him.*

EDDIE. That's the thanks I get? Which I took the blankets off my bed for yiz? You gonna apologize to me, Marco! *Marco!*

FIRST OFFICER, *in the doorway with* MARCO. All right, lady, let them go. Get in the car, fellas, it's over there.

RODOLPHO *is almost carrying the sobbing* CATHERINE *off up the street, left.*

CATHERINE. He was born in Philadelphia! What do you want from him?

FIRST OFFICER. Step aside, lady, come on now . . .

The SECOND OFFICER *has moved off with the two strange men.* MARCO, *taking advantage of the* FIRST OFFICER'S *being occupied with* CATHERINE, *suddenly frees himself and points back at* EDDIE.

400   MARCO. That one! I accuse that one!

EDDIE *brushes* BEATRICE *aside and rushes out to the stoop.*

FIRST OFFICER, *grabbing him and moving him quickly off up the left street.* Come on!

MARCO, *as he is taken off, pointing back at* EDDIE. That one! He killed my children! That one stole the food from my children!

MARCO *is gone. The crowd has turned to* EDDIE.

EDDIE, *to* LIPARI *and wife.* He's crazy! I give them the blankets off my bed. Six months I kept them like my own brothers!

LIPARI, *the butcher, turns and starts up left with his arm around his wife.*

EDDIE. Lipari! *He follows* LIPARI *up left.* For Christ's sake, I kept them, I give them the blankets off my bed!

LIPARI *and wife exit.* EDDIE *turns and starts crossing down right to* LOUIS *and* MIKE.

EDDIE. Louis! *Louis!*

LOUIS *barely turns, then walks off and exits down right with* MIKE. *Only Beatrice is left on the stoop.* CATHERINE *now returns, blank-eyed, from offstage and the car.* EDDIE *calls after* LOUIS *and* MIKE.

EDDIE. He's gonna take that back. He's gonna take that back or I'll kill him! You hear
410   me? I'll kill him! I'll kill him! *He exits up street calling.*

There is a pause of darkness before the lights rise, on the reception room of a prison. MARCO *is seated;* ALFIERI, CATHERINE, *and* RODOLPHO *standing.*

ALFIERI. I'm waiting, Marco, what do you say?

RODOLPHO. Marco never hurt anybody.

ALFIERI. I can bail you out until your hearing comes up. But I'm not going to do it, you understand me? Unless I have your promise. You're an honorable man, I will believe your promise. Now what do you say?

MARCO. In my country he would be dead now. He would not live this long.

ALFIERI. All right, Rodolpho—you come with me now.

RODOLPHO. No! Please, Mister. Marco—promise the man. Please, I want you to watch the wedding. How can I be married and you're in here? Please, you're not going to do anything; you know you're not.

420

MARCO *is silent.*

CATHERINE, *kneeling left of* MARCO. Marco, don't you understand? He can't bail you out if you're gonna do something bad. To hell with Eddie. Nobody is gonna talk to him again if he lives to a hundred. Everybody knows you spit in his face, that's enough, isn't it? Give me the satisfaction—I want you at the wedding. You got a wife and kids, Marco. You could be workin' till the hearing comes up, instead of layin' around here.

MARCO, *to* ALFIERI. I have no chance?

ALFIERI *crosses to behind* MARCO. No, Marco. You're going back. The hearing is a formality, that's all.

430   MARCO. But him? There is a chance, eh?

ALFIERI. When she marries him he can start to become an American. They permit that, if the wife is born here.

MARCO, *looking at* RODOLPHO. Well—we did something. *He lays a palm on* RODOLPHO's *arm and* RODOLPHO *covers it.*

RODOLPHO. Marco, tell the man.

MARCO, *pulling his hand away.* What will I tell him? He knows such a promise is dishonorable.

ALFIERI. To promise not to kill is not dishonorable.

MARCO, *looking at* ALFIERI. No?

ALFIERI. No.

440   MARCO, *gesturing with his head—this is a new idea.* Then what is done with such a man?

ALFIERI. Nothing. If he obeys the law, he lives. That's all.

MARCO, *rises, turns to* ALFIERI. The law? All the law is not in a book.

ALFIERI. Yes. In a book. There is no other law.

MARCO, *his anger rising.* He degraded my brother. My blood. He robbed my children, he mocks my work. I work to come here, mister!

ALFIERI. I know, Marco—

MARCO. Is there no law for that? Where is the law for that?

ALFIERI. There is none.

450   MARCO, *shaking his head, sitting.* I don't understand this country.

ALFIERI. Well? What is your answer? You have five or six weeks you could work. Or else you sit here. What do you say to me?

MARCO *lowers his eyes. It almost seems he is ashamed.* All right.

ALFIERI. You won't touch him. This is your promise.

Slight pause.

MARCO. Maybe he wants to apologize to me.

MARCO *is staring away.* ALFIERI *takes one of his hands.*

ALFIERI. This is not God, Marco. You hear? Only God makes justice.

MARCO. All right.

ALFIERI, *nodding, not with assurance.* Good! Catherine, Rodolpho, Marco, let us go.

CATHERINE *kisses* RODOLPHO *and* MARCO, *then kisses* ALFIERI's *hand.*

CATHERINE. I'll get Beatrice and meet you at the church. *She leaves quickly.*

MARCO *rises.* RODOLPHO *suddenly embraces him.* MARCO *pats him on the back and* RODOLPHO *exits after* CATHERINE. MARCO *faces* ALFIERI.

460   ALFIERI. Only God, Marco.

MARCO *turns and walks out.* ALFIERI *with a certain processional tread leaves the stage. The lights dim out.*

The lights rise in the apartment. EDDIE *is alone in the rocker, rocking back and forth in little surges. Pause. Now* BEATRICE *emerges from a bedroom. She is in her best clothes, wearing a hat.*

BEATRICE, *with fear, going to* EDDIE. I'll be back in about an hour, Eddie. All right?

EDDIE, *quietly, almost inaudibly, as though drained.* What, have I been talkin' to myself?

BEATRICE. Eddie, for God's sake, it's her wedding.

EDDIE. Didn't you hear what I told you? You walk out that door to that wedding you ain't comin' back here, Beatrice.

BEATRICE. Why! What do you want?

EDDIE. I want my respect. Didn't you ever hear of that? From my wife?

CATHERINE *enters from bedroom.*

CATHERINE. It's after three; we're supposed to be there already, Beatrice. The priest won't wait.

470   BEATRICE. Eddie. It's her wedding. There'll be nobody there from her family. For my sister let me go. I'm goin' for my sister.

EDDIE, *as though hurt.* Look, I been arguin' with you all day already, Beatrice, and I said what I'm gonna say. He's gonna come here and apologize to me or nobody from this house is goin' into that church today. Now if that's more to you than I am, then go. But don't come back. You be on my side or on their side, that's all.

CATHERINE, *suddenly.* Who the hell do you think you are?

BEATRICE. Sssh!

CATHERINE. You got no more right to tell nobody nothin'! Nobody! The rest of your life, nobody!

480   BEATRICE. Shut up, Katie! *She turns* CATHERINE *around.*

CATHERINE. You're gonna come with me!

BEATRICE. I can't Katie, I can't . . .

CATHERINE. How can you listen to him? This rat!

BEATRICE, *shaking* CATHERINE. Don't you call him that!

CATHERINE, *clearing from* BEATRICE. What're you scared of? He's a rat! He belongs in the sewer!

BEATRICE. Stop it!

CATHERINE, *weeping.* He bites people when they sleep! He comes when nobody's lookin' and poisons decent people. In the garbage he belongs!

EDDIE seems about to pick up the table and fling it at her.

490 BEATRICE. No, Eddie! Eddie! *To* CATHERINE. Then we all belong in the garbage. You, and me too. Don't say that. Whatever happened we all done it, and don't you ever forget it, Catherine. *She goes to* CATHERINE. Now go, go to your wedding, Katie, I'll stay home. Go. God bless you, God bless your children.

Enter RODOLPHO.

RODOLPHO. Eddie?

EDDIE. Who said you could come in here? Get outa here!

RODOLPHO. Marco is coming, Eddie. *Pause.* BEATRICE *raises her hands in terror.* He's praying in the church. You understand? *Pause.* RODOLPHO *advances into the room.* Catherine, I think it is better we go. Come with me.

CATHERINE. Eddie, go away, please.

500 BEATRICE, *quietly.* Eddie. Let's go someplace. Come. You and me. *He has not moved.* I don't want you to be here when he comes. I'll get your coat.

EDDIE. Where? Where am I goin'? This is my house.

BEATRICE, *crying out.* What's the use of it! He's crazy now, you know the way they get, what good is it! You got nothin' against Marco, you always liked Marco!

EDDIE. I got nothin' against Marco? Which he called me a rat in front of the whole neighborhood? Which he said I killed his children! Where you been?

RODOLPHO, *quite suddenly, stepping up to* EDDIE. It is my fault, Eddie. Everything. I wish to apologize. It was wrong that I do not ask your permission. I kiss your hand. *He reaches for* EDDIE'S *hand, but* EDDIE *snaps it away from him.*

BEATRICE. Eddie, he's apologizing!

510 RODOLPHO. I have made all our troubles. But you have insult me too. Maybe God understand why you did that to me. Maybe you did not mean to insult me at all—

BEATRICE. Listen to him! Eddie, listen what he's tellin' you!

RODOLPHO. I think, maybe when Marco comes, if we can tell him we are comrades now, and we have no more argument between us. Then maybe Marco will not—

EDDIE. Now, listen—

CATHERINE. Eddie, give him a chance!

BEATRICE. What do you want! Eddie, what do you want!

EDDIE. I want my name! He didn't take my name; he's only a punk. Marco's got my name—*to* RODOLPHO: and you can run tell him, kid, that he's gonna give it back to

520 me in front of this neighborhood, or we have it out. *Hoisting up his pants.* Come on, where is he? Take me to him.

BEATRICE. Eddie, listen—

EDDIE. I heard enough! Come on, let's go!

BEATRICE. Only blood is good? He kissed your hand!

EDDIE. What he does don't mean nothin' to nobody! *To* RODOLPHO. Come on!

BEATRICE, *barring his way to the stairs.* What's gonna mean somethin'? Eddie, listen to me. Who could give you your name? Listen to me, I love you, I'm talkin' to you, I love you; if Marco'll kiss your hand outside, if he goes on his knees, what is he got to give you? That's not what you want.

530   EDDIE. Don't bother me!

BEATRICE. You want somethin' else, Eddie, and you can never have her!

CATHERINE, *in horror.* B.!

EDDIE, *shocked, horrified, his fist clenching.* Beatrice!

MARCO *appears outside, walking toward the door from a distant point.*

BEATRICE, *crying out, weeping.* The truth is not as bad as blood, Eddie! I'm tellin' you the truth—tell her good-by forever!

EDDIE, *crying out in agony.* That's what you think of me—that I would have such a thought? *His fists clench his head as though it will burst.*

MARCO, *calling near the door outside.* Eddie Carbone!

EDDIE *swerves about; all stand transfixed for an instant. People appear outside.*

EDDIE, *as though flinging his challenge.* Yeah, Marco! Eddie Carbone. Eddie Carbone.

540   Eddie Carbone. *He goes up the stairs and emerges from the apartment.* RODOLPHO *streaks up and out past him and runs to* MARCO.

RODOLPHO. No, Marco, please! Eddie, please, he has children! You will kill a family!

BEATRICE. Go in the house! Eddie, go in the house!

EDDIE—*he gradually comes to address the people.* Maybe he come to apologize to me. Heh, Marco? For what you said about me in front of the neighborhood? *He is incensing himself and little bits of laughter even escape him as his eyes are murderous and he cracks his knuckles in his hands with a strange sort of relaxation.* He knows that ain't right. To do like that? To a man? Which I put my roof over their head and my food in their mouth? Like in the Bible? Strangers I never seen in my whole life? To come out of the water and grab a girl for a passport? To go and take from your own family like from the stable—and never a word to me? And now accusations in the bargain! *Di-*

550   *rectly to* MARCO. Wipin' the neighborhood with my name like a dirty rag! I want my name, Marco. *He is moving now, carefully, toward* MARCO. Now gimme my name and we go together to the wedding.

BEATRICE *and* CATHERINE, *keening.* Eddie! Eddie, don't! Eddie!

EDDIE. No, Marco knows what's right from wrong. Tell the people, Marco, tell them what a liar you are! *He has his arms spread and* MARCO *is spreading his.* Come on, liar, you know what you done! *He lunges for* MARCO *as a great hushed shout goes up from the people.*

MARCO *strikes* EDDIE *beside the neck.*

MARCO. Animal! You go on your knees to me!

EDDIE *goes down with the blow and* MARCO *starts to raise a foot to stomp him when* EDDIE *springs a knife into his hand and* MARCO *steps back.* LOUIS *rushes in toward* EDDIE.

LOUIS. Eddie, for Christ's sake!

EDDIE *raises the knife and* LOUIS *halts and steps back.*

EDDIE. You lied about me, Marco. Now say it. Come on now, say it!

560   MARCO. Anima-a-a-l!

EDDIE *lunges with the knife.* MARCO *grabs his arm, turning the blade inward and pressing it home as the women and* LOUIS *and* MIKE *rush in and separate them, and* EDDIE, *the knife still in his hand, falls to his knees before* MARCO. *The two women support him for a moment, calling his name again and again.*

CATHERINE. Eddie I never meant to do nothing bad to you.

EDDIE. Then why— Oh, B.!

BEATRICE. Yes, yes!

EDDIE. My B.!

He dies in her arms, and BEATRICE *covers him with her body.* ALFIERI, *who is in the crowd, turns out to the audience. The lights have gone down, leaving him in a glow, while behind him the dull prayers of the people and the keening of the women continue.*

ALFIERI. Most of the time now we settle for half and I like it better. But the truth is holy, and even as I know how wrong he was, and his death useless, I tremble, for I confess that something perversely pure calls to me from his memory—not purely good, but himself purely, for he allowed himself to be wholly known and for that I think I will love him more than all my sensible clients. And yet, it is better to settle for
570   half, it must be! And so I mourn him—I admit it—with a certain . . . alarm.

CURTAIN

(1955)

QUESTIONS

1. Explain the role of Alfieri, the lawyer. In what ways is his role akin to that of the chorus in *Oedipus the King* (see p. 1153)?

2. Discuss how Eddie Carbone's protective behavior conceals hidden emotions for Beatrice and Catherine.

3. Define Beatrice's role in the family. If she recognizes Eddie's deep feelings for Catherine, why doesn't she make her own feelings more forcefully explicit?

4. What are the gender roles and traditional attitudes toward gender that trap the characters?

5. What does Eddie mean when he says to Marco, "I want my name"?

6. Discuss the way immigrants are treated by different characters in the play.

7. Explain why this play might be seen as an American tragedy.

Writing Topics for Drama

1. Discuss the nature of jealous love in *A View from the Bridge*, showing how it leads to destruction beyond the jealous individual.

2. Discuss Alfieri's role as narrator. What seems to be his primary function? In what ways can he be considered a commentator, a character who affects the actions, a conscience, a confidant, and/or a modern Greek chorus?

3. Analyze Alfieri's opening and closing speeches in *A View from the Bridge*. What moral issues are suggested when Alfieri says that he will mourn Eddie Carbone "with a certain . . . alarm"?

4. Examine the relationship of Rodolpho and Catherine in *A View from the Bridge*. Consider whether or not Rodolpho is truly trustworthy and Catherine as innocent as she seems.

5. Analyze the roles of gender, race, and class in the denouement of *A View from the Bridge*.

6. How does Miller portray masculinity and courtship? Discuss whether his portrayal is realistic in its depiction of time and place, or does it represent a more universal portrait?

7. Discuss whether you think that *A View from the Bridge* is a tragedy of the common man.

8. Considering the role "snitching" plays in *A View from the Bridge* and when the play was written, consider how this play might be seen as commenting on the McCarthy era in American history.

PART 3: PEOPLE IN LOVE
CROSS-GENRE DISCUSSION AND WRITING TOPICS

1. What insight do Hopkins's essays "The Marriage of True Minds" and "Romantic Love After the Middle Ages" offer on the reasons romantic love is so often sought outside marriage, and how do they illuminate Chekhov's "The Lady with the Dog," Chopin's "The Storm," and Miller's *A View from the Bridge*?

2. How do Solomon's essays "I Love You" and "Romantic Love" reveal and illuminate the emotions and behavior of the lovers in Chekhov's "The Lady with the Dog," Browning's "Meeting at Night," and "Parting at Morning," Donne's "The Good-Morrow," Chopin's "The Storm," and Lawrence's "The Horse Dealer's Daughter"?

3. Identify and compare the kinds of trials and the purposes they serve that lovers must undergo in Apuleius's "The Myth of Cupid and Psyche," de Beaumont's "Beauty and the Beast," and Browning's "Meeting at Night."

4. Why does love turn destructive for the Knight in Keats's poem "La Belle Dame sans Merci," the Lady in Bulfinch's folktale and Tennyson's poem "The Lady of Shalott," the speaker in Browning's poem "Porphyria's Lover," and Eddie Carbone in Miller's play *A View from the Bridge*?

5. What role does setting play in helping or impeding love's progress in Apuleius's "The Myth of Cupid and Psyche," the Chinese folktale "Faithful Even in Death," Lawrence's "The Horse Dealer's Daughter," Chopin's "The Storm," Mansfield's "A Dill Pickle," Rukeyser's "Waiting for Icarus," or Eliot's "The Love Song of J. Alfred Prufrock"?

6. Love can be portrayed humorously. Explain the role of humor in Breton's poem "Free Union" and Marvell's poem "To His Coy Mistress."

7. People in love often struggle with the desire to remain in control of themselves and the scary feeling of "losing themselves" that love often generates. Examine how this struggle is portrayed in Ovid's "The Myth of Pygmalion," Lawrence's "The Horse-Dealer's Daughter," Bishop's "One Art," Rukeyser's "Waiting for Icarus," Hughes's "Lovesong," and Miller's *A View from the Bridge*.

8. Compare the versions of the story of the life and death of the Lady of Shalott as told by Bulfinch in the myth "The Lady of Shalott" and Tennyson in the poem "The Lady of Shalott." What elements of the story are adapted by Alfred, Lord Tennyson in his poem? In what way do their differences change the thrust of the outcome? Explain which one you prefer.

9. In what ways does one view a former lover or a deceased lover? Compare attitudes toward the "lost loved one" as portrayed in Mansfield's story "A Dill Pickle," Birtha's story "In The Life," and Bishop's poem "One Art."

10. Drawing on the various selections in Part 3: People in Love, make a list of the similes and metaphors used to convey the ineffable nature of love. Which ones do you think are the most successful? Explain why they work so well.

11. In writing about the Grimms's folktale "Snow-White," Gilbert and Gubar relate Tennyson's "The Lady of Shalott" to the predicament of the stepmother in their essay "Snow White and Her Wicked Stepmother." In noting that women's art "is an art of silence," they write, "The Lady of Shalott must weave her story because she is imprisoned in a tower as adamantine as any glass coffin, doomed to escape only through the self-annihilating madness of romantic love (just as the Queen is doomed to escape only through the self-annihilating madness of her death dance), and her last work of art is her dead body floating downstream in a boat." Using Gilbert and Gubar's essay as a point of departure, write an essay that examines the validity of Gilbert and Gubar's comments.

Sir Edward John Poynter (1836-1919). *Orpheus and Eurydice* (1862). Painting. Fine Art Photographic Library, Ltd.